The Adams Papers

RICHARD ALAN RYERSON, EDITOR IN CHIEF

SERIES II

Adams Family Correspondence

Adams Family Correspondence

RICHARD ALAN RYERSON, *EDITOR*

JOANNA M. REVELAS, *ASSISTANT EDITOR*
CELESTE WALKER, *ASSOCIATE EDITOR*
GREGG L. LINT, *SENIOR ASSOCIATE EDITOR*
HUMPHREY J. COSTELLO, *EDITORIAL ASSISTANT*

———— ☆ ————

Volume 6 • December 1784–December 1785
Index

THE BELKNAP PRESS
OF HARVARD UNIVERSITY PRESS
CAMBRIDGE, MASSACHUSETTS
AND LONDON, ENGLAND
1993

Funds for editing *The Adams Papers* were originally furnished by Time, Inc., on behalf of *Life*, to the Massachusetts Historical Society, under whose supervision the editorial work is being done. Further funds were provided by a grant from the Ford Foundation to the National Archives Trust Fund Board in support of this and four other major documentary publications. In common with these and many other enterprises like them, *The Adams Papers* has continued to benefit from the guidance and cooperation of the National Historical Publications and Records Commission, chaired by the Archivist of the United States, which from 1975 to the present provided this enterprise with major financial support. Important additional funds were supplied by The Andrew W. Mellon Foundation, The J. Howard Pew Freedom Trust and The Charles E. Culpeper Foundation through the Founding Fathers Papers, Inc.

Library of Congress Cataloging-in-Publication Data (Revised for vols. 5–6)
Adams family correspondence.
  (The Adams papers. Series II, Adams family correspondence)
  Vols. 3–4: L. H. Butterfield and Marc Friedlaender, editors.
  Vols. 5–6: edited by Richard Alan Ryerson et al.
  Includes bibliographical references and indexes.
  Contents: v. 1. December 1761 – May 1776–v. 2. June 1776 – March 1778–[etc.]– v. 5. October 1782 – November 1784–v. 6. December 1784 – December 1785.
  I. Butterfield, L. H. (Lyman Henry), 1909–1982. II. Friedlaender, Marc, 1905–1992. III. Ryerson, Richard Alan, 1942–　　. IV. Series: Adams papers, Series II, Adams family correspondence.
E322.1.A27   929'.2   63-14964
ISBN 0-674-00400-0 (v. 1–2)
ISBN 0-674-00405-1 (v. 3–4)
ISBN 0-674-00406-X (v. 5–6)

Contents

Descriptive List of Illustrations

1. WESTERN SUBURBS OF PARIS (INCLUDING AUTEUIL AND PASSY) IN
THE EIGHTEENTH CENTURY   4

Molière, Boileau, and Rousseau were but a few of the famous
authors, artists, and political figures who made their homes in the
elegant western suburbs of Paris during the seventeenth and eighteenth centuries. Both in Passy, in daily working sessions with
Jefferson and Franklin at the Hôtel de Valentinois, and in Auteuil,
where he resided reunited with his family, John Adams finally
escaped "the putrid streets of Paris" and found his situation "the
best I could wish for" (*Diary and Autobiography of John Adams*, vol.
3:171). Abigail Adams reiterated her husband's sentiment in a letter
to her sister Mary Cranch. "The house we have taken is large,
commodious, and agreeably situated, near the Woods of Bolign,
which belong to the King, and which Mr. Adams calls his park, for
he walks an hour or two every day in them" (5 September 1784, vol. 5).

The vast Bois de Boulogne of approximately 2,200 acres is on the
western border of Passy and Auteuil, which are now part of the 16th
arrondissement of Paris. The forest was enclosed in 1556, and in the
seventeenth century Colbert converted it into a Royal Hunt. Louis
XIV opened the park to the public, but it was not until the Regency
that great houses like Bagatelle and La Muette were built. The Bois
de Boulogne was at its height of fashion during the Adamses
residence at the Hôtel Rouhault in Auteuil (René Sédillot, *Paris*,
Paris, 1962, p. 174, 208–209).

This illustration is a detail from *Plan of Paris and its Environs*, by
Jean Rocque, London, 1792, based on earlier surveys of Abbé Dela-
grive.

Courtesy of the Bilbliothèque Historique de la Ville de Paris.

2. VUE DU THÉÂTRE FRANÇAIS   37

Le Théâtre Français, also known as La Comédie-Française, was
founded in 1680, during the reign of Louis XIV, and made its newest
home in 1782 on the former site of the Hôtel de Condé, near the
Palais du Luxembourg. This majestic theater-temple, with eight
doric columns adorning the facade and porticos creating arcades or
galleries along its sides, was the design of royal architects Charles
de Wailly and M.-J. Peyre. Although far from the center of Paris,
the new structure was quite an improvement on the cramped
quarters occupied by the royal troupe at the Palais des Tuileries in
the 1770s. Abigail Adams, impressed by the theater after attending

many performances there with her family, described the building in detail to her niece Elizabeth Cranch and exclaimed: "Fancy, my dear Betsey, this house filled with two thousand well-dressed gentlemen and ladies! The house is large enough to hold double the number. Suppose some tragedy to be represented which requires the grandest scenery and the most superb habits of kings and queens, the parts well performed, and the passions all excited, until you imagine yourself living at the very period." Fire destroyed the theater in 1807, but it was rebuilt in the same neoclassical style and survives today as Le Théâtre de l'Odéon. (Luc Vincent Thiéry, *Almanach du Voyageur à Paris*, Paris, 1784, p. 584–588; Howard C. Rice Jr., *Thomas Jefferson's Paris*, Princeton, 1976, p. 68–70; Abigail Adams to Elizabeth Cranch, 3 January 1785, below.)

The illustration, a Née engraving after the work of Jean Baptiste Lallemand, is from Jean Benjamin de Laborde and others, *Description générale et particulière de la France . . .*, 12 vols. [called *Voyage pittoresque de la France . . .*, after vol. 4], Paris, 1781-[1796], vol. 10, *Monuments de Paris et des environs*, plate no. 74.

Courtesy of the Boston Athenæum.

The editors are aware of two likenesses of Adrienne Françoise de Noailles (1759–1807), who married the sixteen-year-old Gilbert du Motier, the Marquis de Lafayette (1757–1834), in April 1774, when she was fourteen. Both, unfortunately, appear to be at least a decade removed from 1784-1785, when the Adamses knew the Marquise in Paris. The first likeness, an ivory miniature by an unknown artist made about the time of Adrienne's marriage, is reproduced here. The second, a portrait of unknown date, shows a rather pensive woman who looks to be at least in her mid-thirties, and had perhaps already experienced the strain of seeing her husband flee from revolutionary France, only to be imprisoned by the Austrians for several years in the 1790s (this is reproduced in André Maurois' *Adrienne, The Life of the Marquise de La Fayette*, N.Y., 1961, following p. 284).

The ivory miniature of the Lafayette children reproduced here is also by an unknown artist. It shows Anastasie (1777–1863), Georges Washington (1779–1849), and Virginie (1782–1849), with a bust of their father on a pedestal inscribed: "Dans tous les coeurs son mérite le place." It is thought to date from about 1786, when the children were about eight, six, and three years of age (Howard C. Rice Jr., *Thomas Jefferson's Paris*, Princeton, 1976, p. 63, 144).

Madame Lafayette was of an old and wealthy noble family, the daughter of Jean de Noailles, Duc d'Ayen, and Henriette d'Aguesseau. Members of the Noailles family had been prominent courtiers and military officers for over a century, and Henriette's grandfather had been a chancellor. The five Noailles daughters were raised in the heart of Paris by an intensely religious mother, and Adrienne, the second oldest, seems never to have gone out much in society, either before her early marriage or after it. To the end of her life it was her family, first her mother and her sisters, then her husband and children, who defined her social world. Making allowances for large differences in cultural background and social standing, Madame Lafayette's youth, adult life, and attitudes toward family and society resembled those of Abigail Adams in several important respects.

It is therefore not surprising that Madame Lafayette made a most favorable impression upon both Abigail Adams and her daughter from their first meeting in the fall of 1784. On this occasion and every other in which they mention her, the Adamses saw exactly those virtues in the Marquise which they found lacking in many European ladies, and in many of their countrywomen living in Paris: an easy amiability, a devotion to her mother and sisters, her husband and children, a dislike of gambling, large social gatherings, and all manner of show, and a remarkable simplicity in dress.

When Abigail Adams first invited Madame Lafayette to a large dinner at Auteuil, given mostly for Americans, the Marquise attended, and Abigail observed that: "there is not a Lady in our Country who would have gone abroad to have dined so little drest." Several American ladies, "Glittering with diamond watch Chains girdle Buckles &c.," were shocked at her plain attire, but Madame Lafayette "was no ways ruffled by her own different appearence" (to Mary Cranch, 9 December 1784, below; and see Abigail Adams 2d, *Journal and Correspondence*, 1:30–31, 32, 33). Each meeting thereafter convinced Abigail and her daughter that in Madame Lafayette they had found a friend of real virtue, who ignored the profligate manners and material show that so disturbed them in France, and later in England. By the time of their departure from Auteuil, Adrienne de Noailles de Lafayette was the Adams women's closest female friend in France.

The two older Lafayette children, Anastasie and Georges Washington, also delighted Abigail Adams when she met them in February 1785: "Madam la Marquise . . . has two very pretty children. . . . The Eldest daughter is 7 years old and Gorge Washington about 5. After dinner miss and master are always introduced to the company, both of them Speak English, and behave very pretty" (to Mary Cranch, 20 February 1785, below). On the same occasion, Abigail Adams 2d observed: "The fondness that Madame la Marquise discovers for her children, is very amiable; and the more remarkable in a country where the least trait of such a disposition is scarce known. She seems to adore them, and to live but in them. She has two that were presented to us; they both speak English, and sing it; the Marquis appeared very fond of them likewise" (*Journal and Correspondence*, 1:49).

An extensive correspondence survives, primarily in the Adams Papers, between the Marquis de Lafayette and John Adams (from 1778 to 1825), and John Quincy Adams (from 1785 to 1834), as well as a more modest exchange between Georges Washington Lafayette and John Quincy Adams (from 1834 to 1839). The only extant correspondence between an Adams and Madame Lafayette, however, is that with John Quincy Adams, 1795–1796, and 1802, again in the Adams Papers.

Courtesy of private owners.

5. AUTEUIL AND PASSY, FROM THE ISLE DES CYGNES, CA. 1785   110

From August 1784 to May 1785, John and Abigail Adams and their children John Quincy and Abigail took up residence in Auteuil, just four miles from Paris, at the Hôtel Rouhault. The spacious new home with its beautiful sprawling gardens delighted the Adams family. Its opulence is described in great detail in Abigail Adams' letters in these volumes. Writing to her niece Elizabeth Cranch, she incredulously described one of the rooms: "Why my dear you cannot turn yourself in it without being multiplied 20 times. Now that I do not like; for being rather clumsy and by no means an elegant figure, I hate to have it so often repeated to me. This room is about ten or 12 foot large, is 8 cornerd and pannelled with looking Glasses . . . festoons of flowers are round all the Glasses, a Lusture hangs from the cealing adornd with flowers, a Beautifull Soffa is placed in a kind of alcove with pillows and cushings in abundance the use of which I have not investigated. In the top of this alcove over the Soffa in the cealing is an other Glass . . . The looking Glasses in this house I have been informd cost 300 thousand liveres" (Abigail Adams to Elizabeth Cranch, 5 September 1784, vol. 5; for a full and colorful account by Abigail Adams of the Adams household at Auteuil, see Howard C. Rice Jr., *The Adams Family in Auteuil, 1784–1785*, Boston, 1956).

The view shown in this illustration is from the Isle des Cygnes, now called the Allée des Cygnes (Swan's Walk), with Auteuil on the left and Passy on the right. This islet divides the Seine just west of Chaillot and the Ecole Militaire. During the Restoration it was built up on the riverbed and is now, as it was in the eighteenth century, enjoyed as a popular promenade (Larousse, *Grand dictionnaire universel*). The engraving by Jean-Jacques Le Veau is from Jean Benjamin de Laborde and others, *Description générale et particulière de la France . . .*, 12 vols. [called *Voyage pittoresque de la France . . .*, after vol. 4], Paris, 1781-[1796], vol. 7, plate no. 37.

Courtesy of the Boston Athenæum.

6. "BOTH OF THEM WERE KILLED BY THEIR FALL, AND THERE LIMBS EXCEEDINGLY BROKEN"

ABIGAIL ADAMS 2D TO LUCY CRANCH, 23 JUNE 1785   184

During the early 1780s, the nascent science of ballooning captured public attention in Europe and America. In August 1783, John Quincy Adams attended the first public launching in Paris of a gas balloon (*Diary*, 1:187), and his Diary in August and September contains numerous articles on ballooning copied from the *Journal de Paris*. John Adams, writing to Abigail Adams on 7 September 1783 (above), contemplated useful transportation by balloon: "The moment I hear of [*your arrival in Europe*], I will fly with Post Horses to receive you at least, and if the Ballon, Should be carried to such Perfection in the mean time as to give Mankind the safe navigation of the Air, I will fly in one of them at the Rate of thirty Knots an hour."

In November 1783, the popular young scientific lecturer Jean François Pilâtre de Rozier and the Marquis d'Arlandes made the first free flight, rising from the Château de la Muette at Passy and traveling about six miles over Paris in about twenty-five minutes. And in September 1784, Abigail Adams 2d recorded the family and "eight or ten thousand" others viewing a balloon ascend from the Tuileries. Rising sometime after eleven in the morning, it traveled to "Bevre [*Bruay?*], fifty leagues from Paris," by six in the evening (Abigail Adams 2d, *Journal and Correspondence*, 1:18–19; see also John Adams, *Diary and Autobiography*, 3:xiii, illustration facing p. 289).

The enthusiasm for ballooning diminished after its first fatal accident, in June 1785. Pilâtre de Rozier and Dr. Pierre Ange Romain crashed on the French shore while attempting to cross the English Channel. The gas balloon of their *aéro-montgolfier*, a two-balloon hot air and gas contraption, exploded, and they fell over a thousand feet to their deaths. Thomas Jefferson commented, "This will damp for a while the ardor of the Phaetons of our race who are endeavoring to learn us the way to heaven on wings of our own" (to Abigail Adams, 21 June 1785, below). Abigail Adams 2d described the accident in a letter to her cousin Lucy Cranch: "There has lately [*been*] a most terible accident taken place by a Balloons taking fire in the Air in which were two Men. Both of them were killed by their fall, and their limbs exceedingly Broken. Indeed the account is dreadfull. I confess I have no partiallity for them in *any* way" (23 June [*1785*], below).

This illustration is from Jean Paul Marat's *Lettres de l'observateur Bon-Sens, a m. de * * *, sur la fatale catastrophe des infortunes Pilâtre de Rosier & Romain, les aéronautes & l'aérostation*, London, 1785. Marat, prior to attaining fame and martyrdom in the French Revolution, studied medicine and wrote on various branches of the sciences without much success. See also Hoefer, *Nouv. biog. générale*; and Larousse, *Grand dictionnaire universel*.

Courtesy of the Houghton Library, Harvard University.

7. PRINCESSES CHARLOTTE, AUGUSTA, AND ELIZABETH, ABOUT 1784, BY

THOMAS GAINSBOROUGH   191

This portrait shows King George III and Queen Charlotte's three eldest daughters, the Princess Royal, Charlotte (1766–1828), Princess Augusta (1768–1840), and Princess Elizabeth (1770–1840). Thomas Gainsborough painted the portrait at the request of the princesses' brother George, Prince of Wales (later George IV). The portrait was completed in time to be shown, along with seventeen other works by the artist, at the 1784 exhibition of the Royal

Academy. A dispute arose when Gainsborough requested that the Academy depart from custom (where full-length portraits were hung above the height of doorways), and not hang the picture of the princesses above five and a half feet. He wrote that he had "painted . . . in so tender a light . . . the likenesses and work of the picture will not be seen" at the higher level. If the Academy did not consent, he would "beg the rest of his pictures back." The Hanging Committee refused the request and had his other pictures removed. Gainsborough did not exhibit again at the Royal Academy. (Jack Lindsay, *Thomas Gainsborough, His Life and Art*, N.Y., 1980, p. 162–163; Christopher Hibbert, *George IV, Prince of Wales, 1762–1811*, N.Y., 1972, p. 41, 259; Mary Woodall, *Thomas Gainsborough, His Life and Work*, N.Y., 1949, p. 80–81.)

The three sisters were quite close to each other, deeply loyal to their father through all his difficulties to the end of his life, and strongly sympathetic to their eldest brother, George, who was permanently estranged from his father by the mid-1780s. Despite their strong family feelings, they sometimes chaffed under the demands of royal etiquette. Augusta objected at an early age to being so often on display to the British public, the very duty that elicited Abigail Adams' sympathy for Queen Charlotte and her daughters upon her first presentation to them (Stanley Ayling, *George III*, N.Y., 1972, p. 222; Abigail Adams to Mary Cranch, 24 June, and to Charles Williamos, 1 July 1785, both below).

By the 1790s, the princesses looked to the Prince of Wales for support in achieving a difficult objective: marriage. Their father apparently felt that no British suitor was good enough for them, and he was so attached to them that he resisted the suit of any foreign prince who would take them away. George III did consent to Charlotte's marriage to Frederick I, Duke (and later King) of Würtemberg, in 1797, and his fear of losing a daughter proved justified. Charlotte never saw her father again, and her husband's alliance with Napoleon after 1805 placed her in the camp of Britain's enemies for a decade. Elizabeth did not marry until 1818, after her father had lost his reason. Augusta, along with two of the three younger princesses, remained unmarried.

This portrait and others, along with literary testimony, give a highly favorable impression of the appearance of the three princesses and of their many siblings. Gainsborough was said to be "all but raving mad with ecstacy in beholding such a constellation of youthful beauty" (Ayling, *George III*, p. 221; Hibbert, *George IV*, p. 259). Abigail Adams was more restrained in her praise of Princesses Charlotte and Augusta upon first meeting them, in June 1785: "They are pretty rather than Beautifull, well shaped with fair complexions and a tincture of the kings countanance. The two sisters look much alike." But she found both princesses affable, relaxed, and even "compassionate" (to Mary Cranch, 24 June 1785, below). Abigail Adams 2d also was not greatly impressed with the royal family on this first visit to Court (to John Quincy Adams, 4 July 1785, below), but by her third visit to St. James's, she came to admire Charlotte, the Princess Royal, finding a "dignity, grace, and affability, with a certain degree of steadiness which I like, in her manners" (*Journal and Correspondence*, 1:81 [3 November 1785]).

All the Adamses soon liked George III as well. Queen Charlotte was another matter. Both Abigail and Abigail 2d felt that she, alone among the royal family, was embarrassed to meet them, and was hostile to their presence at Court (Abigail Adams to Mary Cranch, 24 June; Abigail Adams 2d to John Quincy Adams, 4 July, both below). But when Abigail Adams judged the Queen "not well shaped or handsome" (same), she was simply echoing a view common to many English observers, from the day of Charlotte Sophia's arrival in England for her marriage to George III in 1761, to twentieth-century historians of the Hanoverian monarchy (see Ayling, *George III*, p. 83–84).

Courtesy of Her Majesty Queen Elizabeth II.

8. ABIGAIL ADAMS 2D, JULY 1785, BY MATHER BROWN   217

This large portrait, long in the possession of members of the Adams family, is now owned by the Adams National Historic Site in Quincy, where it hangs in the large parlor. Its artist was the popular young portrait painter Mather Brown (1761–1832), a native of Boston and a student of Gilbert Stuart in America and of Benjamin West in London. Its date and place of execution are given by its sitter, in a letter of 4 July 1785 (below) to her brother John Quincy Adams: "By the way, I must not omit to tell you, what a rage for Painting has taken Possession of the Whole family. One of our rooms has been occupied by a Gentleman of this profession, for near a forghtnight. . . . [Mr. Brown] was very sollicitous to have a likeness of Pappa, thinking it would be an advantage to him, and Pappa Consented. He has taken the best likeness I have yet seen of him, and you may suppose is very Proud, when so many have failed before him. Mama has set for hers, and I, followed, the example. It is said he has taken an admirable likeness of my Ladyship, the Honble. Miss Adams you know. It is a very tasty picture I can assure you, whether a likeness or not. Pappa is much pleased with it, and says he has got my character, a Mixture of Drolery and Modesty."

Of the three portraits which Abigail Adams 2d refers to here, only that of herself survives. It is the first of two known likenesses. The second, a portrait by John Singleton Copley executed sometime between 1785 and 1788, owned first by John Quincy Adams, then by Abigail and John Adams, and after John's death by Abigail Adams 2d's daughter, Caroline Smith de Windt, was perhaps destroyed in the 1862 fire that consumed the de Windt home, and so many of the letters written to Abigail Adams 2d. Caroline de Windt had an engraving of the Copley portrait made for the frontispiece of her first volume of her mother's *Journal and Correspondence* (1841).

Compared with the engraving of Copley's work, Mather Brown's portrait is the more revealing likeness, conveying the poignancy of a sensitive and reserved young woman who had, as her father observed, an element of "Drolery" mixed with her modesty. Brown also conveys a certain wistfulness, perhaps partly a reflection of

Abigail 2d's difficult decision, which she was making just at this time, to terminate her relationship with Royall Tyler. A loyalist merchant from Boston living in London grudgingly described young Abigail as having "an agreeable look," though he did not "like the breed or name" (Thomas Aston Coffin to Mary Aston Coffin, 3 August 1785, Coffin Papers, MHi).

Mather Brown's portrait of Abigail Adams was thought for several years to be the "Portrait of a Lady" now owned by the New York State Historical Association, in Cooperstown, N.Y., but recent scholarship has cast grave doubt on the attribution of both the artist and the subject of that painting (Andrew Oliver, *Portraits of John and Abigail Adams*, Cambridge, 1967, p. 47, illustration on p. 51, 53–54, 244; Abigail Adams 2d to John Quincy Adams, 4 July 1785, note 29, below; Dorinda Evans, *Mather Brown, Early American Artist in England*, Middletown, Conn., 1982, p. 195).

Brown's 1785 portrait of John Adams is also lost, but a second one survives, completed in March 1788 for Thomas Jefferson, and now owned by the Boston Athenæum (*Portraits of John and Abigail Adams*, p. 47–53, 244, illustration on p. 50). Brown also made a portrait of Thomas Jefferson, in the spring of 1786, for John Adams. John Adams' opinion of Brown's 1785 portraits, particularly that of himself, may have been more complex than Abigail 2d allows in the passage quoted above. Writing in her journal, evidently in early September, and referring to paintings that were almost certainly those by Brown, she records: "we had some conversation upon the pictures below. Papa said they were spoiled; he was not at all content with his own, yet thought it the best that had ever been taken of him. No one had yet caught his character. The ruling principles in his moral character, were candour, probity, and decision. I think he discovered more knowledge of himself than usually falls to the lot of man; for, from my own observation, I think these are characteristic of him; and I add another, which is sensibility. I have never discovered a greater portion of candour in any character. I hope if I inherit any of his virtues it may be this; it is a necessary attendant through life. . . . and in the mind of a woman, I esteem it particularly valuable" (*Journal and Correspondence*, 1:80–81).

At some time in the late 1780s, Mather Brown also made a portrait of Col. William Stephens Smith, who would marry Abigail Adams 2d in June 1786 (Katherine Metcalf Roof, *Colonel William Smith and Lady*, Boston, 1929, p. 334–336, and illustration facing p. 336).

Courtesy of the U.S. Department of the Interior, National Park Service, Adams National Historic Site, Quincy, Massachusetts.

---

9. SARAH KEMBLE SIDDONS AS DESDEMONA   367

Sarah Siddons (1755–1831), considered to be Britain's finest tragic actress, enraptured the public and critics in London and smaller cities through the last quarter of the eighteenth century. Abigail Adams, though initially unimpressed with English theater, became an enthusiastic fan. In a letter to Thomas Jefferson (12 August 1785, below), she wrote, "after having been accustomed to [the theater] of France, one can have little realish for the cold, heavy action, and uncouth appearence of the English stage. . . . I know not how a Siddons may reconcile me to English action but as yet I have seen nothing that equals Parissian ease and grace." The Adamses saw Sarah Siddons play Desdemona in *Othello* on 17 September 1785, and the following day Adams wrote to William Stephens Smith (below), quoting Milton: "I was last Evening . . . at Drury Lane and Saw for the first time Mrs. Siddons. Grace was in all her steps heaven in her Eye/ And every Gesture dignity and love." Abigail Adams 2d was equally enthusiastic: "Altho I saw her under many disadvantages, the part not being such as I shold have chosen, and her present situation [*Siddons was six months pregnant*] renders it impossible for her to Play so well, as formerly, yet I think She answered my expectations. I did not go into fits, nor swoon, but I never was so much pleased with any person I ever saw upon any theatre" (to John Quincy Adams, 24 September 1785, below; see also Abigail Adams 2d, *Journal and Correspondence*, [3]:198).

The engraving, by C. Sherwin, was done in 1785 for the publisher John Bell. It appeared in the 1788 edition of *Bell's Edition of Shakspere*, London, 20 vols. John Bell (1745–1831) produced inexpensive, attractive volumes of broad appeal. Abigail Adams 2d owned *Bell's Edition: The Poets of Great Britain complete from Chaucer to Churchill*, London, 1777–1782, 109 vols. (see Abigail Adams 2d to John Quincy Adams, 4 July 1785, below).

On Sarah Siddons and John Bell, see *DNB*.
Courtesy of the Trustees of the British Museum.

10. "NEVER WAS THERE A YOUNG MAN WHO DESERVED MORE A SEVERE PUNISHMENT THAN YOURSELF"

ABIGAIL ADAMS 2D TO JOHN QUINCY ADAMS, 27 NOVEMBER 1785 468

Thus begins one of the liveliest letters by Abigail Adams 2d, begun on 27 November 1785 to the young man who had recently become her favorite correspondent, her brother John Quincy Adams. The correspondence began in May 1785, with John Quincy's departure from France for America to complete his education, and young Abigail's nearly simultaneous departure for London with her parents. Saddened by their separation after a most enjoyable year spent together in Auteuil and Paris, sister and brother faithfully wrote one another long and vivid accounts of their activities, filled with incisive portraits of the people they met, for the remainder of the year. But delays in transatlantic communication and difficulties in routing their first letters through France at times caused them nearly as much frustration as their parents had known during the war years.

When Abigail 2d began this letter, it had been almost three months since she last received letters from John Quincy bringing her news of his arrival and stay in New York. Later in the course of this letter Abigail 2d acknowledged the receipt on 29 November of her brother's letters of 1 and 8 August, the last finished on 19 August in New Haven. As December began she had not yet heard from him of his arrival in Boston at the end of August, although the Adamses had received other letters from Boston, coming on different ships, dated from as late as October. Thus she could write, on the page illustrated here: "a few weeks have elapsd since, without my writing a word [*her last letter, of 18 October*], to you, but you have not any shawdow of complaint to make, and I do not even think it proper to make any apology to you."

Complaints to one another for being poor correspondents, and then apologies when letters did arrive, particularly by John Quincy Adams, appear in many of their letters, from May to December 1785 (all of which are printed below), but neither brother nor sister remained bothered for long. John Quincy would soon turn to a fairly sober, unfailingly articulate and perceptive description of the several communities through which he passed, from northern France to eastern Massachusetts. Abigail 2d did the same, less incisively, but with many interesting observations, for the one large community in which she lived, London.

As this letter shows, young Abigail often engaged in jesting humor, and even outright teasing. Beginning with the last lines on the page reproduced here: "I met a Lady . . . who knew you in Stockholm. Now what think you young Man. Does not your heart go pitepat, now bounce, as if it would break your rib," she continued: "Nor do you know how many of yours adventures She confided to me. No matter what they were, I well remembered with how much pleasure you used to speak of Sweeden, and how many encomioums you passed upon *some* Ladies there."

The passage is young Abigail at her best, displaying that playful humor found in some measure in most of her letters to her cousin Elizabeth Cranch, beginning in 1779 (appearing throughout vols. 3–6), and later to her brother John Quincy. This letter gives us an enticing hint of whatever John Quincy Adams may have been thinking and doing during the five weeks he spent in Stockholm, November–December 1782, beyond the few names of officials and merchants that he met (JQA, *Diary*, 1:159–162; John Quincy Adams to John Adams, 1 February 1783, printed in vol. 5). For a striking confirmation of her hint, see John Quincy Adams to Alexander H. Everett, 19 Aug. 1811 (Everett-Peabody Papers, MHi), quoted at illustration no. 8, vol. 5.

In all her letters to John Quincy Adams, Abigail Adams 2d showed the same keen interest in her family's more private life in London during the summer and fall of 1785. Many of her letters convey information found nowhere else in the Adams Papers. In 1785, Abigail Adams 2d played a role that she had never played before—and after her marriage, in June 1786, would never play again—that of principal chronicler of the daily life of the Adams family.

From the original in the Adams Papers.

VOLUME 6

Family Correspondence

1784–1785

Adams Family Correspondence

Cotton Tufts to Abigail Adams

My Dear Cousn   Weymouth Decr. 1. 1784

Your letter from Autueil near Paris of Sept. 8 gave me great Pleasure as it assured me of Your safe Arrival in France and of Your being
once more in a Family State with the dear Partner of Your Life—whose
arduous Labours and pressing Cares will be greatly alleviated, a
Happiness which He has undoubtedly long wished for; and which
the peculiar Scituation of Things prevented. May You both enjoy
every Good. But I find by Your entertaining Account of Your Family
Appendages, that We must not look for it in Paris, to be held in
Duress is painfull, whether held by Servants by Lords or Crownd
Heads, it matters not. Custom may as effectually produce it when
under the Sanction of a soveregn as an express order from him, and
every one that has to do with a foreign Court I suppose must wear
Shackles. I take it to be a matter of Course and so it becomes
tolerable. I remember a Story of Doctor Busby[1] a famous Schoolmas-
ter in England. A Frenchman strolled into his School, the Dr. ordered
his Scholars to set him upon a Wooden Horse and gave him a
Flogging for his Impertinence. The Frenchman went off swearing and
as soon as possible seized upon a Pen wrote a Challenge to Dr. Busby
and sent it by a Porter. The Porter entred and presented the Note.
The Dr. upon reading it, immediately orderd the same Discipline to
the Porter. The Porter filld with Rage sought his Employer with a
Determination of Revenge. But upon comparing Notes they found
themselves both in the same Predicament and parted in good Nature.
I am sorry to find that foreign Customs and Manners are so rapidly
gaining Ground amongst us. I am told that a Mrs. Haley is forming
her Family much upon the Plan represented in Yours. You may easily
guess what Influence her Example and that of a few others will
produce.

You will find by my Letter to Mr. Adams[2] that agreeable to his

Power and Instructions given me I have bargaind for some Salt Marsh and propose in a Day or two to treat with James Thair for the Pasture, but am of the Opinion, that his Interest will be more effectually served by laying out spare Moneys in public Securities. Our consolidated State Notes have risen to 8/ and 9/pr £ whilst the final Settlement Certificates given to the Army fetch but from 2/10 to 3/4, Loan office Continental Notes 6/8pr £—these however will rise. As the Difference of Exchange, is at present with London, there would an Advantage arise to you in having Bills drawn on you and [placing?] Your Money in any Productive Interest here, Bills being 6 P Cent above par. If You should have Cash to spare.

I have mentioned also the Necessity of putting a New Roof on Your House in Boston, and am of opinion it would be best to raise it even with the adjoyning Buildings. Green has raised his since You went away.

Pheebe has been exceeding attentive to the Preservation and cleanliness of Your House and Houshold Stuff, and Your Farm is well managed by Pratt at present. He has asked me to refund part of a Town Tax paid by him, alledging that You gave him assurances that he should pay no more than his Tax of the Customary and ordinary Taxes of the Town, but such part as should be laid for payment of past Debts should be remitted to him.

Masters Charles and Thos. were well last Week. A Dancing School is kept at Haverhill through the Winter Evenings. Mr. Shaw mentioned it the other day in a Letter and [I] have advised him to send them and have furnished him with Money for the Purpose. I hope it will meet [with] Yours and Mr. Adams Approbation. I conceive that it will be much better for them to acquire the Art, at least so far as to give them a proper Air before they enter College rather than Afterwards. The only Objection to Charles's attending the School must be, the taking off his Attention at a Time, when the closest Application was necessary in order to fit him for an honorable Admission in to College next Year, but I flatter myself his Uncle will take Care that he does not receive any Injury. . . . .[3] I have been your Almoner and witness to the Pleasure and Joy springing from the Widows Heart.[4]

Brother Quincy[5] has been confined with the Rheumatism and in severe pain for some Days past, but seems to be somewhat Better. Mrs. Tufts's Cough still continues, otherwise in her former State. She begs to be remembered to You and Mr. Adams. Sometimes she mourns for the Climate You reside in, fearing the ensuing Winter with anxious Dread, having suffered so much in the last. Pray give me what Politics You may be acquainted with and may communicate, for I cannot expect much from my Friend, whose Correspondence is so large as to allow but a small Portion to my Share. Pray remember us to Cousin Nabby, her Health and Happiness will We hope suffer no Diminution from her Tour abroad. Cousin John I hope We shall eer long see at Cambridge.

Adieu. May the best of Heavens Bless and attend Yours.

Cotton Tufts

RC (Adams Papers); addressed: "Mrs. Abiga. Adams Paris"; endorsed: "Dr. Tufts December 1 1784." Slight loss of text where the seal was removed.

[1] Richard Busby (1606–1695), headmaster of Westminster School, taught a host of celebrated political, religious, and cultural figures of the Restoration, including John Dryden and John Locke (*DNB*).

[2] Of 26 Nov., above.

[3] Thus in MS.

[4] For the several widows who received alms from Tufts at AA's direction, see AA to Tufts, 18 June, above.

[5] Norton Quincy.

Abigail Adams to Elizabeth Cranch

No. 3

My dear Betsy   December 3. 1784

I had my dear Girl such an obligeing visit from you last Night,[1] and such sweet communion with you that it has really overcome the reluctance which I have for my pen, and induced me to take it up, to tell you that my Night was more to my taste than the day, altho that was spent in the company of Ambassadors Barons &c. and was one of the most agreeable parties we have yet entertaind.

I do not recollect that I once mentiond to you during all your visit, the company of the day, nor any thing respecting the Customs and habits of the Country where I reside. I was wholly wrapt up in inquiries after those Friends who are much dearer to me, and who are bound faster to my Heart, I think for being seperated from them. And now my dear girl I have told you a truth respecting the pleasure your company afforded me, and the pleasing account you gave me of our own dear Friends and Country. I suppose your curiosity is a little raised with respect to the Company I mentiond. I could write you an account every week, of what I dare say would amuse you, but I fear to take my pen least I should give it a Scope that would be very improper for the publick Character with which I am connected, and the Country where I reside.

3

I. WESTERN SUBURBS OF PARIS (INCLUDING AUTEUIL AND PASSY)
IN THE 18TH CENTURY

See page vii

It is necessary in this Country for a Gentleman in a publick Character to entertain Company once a week, and to have a Feast in the Stile of the Country. As your uncle had been invited to dine at the Tables of many of the foreign ministers who reside here, it became necessary to return the civility, by at least giving them as good dinners, tho it could take 2 years of an American ministers Sallery to furnish the equipage of plate which you will find upon the tables of all the Foreign ministers here; Monsieur D'Ambassodor de Sweed was invited together with Mr. d'Asp the Secretary of Legation, the Baron de Geer and the Baron de Walterstorff, two very agreeable young Noble Men who Speak english. The Sweedish Ambassodor is a well made genteel Man very polite and affable, about 30 years old. Mr. Jefferson and Dr. Franklin were both invited but were too sick to come out. Col. Humphries Secratary to the American Embassy and Mr. Short private Secratary to Mr. Jefferson, Mr. Jackson and Mr. Tracy Mr. and Mrs. Bingham Dr. Bancroft and Chevalier Jones made up the company.[2]

Col. Humphries is from Connetticut a dark complextion Stout well made Warlike looking gentleman of about 30 years old, you may read in his face industery probity and good Sense. Mr. Short[3] is a younger Man, he is but just arrived from Virginna, appears to be modest and Soft in his Manners. Mr. Jackson and Tracy you know. Dr. Bancroft is a Native of America. He may be 35 or 40 years old. His first appearence is not agreeable, but he has a smile which is of vast advantage to his features enlightening them and dispelling the Scowl which appears upon his Brow. He is pleasent and entertaining in conversation, a Man of literature and good Sense. You know he is said to be the Author of Charles Wentworth.[4] Chevalier Jones you have heard much of. He is a most uncommon Character. I dare Say you would be as much dissapointed in him as I was. From the intrepid Character he justly Supported in the American Navy, I expected to have seen a Rough Stout warlike Roman. Instead of that, I should sooner think of wraping him up in cotton wool and putting him into my pocket, than sending him to contend with Cannon Ball.

He is small of stature, well proportioned, soft in his Speach easy in his address polite in his manners, vastly civil, understands all the Etiquette of a Ladys Toilite as perfectly as he does the Masts Sails and rigging of a Ship. Under all this appearence of softness he is Bold enterprizing ambitious and active.

He has been here often, and dined with us several times. He is said to be a Man of Gallantry and a favorite amongst the French

Ladies: whom he is frequently commending for the neatness of their persons their easy manners and their taste in dress. He knows how often the Ladies use the Baths, what coulour best suits a Ladys complextion, what Cosmecticks are most favourable to the skin. We do not often See the Warriour and the *Abigail* thus united.[5] Mr. and Mrs. Bingham bring up the rear, both of whom are natives of America. He is about 25 and she 20.[6] He is said to be rich and to have an income of four thousand a year. He married this Lady at Sixteen, She is a daughter of Mr. Willing of Philadelphia. They have two little Girls now with them, and have been travelling into England Holland and France. Here they mean to pass the winter in the gaietys and amusements of Paris. Tis Said he wishes for an appointment here as foreign Minister, he lives at a much greater expence than any American minister can afford to. Mrs. Bingham is a fine figure and a Beautifull person, her manners are easy and affible but she was too young to come abroad without a pilot, gives too much into the follies of this Country, has money enough and knows how to lavish it with an unspairing hand. Less money and more Years may make her wiser, but She is so handsome she must be pardoned. Mr. and Mrs. Church are here too, alias Cartar. Mrs. Church is a delicate little woman. As to him, his character is enough known in America.[7]

December 13

Since writing the above I have had the pleasure of receiving your obliging Letter of September 26. I believe I wrote you a Letter of nearly the Same date[8] in which I think I must have satisfied some of your particular inquiries respecting House Gardens and appartments, and if it will be any Satisfaction to you to know where this Letter is written, I will tell you; in your Cousin Jacks Chamber. He is writing at his desk and I at a table by the fire. It is customary in this Country to live upon the second floor. There are a Row of Chambers the length of the House which all look into the Garden, into the first which makes one corner of the House I am now writing. It is [lined?] in the Same manner as if it was paper, with a [flowered?] white chinzt, the bed, curtains, window curtain, and Chairs, of the Same. A Marble mantletree over which is a looking Glass in the fashion of the Country, which are all fixed into the walls, it is about four foot wide and 5 long. Then their is between the windows a handsome Bureau with a Marble Top, the draws gilded like trimming them with a broad gold Lace, and another looking Glass like that I have just mentiond; there is a little appartment belonging to this Chamber about as larg as your Library; which has a Soffa of red and white copper plate and 6 chairs of the Same. This too looks into the Garden and is a pritty summer appartment. Between this Chamber and the Next is the stair case upon the other side of which is the Chamber in which we all associate together when we are not in our seperate rooms. This is properly Your uncles Room, because there he writes and receives his forenoon company. This Chamber has two large glasses and furnished much in the same stile with the one I have discribed, the furniture being red and white. Next to that is a Chamber calld an antichamber paperd with a blew and white paper one glass only and one window. [Out of?] this going into my lodging Chamber which is large and furnishd in the same stile with the others only that the figures are all chinese, [. . .] horrid looking creatures. Out of my chamber all in the same row is a little Room for a dressing room and one of the same kind next to it, which is in warm weather my ⟨dressing⟩ writing room, having 2 little Book cases and a small Escriture. Next to that is the *Delicious* little appartment which I formerly told you of: and then your Cousins Nabbys appartment which makes the other corner of the house. There are very Clever apartments up the second pair of stairs over these chambers, but they are out of repair. Their are two wings in which there are a number of Chambers, one of which Ester and Paulina keep in, allways having a fire to themselves. Who say you is Paulina? Why she is Your cousins Chamber Maid and our Hair Dresser. Every Lady here must have a female Hair dresser, so these Girls serve an apprentiship to the buisness like any other trade, and give from 5 to 8 Guineys for their lerning. Then they are qualified to dress a Lady, make her bed, and sew a very little. I have however got this to lay asside some of her airs and to be a very clever girl. Whilst Ester was sick she was as kind to her and as carefull, as if she was her sister, watching with her night after night. The Cook too, upon this occasion was very kind. And Paulina has under taken to learn Ester to dress Hair, which will be a vast advantage to me if as I fear, I should be obliged to go away this winter.[9] It is very unpleasent to break up a house, to part with ones servants and to set all affloat, not knowing where your next residence will be.

What a Letter this? I hope it is sufficiently particular to satisfy all your curiosity, but do not shew it as a specimin of Aunt A's abilities. Enter Miss Paulina, Madam vous alléz faire mettre des papillottes a vos Cheveux aujourd'hui? Il est midi. Oui. Je viens, so you see my pen must be laid asside for this important buisness. I commonly take a play of Voltaire or some other French Book to read, or I should have no patience. The buisness being compleated I, have a little advice to give you respecting the French [language?] You had begun to learn it before I left America. Your good pappa many years ago gave me what is called a little smattering of it, but Indolence and the apprehension that I could not read it without a preceptor made me neglect it. But since I came here, I found I must read french or nothing. Your uncle to interest me in it, procured for me Racine, Voltaire Corneille and Cribillons plays, all of which are at times acted upon the French Theater. I took my dictionary and applied myself to reading a play a day, by which mean I have made considerable progress, making it a rule to write down every word which I was obliged to look. Translating a few lines every day into english would be an other considerable help and as your pappa so well understands the language he would assist in inspecting Your translation. By this means and with the assistance of the Books which You may find in the office you will be able to read it well in a little while. Do you look in the office for Racines plays and Voltaires and engage in them I will answer for your improvement, especially that volum of Voltaire which contains his Zaire, and Alzire, the latter is one of the best plays I ever read; there is a commedy of his called Nanine which I saw acted.[10] I wish my dear I could transport you in a Baloon and carry you to the Stages here: you would be charmed and enchanted with the Scenerary the Musick the dresses and the action.

An other time I will discribe to you all these Theaters. At present I am shortned for time. Mr. Jackson and Mr. Tracy talk of going on thursday, and Say our Letters must be ready. They will be out here tomorrow morning, and I have not written to more than half the Friends I designd to. Give my Love to cousin Lucy and tell her she is indebted to me a Letter. How is Aunt Tufts. You did not say a word about her. My duty to her, I will give her some account of some pretty place that it is probable I shall visit before long. Who is [now living?] ⟨there⟩ at Weymouth? And are they like to settle any body?[11] How does Mr. and Mrs. Weld.[12] I had a visit from Mrs. Hay since I have been here. She is in France at a place called Beaugenci about a 100 miles from Paris. I have had several Letters from her. She was well about 10 days ago.[13]

Let Mrs. Feild know that Ester is very happy and contented, that I have not been able in France to procure for her the small pox as I expected; she has not been exposed living out of Paris and in Paris it is not permitted to innoculate. I made inquiries about it of a physi-

8

cian. If I should go to London again I shall there endeavour that she has it. She and my other Chamber Maid keep in a chamber by themselves. One of them makes the Beds and the other sweeps the Chambers which is all they have to do in the [stirring?] way from monday morning, till Saturday night. When Ester was well, she undertook with Palina to wash and do up my muslin and lawn, because they batterd it to death here. She is cleverly now, tho she had a severe turn for a week. John has not had very good Health, he was sick soon after he came here; but is pretty smart now, and an honest good servant. John always waits upon me when I dine abroad and tends behind my chair as the fashion of this Country is always to carry your servants with you. He looks very smart with his Livery, his Bag and his ruffels and his Lace hat. If possible I will write to Germantown, but I neglect writing when I ought, and when I feel roused I have so much of it to do; that Some one has cause to be offended at my neglect; and then I never know when I once begin how to come to that part which bids you adieu, tho beginning and end I can always assure you of the affectionate Regard of Your Aunt

Abigail Adams

RC (MSaE:Abigail Adams Letters); endorsed: "Letter from Mrs. A Adams to Miss Eliz. Cranch France Decr. 3. 1784 No. 3."

[1] This visit was AA's fantasy; she did not receive Elizabeth Cranch's only known letter to her of this period, dated 26 Sept., until shortly after 3 Dec. (see text under 13 Dec., below).

[2] The Adamses gave this dinner on 2 Dec. (AA2, *Jour. and Corr.*, 1:35–36). The Swedish minister was Erik Magnus, Baron de Staël Holstein, who represented his nation in Paris from 1783 to the mid-1790s. Per Olof von Asp, secretary of the Swedish mission, had been Sweden's chargé d'affaires at The Hague in Sept. 1782, when JA first met him. Baron von Geer had been Sweden's envoy to the Netherlands, 1775–1779. Ernst Frederik von Waltersdorff, a Danish diplomat in Paris, had known JA since May 1783. JA, *Diary and Autobiography*, 3:8, 128; *Repertorium der diplomatischen Vertreter aller Länder*, 3:408, 411.

[3] William Short, age 25 in the fall of 1784, was beginning a decade of distinguished diplomatic service that took him to The Hague and Madrid, in addition to long periods in Paris, but always in a subordinate or coordinate position to Jefferson, JA, William Carmichael, or Thomas Pinckney. Short, a founding member of America's first ΦBK

chapter, at the College of William and Mary, was Jefferson's close friend from 1781, transacted legal business for him, and served on Virginia's executive council. *DAB*; see also Jefferson, *Papers*.

[4] Dr. Edward Bancroft, a native of Massachusetts, was a natural historian, inventor, novelist, speculator, and spy. He had been an associate in diplomacy of Benjamin Franklin and Silas Deane, and in business speculation of Deane, since 1776, but was also a double agent for Britain, from the same date. JA had disliked Bancroft, whom he regarded as an immoral, irreligious, loose-tongued speculator, from their first meeting in France in April 1778, but he did not suspect the doctor's treason, which only came to light in 1890. Dr. Bancroft published his three-volume novel, *The History of Charles Wentworth*, anonymously in London in 1770. The Adamses owned this work by 1774. See vol. 1:138; JA, *Diary and Autobiography*, vols. 2–4, esp. 4:71–72, note 3; JA, *Papers*, vols. 6–8, esp. 6:14, note 3.

[5] Abigail, in 1 Samuel 25, persuaded an angry David, through gifts and entreaties, not to attack her arrogant husband, Nabal, who

had offended David's men. Nabal died soon thereafter, and David married Abigail. John Paul Jones was a short man with fine features, but his delicate appearance in 1784 may have been due in part to poor health, which plagued him for the remaining eight years of his life. JA and Jones were never warm friends, but JA did respect Jones' naval achievements. See JA, *Diary and Autobiography*, 2:370–371; 4:125, 165–166; Mrs. Reginald [Anna Farwell] de Koven, *The Life and Letters of John Paul Jones*, 2 vols., N.Y., 1913, 2:215, 285; Samuel Eliot Morison, *John Paul Jones, A Sailor's Biography*, Boston, 1959, p. 177, 200–201, 437.

[6] Anne Willing Bingham was twenty, but William Bingham was thirty-two in 1784 (*DAB*).

[7] John Barker Church, an Englishman, had gone to America under the name John Carter, where he had worked with Jeremiah Wadsworth to supply Rochambeau's army (*JQA, Diary*, 1:297, 310, and note 2). Angelica Schuyler Church, daughter of Gen. Philip Schuyler and Catherine van Rensselaer of New York, and sister-in-law of Alexander Hamilton, was Church's wife (Mary Gay Humphreys, *Catherine Schuyler*, N.Y. 1897, p. 1, 48, 52, 180, 191).

[8] That of 5 Sept., above.

[9] See AA to Mary Cranch, 9 Dec., below.

[10] The "office" was JA's study in Braintree. The plays of Racine and Voltaire, in editions published in the early 1770s, are listed in the *Catalogue of JA's Library*.

[11] Mary Cranch to AA, 6 Nov., note 3, above, identifies the Hazlitts, occupants of the Weymouth parsonage. The town had not yet settled a new minister to replace AA and Mary Cranch's father, Rev. William Smith.

[12] Probably the Rev. Ezra Weld, pastor of the Middle Parish in Braintree, and his wife, Abigail Greenleaf Weld (vol. 1:206; *Braintree Town Records*, p. 882).

[13] See Katherine Hay to AA, 17 Dec., below.

Abigail Adams to Benjamin Franklin

Auteuel December 3 1784

Mrs. Adams'es Respectfull Compliments to Dr. Franklin, is much obliged to him for the oil he was so kind as to send her, and is very sorry that his indisposition deprived her of the Honour of his company to dinner.[1] Mrs. Adams takes the Liberty of recommending a Sedan Chair, by which the inconvenience arising from a Carriage might be avoided.

RC (PU:Franklin Papers); addressed: "To Honbll. Dr. Franklin Passy"; docketed: "Dec. 3d. 1784."

[1] On 2 Dec., Franklin, suffering from gout and "stone," wrote to JA to decline his invitation to dinner, "which he should accept with Pleasure, but that he finds himself oblig'd to renounce dining abroad, his Malady rendring it on many accounts extreamly inconvenient to him" (NN: Franklin Papers). On this same date, the Adamses gave a dinner for the Swedish minister and several other diplomats (AA to Elizabeth Cranch, 3 Dec., above).

Elizabeth Smith Shaw to Abigail Adams

My Ever dear Sister   Haverhill Dec. 5 1784

I have not seen your Letter to Sister Cranch[1] as yet, and cannot tell how you like your present Situation—the People—their Language—

nor their manners. But I suppose all "is sweet" now the dear chosen Partner is by. I think I will not allow Cousin Nabby to be a proper Judge. She will pardon me I hope. She views things through an unpleasing medium—she neither feels, nor wishes to be interested in the Objects arround her.[2] Mr. Thaxter says she cannot be more disgusted with European manners than he was at first, but before he returnd they became familar, and much more agreeable to him. What will not Use, and Custom do?

Your Sons enjoy a fine state of Health, and are very happy in an addition to their Uncles Scholars, a Samuel Walker of Bradford—a very clever obliging Lad, he has a something that seems as if he was Billy Cranch, he is very attentive to all of us, which I did not expect, considering he never was used to polite Company. But there is a natural Benevolence in some tempers, and they cannot help being polite—for Politeness is nothing more, than acquired benevolence, displaying itself under certain modifications.

There is a Mr. Le Blanch, who keeps a dancing School in Madam Bernards House. He has *1 and* 20 Scholars, and your two Sons, and Betsy Smith attend him upon tuesday in the afternoon, and Wednesday in the forenoon. I thought it would be a fine Opportunity for Your Children, which you would rejoice in, and so we ventured to send them, but not without consulting Dr. Tufts upon it.[3] The Charge is 2 Dollars entrance and five Dollars a quarter, he will keep two quarters.

Mrs. Marsh is confined, poor Lady, with a bad humour in her Legs. Judge Seargants Family are well. Miss Peggy White seems more chearful, and composed—I hope will soon recover. But how are her Parents dissappointed, how are their pleasing prospects of their Daughters usefulness dashed to pieces. When I was at Braintree I went to see your Mother Adams. She wept plentifully at the mention of her absent Children, fears she shall never live to see you all again.

Write to me my dear Sister as often as You can. If it is but a line it will do me good. Mr. Shaw desires you would accept his most affectionate Regards. If you should have an Opportunity to procure me some Lace I wish you would not forget it. I fear you will not be able to read this wretched scrawl, but it must go, for Mr. Thaxter sups here this Eve upon the remainder of Thansgiving Pyes, and tomorrow he is going upon a visit to his Friends at Hingham and will take this with him. May it have a safe, and speedy conveyance, to a beloved sister, from a most affectionate One   Eliza Shaw

Our best regards attend Mr. Adams, Yourself—Your Son and Daughter. Betsy Smith, my little ones send their duty to Aunt, and thank her for their Book.

RC (Adams Papers); addressed: "To Mrs Abigail Adams"; endorsed: "Mrs Shaw December 5 1784."

[1] Of [5 *Sept.*], above.

[2] Elizabeth Shaw refers to a letter from AA2 to her that has not been found; writing to Mary Cranch on 23 [28?] Nov. (DLC:Shaw Family Papers), she remarks: "I have no Letter from [AA], but one from Cousin Nabby, and by that I find she is greatly dissatisfied with France—and with the People she finds there." For AA2's first reactions to France, see her letters to Elizabeth Cranch and Lucy Cranch, both 4 Sept., above.

[3] See Cotton Tufts to AA, 1 Dec., above.

Mary Smith Cranch to Abigail Adams

Dear Sister   Braintree December 6th 1784

I yet do not know that you have receiv'd one of the many Letters I have sent you but hope you have all. I too well know the pleasure of receiving intelligance from my absent Friends, to let one vessail Sail without carring Some Token of Sisterly remembrance from me if I know of the oppertunity Soon enough. *I* have not an Idea that I shall inhance the value of my Letters, by withholding them. I will never dissapoint the Freind I Love in this way.[1] If Scott is arriv'd I hope you have *all* receiv'd Letters which will give you pleassure, and Some of them by there quallity as well as quantity make up for all Seeming—omissions.[2] I have my Dear Sister receiv'd your Letter Dated September 5th and most heartily long to Strole with you in your Beautiful Garden, but I do not fancy your House Grand as it is, nor your Pack of Servants nor the Company of your French Ladies, if they are all Such as you have describ'd one of them, but I do not believe they are. It would be very unfair to form a judgment of the American Ladies by an Aunt Edwards who's manners was She in France would be much Like the Ladys you Saw at the Doctors, and we know Mrs. Edwards is not a bad woman.[3]

Billy has receiv'd a Letter from Cousin John[4] giving him Some hopes that he may yet be his Class-mate. He will answer his quistions. The Governors of the College have voted to receive him into any Class that he shall be found quallified for, and in consideration of the great Services Mr. Adams has done his Country will admit him without the Custumary Fees. Give my most Tender and affectionate Love to him and tell him he will be receiv'd by his uncle and aunt Cranch with an affection truly Parental, and Shall not want for any attention that we can give him and that he will only leave one Sister to gain two.

Old Coll. Thayer has lost his wife, and a dreadful loss it is to the whole Family.[5] Doctor Fogg was married about a month ago.[6]

Has any Body told you that Mrs. Otis is like to increase—! Tis true I assure you.[7]

Poor Mr. Palmers Family are likely to be greatly distress'd I fear. Germantown has Shifted owners till the Whole of it with all the Building is fallen into the Hands of Major Swan and Mr. Parkers Creditors, and is now to be sold. What will become of them I know not. We are greatly distress'd about them.[8]

I fear this will be the last letter I shall be able to send you this winter. I hear of no more vessails for Europe till Spring. We are in dayly expectation of Some from you. I wish you was in London, we hear much oftener. I had a Letter from Sister Shaw last Week.[9] She had recover'd her Health finely, She Says. The children were all well. They have a dancing School at Haverhill. Your Sons are Figuring away I hear. Mr. Shaw has Sent Betsy Smith to it. This will please her mama. Lincoln Friends were all well last week.

Present my best wishes to Mr. Adams and my dear Cousins and accept the warmest affection of your Sister   Mary Cranch

Your Mother Hall and Brother Adams's Family are well. I was there last week.

RC (Adams Papers); addressed, probably by Elizabeth Cranch: "Mrs Abigail Adams"; and possibly by Royall Tyler: "Auteul, pres de Paris. Pr. favr. of Mons. de Valnais"; endorsed: "Mrs Cranch December 26 1784." AA's endorsement is misdated; the dateline clearly reads "December 6th."

[1] Given her emphasis upon the initial "I" in the first of these two sentences, Mary Cranch may intend here a reflection upon Royall Tyler, who wrote few letters to AA2 after her departure for Europe.

[2] Capt. Scott took Mary Cranch's letters of 3 and 10 Oct., and perhaps those by Elizabeth Cranch, 26 Sept., and by Joseph Palmer, 29 Sept., all above.

[3] Perhaps their aunt, Sarah Smith Edwards (1704–1775), although Mary Cranch's use of the present tense makes this quite uncertain.

[4] Not found.

[5] Rebecca Miller Thayer died on 3 Dec. (*Braintree Town Records*, p. 816, 865).

[6] Dr. Daniel Fogg married Susannah

Thayer on 29 Oct. (same, p. 868).

[7] Mary Cranch here repeats the news she had reported on 3 Oct., above.

[8] Gen. Joseph Palmer had fallen deeply into debt by this date, and by 1786 he had left Germantown for Charlestown and then Dorchester. He soon established a successful salt works on Boston Neck to replace the numerous manufactories that he had had to abandon in Germantown—of glass, chocolate, and spermaceti candles, as well as salt—but his health was broken and he was unable to recoup his losses before his death in 1788 (*DAB*; Pattee, *Old Braintree and Quincy*, p. 486–490).

[9] Elizabeth Shaw to Mary Cranch, 23 [28?] Nov. (DLC: Shaw Family Papers).

Abigail Adams to Mary Smith Cranch

No. 4.

My dear Sister ⟨*Auetuel*⟩ Auteuil[1] December 9. 1784

Your Letter by way of Amsterdam[2] had a quick passage and was matter of great pleasure to me. I thank you for all your kind and Friendly communications, by which you carry my imagination back to my Friends and acquaintance; who were never dearer to me than they now are, tho distanced so far from them.

I have really commiserated the unhappy Refugees more than ever, and think no severer punishment need to be inflicted upon any mortals than that of banishment from their Country and Friends. Were it my case, I should pray for death and oblivion. The consolations which Bolingbrooke[3] comforted himself with would afford me little Satisfaction, for tho the Same Heavens were Spread over me, and the Same Sun enlightned me; I should See the Heavens coverd with darkness and the Sun bereft of its Splendour.

We reside here at this village 4. miles distant from Paris. It is a very agreable summer situation but in winter I should prefer Paris on many accounts, but upon none more than that of Society. The Americans who are in France and with whom I have any acquaintance all reside in Paris. They would frequently fall in and spend an Evening with us. But to come 4 miles unless by particular invitation is what they do not think of, so that our Evenings which are very long, are wholly by ourselves. You cannot wonder that we all long for the Social Friends whom we left in America, whose places are not to be supplied in Europe. I wish our worthy and Sensible Parson could visit us as he used to in America, his Society would be very precious to us here.

I go into Paris sometimes to the plays of which I am very fond, but I So severely pay for it, that I refrain many times upon account of my Health. It never fails giving me a severe Headack, and that in proportion as the House is thin or crowded, one 2 or 3 days after ⟨*I suffer*⟩. We make it a pretty general rule to entertain company once a week, (I do not call a transient Friend or acquaintance dining, by that Name). Upon those occasions our company consists of 15 18 or 20, which commonly costs us as many guineys as there are persons. You will naturely be surprizd at this as I was when I first experienced it, but my weekly Bills all of which pass through my Hands and are pay'd by me; convince me of it. Every American who comes into Paris, no matter from what State, makes his visit and pays his respects to the American ministers, all of whom in return you must dine. Then there is the foreign ministers from the different Courts who reside here and some French Gentlemen. In short there is no end of expences which a person in a publick Character is obliged to be at. Yet our Countrymen think their ministers are growing rich: believe me my dear Sister I am more anxious for my Situation than I was before I came abroad. I then hoped that my Friend in his advanced years would have been able to have laid up a little without toiling perpetually, and had I been with him from the first, he would have done it, when the allowence of Congress was more liberal than it now is. But cutting of 500 [*guineas*] at one blow, and at the same time encreasing our expences by removeing us from place to place is more than we are able to cope with, and I see no prospect but we must be loosers at the end of the year. We are now cleverly sittuated, I have got a Set of Servants as good as I can expect to find, Such as I am pretty well satisfied with. But I apprehend in the Month of Janry that we shall be obliged to give up our House dismiss our servants and make a journey to England. This is not yet fully agreed upon but I suppose the next Letters from the court of England will determine it, and this has been Mr. Adams'es destiny ever since he came abroad.[4] His Health which has sufferd greatly in the repeated attacks of the fevers he has had, obliges him to live out of cities. You cannot procure Genteel Lodgings in Paris under 25 and 30 Guineys a month, which is much dearer than we give for this House, besides the comfort of having your family to yourself. When I Speak of 25 and 30 Guineys per month not a mouthfull of food is included.

I have too little exercise here which I find the want of. My domestick buisness is so different and my family cares so lessned that unless I ride I have no excersise. The Cooks department relieves me from every care of that kind, and cleaning house is performd by Men Servants so that poor Esther has really had a fit of sickness lately merely for want of due excercise. After she came to Auteuel she grew very fat and enjoy'd the best Health that she ever had, but got herself so crowded in concequence of it, that She was seized with a pleurisy. But she is recovering now and I will make her contrive some way to prevent the like again from the Same cause; She is perfectly contented and happy.[5]

As to Speaking French I make but little progress in that, but I have accquired much more facility in reading it. My acquaintance with French Ladies is very small. The Marquise Fayette[6] was in the Country when I first came and continued out untill November. Immediately upon her comeing into Paris I calld and paid my compliments to her. She is a very agreeable Lady, speaks english tollerably easy. We sent our servant as is the custom with our Names into the House to inquire if she was at Home. We were informd that she was not. The Carriage was just turning from the Door when a servant came running out to inform us that Madam would be glad to see us, upon which Mr. A carried me in and introduced me. The Marquise met me at the door, and with the freedom of an old acquaintance and the Rapture peculiar to the Ladies of this Nation caught me by the hand and gave me a salute upon each cheek, most heartily rejoiced to see me. You would have supposed I had been some long absent Friend, whom she dearly loved. She presented me to her Mother and sister who were present with her, all setting together in her bed room quite in the family way, one of the Ladies was knitting. The Marquise herself was in a chintz polinee. She is a middle siezd Lady Sprightly and agreeable, professes herself strongly attached to Americans. She supports an amiable Character, is fond of her Children; and very attentive to them, which is not the General Character of Ladies of high rank in Europe. In a few days she returnd my visit, upon which we sent her a Card of invitation to dine. She came, we had a large company. There is not a Lady in our Country who would have gone abroad to have dined so little drest, and one of our fine American Ladies who sat by me whisperd me; good Heavens! how awfully she is drest. I could not forbear returning the whisper which I most sincerely despised, by replieing the Lady's rank sets her above the little formalities of dress: she had on a brown flowence gown and peticoat which is the only Silk except Sattins which are worn here in Winter, a plain double Gauze hankerchief a pretty cap with a white ribbon in it, and lookd very neat. The Rouge tis true was not so artfully laid on as upon the faces of the American Ladies who were present, whilst they were Glittering with diamond watch Chains girdle Buckles &c. The Marquise was no ways ruffled by her own different appearence. A real well bred French Lady has the most ease in her manners that you can possibly conceive of, it is studied by them as an Art, and they render it Nature. It requires some time you know, before any fashion quite new becomes familiar to us. The dress of the French laidies has the most taste and variety in it, of any I have yet seen, but these are topicks I must reserve for to amuse my young acquaintance[7] with. I have seen none however who carry the extravagance of dress to such a height as the Americans who are here, some of whom I have reason to think live at an expence double what is allowed to the American ministers. They must however abide the consequences.

Your Letters date Sepbr. I received,[8] one of which gave me pain and mortification, because it shewd a want of delicacy and Honour, where I wished to have found both. I did with it as you requested. If I had written immediately upon the receipt of it, I should have exprest myself with a warmth that I might afterwards have repented. Time has made me consider it, as an imprudent triumph over mortification, but if I had been here, well as I wish to think of . . . . and happy as I hope to see . . . . I should have prevented so explicit an answer. But you know, who never does any thing by halves. Any family unhappiness would Soon put a period to the days of a person whose warmth of passions are meliorated and Softned by time, whose Health is infirm and whose great publick exertions in the most hazardous times have batterd and impaired the fabrick.[9] Mr. Jefferson has been sick and confined to his house for six weeks. He is upon the recovery tho very weak and feeble.[10] Dr. Franklin is much afflicted with the Stone, which prevents his going abroad unless when the weather will permit him to Walk.

December 12 1784

Do you say that Scott has arrived in England, said I to my Friend when he returnd from Paris, and that Mr. Tracy and Jackson have received their Letters by the post and that we have none, how can this be? News too of Mr. Smiths arrival. Emelia lookd sad but said nothing. Six months and not one line was hard accounting for. The last pacquet which I received from you, as there were no Letters for her, I kept the knowledge of it wholy from her.[11] Thus past the day and the next which followed, but in the Evening a letter was brought for JQA. from London from Charles Storer,[12] informing us that he had received sundry large pacquets from America. Not being able to find a private conveyance he had sent them by the New dilligence lately set up, which past once a week from ⟨Dover⟩ Callis to Paris. It was Evening no sending in that Night, because a servant could not get them. There was nothing to be done but wait patiently untill the next morning. As soon as Breakfast was over the Carriage was orderd and Mr. JQA. set of for Paris. About two oclock returnd, and was met with *a well*, have you found the Letters? Yes he had heard of them but could not procure them; they refused to deliver them at the post office, because he had carried no proof that the Letters belonged to the family. He might be an imposture for ought they knew, and they were answerable for them. He Scolded and fretted, but all to no purpose. They finally promised to send them out in the Evening to our Hotel. O how provokeing. About 8 in the Evening however they were brought in and safely deliverd to our great joy. We were all together, Mr. A in his easy Chair upon one side the table reading Platos Laws.[13] Mrs. A upon the other reading Mr. Saint Johns Letters.[14] Emelia setting upon the left hand in a low chair in a pensive posture. Enter JQA. from his own room with the Letters in his Hand, tied and seald up as if they were never to be read, for Charles had put half a dozen new covers upon them. Mr. [A] must cut and undoe them leisurely each one watching with eagerness, finnally the originals were discoverd: "Here is one for you my dear, and here is an other, and here Miss Nabby are 4, 5 upon my word six for you and more yet for your Mamma. Well I fancy I shall come of but slenderly, one only for me." "Are there none for me, Sir?"[15] says Mr. JQA erecting his Head and walking away a little mortified.

We then began to unseal and read, and a rich repast we had; thank you my Dear Sister for your part of the entertainment.[16] I will not regreet sending my journal uncooth as I know it was. To Friends who so nearly interest themselves in the welfare of each other, every event as it passes, becomes an object of their attention. You will chide me I suppose for not relateing to you an event which took place in London, that of unexpectedly meeting there my long absent Friend, for from his Letters by my son I had no Idea that he would come. But you know my dear sister, that poets and painters wisely draw a veil over those Scenes which surpass the pen of the one and the pencil of the other. We were indeed a very very happy family once more met together after a Seperation of 4 years. For particular Reasons we remained but one day in England, after the arrival of Mr. A. We set of a Sunday Morning as I believe I have before related, in a Coach and our two servants in a post Chaise. As we travelled over the same part of the Country which I had before described in my journey up to London, I was not particular in relateing my journey to Dover. We were about 12 hours in crossing to Calais.

The difference is so great between travelling through England and through France, that no person could possibly immagine that these countries were Seperated only by a few Leagues. Their Horses, their Carriages their postilions their Inns! I know not how to point out the difference, unless you will suppose yourself a stranger in your own Country first entertaind at Mr. Swans then at Gen'll Warrens and next at Brackets Tavern.[17] Such is the difference I assure you. From Calais to Paris you pass through a number of villages which have the most misirable appearence in general, the Houses of the pesants being chiefly low thatchd Huts without a single Glass window. Their Feilds were well cultivated and we saw every where women and children Labouring in them. There is not however that rich Luxurience which Beautious England exhibits, nor have they ornamented their feilds with the Hedge; which gives England a vast advantage in appearence over this Country. The place most worthy of Notice between Calais and Paris, is Chantilly where we stoped one day, but as I was so much fatigued with my journey I made no minuts of what I saw there, tho richly worth a particular discription. I must therefore request the favour of Mr. JQA to transcribe a few incorrect minuts from his journal which will give you some Idea of what we saw there.[18] I have not a wish to repeat this journey in the winter Season, but I greatly fear we shall be obliged to, as England does not chuse to Treat in France. This however you will not mention at present, as I cannot yet assure you what will be the result of the last dispatches sent to that Court.

This is the 12 of December and a severer snow storm than the present, is seldom seen in our Country at this Season. I was pleasd at the appearence because it lookd So American, but the poor French man will shrug his shoulders.

Your sattin I shall deliver to Mr. Jackson requesting him to forward it to you, and desireing your acceptance of it as a small token of my affection. There is a very great difficulty in sending any thing from Paris, there is no water Carriage, and such a train of custom House officers inspecting your Baggage that nothing escapes them. You are constantly in danger of having your things taken from you. You wrote me respecting a Carpet.[19] In France they are very little used and nothing to be had here of the kind but tapestry. I do not know their prices in England, but I should judge you would suit yourself better in America and full as cheep. Mr. Smith can inform you with respect to every article better than I am able to, because I tarried there so little time. I would send my dear Mother some token of my Regard towards her and remembrance of her, if it was not attended with so much difficulty. I have inclosed to you two Joes,[20] one of which I request you to lay out for her in such things as she may want, and the other for Louissa. I give you the trouble of both, in one case the money might be expended in the family and in the other, I need not add.[21]

I thank you most sincerely, and so does Mr. Adams for all your kind attention to our Worthy Parent, and he requests that she may not want for any thing which may render the remainder of her days comfortable. If you find her in want of any comfort procure it for her, my dear Sister, and Dr. Tufts will be so good as to Supply the money chargeing it to Mr. Adams. If I should not be able to write to Dr. Tufts at this time will you desire him to give Pheeby 7 pd of sugar and a pd of tea on my account as a present, and let her know that I am pleased with her care, and that I send my Love to her and Respects to her Husband. All my good Neighbours too, Remember me to them. With regard to any linnen which Charles and Tommy may want, I think it best to purchase it in America. You kindly offerd to take that Charge from Sister Shaw and my cousins[22] told me they would make it. You will draw upon Dr. Tufts for the money. Should their cousin return to America in the spring, as he wishes to, I shall then have an opportunity of sending them some little articles which I now wish to; but dare not subject a Gentleman to the loss of his Baggage on my account.[23] I feel very loth to part with my son and shall miss him more than I can express, but I am convinced that it will be much for his advantage to spend one year at Harvard, provided he makes, as I have no reason to doubt; a suitable improvement of his time and talants. The latter the partiality of a Mother would say, no young fellow of his age can boast superiour, yet their are many Branches of knowledge in which he is deficient, and which I think he will be best able to acquire in his own Country. I am sure he will acquire them with more pleasure to himself, because he will find there companions and associates. Besides America is the Theater for a young fellow who has any ambition of distinguishing himself in knowledge and Literature, So that if his Father consents[24] I think it not unlikely that you will see him in the course of next summer. I hope I shall follow him the next Spring. Europe will have fewer Charms for me then, than it has at present.

Our dear Sister Shaw, I tremble for her Health. Heaven preserve the good creature. My Love to Mr. Cranch, I hope he enjoys good Health. Love to Cousin Billy. I fancy he will have his cousin J Qu As company one year at least in colledge. The ⟨young⟩ gentleman who lives in your family I hope you will Gaurd and Guide advise and counsel. I was happy to find he improved upon his situation. What a source of anxiety has it been to me!! More I pray than it ever may again. There are certain requisites which Mr. A. thinks necessary in the Character of a Man to whom he would be willing his daughter should be united. I have never told him that they were not the original Growth of a certain Soil.[25] I have done all in my power to plant them there, and hope they may be so cultivated as to appear deep rooted ⟨*there*⟩. Remind him often of the expectations of his Friends, remind him of what he hopes one day to be, tell him the Eyes of the World are more than ever fixed upon him, and that he stands not immoveable; if this should be necessary: which I hope it will not.[26]

I know not how to bid you adieu. You did not say a word of Uncle Quincy. How does he do? My duty to him, tell him if Mr. A was in Braintree he would walk twice a week to see him. Madam Quincy too, how is she. My Respects to her, and to Mr. Wibird who I think misses me as much as I do his Friendly visits.

Emelia is constantly at her pen so there is no need of mentioning her. I must bid you good by, for I have got a prodigious Letter to write to cousin Betsy, besides half a score more. My paper too bids me tell you that I am most[27] affectionately yours   A A

RC (MWA:Abigail Adams Corr.).

[1] The spelling of "Auteuil" was corrected by JQA.

[2] Either Mary Cranch to AA, 7 Aug., above, or an August or September letter that has not been found. See Mary Cranch to AA, 3 Oct., postscript, above.

[3] Henry St. John, 1st viscount Bolingbroke, England's brilliant Tory opposition writer, lived in exile in France, 1714–1723, where in 1716 he wrote his "Reflections Upon Exile," and where he was in self-imposed exile again for some years after 1735. Several volumes of his political tracts, letters, and miscellany, published between 1748 and 1778, are in JA's library. *DNB; Catalogue of JA's Library.*

[4] Anglo-American relations had remained strained since the signing of the peace in Sept. 1783, and from the outset of their mission, JA, Franklin, and Jefferson recognized the difficulty of bringing Great Britain, which was reasonably satisfied with its American trade, to any commercial agreement that would have important advantages for the United States (see JA to Joseph Palmer, 26 Aug., MSaE:Benjamin Pickman Coll., and to Thomas Cushing, 27 Aug., LbC, Adams Papers; and JQA to Richard Cranch, 6 Sept., MeHi).

Nevertheless, the commissioners communicated their eagerness to negotiate a commercial treaty to David Hartley on 31 August. Following Hartley's recall to England in Sep-

tember, they repeated this overture to John Frederick Sackville, 3d duke of Dorset, Britain's ambassador to France, on 28 October. On 24 Nov., Dorset replied that the British ministry was ready to negotiate, but preferred that the United States send a properly authorized envoy to London to negotiate the treaty (*Dipl. Corr., 1783–1789,* 1:503–504, 515–516, 542–543).

After some hesitation, the commissioners replied on 9 Dec. that if Britain "intended that the United States should send a public Minister to reside constantly at the Court [*of St. James's*]," they were not authorized to play that role, but they would transmit the request to Congress. If Britain "intended only that the proposed negotiation should be concluded in London," however, they had the authority "not only to treat but to conclude upon all the Subjects in question" in that city (same, 1:543–544).

The commissioners' hesitation was due to their reluctance to travel to London, both because of the attendant expense at a time when all three felt that their salaries were inadequate to the performance of their duties even in one location, and because of Franklin's and Jefferson's ill health. Further complicating the picture was Franklin's longstanding request to Congress to be relieved of his post so that he could return to America.

For his part, however, JA clearly understood

that America's only chance at securing a satisfactory commercial treaty, as dubious as that chance might be, lay in sending a minister to Britain. And he knew that he was the logical, but not the inevitable choice (see JA to Cotton Tufts, 15 Dec., Adams Papers). On 15 Dec. the commissioners sent copies of Dorset's 24 Nov. letter, and of their reply of 9 Dec., to the president of Congress, virtually without comment (*Dipl. Corr., 1783–1789*, 1:544–545); but in letters to Massachusetts congressmen Elbridge Gerry (12 Dec., LbC, Adams Papers) and Samuel Osgood (13 Dec., NHi:Osgood Papers), JA insisted on the necessity of the American commissioners' going to London. And in letters of early 1785 he wrote of the need to post an American minister there. In these letters, however, JA offered no opinion on proper candidates for that post, and he gave no explicit indication that he wanted to fill it himself. His most candid recorded expression of his belief in his suitability for the position was in his 15 Dec. letter to Cotton Tufts.

Thus when AA, in this letter, anticipates moving to London in January, it was because the commissioners thought that the British ministry might accept their second offer, in their 9 Dec. letter to Dorset, and invite them to begin negotiations immediately. See also JA, *Diary and Autobiography*, 3:177–178, note 1.

⁵ This paragraph is omitted from AA, *Letters*, ed. CFA.

⁶ Adrienne de Noailles, the Marquise de Lafayette. AA2 also records the Marquise's first meeting with AA and AA2, in an undated journal entry following that of 28 Oct., and preceding that for 7 November. The first dinner that she attended at the Adamses', mentioned below, occurred on 18 Nov., and she was the only non-American present (AA2, *Jour. and Corr.*, 1:30–31, 32, 33). Further references to the Marquise de Lafayette, of whom both AA and AA2 became quite fond, appear in AA2's journal from February to May 1785.

⁷ Presumably Elizabeth and Lucy Cranch.

⁸ Not found; see note 2.

⁹ All of this paragraph up to this point is omitted from AA, *Letters*, ed. CFA. The person (or persons) whose behavior gave AA "pain and mortification" has not been identified, and she, in dealing with the letter containing the distressing news "as you [*Mary Cranch*] requested," presumably destroyed the evidence. The concluding sentence of

this passage suggests that the problem would have upset JA as deeply as AA.

¹⁰ See AA to Cotton Tufts, 8 Sept., and note 4, above.

¹¹ The text from "Emelia looked sad" to this point is omitted from AA, *Letters*, ed. CFA.

¹² Not found. On 15 Dec., JQA received a letter from Storer dated 7 Dec. (JQA to Storer, 16 Dec., Adams Papers); the letter to which AA refers here was probably written about 1–4 December.

¹³ Several editions of Plato's works, in Greek, Latin, French, and English, are in JA's library at the Boston Public Library (*Catalogue of JA's Library*). See AA to Royall Tyler, 4 Jan. 1785, note 1, below.

¹⁴ See note 3.

¹⁵ The editors have supplied the quotation marks in this sentence, and have moved the question mark which follows "mortified" in the MS to "Sir."

¹⁶ Mary Cranch to AA, 3 Oct., and perhaps also Mary Cranch to AA, 10 Oct., both above.

¹⁷ James Swan's house in Dorchester, James Warren's house on Milton Hill (formerly Gov. Hutchinson's country seat), and James Brackett's tavern just south of Braintree (Quincy) center, a short walk from the Adams' house (the JQA birthplace). The first two were country seats of the well-to-do; the last a long-established country inn. See JQA, *Diary*, 1:313; Pattee, *Old Braintree and Quincy*, p. 168–169.

¹⁸ JQA to Mary Cranch, 12 Dec., below; see also AA2, *Jour. and Corr.*, 1:11–14.

¹⁹ Mary Cranch to AA, 7 Aug., above.

²⁰ "Johannes" or "Joes" were the terms used for the Portuguese gold coin, the dobra de quatro escudos. The gold dobra and the silver Spanish piece of eight were the most widely circulated coins in the Americas (John J. McCusker, *Money and Exchange in Europe and America*, Chapel Hill, 1978, p. 300).

²¹ AA probably feared that any money given to her young niece, Louisa Catherine Smith, would be spent by her mother; see Elizabeth Shaw to AA, 26 March, note 3, above. She apparently also had doubts about giving money directly to JA's mother, Susanna Boylston Adams Hall; see Mary Cranch to AA, 25 April 1785, below.

²² Elizabeth and Lucy Cranch.

²³ The previous paragraph, and this paragraph to this point, are omitted from AA, *Letters*, ed. CFA.

²⁴ Because JA was eager, long before this

date, to have JQA complete his education in America (see Cotton Tufts to AA, 26 Nov., note 3, above), AA may mean that JA would have to consent to losing his son's valuable services as a secretary.

[25] It would appear that AA's memory fails her here; in Dec. 1782 she quite candidly admitted to JA that certain virtues upon which

he insisted in a son-in-law were not at first evident in Royall Tyler, but that he was acquiring them (AA to JA, 23 Dec. 1782, above).

[26] This paragraph is omitted from AA, *Letters*, ed. CFA.

[27] This paragraph, to this point, is omitted from AA, *Letters*, ed. CFA.

Abigail Adams 2d to Elizabeth Cranch

N 4.

Paris December 10 1784

You can judge of my impatience my Dear Cousin, the last week when we heard from Mr. Storer who informed us that he had forwarded some days before a large packet of letters from America to my Pappa, by a *diligence* established for transporting letters and packets from London to Paris, and he supposed it must have arrived some days before we should receive his letter. The next Morning my Brother went to Paris and Mamma and myself were anticipating the pleasure we should receive from his return, but to our disappointment he came without the letters. The People who received them in Paris, were officers perhaps de la Roy, and they pretended that they could not deliver them, to any person except where they were directed. They knew not but he was deceiving them, and that they would send them to us at Auteiul in the Eve. How provoking was this answer, to us so greatly interested in the Contents. The truth of the matter was I suppose that they had not sufficiently inspected them, for when we received them we found every seal had been opened, and seald again, but in a manner as not to conceal it. This is often the case, and there is no avoiding it, in this Country.[1] With respect to politicks it will sometimes put people upon their Gaurd, but in domestick matters the knowledge they can get is of no importance. Let it not influence any of my friends. Perhaps we shall soon be in London, where there will not be this dainger. We have some expectation of spending some Months in London. Pappa thinks he shall be obliged to go, and he determines in all his journeys, to take his family with him. It would indeed be very disagreeable to be in a strange Country without him.

I am obliged to you my Dear Eliza for more letters than I have received from any one of my friends. I have never omitted answering them, which will I hope induce you to continue your frequent communications. Any thing is pleasing to me now, and your letters my Dear will always afford me entertainment and gratification.

Poor Braintree, seems to fall away strangly. There will be nothing left I fear by the time I return but uninhabbited houses. I suppose, I shall soon be informed by my letters from thence that my friend Eliza Cranch has added to the Number who have left it. Perhaps by following the example of E[lizabeth] Q[uincy].[2] I beg you would be the first to give me this information. It is an event in which I shall ever feel interested, as I shall never cease to Love and esteem you. I think however you had better remain an inhabitant, even should you follow the example of EQ, as I think it is a pitty that so prety a place should be deserted.

Believe me my Dear Eliza I can never loose the recollection of the Eve you speak of, nor can I ever describe ⟨*the* [. . .]⟩[3] what I then suffered. I sometimes fear it was ominous of some future dreaded event. I can never reflect upon it with calmness of mind.

I confess my Dear that I do not feel influenced by a great Share of *disinterested benevolence*, nor can I suffer you to give me credit for what I do not deserve. The appologies that you make for your letters are the only uninteresting parts of them. I will request that in future you will spare them, and fill your paper, with what you stile uninteresting, which I assure you I find quite otherwise. I will answer your *trifling* questions. Some persons would stile them very important, but your mind being usually employd, upon things of higher consequence, you thought perhaps some apology necessary. I rise in the Morning between eight and nine oclock. As soon as I go out of my chaimber I set down to the Breakfast table, where I make tea for my Mamma, Brother and myself. My Pappa always breakfasts upon Chocolate. When we have finished breakfast I wash the tea things and ring the bel for John B[riesler], to take the plates and the fragments of toast and bread, which we have left. When I have dismissed the things I employ myself either in reading Moliere, in French, or in translating Telemaque,[4] from french into English, I have got into *Livre* 4—or in writing letters to America, and sometimes in Working, which I am not like to forget I assure you, as I find it quite as necessary here as I ever did in Braintree, till twelve or one oclock, when I repair to our dressing room and *Pauline* my ⟨*Mammas*⟩ Chaimber Maid, dresses my head. The time appropriated to this business, I either talk French to her or read French. We dine at two oclock in general, and we eat and drink in the same manner that we did in America. Our table is laid for 4 persons, each has two plates, the one soup the other a flat plate, a knife, fork, and spoon to each. In each plate is laid a Napkin and a peice of bread. We have every day a soup and a peice of *bouilli*[5] with as many other things as our Cook pleases to give us. Pappa and Mamma have each a servant behind their Chairs, who, tend the table. It is the Custom in this Country to have a servant to each Person. If you have a company of twenty People they each bring with them a servant to tend upon themselvs, but they do not dine in your Kitchen, which would be rather an inconvenience. But you allow them 3 livres, I think it is for their dinner, which they get at some place or other. We never have but one course and a desert unless we have company, then the custom of the Country obliges us to have two. After we have dined, we retire to our chaimber up stairs which we Live in, and if my Pappa does not walk in the Morning he with my Brother take a walk of five or Six miles, which is my Pappas daily practice. By half after four oclock it is dark. Between five and six, we drink tea. After tea I take a stove and go to my chaimber, and write or translate again. About nine oclock, when I have made myself pretty cold, and my Brother has tired himself with his studys and my Pappa read till his eyes are tired and my Mamma in a disposition to amuse herself by playing a game of Cards, we play, a game or two for amusement, an hour perhaps or more, till it is time to retire for the night. Pappas hour is a little after ten. My Brother and my self generally have a little conversation after-wards. And when it pleases us, we retire to our several chambers. We see but little company, and visit much less. We sometimes dine out, but seldom. We have company generally once a week, sometimes not so often. Now judge you Eliza whether I find so much amusement and entertainment as you have supposed. Oh how I should now enjoy that social friendly intercourse which we have in our friendly circles in America. But alas it is not found here.

The dress of the Ladies here, is more agreeable than in Either England or America. We in America coppy the English. There is more taste more variety, and more ease here than in England. Their cloaths are not richer or more expensive except upon account of the variety one is obliged to have. They wear at Present very little trimming, if any, and the people of highest rank dress least. I have had two or three dresses made since I have been here, and not the least triming upon either. For my own part I like it much.

Mr. Smith carried with him to America two hats of the newest taste in England, then, they were excessively stif. I had one of the same fashion in England, not tho because I was pleased with them, but there was no others worn. When I came to France, I found the same kind of hats, but made in a manner much more agreeable to the Eye. They trim them much prettier and give them an airiness that is very prety. If it was not so very dificult I would sometimes send my friends, some things that might be agreable to them to receive, but from hence it is impossible. There is no conveyance to England but by private persons except for letters, and I have not found any person as yet who I could ask this favour of. Mr. Jackson and Tracy, go soon, but it is a long time before they go to America. I expect that my Brother will go as soon perhaps as they will. By him I shall have an opportunity which I shall take advantage of. Remember me to every body who inquires after your friend   A Adams

RC (MHi:C. P. Cranch Papers); docketed: "Letter from Miss A Adams to Miss Eliz Cranch, Paris, Decr 10 1784."

[1] Compare this with JQA's experience in Russia (JQA to AA, 30 July 1783, above).

[2] Elizabeth Quincy had married Benjamin Guild on 27 May.

[3] One or two words are too thoroughly struck out to be legible. The editors do not know either the date or the nature of this upsetting event.

[4] *Les aventures de Télémaque*, published in 1699, was a didactic novel by Fénelon, written shortly after he was dismissed from his post as tutor to Louis, Duc de Bourgogne, son of the dauphin, and father of Louis XV (Hoefer, *Nouv. biog. générale*).

[5] AA2 first left a blank space, and then filled in this word for boiled or stewed meat.

John Quincy Adams to Mary Smith Cranch

Auteuil December 12th. 1784

My Mamma has desired me, My dear Aunt, to give a Copy of a few cursory minutes, that I took at Chantilly of the Prince de Condé's Seat there.[1] They are very incorrect and confused, but I dont love to make apologies, and will therefore give them such as they are, and trust for the rest in your Candour.

Chantilly is the seat of the Prince de Condé, and is perhaps the most magnificent, and most elegant place of the kind, in the world. It took us from 9 in the morning to 2. afternoon to see it imperfectly; we saw an immense variety without seeing all. We first went through the Stables. A very magnificent piece of Architecture; so much so, that it has been said, that the Prince de Condé's horses, were lodged more superbly, than two thirds the kings in Europe. It was built by one of the Princes, who had made a very large fortune, by the System, which turned every thing topsy turvy in France, in the beginning of the present Century.[2] There is place for 240 horses, and there are almost always 160, or 170 there. In the same building are about 150 dogs for hunting Stags; an amusement of which the Prince is very fond. The next thing we saw was a theatre, upon which the Prince himself plays with his Courtiers every Sunday while he is at Chantilly, from Octr. to January. Near this is the armoury, where the armour of the great Condé, and of many others are shewn, among which is that of the famous Maid of Orleans. These Pieces of old iron, the intrinsic value of which is very little more than nothing are looked upon by some People, as inestimable. The castle we had not time to see it is almost surrounded by a large pond of water, in which there is vast number of Carps so tame, that you may take them in the hand. The garden is very large, and has in it a variety of flowers, and a number of fountains from which the water spouts up ten feet high. There is also an English Garden as they call it, because in the English taste, and in it is a little farm with a mill. There are two or three buildings which appear on the outside to be small huts or cottages, but are furnished within, in the most elegant and splendid manner imaginable.[3] One of them the present Prince built in 1782 for the reception of the grand Duke of Russia, and gave him an entertainment in it. Opposite the Garden is a Ménagerie where there are a few curious birds, and some wild beasts, but this is not equal to the rest and I think it would be as well if it was not shown at all, as there is at Versailles a very extensive Ménagerie, and this must suffer by the Comparison. There are besides all this two buildings, one of which is called *pavillon de Venus* and the other, which is built in imitation of the Chinese manner, *pavillon Chinois*; they are both very elegant, but are not otherwise Remarkable. The Castle appears to be an ancient building, and is said to contain a number of very fine Pictures, but we had not the time to see it.

Besides the pavillon de venus, is a small statue of Cupid. Not represented with mischievous instruments as he commonly is, nor with wings, not with a bandage round his eyes. He is Standing in an easy posture, and holds in one hand a flaming heart. The Inscription under him is very pretty it is as follows. / I give it in French; because it would lose by a translation, and you will be able to understand it in the original.

> N'offrant qu'un coeur à la Beauté,
> Ausse nud que la *Verité*.
> Sans armes, comme *l'Innocence*

Sans ailes, comme la *Constance*
Tel fut *l'Amour*, au siécle d'or
On ne le trouve plus mais on le cherche encore.

If this last line surprises you, you will remember that it was written in France, where the assertion will doubtless hold good and the writer probably thought it was every where as it was in his own Country. I think it will do very well to be in the Garden of a Prince, who can certainly know nothing at all about l'Amour.

I am, my dear Aunt, your obliged Nephew and humble Servant.

J. Q. Adams

RC (MWA:Abigail Adams Corr.).

[1] The Adams family visited Chantilly, twenty-five miles north of Paris, on 13 Aug. (JQA, *Diary*, 1:208). The town was best known for its chateau and park, which passed to the House of Condé in 1632. The first Prince de Condé to reside at Chantilly was Louis II de Bourbon (1621–1686), called the great Condé, whose fame rested on his military genius. The Prince de Condé mentioned in this letter is his direct descendant, Louis Joseph (1736–1818), who had distinguished himself in the Seven Years War (Larousse, *Grand dictionnaire universel*; Hoefer, *Nouv. biog. générale*).

[2] The stables were built from 1719 to 1735 by Louis Joseph's father, Louis Henri, Duc de Bourbon (Larousse, *Grand dictionnaire universel*).

"The System" was a financial scheme set up by the Scottish economist John Law under the Regency in 1716. Law's System, in its initial form, the Banque Générale, issued paper money redeemable for a fixed amount of coin and offered loans at low rates, thus increasing the supply of money and encouraging French industry. The System took control of France's non-European trade, became the dominant creditor to the State, and assumed the function of receiver-general in tax collection. Speculation in the System soon became frantic, and the boom, called the "Mississippi bubble," burst in 1720 when stock-holders started to demand their paper gains in specie, and Law attempted to impose regulations limiting its ownership. Popular opposition forced the government to withdraw a decree that would have gradually reduced the value of bank notes, but the System, Law, and many investors were ruined. *Cambridge Modern Hist.*, 6:168–176; DNB.

[3] AA2 gives a more detailed description of the interior of one of these cottages in her journal: "It had the appearance, on the outside, of a little dirty place, with old windows and little doors, with every appearance of rustic simplicity—when, to our surprise, we were shown into an elegant apartment, with pictures and paintings; the furniture of pink silk, trimmed with a deep, rich silver fringe and tassels; in the centre was a table with a set of Sevres China—white, with a gilt edge" (*Jour. and Corr.*, 1:13–14).

Abigail Adams to Elizabeth Smith Shaw

My dear Sister   Auteuil December 14th 1784

I know your good will to have written to me if you had been able. It gives me pain to hear that you were not. Hearing of your indisposition was the only alloy to the pleasure I experienced when my last pacquet arrived. I fear you are not sufficiently carefull of your Health. Let me beg of you, and if you will not hear, Let me desire Mr. Shaw to assert the authority of a *Husband*[1] and forbid your ever touching *wet* Cloaths, or Ironing, which is but a slow poison for you in Your state of Health. You know my sister that you were not the production of sound Health, but that the infirmities of the Parent[2] have been visited upon the Child, and that your constitution is heriditarily feeble. Let me read you a medical lesson from a favorite Author, Buckhan, who says more consumptive patients date the beginning of their disorders from wet feet; damp Beds, Night air, wet Cloaths or catching cold; than to any other especially after the body has been overheated. As to the Regimin for people of weak lungs; he advices to Milk light food fruits &c and to riding even long journeys to a voyage at sea, but for the latter I imagine you will have no inclination.[3]

From the interest you take in every thing which concerns your Friends, I hear you inquiring how I do? How I live, whom I see? Where I visit, who visits me? I know not whether Your curiosity extends So far as the coulour of the House which is white stone, and to the furniture of the Chamber where I sleep. If it does you must apply to Betsy Cranch for information whose fancy has imployd itself so Busily as to seek for intelligence even in the minutias; and altho they look trifling upon paper, yet if our Friends take an interest in them that renders them important, and I am the rather tempted to a compliance from the recollection, that when I have received a sentimental Letter from an absent Friend, I have passt over the sentiment at the first reading, and hunted for that part which more particuliarly related to themselves.

This Village where we reside is four miles from Paris, and is famous for nothing that I know of, but the learned Men who have inhabitted it. Such was Boileau, Mollire, ⟨*d'Auguisson*⟩ d'Aguesseau[4] and Helvitius. The first and last lived near this Hotel, and Boileaus garden is preserved as a Choice relict. As to my own Health it is much as usual. I suffer through want of excersise, and grow too fat. I cannot persuade my self to walk an hour in the day in a long entry which we have merely for exercise, and as to the Streets they are continually a Quagmire; no walking there without Boots or Wooden Shoes, neither of which are my feet calculated for. Mr. Adams makes it his constant practise to walk several miles every day without which he would not be able to preserve his Health; which at best is but infirm. He professes himself so much happier for having his family with him, that I feel amply gratified in having ventured across the ocean. He is determined that nothing but the enevitable Stroke of Death shall in future seperate him; at least from one part of it, So that I know not what climates I may yet have to visit. More I fear than will be agreeable to either of us.[5] Master John, who is a Man in most respects: all I may say but age; wishes to return to his own Country, and to become a while a resident in your family; that he may acquire what ever knowledge is necessary, for spending one year at Harvard Colledge. I know not how I shall part with him, for he is companion; assistant interpreter &c. Yet he lives a recluse life for a young fellow of his age, he has no companions of his own, and never stirs out unless to accompany his Mamma or Sister. The consideration alone of his advantage will prevail with us, but we shall make a great Sacrifice in doing it. My other dear Lads are well I hope and good and dutifull. I have got their profiles[6] stuck up which I look at every morning with pleasure and sometimes speak to; as I pass, telling Charles to hold up his Head. My little Cousins too, I hope are well. Can they say Aunt Adams yet?

If you want to know the manners and customs of this Country, I answer you that pleasure is the buisness of Life, more especially upon a Sunday. We have no days with us, or rather with you, by which I can give you any Idea of them, except commencment and Elections. We have a pretty woods within a few rods of this house which is called the Bois ⟨Beloing⟩ Boulogne. This is cut into many Regular Walks, and during the Summer Months upon Sundays, it looked like Boston and Cambridge Common upon the publick Days I have mentiond. Paris is a Horrid dirty City, and I know not whether the inhabitants could exist, if they did not come out one day in the week to Breath a Fresh air. I have set at my window of a Sunday and seen whole cart loads of them at a time. I speak literally, for those who neither own a Coach, nor are able to hire one, procure a cart, which in this country are always drawn by Horses. Sometimes they have a peice of canvase over it. Their are benches placed in them, and in this vehicle you will see as many well drest women and children as can possibly pile in, led out by a Man or drove just at the entrance of the wood they descend. The day is spent in musick danceing and every kind of play. It is a very rare thing to see a Man with a Hat any where, but under his Arm, or a Women with a Bonet upon her Head. This would brush of the powder, and Spoil the elegant *tupee*. They have a fashion of wearing a hood or veil either of Gauze or silk. If you send for a Tailor in this Country, your servant will very soon introduce to you a Gentleman full drest in Black, with his Head as white as a Snow Bank, and which a Hat never rumpled. If you send to a Mantua Maker she will visit you in the same stile, with her silk gown and peticoat, her hood in ample order, tho prehaps she lives up five pair of Stairs and eats nothing but Bread and water, as two thirds of these people do. We have a Servant in our family who dresses more than his young Master, and would not be *guilty of tending table* unfriz'd upon any consideration. He dresses the Hair of his young Master, but has his own drest by a Hair Dresser. By the way I was guilty of a sad mistake in London. I desired the Servant to procure me a Barber; the fellow staird, was loth to ask for what purpose I wanted him. At last he said you mean a Hair Dresser Mam, I believe. Aya says I, I Want my Hair drest. Why Barbars Madam in this country do nothing but Shave. When I first came to this Country I was loth to submit to Such an unnecessary number of Domesticks as it appeard to me. But I soon found that they would not let me do without them, because every one having a fixed and settled Department; they would not lift a pin out of it: all tho two thirds of their time they had no employment. We are however thankfull that we are able to make 8 do for us, tho we meet with some difficulties for want of the ninth.

Do not Suppose from this that we live remarkably nice. I never put up in America with what I do here. I often think of Swifts High Dutch Bride who had So much Nastiness and So much pride.

With regard to Cloathing for the Children, the distance I am at from a sea port makes it very difficult to send any thing to them. Their Brother has written to the Hague to have a trunk of Cloaths sent home which he has out grown.[7] If they arrive some will answer for one and some for the other, and what ever else they want You will be kind enough to provide for them drawing upon Dr. Tufts for the money. Mr. Tracy and Jackson assure me they shall set of for London a thursday, and that they will be here tomorrow to take leave. Remember me to Mr. Thaxter. How does he, I think he ought to tell me himself. Alass poor Mrs. White. I am grieved for her, to every body remember me. Your best Friend be sure. My paper is too short, but I dare not take an other sheet. I must find room to say your[8]   A A

RC (DLC:Shaw Family Papers).

[1] AA wrote "*Husband*" in larger letters than other words in the text.

[2] Elizabeth Quincy Smith died at age 53 in 1775, after repeated illnesses (vol. 1:148, 169, 284, 287–289). Rev. William Smith also suf- fered serious illnesses years before his death at age 76 in 1783 (vol. 2:130; 3:376–377; AA to JA, 20 Sept. 1783, above).

[3] The opening paragraph is omitted from AA, *Letters*, ed. CFA.

[4] JQA made this correction. Henri François d'Aguesseau was a prominent magistrate and legal reformer under Louis XV (Hoefer, *Nouv. biog. générale*).

[5] See AA to Mary Cranch, 9 Dec., and note 4, above. The remainder of the paragraph is omitted from AA, *Letters*, ed. CFA.

[6] These "profiles," perhaps silhouettes, of CA and TBA have not been found.

[7] Elizabeth Shaw, in her letter of [*ca. 15*] Oct. to AA, above, mentioned altering clothing for CA and TBA to see them through the winter. See the inventory of JQA's clothing and books sent to Boston from The Hague, made out by Christian Lotter on 6 Nov. (Adams Papers).

[8] The closing paragraph is omitted from AA, *Letters*, ed. CFA.

John Quincy Adams to William Cranch

Auteuil near Paris December 14. 1784

I have been so much taken up these four or five days, in copying both for my Pappa and Mamma, that I have not been able to write at all for myself. I expected that Mr. Tracey and Mr. Jackson would not leave Paris till next Monday, but I dined with them this day, and they seem determined upon setting out the day after to morrow: I shall see them to morrow for the Last time, and have therefore only this evening and morning for writing.

You can imagine what an addition has been made to my happiness by the arrival of a kind, and tender mother, and of a Sister who fulfills my most sanguine expectations. Yet the desire of returning to America still possesses me. My Country has over me an attractive power which I do not Understand. Indeed I believe that all men have an attachment to their Country, distinct from all other attachments. It is imputed to our fondness for our friends, and relations; yet I am apt to think I should still desire to go home, were all my friends and relations here. I cannot be influenced by my fondness for the Customs and Habits of my Country, for I was so young when I came to Europe, and have been here so long; that I must necessarily have adopted many of their customs.

But I have another Reason, for desiring to return to my native Country. I have been such a wandering being these seven years, that I have never performed any regular course of Studies, and am deficient on many Subjects. I wish very much to have a degree at Harvard, and shall probably not be able to obtain it, unless I spend at least one year there. I therefore have serious thoughts of going in the Spring so as to arrive in May or June; stay a twelve-month at Mr. Shaw's; (who I hope would be as kind to me, as he has been to you and is to my Brothers) and then enter college for the last year, so as to come out with you. I imagine that with steady application I might

in one year, acquire sufficient proficiency, in all the Sciences necessary, for entering the last year. . .[1] however I know not whether I shall
do any of these things, for it is still very uncertain whether I shall
return next Spring or not.

I have been this day to see one of the greatest curiosities that P[aris
contains]. The abbé L'Epée, Who for many years has made his sole
employment, to alleviate, the unhappy fate of that unfortunate class
of human beings the Deaf and Dumb.[2] He teaches all, indiscriminately, and whoever desires to be instructed in his method, has only
to present himself, and not pretend to offer any recompense because
that would give offence. Oh! how consoling it must be to these
Europeans, that they are able to say that there still are such Characters who devote all their time, to assist the unfortunate! The name
of such a man deserves to be transmitted to Posterity, more than all
the Kings in Europe. His success has been astonishing, he teaches
the deaf and dumb, not only to converse with each other by signs,
but to read and write, and comprehend the most abstracted meta-
physical Ideas. He has published a book, which contains his complete
System. I would send it you, but it is in French, which you do not
understand I suppose sufficiently to read it. When the Emperor was
here, he went to see the Abbé, and was so pleased with his School,
that when he returned to Vienna, he wrote him a very flattering Letter
and sent him a gold box, containing a medal with his Picture.

Your Mamma in one of her late Letters[3] desired I would get a
Violin, for you. Will you accept of that I left at home? My Mamma
tells me that Mr. C. Warren had it when she came away; but if he
has sailed for Europe, as he intended, he probably left it. I shall never
make any use of it, for I have not touched a violin Since I left
America: and I fansy I should not be able to get so good a one for
you here.

Believe me to be, my Dear Cousin, your sincere Friend

J.Q.Adams

RC (Private owner, N.Y., 1957); addressed: "Mr. William Cranch. Cambridge.
Massachusetts"; endorsed: "J.Q.A. Auteuil. Decr. 14 1784." Printed in the N.Y. *Ex-
aminer*, 20 Dec. 1855. Some damage to the text where the seal was torn away. Missing
words supplied from newspaper copy..

[1] Elipses in MS. On JQA's plans to enter
Harvard, see Cotton Tufts to JA, 26 Nov., and
note 3, above.

[2] The seventy-two year old Charles Mi-
chael, Abbé de L'Epée, had just published the

third edition of what JQA, below, calls "his
complete System": *La veritable manière
d'instruire les Sourds et Muets* (1784), and
was working on a dictionary of manual signs
for the use of deaf mutes, which was com-

pleted after his death. The Austrian emperor, Joseph II, sent a cleric who learned L'Epée's system of instruction and returned to Vienna to establish that city's first school for teaching deaf mutes. Hoefer, *Nouv. biog. générale.*

[3] Letter not found.

Katherine Hay to Abigail Adams

Beaugancy[1] Decer. 17 [1784]

Permit me My Dear Madam to express my warmest gratitude for your kind attention, in conveying me Intelligence that I am so much Intrested in. Your second letter[2] entirely reliev'd my Mind from the anxiety your former letter had excited. I had the pleasure of receiving a packet of letters from America By Capt Scott the Evening before yours of the 10th. instant came to hand. They were replete with every pleasing account that cou'd rejoice my Heart.

I partook of your pleasure and feasted with you, nothing cou'd render the seperation from our friends tolerable but the Aid of pen Ink and paper, and I every Hour of my life Bless the Inventon.

I am now alone my Dear Madam seperated from all that is Dear to me on Earth, Freinds that have my thorough love amity, confidence and esteem, if my Husband cou'd be with me it wou'd in some degree compensate for the loss of such near connexions. But *Alass* Heaven, has ordain'd otherways, I must live alone the greatest part of my Life, and friends are rare to be found. I do not mean to complain for it is my constant study to Build contentment in my own Breast. And pardon me for naming unavoidable Evils, my feelings overflow'd this instant and it was impossible but to drop some on the paper.

I can give you nothing New and entertaining from hence, my apartment with a constant fire I have made tolerable. And my Cheif employment is my French, which if I attain, I shall think will fully repay me for any inconveniency I may meet with. I am by no means eligibly situated however the Winter will soon pass away and I shall make the Best of it.

I am rejoic'd with the Idea of seeing Mr. Jackson I hope I shall not be disappointed. I often wish I had taken my Winter residence near you, it wou'd have afforded me much pleasure. Your observations are very just in giving the preference to the purity of manners in our Country no Doubt these old Countrys have arriv'd to the highest pitch of improvment and refinement which will excite our admiration, but they too often Sacrafice all the finer feelings of the Soul to fashion Etiquette parade and ceremony. I own my path has been chequer'd with much pleasure since I have been in Europe but nothing has charms for me to Balance the delightfull society I left in my own Country. Freindship and sincerity are only knon here by Name. My only fear is on my return I shall find a change in their Manners for travellers too often transplant the follys of other Countrys instead of their Virtues. I have ever been a conformist to fashion because I think it a civility due to a Country from a Stranger, excepting where it interferes with our principles, in that case, we have an undoubted right to dissent without any Breach of politness. In your situation you will find conformity to fashion Necessary, and often convenient, the Multiplicity of Visits that you must receive and repay wou'd be tedious to a degree without the ceremony of a Card.

I was much entertain'd with your descrip[tion] of a Court Introduction. I think you so goo[d] at de[scribing? th]at I shall be always entertain'd ⟨at⟩ w[ith] any [thing you?] may think worth relating. I find [it?] difficult [to] write to America from Hence. I will Beg the favour of you to mention that I am well to Mrs. Shaw when you write, she is so near my Mother she can easily acquaint her with it.[3]

I join with you in wishing for a little more sunshine however I find the weather vastly more agreable than in England. I have as yet enjoy'd my Health exceedingly well and Mrs. M[ather] I think seems perfectly recover'd.

How do you succeed in your French My Dear Madam I wish to know. My Best respects to Mr. Adams and Family, Mr. and Mrs. M[ather] Join. Is Mr. Storer in Paris yet? I shall be always happy to hear from you My Dear Madam.

With great esteem your Obliged Freind & Servt.   K Hay

RC (Adams Papers); addressed: "A Madame Madame Adams a la Maison de M. le Comte de Rouhaut á Auteiul près Paris"; stamped: "BEAVGENCY"; endorsed: "Mrs Hay December 17. 1784." Some loss of text where the seal was cut out.

[1] Katherine Hay had traveled to Beaugency, on the bank of the Loire River near Orleans, in late October with Samuel and Margarette Gerrish Mather. See Katherine Hay to AA, 1 Nov. (Adams Papers).

[2] Not found, but evidently dated 10 Dec. (see the following sentence in the text). AA's first letter to Katherine Hay, also not found, was probably dated ca. 10 November. In it, AA apparently informed Hay that three American ships were missing. Hay was alarmed by this because her brother, William Farnham, had recently sailed for Boston on board Capt. Callahan's packet *Gloucester*. However, he arrived after a passage of forty days on 23 or 24 Sept. (Katherine Hay to AA, 18 Nov. [Adams Papers]; John J. Currier, *History of Newburyport, Mass.*, Newburyport, 1909, 2:260–261; *Independent Chronicle*, 30 Sept.).

[3] Sibyll Angier Farnham lived in Newburyport (*Vital Records of Newburyport, Mass.*, Salem, 1911, 2:626; also, *Sibley's Harvard Graduates*, 10:364–366).

Abigail Adams to Elizabeth Cranch

No:4

My dear Betsy   Auteuil, January 3, 1785

I am determined not to neglect my pen for so long an interval as I did before your last Letters; for then I always go to it with reluctance. Mr. Appleton came here this Day week; from London, and as he thinks he shall return before Captain Young sails, I am induced to proceed to the fulfilment of my promise,[1] and attempt a Description of the French Theater. I have from time, to time, survey'd it with as much accuracy as I am capable of, that I might be able to render my account intelligible. If I fail in architecture, your lively imagination must supply my deficiency.

This superb Building, the French Theater, is situated near the Palace of Luxembourgh, and was Built by Messrs. De Wailly and Peyre the ablest Architects of the King.[2] This Monument is open on every side, and is in the form of a parallelogram (for this figure see the Preceptor,[3] plate 1st in Geometry, Figure 9, B.D.). This is surrounded with porticos which form galleries, by which means you go up and come down under cover. The front, where you first enter, is simple but noble, and announces its Majesty by a perystyle, or a circular range of pillars jutting out, Decorated with Eight collumns in the Doric order, you ascend to it by nine large stone stairs. The back is ornamented with partitions, and the whole is covered by an Attic, which term signifies having the Roof concealed, and is a peculiar kind of base, used sometimes in the Ionic and Doric orders. Under this porch there are three doors, each of which introduce you into a Hall, decorated with collums in the Tuscan order (for this order see the Preceptor). These sustain an arched roof. In front of the middle Door; and at the bottom of the Hall, there is a marble statue of Voltaire. The doors which open upon both sides of this statue, serve as an entrance into a large entry, which was designd as a safe retreat in case of fire. Accordingly it communicates with the highest Galleries as well as the pit, the orchestra and the stairs of all the Boxes. In this entry you are presented with two great flight of stairs opposite each other, which conduct you equally to the first stage or two galleries in Collonade, a series of pillars disposed in a circle, which communicate with the entry of the first Boxes, and through them into the great public retiring room. This Room is

2. VUE DU THÉÂTRE FRANÇAIS
See page vii

decorated in the doric order of a new invention. It represents a Hall in the Italian form square at the bottom and octagon (which is a plain figure consisting of Eight equal sides and angles), at the first entablature (that is at the first frieze and cornice of the pillars,) and circular at the top which supports the cupola, which signifies a dome, the hemispherical summit of a building. This Hall is concecrated to the memory of the great Men, who have renderd the French Theater illustrious; accordingly you find their Marble Busts placed round it. Moliere, as the Father of commedy, has his seat over the Chimny, and upon the right hand is Piron and Voltaire, Racine and Regnard, upon the left Crebillon, *Nericault Destouches*, *Pierre Corneille*, Dufresny.[4] Over the Doors are the medallions of Plautus, Terence, Sophocle, and Euripides. This hall is enlightned by six large Lustures, each of which holds 50 lights, they are of great service to the entry which communicates with it. To compare great things with small, imagine yourself in the gallery of the cupola of Dr. Coopers meeting House, and this cupola under the covering which I have described. It has as many small doors just large enough for one person to enter at a time: as there are boxes within, open one of them, and it introduces you into the first Boxes of the great Theater. Look above you and you will see 3 galleries divided into Boxes in the same manner as the first. Look below you, and you will see what is called the Amphitheater, in which are two rows of benches, advanced sufficently forward to give the spectators an equal chance of seeing. You must never loose sight of the perfect circular figure of the House and that taking off a quarter part of your circle for the Theater, you leave the other three quarters, for the spectators who all necessarily face the theater; below the Amphitheater, is the pit upon the first floor; and here are rows of benches, that every person may sit down; between the pit and the theater; is the orchestra. The Musisians when sitting, have their heads just even with the floor of the Theater. The inside of the Boxes are coverd with green velvet, and cushions of the same. The first Boxes will hold six persons, but 4 are sufficient for comfort. The front of the Boxes, which resembles the Gallery of a meeting house, is ornamented with Drapery, and the second galleries, which are advanced a little forward of the first, are adornd with garlands of flowers, and fruits in Relievo, which you know is the seeming prominence of a figure in sculpture. Above the uppermost Boxes are 12 bendings in the vault, which is supported by 12 pilasters. The 12 signs of the Zodiac ornament these arches, which are all in arabesk sculpture. Before the scene are four pillars adorned, with

Caryatides, as large as life. This is an order of columns under the representation of women, cloathed in long robes and serving to support entablatures; for a figure of this kind, look in the Preceptor to the Corinthian order, and for the arabesk which adorns the vault, look to the composite order against the term foliages, a a. Over the top of the stage is the Lyre of Apollo, supported by Melpomene, who represents the tragick Muse, and holds a dagger in her hand, and Thalia, the Comick Muse, who has a mask in hers. These figures are in sculpture and large as life. The inside of this Theater is painted a sky blue, and the ornaments are all white. From the middle of this vault hangs a prodigious Lustre, containing I imagine two hundred lights.[5] There is over this Lustre in the arch of the Ceilling, a circle, prehaps 40 foot in circumference which is inlaid with some shining metal and reflects back the lights in such a manner that I have easily read the finest print as I set in the Box. The floor of the stage is lighted by two rows of lamps which are placed upon it just before the orchestra; and are so constructed as to be drawn below it, whenever the part acted requires that it should be night. Fancy, my dear Betsy this house filled with 2000 well drest gentlemen and Ladies! The house is large enough to hold double the number. Suppose some tragedy to be represented which requires the grandest scenery, and the most superb habits of kings and Queens, the parts well performed; and the passions all excited, until you imagine yourself living at the very period; and witnessing what you see represented, or, in the Words of Pope,

> "Live o'er the scene, and be what you behold."[6]

Can you form to yourself a higher repast, or one more agreeable to your taste? To my dictionary and the Preceptor I am indebted for the explanation of the terms of Architecture; and, like many other preceptors; whilst I have endeavourd to instruct, I have found my own knowledge increased, for I should never have comprehended half the Beauties of this Theater, if I had not attempted a description of them to you.

Since I began this Letter, yours of November 6 reached me.[7] You was at Germantown assisting a worthy family whose various and complicated distresses would furnish sufficient materials for a tragick muse. The Book of fate is wisely closed from the prying Eye of man, or "who could suffer Being here below." My affectionate regards to them. My paper calls upon me to close, and to assure you, whilst I have sufficient space of the affection of your Aunt,   AA

39

RC (Private owner, 1991).

[1] See AA to Elizabeth Cranch, 3 Dec. 1784, above.

[2] Charles de Wailly and Marie Joseph Peyre (Hoefer, *Nouv. biog. générale*).

[3] Robert Dodsley, *The Preceptor; containing a general course of education . . .*, 2 vols., London, 1748, with numerous later editions. A copy of the 1764 edn. is in JA's library at MB (*Catalogue of JA's Library*); a copy of the 1783 edn. is in MQA.

[4] These dramatists, in addition to Voltaire, Racine and Corneille, were Alexis Piron, Jean-François Regnard, Prosper Jolyot de Crébillon, Philippe Nericault Destouches, and Charles Rivière Dufresny.

[5] Starting with the second paragraph until this point, this highly detailed description of the French Theater is translated verbatim from Luc Vincent Thiéry, *Almanach du voyageur à Paris*, Paris, 1783, pp. 584–588. A copy of the 1784 edn. is in JA's library (*Catalogue of JA's Library*).

[6] "Live o'er each scene, and be what they behold," line 4 of the "Prologue to Mr. Addison's Cato."

[7] Adams Papers. This letter closely resembles Mary Cranch to AA, 6 Nov. 1784, above.

Abigail Adams to Charles Storer

My dear Charles   Auteuil Janry 3. 1785

You bring me much deeper in Debt than I was aware of,[1] but thus it often happens to those who are irregular in their accompts: nor is it in my power to detect you in a wrong Charge as my Receipts are all in America; I will therefore submit to your statement, and plead insolvency. There is not a little due to you too, on the score of acknowledgment for your adroitness in executing the several comissions with which I have charged you since my arrival here.[2] I can only say to you come to Auteuil and the Cordial reception you shall meet with here; shall testify to you how much I esteem and Love you. The House indeed is not calculated for a winter Habitation, and the present unrepaired state in which it now is, proclaims the poverty of its owners. Before we came here, we were assured that every necessary repair should be made to our satisfaction, but from week to week the promises failed, and last week we were requested to pay no more Rent to the owners as the House was attached, and taken by execution, so that this once elegant Building will not bear the term which you apply to it, for neither House or furniture in its present state is really fit for a publick minister to live in. I have had one Chamber furbishd up for you some time ago. We do not want for House Room such as it is, and such as it is, you will be welcome to a part of it.

As to my observations upon the Beau Mond, which you request of me, they are such I suppose as accrue to every person who thinks and reflects. Objects appear different, according to the different positions in which they are placed, or the point from which you view them. Dukes and Duchesses, Lords and Ladies, bedizened with pomp, and stuck over with titles, are but mere flesh and Blood, like their fellow worms, and sometimes rather frailer. He who possesst the greatest riches, and what was far better, the most extensive knowledge, who had exhausted Nature and art in the gratification of all his passions, pronounced upon the whole: vanity of vanities, all is vanity![3] Nor have any of his successors been able to make a more judicious estimate of the whole circles of pleasures. Their are many customs in this Country worthy a transplantation to the Soil of America and there are others which would lead me to repeat in the words of the Church Service, "Good Lord Deliver us" "Good Lord save thy people."

I enclose to you a Letter[4] which I beg you to forward by the first vessel which sails for America. My best Regards to Mr. and Mrs. Atkinson, whose Friendly kindness towards me whilst in London is not forgotton by me. I am sorry to hear Mrs. Atkinson is so unwell, I hope the air of her native Soil will prove more favourable to her. The Great folks upon Your Side the Water, keep us yet in uncertainty. I rather begin to think that we shall be saved the trouble of a winter journey, for which I have no realish. The Duke of Dorset who is vastly civil to Mr. A. gave him to understand that he hourly expected a replie.

I have often heard it said, that their is more art in concluding a Letter genteelly than in writing one handsomely. If I can make no pretentions to either of these, I can to the Sincerity with which I subscribe myself affectionately Your Friend.   Abigail Adams

RC (Adams Papers); addressed in JQA's hand: "Mr. Charles Storer No. 7. Basinghall Street London. England"; endorsed: "Portia to Eugenio. 3d. January. 1785." See also AA to Storer, 28 April 1783, descriptive note (above).

[1] See Storer to AA, 22 Nov. 1784, above.
[2] AA requested "half a pound of the best red Peruvian Bark, and four ounces of Castor Oil" (JQA to Storer, 23 Nov. 1784, Adams Papers). See also Storer to AA, 22 Nov. 1784, note 5, above.
[3] Ecclesiastes 1:2.
[4] Not identified.

Abigail Adams to Cotton Tufts

Dear Sir   Autieul Jan'ry 3 1785

In a Letter which Mr. Tyler wrote me not long since[1] he informd me that Mr. Alleyne was about parting with his House and Farm and that he would sell it reasonably, but did not Say for what Sum.[2] If Mr. Alleyne is really in earnest, and means to part with it, Mr. Adams requests You to see it, and to estimate what you think, to be the real

Worth of it, to inspect the House; and buildings &c and if it falls within or about two thousand pounds Sterling, he empowers you to Close the Bargain for him and draw Bills upon him for the payment, but if it is not to be had for that Sum, or under, we must give up the thoughts of it, and content ourselves to return again to our small Cottage. If it is not to be had Mr. Adams would be glad that no mention may be made of his intention respecting it. I am very desirous of having it, and have; I own persuaded Mr. Adams to attempt it. "It is a bold Stroke for a Wife." Mr. Adams has Some Money due to him; which he was able to save when Congress allowd him 25 hundered a year,[3] and he has some furniture at the Hague[4] which is or ought to be very valuable; and which I had much rather he should part with; than not be able to pay for this place. As to saving any thing upon the present establishment, I find it impossible, unless we submit to meannesses which neither of us are inclined to whilst a copper of the Salary remains unexpended: it is rather hard that a person should be placed in such a situation, as to be necessitated to expend all his income without regard to old age which is approaching fast, or to a family whose circumstances would have been very different in all probability, if private business had not been relinquished for publick service. Dr. Franklin has really been in a less expensive department than Mr. Adams, for he has been fixd to one spot, where as Mr. Adams has been obliged to make no less than ten different journeys to and from France since he came last abroad.[5] No person who has never travelled 500 miles upon paved roads can form any Idea of the injury which it is, both to a Carriage and baggage. Mr. Adams purchased a Carriage in England perfectly New and made for travelling, the wheels of which lookd firm enough to stand for Years, Yet we had not been here a month before we were obliged to have intire new wheels.

Last Saturday was New Years Day. As *we experienced* I will give you a short history of the parade of the Day. The Secratary of the King sends notice to all the Ministers that his Majesty holds a Court to receive the Compliments of all the Foreign ministers. Upon this occasion also all officers civil and Military pay their compliments to all the Royal family every branch of which are with their train, in different appartments. This however is allways the case, so that upon every twesday the ministers have to make the tour of the whole Court. There is a high Mass held in the Chappel upon this day where all the Royal family attend, with the Chevaliers of the order of the St. Esprit, in their Robes. His Majesty Creates these Knights upon this day which Ceremony is perform'd by the Kings putting a blue ribbon over their necks and shoulder. Their Robes are immensely rich, one of them told Mr. Adams that his Robe cost him sixteen thousand livres.[6] Upon this occasion there are *Etrennes* as they are termd to all the servants, and for the curiosity of it I enclose you a list, which every minister has as regularly as if they were all his creditors, as indeed they are. Yet here is one amongst a thousand other expences of which our Countrymen have no Idea, but which habit and custom have made as absolute as the Laws of the Meads and Persians.[7] Therefore of what avail would it be to complain? or execrate and detest the Custom? If you Should chance to omit or forget one of these Harpies, he will follow you to Auteuil or to Paris and demand his due. Besides these: there are all the Servants of ones own family; the Clerk of the Parish; the Newspaper Carrier. In short I know not yet where it is to end.

I know not whether I shall be able to content myself to tarry out my two years, my Heart and Soul is more American than ever. Yet we are a *family by ourselves*. We do not even see so much Company as would be agreeable to me, that is provided I could See it in my own way, in a rational Conversable Friendly Stile. But every Country has its customs and manners peculiar to it. You inquire how commercial matters proceed? There has nothing very material taken place Since Mr. Adams wrote you. The Loan which Mr. Adams procured in Holland is the only resource which Supports the Faith and credit of the united States, for he is obliged to draw from thence money to pay the interest which is due to this Court and for which they are continually dunning Dr. Franklin. And tho C[ongre]ss expected that Mr. Jefferson and Col. Humphries would receive their salaries here, let me whisper it to you, that neither of them could get a Farthing and Mr. A has been obliged to draw upon his Bankers in Holland to supply them, even he who once wrote it as a criminal Charge against a certain person to C[ongre]ss, that "he had said he would go to Holland and see if he could not make the united states less dependent upon France,"[8] and who during the times of our greatest distress in that Country; threatned to with hold the Salary which was then paid here. This Same Gentleman is now obliged to apply for his own from that very Country and through that Same person: which I think is a little sweet and innocent revenge. Will our Country make any provision for the payment of their Foreign debt, do they not feel that interest is a Canker Worm? And do they not feel for those who in their Names have become responsible for them? If the Foreign debt was once consoladated and the interest paid, we might have credit enough in Holland to procure the principal which is due to this Court, and which the politician of America and the independant Spirits Say, they would do as soon as it becomes due. But if our Countrymen will do nothing towards collecting where with to pay even the Interest, but are remitting millions of dollors to England for mere trumpery, where in future can they look for credit?

I hoped my dear sir to have heard from you before now. Letters from my Friends are a cordial to my Soul. Are you like to Settle any body with You?[9] I feel an interest in and a Regard for a people over whom my dear and honourd parent so happily presided for many years. How do my sable Tennants, and my white ones too.[10] I am so habituated to talk in the singular stile, that I forget it should be plural, but if we should be so happy as to procure the place I wish for, I will use my utmost endeavours to prevail upon my Friend; and convince him that Agriculture is the only thing for him the remainder of his Life. The commercial commissions compleated, I will most joyfully quit Europe for ever. If they should be equally fortunate with the treaty of peace, perhaps Congress may be induced to reward their ministers by a vote of thanks, which they have never yet done. The only recompence afforded them for the extensive territory secured to them; and their fisheries, was to curtail their Salleries 500 pounds.

Sir do you envy an American Minister his Station? It has but one Charm for me; that of doing good to ones Country, and virtue in this as in many other departments must be its own Reward.

My best Regards to my worthy Aunt. How is her Health? And to your son be so good as to present my Love and tell him I advise him to get married, for a Man makes but a poor figure solo.

Mr. Adams my son and daughter desire to be affectionately Rememberd to your family. Believe me Dear Sir most affectionately Yours

Abigail Adams

ENCLOSURE

Salle des Ambassadeurs.

1. Louis to the Suisse.[11]	_____1.
2. Do. to each of the Coffee-Men.	2._____2.
At the Oeuil de Boeuf[12]	1. Louis to each of the Suisse's____2.
At M: de Vergennes's.	
1. Louis to the Porter.	1. Do. to the Livery_____2.

2. Louis to each of the Valet de Chambre's,		4.
M: de Rayneval's Porter	1. Louis	1.
Mr. Secqueville's Servant	1. Louis	1.
Mr. Tolozan's _____	Do.	1.
Mr. La Live de la Briche's	Do.	1.
Marechal de Castries's Porter.	Do.	1.
Marechal de Ségur's. Do.____	Do.	1.

17.
Louis d'or's.

RC (Adams Papers); one enclosure, in JQA's hand.

[1] Not found.

[2] AA had been interested in the farm of Thomas(?) Alleyne of Braintree since March 1782 (vol. 4:295–296, 315–316).

[3] That is, £2500 sterling, JA's salary from Oct. 1779 to March 1784 (*JCC*, 15:1143–1144; 26:126).

[4] See the inventories of household goods at The Hague, made on 14 May and 16 Oct. 1782, by John Thaxter, and on 22–24 June 1784, by Marie Dumas (Adams Papers, all filmed at 14 May 1782).

[5] AA is evidently counting each one-way journey that JA took from one country to another; JA did in fact take ten of these journeys, between France, the Netherlands, and England, between July 1780 and Aug. 1784. See JA, *Diary and Autobiography*, 4:263–265.

[6] JA records seeing the Chevaliers du St. Esprit in June 1778 (*Diary and Autobiography*, 2:316; 4:130–131), and again in May 1780 (to AA, 15 May 1780, vol. 3:347).

[7] Daniel 6:8.

[8] AA quotes, only slightly inaccurately, from Benjamin Franklin to the president of Congress, 9 Aug. 1780 (Wharton, ed., *Dipl. Corr. Amer. Rev.*, 4:21–25). For a full discussion of AA's first reaction to this letter, in the summer of 1781, see vol. 4:154 and notes 3 and 4, 162–192 passim.

[9] See AA to Elizabeth Cranch, 3 Dec. 1784, and note 11, above.

[10] AA's black house tenants, Phoebe and William Abdee, and the white tenant of the Adams' farm, Matthew Pratt. Three women are recorded as marrying a Matthew Pratt in Braintree: Lydia Hunt in 1765 (Matthew Pratt Jr.), Sarah Jones in 1774, and Mary Niles in 1784 (*Braintree Town Records*, p. 873, 878, 885).

[11] Porters or doormen.

[12] The Salle de l'Œil de Boeuf, named for its oval window, was an anteroom both to the private apartments of Louis XVI, and to the Great Hall at Versailles.

Abigail Adams to Royall Tyler

My Dear sir   [4 January 1785][1]

Half the pleasure of a Letter consist in its being written to the moment and it always gave me pleasure to know when and Where Friends received my Letter. Know then sir that this fourth of Janry 1785 of which I give you joy, I was sitting by my fire side at one end of a table and at the other my best Friend studying his favorite Author Plato.[2] I was a reading a French comedy called the, procurerer which

I saw acted a few evenings ago and was at that part in which Aristes who is the Attorney says,

> D'ailleurs, j'ai voulu voir Si, Sous ce vêtement,
> Un homme ne pouvoit aller droit un moment,
> Si cette Robe etoit d'essence corruptible
> Si l'honneur avec etoit incompatible[3]

when John Brisler entered with two large packets in his hand, upon which I cried from America I know from America and seizd my sizer to cut them open. Emelia and her Brother went to Paris this afternoon and have run away to some play I fancy by their not being yet returnd, so that we had the reading of our Letter wholly to ourselves. Hers I have tuckd away with an intention of teazing her a little. This packet is dated November 6th. and is the second received from you since my arrival.[4] I wrote to my Friends about 10 days since, but only a few line to you[5] as I wished to set down and write you a long Letter, but the receipt of this 2d Letter has determined me to Seaize my pen this very moment and thank you for both your excellent Letters. To discribe to you the pleasure that a packet from America gives me, I must take a theatrical Stile and Say it is painted upon my face it Sparkles in my Eyes and plays round my Heart. News that is not what I want, politicks well enough by the by. I Love to hear every domestick occurrence then I live with you tho absent from you, and your paper of occurrences I approve much. It is not my fault that Cap. Lyde did not take my Letters, I sent them to London with orders to be put on board of him, but Mr. Tracy gave them to some other Captain. London is the best and only way of safety by which you may convey Letters or to Amsterdam. I write by no other way than London; direct there to Mr. Cranchs Friend Mr. Elworthy.

You and the rest of my Friends seem to think me engaged in a round of pleasures and amusements. I have pleasures and I have entertainments but they are not what the Beau Mond would esteem such. I never was more domestick or studious in my Life. I will tell You how, and give you a journal not in the stile of Swift, but of my own. We rise in the morning, not quite so early as I used to when I provided the turkies and Geese we used to Feast upon, but as soon as my fire is made and my room cleaned I then repair to Emelias Chamber and rouse her, from thence knock at my sons door, who always opens it with his Book in his hand: by that time we are all assembled to Breakfast, after which Mr. A sets down either to writing or reading, I to prepareing work for my Chamber Maids or sewing myself, for I still darn stockings, my son retires to his Chamber to his studies and translations of Horace and Tacitus,[6] Emelia to her room to translating Telemack. In this manner we proceed till near 12 oclock when Mr. A takes his cain and hat for his forenoon walk which is commonly 4 miles, this he compleats by two. The Ladies at 12 repair to the toilite where some Author employs their dressing hour. At 2 we all meet together and dine, in the afternoon ⟨I⟩ we go from one room to an other sometimes chat with my son or make him read to me. Emelia in the same manner works reads or plays with her Brother which they can do together in a game of Romps very well. The afternoon here are very short and tea very soon summons us all together. As soon as that is removed the table is coverd with mathamatical instruments and Books and you hear nothing till nine oclock but of Theorem and problems besecting and desecting tangents and Se[quents?][7] which Mr. A is teaching to his son; after which we are often called upon to relieve their brains by a game of whist. At 10 we all retire to rest, and this is the common method in which we spend our time varying sometimes by receiving and sometimes by going into company. Ten oclock and these young folks not returnd, a dark stormy night too, but then there are Lamps from Paris here which enlightens the road. This is a very pretty ride in agreeable weather, for upon your right hand you have the River Sein; Ceasar barks and the gate bell rings which announces the return of the Carriage. Now for a little pleasure of which you shall have the whole History. Enter Miss A, "What are you cold?" Enter Mr. JQA with a set of Mathamatical instruments, "Pray what Spectacle have you been at to Night?" "A Variety, into the palais Royal. I have seen ⟨the⟩ du palais du bon goüt l'Intendant comedien malgre lui; le Mensonge excusable, et le nouveau parvenu."[8] Now what had I best do, give her these letters to night which will keep her up till 12 or give them for her Breakfast to morrow morning? "Hem, come take of your Cloak and I will give you an etrennes"; which in plain english signifies a new Years Gift. Off went the Cloak in an instant, then I delt out the letters one by one, at every one Miss calling out for more, more untill I had exhausted the bugget; but so secret and so affraid that one can hardly get a peep at a single line. I believe you will think by my thus trifling that I am tinctured with the frivolity of the Nation. Manners are very catching I assure you, and dissagreeable as I found many customs when I first came here, 5 months habitude have made them less so.

For instanc when I dine abroad I am not so grosely offend at seeing a Gentleman take a partridge by the leg and put it to his Nose to see if it is in a condition to offer to the Ladies, because I have learnt that this is politeness instead of incivility. Nor do I look with so much amazement when I see a Lady wrapturously put her Arms round a Gentleman and Salute him first upon one cheeck and then upon the other, I consider it as [a] thing of mere course. I can even see that the Rouge gives an additional splendour to the Eyes: I believe however there are some practices which neither time nor Custom will ever make me a convert to. If I thought they would, I would fly the Country and its inhabitant[s] as a pestilence that walketh in darkness and a plague that waisteth at noon day.[9] I believe you need be under no apprehension respecting a young Lady of your acquaintance, who has never yet found her self so happy in Europe as America, and who I dare say will ever find in herself a preference to the manners of her Native Country. She has had an ernest desire to spend half a Year in a celebrated Convent in Paris for the purpose of acquiring the Language perfectly, but her Father entertained not so favourable an opinion of those abodes as some who have placed their Children there, and thought that the advantages arising from speaking the Language perfectly would never compensate for one less strickt Idea either of Modesty or Manners. I pretended not to judge in this Case. There is a certain saying not the less true for being often repeated, that habit is second nature. The Phythagorian doctrine of Reverence-ing thyself is little practised among the Females of this Nation; for in this Idea if I comprehend it aright is included an incorruptable virtue joined to the strickest modesty. There is so little Regard paid here to the conjugal union that it naturally introduces every kind of licentiousness. The distinction of families is the corrupt Source from whence the pestilential Streems issue. The affections of the Heart are never traced. The Boy of ⟨12⟩ 14 or ⟨13⟩ 15 is married to the miss of 10 or 11, he is sent upon his travels and she confined in a convent. At 20 or 21 he returns and receives his wife; each of them perhaps cursing their shackels. Dispositions and inclinations varying, he seeks a mistress more pleasing, and she a Gallant more affectionate and complasant. Or if it is thought necessary to perpetuate the family titles and estate perhaps a year or twos fidelity is necessary upon the Ladys part, and it is esteemed a sad misfortune when more than two or 3 children fall to the share of a family. The young Ladies of a family are gaurded like the Hesperian fruit and never sufferd to be in company without some watchfull dragon. They have no Idea of that sure and only method of teaching them to reverence themselves which Prior so beautifully discribes—

⟨*Let all their ways be unconfined*⟩
Be to her faults a little blind,
Be to her virtues ever kind
Let all her ways be unconfine'd
And clap the padlock on her mind.[10]

Yet dissolute as the manners of this people are said to be they Respect virtue in the Female Character almost to Idolating and speak of a Lady whose Character is unblemished and some such there are even here, as the Phoenix of the age. A Gentleman carries his Galantry to such a pitch here that altho he knows that his Lady has her Lover, yet if any person dares to insinuate the least reflextion upon her honour, nothing but blood can wash it out. I have had a Rouncounter related to me which happend last year at the opera where they frequently have Mask Balls. The Count D Artois the kings youngest Brother taking a fancy to a Lady in a Mask and supposeing her a Lady of pleasure used some familiarity with the Lady which she resented. Feeling his Rank he gave her a Box on the ear, upon which he was instantly seizd and his Mask torn of. The Lady proved to be the sister of the Duke de Bourbon. This being an offence for which even the kings Brother could not ⟨*repair*⟩ attone by asking pardon, he was challenged by the Duke they fought and the Count was wounded.[11] Are not these things lessons to our Country to avoid family titles and every distinction but those which arise from Superiour Merit and Virtue: to cut of the Hydra headed Cincinnati and every appendage which pertains to it. The Heraditary Monster is already ⟨*distroyed*⟩ routd, but who sees not others which in time may grow to be equally distructive? The most fatal poison is that Secreet kind which distroys without discovery.

I can offer you no advise, at this distance but such as you already have upon paper and if as you are pleased to say you feel disposed at all times to attend to it, I flatter myself it has ever been of that kind which will promote both your honour and Reputation, for which you may be assured I am not less solicitious when I view you with more confidence as the person to whose care and protection I shall one day resign a beloved and only daughter. Industery integrity frugality and honour are the Characteristick Virtues which will recommend and ensure to you parental Regard and Fraternal affection and which will continue to you the Friendship the Esteem and the Maternal Regard of

A Adams

Dft (Adams Papers).

[1] Possibly 3 Jan.; see AA to Lucy Cranch, [5] Jan., note 1, below.

[2] Whether JA really did hold this high opinion of Plato in January 1785, and if so, when he first formed it, is not known to the editors, but it did not endure. He may have begun his first serious study of the philosopher in the fall of 1784 (AA to Mary Cranch, 9 Dec. 1784, and note 12, above), and over the next year or two he evidently read through all the dialogues. In 1786, JA briefly summarized what he regarded as the major lessons of Plato's political dialogues in the first volume of his *Defence of the Constitutions of the United States.*

Three decades later, in response to a sweeping denunciation of Plato by Thomas Jefferson, JA described this period of study and its surprising outcome: "Some thirty Years ago I took upon me the severe task of going through all his Works. With the help of two Latin Translations, and one English and one French Translation, and comparing some of the most remarkable passages with the Greek, I laboured through the tedious toil. My disappointment was very great, my Astonishment was greater and my disgust was shocking. . . . his Laws and his Republick from which I expected most, disappointed me most" (JA to Jefferson, 16 July 1814, DLC:Jefferson Papers; printed in Lester J. Cappon, ed., *The Adams-Jefferson Letters*, 2 vols., Chapel Hill, 1957, 2:437). Five editions or translations of Plato survive in JA's library, including one complete edition in parallel Latin and Greek columns, a complete French translation, with some marginal comments by JA, and English and French translations of the *Republic* (*Catalogue of JA's Library*).

[3] This passage is from Philippe Poisson's *Le Procureur arbitre, comedie en vers* (ii, 54–57), which was first performed in 1728.

[4] Tyler's most recent extant letter was to JA, 27 Aug. 1784, above.

[5] Not found.

[6] JQA pursued a keen interest in both authors into adulthood, and was translating various odes of Horace into his seventies. Several of JQA's translations of Horace and Tacitus made in the 1780s survive in the Adams Papers (see Adams Papers, M/JQA/30, 42, 44, and 45, Adams Papers, Microfilms, Reel Nos. 225, 237, 239, and 240).

[7] This word appears to be corrected from either "segments" or "secants."

[8] The editors have supplied all the question and quotation marks in this passage, and in the two following sentences. See AA2, *Jour. and Corr.*, 1:39–40; and JQA, *Diary*, 1:212, and note 3, which gives the authors, exact titles, and publication data for these four plays.

[9] Psalms 91:6, somewhat altered.

[10] Matthew Prior, "An English Padlock," lines 79–82, somewhat altered, with lines 79 and 80 interchanged.

[11] This event actually occurred on mardi gras, 3 March 1778 and involved the Duc de Bourbon's wife. Charles Phillipe, the Comte d'Artois became Charles X of France in 1824. Hoefer, *Nouv. biog. générale.*

Abigail Adams to Lucy Cranch

My dear Lucy Auteuil, 24 [5] January, 1785[1]

I HOPE you have before now received my letter, which was ordered on board with Captain Lyde, but put on board another vessel, because it was said she would sail first.[2] By that you will see that I did not wait to receive a letter from you first. I thank you for yours of November 6th,[3] which reached me last evening; and here I am, seated by your cousin J.Q.A.'s fireside, where, by his invitation, I usually write.

And in the first place, my dear Lucy, shall I find a little fault with you? A fault, from which neither your good sister, nor cousin Abby, is free. It is, that all of you so much neglect your handwriting. I know that a sentiment is equally wise and just, written in a good or bad hand; but then there is certainly a more pleasing appearance, when the lines are regular, and the letters distinct and well cut. A sensible woman is so, whether she be handsome or ugly; but who looks not with most pleasure upon the sensible beauty? "Why, my dear aunt," methinks I hear you say, "only look at your own handwriting." Acknowledged; I am very sensible of it, and it is from feeling the disadvantages of it myself, that I am the more solicitous that my young acquaintance should excel me, whilst they have leisure, and their fingers are young and flexible. Your cousin, J.Q.A., copied a letter for me the other day, and, upon my word, I thought there was some value in it, from the new appearance it acquired.[4]

I have written several times largely to your sister, and, as I know you participate with her, I have not been so particular in scribbling to every one of the family; for an imagination must be more inventive than mine, to supply materials with sufficient variety to afford you all entertainment. Through want of a better subject, I will relate to you a custom of this country. You must know that the religion of this country requires abundance of feasting and fasting, and each person has his particular saint, as well as each calling and occupation. To-morrow is to be celebrated, *le jour des rois*. The day before this feast it is customary to make a large paste pie, into which one bean is put. Each person at table cuts his slice, and the one who is so lucky as to obtain the bean, is dubbed king or queen. Accordingly, to-day, when I went in to dinner, I found one upon our table. Your cousin Abby began by taking the first slice; but alas! poor girl, no bean, and no queen. In the next place, your cousin John seconded her by taking a larger cut, and as cautious as cousin T——[5] when he inspects merchandise, bisected his paste with mathematical circumspection; but to him it pertained not. By this time, I was ready for my part; but first I declared that I had no cravings for royalty. I accordingly separated my piece with much firmness, nowise disappointed that it fell not to me. Your uncle, who was all this time picking his chicken bone, saw us divert ourselves without saying any thing; but presently he seized the remaining half, and to crumbs went the poor paste, cut here and slash there; when, behold the bean! "And thus," said he, "are kingdoms obtained;" but the servant, who stood by and saw the havoc, declared solemnly that he could not retain the title, as the laws decreed it to chance, and not to force.

How is General Warren's family? Well, I hope, or I should have heard of it. I am sorry Mrs. Warren is so scrupulous about writing to me. I forwarded a long letter to her some time since. Where is Miss Nancy Quincy? Well, I hope. We often laugh at your cousin John about her. He says her stature would be a great recommendation to him, as he is determined never to marry a tall woman, lest her height should give her a superiority over him.[6] He is generally thought older than your cousin Abby; and partly, I believe, because his company is with those much older than himself.

As to the Germantown family, my soul is grieved for them. Many are the afflictions of the righteous.[7] Would to Heaven that the clouds would disperse, and give them a brighter day. My best respects to them. Let Mrs. Field know, that Esther is quite recovered, and as gay as a lark. She went to Paris the other day with Pauline, to see a play, which is called "Figaro."[8] It is a piece much celebrated, and has had sixty-eight representations; and every thing was so new to her, that Pauline says, "Est is crazed."

Affectionately yours,   A.A.

MS not found. Printed from AA, *Letters*, ed., CFA, 1840, p. 275–278.

[1] The supplied date is derived from AA's statement, below, that "to-morrow is to be celebrated, *le jour des rois*" or ephiphany, the 6th of January. The current location of the recipient's copy, which was privately owned earlier in this century, is unknown. The dateline probably read "Jany 4," with a superscript "y" that was misread as a "2." The "4," which is validated in several auction catalogues (Adams Papers Editorial Files), is probably AA's error. It may, however, be the correct date, because the arrival of the letters from America and AA2's and JQA's evening at the theater may have occurred on 3 Jan. (see AA to Mary Cranch, 7 Jan., below; JQA, *Diary*, 1:214, note 1 to the first entry for 4 Jan.; AA2, *Jour. and Corr.*, 1:39–40).

[2] The letter is that of 5 Sept. 1784, above.

[3] Not found.

[4] This may be AA to Mercy Warren, 5 Sept. 1784, above, completed only on 12 Dec.; this is the only extant AA letter of the period in JQA's hand.

[5] Probably JA's cousin, the merchant Thomas Boylston.

[6] Ann (Nancy) Quincy was nearly four years JQA's senior. When she married the Rev. Asa Packard of Marlborough, Mass., in 1790, JQA wrote to AA: "thus you will perceive your *darling* project for the advancement of your Son blasted even before the bud. Indeed Madam I hope you will not think the worse of your Son, if he assures you that he never will be indebted to his wife for his property" (14 Aug. 1790, Adams Papers). AA replied on 20 Aug.: "I approve your spirit, I should be ashamed to own him for a son who could be so devoted to avarice as to marry a woman for her fortune. . . . I always loved Nancy Quincy from a native good humour and honesty of heart which she appeared to possess, but I never was in earnest in ralying [railying?] you about it" (Adams Papers).

[7] Psalms 34:19.

[8] Beaumarchais' *Le mariage de Figaro* received its first public performance at the Théâtre Français in April 1784, after strong royal opposition to its production. JQA, and

probably other Adamses, had seen it on 3 September. The play's potentially revolutionary theme, centering on the triumph of clever and virtuous servants over their slow-witted and venal aristocratic masters, made it an instant sensation in Paris, and soon thereafter throughout much of Europe, especially after Mozart and Da Ponte transformed it into an Italian *opera buffa* in 1786. See Hoefer, *Nouv. biog. générale*; JQA, *Diary*, 1:210, 233–234.

Abigail Adams to Mary Smith Cranch

No. 5.

My Dear Sister   Auteuil Janry 7 1785

Your kind Letter of November 6, I received the 4 of Jan'ry. I hope you have received my September Letters which were so unfortunate as to be put on Board a vessel which Mr. Tracy thought would convey them sooner than Lyde, but which I find had not reach'd you when you wrote me; by Mr. Jackson who left Paris in December I wrote 12 Letters[1] which were to be put on Board Captain Young, one of the packets addresst to Mr. Cranch, in which was a peice of sattin for you; and Some Money which I requested you to dispose of, I desired Captain Young by a card, which I wrote to him; to put that into his trunk and to deliver it himself: which I hope he has done. Mr. John Appleton has ben here for 3 weeks, and I expect him with other Company to dine with us to day: he will go on twesday to London[2] and I am very desirious of getting my letters ready to send by him.

I wrote you so lately that I have nothing material to entertain you with: even the common topick of conversation, the Weather, were I to discribe it as I find it, would rather Serve to make you gloomy than Cheerful, yet the present Beautifull Sunshine which invigorates my Heart, almost tempts me to pass over, the last ten days of fog and clouds and rain, and the ten which will probabily succeed according to the custom of the present Winter, this one Days clear Sky. I think I had rather feel our severe frosts, and see our hills and Feilds glittering and sparkling with Snow; in the clear Sun beams; and the delightfull azure which paints our Sky; than this more temperate climate; which has so much more Shade than light. The parisians have certainly a better excuse for continually seeking amusements; than our Country will be ever able to produce. The suicide which is so frequent in London I have heard attributed to the everlasting fogs of that Island. There is no object in nature so exhilarating to the Spirits, or so invigorating to the animal as well as the Natural World, as that Glorious Luminary which was worshiped by the Heathens as a deity, and is truly one of the most magnificent productions of the Great architect.

I am sorry to find that there is such a prodigious Dearth of Clerical Genius in our Country as to tempt, one church to rob an other. I have no personal acquaintance with the Gentleman who is called to set in the seat of the late Dr. Cooper, to supply his place will be no easy matter. There are some stars which shine best in their own Hemisphere, and I rather think from the Character I have heard of that Gentleman, that his wisest course would be to imitate those stars which are fixed.[3] The Church over which our dear parent so happily presided, have my good wishes for their prosperity, and I feel an affection towards them, not for having my birth amongst them but because they are the Sheep of a Shepherd who was every way dear to me.

With those Letters which went by Captain Young was one to Mr. Cranch; from the Dutch Merchants; which they enclosed to Mr. Adams with bitter complaints; that they had not received any letters from Mr. Cranch for a long time: they had received remittances; but they know not the state of their affairs: what goods remained unsold, nor what best suited the American Market. Mr. Cranch will look into these matters and satisfy them; as soon as possible.[4] There is such a crumbling to pieces of the merchants every where, that I suppose they feel allarmed. Unless the price of goods rise with you, they that have the least to do with trade are the best off. I should think myself very well off to purchase goods here as I could in America. Every article which goes into Paris pays a heavy Duty. From thence I am obliged to supply myself. In the Seaports and the manufacturing towns I suppose they are more reasonable. The few articles I left at home, I am very glad I did not part with.

Mr. Adams desires to be rememberd both, to Mr. Cranch and the rest of the family. Continue to write to me by every opportunity, and believe me most tenderly and affectionately Your Sister

Abigail Adams

RC (MWA:Abigail Adams Corr.); addressed in JQA's hand: "Mrs. Mary Cranch Braintree near Boston Massachusetts."

1 Six Adams letters carried by Jonathan Jackson to London, dated from 3 to 14 Dec., appear above; three were by AA. All other extant Adams letters of December sent from France were by JA, except JQA to Charles Storer, 16 Dec. (Adams Papers).

2 John Appleton did not leave Paris on Tuesday, 11 Jan., but on 19 Jan. (JQA, *Diary*, 1:216), giving AA until that date to complete her letters to America.

3 On Rev. Peter Thacher, see Mary Cranch to AA, 6 Nov. 1784, note 5, above.

4 JA's letter to Cranch of 13 Dec., which forwarded the van Heukeloms' letter has not

been found; but see Messrs. van Heukelom to JA, 27 Oct. (Adams Papers), JA's reply of 11 Dec. (LbC, Adams Papers), Richard Cranch to JA, 3 June 1785, below, and Mary Cranch to AA, 19 July, note 14, also below.

Abigail Adams to Elizabeth Smith Shaw

My Dear Sister   Auteuil January 11 1785

I was doubly rejoiced to receive a Letter from you[1] not only on account of the pleasure which I usually enjoy from your pen: but because it informd me of your recovery from a dangerous illness. In a Letter which I wrote you the latter part of December,[2] I have given you a long lesson respecting your Health: which altho it might savor something of the Quack, and a little of the Authority of Eldership, Spoke not my Heart, if it manifested not the tender solicitude of a Sister anxious for the Health of one deservedly Dear to her. I must therefore repeat to you; not to encumber your family beyond your Strength. A life of ease, and gentle excercise, is absolutely requisite for you: a tranquil State of mind, which has much to hope and nothing to fear. A different Situation would remove you, much sooner than Your Friends wish, to a state greatly Superiour to that which you now possess. I own myself so selfish that tho I doubt not of your qualifications for it, I hope to see you remain many years subject to the incident infirmities of Mortality, and like your fellow Mortals grow Grey and wrinkled here, before you Bloom afresh in the regions of immortality. I am not a little rejoiced that my Letters proved so benificial to you as you describe, and that I was capable of serving you, tho so far removed from you. A sudden exhilaration of the spirits, has proved of vast service in many disorders. I have experienced the benifit myself. Your family narrative afforded me pleasure because it related those calamities which were happily past, and displayd a more pleasing picture.

I am rejoiced to find that my Sons have been bless'd with so large a share of health since my absence, if they are wise they will improve the rigor of their early Days, and the Bloom of their Health in acquiring such a fund of learning, and knowledge, as may render them usefull to themselves, and benificial to Society, the great purpose for which they were sent into the World. That knowledge which is obtain in early Life becomes every day more usefull, as it is commonly that which is best retaind. To be Good, and do Good, is the whole Duty of Man, comprized in a few words; but what a capacious Field does it open to our view? And how many Characters

55

may grow from this root, whose usefull branches may shade the oppressd; May comfort the dejected: may heal the wounded: may cure the sick, may defend the invaded; may enrich the poor. In short those who possess the disposition will never want employment.

How justly did you describe my Ideas; when you said "a parents thoughts flew quick."[3] Mine, I own, had outstriped that passage; I would not, that a son of mine, should form any sentiments with respect to any female, but those of due decorum, and a general complasance, which every Youth acquainted with good manners, and civility will practise towards them, untill years have matured their judgment, and learning has made them wise. I would; that they should have no passion but for Science, and no mistress but Literature: "so shall discretion preserve them and understanding keep them. If they incline their ears to wisdom and apply their Hearts to understanding."[4]

The age of the Young Lady relieved me from some anxiety, especially as I have since heard that she has much older admirers.[5] Charles's disposition, and sensibility will render him more liable to female attachments, than the Young Hercules who sits beside me, and who like many other Youths pretends to brave the danger which has never assaild him; but who in time, like that Hero, may find an Omphalia to bring him to the distaff, but who, at present is much better occupied with his Horace and Tacitus.[6]

I thank you for all your kind Maternal care towards my sons. I hope they will be both sensible of it; and gratefull for it, and that both their uncles and your advice to them will not fail to have a due influence upon their conduct.

I suppose every Letter I write; you will expect that I should give you some account of the amusements I have; and the curiosities I see; there are enough of each in Paris to employ my pen. But of the amusements, the theaters are those only which have yet occupied me; the description of which I must reserve for my Young correspondents.[7] As there are a variety of cuorisities I shall endeavour to adapt the account of them to the different tastes of my Friends; I am going this afternoon to visit the Enfans trouvés, which at my return I will recount to you because I know your Benevolence will lead you to rejoice in an institution calculated to save from Death and wretchedness, those helpless Indigent Beings brought into existance by criminality; and owned by no one.

I have returned from my visit to the Hopital des enfans-Trouves, and truly it is a painfull pleasing sight. This House was built in the

Reign of Louis 14th. in the year 1747.[8] It was built by a decree of the king and is under the direction of Eight administrators, and is Superintended by Nuns, or charity sisters as they are call'd. We were shewn into a Room Large and airy which contain about a hundred cribs, cradles they call them, but they are more properly cribs, as they are fixd all round the room and are not moveable. Through the middle of the appartment are two more rows the length of the Room, which was I am almost tempted to say the cleanest I have seen in France. Every bed was white linnen, and every child in them appeard neat, and with cloathing that lookd comfortable. I observed too; the large quantitys of necessary linnen which hung at fires in the different rooms, which like every thing else which I saw here; was very white and clean. The rooms too were sweet, which was an other proof of the attention of the Nurses. There were numbers in the Arms; great numbers a sleep; and several crying, which you will easily credit, when I tell you; that this is but the Eleventh day of the Month, and the Charity sister who appeard an intellegent well bred woman informd us; that two hundred had been brought in since the year commenced. Whilst I stood talking with her there was one brought in which appeard to be 3 months old. They generally receive at this House Six thousand a year, (there is an other House of the same kind.) Last year she told us that five thousand five hundred were lodged there, and that House had sent into the provinces 15 thousand which were now at nurse: they keep them out untill they are 5 years old. Children are received here at any hour of the Day, or Night, in the day they are brought in at the door, and in the Night the Nuns watch to receive them. There are certain parts of Paris which are appropriated to this purpose, and small Boxes which may be drawn out from under a cover; in which the child is deposited, and the person who finds it Carries it to this House; where they are received without any further form or declaration from the Commissary of the quarter than naming the place the Day and Hour when the child was found. The person is not obliged to relate any other circumstance. They have always four wet nurses in each appartment for the youngest and weakest of the children: but as fast as they can provide accommodations for them in the Country, they are sent there: where the Air is purer and better than in Paris. The Governess told us that about a third of them died, notwithstanding all their care and attention, that they were sometimes so chill'd with the cold; and so poorly clad that they could not bring them to any warmth, or even make them swallow.

"Where can they hope for pity, peace or rest
Who move no softness in a parents Breast."

The Hôpital de la pitié which joins upon this is the place where they are received when they return from the Country. There they are taught to read and write, the Boys to knit, and the Girls to sew and make lace. When they have made their first communion which is from 10 to 12 years of age they are put to trades. They have a church which belongs to the Hospitals, but I had not time to see it. Whilst we approve the Charatable disposition, and applaud the wise institution which alleviates the fate of helpless innocence; can we draw a veil over the Guilty Cause, or refrain from comparing a Country grown old in Debauchery and lewdeness with the wise Laws and institutions of one wherein Mariage is considerd as holy and honourable, wherein industry and sobriety; enables parents to rear a numerous ofspring, and where the Laws provide a resource for illegitimecy by obliging the parents to a maintenance; and if not to be obtaind there, they become the charge of the town or parish where they are born: but how few the instances of their being totally abandoned by their parents? Whereas I have been credibly informd that one half the Children anually born in that immense City of Paris, are enfans trouvés.

Present my Regards to Mr. Shaw, to whom I will write if I have time. Pray has Mr. Allen carried home his Lady yet?![9]

I believe Mr. Thaxter has forgotton that I was formerly a correspondent of his, but I design soon to remind him of it. I hear of his success with pleasure; you will not fail to remember me to your Venerable Neighbour at the foot of the Hill, and all her Worthy family. I feel for the sore calimity of Mrs. White: by how many instances are we taught, not to place our affections too firmly upon earthly objects. How doatingly fond was this good Lady of her children, and she had reason to be fond, for they were both amiable and good. To Judge Sergant and family present my Regards. Honest, Modest Mr. Flint shall not be forgotten by me. The air of Haverhill Hill is too keen for him, he should live below it. Mr. Adams by me, presents his affectionate Regards to Mr. Shaw and my worthy Sister, to whom I tender the compliments of the New Year. May this and many succeeding ones find her happy is the ardent wish of her affectionate Sister

Abigail Adams

Will my sister accept a peice of sattin for a peticoat, which if I can smuggle into England in the form of a large Letter; will I hope go safe to her hand. There is a trunk of Cloaths sent from the Hague for the Children[10] which you will be so good as to let me know when they arrive. Whatever is out grown you will dispose of as you think best and if there is any thing which will serve Mrs. West, who prehaps may be more needy than some others, you will be so good as to give them to her but dont mention my name, as they are all at your disposal.

RC (DLC:Shaw Family Papers).

[1] That of [*ca. 15*] Oct. 1784, above.

[2] 14 Dec. 1784, above.

[3] AA rephrases Elizabeth Shaw's speculation, in her [*ca. 15*] Oct. letter, that AA would be concerned that CA might take a premature interest in Nancy Hazen, who had come to live with the Shaws, and to whom AA refers in the next paragraph.

[4] Proverbs 2:11 and 2:2.

[5] The source of AA's information is not known to the editors, but Elizabeth Shaw mentions one of Nancy Hazen's admirers, a William Osgood, in her letter of 30 Jan., to Mary Cranch (DLC:Shaw Family Papers).

[6] In Greek mythology, Omphale was a Lydian queen who bought Hercules' labor for a year. Alexandrian poets and Ovid, in his *Heroides*, portray Hercules performing domestic chores, and Omphale bearing Hercules a son. *Oxford Classical Dictionary*.

[7] See AA to Elizabeth Cranch, 3 Jan., above.

[8] AA2, in her description of this institution (under 12 Jan.) helps to explain AA's chronological error: "Louis 14th, by a declaration of an order of his council, authorized the establishment of this hospital, ... This house was built in the year 1747" (*Jour. and Corr.*, 1:41).

[9] Rev. Jonathan Allen of Bradford, Mass., would marry Elizabeth Kent of Charlestown, AA's first cousin, on 11 Dec. 1785 (JQA, *Diary*, 1:369, note 1).

[10] See the inventory of JQA's clothing and books, 6 Nov. 1784, Adams Papers.

Mary Smith Cranch to Abigail Adams

My Dear Sister   Braintree Janry 16th 1785

Not one line from my dear Sister have I reciev'd sinc last September. What can be the reason? I hope the letters we have written to you are all come safe to your Hands and that you have had no great expence in geting them. We have done all we could to prevent it. John Cranch tells us of a large Pacquit coming from the Hague by the English Ambassador which Mr. Elworthy sent to you. I hope one of them was mine the first I sent you.[1] It was directed to be sent to London but Uncle Smith thought you would be at the Hague and sent it to Holland.

I long to know what you have been doing since you wrote last. What you have seen and whether you can speak French glibly. Where Cousin Nabby is, whether in a Nunnery or not. If She is how She likes it. What success my dear Brother meets with, and above all when you will come Home. Indeed my Sister Braintree is a dull place without you. I missd you Sadly in the Summer, but this Winter much more. Mr. Cranch keeps in Bostoon as usual, but he has mov'd his Lodgings to a Brother of the Mr. Fosters[2] where he was when you went away. He is now well accomidated with room enough. The People neat sensible and obliging. We have been blessed with Health, excepting little indispositions ⟨*now and then*⟩ some times. I have had more Rhumatick Pains this winter than I ever had in my life. Betsy has not had one of her Ill turns since you went away, I hope She has out grown them. I heard last week from Haverhill. They were all well. Sister Says you said you should send the children some stockings. Charles is in want of some. I have bought two pair for him. Your Mother Hall is well, desires I would give her Love to you all. Our Germantown Friends affairs are yet in a bad way, and Cousin Jo[3] is again shut up in Boston. He open'd a shop in town. He had goods of Mr. Swan and others upon commission, but he could not do business enough to pay his rent and support his Family and make payments as they expected. Mr. Swan more careful than the others Siez'd every thing he had in his Shop which oblig'd him to Shut up. I pity them from my Heart. What can they do next. The House is strip'd of almost all the furniture. You may remember a consignment of about four Hundred pound Sterling that Mr. Bond Who married Hannah Cranch sent him. I fear he will lose the greatest part of it. He happen'd to come to Boston just as he shut up,[4] part of his goods were among those that Mr. Swan took. Most of them were Sold and the Money Spent. He has got part of the Firniture made over to him. Their distresses are very great and will be greater I fear.

Mr. Bond is a little sprilly kind good natur'd sensible Man. They hop'd to have seen you in the West.[5] You would be diverted to hear him give an account of the Preparations that were made to recieve you. Their Houses were all set in order, and new cloaths purchased to waite upon your Ladyship in. John Cranch had his Hair dress'd and Powder'd a thing which was never done but twice before in his life. A new Hat was procur'd and a pair of Buckels were put into his shoes which had not been fastend with any thing but shoe strings for Seven years before. John Palmer had a new coat &c. and was greatly concern'd least the Lane leading to his House should not be wide enough to admit your carriage to come up to the Door. But poor Creatures how you dissapointed them by landing at Dover. If you should go to England again you must if you can, make them a visit.

Mr. Thacher was installed on wednesday last, and on thursday evening he married Judge Quincy to Miss Gerrish.[6] I expect to see a pompous account of it in the news Paper. I was in Boston yesterday.

All our Freinds were well. Mrs. Otis and Mrs. Guild are in a very thriving State.[7] The Doctor and Aunt Tufts are well. Aunt has had her Health better than common this winter. Lucy[8] has been with her for above a month. You never saw such a fine winter as we have had thus far. We have had fine slaying for Six Weeks without any interuption. Snow enough and not a Bank to be Seen. You may turn out of the road better than in Summer.

Mr. Tyler had determin'd to carry all our Children to Haverhill this week in his sleigh but the court sets in Boston and will prevent him he thought, it would have been up. His business I think increases and as far as I can judge he attends it with steadiness. He has his share at this court. Billy is now at home and will write to cousin John if the vesel does not sail too soon for him. He is Studous and behaves well, is determin'd to study Law if he lives to come out of College, hopes for the Company of his Cousin next spring. Your Neighbours are all well, and desire to be remember'd to you. Mrs. Quincy sends her Love to you. Uncle Quincy has been confin'd to his chamber above two months with the Rhumatism in his Hip and Leg. He is better but not down Stairs yet. I frequently visit him. He sends his Love too, and indeed I do not know Who does not, so pray excuse me for the future from particularizing. I am out of all patience with my Letters. They are all narritive, do not expose me to any body. Pray find some way to let me hear[9] from you oftner. Rem[ember] me kindly to Mr. Adams and my Cousins and believe [me at all?] times your affectionate Sister.

RC (Adams Papers); slight damage where the seal was cut away.

[1] Probably Mary Cranch to AA, 7 Aug. 1784, above; see Mary Cranch to AA, 3 Oct., postscript, and AA to Mary Cranch, 9 Dec., note 2, both above.

[2] Perhaps a brother of Joseph Foster, the State Street merchant who was a passenger with AA on the *Active* in June-July 1784 (see vol. 4:348, note 11; JA, *Diary and Autobiography*, 3:164; AA to Mary Cranch, 6 July 1784, above).

[3] Joseph Pearse Palmer.

[4] Comma supplied.

[5] That is, the West Country of England. The persons appearing in this paragraph lived in Devon, near the ports of Plymouth and Exeter. In July-Aug. 1787, AA, JA, and AA2 visited several Cranches and Palmers in this area, including Joseph Cranch of Axminster, nephew of Richard Cranch, and John Palmer of Horsham, nephew of Gen. Joseph Palmer. See JA, *Diary and Autobiography*, 3:203-210; AA2, *Jour. and Corr.*, 1:85-89; and particularly AA to Elizabeth Cranch, 1 Oct. 1787 (Adams Papers), which describes John Cranch's dress and manners, and the impossibility of reaching John Palmer's farmhouse by coach.

[6] Edmund Quincy IV, then age 81, married Anna Gerrish, who was in her sixties, on 13 Jan. 1785. The *Boston Gazette* of 17 Jan. carried an account of Rev. Peter Thacher's installation at the Brattle Square Church, and a brief notice of the Quincy-Gerrish wedding.

[7] Both women, AA's cousins, were pregnant. Elizabeth Quincy Guild gave birth to Benjamin Guild Jr. on 8 May 1785.

[8] Lucy Cranch.

[9] Mary Cranch wrote the text after "hear" in the left margin.

Abigail Adams to John Shaw

Auteuil Janry. 18 1785

I find Sir, what I never doubted; that you are a Gentleman of your word: I thank you for the agreeable proof which you have given me of it,[1] and that I may not be wanting in punctuality I have taken my pen[2] to discharge the debt which I acknowledge is due to you. Amongst the publick Edifices which are worthy of notice in this Country are several Churches. I went a few days Since to see three of the most Celebrated in Paris.[3] They are prodigious Massess of Stone Buildings, and so surrounded by Houses which are seven story high that the Sun seldom enlightens them. I found them so cold and damp that I could only give them a very hasty and trancient Survey. The Architecture, the Sculpture, the paintings are Beautifull indeed, and each of them would employ my pen for several pages, when the Weather will permit me to take a more accurate and critical inspection of them. These Churches are open every day, and at all times of the Day, so that you never enter them without finding preists upon their knees, half a dozen at a time, and more at the Hours of confession. All kinds of people and all ages, go in without Ceremony, and regardless of each other, fall upon their knees, cross themselves say their pater nosters, and ave Marias, silently and go out again without being noticed, or even seen by the priests whom I found always kneeling with their faces towards the Alter. Round these churches (for they have not pews and Galleries as with us; Chairs alone being made use of) there are little Boxes, or closets, about as large as a Centry Box, in which is a small grated window, which communicates with an other closet of the same kind. One of them holds the person who is confessing, and the other the confessor, who places his ear at this window, hears the crime, absolves the transgressor,[4] and very often makes an assignation for a repetition of the Same Crime, or prehaps a new one. I do not think this a breach of Charity, for can we suppose that of the many thousands whom the Religion of the Country obliges to Celibacy, one quarter part of the number can find its influence sufficently powerfull; to conquer those passions, which nature has implanted in Man, when the gratification of them will cost them only a few livres in confessions. The Priest who is known to betray his trust, or devulge any thing committed to him in confession; is punished with Death.[5]

I was at the Church St. Rock[6] about ten oclock in the morning, and whilst I was there, about three hundred little Boys came in from some Charity Seminary which belongs to that Church; they had Books in their Hands. They followed in each other in regular order, and fell upon their knees in rows like Soldiers in rank and file. Their might be 50 other persons in the Church at their devotion. Every thing was still and Solemn throughout this vast edifice. I was walking with a slow pace round it, when all at once, the drear Silence which Reignd was suddenly broken by all these Boys at one instant Chanting; with loud voices which made the dome ring; and me spring, for I had no apprehension of any Sound. I have never been to any of these Churches upon a Sunday, when the weather is warmer I design it, but their Churches seem rather calculated to damp Devotion than excite it. I took such a cold there; as I have not had since I have been in France before. I have been several times to the Chaple of the Dutch Ambassador; and should go oftner, if I could comprehend the discourses which are all in French. I believe the American embassy is the only one to which Chaplings are not allowed. Do Congress think that their Ministers have no need of Grace? Or that Religion is not a necessary article for them. Sunday will not feel so to me, whilst I continue in this Country. It is High Hollyday for all France.

We had a visit the other day from no less a personage than Abbe Thayer in his Habit, who has become a convert.[7] His visit I suppose was to me, for he was a perfect stranger to Mr. Adams. He told us that he had spent a year at Rome, that he belonged to a Seminary of St. Sulpice in Paris; that he never knew what Religion was untill his conversion, and that he designd to return to America in a year or two, to see if he could not convert his Friends and acquaintance. After talking sometime in this Stile he began to question Mr. A. if he believed the Bible, and to rail at Luther and Calvin, upon which Mr. A took him up pretty short, and told him that he was not going to make a Father confessor of him, that his Religion was a matter that he did not look upon him self accountable for, to any one but his Maker, and that he did not chuse to hear either Luther, or Calvin treated in such a manner.

Mr. Abbe took his leave after some time, without any invitation to repeat his visit.

With respect to our interest at Medford what ever is necessary to be done[8] for our mutual benifit, you will be so good as to direct performd. I am glad that the old Tennant did not go off, untill death removed him.[9] The account you give of your Nephews is vastly pleasing to their, and Your affectionate Friend.[10]   A Adams

RC (DNDAR); addressed in JQA's hand: "The Revd. John Shaw Haverhill Massachusetts"; endorsed: "Jan 18th 1785." Dft (Adams Papers), originally identified as written to Cotton Tufts, dated [1784], and filmed under that date (Adams Papers, Microfilms, Reel No. 363).

[1] John Shaw to AA, 15 Oct. 1784, above.

[2] At this point the draft completes this sentence: "without any previous preparation of Subject to entertain you with."

[3] The draft sentence begins: "I went last week," and AA2 records visiting Notre Dame and St. Sulpice with her parents on 12 Jan. (*Jour. and Corr.*, 1:41). The third church was St. Roch.

[4] The rest of this sentence is not in the draft. The text from "I do not think" to "a few livres in confessions" is written at the end of the draft, with no indication that it was to be inserted at any point. In place of the last sentence in this paragraph, the draft has "From hence come ⟨those⟩ many of those foresaken beings call'd enfans trouves which I have described in my Letter to Mrs. Shaw" (AA to Elizabeth Shaw, 11 Jan., above).

[5] This sentence is omitted from AA, *Letters*, ed. CFA.

[6] St. Roch, on the Rue Saint Honoré, a little north of the Tuileries Gardens, was built in the 1650s, with alterations to 1740 (Larousse, *Grand dictionnaire universel*).

[7] John Thayer, born in Boston in 1758 and related to the Thayers of Braintree, preached as a Congregationalist in Boston during the War for Independence. In 1781 he traveled to France, where he offered to become Benjamin Franklin's personal chaplain. Franklin declined. In 1783 Thayer converted to Roman Catholicism. He completed his theological studies at the Séminaire de St. Sulpice in 1787, was ordained, and in 1790 returned to America, where he proselytized for over a decade, from Massachusetts to Kentucky. He spent his last years in Limerick, Ireland, where he recruited young clerics to go to New England (*DAB*).

[8] At this point the draft adds: "by way of repairs." The Medford interest was the farm left by Rev. William Smith to AA and Elizabeth Shaw. John Shaw had reported the death of tenant Benjamin Teel (or Teal) in his letter of 15 Oct. 1784, above.

[9] At this point the draft adds: "tho we may meet with some Difficulty in getting the Rent."

[10] In place of this sentence the draft has: "I hope you will continue from time to time to write to [your] affectionate Friend and sister." This paragraph is omitted from AA, *Letters*, ed. CFA.

Abigail Adams to Hannah Quincy Lincoln Storer

MY DEAR MADAM,   Auteuil, 20 January, 1785

For your kind congratulations upon my arrival in Europe,[1] receive my thanks. Those only, who have crossed the ocean, can realize the pleasure which is felt at the sight of land. The inexperienced traveller is more sensible of this, than those who frequently traverse the ocean. I could scarcely realize that thirty days had removed me so far distant from my native shore; but the new objects which surrounded me did not efface from my remembrance the dearer ones which I left behind me. "And is this the country, and are these the people, who so lately waged a cruel war against us?" were reflections, which did not escape me amidst all the beauty and grandeur, which presented themselves to my eyes. You have doubtless heard from my friends, that I was pleased with England, and that I met with much civility and politeness there, and a large share of it from your connexions.[2]

I am now resident in a country, to which many Americans give the preference. The climate is said to be more temperate and mild. I can pass no judgment by comparison, but that there are more fogs in both, than are agreeable to me. A North-American, however, has no right to complain of the rigor of a climate, which, in the middle of January, is as mild as our May; though I think the fall of the year was near as cold as ours.[3]

Do you know, my dear Madam, what a task you have set me? a description of ladies!

"Catch, ere she change, the Cynthia of this minute."

To a lady of Mrs. Storer's discernment, the mere superficial adorning of the sex would afford but little satisfaction. Yet this is all I shall be able to recount to her. A stranger in the country, not only to the people but to the language, I cannot judge of mental accomplishment, unless you will allow that dress and appearance are the index of the mind. The etiquette of this country requires the first visit from the stranger. You will easily suppose, that I have not been very fond of so awkward a situation as going to visit ladies, merely to make my dumb compliments, and receive them in return. I have declined visiting several personages, to whom Mr. Adams would have introduced me, upon this account. An acquaintance with a gentleman by no means insures to you a knowledge of his lady; for no one will be so ill-bred as to suppose an intercourse between them. It is from my observations of the French ladies at the theatres and public walks, that my chief knowledge of them is derived.

The dress of the French ladies is, like their manners, light, airy, and genteel. They are easy in their deportment, eloquent in their speech, their voices soft and musical, and their attitude pleasing. Habituated to frequent the theatres from their earliest age, they become perfect mistresses of the art of insinuation and the powers of persuasion. Intelligence is communicated to every feature of the face, and to every limb of the body; so that it may with truth by said, every man of this nation is an actor, and every woman an actress. It is not only among the rich and polite, who attend the great theatres, that this art is acquired, but there are a dozen small theatres, to which all classes resort. There are frequently given pieces at the opera, and at the small theatres, where the actors speak not a single word, but where the action alone will delineate to you the story. I was at one of this kind last evening. The story is too long to relate here; but there was a terrible sea-storm in it; the rolling of the sea, the mounting of the vessel upon the waves, in which I could discern a lady and little child in the utmost distress, the terrible claps of thunder and flashes of lightning, which flew from one side of the stage to the other, really worked me up to such a pitch, that I trembled with terror. The vessel was finally dashed upon the rocks, and the lady and child were cast on a desert island.

The dancing on the stage is a great amusement to me, and the dresses are beautifully fanciful. The fashionable shape of the ladies here is, to be very small at the bottom of the waist, and very large round the shoulders,—a wasp's,—pardon me, ladies, that I should make such a comparison, it is only in shape, that I mean to resemble you to them. You and I, Madam, must despair of being in the mode.

I enclose to you the pattern of a stomacher, cape, and forebody of a gown; different petticoats are much worn, and then the stomacher must be of the petticoat color, and the cape of the gown, as well as the sleeves. Sometimes a false sleeve is made use of to draw over the other, and, in that case, the cape is like the gown. Gowns and petticoats are worn without any trimming of any kind. That is reserved for full dress only, when very large hoops and negligees, with trains three yards long, are worn. But these are not used, except at Court, and then only upon public occasions; the Queen herself, and the ladies of honor, dressing very plain upon other days. Abby has made you a miniature handkerchief, just to show you one mode; but caps, hats, and handkerchiefs are as various as ladies' and milliners' fancies can devise.[4]

Thus Madam, having displayed the mode to you, be so good as to present Mr. Adams's and my regards to Mr. Storer, and, in one word, to all who inquire after your affectionate friend,   A. Adams

RC not found. Printed from AA, *Letters*, ed. CFA, 1840, p. 271–275. Dft (Adams Papers); dated [*ca. 15 January*]. The Dft is incomplete and about one third shorter than the printed text, which must have been based on the RC or a copy made from it. Two cases of material in the Dft that is not in the printed text are noted below.

[1] Not found.

[2] Charles Storer and Elizabeth Storer Atkinson, two of Hannah Storer's stepchildren.

[3] In the draft, AA adds that the fall was said to be "not so pleasant as usual." She also wrote that in "the middle of Janry the grass is as green as it commonly is in May with us," and reported just one snowfall "which might be 6 inches deep," probably from the snowstorm of 12 December, mentioned in her letter of 9 Dec. 1784 to Mary Cranch, above.

[4] In her draft AA added: "No such thing as a quilted peticoat to bee seen and Scarcly an Apron of any form or fashion."

Abigail Adams to Mary Smith Cranch

No. 6.

My Dear Sister   Auteuil February 20. 1785

Your last favour which was dated in December came to hand in Febry.[1] If Capt. Young has arrived safe, my Friends will find a sufficent number of Letters there, to convince them that I have been mindfull of them. It was no fault of mine that Capt. Young was detaind Months after I hoped that he was in America. Concequently my Letters must lose a large part of their value by being of an old date, for they are not of a quality to grow better for age. Yet they spoke not my heart if they bear not strong traits of that which time can neither injure; or impair.[2]

This Day 8 Months I sailed for Europe since which many new and interesting Scenes have presented them selves before me. I have seen many of the Beauties and some of the Deformities of this old World. I have been more than ever convinced that there is no Sumit of virtue, and no Depth of vice which Humane Nature is not Capable of riseing to, on the one hand, or sinking into on the other. I have felt the force of an observation which I have read, that "daily example is the most subtle of poisons." I have found my taste reconciling itself to habits customs and fashions, which at first disgusted me. The first dance which I saw upon the Stage shoked me, the Dress'es and Beauty of the performers was enchanting, but no sooner did the Dance commence, than I felt my delicacy wounded, and I was ashamed to bee seen to look at them. Girls cloathd in the thinest Silk: and Gauze, with their peticoats short Springing two foot from the floor poising themselves in the air, with their feet flying, and as perfectly shewing their Garters and draws, as tho no peticoat had been worn, was a sight altogether new to me. Their motions are as light as air and as quick as lightning. They balance themselves to astonishment. No description can equal the reality. They are daily trained to it from early infancy, at a Royal academy instituted for this purpose.[3] You will very often see little creatures not more than 7 or 8 years old as undauntedly performing their parts as the eldest amongst them. Shall I speak a Truth and say that repeatedly seeing these Dances has worn of that disgust which I first felt, and that I see them now with pleasure. Yet when I consider the tendency of these things, the passions they must excite, and the known Character, even to a proverb, which is attached to an opera Girl, my abhorrence is not

3. MADAME LAFAYETTE, ABOUT 1774
See page viii

4. THE LAFAYETTE CHILDREN WITH A BUST OF
THEIR FATHER, ABOUT 1786
See page viii

lessned, and neither my Reason or judgment have accompanied my Sensibility in acquiring any degree of callousness. The art of dancing is carried to the highest degree of perfection that it is capable of; at the opera. The House is neither so grand, or Beautifull architecture as the French Theater, but it is more frequented by the Beau Mond, who had rather be amused than instructed. The Scenary is more various, and more highly decorated, the dresses more costly and rich. And O! the Musick vocal and instrumental, it has a soft persuasive power and a dying dying[4] Sound. Conceive a highly decorated building filled with Youth, Beauty, Grace, ease, clad in all the most pleasing and various ornaments of Dress which fancy can form; these objects Singing like Cherubs to the best tuned instruments most skilfully handled, the softest tenderest Strains, every attitude corresponding with the musick, full of the God or Goddess whom they celebrate, the female voices accompanied by an equal number of Adonises. Think you that this city can fail of becoming a Cytherea[5] and this House the temple of Venus?

"Where Musick Softnes, and where dancing fires"[6]

it requires the immortal Shield of the invincible Minerva to skreen youth from ⟨*being wounded by*⟩ the arrows which assail them upon every side.[7] How many of them resemble the Simple youth which Solomon describes as void of understanding, and when he drew the picture of his H[ear]t he drew the portrait of a Par[isia]n. She Caught him says the wise king, and kissed him with an impudent face.[8] How often have I seen this upon the Stage?

As soon as a Girl sets her foot upon the floor of the opera, she is excommunicated by the Church and denied Burial in holy ground; she conceives nothing worse can happen to her, all restraint is thrown off and she delivers herself to the first who bids high enough for her. But let me turn from a picture of which the outlines are but just sketchd. I would willingly veil the rest as it can only tend to excite sentiments of Horrour.

March 13. 1785

You will see by the former date that my Letter has lain by me some time. Mr. Pickman of Salem who is going to London has promised to take this with him, and will carry it himself if no opportunity offers before to America. We are all well, some prepairing for America,[9] and others longing for the time of their departure there. What a sad misfortune it is to have the Body in one place and the Soul in an other. Indeed my dear sister I hope to come home the Spring after the present. My acquaintance here is not large nor ever will be. Then what are dinners and visits of ceremony, "compared with the Feast of Reason and the flow of Soul."[10]

I have dined twice at the Marquiss Fayette with a large company[11] some of whom I was acquainted with, and others that I never saw before, and tomorrow are to dine here Mr. Brantsen the Ambassador extrodonary from Holland[12] the Chevlr. Luzern late minister in America Marquiss de la Fayette and Lady, Mr. W. T. Franklin late Secretary to the American commission, Col. Humphries our present Secretary, and Mr. Williamos[13] a worthy clever gentleman who has been very Friendly to us. Mr. Jonathan Williams[14] a Bostonian who very often comes to have a social talk about all our old Friends and acquaintance in Boston, the Chevlr. Jones,[15] Mr. Bingham and Lady, a Mr. and Mrs. Rooker[16] and Mrs. Rookers sister lately from New York. Strangers to me, but all strangers from every part of America visit the American Ministers, and then are invited to dine with them. The Duke de la Vauguyon was invited also, but not hearing from him suppose him not in Paris, at present. He was late minister from this Court to Holland. Madam la Marquise F. is a very agreeable Lady, and has two very pretty children. The 3[d,] Virgina I have never seen, it is in the Country. The Eldest daughter is 7 years old and Gorge Washington about 5. After dinner miss and master are always introduced to the company, both of them Speak English, and behave very pretty.[17] Madam Fayette has promised to bring me acquainted with her Mother the Dutchess de Noailes who is now at Versailles waiting for the Birth of a prince or princess which is daily expected,[18] and as she is one of the Ladies of Honour to the Queen her attendance is indispensable.

I find by a late Letter from Charles Storer[19] that Mrs. Atkinsons going to America will be defered for some time as she daily expects to be confined, and she will not let him come away tho we have constantly expected him for months untill She gets to bed. Mrs. Hay and I correspond ⟨once in a while⟩ some times. I had a letter from her a few days since when she was well.[20] She is at a place calld Beaugency.[21] I have Scarcly room left to say that I am Your affectionate sister   A.A

RC (MWA:Abigail Adams Corr.).

[1] Mary Cranch's letter of 6 Dec. 1784, above, probably arrived on 6 Feb. (JQA, Diary, 1:220).

[2] The opening paragraph is omitted from AA, *Letters*, ed. CFA.

[3] The Académie Royale de Musique et de

Danse, or Paris Opéra, gave performances of 17th- and 18th-century opera, primarily French, and of ballet, at the opera house built in 1781 near the Porte St. Martin, one of the northern gates of Louis XIV's wall around Paris (Rice, *Jefferson's Paris*, p. 44–45).

[4] Thus in MS.

[5] In Greek mythology this island off the south coast of Greece was the birthplace of Aphrodite (Venus).

[6] With slight modification this quotation is taken from Alexander Pope, "The Rape of the Lock," canto 1, line 76.

[7] The remainder of this paragraph is omitted from AA, *Letters*, ed. CFA.

[8] Proverbs 7:7, 13.

[9] That is, JQA.

[10] Alexander Pope, "The First Satire of the Second Book of Horace," line 128.

[11] These dinners were given on 21 Feb., and 7 March; for detailed accounts, see JQA, *Diary*, 1:225, 230; AA2, *Jour. and Corr.*, 1:49–50, 52–53.

[12] JA had known Gerard Brantsen, the Dutch minister plenipotentiary to France from late 1782, and ambassador extraordinary from 1783 to 1787, since April 1782 (*Diary and Autobiography*, 3:1, 14; and see JQA, *Diary*, 1:184).

[13] The Swiss-born Charles Williamos, who had traveled widely in America, was close to the Adamses and Jefferson in 1784–1785 (JQA, *Diary*, 1:232–233, note 1).

[14] Jonathan Williams Jr., Benjamin Frank-lin's great-nephew, acted as American agent in Nantes; JA had known him since 1778 (see JA, *Diary and Autobiography*, vol. 4; JA, *Papers*, vols. 6–8).

[15] "Jones" is smudged and nearly illegible; AA may have attempted to erase and write over a name here. Neither JQA nor AA2 mention John Paul Jones' presence at the Adamses on 14 March (JQA, *Diary*, 1:235; AA2, *Jour. and Corr.*, 1:56).

[16] Mr. and Mrs. John Rucker had visited the Adamses on 11 March; John Rucker was a partner in Robert Morris' New York commercial house (JQA, *Diary*, 1:233, and note 2).

[17] The three Lafayette children mentioned in this passage were Anastasie, the eldest, Georges Washington, and Marie Antoinette Virginie, still an infant, AA's "3[d,] Virginia I have never seen." See JQA, *Diary*, 1:225, note 1.

[18] This was to be Louis Charles, born on 27 March. He became the dauphin upon the death of his older brother, Louis Joseph, in June 1789. The royalists declared him to be Louis XVII upon the execution of his father in 1793. He apparently died in prison in 1795, but several pretenders advanced the tradition that he had escaped from France. Hoefer, *Nouv. biog. générale*.

[19] Probably Storer to JQA, 2 March (Adams Papers).

[20] Letter of 7 March, below.

[21] This paragraph, to this point, is omitted from AA, *Letters*, ed. CFA.

John Adams to Cotton Tufts

Dr Sir   Auteuil near Paris March 5. 1785

Last night I received yours of 1 Jan.[1] and immediately accepted the Bill for 50 £. St. payable in London. Whenever you draw upon me, you may draw payable in London, Amsterdam or Paris, as you shall find most beneficial. I accepted the Bill with Pleasure, as the purchases you have made are much to my Taste. I consent too, very readily to your raising my low House.[2] It has need of it. If Verchilds Pasture, which lies between me, can be purchased, I wish you to do it. You may continue to purchase, such Scraps of Marsh or Woodland as are to be sold at reasonable Rates and draw upon me. Mrs. A. I believe has hinted a larger Purchase[3] but I could not get through it without running in debt, or Selling my Furniture, or both, and I love to feel free. So I had rather you should go on, in the small Way.

My Love to your Lady and son and all Friends particularly Uncle Norton [*Quincy*]. John Adams

RC (Adams Papers).

[1] Not found.
[2] On Tufts' purchases, see Tufts to JA, 26 Nov. 1784, note 2, above. The same letter discusses raising the roof of JA's Boston house.

[3] The farm of Thomas(?) Alleyne (see AA to Tufts, 3 Jan., above; AA to Tufts, 8 March, below).

Katherine Hay to Abigail Adams

My Dear Madam Beaugency March 7th. 1785

I intended writing you before this but have been waiting very impatiently for letters from Mr. Hay, (but hitherto in vain) as they will fix the time of my leaving France. I have expected my next letter to you wou'd be to ask the favour of you to take a lodging for me, but I am now under the Necessity of troubling you very unexpectedly upon an affair that has given me a good deal of uneasiness.

It was fix'd when I came to this Country that I shou'd draw a Bill on my Freind in England, if I shou'd want more Money than I brought with me. January last I found I shou'd be Oblig'd to Draw for Money by February, at that time a quarter wou'd be due for my Board accordingly. I try'd to get Money here for my Bill on London, but it was impossible. Mr. Mather advis'd me to write to a Mr. Graff in Paris, and get him to Negociate the Bill for me. This Mr. Graff Mr. Storer recommended to me for Cambrick or laces and every Article in the Linin way; we lay'd out some Money at his Magazin, and he appeared much of the Gentlemen, was very polite to us while in Paris. He came every Day to see us, and offer'd his service for any commission when we got into the Country. From this knowledge of Mr. Graff, without any doubt, I drew a Bill on my friend in London payable to Mr. B Graff for £30. Sterling at 7 Days sight, enclos'd it to Mr. Graff, desiring him to get me the Money for it, and send it to me, by a rescription on the financier of this place. He immediately answer'd my letter with all possible politness and attention, and told me he had taken the Bill himself, and wou'd send me the Mony in the way I propos'd or some other way very soon. In about a Week after he wrote me a friend of his that was a going to Bordeax had taken charge of 30 louis d['O]r, and would pay them to me at this place and desir'd me to acknowledge the receipt of them in due time;—I waited 10 or 12 Days and heard nothing of his friend nor Mony (in the mean time I receiv'd a letter from my friend in London acquainting me he pay'd my Bill the 30th. Janry.). I then wrote to Mr. Graff acquainting him that I had not receiv'd the Money and I was in want of Money, and wou'd be much Oblig'd to him to send it as soon as possible. I every Day expected an Answer. I waited 10 Days without hearing a Word. I then wrote the second letter, this is the 8 Day and I have not heard a word of him.

Mr. Mather thinks that he heard your son say he knew him, however I must beg the favour of you to Intercede for me with your son, and get him to go [*to*] Mr. Graff and know if he is alive, for I cannot help thinking he is Dead; if he is in existance, will he be so good as to let him know that I have not receiv'd the Money and have wrote him two letters to that purpose, that perhaps have miscarried (tho' it is hardly possible that two letters shou'd miscarry) and that the delay has put me into a very disagreeable situation.[1] I am reduc'd to my last Crown for pocket Money. I have been Oblig'd to ask Mr. Mather to pay my Board for me that was due last Month. Six Weeks has elaps'd since I first sent him the Bill, and I suppos'd I shou'd have reciev'd [the?] Money in [8?] or 10 Days.

Shou'd their be any trouble or difficu[lty. . .] matter, (which I hope not and am ready to think its oweing to something that I cou'd not foresee,) will you be so good as to shew Mr. Adams the letter Ask his advice what steps I shou'd take. I wish Mr. Graff wou'd pay your son the Money and he wou'd give him a receipt for it. If I cou'd get it, into your hands I shou'd be quite contented. I would give a Bill upon Paris for it. Will you be so good as to write me my Dear Madam as soon as you know what is the Difficulty.[2]

I must rely on your goodness and candour to excuse the frequent favours I ask of you. I can only say I shall ever be ready to serve you or yours. My Best respects to Mr. Adams Miss Adams and Mr. A—Junr. in which Mr. and Mrs. Mather Joine.

With great esteem Dear Madam your Oblig'd freind and Servt.

K Hay

Mr. Graffs Direction Magazin de Dentelles Rue de Deux Portes St Sauveur.

PS This Week receiv'd a letter from Mrs. Atkinson, she has been in very bad Health all the Winter and in a way of having an addition to her Family.

RC (Adams Papers); addressed: "A Madame Madame Adams a la Maison de M. le Comte de Rouhaut á Auteuil prés Paris"; stamped: "BEAVGENCY"; endorsed: "Mrs Hay March 6th 1785."

¹ JQA briefly records visiting P. B. Graff, a Paris clothier, with his mother, "upon some business for Mrs. Hay," on 12 March (*Diary*, 1:233).

² AA evidently replied to this letter on 13 March (not found), to which Katherine Hay in turn replied on 26 March (Adams Papers).

In that letter, she told AA that Mr. Graff had also written to her on the 13th, and sent her a bill which she cashed immediately. Although Graff's letter "was full of Apologies, and mentions not a word of seeing you," Mrs. Hay was convinced that he had written to her because of AA's and JQA's intervention.

Abigail Adams to Elizabeth Cranch

No 5

My Dear Betsy   March 8th. 1785 Auteuil

There is a Gentleman by the Name of Blakney¹ a Philadelphian who is with other company to dine here to day and on Monday is going to England. I think to charge him with a Letter or two, tho I know not of any present conveyance unless Young is yet there, who has been going every week, ever since December, and who has, as my Friends will find, Letters on board written in that month, which is very discouraging. I could write by way of New York monthly, but I am loth to load my Friends with a postage. If Mr. Gerry continues there I shall some times take the freedom of covering a Letter to him, and getting him to forward it by a private hand.² And my Friends may in the same manner enclose at any time under cover to Mr. Jay who is minister for foreign affairs directed to your uncle which Letters have a right to come as far as the packet, without postage, and from thence will not be more expensive nor indeed so much so, as those which come by way of England. Never omit writing for want of Subjects, every thing and every object is interesting to me, ten thousand times more so than any thing which I can write you from hence, because I had almost Said I love; every thing and every body in that Country. Tell me when you begin to garden. I can brag over you in that respect, for our flower pots were set out in February and our garden began to look smilling. The orange Trees were not however brought out of the House, and it was very lucky they were not, for since this month commenced came a nipping frost very unusual at this season, and stiffend all our flower roots. I really fear they are kill'd. O Betsy how you would delight in this Garden. As to the House it is large and with 20 thousand livers expence in repairs and furniture would be very elegant and fit for a minister to live in, but as it is, let it pass, it is as good as we can afford, and is a fine clear air. The Garden too is much out of repair and bespeaks the too extravegent provision of its owners who are not able to put it in order. The Garden is however a fine walk in summer and the beautifull variety of flowers would tempt you to tan yourself in picking and trimming them. The garden has a number of statues and figures, but there is none which pleases me more than one of a Boy who has robed a bird of her nest of young; which he holds in one hand and in the other the old bird, who has laid hold of his finger with her Bill and is biteing it furiously, so that the countanance of the lad is in great distress between the fear of loosing the young and the pain of his finger.

Cousin Nabby says Mam, the company are come some of them. Well then go down and entertain them, for I will finish my Letter to Betsy. There is amongst them a Mr. Pickman of Salem, to whom Mr. Tracy gave a Letter of introduction. Do you know him? I have never seen him yet. He calld and left his Name one Day and his address. Your cousin Jack returnd his visit but not being at home, he also left a card, and we sent him an invitation to dine here to day. That is the form and process in this country. There is a Mr. Williamos here who was in Boston after I left it. He is a Swiss by Birth, a very clever sensible obligeing man, who is a very great intimate at Mr. Jefferson's, which alone would be sufficient to recommend him. He dines here to Day and Col. Humphries our Secretary, a Mr. Waren[3] a Carolianian and Miss Jefferson from the Walls of her convent[4] does us the favour of a visit to day. Those form our Society for this day. O, could I transport you and your Dear family how much it would enhance the pleasure. Mr. T—r[5] too should assist at table as he is very handy that way, but his Carveing abilities would be almost useless here as the provision seldom wants any thing more than shaking to peices. I have got a long Letter begun to your Mamma[6] and I have had some thoughts of changing the address and sending it to you, only I owe her one and not you. Tell Lucy I would give a great deal for one of her Cats. I have absolutely had an inclination to buy me some little Images according to the mode of this country that I might have some little creatures to amuse myself with, not that I have turnd worshiper of those things, neither.

There is not one creature of you that will tell me a word of our good parson.[7] How does he do? Alass he deserves it, for being a simple individual. I will however remember him and tender him my Respects.

I design to get my other Letters ready to send on, about the middle of the week, but if this should have the Luck to get a passage as soon as it arrives in England, why it may possibly travel along accompanied only, with one to Dr. Tufts and an other to Mrs. Feild[8] which is all I have had leisure to get ready. Your cousin John thinks very much of it that none of his Friends have written to him.[9] Remember me to all my dear Friends. I can name none in particular but your good Parents. I have vanity enough to think it would take all the rest of my paper to enumerate them.

I have written you all this, to shew you how to triffle and as it is unworthy of a copy and written in great haste I must apoligize for its inaccuracy.

Believe my dear Girl affectionately yours,   A A

I darnt send my Elder Sister such a hasty scrip, besides I may venture to triffel with the daughter when her Mamma requires a steadier pen.

RC (MB); docketed in an unknown hand: "Letter from Mrs. A. Adams. to Miss Eliz. Cranch Mar. 8. 1785. France. (No. 5)." The name "John" appears to the right of the docket.

[1] John Bleakley (JQA, *Diary*, 1:227, 230).

[2] Elbridge Gerry attended Congress in New York, 31 Jan. to 1 March, and 12 July to 4 Nov. 1785 (Burnett, ed., *Letters of Members*, 8:lxxxvii). No letter from AA to Gerry in 1785 is known to the editors.

[3] JQA has "Mr. Waring"; this may have been Dr. Thomas Waring of South Carolina (JQA, *Diary*, 1:216, and note 2, 230).

[4] Martha Jefferson, age twelve, had accompanied her father to France and would remain there, receiving her education at the Abbaye Royale de Pentemont, a fashionable Paris convent school, until April 1789, shortly before her return with her father to America (Jefferson, *Papers*, 7:364, 410–411; 14:356–357; 15:490–498, 560–561).

[5] Probably Royall Tyler; see AA to Tyler, [*post 14 June 1783*], above.

[6] Of 20 Feb., above, finished on 13 March.

[7] A "+" appears above the line at this point. Written in lighter ink, it was probably not inserted by AA. The "good parson" is Rev. Anthony Wibird.

[8] AA's letter to Esther Field's mother has not been found; her letter to Cotton Tufts is immediately below.

[9] The last extant letter received by JQA from anyone in America, except for his mother and sister, is that from Elizabeth Cranch, May 1781 (vol. 4:146–148). Following his 17 March 1782 reply to Elizabeth (vol. 4:297–299), the only extant JQA letters to anyone in America outside his immediate family are those to Richard Cranch, 6 Sept. (MeHi), to Mary Cranch, 12 Dec., above, and to William Cranch, 14 Dec. 1784, also above. See AA to Mary Cranch, 9 Dec. 1784, above; and JQA, *Diary*, 1:214.

Abigail Adams to Cotton Tufts

My Dear Sir   March 8th. 1785

Mr. Adams received last Evening a Letter from you dated January 1st,[1] in which you inform him of some little purchases which are very agreeable to him. I wrote you by his consent in January respecting Mr. Alleynes Farm. I suppose my Letters have not yet reachd America, as Captain Young has been detained Months in England longer than was expected. We are a little alarmed at the Hazard we have run, because we find it impossible upon the present Establishment to save any thing from it. I believe I mentiond to you that with the assistance of my son I had kept a Regular account of all our expences. And I am sure you will suppose that we live very differently from what we really do, when I assure you that I am obliged to Economize not to be in debt at the close of every Month; if Congress would place us where we were at first, we might get through the purchase of the place, but as that is yet dubious and our sons are going into College which will be attended with a large expence, we are fearfull of being involved in difficulties, and tho it is an object very desirable to us, we fear we shall be obliged to give up the Idea of it. If Mr. Alleyne however should be as dilatory as he has hitherto been, I will not dispair, if our former request have not reachd you so as to have taken decisive measures. You will go no further at present than to make inquiries what it may be had for, and what you really think the value of it, which you will be so kind as to transmit to us. I recollect a story of a minister of Queen Elizabeths whom she one day visited, and observed to him that he had a very small and indifferent House. May it please your Majesty said the minister, the House is big enough for the Man, but you have made the Man too big for the House.

As to the Medford Farm you will be so kind as to have every thing done which will be for the benifit of it. We have so perfect a confidence on your judgment with regard to all these matters that we scarcly wish to direct about them, and Mr. A has been so long a statesman that I cannot get him to think enough upon his domestick affairs. He loves to have every thing as it should be, but does not wish to be troubled about them. He chuses I should write and think about them and give directions. Tho I am very willing to releive him from every care in my power, yet I think it has too much the appearence of weilding instead of sharing the Scepter.

I cannot Sir give you any very promising account with Regard to the Treaties of commerce. Prussia have compleated theirs all to signing. As to England they appear as much infatuated as ever, no answer has been as yet sent to the information which our ministers gave them in December, that they were ready to go to England and treat with them.[2] I have heard that our Merchants are very Angry that the ministers do not Treat, and that they reflect upon them. What more can be done than to inform the Courts of their powers, and to offer them term of treatys. They cannot compel nations into treaties. England is very sour and bitter haughty and imperious, and I hear abuses America upon every occasion. Time was you know Sir, when

an amicable treaty might have been made with England very favourable to Am[erica], and you know to what intrigues it was oweing th[at
the?] Commercial powers were taken from the person in w[hom] they
were first invested;[3] but Time past, can not be recalled, as our
Country Men now feel, and as was then predicted.

Mr. Jays acceptance as minister for Foreign affairs[4] gives us hopes
that his wisdom and integrity will have a happy influence upon our
affairs. Mr. Adams's Colleigue Mr. Jefferson is an Excellent Man.
Worthy of his station and will do honour to his Country. He has been
sick all winter and is now far from being well. Dr. Franklin goes not
out at all. Remember me sir to my dear good Aunt and to your son
and Neice.[5] My Heart always overflows when I think of all my dear
Friends in America, in the first of that Number I hold you and yours
and such I hope you will ever c[onsi]der your affectionate

A Adams

RC (Adams Papers); addressed by JQA: "Honble. Cotton Tufts Esqr. Boston
Massachusetts"; endorsed: "Mrs. Adams Lettr. March 5th"; in another hand?: "recd.
by Dr. Clarke May. 17. 1785." Some damage to the text where the seals were torn
away, and along one edge.

[1] Not found. JA's letter to Tufts of 5
March, above, acknowledges receipt of the
letter.

[2] See AA to Mary Cranch, 9 Dec. 1784,
note 4, above.

[3] Congress' decision, in July 1781, to re-
voke JA's sole power to negotiate a commercial treaty with England (see AA to Tufts, 3
Jan., and note 8, above; JA, *Diary and Autobiography*, 3:104, and note 1).

[4] Congress elected John Jay secretary of
foreign affairs in May 1784, just as he was

preparing to return to America (*JCC*, 26:354–
355). Jay assumed his office on 21 Dec. 1784,
and formally notified JA, Franklin, and Jefferson of his acceptance on 14 January (Jefferson, *Papers*, 7:606). JA, who had expressed his
concern to Jay on 15 Dec. over whether he
would accept the office, warmly congratu-
lated him on 9 March (PCC, No. 84, V, f.
363, 371).

[5] Probably a daughter of Dr. Cotton Tufts'
brother, Dr. Simon Tufts, and his first wife,
Lucy Dudley Tufts, who died in 1768.

Abigail Adams to John Thaxter

My Dear Sir   Auteuil March 20. 1785

To what cause shall I attribute your silence, that not a line has
reachd me since I arrived in Europe? Altho I have not written to you
since my arrival, yet as a Friend and former correspondent I feel
myself entitled to your remembrance. I have heard from others of
your welfare and pleasing prospects, in which be assured no one more
sincerely rejoices than your Friend.

My son too complains that altho he has repeatedly written to you,
and other Friends, he has not received a line in reply. He hopes soon
however to refresh the memory of them, by his return to America,

where he flatters himself he shall be kindly and cordially received notwithstanding their failure in literary testimonies of remembrance.

It is with no small regret that I see the day speedily hastning, which is again to seperate me from this Branch of my family, but I do not consult my own pleasure or satisfaction which must necessaryly suffer a diminution; but the future benifit and prospects of a Youth just Launching into the world. An American breize will be more likely to set him forward on his Voyage with less danger to his passage than the European gales, which too often wreck the adventurous Passenger, and always hazard his safety.

But to quit Allegory, it is in complience with his own requests, that both his Parents have consented to his return. A Year spent at Harvard with diligent application may qualify him to commence the study of the Law, and prepare him for a usefull Citizen in his native Country. You and the rest of our Friends I hope will aid him, by your advice and counsel, and from his present disposition and inclinations, I think he will not willingly give them any cause of displeasure.

You may posibly think it much out of season, if I should now congratulate you upon your return to your native Country, but I never before could do it, with such a firm persuasion of the utility of it, or paint to myself the amaizing difference which subsists between those Countries which have passt the Zenith of their glory, saped by Luxury, and undermined by the rage for pleasure, and a Young a flourishing a free, and I may add, a virtuous Country uncontrouled by a Royal Mandate, unshackled by a military police, unfearfull of the thundring anathamas of Ecclesiastic power, where every individual possest of industery and probity, has a sure reward for his Labour, uninfested with thousands of useless virmin, whom Luxery supports upon the Bread of Idleness, a Country where Virtue is still revered; and modesty still Cloaths itself in crimson. But you have lived too long in Europe to require any description from my pen, and I dare say have too often contrasted the difference not to wish a long long youth to America.

Do you expect from my pen a detail of politicks? I can only tell you, that neither England or Spain will enter into any treaty here; Prussia is the only power with whom a final treaty is closed. Other Courts move so slowly that no buisness is yet concluded with them. We hear daily and bitter complaints of the British temper and disposition towards America, but it is not the Mercantile Clamour of a people which designates the sense of the Cabinet. We suffer for want of a Minister there. You know it is the policy of . . . .[1] to prevent an exchange of ministers with the British Court, but the invitation from St. James to Congress to send a minister and the late appointment of Mr. Temple as consul General,[2] are proofs that they are not so indifferent with regard to a connection with America as Refugees and others pretend. You are too well acquainted with Courts not to know, that you must look behind the scenes to discover the real Characters of the actors, and their naturel appearence, whilst the World see no further than the Stage, without once conceiving that all Courts are James'es.

The ministers have received Authentic accounts that an American vessel has been Captured by one of the Emperor of Morocas Corssairs. He has not sufferd the Men to be enslaved, as those which are taken from other Nations are, but has informed the Ministers that he will release them as soon as Congress will send a person to treat with him, and that he is ready to enter into an alliance with America upon the same footing with other Nations, which you know is with Cash in hand, but as the Ministers here have no Authority upon that score, they are much perplexed what course to take.[3] Some are for making war upon these people as pirates, but England France and Holland treat and pay, would it not be folly and madness in America to Wage War? Mr. A's dutch loan has succeeded so well that there is cash enough to treat with, provided Congress think proper. The words which were once represented as so reprehensible, viz. "I will go to Holland and see if I cannot make America less dependant upon France," have been literally accomplishd, in more instances than one, for not a single stiver is to be had any where but in Holland, even the interest due to this Court is drawn from thence.[4] But what does our Country design. Interest is a canker worm which will knaw to the vitals, and to borrow abroad even for the payment of interest they will find very bad policy.

On Monday last I dined with the Dr. [*Franklin*][5] who has always been vastly social and civil to me. He looks in good Health, but is much afflicted with his disorder which prevents his riding or walking. He tells me that he is fully determined to go out to America in the spring, but I think whatever his inclination may be, his infirmities will prevent him. Mr. Jefferson too has been sick these four months. Mr. A is very happy in him. As to Col. Humphries he looks Built for duration.

Pray make my affectionate Regards to all your family and tell me how they do. I cannot in future suffer either Courts or Writs to Rival me in your Regards, nor will I give place to any female but a wife.

Be not alarmed at the word, Since you will find the reality a very necessary ingredient in your future portion of happiness. At least that is the opinion of one who has had twenty Years experience in the Connubial State. A greater felicity than a happy union cannot therefore be wished you by your affectionate Friend   Abigail Adams

Be so good as to present my Respects to Judge Sergent and family. Emelia joins in affectionate Remembrance to you.

RC (MB); endorsed: "Mrs. Adams March 20th. 1785." Dft (Adams Papers); notation in JQA's hand: "To J. Thaxter. May 1785"; originally filmed under May 1785, Adams Papers, Microfilms, Reel No. 364.

¹ AA probably intended Vergennes, the French foreign minister. Many French and British merchants were also cool toward Britain exchanging ministers with the United States.

² John Temple was appointed the first British consul general in the United States on 5 Feb., presented his commission to John Jay on 24 Nov., and was formally accepted by Congress on 2 Dec. 1785 (*JCC*, 29:886, 897–898).

³ JA discusses this issue at length in his Diary for 19 and 20 March (*Diary and Autobi-ography*, 3:173–175).

⁴ JA had negotiated the most recent Dutch loan on 9 March 1784 (same, 3:168, note 1). For the quotation, see AA to Cotton Tufts, 3 Jan., note 8, above.

⁵ Both AA2 and JQA place the most recent Adams visit to Franklin's for dinner on Thursday, 17 March, and give details of that occasion. The Adamses had entertained several guests on Monday, 14 March, but the ailing Franklin probably did not attend (AA2, *Jour. and Corr.*, 1:56–57; JQA, *Diary*, 1:235–237).

Cotton Tufts to Abigail Adams

Dear Cousin   [*11 April 1785*]¹

I have not received any Letter either from Mr. Adams or from you since Yours, just after your Arrival at Passy.² We are solicitous to hear, from You—and I flatter myself that We shall for the future have more regular Intelligence. We have had much to do in the Electioneering Way. So far as we can judge from Accounts from different Parts of the Country, Mr. Bowd[oi]n will be elected Governor. Am doubtful whether the Lt. Governor is elected by the People. Had Your nearest Friend been here, No Struggle would have arisen who should have been the first Magistrate. I think there would have been a Unanimity. Mr. H[ancock] and his Adherents struggled hard to introduce Mr. C[ushin]g.³

Bror. Cranch and Sister, Betsey and Lucy are all well. Mr. P[alme]r is reduced to a deplorable Scituation as to Estate. German Town is advertised f[or sale?]⁴ and he still possesses his State for planning. His Daughter B[etsy] is I fear in a Hectic State.⁵ I had no expectation [of] writing a Line to you, But Mr. Smith presenting to me this Letter⁶ and informing me that Col. Norton who will probably be the Bearer of this, will not go on Board untill half an hour hence I could not resist the Impuls of writing. Love to Cousins. More hereafter. Your Affectionate Frd. & Kinsman   Cotton Tufts

RC (Adams Papers); addressed: "Mrs. Adams at the Honble. John Adams Esqr. Boston favd. by Capt. Grant with A Box"; marked: "⟨*Postage 12d*⟩"; endorsed: "Mrs Fitchs Letter."

Tufts wrote this letter on the blank third sheet of Mary Fitch's brief letter to AA, dated "Kingston Jamaica Jan. 11th. 1785" (Adams Papers). Fitch sent her letter with "a small Box, which contains [three?] Potts of our Country preserves and two Bottles of Cayan Pepper," to AA in Massachusetts as a token of her appreciation for the "polite Attention" which JA and JQA had paid to her and her husband, Eliphalet Fitch, one of JA's Boylston relations, in Europe in 1783 (see JA to JQA, 12 June 1783, above; JA, *Diary and Autobiography*, 3:134; JQA, *Diary*, 1:175, 204). Isaac Smith Sr. gave the letter and box to Cotton Tufts, who wrote the following postscript to Fitch's text: "April 11. 1785. I have broke open this Letter and finding that it communicates sweet Things, which as You cannot reep the Advantage of them, personally, consulting Your Disposition I shall take the Liberty to give Your Friends a Taste of them." Then, after adding the text printed here, Tufts entrusted the letter to Col. Beriah Norton. See Tufts to AA, 19 April, below.

[1] Dated from Tuft's postscript to Mary Fitch's letter of 11 Jan. to AA; see the descriptive note.

[2] Of 8 Sept. 1784, above.

[3] John Hancock abruptly resigned the governorship on 29 Jan., in a winter of increasing economic distress, political controversy, and social discord. He was succeeded by his protégé, Lt. Gov. Thomas Cushing, but Cushing was defeated by James Bowdoin in the spring, and the Hancock forces were out of office until the spring of 1787. See Tufts to JA, 11 March (Adams Papers); William M. Fowler Jr., *The Baron of Beacon Hill, A Biography of John Hancock*, Boston, 1980, p. 255–261.

[4] The bracketed text here and below was lost by the cutting away of the seal; for the inserted text, see Mary Cranch to AA, 25 April, below.

[5] Whatever medical problem she had in 1785, Elizabeth Palmer, daughter of Gen. Joseph Palmer, survived it to marry Joseph Cranch in 1790.

[6] Mary Fitch to AA, 11 Jan. (Adams Papers); see the descriptive note.

Abigail Adams to Mary Smith Cranch

No. 7.

My Dear Sister   Auteuil April 15 1785[1]

There is a Young Gentleman going from Passy in the pacquet for New York. His Name is Chaumont, the Son of a Gentleman whose Name is well known in America. I have met him once or twice at Dr. Franklin: whose next Neighbour he is, and he has once dinned here: the Ministers have intrusted him with publick dispatches of importance to Congress. He appears a modest agreeable Young Gentleman. He proposes visiting all the States and has requested Letters of introduction from Mr. Adams, which he has given him, to some of our Boston Friends who will be kind enough to notice him.[2] All foreigners who have visited America speak in the highest terms of the Hospitality of the people of Boston, and with reason, for I do not believe that it is exceeded, if equald: in any part of the World. Mr. Chaumont speaks english tolerably, so that he will have that advantage, over many others of his Nation. Nothing can be more dissagreeable than liveing in a Country, the language of which you cannot speak.

He has requested me to give him Letters but as I expect my son will sail in the next pacquet, I have not been very solicitious to write this way, as it is probable the Letters will be very old before they reach you.

I have not heard from my American Friends since December, but as the Spring opens I begin to have my usual impressions that there are some Letters on their way. If my Friends have any thing pressing at any time which they wish to communicate by covering to Mr. Jay who is Minister of foreign affairs; or to Mr. Gerry whilst he is at Congress it will come more speedily by the pacquets; I have writen by way of England when ever a private opportunity has offerd of conveying Letters from hence; most of the Americans who have past the winter in Paris, have left it, and are going, so that I fear we shall be very *trist*, especially when Master JQA leaves us. In proportion as a person becomes necessary to us we feel their loss: and in every way I shall feel his absence: I dare not trust myself with thinking upon the Subject. He is now at a time of Life when it is necessary for him to Regularly compleat his Education at some Seminary: that he may go into the Study of the Law which he proposes; we expect he will be at Home before his Brother enters Colledge: but if he should not, so that I should be able to write by him concerning Charles: I must request you to take care to provide what ever is necessary for him, and to have the Same care of him, that I would take for Yours, in the like circumstances. Whatever expences occur you will apply to Dr. Tufts, and consult with him in all things with respect to him. Mr. Adams and I both think that in order to prevent confusion all money Matters should pass through the hands of the Dr, and that he should make the necessary draughts upon Mr. Adams here, both for our sons in America and that which is going out, always remembring that there is to be no extrodanary expences on account of the publick Character which Mr. Adams sustains, because he is not half so able to bear them, as he would have been if he had been only a private citizen. In short I am weary of being obliged to eat and drink up all we have.

This is very easily done, and have company no oftner than once a week neither: I dare say we should be able to live, and I hope educate our children in America. We shall do no more here, and must excercise a frugality to accomplish that; which is thought meaness here. A Minister who cannot keep a train of Servant[s], a publick table &c. is thought very little off. The Spanish Ambassodor Count d'Aranda has no less than Seventy 50 of whom are Livery and the British minister the Duke of Dorset who was invited to dine here to day, but was prevented by our inviting him upon one of the days in which he gives publick dinners: he has a train of 50 servants 25 of which are in Livery and lives in every other respect answerable to that Retinue, and So does every other foreign minister who resides here.[3] It would be vastly more to my taste, and much more to my satisfaction to return to my own Country and live in that social Friendship and that Simplicity in which I formerly rejoiced. I take no pleasure in a life of ceremony and parade. I had rather dine in my little room at Braintree with your family and a set of chosen o[ld] Friends, than with the Marquisses Counts and countesses Abbes and Great folks who dine with us to day.[4] Madam de la Fayette, I will however except. I should always take pleasure in her company. She is a good and amiable Lady, exceedingly fond of her Children and attentive to their education, passionatly attached to her Husband!!! A French Lady and fond of her Husband!!!

Remember me to all my Dear Friends in America. Tell Cousin Betsy, that I have procured of our gardner a parcel of Beautifull flower seeds for her, which I design sending her by her cousin, and that she must new Name them, calling them after our family. It is a fine season now a little too dry, but I have got some pots of flowers with which the gardner has presented me, now flourishing in my Chamber, and the peach blossoms are just shewing themselves. They complain here that it is very cold for the season. We are all well. Pray is Mrs. Otis a Mother yet? I want to hear; has Mr. Cranch forgot us that we see not his hand writing? Regards to Mr. Tyler. I hope he is very buisy and to great purpose.[5] My paper calls upon me to close. Most affectionately and tenderly Yours   Abigail Adams

RC (MWA:Abigail Adams Corr.); addressed in JQA's hand: "Mrs. Mary Cranch. Braintree near Boston Massachusetts."

1 The body of this letter may have been written, or at least drafted, on 14 April; see note 4.

2 Jacques Donatien Le Ray de Chaumont (later known in America, where he lived after 1800, as James Le Ray) was the son of the owner of the house in Passy in which Benjamin Franklin lived, rent-free, for nine years,

and which JA shared with Franklin in 1778–
1779. JA and JQA had known young Chaumont since 1778; AA met him on 17 March
1785, if not earlier, at Franklin's. Chaumont
left Paris for Lorient and the New York packet
on 14 April. JQA would travel with Chaumont
from New York to Boston in August, and
would correspond irregularly with him to
1821. See JQA, *Diary*, 1:236, and note 2, 249,
298–318 passim.

On 14 April, JA wrote letters of introduction
for Chaumont to Samuel Adams (NN),
Thomas Cushing, John Hancock, Samuel Allyne Otis (all LbC, Adams Papers), and William Tudor (MHi).

³ In February, JQA had commented on the
servants, equippage, and other trappings of
wealth and power displayed by the Conde
d'Aranda, and had recorded the Duke of
Dorset's expression of disgust at the ceremony of court life (*Diary*, 1:224, 225–226).
AA2 made similar observations on Aranda's
and Dorset's households in April (*Jour. and
Corr.*, 1:71).

⁴ AA may be referring to the dinner which
the Adamses gave on 14 April, for the Lafayettes, the Count and Countess Doradour,
the abbés Chalût and Arnoux, Daniel Hailes,
the secretary of the British embassy, and
Count Sarsfield (JQA, *Diary*, 1:249).

⁵ Royall Tyler was in Braintree, maintain-
ing his social ties with the Cranches, and by
mail with the Shaws and the young Adamses
in Haverhill. On 20 March, Elizabeth Shaw
reported to Mary Cranch (DLC:Shaw Family
Papers) that the previous week they had received a letter from Tyler, "accompanied by a
genteel Present, of a Morocco Pocket-Book to
Mr. Charles, and an elegant Set of Geograph-
ical Cards for Mr. Thomas; informing us at
the same time that he had made several attempts to make us a Visit, but that all had
proved ineffectual, and must therefore give it
up for the Present. I hope however when the
soft Season is further advanced, and the roads
are become good, both Mr. Tyler, and my
Cousins will be more fortunate. It would have
given me pleasure to have seen them here."

Cotton Tufts to Abigail Adams

Dear Cousin   Weymouth April 19. 1785

It is now a violent Snow Storm (PM) and I hope it will be the last
for this Spring, for the Snow has been on the Earth through the
Winter and from January to the first Instant the Sledding has continued; on the 26th. of March I rode to Abington, from Mr. Williams's
Meeting House,¹ in one of the Roads for near two Miles the Snow
was level with the Walls and the Crust so hard as to bear my Horse,
the Snow supposed to be 2 1/2 Feet upon a Level at that Time. On
the 10th. of this Month Your Sister Shaw writes, Ice continues in our
River over which People pass and repass &c.² The Weather however
has not been so cold through the Winter as in some former Seasons.

Last Week Mr. Smith handed me a Letter from a Mrs. Fitch of
Jamaica directed to You and informed me what he supposed it related
to. I took the Liberty to open it, write a few Lines in it sealed it and
as Col. Norton was just then going to Europe committed it to him.
I found Mrs. Fitch as an Expression of Gratitude for the Kindness
and Civilities shewn by Mr. Adams to Mr. Fitch and herself when in
Europe had sent you some Sweet Meats and Cuhen.³ I advised Mr.
Smith to distribute them among Your Friends, but afterwards finding
that they consisted of several Parcels, packed up in great order and

no Danger of spoiling, Your Sister Cranch thought it best to let them laiy untill We had Your Directions and She will accordingly write to You therefor.

I have wrote both to Mr. Adams and to You 3 or 4 Letters since You left America. Cap. Young arrived last Wednesday and brot sundry Letters for Haverhill and Braintree[4] also One for me from Mr. Adams of Dec. 15. 1784 in which he makes no Mention of his or Your having received any from me. Should some Things be repeatedly mentioned Youll excuse it, as I am in doubt whether my Letters reach my Friends and for want of some sure Conveyance I think it prudent to withhold many Things which I wish to communicate.

21st.

I just received Yours of January 3d. which affords me much entertainment and Pleasure. Your Scituation methinks is Curious, to be obliged to appear in high Life in Europe (and indeed almost any where else) and submit to all its Follies is I suspect laying Nature upon the Wreck but as You justly observe when Necessity calls it is best to obey with Patience.

I received a Letter from your Brother Shaw the other Day. Your two Sons are in Health. They have besides their Studies attended a Singing and Dancing School through the Winter. I took Occasion upon Mr. Shaws consulting me with respect to their attending the dancing School, to express some sentiments relative to Master Charles's Attention being engaged to his Studies, the Expectation of his entring at our University next Commencement and my Wish that He might be so fitted as to enter with Honor to his Instructor and to himself. I received an agreable Answer Viz. "If Master Charles has his Health and pursues his Studies as Well as he has done I doubt not but he will enter College with Reputation to himself and his Instructor." I am pleased with the Intention of Mr. Adams's sending Master John to our University, I am of Opinion, the sooner he sends him the greater will be the Advantage. If there is any particular Branch of Learning that he may be unacquainted with and necessary for his Admission to an advanced Station, he may be placed under some of the Professors or some eminent Instructor for a short Time previous thereto if thought best. I cannot but urge the Expediency of his residing a Year and an half or two Year[s] at the University, he may be of great Service to his Brother Charles and he will have the Company of his Cousin Cranch, a sober amiable and studious Youth.—It is reported here that Miss Nabby is to return with Your

86

Son.[5] Would it not be best for her to defer it untill You return which I presume will not exceed another Year for I am pretty Certain You will by that Time be well tired of Europe. And by that Time I hope Mr. Adams will have compleated the necessary Treaties in Europe and that We shall once more have the Pleasure of seeing You all at Braintree.

I last Week went to Medford, leased the Farm at £40 Per Annum to Benj. Teal a Nephew of the Old Tenant. The Farm Buildings and Fences are all in bad Order. Repairs must soon be made. The House at Boston I have contracted with a Carpenter to take down the Roof (which is rotten) and raise it one Story higher. Belcher is going out of the House at Braintree. Turner the Stocking Weaver is coming in. I know not what to do with this House, the South End of it is going to Wreck and Ruin. Real Estates in the Country are Sunk greatly in Value, they afford but little Profit. This is a Subject if Time permits I shall enlarge upon in some future Letter.

Pheobe and Abdy is still in your House, she takes good Care of it. Notwithstanding her Attention, somethings will suffer. I call'd in this Week and took a general View. Some of the Woollen Articles, and especially some of Mr. Adams Cloaths, that will not answer for the Children, had they not better be disposed of? However Your Sister will write You more fully upon this. I have now and then a little Trouble to keep down the Spirit of the African and reduce it to a proper bearing, but upon the whole I generally succeed.

The Farm under the Care of Mr. Pratt is conducted as heretofore. I have made an Addition to it of 20 Acres bott of James Thayer and between 2 & 3 Acres of Salt Marsh bott of Davd. Bass of which I suppose You have received Information by this Time as I drew a Bill on the 5th. January on Mr. Adams for £50, in favour of Mr. Elworthy on Account of the Purchases. On Settling with Mr. Pratt he claimed a Remission of such Part of the Town Taxes as exceeded the ordinary Taxes of the Town, this he said You agreed to, and as I had hitherto found him honest, I allowed it, But wish You to write in Your next what lies in Your Mind with respect to it.

I have not had an Opportunity to negociate any thing relative to Allens Farm, but shall attend to it as Opportunity presents.

29.

You kindly enquire after the State of our Parish. I wish I could give You a pleasing Account, but we are still unsettled. We have made several unsuccesful Attempts. Two have been called and have refused, Viz. Mr. Shuttleworth, and a Mr. Packard.[6] Their Refusal perhaps, may prove in the Issue advantageous. But Time must settle the Minds of contending Parties and I hope Time and Patience will bring us a good Man.

May 1. Sunday Evening 12°

I need not tell You my Letters are wrote in haste, they sufficiently shew it, besides my Eye sight is so weak that I suffer much by writing. I can only add that Mrs. Tufts presents her Love to You Mr. Adams and the Children, a Turn of the Cholic kept her Low through the fore part of the Winter but she is now in her former State, begins to think of getting into her Chaise and take an Airing. Lyde I am informed will sail to Morrow and hope to forward this seasonably in the Morning, and trust it will reach You in London. With Love and Affection to Mr. Adams, Yourself and Children I am Yr Affectionate Kinsman

C. Tufts

RC (Adams Papers); endorsed by AA2: "Dr Tufts April 19."

[1] Probably the South Congregational Church of Weymouth, of which Simeon Williams was minister from 1766 to 1818 (*Sibley's Harvard Graduates*, 16:272–273).

[2] On 20 March, Elizabeth Shaw wrote Mary Cranch: "The Ice has longer held in Our River [*the Merrimack*] than for many years past, it is said there is 3 feet of Snow now upon the Ground, caked into a sort of ice. I do not know but it will be June before it is all melted" (DLC:Shaw Family Papers).

[3] Preserves and cayenne pepper; see Tufts to AA, [*11 April*], descriptive note, above.

[4] The letters written in Dec. 1784, and probably several of AA's letters of early January, all above (see AA to Elizabeth Cranch, 3 Jan., above; Mary Cranch to AA, 25 April, below).

[5] The source of this rumor is not known to the editors. In her letter of 30 April to Mary Cranch, below, Elizabeth Shaw assumed that neither AA nor AA2 would be returning to America in the near future.

[6] Probably Samuel Shuttlesworth, Harvard 1777, and Asa Packard, Harvard 1783 (*Harvard Quinquennial Cat.*, p. 197, 199).

John Adams to Cotton Tufts

Dear Sir   Auteuil April 24. 178⟨4⟩5

It was yesterday only that I received your Favour of Nov. 26, which contains many Things which you mentioned in a posteriour Letter which I have answered.[1]

I am glad you purchased the Pasture and Marsh.[2] I accepted your Bill at sight and it was paid to Mr. Elworthy at sight fifty Pounds. I wish you to repair the House in Boston, and to go on purchasing Bits of Marsh and Wood, if you can find them at moderate Prices, but I am not zealous about this. You may draw upon me, to the amount of Three hundred Pounds when you please, and also to pay for Veseys Place if he will sell it reasonably, and provided you can obtain a good

Profit upon Exchange. With this purchase I Stop my Land Projects, but poor as it is, it lies so situated that I wish it added to my little territory.

My Son John Quincy will embark in the Packet at L'Orient, for New York, and will be with you before Commencement I hope, perhaps he will deliver this.[3]

Charles as well as John I hope will enter Colledge this summer and I hereby place them both under your Superintendence. I pray you to pay all their Bills and draw upon me for the Moneys necessary. It is my Intention that both of them shall be accountable to you for their Expences of every kind, and receive nothing but by your Order. They must be as frugal as possible, otherwise I shall find the Utmost difficulty to get along with them.

Dr. Franklin has been soliciting for Years, to get his Grandson appointed a Minister abroad,[4] Supposing no doubt that his own Services, would prevail: I know too well the Character of my Countrymen, to believe that they will thus impute the Merit of the Parent to the Offspring, and therefore instead of proposing my son for publick Employments, I am Sending him to qualify himself for private ones. I might retain him as my private Secretary, But I will not educate him in such a state of Dependence upon Congress nor my self. He shall Stand on his own Legs, place himself on a Level with the Youth his Contemporary Countrymen, and become a Town Meeting Man first, if he ever wishes for public Employment.

You ask my Opinion concerning the 4th Article of the Treaty of Peace. I wish to avoid being quoted upon these Points. I cannot See the Propriety of the Legislatures interfering. If a Jury determine the Interest to be a bona fide debt, there is no Remedy. An Explanation will never be obtained unless a Minister should be sent to London, if then. We have written and demanded long since, but have no Answer from the British Ministry. In short they are determined not to treat in France. These Interferences of the Legislatures will be construed Violations of the Treaty and the great Posts upon the Frontier will be pretended to be held against Treaty for this Reason. But the little Interests of Individuals in such Governments as ours, will if We are not cautious, disturb publick Interests of infinitely greater Magnitude, and involve our Reputation and even our public Faith.

Whether England and France can import Timber and Lumber from Denmark cheaper than from America I know not. I dont believe they can. But if they could they should consider how they are to pay. There is a great difference between paying Cash and paying in Produce and Manufactures.

Shewing what I had written to Madam she has made me sick of purchasing Veseys Place. Instead of that therefore you may draw upon me, for two hundred Pounds at as good an Exchange as you can obtain and lay it out in such Notes as you judge most for my Interest, so that the Interest may be a little Fund for assisting you in paying the Expences of the Education of my Children. Indeed if you See a Prospect of making any considerable Advantage in this Way, for me, you may draw upon me for more.

My regards to you Lady & son, and believe me with great Affection your Friend   John Adams

RC (Adams Papers), endorsed: "John Adams Esq Letter April 24th 1785. recd. Aug. 29"; docketed, also by Tufts: "recd. Aug. 29, 1785."

[1] On 5 March, above, JA answered Tufts' "posteriour" letter of 1 Jan. (not found).

[2] See Tufts to JA, 26 Nov. 1784, and note 2, above.

[3] JQA did deliver this letter (see JQA, *Diary*, 1:312–315, 318; the docketing in the descriptive note; and Tufts to JA, 6 Oct., below).

[4] JA had first objected to Franklin's efforts to promote William Temple Franklin when the Doctor arranged, in Oct. 1782, to have his grandson named secretary to the peace commission without JA's prior approval (JA, *Diary and Autobiography*, 3:38–39, and note 3, 102–103). On 22 July 1783, Franklin wrote R. R. Livingston, secretary for foreign affairs, that young William was qualified to head a mission, and informed Livingston that both Swedish and Danish officials had asked him whether his grandson might not be named an envoy to their courts (Wharton, ed., *Dipl. Corr. Amer. Rev.*, 6:586). And on 27 June 1784, JA wrote to Elbridge Gerry that he suspected Franklin of trying to secure his grandson's succession to his mission at Versailles when he returned to America. Franklin's suggestion of Sweden as an appropriate post for William, JA wrote, "is only a stalking Horse" (LbC, Adams Papers). William Temple Franklin never did receive another diplomatic appointment.

Elizabeth Cranch to Abigail Adams

My dear Aunt   Braintree April 25th. 1785

How shall I express to you the grateful Sense I feel, for your kind remembrance and attention in favouring me with such charming Letters? I find indeed that I cannot do it as I wish; if you know my heart, tis unnecesary to say more. I have written so much to Cousin Nabby, that I find it difficult to find a Subject for another Letter.[1]—I have informed her of all my *past adventures*; but have not told her of any of my intended employments or amusements; You know my dear Aunt how fond my good Papa is, of gratifying all the wishes of his Children; I have long felt a very great inclination, to learn musick; it has ever been Papa's desire that I should; the expence of it, only, has prevented; He has lately purchas'd me a good second hand Harpsi-chord, and has determin'd to let me have a few months instruction from Mr. Selby;[2] I know not how well I shall succeed; but I hope after a *little* instruction, (and it can be *but* a *little*) by practise, and attention, to make some progress in this Art.—I am so (I believe, *passionately*) fond of Musick, that I shall improve the time, to the best advantage, that I am able to. It would amuse many a solitary hour, and soothe perhaps, many a sad one. Do you recollect my dear Aunt the use Lady G.[3] made of her Harpsichord? May-hap in *process of time*, mine may answer a like serviceable purpose.—I shall board where my Papa does; at a Mr. Forsters [*Foster's*]—a very agreable good Family. How do you think Ma'am I shall, *live two months* in Boston? I shall be quite a rustick Lass among the polishd Belles of Boston, I intend however to be happy; and I hope from that seat of bussiness, and amusements, to find some things that may afford you more entertainment, than tis possible for me to offer you from this un-varied scene; I propose to go abroad among my Friends, to mix in all the agreable Circles, which my station will, with propriety, admit me to, and it will be my endeavour to improve every event, and every occurence, to some advantage, either to myself or friends.

I believe it will be good for me to change this scene, which has been so long continually before me; not that the present is unpleas-ing, for I do not expect to find an equal proportion of pleasure any where else; but because the mind is apt to contract; to be biggoted to certain forms and opinions by being always confined to a certain spot, to a particular Set of accquaintance.——In the course of a few weeks I expect to leave Braintree; it will be with regret just at the approach of the finest Season; but the hope of improvement, will overcome this reluctance. I intend to rise very early, and take a walk every pleasant morning in the Mall; it is near my Lodgings, and has been much improved within this past year; they have made a fine Gravel Walk, that will prevent my damping my feet. There I expect to ruminate, and reflect: and while I enjoy the freshness of the morning breeze, with health and calm contentment for my compan-ions, I hope to feel my heart rise, in grateful adorations to that good Being, from whose benificent hand I recieve all my happiness.

I thank you my dear Aunt for your directions with regard to my learning French;[4] I shall implicitly follow them. I am determined to read *nothing* but French while I am in Boston. My work will be to make Shirts for my Cousin's Charles and Tommy, which I am going about directly, as they are in much want of them. There last Linnen wore very badly. Every attention which it is mine or my Sisters power to afford them, we shall be happy to offer. I have written to each of them,[5] but cannot recieve any reply to my Letters. These *young Men* dont love writing. My Brother is quite defficient in this respect, and troubls me by his neglecting it. Time will remedy this error. With inexpressible Satisfaction, *I think,* I yet, see him innocent and good; his conduct has not yet cost me one Sigh. I pray heaven, it never may. He knows he is tenderly belov'd by Parents and Sisters, and he knows how deep would be the wound in their Hearts, should he become a Votary to Vice. Independant of these reasons, ('tho to a good mind *they* would be very powerful incentives to Virtue) I hope and trust, he has a higher principle, firmly fix'd, and conscienciously adhered to.

I have indeed made out a long Letter without thinking of it; You will know, my Aunt if this Letter reaches you soon, what is like to be my employment for some months to come, if no unforeseen event should oblige me to alter my Plan.

If you accept this prattle as a testimony of undissembled affection and grateful remembrance; It will have answerd the intent with which it was written. Will you make my most respectful and affectionate regards acceptable to my honoured Uncle, and believe me to be your truly affectionate and oblig'd Neice   E Cranch

RC (Adams Papers); endorsed: "E Cranch April 25 1785."

[1] No letter from Elizabeth Cranch to AA2 has been found.

[2] William Selby was a British-born composer and choral director, and an organist at King's Chapel. JQA would hear Selby's music on 4 July 1787 (*Diary*, 2:249, and note 2; *DAB*).

[3] Almost certainly a reference to Charlotte Grandison, a character in Samuel Richardson's *The History of Sir Charles Grandison.* She was the sister of Sir Charles and was usually referred to as "Lady G." See also, Elizabeth Cranch to AA, 5 Sept., below.

[4] AA to Elizabeth Cranch, 3 Dec. 1784, above.

[5] Letters not found.

Mary Smith Cranch to Abigail Adams

N1:85[1]

My Dear Sister   Braintree April 25th 1785

I reciv'd your September Letters a little while after I sent off my November ones, and a Feast they were to me. Mr. Storer inform'd us of your leaving England, any thing further was all conjecture. We have not had one chance of Sending to you this winter except by the way of Amsterdam last week: but as I thought you would get a Letter sooner from England, and Capn. Lyde was to sail soon, I would wait and Send by him. Doctor Tufts met with Colln. Norton in Boston who was going Passenger in the Amsterdam Vessal and was to be landed or left in the Downs. By him he wrote a short Letter he had not time for more. I should have done the same had I known of the opportunity in Season.

Your December and January Letters we reciev'd the 13th. of this month. I need not decribe the pleasure we felt upon being inform'd of your welfair after a tedious interval of Six month. Had you been in England we could have heard from you often. There have been many Letters from thince in the course of this winter. We reciev'd your December Letters almost a week before we knew we had later ones on board the Ship. Mr. T[yler] reciev'd only one from Emelia, Dated September in the first Pacquit.[2] He look'd very cross. It was nothing but a scolding Letter he said. I told him I was very glad of it. Such an one was all he deserv'd, and that had my Cousin possessed my Spirit he would not have had one. I told him also that my last date was the 12th of December.[3] That [*Captain*] Scot had arriv'd, and that you had receiv'd the Letters sent by him, but I refused to read him that part of your Letter in which you so Pictures[q]uely decribe the reception of them. Ask'd him whether after setting such an example of neglect and exerciseing the Power he knew he had to give Pain, He thought he ought to expect any more. He was nettled and I design'd he should be. I had no doubt but he had more on Boad ship, but it was hard, that one should suffer so long Such *Cruel* Suspence and the other none. He was gone to Plymouth Court when we reciev' his Pacquit, and did not come home till the last of the Week. He stay'd at home and pouted away all Sunday. Monday morning He sent a messanger to Deacon Storers to inquire if he had not reciev'd a Pacquit for him. The man return'd about Noon with a volume of Letters for him and several for others. I gave him yours to him Which was inclosed in Mr. Cranchs.[4] I have read both Mr. Adams's and yours, and have heard parts of Emelias, and you may if you please assure her that he never fails of reading that part in one of them, wherin She tells him that Mrs. Hall[5] told her Papa that Mr. T. was a very handsome Man.

We thought for a long time that you were in England. We had some accounts that made it probable you would be there, and concluded you were ingag'd in a round of company and amusements, but by your Letters I find that Some of our Social evening[s] would have been a cordial to you. This winter has been indeed a Solotary one to me. There never has been a time since I liv'd in Braintree, when I should have miss'd your Company so much as since you left us. Your Supporting presence and kind assistance, through the goodness of Providence, I have not needed as in times past. I have had much of the Rhumatism this winter but have not been confin'd to my Chamber above three or four Days. Betsy has had her Health much better than usual, not one turn of the pain in her Stomach that used to afflict her so.

Mr. Cranch has been as usual in Boston except Sundays all winter. Billy at College and Betsy or Lucy have been either at Weymouth or Germantown. Mr. T but little at home.—He is very fond of being drove about in a Sliegh you know, and we never had finer roads for it than the last winter, nor did it ever continue longer. The poor Cattle and Horses would tell us so if they could speak, both Beast and Man were tir'd of it. Mr. T has been rather unlucky in his plans for the sleighing season. In the beginning of it, he took a Gay Horse of Thomson Baxters to keep for the use of the Sleigh. He had not used him above three times before he lamed him so much that he could not use him again the whole winter and was oblig'd to keep him, and hire another, for the Sleigh could not go with one: and ours made so poor a Figure by the side of his, that he would not do by any means. But this is not all. About the middle of March the lame Horse was thought well enough to be return'd, and Mr. T was very loth to be at the expence of keeping him so long for nothing. He was determin'd to have one ride with him before he put him home. He invited us Ladies to go to Germantown with him. The Horse was so fat and so Gay that we were affraid: but Mr. T could not think there could be any danger. We Ventur'd. The Snow was in some places quite gone tho much bankd in others. We got as far as Deacon Webbs Bridge. It was bare. The Horses were obstinate and would not draw. It was a dangerous place. We got out, and left Mr. T and John in. Mr. Vessy happen'd to be ingag'd. They whip'd but all to no purpose. They got out. Mr. T whip'd and John push'd behind, and we three stood in the wet to see what the result would be. After much Flagilation they started and went like the wind. Mr. T being out, had no command of the Horses. The Lane between Mr. Mashes [*Marshes?*] and Mr. Vesseys was much bank'd. The Sleigh was immediately overset. The Horses ran Scraping the Top of it against the Fence till they tore it all to peices. Thus ended the Sleighing for the winter. The Glass lamps happen'd not to be on and the Glasses in the Back and Sides were not broke. Mr. T had depriv'd the Sleigh of its Gloomy appearence by rendering it light both by day and night.

I am really greiv'd that your Friend Should Sacrifice his Health and spend all the best of his days in the service of his Country and yet not be able to lay up enough to admit him to spend the evening of them in retirement and repose. Dearly as I love you and much as I miss you I most Sincerly wish you had been with him from his first going abroad. I dare say he is now more than ever sensible how necessary you are to his Health and Happiness. The more important the Business is in which a Man is ingag'd the more he stands in need of a Sensible prudent and discreet companion, and he never will make so good a Figure without as with such an one. Turn your thoughts to our worthy Parson.[6] I need not bring an other Instance.

Mrs. Hall looks in fine Health considering her age. I told her soon after you went a way that if She wanted any thing and would be so good as to apply to me I had orders to supply her. She said she did not want any thing. I sent Betsy one day this winter to bring her to dine with me. As she was comeing she told Betsy She heard you had left orders with Doctor Tufts to give your poor Neighbours and a number of widows something at Thanksgiving. She took it very hard that She was not among the number. She was sure nobody was poorer than she was. That she had nothing that she could command, "That every thing she had was in Mr. A's Hands." Betsy told her that the Doctor would have thought he should have insulted her if he had done it in that way. That she knew I had orders to supply her with every thing she wanted, and that she was Sure that her uncle and aunt wish'd her to have every thing for her comfort. I did not know of this till after she was gone or I should have talk'd with her upon the matter. As soon as I reciev'd your Letters I went to see her, and told her I had again reciev'd orders to supply her with any thing She might want and ask her to let me know what she wish'd for. She said as before, that she did not want any thing. I did not tell her, you had sent me money to lay out for her, for the reason you gave for not sending it immediately to her.[7] She was very warm. She said she thought very hard of it that you did not leave her something when you went away that she could have commanded and done what she pleas'd with. That Mr. A had all she was worth in the world in his Hands. That she had not ask'd for any Interest for twenty four years.[8] That she could not now earn her living. That she was a burthen upon her son,[9] not that he complain'd She said, but she was sure she was. That you was very kind to her while you was here. That you did not let her want for any thing. But to ask for any thing of Doctor Tufts or me, was so like beging that She Could nor would not. I ask her why she did not tell you so before you went away. She[10] did not think You would have gone so soon. I told her I knew you wish'd her to have every thing in that way that would make her happiest. That I should let you know her mind. I thought it would be best to give her the money you sent, taking a recept for it. I did not give it to her then, thinking it best to wait till I should recieve another Letter, and then tell her that you had sent it to her. I ask'd the Doctors advise. He thought so too. I have now reciev'd another and shall give it to her as soon as I can see her and shall wait your orders before I offer her any thing further.

I shall dispose of the money for Louisia as I think best. She is well and so they were all. We have no very good accounts of her Papa. Some people from the place where he is say that he is out of business and does not behave well.[11]

I had a Letter from Sister Shaw last week. She is well. Your Sons also. They are very good children. Cousin Charles will enter College without doubt Mr. Shaw thinks. Tommy *pulls up* his uncle says.

I shall be gratified, when they are where I can be of use to them and repay some of the obligations I am under to their Parents. I fear you will think Cousin John so necessary to your Happiness that you will not part with him. From the accounts I have of him I do not wonder you wish to detain him with you, but our own pleasures are soon given up when we cannot enjoy them without injuring our children. To know that they are great and good will give us the most Satisfaction, be they where they will. I want more than I can express to see him, Sweet Youth! I could have shed Tears at your description of his walking away a little morftified upon not finding any Letters for him among those he had taken so much pains to procure.[12] It shall not be so again. He will have enough this time to make up his dissapointment. I shall thank him for mine. His uncle is much pleass'd with those to him[13] and will not fail to answer them. His cousins will remember him also. If I have time I shall write to Cousin Nabby. Dear Girl she does not know how anxious I am for her Happiness.

I fear my dear sister your Health will suffer greatly for want of exercise. I hope soon to hear you are in England. You will be then able to walk, as tis the Fashion to do so there, unless your rank Should render your Feet useless. There are a thousand things which I want to ask you, and want to tell you that the distance renders improper, as Letters are so liable to be open'd. When you get to London we shall do better. Mr. A mentions his design of returning to his own country Soon, but I suppose he did not then know of his appointment to the Court of Great Britain. This I fear will retard your return but if you are there I shall feel as if you were half way home.

Thank you my dear sister for the sattin you sent me. Tis a beautiful colour. I shall never veiw it but as a Token of the Tender affection of my sister. Uncle Quincy has been confind to his chamber with the Rhumatism in his hip and Leg ever since the beginning of November. He came down Stairs last week but has not been out of the House yet. He has been very sick part of the time. My visits when I was able to go out have been divided between him and the distress'd Family at Germantown. The latter have been so long the Tool-ball of fortune that they are almost wore out. The Farm The Great House and all the Land except thirty acres, Has by Some negotiations have fallen into the Hands of Major Swan. The remainder Mr. Guild attach'd as Mr. Parkers property and they have been all advertiz'd for Sale. The Family have been in expectation of being oblig'd to move they knew not where this whole winter. What will yet be done they know not. Mr. Guilds affairs are so involv'd with Mr. Parkers, that every thing he has in the world is attach'd, all the Furniture, and all her[14] fortune in the Hands of the Executors. I hope she has not been so romantick as not to secure it. She was advis'd to do it before she was married, but she would not. Poor Creature, I went to see her last week; she looks as if she would sink into the earth. She lays in, this month. Mrs. Quincy is with her. She has charming spirits you know. Nancy will pine all the Flesh off her Bones.

The Doctor wrote you that Mrs. Fitch had sent you a Box of Sweetmeats from the West Indias, and that he had desir'd uncle Smith to divide them among your Friends. He told me of it and desir'd me to see to its being done, but when I came to unpack the Box I found a Pot holding about two Quarts, mark on the cover Green citron and two others holding one Quart mark'd I know not what. They were rub'd out—and two pint Bottles of Cayenne. I did not open them as I thought it best to let them remain unopen'd till I heard from you. They are so well secur'd that I think they will keep a long time. Had they been articles that would have perish'd soon I should not have scrupled useing them, but as they are not, I chuse you should have the direction of them your self. Billy is under great obligations to his uncle, for the kind present of Books which he has made him. Be so kind as to present him my thanks also, but as he is not in present want of any, we shall wait till Mr. Adams returns. He will recieve them with double pleasure from the Hands of his uncle.

At present we hardly know what will be of the most advantage to him. If he should Study Law as he now seems determin'd too do, Law Books would be most acceptable.

The Violin cousin John is so kind as to give Billy is gone a Voyage to Cape Francois.[15] Whether it will be benifited by it I cant say. I ask'd to borrow it till Mr. Cranch could meet with one for Billy as I supposed he would not carry it with him when he went, but his mama thought it would be an amusement to him and advis'd him to take it. "Then let me Buy one mama." I found how the matter Stood so said no more about it. I thought you would have been as willing I should have it as that it should go a voyage.

Aunt Smith[16] would take it kind in you to write to her. She Says her Hands are too lame to hold a pen or she would write. Uncle open'd the Pacquit directed to him and was almost affronted that he had not one line. He talk'd of Sealing the cover and Sending it back a Blank paper.

Our Neighbour Mrs. Bass has been confin'd the whole winter by bad managment of the shingles which she had in the beginning of it. She was in Boston. Was taken with a pain in her hip, thought it was the Rhumatism, advis'd with a Doctor. He order'd a Blister upon it. She came home, her Hip Broke out. She did not know what it was. She put on the Blister in the midst of them, but a dreadful peice of work she had with it. The irrupttion spread half round her and a great Blister as big as your hand besides did not help the [naturaler?] Irritabillity of her Temper. She was seizd as soon as they began to heal with such Spasms in that side as if possible exceeded Betsy Winstows [*Winslows?*].[17] They lasted a month. I had no expectation of her Life, but she is now much better, I think. I have seen enough of this dissorder to dread it.

Mrs. Field is made quite happy by hearing from Ester. She is well and so are all your Nieghbours.

Captain Brackit has lost that pale delicate little Daughter of his. Scattering the Kings-Evil[18] which she had in her neck was the cause. Fanny Nash we fear will not live long. She is in a consumtion. Captain Jo. Baxter is going to marry Deacon Arnolds Widdow, much against her Friends advice, but of how little avail is this in such cases. But tis very hard when we think we see our Friends connecting themselves in a manner that will make their future Days unhappy, to be silent.

I have heard so much of the fine climate of France, that the account you give me of the Gloom appearence of the winter Surprises me. Give me a warm House and an american winter I say.

There are a number of things in your House which I think will be usefull for your Sons at college. They will want Sugar and Tea. There is one cannester unoppend and a little Breakfast-Tea in another. The Bag of Pepper Docr. Tufts thinks had better be sold. It will loose its strength. We find it necessary to open and shake the woolen Cloaths in your House very often. The Moths have got into the Hair of the trunks. We have order'd them to be keept Brush'd. I have at present a violent cold but as soon as tis better, I shall make a thorough rummage and pin all the woolens up close in Sheets. There is no other way to preserve them. Are there none of those cloaths that will do to be alter'd for Cousin Charles? The Fashon may alter so much, that Mr. Adams will not chuse to wear them. Cousin Charles is grown very tall I am told. I bought three pair of stockings for him last winter. Sister Shaw Says they must have more this Spring. I cloth'd them in Lamb-Skin for winter. Sister writes me that they did not put on their new Shirts till January, but that the Linnen was so poor that by the Time they had been wash'd twice or three times she had to mend them from one end to the other. I have I think got them a very pretty Piece of Linnin, and have sent for their measure. The children will make them as soon as they recieve them. I disign to take care of Cousin[s] washing when he becomes a Collegian. I can then mend them in Season.

Mr. Thacher is settled at Doctor Coopers, and is become quite [*an*] old story. Many of the People are gone to the old Brick.[19] By the way they have made a very elligant house of it and have got an organ in it. Have you read Doctor Cha[u]ncys Book, which was publish'd in England last Summer? It has been much talk'd of there. It has been republish'd here, but instead of making a noise as it was thought it would, it has silenc'd every body. There has not been one attempt to answer that I can hear off. True or not, tis most admirable done.

Weymouth are in an unsettled State yet and like to be so for any thing that appear at present. They have behaved oddly this winter, and treated the Doctor Shamfully, and all because he would not vote for a man he did not like.

I hear that Lyde is to sail next Sunday. Mr. T would not write till the Court which began to set ⟨*excepting two days last week*⟩ this week was over, so that unless he writes in Boston which I should think he may, he will not write by this vessel. I dont know how it is with you, but I had rather have a Letter by every vessel than a volume at a time, and that but seldom. I wish you could see him when he is writing. Shut up in his chamber for a week together with about forty Books round him: I told him one day, that one Letter warm from the Heart and sent *in Season* was worth all of them. I ask'd him also what excuse he could make for his neglect. He said he should make none. I confess I felt too much to answer him. I will not take another Sheet. Som thing shall be left for the next vessel. Love to Mr. Adams and cousins. Adieu, may you be happy prays your affec Sister

M Cranch

RC (Adams Papers); endorsed at the top of the first page: "Mrs Cranch."

[1] This is Mary Cranch's second letter of 1785 to AA; the first is dated 16 Jan., above.

[2] Not found.

[3] AA to Mary Cranch, 9 Dec. 1784, above, was finished on 12 December.

[4] AA to Royall Tyler, 4 Jan., is above; no letter to Richard Cranch for this period has been found.

[5] "Hall" may have been corrected from, or to, some other name. No letter from Susanna Boylston Adams Hall to her son, JA, has been found.

[6] Rev. Anthony Wibird.

[7] See AA to Mary Cranch, 9 Dec. 1784, and note 21, above.

[8] JA's father, Deacon John Adams, had died in May 1761. Under the terms of his will, dated 8 Jan. 1760, and proved on 10 July 1761 (JA, *Papers*, 1:33–38, 51–53), Susanna Boylston Adams was to receive one-third of the income from the Deacon's estate, and one third of his personal estate. JA and his brothers, Peter Boylston and Elihu, received particular bequests of real estate, and were expected to support their mother from the income of those bequests.

[9] Peter Boylston Adams of Braintree, Susanna Boylston Adams Hall's only surviving son in America, with whom she lived after John Hall's death in 1780.

[10] Mary Cranch wrote quotation marks before "She."

[11] AA's brother, William Smith Jr., may have been in New York state, where later in the year he would be tried and acquitted for passing forged notes. See Mary Cranch to AA, 10 Dec., below, and 22 March 1786 (Adams Papers).

[12] See AA to Mary Cranch, 9 Dec. 1784, above, under 12 December.

[13] JQA's last known letter to Richard Cranch is 6 Sept. 1784 (MeHi); his 12 Dec. 1784 letter to Mary Cranch is above.

[14] Elizabeth Quincy Guild. Her husband Benjamin Guild, like many Boston merchants, suffered a serious business failure in 1785 (see Mary Cranch to AA, 19 July, below; JQA, *Diary*, 1:315).

[15] See JQA to William Cranch, 14 Dec. 1784, above. James and Mercy Warren's son Charles had gone to Cap-Français (now Cap-Haitien) in Ste. Domingue for relief of his tuberculosis (JQA, *Diary*, 1:313–314). The fate of JQA's violin is not known.

[16] Elizabeth Storer Smith; "uncle" shortly below is her husband, Isaac Smith Sr.

[17] Perhaps Elizabeth Winslow, daughter of the late Rev. Edward Winslow, the Anglican minister who preached in Braintree for the Society for the Propagation of the Gospel from 1763 to 1777, and then served as a chaplain for the British navy at Newport and New York until his death in 1780 (vol. 1:154, note 1; *Sibley's Harvard Graduates*, 11:97–107).

[18] Scrofula, a chronic enlargement and degeneration of the lymphatic glands, which was traditionally believed to be curable by the touch of a king or queen (*OED*: "King's evil"; "scrofula").

[19] The "Old Brick" was the First Church of Boston, located on Washington (Cornhill) Street, near the old State House, and fairly close to the Brattle Square Church (Annie Haven Thwing, *The Crooked & Narrow Streets of the Town of Boston 1630–1822*, Boston, 1920, map opposite p. 78). Mary Cranch had voiced her reservations about Peter Thacher succeeding Samuel Cooper at the Brattle Square Church in her letter of 6 Nov. 1784, to AA, above.

Elizabeth Smith Shaw to Abigail Adams

My Dear Sister   Haverhill April 25th. 1785

Not to hear one word from Novem. to April seemed a very long space of Time, to One solicitous for the Welfare, and deeply interested in every-thing relative to, or that can affect the Happiness of a much loved Sister. I have this Week been made happy by receiving two charming Letters from you.[1] It was a Repast my very Soul thirsted after. And as I am informed that a Vessel is to sail the last of this Month, I wish to improve this Opportunity of Writing to you, as I flatter myself you will be gratified by hearing from me. Altho' my Letters cannot boast of the same *excellencies*, as those I receive, yet I may venture to say, they are not presented with less love, and tender Affection. I thank you my Sister for your kind solicitude for my Health. Be assured I received it just as you intended, as an effusion of your Love, and Benevolence, and I never entertained even in younger Life, an Idea that *You* wished to assert the superiority of eldership. If at any time your Counsel and Advice, ever opposed my Inclination, I always believed it to arise from the heighth of goodness, and from too great an Opinion of, and Love for me.—Let me assure you I have acted agreeable to your Injunctions, though I cannot say it was without Mr. Shaws interposition, and have not Ironed or touched the wet Cloaths this Winter. I have been obliged to content myself by employing my Time in a Way that would expose my Health less, and I hope as useful to my Family: As we have had twelve in it all Winter,[2] I find there is suffcent sewing, and no occasion for my being idle. My Health this Spring is much as usual, I have no Cough, but my Lungs are still weak. When I see how many hardships Others can endure I am almost tempted to repine at my own feeble Constitution, but that would be opposite to that Humility of Heart which makes happy. Gratitude for present Mercies, and cheerful Resignation to the dispensations of Providence in all time to come is a Temper of Mind I would wish devoutely to cultivate.

Your Children are still in fine Health, they have been two Quarters to dancing School, and they both dance excellently, but Mr. Charles exquisitely. You know what an Ear he has for Musick, and that has been of Great advantage to him in his movements. He is graceful in all his motions, and attitudes, he, as if his Profile had been faithful to the maternal charge, has held up his head much better than formerly. At the close of each Quarter the[y] have had a Ball, in our new assembly Room, and Mr. Charles had the honour of opening it, with a Minuet, with Miss Sally White.³ I find the Misses all like to have him for a Partner. Mr. Le Blanch closed his School with a publick Ball the 15 of this Month, and now Mr. Charles having improved by the Graces, must pursue after their Mistress Literature, with greater diligence than ever, for it is but a few Months now, before Mr. Shaw expects to offer him, with Mr. Samuel Walker, at the University of Cambridge, where I hope neither Preceptor, nor Scholar will have the mortification of a Refusal.

Thomas is a very good Child, he does not want for fondling over because your are absent, he has many a kind stroke, and kiss upon that account. Miss Nancy often makes me think of your Jenny's behaviour to Tommy, the pleasantness and innocence of two little Children. I think his natural roughness is much worn of, and he never thinks of seting down out of his School Room, but with us.

I have not received the Trunk of Cloaths you mention yet, but hope to, before I make their Summer wear, for Cousin Charles has out-grown all his, and Thomas must have them. I have made them both Winter Coats and waistcoats of cloth couloured Lambskin. It was Mr. Charle's Taste. Tommys uniform blue coat and Jacket, and [I?] shall carry to Braintree. I believe they both will make a very good coat for his Cousin Boylstone. What they have not out-grown, I have mended so that they are not worth much. I shall endeavour to distribute their cloaths so as to do as much good as possible, or in other words, I shall act as I think my Sister would. I believe the Linnen which was made up for my Cousins before you embarked was damaged, for they did not put them on till the middle of January, and they are now mended more than you would wish to see them. I sent Last week to have Linnen purchased for them and it is accordingly done. So you need not think the poor Boys will suffer. For I shall always take unspeakable pleasure in serving them, while their dear native Gaurdians are absent.—Judge Seargants [*Sargeant*] Family are well. Mr. Payson was married to Mrs. White a month ago, and I have made the wedding Visit, and found them as fond a Couple as you would chuse to see in the honey-Moon.—Dear Venerable Mrs. Marsh has been confined to her room, and cheifly to her Bed, ever since September, but as meek, and resigned as Patience itself. Faith, Hope, and humble Zeal asswages her Pain, and lightens the weight of her heavy Sufferings.

I have most got to the end of my paper, and have not said half what I intended. I have not thanked You for your account of Enfans

Trouves, I indeed lament the Cause, while I am pleased with the Institution. I think that country that will admit 52 thousand unmarried Women to enter their Names at the police for abandoned purposes, ought certainly to make ample provision for such a spurious Offspring.

RC (Adams Papers).

[1] Of 14 Dec. 1784, and 11 Jan., both above.

[2] The family included four Shaws, CA, TBA, Samuel Walker, Nancy Hazen, Betsy Smith (daughter of AA's brother William), and for extended periods, either Betsy or Lucy Cranch, plus a few servants.

[3] Sarah, daughter of Samuel White of Haverhill (JQA, *Diary*, 1:373).

Abigail Adams to Cotton Tufts

Dear Sir   Auteuil [26 *April*] May 2d. 1785[1]

It was not untill the 21 of April that your Letter of December 1st. reach'd me, tho forwarded by Mr. Elworthy the 2 of Feb'ry. Where it has lain ever since I cannot divine, as many letters from all quarters come to us weekly. The contents of yours were not so political as to have made it necessary to have detaind them so long, four hundred and fifty thousand livres anual Salary to the intendant of posts for decyphering and Copying Letters one would think a sufficient Sum to render them expert at the buisness.[2]

This Letter I trust will be deliverd you by my son[3] whose departure from hence will be Soon. You will easily believe that we make a Sacrifice of our present enjoyment in consenting to his return without us. Indeed he has been so usefull that I know not what his Father will do without him, as close application to writing is become so injurious to him that he never applies himself a few hours together to his pen without Suffering for it, and there is So much Copying to do for a person in publick Life, that I think he cannot do without a secretary. But neither Mr. Adams or I are willing that our Sons should be brought up without a regular Education and some profession or Buisness by which they may honestly earn their Bread. For this purpose we have thought it best, that he should return to America and pass a Year or more at Colledge, and by obtaining a degree there be able to rank amongst his fellow citizens. Altho so long in Europe I think I may with confidence Say, that he will carry Home neither the vices or Fopperies of it. Tho he has been a Witness to the pomp and Splendour of Courts, he is I hope Republican enough to leave these Ideas in their native Soils, and to exhibit an example of prudence and frugality which he knows to be very necessary for him in order to the compleation of his and his Brothers Education. I recommend him Sir to your Friendship your care and patronage, as well as his Brother who I Suppose will enter Colledge this Year. Mr. Adams has written you upon this Subject[4] and requested you to take the charge upon you of Supplying their expences and drawing upon him for the discharge of them. I am sensible it is an important Charge, because merely paying their Bills is not all we ask of you. We beg you to counsel and advise them as Children of your own, and we hope and trust that they will not give you any unnecessary trouble. I know that your Family is not calculated to receive them at the vacancies.[5] I have therefore requested Mr. and Mrs. Cranch to let them make their House their Home, and Mrs. Cranch will be kind enough to take care of their linen and cloathing, for I would not over burthen one Friend. It is uncertain whether my son JQA, will be admitted to Colledge this year. The Gentlemen who examine him will judge of his qualifications and advise him with regard to his Studies, which we think if he does not enter colledge at present, he had better persue at Haverhill under the care of his uncle.[6] You will find by conversing with him, that in many branches of knowledg he has few superiours of his age, and he has a habit of Study and application which I hope will not quit him by a Change of climate.

With regard to our family affairs Mr. Adams has written you upon them, he has however directed me to enlarge to you upon the subject of Bills, and to request you to invest 3 or four hundred pounds sterling in them, and in that kind which you shall judge most for his advantage. I should think it might not be amiss to invest one hundred pounds in the Army certificates[7] which tho not so valuable at present, will become so in time. But all this we leave to your judgment. I see by the publick papers that there had been some frauds practised in alterations of figures. You will not let that matter escape you I dare say. And you will be so good as to inform Mr. Adams whether it would be best to make larger purchases if he should find himself able. But of that I despair unless Congress should see fit to place the Salaries upon the former footing, nor then neither if as I have reason to apprehend Mr. Adams should be sent to England, where it is Still more expensive liveing than here. If we had a private fortune which we could afford to add, to what Congress allow, we might then be in Some measure upon a footing with the publick ministers of other powers, but it would then be, as it is now, a dissagreable Life to me. My happiness has ever been in a domestick State, in the Society of my Friends, rather than the World. In these European Countries you must either engage in a Life of dissipation and amusement, company and play continually, or you must live a retired one without any intimates, and See company only in a ceremonious Way. There are very few Foreign Ministers here who do not expend their Salarys their private fortunes and run deep into debt besides, unless like the Count d'Aranda the Spanish minister, they have the income of a prince. Judg you Sir whether Seperate from the Idea of serveing ones Country, any satisfaction or pleasure is to be derived to persons feeling, and thinking as we do. Few Ministers it is true have ever met with more Success than has Crownd Mr. Adams's endeavours for the publick Service, but I wonder now, much more than I did before I came abroad; how he has lived through the perplexing Scenes he has had to encounter: twice it has very nearly cost him his Life,[8] and if he should be as I fear he will appointed to England he will not have a less thorny road to tread than those which he has already past. There are many difficulties and perplexities to adjust in order to bring England and America yet together even in a commercial intercourse. The passions of both Nations instead of being cooler, appear more irritable every day: Greivious words Stir up Wrath, and perhaps our Countrymen are not sufficently aware that it is the wish of some other nations to keep us still at varience, or that the *Friendship* of *Nations* is only an other Word for interest. Mr. Adams has been so long abroad, and so largly engaged in the Field of politicks, so accustomed to "look quite through the deeds of Men," and haveing himself no other views or desires, but those of promoteing the welfare of his Country, and laying a foundation for its permanant Glory and happiness that I think he would be more likely to succeed in England than a New Hand. I cannot therefore oppose it should he be appointed, but at the same time I must solicit to return to America next Spring unless some important unfinishd negotiation Should oblige us to a longer Stay. I think from the conversation which Mr. Adams had yesterday with Mr. Hales the British Charge des affairs that if he was in England he would be like to Succeed in obtaining the Frontier Post[s], and bringing matters upon a more amicable footing. Here neitheir England or Spain will treat, and no great object can be accomplishd. If he does not Succeed in England, America will know better than now; what course to take. Mr. Adams met Mr. Hales at dinner at Count Sarsfields[9] and fell designedly into conversation with him upon the Subject of the Frontier Posts. He ask'd him what could be the reason of the delay to surrender them. Mr. Hales replied that he could not pretend to say precisely, but he had no doubt it was the private interest of some individual officer or Trader which had heitherto studied pretences, and excuses for delay, but that he might depend upon it, there were no thought at Court, or in the Nation, of holding these posts; he said Mr. Pit was a man of the most perfect Moral Character, and of the highest Sense of publick and private honour, and would abhor every Idea of voilating the National Faith. He askd Mr. Adams if he did not think Mr. Pit a wonderfull young Man? He replied that he did, and that he had often seen with Surprize his firmness and coolness and his perfect command of himself, qualities in which he had shewn him self superiour to all his Rivals, that he seem'd to be the Man for the Salvation of the Nation if it was yet in a Salvable State, but that he did not appear to be sufficiently sensible how large a share America must have in assisting him to Save it, that he would finally miss his object, and fail in all the great projects if he did not place the intercourse with America upon a proper footing. Mr. Hales laughd and said it was very true; and as soon says he as we have Settled with Ireland,[10] we will take you in Hand, and settle with you, upon honest and generous terms, but it is dangerous attempting too many things at once. This Mr. Hales appears to be a well informd sensible Man, he supports a good Character here. His Grace the Duke of Dorset I have not yet seen, but expect that honour soon, as he is to dine here this week, together with Mr. Hales and other company. Mr. Adams has dined with the Duke several times who has always been very civil and gracious to him. He lives very magnificiently here, the British court allow him a salary of nine thousand some say ten a year, but tis said he spends that, and his private fortune too. He keeps a publick table twice a week, and tho a sensible Man is a lover of pleasure, and some say, of Play too.

[*27 April*]

Company comeing in I broke of my writing, last evening. Mr. Jefferson came in from Paris and informd us that the March packet had arrived and that he had received some Letters, one of which from Mr. Gerry ⟨*informd*⟩ acquainted him that Congress had appointed Mr. Adams Minister to London.[11] This is an event tho not unexpected, from the late Letters which have been received, yet an event which will load with cares and anxieties the Head and Heart of my Friend, subject him I suppose to many censures, and no small share of ill nature. I hope each State will do all in their power to render the burden as light as they can, by stricktly adhereing to the National Faith and honour pledged by the Treaty, that they will suffer no undue warmth to prevail, or the intrigues of any Nation to blind their eyes to the prejudice of their own.

The Spring is opening now in great Beauty, and Auteuil begins to look Charming. The exchange of climate must be for the worse. I shall regreet that, and the loss of Mr. Jeffersons Society. In some respects I shall find myself happier in England. I expect that we shall necessarily be subject to much more company, and concequently more expence, but I will not be over anxious. Our Country will not forget their best Friends, and our Children I hope will be qualified to earn their Bread.

What ever you find necessary to be done in our private affairs, you will do, tho you have not immediate opportunity to inform us of it. With Regard to Mr. Pratt, you will do what you think just and reasonable. And be so good as to add to the list of the poor the wife of John Hayden, the old Man who lives by the meeting house. 2 dollors to her, but at different seasons of the Year. I wish it was in my power to enlarge the sums, and increase the number. I reflect upon this trifle with more pleasure than all the Sums I am necessatated to spend here.

My most affectionate Regards to my Aunt and cousins. Pray sir continue to write to me. Writing to my Friends and Receiveing Letters from them; is one of the highest pleasures I enjoy here. I know not when we shall be obliged to leave this Country, as no official account has yet reachd us, nor any commission, but I suppose Congress see so fully the necessity of adjusting their affairs in England, that they will not delay the Matter. Your next Letters you will address to London and to Mr. Adams as Minister there. Nabby sends her duty to you and my Aunt. She is well, and a Good child. I hope she will ever be a happy one, and to this purpose sir I wish you to give advise to a Young Friend of hers,[12] when ever you see it necessary. I was not without anxiety, as every thoughtfull young person must be, when they are going to connect themselves for Life, when I changed a Single for a Married State. I need not say to you Sir that my own union has been of the happiest kind, but I am not the less desirious that my daughters should prove so too, tho I have had more fears and more anxieties for her than ever I felt for myself. This Sir is between ourselves. I will leave my Letter open untill my Son goes and possibly I may fill my paper.

May 10th

Mr. Adams has received his commission and we must hasten to arrange our affairs as soon as possible. We talk of going the 20th. I hope however not quite so soon, tho the nature of the Buisness is such as requires an immediate attention, and we shall make no unnecessary delay. Mr. Adams is full of anxiety. If he does not succeed it will not be oweing to any want of application or endeavours for the publick service. The Duke of Dorset has been so polite as to tell him, that either in a publick or private capacity he should be happy to serve him. Mr. Smith the Secretary of Legation[13] has not yet arrived. Dr. Franklin has received leave to return and talks of going out in july, but with his disorder I cannot conceive how he will bear a voyage.

By my son I have sent you 50 pounds Lawfull Money,[14] part of which is money which I brought with me, but not passing neither here or in England I thought it best to return it, to America. With this money which I call mine I wish you to purchase the most advantageous Bills and keep them by themselves. If hereafter I should be able to add to it, I may establish a little fund for my pensioners.

My Son will give you all the politicks of the Day. Yours   A A

PS. As there is a communication between the Medical Society of Paris and Boston I thought it might not be amiss for the improvement of one of its members[15] to communicate the inclosed, as a Specimen for his future practise. It is usual for Physicians when they attend any person of character to write daily as you see, and very particularly the Symptoms of their paitients. A Lady who is my Neighbour being very sick, I sent frequently to inquire after her and have a collection of such kind of Billets in replie.

RC (Adams Papers); endorsed: "Mrs. Abigl. Adams May. 1785 recd. Aug. 29."; and "Recd. Aug. 29. 1785."

[1] "May 2d. 1785" is written in a different pen point than both "Auteuil" and the first section of the text, which was written on 26 April (see note 9). It does not appear that any part of this letter was written on 2 May, which was the day on which JA received his commission to the Court of St. James's (JQA, *Diary*, 1:259–260).

[2] See AA2 to Elizabeth Cranch, 10 Dec. 1784, and note 1, above.

[3] See JA to Tufts, 24 April, note 3, above.

[4] JA to Tufts, 24 April, above.

[5] Lucy Quincy Tufts was in poor health,

and not able to care for JQA and CA during their school and college vacations.

[6] Rev. John Shaw.

[7] Final settlement certificates given to army troops in lieu of cash; freely bought and sold by investors.

[8] AA refers to JA's two serious illnesses in Europe: in Aug.-Oct. 1781, in Amsterdam; and in Sept.-Oct. 1783, in Paris (vol. 4:224, and note 3; JA, *Diary and Autobiography*, 3:143–144; JA to AA, 14 Oct. 1783, above).

[9] The Adamses—at least JA and JQA—dined at Count Sarsfield's on 25 April (JQA, *Diary*,

1:255). The secretary of the British embassy was Daniel Hailes; he had dined with the Adamses on 14 April (same, 1:249).

[10] In Jan. 1785, at a time when Ireland was in great economic distress, the Pitt ministry proposed a new Anglo-Irish commercial relationship. Resistance from merchants in northern England, and amendments proposed by the Irish Parliament in February, forced Pitt to reconsider his plan. On 12 May, he submitted a heavily revised proposal to the British House of Commons, and this was altered further before passage by both houses of Parliament in July. But the entire proposal was rejected by the Irish Parliament in August, and no further reforms were attempted for several years. AA2 to JQA, 4 July, and note 31, below; Vincent T. Harlow, *The Founding of the Second British Empire*, London, 1952, vol. 1:558–616.

[11] See JA to Richard Cranch, 27 April and note 1, below. The next three paragraphs were written between 27 April and 2 May, the day on which JA received his commission to Great Britain (see note 1, above).

[12] Royall Tyler.

[13] William Stephens Smith, of New York, was appointed secretary of the American legation in Great Britain on 1 March, and arrived in London in May, just before the Adamses. The Adamses first learned of his appointment on 29 April. See JA, *Diary and Autobiography*, 3:177, note 1, 183–184, note 3; JQA, *Diary*, 1:258, and note 1.

[14] Massachusetts paper currency.

[15] AA refers to Tufts himself. AA's ailing neighbor was Madame Helvétius. When AA first heard of her illness and inquired how she was doing on 11 April, she "received a curious handbill for answer" (JQA, *Diary*, 1:248), probably the first of the enclosed "billets" referred to below. These items have not been found.

John Adams to Richard Cranch

Dear Sir   Auteuil April 27th. 1785

Last Evening, Mr. Jefferson, my worthy Friend called upon me to shew me a Letter from Mr. Gerry which came by the March Packet,[1] in which it is said that Mr. Adams is appointed to London, so that I suppose you will have no more occasion to write to me, but in that way.

It will be pleasanter in some respects to me and my Family to be in England, than in France, or Holland, but it will be more expensive, more laborious, and what is of more consequence to my Feelings more difficult to give Satisfaction to my Countrymen. I know not whether I shall meet a candid or even a decent Reception in England. It is not to be expected that I should be cherished and beloved, but I may be more likely to succeed, if it is true as a Gentleman from London once told me, at the Hague, about a year ago. "Sir, says he, I certainly know there is no Man in public Life whom the English fear so much as you."[2] They have however less cause to fear from me, than some others because, I confess that although I would contend for my Country's Rights against them, as much as any Man, yet my System of Politics is not so hostile to them, nor so subservient to the Views of some of their Enemies as some others.[3]

Congress I see are aroused, at the Conduct of the English, and are about to act, with Spirit and Dignity. They shall be seconded, as far

5. AUTEUIL AND PASSY, FROM THE ISLE DES CYGNES, CA. 1785

See page x

as may depend upon me, to the Utmost of that little Prudence and Fortitude which remains in me, and I confess I do not yet despair, entirely of Success. I shall find no where so fine a little Hill, so pleasant a Garden, so noble a Forest and such pure Air and tranquil Walks, as at Auteuil: But although my Health is dear to me, the Public Peace, and Prosperity are dearer.

Would you believe that my young Secretary should prefer Harvard Colledge, and the Bar at Boston to the Delights of England? I see with Pleasure that he does. He carries my Affections and best Wishes to you and Sister Cranch and your Children.

I shall part with Mr. Jefferson, with great Regret, but as he will no doubt be placed at Versailles, I shall be happy in a Correspondence of Friendship, Confidence, and Affection with the Minister at this Court, which is a very fortunate Circumstance, both for me, and the public.

My Love to Uncle Quincy, Mr. Wibert, and Mr. Palmers Family; my Duty to my Mother and Brother, and regards to Mr. Tyler.

If I should not be able to accomplish any Thing in England, I shall come home the next Spring. I consider this Appointment as critical, and decisive to me if my Health can Sustain the Anxiety, I shall be happy. You must watch over my Boys, in their Orphan State and advise and admonish them when you have opportunity. Your affectionate Brother.

LbC in JQA's hand (Adams Papers).

[1] Gerry to Jefferson, 25 Feb., in Jefferson, *Papers*, 7:651–652.

[2] The speaker has not been identified.

[3] JA undoubtedly intends Benjamin Franklin, and all Americans whom he believed were under strong French influence.

Catharine Louisa Salmon Smith to Abigail Adams

My Dear Sister   Lincoln April 27 1785

Your kind Letter of the 15th. December[1] came to me last week, and should I pretend to describe the innate Plesure I felt on the perusal, words would be wanting in the description. I most ardently wish to see you, and hope it will not be many years before I shall have that pleasure.

I realy wish that those customs you speak of were indeed adopted here. I have more reason to wish it than many others, haveing been too much used to be considered as a Species apart from the Lords of the Creation. There are very few but what wishes it, yet have not resolution to bust those Magick fetters which that tyrant Custom has shackeled them with.

You must not expect news from the shades of Lincoln. I know but very little of what passes in the gay world. My imployments or diversions do not often extend beyond the little circle at my own fire side. I am indeed so vain as to think that nothing I can say will afford more satisfaction to you than to tell you we are in fine Health, my little Girls and Boys are very good, and I have had nothing to interrupt my Domestick peace and tranquility. I have the inexpressible happiness to see my little tribe reward and justify my cares, by paying a strict attention to what I injoin upon them. I [look?] forward with many pleasurable ideas. You may judg with what pleasure I go through the task of instructing them (for I have no schools to send them to) when I hear them commended for their good behaveour by every mouth. You will say I write with the partiality of a fond mamma, but you I hope will excuse it.

We have had the most severe Winter and Spring that I ever remember—the Snow so deep that the Roads have been impassable for two months past. Never was such a time known in this part of [the] Globle before. Yesterday I went to Concord, the first time I have been in a Chaise for more than Six months.

Mr. Smith I have seen but once since I came to Lincoln. It grieves me to say that fame speaks him to be the same he has been for many years.

Judg Russell[2] and the Ladies I saw last Sunday. They Present their regards. The Children send their most humble Duty.

Remember me to Mr. Adams Miss Nabby and M[r. John?] and beleive me ever Your most obliged and affectionate Sister

Catharine L. Smith

Louisa[3] is grown very tall, and has injoyed a good state of health ever since she has been here, excepting now and then a pain in her side and shoulder.

RC (Adams Papers); slight damage to the text at a tear, and where the seal was cut away.

[1] Not found.

[2] Judge James Russell occupied the Lincoln estate which his son Charles had inherited from James' brother Chambers in 1766; see Catharine Smith to AA, 26 Oct., and note 3, below.

[3] Louisa Catharine Smith.

Mercy Otis Warren to Abigail Adams

Milton Hill April 30th. 1785[1]

After long Expecting that Pleasure I was Gratifyed about four days since by the Receipt of a very agreable Letter from my Friend.[2] I have so long answered in the Negative, when in all Company, the question is asked "No Letter from Mrs. Adams, your particular Friend," that I have been obliged to make many apologys for your silence, to prevent some unfavorable Construction.

I find by yours that you are not yet a European Lady, that the splendor of a Court dos not obliterate the undissembled Pleasure of sociallity in a Private Circle of *Friends*. You seem to wish for the afternoon interviews of your Country, which Custom has rendered an agreable hour. I assure you we miss you much at the little tea *parties*. This is a pleasure Ridiculed by Frenchmen. Yet perhaps it is as Rational an amusement as a Rope Dancing, a puppet show or an opera.

In the Ramblings of the Vissionary slumber, I often Visit the European shores where I have an Interest separate from my Friends at Auteiul.[3] But I more frequently transport them all to the summit of Milton, or its Neighbouring hills. When I awake I wish to Realize the Phantom. Yet I acknowledge more for my own than for their sakes.

I think you must be Exceedingly happy, though I beleive more from your Domestic than your Public Connexions. The affections of the Former are strengthened by time, while the Parade of the latter Fatigues and the Glare of Grandeur pall, upon the Eye, and after a Certain age Even Novelty dos not posses Charms sufficient to wean us from the local Attachments of Earlier life.

I do not wonder you are pleased with the Theatrical Entertainments. The Refined and Elegant Compositions must improve the Taste, while the lively Representation of Character, and the Exhibition of Great Historical Events lay open a wide Field of amusement to the Reflecting mind. And I think your situation has been peculiarly advantagous, as you Could retire to the sequestered Villa, without the interruption of thought by the bustle of a Crowd to push away the agreable images.

I Expect your next will be dated from England. I think it must be more agreable to you in many respects than France. I dare say you

113

will be very happy there, though that Nation have not discovered Either a wise or a Friendly disposition towards the Americans in General since the Conclusion of the Peace. Perhaps the treaties of Commerce may put the two Countrys on a more amicable Footing. I beleive it unfortunate that this was not done Earlier. I wish we were wise Enough to render ourselves wholly independant. But the foolish passions of mankind will forever prevent. You know it has long been my opinion that the Human Race were made for slaves, for in all ages whatever advantages Valour Virtue or Fortune throws into ⟨*their*⟩ our hands, they are Generally bartered away for the Gratification of our own Vanity, or the agrandizement of a few individuals who have not Enough to Facinate the undistinguishing Multitude.

I fear the Conduct of our own Country will stand upon record as a striking Example of the truth of this Observation. We have Goverments of our own Forming, Magistrates of our own Electing, but without Confidence in their abilities, or Energy and Decission on their part to acquire or sucure it. The Bostonians are wrangling with British Factors, Yet runing mad for their Commodities. The Narrow scale of their Politics is a Contrast to the spirit of this People previous to the Late Hostilities.

But why do I touch on a Political subject in a Letter to a Lady who has announced her determination, to Relinquish the Theme. I will ask Pardon for introducing it, when I have told her I know of another, who most ardently wishes that neither she or her Connexions had Ever been Engaged in the thorny Path. It is doubtless best for man that he cannot look into the Page of Futurity. A kind of apathy might overspread the World that might be Fatal to the Exertions of the mind. Yet few Revolutions that take place are Favorable Either to the Virtue or the Happiness of Mankind, and Even in those singuler instances when salutary Effects have resulted to the Public, most of the leading Characters who Early Embarked in the struggle have been rendered miserable, Either by the sacrifice of Fortune and Friends, the Fickleness and ingratitude of their Country, or the Machinations of a few individuals who would never have been brought into Consideration but from the Convulsions of the times. This is not a trait peculiar to America. It is the story of Man. Past ages bear testimony of its authenticity, and Future Events will Convince the unbeleiving. But I hope my dear madam that Neither you nor yours will Ever Reallize it from painful Experience.

I thank you for your Friendly inquiries after my sons, and as you particulerized all but one, I will take them in the same order.[4] The youngest is a very diligent student under the tuition of Mr. Strong of Northhamton. Harry I beleive is not too Gay for his years. Enjoys tolerable Health, but thinks it is necessary to Get into bussiness, in order to be thrifty Either in purse or in flesh. He is at present at home, waiting the Return of his Brother Charles from Cape Francois [*Cap-Français*], where he has spent the winter with much advantage to his Health. If, as we flatter ourselves his Recovery should be perminent, these two youths mean to take the manssion, the stores &c. &c. go into Bussiness at Plimouth, as that Decayed Village begins again to hold up its Head. The unfortunate wounded officer thanks Every one who inquires after him, and desires particuler respects to Mr. and Mrs. Adams.

There is yet one whom you have seen several Months since I had that pleasure. But we hear often from Lisbon where he means to Reside Yet for a time, but with a preference to his Native Country that gives me Pleasure, and an attachment unusual in a young Gentleman who has lived so long in the European World. He loves both the People and the Manners of America, better than those of any other Place. I hope None of my Friends Either young or old will stay[5] abroad long Enough to be weaned.

Are the Ladies in England[6] all Gamblers, and the Gentlemen all pleased with the accomplishment: It is a new thing to us for any one who has a Claim to Character, to Go from the Dining, to the Card table, and sit till Near midnight Painfully agitated least she rises with fewer Guineas in her poket than when she set down. It is not many years since such a Conduct would have been deemed almost un-pardonably disgracful in the heedless Youth of the other sex.

You will have so many letters to read from sisters Neices sons &c. that a protraction of this Can very well be dispenced with. Yet I shall Claim a full share in the returns.[7]

Mr. Warren would like very well to take a Veiw of the agricultural improvments in England. But rather think[8] it is too late for him to Visit Europe. Though he sometimes talks of running to Lisbon to spend a few weeks with a Beloved son, but this is the sugestion of a fond Moment, that I believe will never be Executed.

Mr. John I understand is Coming to America. My love to Him. Tell him he must by no means make himselve a stranger at Milton, but Consider it as one of his homes at least.

It seems as if you was Rather nearer by Coming to England. If it appears so to you we shall have the Pleasure of Hearing oftener from you. Do you think it will be saying too much if I tell you none will

115

be more Gratified with this Circumstance than your affectionate
Friend   M Warren

RC (Adams Papers); endorsed: "Mrs Warren April 30 1785." Tr (MHi:Mercy
Warren Letterbook). This letterbook is a selected and somewhat edited set of
transcriptions, many of which are evidently based upon drafts that have not been
found. None of the Trs are in Mercy Warren's hand, but they may have been done
in the last years of her life (see vol. 1:93–94, note 1). The editors have noted only
major differences between the Tr and the RC.

[1] The transcript is dated 24 April.

[2] AA to Mercy Warren, 5 Sept. 1784, above, finished on 12 December.

[3] The transcript confirms that Mercy is here referring to her son Winslow, then in Portugal; see below.

[4] Mercy Warren reports on her sons in a somewhat different order than AA inquired about them (AA to Mercy Warren, 5 Sept. 1784, above). George Warren, then reading law with Caleb Strong, was eighteen. Henry Warren was twenty-one; Charles Warren was twenty-three. "The unfortunate wounded officer" was James Warren Jr., age twenty-seven, who was injured in a naval battle in

1779, and lost a leg. AA had not mentioned Winslow Warren, age twenty-six, whom Mercy discusses in the following paragraph, probably because she had seen him in London in July 1784 (AA to Mary Cranch, 6 July 1784, above). See Alice Brown, *Mercy Warren*, N.Y., 1896, p. 38, 39, 47, and 278.

[5] The transcript concludes this paragraph: "long enough abroad to wean them from their native country: yet you will all find a remarkable change of manners when you return."

[6] The transcript has "Europe."

[7] This paragraph is not in the transcript.

[8] The transcript has "but thinks."

Elizabeth Smith Shaw to Mary Smith Cranch

My Dear Sister   April 30th. 1785

I have but a moments time to write you a Line, and send you by
Mr. Allen the measure of Charles and Thomas Shirts. If you make
them 2 now, each, it will be sufficient. I have indeed been made happy
by receiving 2 Letters from my Sister,[1] but we have none from my
Cousin Nabby. I really commiserate her Situation—look round on
every side, and infelicity must be her present portion.

I suppose Sister, nor Cousin has any thoughts of returning at
present to America. Time may do much upon both sides. A State of
probation we are all in, if we act our parts with fidelity, we shall
receive an ample reward. I should think this would be a motive, to
excite us to great *Circumspection*.

You have my Sister a critical, delicate, part to act. You are at all
times apprized of the necessity of Candor, and impartiality in our
inquires respecting persons, and things. It is not sufficient to hear
only upon one side. I know not anything of the merits of the Cause.
Your own prudence, and goodness of heart, will direct you in the Path
of Duty.—And I sincerely hope it will ultimately tend to the Peace,
Satisfaction, and happiness of all our Families.[2]

Alas, how I lament the unhappy Situation of General Palmer. It seems as if Misfortune had marked him for her own—Those fair Possessions—But when these fail us we must look to the bright realms above, and even in the *midst* of every earthly Enjoyment, it is there we must fix our eye, our affections, and it is there we may place our trust.

The length of Charles Shirt, is a yard and Thomas about 2 inches shorter. I have [no] time now to say more than that I hope soon to see *you* here, but if not I hope to come myself the latter part of May, if it ever grows warm enough to settle the ways.

My Love to all—Ever Yours   E Shaw

RC (DLC:Shaw Family Papers); docketed, probably not in Mary Cranch's hand: "Letter from Mrs Shaw Apl. 30. 1785."

[1] See Elizabeth Shaw to AA, 25 April, note 1, above.
[2] This and the preceding paragraph appear to refer to some difficulty between Royall Tyler and AA2, or at least to express a concern over that relationship.

Hannah Quincy Lincoln Storer to Abigail Adams

May 3 1784 [*i.e. 1785*]

I am, My dear Madam led by Various Motives to take My pen to Scribble a few lines at least by this conveyance. The first is that you May be Sensible of My readyness to Acknowledge the favur[1] you have been pleased to shew Me in Answering My Short letter in such a descriptive Manner as to make it quite *Needless for Me* (to wish) to cross the line to become acquainted with the Mind the form the Manners the Customs dress &c. of the French Ladies.

An other is to Thank you for the receipts patterns &c. And a Third to tell you how much pleasure it Gives Me to hear that you and yours are in health and happy. May the first of Earthly blessings attend you, (at least,) while you are ingaged abroad and "obliged to pay Compliments to those you can't endure." You Now I Suppose often—

"Laugh when your Sad, Speak when yo've Nought to Say
And, for the fashion, when your blyth Seem wae:"

As *Our Magnitude* Must be *diminished* to become a *Wasp*, I am quite content, that the French Ladies shou'd laugh at us, and indulge their taste.

I feel Much Obliged to you good Lady for part of the interesting Story of the Dumb Show. It is indeed very Surpriseing that they can Operate So forcibly upon the human Mind by Mere Shew.

As Mr. Storer is closeing his Letters I have only time to add that all your friends are well, And Betsey G[uild], but alass, She's unfortunate her Husband was, and is involved in Mr. Parkers Affairs. The Story is long and you'll No doubt have it from another quarter. Farewell, and ever belive that you have a friend in her that has the happiness to Subscribe Your Affe[c]tionate   H Storer

P.S. Mr. Storer join's me with the Children in proper regards to Mr. A—ds. Gorge an Polly[2] send a return of their particular regards to you.

RC (Adams Papers); addressed: "Mrs. Adams. Paris"; endorsed: "Mrs Storer May 3d 1785."

¹ Of [*ante 19 Jan.* 1785], above.
² George and Mary Storer were two of Ebenezer Storer's children by his first wife, Elizabeth Green Storer (*Sibley's Harvard Graduates*, 12:208, 213–214).

Abigail Adams to Mary Smith Cranch

My Dear Sister   Auteuil May 8th [*ante* 5] 1785[1]

Can my dear sister realize that tis near eleven Months since I left her. To me it seems incredible, more like a dream than a reality. Yet it ought to appear the longest ten Months of my Life if I was to measure the time by the variety of objects which have occupied my attention. But amidst them all my Heart returns like the Dove of Noah[2] and rest only in my native land. I never thought myself so selfish a being as since I have become a traveller, for altho I see Nature arround me in a much higher State of cultivation than our own Country can boast, and elegance of taste and manners in a thousand forms, I cannot feel intrested in them. It is in vain for me, that here

> "Kind Nature wakes her genial power
> Suckles each herb, & nurtures every flower"

Tis true the garden yeilds a rich profusision, but they are neither plants of my hand, or children of my care. I have bought a little Bird lately, and I realy think I feel more attached to that, than to any object out of my own family animate, or inanimate. Yet I do not consider myself in the predicament of a poor fellow who not having a house, in which to put his Head, took up his abode in the stable of a Gentleman; but tho so very poor he kept a Dog, with whom he daily divided the small portion of food which he earnd. Upon being ask'd why when he found it so difficult to live himself, he still kept a Dog, What Says the poor fellow part with my Dog! Why who should I have to Love me then? You can never feel the force of this replie unless you were to go into a foreign Country without being able to Speak the language of it. I could not have believed if I had not experienced it, how strong the Love of Country is in the humane mind. Strangers from all parts of America who visit us, feel more nearly allied than the most intimate acquaintance I have in Europe. Before this will reach you, you will have learnt our destination to England. Whether it will prove a more agreeable situation than the present, will depend much upon the state of politicks. We must first go to Holland to arrange our affairs there and to take leave of that Court.[3] I shall wish to be moveing as soon as my family lessens, it will be so lonesome. We have as much company in a formal way as our Revenues will admit, and Mr. Jefferson with one or two Americans visits us in the Social friendly way. I shall realy regreet to leave Mr. Jefferson, he is one of the choice ones of the Earth. On Thursday I dine with him at his house, on Sunday he is to dine here, on Monday, we all dine with the Marquis, and on Thursday we dine with the Sweedish Ambassador, one of the most agreeable Men and the politest Gentleman I have met with, he lives like a prince.[4] I know you Love to know all my movements which make me so particular to you.

I wrote to you by the last pacquet which sailed for New York[5] in which letter I requested you to take upon you the care of Charles, after he shall have enterd Colledge, and let him make your House his Home in vacancies &c. Will you also give your Elder Nephew that leave too? At the same time we mean to pay their Board, and every other expence which they may occasion to you. I know however there are many for which you will not be pay'd only by the pleasure you take in doing good, and in sisterly kindness and affection. I hope Charles will be placed with a good Chamber mate, as much depends upon that. I do not desire that you should attend to having their washing done in your family, only be so good as to see that they have a good place at Cambridge for it, provided they should both be in colledge at the same time, which I scarcly expect will take place this year.[6]

I have many affairs upon me at present, what with my sons going away, my own adjustments for a final leave of this Country, many things must pass through my hands. But I am the less anxious to write as your Nephew will tell you all about us. You will think I ought to have written you more now, but I am almost sick of my pen, and

I know you will see what I write to others. I will not however close untill the day before he quits this House.

May 10th.

Tomorrow morning, My son takes his departure for America, and we go next week to England. I have nothing further to add than my Regards to Mr. Cranch and a desire that you would let me hear from you by every opportunity. I shall lose part and the greatest part of American intelligence by quitting France, for no person is so well informd from all the states as the Marquis de la Fayette. He has Established a correspondence in all the states and has the News Papers from every quarter.

Adieu my dear sister and be assured I am most affectionately yours,

A Adams

My Regards to Madam Quincy and daughter to Mr. Wibird to Mr. Alleynes family, and my duty to unkle Quincy.[7]

RC (MWA:Abigail Adams Corr.); addressed by JQA: "Mrs. Mary Cranch. Braintree Massachusetts."

[1] The "8th" was added later (see notes 3 and 4). "No. 8" was written above the dateline, in a different hand.

[2] Genesis 8:8–12.

[3] On 2 May, when JA received his commission to the British court, he also learned that Congress had resolved to appoint a separate minister to The Hague, but had yet to make the appointment or to recall him. For several days JA considered traveling first to The Hague to take formal leave of the Dutch court before going to England, but on 7 May he decided to go to London at once, and not to visit The Hague until he was formally recalled from that court. See JA to the secretary for foreign affairs (John Jay), 4 and 7 May (PCC, No. 84, V, f. 389–392, 397–400; *Dipl. Corr., 1783–1789*, 1:485–487, 489–490); and JA to C. W. F. Dumas, 11 May (LbC, Adams Papers; JA, *Works*, 8:246–248). AA's statement here that the Adamses would first go to Hol-

land suggests that this letter was begun on or before 7 May, and perhaps as early as 4 May (see note 4).

[4] If AA began this letter as early as 4 May, the first two engagements would have been on Thursday, 5 May, and Sunday, 8 May (see JQA, *Diary*, 1:262, 264). The third, dinner at the Lafayette's, occurred on Monday, 9 May (same, 1:264). The last engagement, dinner with the Swedish ambassador, the Baron de Staël Holstein, was certainly that which occurred on Wednesday, 11 May, attended by JA, AA, and AA2 (AA to Elizabeth Cranch, 12 May, below; JQA, *Diary*, 1:265; AA2, *Jour. and Corr.*, 1:71–72).

[5] AA to Mary Cranch, 15 April, above.

[6] This paragraph is omitted from AA, *Letters*, ed. CFA.

[7] This sentence is omitted from AA, *Letters*, ed. CFA.

Abigail Adams to Lucy Cranch

May 7 [5] 1⟨8⟩785 Auteuil[1]

I presume my dear Lucy would be dissapointed if her cousin does not deliver her a line from her Aunt. Yet it is hardly fair to take up an exhausted pen to address a young Lady whose eager serch after knowledge entitles her to every communication in my power.

I was in hopes to have visited several curiosities before your cousin left us; that I might have been able to have related them to my friends; but several engagements in the company way, and some preparation for his voyage; together with the necessary arrangements for our own journey; have so fully occupied me that I fear I shall fail in my intentions. We are to dine to day with Mr. Jefferson. Should any thing occur there worthy of notice it shall be the subject of my Evening pen.

Well my dear Neice I have returnd from Mr. Jeffersons;[2] when I got there I found a pretty large company: it consisted of the Marquis and Madam de la Fayette, the Count and Countess Douradou,[3] a French Count who had been a General in America, but whose name I forget; Commodore Jones, Mr. Jarvis[4] an American Gentleman lately arrived, the same who married Amelia Broom, who says there is so strong a likeness between your cousin, and his Lady that he is obliged to be upon his gaurd least he should think himself at Home and make some mistake. He appears a very sensible agreeable Gentleman. A Mr. Bowdoin,[5] an American also. I ask the Chevalier de Luzerns pardon I like to have forgot him. Mr. Williamos of course as he always dines with Mr. Jefferson, and Mr. Short, the one of Mr. Jeffersons family. As he has been absent some time I name him; he took a resolution that he would go into a French family at St. Germains and acquire the language, and this is the only way for a foreigner to obtain it. I have often wisht that I could not hear a word of English spoken. I think I have mentiond Mr. Short before in some of my Letters. He is about the statue of Mr. Tudor a better figure, but much like him in looks and manners. Concequently a favorite of mine. They have some customs very curious here. When company are invited to dine, if 20 Gentlemen meet, they seldom or ever set down, but are standing or walking from one part of the room to the other, with their Swords on and their Chapeau de Bras, which is a very small silk hat, always worn under the Arm. These they lay asside whilst they dine, but reassume them immediately after. I wonder how this fashion of standing crept in, amongst a Nation who realy deserve the appellation of polite; for in winter it shuts out all the fire from the Ladies. I know I have sufferd from it many times. At dinner the Ladies and Gentleman are mixed, and you converse with him, who sets next you, rarely speaking to a person across the table; unless to ask, if they will be served with any thing from your side; conversation is never general as with us; for when the company quit the table, they fall into tete a tetes of two, and two, when the conversation is in a low voice and a stranger unacquainted with the customs of the Country, would think that every body had private buisness to transact.

[*6 or 7 May*]

Last Evening[6] as we returnd, the Weather being very soft, and pleasent, I proposed to your uncle to stop at the Tuiliries and walk the Garden: which we did for an hour: there was as usual a collection of four or 5 thousand persons in the Walks. This Garden is the most celebrated publick walk in Paris. It is situated just opposite to the River Seine, upon the left hand as you enter Paris from Auteuil. Suppose that upon Boston Neck one side flows the River Seine and on the other hand the Garden of the Tuiliries. There is a high Wall next the street, upon which there is a terace which is used as a winter walk. This Garden has six large Gates by which you may enter. It is adornd with noble rows of Trees straight, large, and tall, which form a most beautifull shade. The populace are not permitted to walk in this Garden, but upon the day of Saint Louis; when they have it all to themselves. Upon one side of this Garden is the Castle de Tuiliries, which is an immence pile of Building, very ancient. It is in one of these Chateaus that the concert spiritual[7] is held. Upon the terrace which borders this Chateau, are six Statues and 2 vases. These vases are large circular spots of water, which are conveyed there from the Seine by leaden pipes under ground. Round the great vase which is in the midst of the parterre are four Groups of white Marble; one represents Lucretia, the story I know is familiar to you. The Parissians do well to erect a statue to her, for at this day there are many more Tarquins than Lucretias. She is represented as plunging the dagger into her Bosom in presence of her Husband. There is an other statue Anchises saved from the flames of Troy, by his son Aeneas who is carrying him out upon his shoulders, leading Ascanius his son by his hand. The 3d. is the Rape of Oryth'a [*Oreithyia*] the daughter of Erectheus king of Athens by Boreas, and the fourth the ravishment of Cybele by Saturn. The two last *very pretty* ornaments for a *publick Garden*. At the end of the Great Alley fronting the largest water peice, which is in the form of an octogone, are eight more marble statues. Upon the right is Hannible counting the rings which were taken from the Chevaliers who were kill'd in the battle of Cannes [*Cannae*]. Two Seasons Spring and Winter are upon the left hand, and a very beautifull figure of Scipio Africanus, near which are the two other

Seasons, Summer and Autumn, and a statue of the Empress Agripina. Over against these are four Rivers Collossus represented sleeping, viz. the Seine, the Loire, the Tiber and the Nile. At the end of the two terraces are two figures in Marble mounted upon winged Horses. One is Mercury and the other Fame, who as usual is blowing a Trumpet. In very hot weather the Alleys are waterd. Under the Trees are Seats and chairs which you may hire to set in for a Sou, or two. There are many plots of Grass intersperced.

Thus you see I have scribled you a long Letter. I hope my description will please you. This is my Eleventh Letter and I have yet several others to write. So adieu my dear Lucy and believe me most affectionately Yours   Abigail Adams

PS. I have sent by your cousin a peice of silk for your sister and you a Gown of which I ask your acceptance. There are 17 yard/2. I would have had a yard half more if I could, but it was all: being 3 quarters wide I believe it will answer.[8]

RC (Adams Papers Editorial Files).

[1] For the assigned dates of the sections of the text, see notes 2 and 6.

[2] JQA places this dinner, with the guests named here, on 5 May (*Diary,* 1:262).

[3] Comte de Doradour had recently lost much of his fortune in a lawsuit, and was planning to settle with his family in Virginia where, he thought, his modest means would be less of a burden than in polite French society. The count planned to sail with JQA in the May packet, but at the last minute he delayed his departure for a month, much to JQA's annoyance. Doradour was soon disappointed with Virginia, and returned to France in 1786 (JQA, *Diary,* 1:249, 256, 262, 265–266; and see Jefferson, *Papers*).

[4] James Jarvis of New York, who had married the daughter of the New York merchant Samuel Broome (JQA, *Diary,* 1:254, note 2, 307).

[5] This was John Bowdoin of Virginia, a member of the House of Burgesses in 1774 (Jefferson, *Papers,* 1:108).

[6] This "Evening" was either immediately following the dinner at Jefferson's on 5 May, or on 6 May when AA and AA2, at least, were in Paris quite late in the day (JQA, *Diary,* 1:262–263).

[7] The *concerts spirituels,* begun in 1725 and held on Sundays and holidays, were originally devoted to sacred music, but the programs soon became thoroughly secular and included both vocal and instrumental compositions. Italian composers were especially favored, but certain French pieces and Haydn symphonies were also popular. Beginning in 1784 the concerts were held in the Salle des Machines, in the northern wing of the Tuileries. AA and AA2 attended one such concert on 2 or 3 April. See Rice, *Jefferson's Paris,* p. 30; AA2, *Jour. and Corr.,* 1:68; JQA, *Diary,* 1:244; and Larousse, *Grand dictionnaire universel.*

[8] The postscript is omitted from AA, *Letters,* ed. CFA.

Abigail Adams 2d to Elizabeth Cranch

Auteuil May 6 1785

I have now before me your two last Letters by [my?] Dear Eliza[1] received by Capt Calliham which I mean to answer before my Brother departs, and this will be in a very few days. You cannot wonder that is an event that I am not at all gratified with. I think of it as little as possible for tis hard to [. . .] the [. . .][2] that he is to be with us by anticipating the lonesomeness of our situation when he Shall be gone. The hope that it is promoting his advantage renders it less Painfull and the idea that he is going home and to all our friends and relations is much less disagreeable than if he were going to a land of Strangers. You have promised to admit him as a fourth Brother.[3] I doubt not that you will find him deserving your regard friendship and esteem.

If you could Eliza be transported into our garden at this time, I think you would enjoy much satisfaction, and I am sure you would confer upon me a great degree of pleasure. At the bottom of it there is a thicket of Lilacs and jasmines, planted to attract the Birds in the spring. They will in a few days be out in blossom, and there is already a Number of Nightingales who have taken their residence in the bushes and every Morning and evening when the weather is warm enough to admit, they Sing to us most beautifully. The scenes I am sure would enchant my Dear Cousin, I never go into the garden without thinking of her. My fancy often places her by my side, and I sometimes even Listen to her raptures upon the surrounding scenes.

But I am going to call your imagination from this rural and romantic picture to a description that will afford ample scope to your fancy. It is of an Opera which has lately appeard and which I have seen, the title is *Panurge dans l'Isle des Lanternes*.[4] It appears that the Lovers in this Island cannot unite themselvs but under the good pleasure of the Goddess who they adore under the name of Lignobie. The actions begins the day consecrated to the *fete* of the Goddess. She is invoked by the whole People to consent to the Marriage of two of the principle inhabitants of the Island who are beloved by their Misstresses as much as they themselvs love them, and replys by the mouth of her Preist that she approves the double marriage, and that they shall be happy, if without ceasing to be faithfull to their Lovers the two Misstresses become equally beloved by a stranger which a tempest shall throw upon their shore. Dispair seizes the minds of every one, not only because it is a new delay but also because that Thunder was never known in their climate and the accomplishment of the oracle appears impossible.

Nevertheless in the midst of their universal discouragement, the Heavens become obscure and they hear at a distance the begining of the tempest. From their particular situation hope springs in every heart, and the joy of the inhabitants augments more and more in proportion as the Storm increases. They discover an unhappy wretch tossing upon the Waves in a frail boat, but his crys only excite their curiossity. They determine finally to retire; he declares in arriving that his name is Panurge. The Lovers interested to bring about the accomplishment of the oracle, load him with caresses. Panurge natureally possessing a good opinion of himself attributes to his Personal attractions the flattery they bestow upon him. He appears in the 2d. act dresst in the fashion of the Country. *Tenire* one of the two Lovers interested to please him, receives him and makes him many compliments. Panurge not only takes them as serious but is persuaded that they are from the mouth of the young *Lanternaise* a true declaration of Love, and he begins himself to find them amiable. The tete a tete is interrupted by *Agarenne* the second Misstress sister to *Tenire*, who feigns to be jealous for a moment, and finishes by affecting a great share of indifferance and gaiety. Panurge attracted by the vivacity of *Agarenne* thinks that she may have more regard to become agreeable to him. Finally the two sisters agree between themselvs, to demand Panurge to explain himself and make a choice. Panurge cannot determine, and they quit him to return to the Ball.

Poor Panurge when left alone complains to Love for not having rendered him less amiable or less *amoureux*. Climéne Wife of Panurg, who the corsaires had taken in the voyage that she had made to meet her husband, and who they had sold as a slave and who served in this capacity the two sisters beloved by Panurge, had a Project to punish the vanity of her husband and at the same time to indeavour to remind him of his first attachment, disguised herself as the Master of the ceremonies, instructs him in what manner he must conduct himself at the Ball, and engages him to decide. Panurge allways uncertain when he sees the two Misstress[es] together cannot pronounce. He at last determines to follow the Consell of Climene and goes to consult the Sibylle. Climene agrees with the four Lovers to change herself with the character of the Sibylle. Panurge in the third act renders himself to the place appointed; he sees the little *Lutins*[5] who reply to him only by ridiculous gestures from which he can comprehend nothing; he interrogates the Sibylle, she even, replys to him at first while concealed from his eyes only by pronouncing the last monosyllable of his demand. She appears finally and recalls to him his first engagements. Panurge cannot deny them, but declares that he determines to break them because that his Wife was Wicked and *ennuyeuse*. The Sibylle takes the part of Climene, brings to the remembrance of Panurge his first promises, and tells him that she has no more those faults which he reproaches her with. She finally discovers herself to him, and Panurge embrases with avidity the occasion which so natureally presents, to dispence with his making a choise that he considered as impossible. The Oracle being accomplished in every point, the Goddess appears in a Great Lanterne and Consents to the marriage of the Lovers, which they celebrate by a general feast.

"The Plan of this peice and the situations are very comique. It has been received with great applause, and has had a great success. The Principle Parts are those of Panurge and of Climene his Wife; that of Panurge is much the most dificult as he is allways in a situation Comique, and as it is necessary to avoid rendering it low by addapting too much buffoonery. Mademoiselle St. Huberti a celebrated actress at the Opera, excelles in the two kinds, which seem to exclude each other. She is as natureally placed in the Part of the Wife of Panurge who amuses herself with the foolishness of her husband, as in that of the Queen of Carthage, in which she has been so generally crowned."

Thus my Dear Cousin I have given you an account of a peice which is much admired, in Paris. I hope it will please you. The scenery and dresses were very curious, as you may suppose in the Island of Lanterns. When a celebrated peice appears at either of the Play houses, there is very soon some Hat or Cap, comes out named after it. Panurge appears in a very large hat as large as an umbrella, and it was not a week before the Milliners had made a hat, which is calld *Chapeau à la Panurge*; it is a straw hat striped with black.

The dansing was superior to any thing you can have an idea of, without having seen it. There were four of the best dansers, all dansing at a time, "each in their kind seemd to dispute the Palm of their art." But I am very sure the Dansing upon the Stage here could not please you at first, for tho it is carried to the greatest Perfection, it is nevertheless divested of every idea of female delicacy and modesty. An American Lady who came to Paris with American ideas of delicacy, told me, and it was my own observation upon myself also, that when she first went to the Opera and saw the dansing, She wanted to conceal herself. But in a very little time she could see it with the rest of the World and admire it as they did.

Be so good my Dear Cousin as to Present my Duty and respects to all my friends to whom they are due. Particularly to your Pappa and Mamma, and beleive me at all times your friend   Amelia

RC (MHi:C. P. Cranch Papers); docketed in an unknown hand: "Letter from Mis A Adams to Miss Eliz: Cranch. France. May 6th. 1785."

¹ Not found.

² Two words on a badly worn fold are illegible.

³ That is, after William Cranch, CA, and TBA.

⁴ *Panurge dans l'île des lanternes*, an opera in three acts with libretto by Etienne Morel de Chedeville and the Comte de Provence and music by André Grétry, opened in Paris on 25 Jan. 1785. The hero was drawn from Rabelais' *Pantagruel*. JQA saw *Panurge* on 25 Feb., the "12th time" it was performed, and was impressed with the music and dancing, but thought the words "very bad" (Larousse, *Grand dictionnaire universel*; JQA, *Diary*, 1:226–227).

⁵ Elves or goblins.

Abigail Adams 2d to Lucy Cranch

N 2.

Auteuil May 6th. 1785

Your agreeable favour¹ my Dear Cousin was received by me some time since. I have defered answering it till my Brother should go, that he should have the pleasure of delivering it to your own hand. He leaves us in less than a week, and tho he is going to many friends and will soon form many acquaintance, he feels himself allmost a stranger to them from having been so long absent and at a Period of Life when a few years makes more alteration in People than any other. You will all tell him Perhaps as the Chavalier de la Luzerne did the other day, he speaks English, but pronounces it as most People who Learn a Language at so advanced an age, "You was little *boa* when you went to America last but now you are great Man."²

Do not in future make me so many apology's for your Letters least they should not compensate for my own, &c &c &c.

You wonder whether I am more pleased with the Gentlemen than the Ladies of this Country. Those Ladies with whom I am acquainted are very amiable and pleasing. I am not a judge of the Gentlemen for I have seen but very few who have not been in America, and those who have resided any time with us, have most certainly imbibed a degree of the manners of our Country, which must consequently flatter and please an American, and lead me to a favourable opinion of them. You know I had not the happiness to please the French Gentleman who I have ever seen in America,³ they thought me reserved and haughty, a character so totally unknown to the Ladies of their own Country that I do not wonder at their disapprobation of those qualities in any other. I am not fond of drawing General characters of People because I think they are seldom just, and I am not qualified I am very sure to form a General opinion of the French, for I have neither Knowledge sufficient of their Language, Country, People, manners or customs. But I beleive one may without danger of deceiving say that Sprightliness vivacity and affability are characteristic of the French Women.

You suppose by the date of your Letter that I had gained a knowledge of the French Language sufficient to enable me to read and speak it fluently. This is more you know than I ever could do in my own Language. And I am told that I am more silent, if Possible, than ever. I wish however that you was not egregiously mistaken, it is not so easy a Matter to acquire a Language Perfectly I assure you. Yet I feel very much ashaimed that I have been in this Country eight Months and have not made a greater Proficiency, till I see People who have been in America or England for several years and can scarce speak enough to make themselves understood. There is nothing easier than to learn to read French, so as to understand it Perfectly, by translating a Page every day from French to English with looking every word in the dictionary, and in three months any Person may insure to themselvs knowledge enough to read the Language. If you have an inclination to Learn it provided you do not understand the Language already, I advise you to this method. It is the same I pursued. At first I found it very tedious but perseverance for some time conquered every obstacle. I can now read with facility to myself any French Book. Mr. Short who came over from America as Private secretary to Mr. Jefferson was so well convinced of the impossibility of acquiring the Language while he lived in a family where he heard nothing but English that he has been for two Months in a French family at St. Germains about twelve miles from ⟨Boston⟩ Paris, and I am told he makes great proficiency. Mr. Jefferson says the French Language Spoken by Ladies or Children is very pleasing, but by Men, it is wretched. It has often been said that there is more softness in the French than English Language, so far as I can judge I am of this opinion.

Tis probable that you know ere this time, that we expect to Leave France soon for England. A residence there will be upon many accounts more agreeable to your Aunt and to me than here, because we know the Language, and shall have many acquaintance. There are some very agreeable American Ladies there from whose society we anticipate much pleasure and sattisfaction, and we Shall have an opportunity of hearing from our friends in America much oftener and sooner than we have here. The manner of Life of most of the People of rank and consideration in Europe, is so very different from our own or what would be agreeable to us, that an acquaintance with them is rather to be avoided than solicited. There is indeed but one alternative, you must either give into their manners and customs, you must be of their card parties in the Winter and of their retirements in the Country in the summer, you must frequent the Plays Opera's Balls and all their amusements, which are necessary for them to pass away their time and absolutely essential to their happiness, every thing in short must be sacrifised to pleasure amusement dress and etiquet, or you must live perfectly retired, and form but few acquaintance. People who have been educated in a manner very different from theirs will be induced from Principle and inclination to pursue the latter path, for they would find themselvs wretched beyond description if obliged to follow such a Life. You will naturally judge from this account my Dear Lucy, that your Cousins acquaintance in the European World is like to be very contracted.

There are some it is true from our Country with educations truly American who have derived pleasure and happiness in the acquaintance they have formed here, and I have know[n] a most amiable American Lady this Winter so absorbed in the pleasures and amusements of Paris as to quit it with tears. Yet this Woman, my Cousin, was possessd of every qualification requisite to have formd as amiable a character as I have ever known, if her attention had been directed to the improvement of her mind instead of Dansing dress and amusements. If she was a friend of mine I should regret exceedingly the sacrifice she has made to European Manners.[4] Mr. Jefferson says no Gentleman or Lady should ever come to Europe under five and thirty years oold, unless they are under very good Gaurdianship—and he is a Man of great Judgement.

Be so good as to Present my Duty respects and remembrance where due, particularly to My Grand Mamma and My Aunt Tufts. To the latter I expect it will be peculiarly acceptable by being presented by my Dear Cousin.[5] Write often to your friend,   Amelia

RC (MWA:Abigail Adams Corr.).

[1] Not found.

[2] Anne César, Chevalier de La Luzerne, the French minister to the United States, 1779–1784, had first met JQA and JA in 1779, when the three sailed to America aboard *La Sensible*. On that voyage, JQA had helped La Luzerne learn English. La Luzerne may have made this remark to JQA on 2 May, when JA and JQA dined with several Frenchmen in Paris; JQA had also seen La Luzerne at the Lafayettes', and at Auteuil, in March. JQA, *Diary*, 1:230, note 1, 235, 241, 259.

³ See the Chevalier de Ronnay to AA, 2 Oct. 1782, and note 3, above. AA2's awkward construction, "who I have ever seen," replaces an illegible erased word or phrase.

⁴ AA2 probably intends Anne Willing Bingham, whom the Adamses saw often with her husband, William, from Sept. 1784 until the Binghams' departure from Paris in April. She appears frequently in AA2's journal as "Mrs. B.", and by Feb.–March in much the same character as the unnamed woman here. The Adamses would see the Binghams again in London. AA2, *Jour. and Corr.*, 1:19, 28–29, 47, 52, 56, 59; JQA, *Diary*, 1:230, 250.

⁵ Both Lucy and Elizabeth Cranch spent much time with their ailing great aunt in Weymouth, Lucy Quincy Tufts, and Lucy was her namesake.

Abigail Adams to Elizabeth Cranch

No 6

Auteuil May 8 1785[1]

Yes my dear Neice, it was a Ceremony[2] that one must study Some time to find out either utility or pleasure in it. I own tho I made one in the procession I could not help feeling foolish as I was parading first up one side of a very wide road, for a mile and half and then turning, and following down a vast number of Carriages upon the other as slow as if you was attending a funeral. By this adjustment you see, one row of Carriages are constantly going up, whilst the others are comeing down, so that each calvicade have a fair view of each other, and this is call'd going to Long Champs.

About the 3d of Feb'ry the Carnival begins. During this time there is great festivity amongst the Parissians, the operas are more frequent, and Mask'd Balls succeed them.[3] The Theaters are crowded, and every place is gay. But upon the 27 of March,[4] or the Sunday upon which the celebration of the passion of our Saviour commences, the Theaters are closed, and continue so during 3 weeks. Lent lasts six weeks, all of which is fill'd up with Church ceremonies, one of which is the Kings washing the feet of a dozen poor Boys, and the Queen as many Girls, after which they give them a dinner in the Palace at which their Majesties and the princiss of the Blood, attend them at table, the princes and Lords carrying the plates.[5] There is an other ceremony which is call'd the day of Branches. The people go very early to mass, before day light and continue a long time at it, after which the Priests go forth preceeded by some Church officer, with a large picture of our Saviour, and an other with a silver cross. The people follow two, and two, Men Women and Children with Branches in their hands, and Book[s] chanting their prayers. They go to kneel and pray before the crusifix one of which is placed upon the Road in every villiage. There are 3 days also when a peice of the *Real* and *true Cross*, as they say is shewn in the holy Chapel of Paris, and every good Catholick kisses it. Then comes holy Sunday when every body goes to Church and the Night it begins the Clergy make a solemn procession into the Halls of the palace at 3 oclock in the morning, and as nothing is performed here without the assistance of the Military, the Commandant of the Watch sends two Companies to escort this procession. But neither the Concert Spiritual which is held three times a week in the Château des Tuileries, nor all the ceremonies of the Church can compensate with the sad Parissians for the absence of the Plays. To fill up the time and vary the Amusement, this parade at Long Champs was invented. It continues 3 days. The place is about one mile from hence. It is a fine plain upon each side of which are rows of trees, like Germantown Woods. Here the Parissians appear with their Superb equipages drawn by six fleet Coursers, their Horses and servants gayly drest. All kinds of Carriages are to be seen here, from the clumsy fiacre to the gilded Chariot, as well as many Gentleman on horse Back and swarms of people on foot. The city Gaurds make no small part of the shew, for the Maré Chaussee[6] as they are call'd are placed along in rows between the Carriages, and are as despotick as their Master. Not a Coach dares go an inch from its rank, nor one carriage force it self before an other, so that notwithstanding there are many thousands collected upon this occasion, you see no disorder. But after all it is a senseless foolish parade, at which I believe I shall never again assist.

Your Cousin who I hope will have the happiness to deliver you this will tell you so much about us, that less writing will be necessary for me than on many other occasions. He cannot however say, that I feel myself happier here than I used to, at the Humble Cottage at the foot of the Hill. I wish the dimensions of that was enlarged, because I see no prospect of a more convenient one; and I hope to rejoice there with my Friends in some future Day. I think I am not unlike the Nun who used once a year to be permitted to make an excursion into the World, half of the Year she diverted herself in recounting the pleasures she had met with and the other half in those which she expected.

I shall have some regret I assure you in quitting Auteuil, since I must leave it for London instead of America, that being the destination which Congress has assignd us. The trees in the Garden are putting on their verdure, and the flowers springing into Life. The Song of the Nightingale too regales me as I walk under the trees whose thick branches intwin'd, form a shade which secures you from the rays of the Sun. I shall mourn my garden more than any other object which I leave. In many respects I think I shall feel myself happier in London, but that will depend much upon our reception there, and the Course which politicks take. If that is not agreable we shall return so much the sooner to America.

It is a long time Since I had a line from you, and I believe I have brought you very deep in debt.

I have sent you some flower seeds. You will not get them early enough for the present Season, but plant and preserve them next year that I may find them blooming when I return, and be so good as to give some of them to Mrs. Warren. Believe me my dear Girl most affectionately Yours   A Adams

RC (MHi:Jacob Norton Papers); addressed by JQA: "Miss Eliza Cranch. Braintree"; docketed in an unknown hand: "L[et]ter from Mrs. A. Adams to Miss Eliz. Cranch. France, May 8. 1785 (No. 6.)."

¹ The "8 1785" is written in a different ink; it was probably added upon the completion of the text.

² Betsy had apparently inquired, in a letter now lost, about the parade out of Paris and along the Allée de Longchamp through the Bois de Boulogne, which was held on three days each year during Holy Week. JA, AA, and AA2 briefly witnessed this affair on 24 March, and AA, AA2, and JQA joined the procession on 25 March, Good Friday, the last and most crowded day of the event. Both JQA and AA2 left vivid descriptions of Longchamp (*Diary*, 1:238, 239; *Jour. and Corr.*, 1:55–56, 62–63). Two years earlier, John Thaxter had devoted an entire letter to AA to this festive occasion (18 April 1783, above). See also the

Descriptive List of Illustrations, vol. 5.

³ JQA saw masked revellers in the streets of Paris on 7 and 8 Feb. (*Diary*, 1:220, 221); carnival week ended on 8 Feb., Shrove Tuesday (AA2, *Jour. and Corr.*, 1:46–47).

⁴ AA is in error here. In 1785, Easter fell on 27 March; the week of *Semaine Sainte* (Holy Week) began on Palm Sunday, 20 March (JQA, *Diary*, 1:238–239).

⁵ In 1785 this event occurred on 24 March. JQA noted it briefly (*Diary*, 1:238); AA2, after mentioning the royal ceremony, gave a highly critical description of a similar washing ceremony at St. Sulpice (*Jour. and Corr.*, 1:61–62).

⁶ Maréchaussée, or mounted constabulary.

Abigail Adams to Elizabeth Smith Shaw

My Dear Sister   May 8th. Auteuil 1785¹

I do not expect to date you any more letters from this place. Delighfull and blooming Garden, how much shall I regreet your loss. The fish pond and the fountain is just put in order, the trees are in blossom, and the flowers are comeing on in succession. The forest Trees are new clad in Green, several beautifull rows of which form arched bowers, at the bottom of our Garden, the tops being cut, so that they look like one continued plain. Their leaves and branches entwine and shade you intirely from the Rays of the sun. It will not be easy to find in the midst of a city so charming a scene.² I shall quit it however with less reluctance on account of my sons absence which would be more urksome to me here, than in a Country the language of which I shall be able to speak without an interpreter, or so much twisting and twirling of my tongue, and then pronouncing badly at last.[3] I expect to be more Scrutinized in England than here.[4] I said I will take heed to my ways[5] is a text of holy writ fruitfull of instruction in all Situations of Life, but speaks more loudly to those who sustain publick Characters.

Your Nephew returns with some expectation, if you give him leave; of becomeing an inhabitant in your family for six months, or more: I hope he will render himself agreable to you and all his Friends. Charles I suppose will have left you before his Brothers return. Tho absent from your family I trust he will not be so from your care, but that both his uncle and you will advise him as you find necessary.[6] I feel myself happy that I have Friends so kind and attentive to my Children that I am not anxious but what they will find good care either in Sickness or Health.[7]

It is so long since I heard from my American Friends that I begin to grow impatient. I had hopes that an other Years wandering would have put an end to our pilgrimage. You can hardly form an Idea how difficult, and expensive it is, to be house keeping, a few Months at a time in so many different Countries. It has been Mr. Adams's fortune ever since he came abroad, not to live a year at a time in one place. At the Hague he has a House and furniture, but they could not be removed 500 miles. Therefore it was necessary to hire a house and furniture here, to buy table linnen; bed linnen, China Glass and plate. Here we have resided 8 months and now we must quit this for England; removals in these Countries is not so easy a matter as in ours, for however well you may pack up your things for the purpose they must undergo so many Scrutinizes, besides paying heavy Duties for passing from one Country, to an other, of which I can give you one instanc which happended a few moments ago. A Gentleman in one of the provinces[8] sent Mr. Adams a present of 5 bottle[s] of wine which he wisht recommended in America, and this was to serve as a sample. The duties which we had to pay upon only those five bottles mounted them up to 3 livres a peice, and the real value of the wine might be nine or ten coppers a bottle, be sure not more. The injury which cloathing sustains in such long journeys upon paved roads is incredible. I fancy I never related to you a droll adventure which happen'd to me on my journey here. My Friends advised me when I came abroad to take my money in Crowns and Dollors, as being the most advantageous for me, but when arrived; I found I could not part with them without much loss, so I concluded to take them with me to France. There were about 200 which I had put into a strong bag and at the bottom of my travelling trunk, they were placed, in the middle of which I had put a large Band Box in which I had packd a very nice Gauze Bonnet 4 Caps hankerchiefs &c. to the amount of about 5 Guineys, which I had made for me, whilst I was in London. The 3d day of our journey I had occasion to open the trunk. I found a prodigious black Dust upon the top. I directed it to be taken out, when o! terible to behold, Dust to Dust, and ashes to ashes, nothing was left of all my riging but a few black rags,[9] so that when I got to Paris, I could not bee seen untill I had sent to the Millinars and bought me a cap. You can carry nothing with any safety but what is upon the top of the carriage.[10]

I hope my Nephew and Niece are well, when I get to England I will send them some Books.[10] I hope I shall be able to suit you in your lace, but fear you will think you could have done better in Boston. You will not fail writing by every good opportunity.

May 10th

Tomorrow morning my son sets out for L'orient from whence he will embark on Board a French pacquet for his Native Land, where I hope he will happily arrive. And next week we commence our journey for England. I mourn more and more leaving this place, for it is daily more Beautifull, and I find too that six months more would make me tolerably expert in the Language. But all things must Yeald to Buisness. The weather continues very dry, and not the least symptom of a change. We hear it is still worse in England where the provisions have risen to an enormus price.

I received a Letter from uncle Smith last week dated 25 of Febry[12] and was happy to find by it, that my Friends were all well. About this season of the Year you used to visit your Braintree Friends. When You meet be sure to talk about us, and that Idea will give me no small pleasure. I send Your lace and hope it will be agreeable to you. There are 10 yard/4. I gave Eight Dollors for it, for which if you please you may give credit. I hope the little peice of blew silk came safe to your hand which I sent by Capt. Young. If you wish me to get you any shoes in England write me word. There are none good under 2 dollors.

Remember me to Mr. Shaw and all my Haverhill Friends, Good Madam Marsh if she is still living,[13] and be assured of the affectionate Regards of Your Sister   Abigail Adams

RC (DLC:Shaw Family Papers). Dft (Adams Papers); incomplete and undated, with the material arranged quite differently from the RC (dated and filmed under [*May 1785*], Adams Papers, Microfilms, Reel No. 364). The editors have noted a few instances of interesting additional material in the Dft.

[1] The "8th" and "1785" appear to have been added later; see AA to Mary Cranch, [*ante 5*] May, note 1, above.

[2] In the draft AA concludes her description of Auteuil with the sentence: "I must not expect for 5000 a Year to be so well situated in London. I hope our Country will think that without any extravagance our expenses are necessarily very great."

[3] At the beginning of the draft, well before giving this same reason for regretting JQA's departure, AA remarks: "A few day[s] more will Seperate my Son from us. On that account I shall less reluctantly quit Paris, for we should find a vacuity in his absence which will call for much amusement to supply his place."

[4] In the draft AA writes more forcefully: "Yet I shall never feel a real freedom of speach whilst I am an Appendage of a publick Character, and I expect to be more scrutinized in England than here."

[5] Psalms 39:1: "I said, I will take heed of my ways, that I sin not with my tongue: I will keep my mouth with a bridle, while the wicked is before me."

[6] The draft adds here: "I hope Tommy is attentive to his Books. Tis probable he will remain with you for several years."

[7] This paragraph is omitted from AA, *Letters*, ed. CFA.

[8] Gazaigner de Boyer, who wrote to JA about wine on 7 and 21 April (Adams Papers). De Boyer lived in Gaillac, probably the town on the river Tarn, about thirty miles northeast of Toulouse.

[9] In the draft AA explains the misfortune more fully: "the Silver had worn through the bag and into the side of the Box and then had mortised to rags every attom of my Gauze."

[10] All the text from this point to the signature is omitted from AA, *Letters*, ed. CFA.

[11] The draft has AA inquiring after her sister's health in the next sentence, and then briefly after her friends, before closing. The material under "May 10th," below, does not appear in the draft.

[12] Not found.

[13] Mrs. Mary Marsh was still alive; JQA would visit her on 3 Feb. 1786 (*Diary*, 1:397).

Abigail Adams to Isaac Smith Sr.

Dear Sir   Auteuil May 8th. 1785

Your Letter by way of Bilboa dated February 25,[1] did not reach me until the 2d. of this Month, yet it was 2 Months later date than any I have received from my Friends, and I feel myself much obliged to you for your information. We had heard by way of New York of the resignation of your Governour, and we have had many conjectures, who amongst all the Canditates will succeed him. We rather thing it will fall upon the Gentleman you named[2] especially if the late Governour gives him his influence. Mr. Adams has written you by this opportunity,[3] and my son will give you all the News. We shall set for London as soon as we possibly can, but what success Mr. Adams will meet with time can only determine; the mission is a very delicate and difficult one.

You did not write me wheather you was a Grandfather. I suppose by this time I may congratulate you upon that event.[4] We have had a mild winter here, but a very dry Spring. There has been no rain worth mentioning for more than 3 Months, which has brought upon this County a serious calamity and such a scarcity of Herbage that the poor people in many places have been obliged to kill their cattle to prevent them starving. But as it must be an ill wind which blows no good to any one, the drought will contribute to silence the provinces and the Clamours which they are making against the commerce of America with the French West India Islands. Supposing that they could supply them themselves, the price of provision is much raisd by the dry season. We should have been very glad of some of the fat Turkies you mention, for a fat one I have not seen since we left America. Geese Ducks and Turkies are very indifferent here, but poor as the latter are we have given more than a Guiney a peice for them stuft with truffels which is the only fashionable way of dressing them here. Poultry and fish are excessive high here as well as in London. We have given three Louisdore's for a turbut, and 10 livres for an Ell. The Capons and poulards of this Country are the best in world. Vegetables and fruit are not so high as in London, but all enormus when compared to Boston Market. The expences of persons in publick Life in Europe even upon the frugal plan in which we live, are beyond the conception of those who have not tried it, and what is worse is, that the importanc of persons is Estimated by the show they make. The inquiry is not, whether a person is qualified for his office, but how many domesticks and horses does he keep? If he is not able to support an army of them, all of whose buisness it is to rob and plunder, he is considerd as a very small person indeed.

Mr. Brantzin the Dutch Minister dined here not long since. He was himself the plainest drest of all the company, but he had an Equipage of six Horses[5] and 5 liveried servants to attend him. An attendance upon Courts cannot be done in the small way, unless a person will submit to be the object of universal Ridicule.

I have no ambition for a Life of this kind and I am sure our Country can have no Idea of the expences. It is my wish to return to America, where frugality and oconomy are, or ought to be considerd as virtues.[6]

Pray sir present my duty to my Aunt in whose better Health I rejoice, and my Regards to My cousins, as well as to Mr. Otis's family and believe me most affectionately Yours   A Adams

RC (MHi:Smith-Carter Papers); addressed by JQA: "Isaac Smith Esqr. Merchant. Boston." Copy (MHi:Smith-Townsend II, E. H. Smith Scrapbook). The copy has several strike-outs and alterations characteristic of a draft, but it is dated "May 9th"; it also has less text than the RC, with two exceptions noted below.

[1] Not found.

[2] Presumably Thomas Cushing, the lieutenant governor and Hancock supporter who replaced Hancock when he abruptly resigned the governorship in January.

[3] Dated 6 May (MHi:Smith-Carter Papers).

[4] See Mary Cranch to AA, 16 Jan., note 7,

above.

[5] The copy finishes this sentence: ". . . six Horses, none but the Royall family are allowed to ride with 8, and four livered servants to attend him."

[6] The copy adds: "and to which necessity will compell us to the practise of them."

Charles Adams to William Cranch

Dear Cousin   Haverhill May the 9th. 1785

I receiv'd your letter of the 27th. of April[1] sometime last week, and as your Chum[2] is going to Cambridge next wednesday I here see fit without more ceremony to give you a small scroll; and you will please to think that you have been at College allmost a year and an half and that between us both four letters have been the production of our Correspondence; now as to your thought's about this matter I do not know them: but for myself I feel quite ashamed, but I shall come and see you one of these days but I beleive not before Commencement, if I get in then I shall be glad. What do you think of it? Why say you how should I know any thing about it in the first place, tell how far you have got. Why I been through Virgil and Tully twice and have got as far as the second of Corinthians. We are all well here and we study in the bedroom as usual two young fellows from Bradford being added to our number, One of whom will be my chum if we get in[3] and who I should be very glad to introduce to you. I shall either send your slate by Leonard or by the post. Now I must leave you and so farewell dear Cousin. Amen Αμην Αμην λεγω σοι[4] Amen from

C Adams to W Cranch

PS Errors excepted.

RC (Private owner, New York, 1957); addressed: "William Cranch Harvard Coledge Cambridg," and "Favoured Honoured and supported by the Honl Mr L W Esqr"; docketed: "C-A H-C May 9 1785."

[1] Not found.

[2] Leonard White of Haverhill, whom CA names below and on the address page (see the descriptive note). White would become a good friend of his Harvard classmate JQA in 1786–1787, and he appears often in JQA's Diary (Diary, 2:237, and index).

[3] Upon entering Harvard in August, CA roomed with Samuel Walker of Bradford, Mass. Shaw's other student from Bradford may have been Ebenezer Webster. See JQA to AA2, 20 Aug., below; JQA, Diary, 1:316, note 3, 393.

[4] Amen Amen I say to you.

Abigail Adams to Mercy Otis Warren

Dear Madam   May 10 1785

I cannot let my son return to America without a few lines to you, nor will I doubt their being acceptable altho it is nine months since I left Home during all which time neither Mr. Adams or I have had the honour of receiving a line either from the General or your Ladyship, altho we have repeatedly written to you.[1] Your Son who is resident in Lisbon and mine who has inhabited France have regularly corresponded[2] by which means I have had the pleasure of knowing that there was one Branch of the Family yet on this side the land of forgetfullness. I left America not a little anxious for the Health of my two young Friends Mr. Charles and Henery, and tho I have heard from them by way of my Braintree Friends, it would have been more agreeable to me to have received the account from the Hand of their Mama. My son has made a wise choice I think in prefering to return to his own country and compleat his education at Harvered that he may become acquainted with the Youth of his own Standing and form connextions in early life amongst those with whom he is to pass his days. An acquaintance and intimacy in your family will be an object with him, and as you and I Love to praise our children and why when deserving should we not? I think you will find him as intelligent as most young Men of his age, and as little tincturd with the vices and follies of Europe. He loves his Studies too well to be much addicted to any thing else. Having spent ten years abroad uncorrupted, I hope he will not be less cautious in his own country where there is little less danger than in Europe. But as he is yet young the advice and Friendship of the ancient Friends of his Parents will ever be usefull to him.

You will hear before this reaches you of the completion of an ancient prophecy of yours, but I do not recollect whether you auguerd good or evil from it.[3] At present there are so many Clouds to peirce, some of them armd with thunder and lightning that I query whether the Electrical Phylosopher himself could devise means to secure a person from the burning flashes. I think too it has been said that when clouds meet from opposite directions the severest tempest ensues. What then can a person expect who stands unshelterd beneath so inclemnant a hemisphere?

But to quit Allegory we are destined to England. An embassy I dare say in which your penetration discovers many difficulties, some arising from one side of the Atlantick and Some on the other. I never could find either sufficient honour or profit to balance the anxiety which I have both seen and felt in the various employments to which my friend has been call'd. His Success and the benifit derived to our Country from that, has given me great pleasure. Whether his usual good fortune in negotiation will follow him in this embassy time must unfold, but it has brought a weight of care and a load of anxiety upon him. I shall feel some Regreets at quitting so agreeable a climate and the delightfull Garden which is just unfolding all its Beauties. My acquaintance with French Ladies is rather small and none that I value much save Madam da la Fayette, who is a Lady with whom you would be much pleased. Her high Rank and family have not made her like most others forget eitheir the Maternal or Domestick Character. She said to me in conversation one day that she dissapr[o]ved very much the Manner in which the conjugal connection was formed in this Country. I was married said she before I was capable of Love. It was very happy for me that my friends made so wise a choice. I made it the Study of my Life to perform my duty and I have always been so happy as to find my pleasures result from the performance of my duty. I am happier says she and I have more reason to be so than many others of my sex and country. They seek their pleasures in dissapation and amusement, they become insipid to them; and they have no resource in Domestick Life. She is passionately fond of America and she has reason to be so, for America has shewn itself passionately fond of her family. The Marquis you know. He is dangerously amiable, sensible, polite, affible insinuating pleasing hospitable indefatiguable and ambitious. Let our Country Gaurd let them watch let them fear his virtues and remember that the summit of perfection is the point of declension. This Gentleman has had the offer of going to America in the quality of minister Plenipotentiary, but he would not accept it because it would forfeit him the right of citizenship.[4] The Apotheose of the ancient Romans is not yet introduced into our Country, but it may follow the Knights of Cincinnatus,[5] as regularly as Statues &c., and these are honours which are paid only to Military Characters, that the people may look to them, and them only as the preservers of their Country and the supporters of their freedom. That they have deserved well of their Country no one will dispute. But no Man or body of Men can Merit the sacrifice of the Liberties of a people for the agrandizement of them or their families. It is not a little mortifying that both the Secretarys of Legation are knights of the order. Col. Humphries is a sensible worthy Man, and I believe abhors the Idea which those who have more maturely traced concequences fear from these family distinctions, but tis dissagreeable laying aside a Badge of Merit, which he sees and feels give him weight and distinction here. Col. Smith is a perfect stranger to us. Col. Humphries gives him a good Character and so does the Marquiss of whose family he has been.

We are told here that Governour Hancok has resignd the Chair!!!— and are much at a loss for his Successor out of the many candidates which will no doubt be upon the list. I hope our state will not get so divided as to fall into unhappy parties. I hear Mrs. Macauly says that she does not find so much Republicanism as she expected. She went there ten years too late. Yet let her serch whatever part of the Globe she pleases, it is not probable that she will find a larger Proportion of it else where. Pray make my Respectfull compliments to her,[6] and remember me to all my Friends of your family. Be assured Dear Madam that frequent communication with you will give real pleasure to your Friend and Humble Servant   A Adams

Dft (Adams Papers); notation by AA: "To Mrs Warren"; docketed by CFA: "To Mrs. J. Warren. Auteuil."

[1] The Warrens' only letters to the Adamses for this period known to the editors are: James Warren to JA, 29 June 1784 (Adams Papers), which AA is perhaps not counting because it followed so closely on her departure for Europe; James Warren to JA, 28–29 Jan. (Adams Papers), which was evidently slow in reaching France; and Mercy Warren's letters of 27 April to JA (Adams Papers), and 30 April to AA, above. AA's only known letter to Mercy Warren for this period was that of 5 Sept. [completed 12 Dec.] 1784, above. JA, however, had written to James Warren on 30 June, and 27 Aug. 1784, and on 26 April (all LbCs, Adams Papers), and to Mercy Warren on 13 Dec. 1784, and 26 April (both MHi:Warren-Adams Coll.), and on 6 May (MB). Six of these letters, dated 30 June and 5 Sept. 1784, and 28–29 Jan., 26 April (to James Warren), 27 April, and 6 May, are printed in *Warren-Adams Letters*, vol. 2.

[2] The Adams Papers contains letters from Winslow Warren to JQA, dated 13 July, and 1 Sept. 1784, and 4 Jan., 1 March, and 29 June; all except the first are from Lisbon. JQA's letters to Winslow Warren have not been found.

[3] In Jan. 1776, JA had proposed to Mercy

Warren that they exchange characterizations of notable people whom they met (JA, *Papers*, 3:397). Mercy Warren responded with enthusiasm, but predicted that she would gain more than he from the bargain, because she believed that he would soon make the acquaintance "not only of the Most Distinguished Characters in America, but of the Nobility of Britain. And perhaps before the Conflict is Ended, with some of those Dignified personages who have held the Regalia of Crowns And Scepters" (10 March 1776, same, 4:51). JA replied, on 16 April, that Mercy Warren would be disappointed in this expectation: "Your Correspondent, has neither Principles, nor Address, nor Abilities, for such Scenes" (same, 4:125). When JA was appointed a commissioner to France, Mercy Warren wrote to AA and asked her to remind JA of her prediction, for she expected that he would keep his part of their original bargain (2 Jan. 1778, vol. 2:377).

[4] The editors have found no evidence that Lafayette sought an appointment as French minister to the United States in the 1780s, but had he been appointed to that post, it seems hardly likely that the two American cities— New York and Hartford, Conn.—and the two

states—Maryland and Massachusetts—that had made him a citizen between September 1784 and February 1785 would have considered his appointment grounds for terminating that honor.

From his return to France in 1782, however, Lafayette had in effect acted as an extra American minister to France, and to Spain, and in February 1783 he sought an appointment as American minister to Great Britain in order to present the peace treaty, once Congress had ratified it, to the Court of St. James's. In letters to America's secretary for foreign affairs, R. R. Livingston, and to George Washington, Lafayette explained that he only wanted to carry out a brief ceremonial mission, and he declared that he had no interest in being America's "Sedentary" minister, a position for which he recommended Alexander Hamilton (Lafayette to Livingston, 5 Feb. 1783 [2d letter], *Lafayette in the Age of the Amer. Rev.*, 5:88–90; Lafayette to Washington, same date, 5:90–93). Both Livingston and Washington concluded that it would be better not to have a foreigner, even the Marquis de Lafayette, make such a presentation to Great Britain.

Meanwhile, both in France, where he consulted frequently with Benjamin Franklin and with the Comte de Vergennes and the French comptroller general Calonne, and on his 1784 tour of America, Lafayette worked tirelessly to promote Franco-American commerce as a counterweight to Britain's growing commercial power in America following the conclusion of peace. In addition to providing strong informal competition to JA as an American diplomat, Lafayette worked in greater harmony with Franklin and his diplomatic objectives than he did with either JA or John Jay, with whom he occasionally had some friction. This fact alone, quite aside from Lafayette's

association with the Society of the Cincinnati (see note 5), seems adequate to explain AA's criticism here. The fullest account of Lafayette's activities in this period is in Louis Gottschalk, *Lafayette and the Close of the American Revolution*, Chicago, 1942, chaps. 15–16; Gottschalk, *Lafayette Between the American and the French Revolution, 1783–1789*, Chicago, 1950, chaps. 3–15; and *Lafayette in the Age of the Amer. Rev.*, vol. 5.

[5] Here AA probably intends a further criticism of Lafayette, the head of the French chapter of the Society of the Cincinnati. The new military order had earned the immediate disapproval of the Adamses, of John Jay and Thomas Jefferson, and even of Lafayette's ally Franklin, as well as that of many other Americans in France. Lafayette, sensitive to their anti-aristocratic criticism, labored to explain the Society to its critics, while urging George Washington to seek the alteration of the Society's rules to eliminate the provision for hereditary membership. Washington supported this change, and hostility to the order, strongest in New England and among civilian servants of America in Europe, soon subsided. But AA's remarks here and her concern, immediately below, that Col. Humphreys and Col. Smith were "Knights of Cincinnatus," demonstrate that republican hostility to the order did not die out quickly. AA probably learned of Col. Smith's membership in the Cincinnati in late April. See JA to Elbridge Gerry, 28 April (LbC, Adams Papers); AA to JA, 11 Feb. 1784, and note 9, above; and Louis Gottschalk, *Lafayette Between the American and the French Revolution, 1783–1789*, chap. 5.

[6] Catherine Sawbridge Macaulay had traveled to America with her second husband, William Graham, in 1784, and visited George Washington at Mt. Vernon in 1785 (*DNB*).

Abigail Adams to Elizabeth Cranch

No 7

May 12th. 1785 Auteuil

Did you ever my dear Betsy see a person in real Life such as your imagination form'd of Sir Charles Grandison? The Baron de Stael the Sweedish Ambassador comes nearest to that Character in his Manners and personal appearence of any Gentleman I ever saw. The first time I saw him I was prejudic'd in his favour, for his countanance

Commands your good opinion, it is animated intelligent sensible affable, and without being perfectly Beautifull, is most perfectly agreeable. Add to this a fine figure, and who can fail from being Charmed with the Baron de Stael?

He lives in a Grand Hotel, and his suite of apartments his furniture and his table are the most Elegant of any thing I have seen. Altho you dine upon plate in every noble House in France, I cannot say that you may see your face in it, but here the whole furniture of the table was burnished and shone with Royal Splendor. Seventy thousand Livres in plate will make no small figure, and that is what his Majesty gave him. The desert was servd in the richest China with knives, forks, and spoons of Gold. As you enter his apartments you pass through files of servants into his antichamber, in which is a Throne coverd with green velvet upon which is a Chair of State over which hangs the picture of his Royal Master. These thrones are common to all Ambassadors of the first order as they are the immediate representatives of the king. Through his antichamber you pass into the grand Saloon which is elegantly adornd with architecture, a Beautifull Lusture hanging from the middle. Settees Chairs and hangings of the richest Silk embroiderd with Gold, Marble Slabs upon fluted pillars round which wreaths of artificial flowers in Gold entwine. It is usual to find in all houses of fashion, as in this, several dozen of Chairs, all of which has stuft backs and cushings standing in double rows round the rooms. The dinning room was equally beautifull, being hung with Gobelin tapestry the coulours and figures of which resembled the most elegant painting. In this room were hair bottom mahogony back chairs and the first I have seen since I came to France, two small statues of a venus de Medicis and a venus de bel—(ask Miss Paine for the other Name,) were upon the Mantle peice, the latter however was the modestest of the kind, having something like a lose robe thrown partly over her.

From the Sweedish Ambassadors we went to visit the Dutchess of D'Anville, who is Mother to the Duke de Rouchfoucault.[1] We found the old Lady sitting in an Easy chair, around her set a circle of Academicians and by her side a young Lady. Your uncle presented us, and the old Lady rose and as usual gave us a Salute. As she had no paint, I could put up with it, but when she approachd your cousin I could think of nothing but death taking hold of Hebe.[2] The dutchess is near 80, very tall and lean. She was drest in a silk chimise with very large sleeves comeing half way down her arm, a large cape, no stays a black velvet Girdle round her waist. Some very rich lace in her chimise round her neck and in her sleaves, but the lace was not sufficient to cover the upper part of her neck which old time had harrow'd. She had no cap on, but a little black gauze Bonet which did not reach her Ears and tied under her chin, her venerable white hair in full view. The dress of old women and young girls in this Country is *detestable* to speak in the French stile. The latter at the age of Seven being cloathed exactly like a woman of 20 and the former have such a fantastical appearance[3] that I cannot endure it. The old Lady has all the vivacity of a Young one. She is the most learned woman in France. Her house is the resort of all Men of literature with whom she converses upon the most abstruse subjects. She is [*of*] one of the most ancient as well as richest families in the kingdom. She askd very archly when Dr. Franklin was going to America; upon being told, says she, I have heard that he is a prophet there, alludeing to that text of Scripture, "a prophet is not without honour" &c.[4] It was her husband who commanded the Fleet which once spread such terror in our Country.

Thus you have my yesterdays entertainment. The only pleasure which I shall feel to day, is that which I have taken in writing you this morning. I forgot to mention to you that several persons of high rank dined with us yesterday, but not one of them can claim a stroke of my pen after the Baron de Stael.

Adieu my dear Betsy your cousin leaves us in a few hours. I will gratify myself in thinking that he is going to his Friends. May heaven Bless him and prosper his Voyage. Yours affectionately   A. A

RC (MHi:Jacob Norton Papers); addressed: "Miss Eliza Cranch. Braintree Massachusetts"; docketed: "Letter from Mrs. A. Adams, to Miss Eliz. Cranch May 10 1785. (France)."

[1] JA had met the Duchess d'Anville and her son upon his first arrival in Paris, in April 1778. The late Duc d'Anville, to whose military career AA refers at the end of this paragraph, had led the unsuccessful French expedition to recapture the fortress at Louisbourg in 1746, and had died, perhaps by his own hand, near the site of Halifax, Nova Scotia. From early reports, New Englanders had feared that d'Anville's expedition would be "a kind of Armada" (JA, *Diary and Autobiography*, 4:42, note 4, 67). The Duchess's son, Louis Alexandre, Duc de La Rochefoucauld, was a leading *philosophe* and friend of America with a keen interest in American state

constitutions. He was killed by a Revolutionary mob in 1792 (Hoefer, *Nouv. biog. générale*).

[2] The daughter of Hera and Zeus, and a cup-bearer to the gods, Hebe was a symbol of youthful beauty.

[3] The words "woman of 20 and the former have such a fantastical appearance" have been made nearly illegible by a badly worn fold. This reading has been confirmed by AA, *Letters*, ed. CFA, 1848, p. 251.

[4] "A prophet is not without honour, but in his own country, and among his own kin, and in his own house" (Mark 6:4; see also Matthew 13:57, and John 4:44).

John Quincy Adams to Abigail Adams 2d

N:1.

Dreux 8 1/2 o'clock.
May 11 [12]. [1785][1]

You will perhaps be surprised, to see that in less than 8 hours I have come 9 1/2 posts.[2] But the Roads, as far as this place, are excellent, and the horses, exceeding sprightly, because, they have very little to do: I did not expect myself, to get to this place, to-night, when I left Auteuil, but my first horses served me much better than, I had hoped. I could have gone with ease, another post and half; but should have found no house to put up at: had I proceeded I must have gone all night, which I did not think necessary.

The roads from Paris here, are vastly agreeable; the ground has not yet, the true tincture of green; but almost all the trees are in blossom, and exhale a fragrance, which would perhaps have had a poetical influence upon me, if my Spirits had not been too low: the dust, was not so inconvenient, as I had feared. Luckily, the wind, blew it all before me, so that very little came into the Carriage. My Cabriolet has held out as well as possible till now: I have not been obliged to have any thing done to it, and I think it is a very good, strong Carriage. It is none of the easiest, and if you see Mr. Randall, present my best Compliments to him, and tell him, I believe, he and his fellow travellers did not want for exercise, after riding a day, in this vehicle: he will understand you, I am sure. Upon the whole, I don't know of any Journey I ever made, that pleased me more, than this would have done, had not all my enjoyments been poisoned by Recollection. You know by experience, what it is to leave, for a long, we know not how long, a time those we love. I shall not there fore describe you my feelings upon this Occasion: you will however easily imagine, that I shall never set down this day, as one of my *happy* days.

The only remarkable place, you pass by between Auteuil and this, except Versailles, is the *Abbaye de Saint Cyr*, which was founded by the famous Madame de Maintenon, who died there in the 84th. year of her age.[3] She was of noble birth, but very poor, so that her Education was not so perfect as perhaps it might have been: when she became the Wife of Louis the 14th. she made this institution, in order to be of service to the young Ladies that might be in the same predicament, that she had been in herself. A Number of young Ladies, are educated in this place at the Expence of the king: in the compleatest manner: but they must be noble: and their Parents must be so poor as not to be able, to give them a proper Education, at their own Expence.

At 4. in the morning I shall depart from this: and, God willing, to-morrow night I will add something to this Letter: which I shall send you immediately on my arrival at L'orient.

Préz-en-Pail[4] May 13th. 8. in the evening

At 4 1/2 in the morning, I left Dreux, and have rode to day 16 Posts. I am now 50 leagues from Paris, and should have gone on further but the Carriage goes so terribly hard, and the roads, are so exceeding Rough, that I am really very tired. To-morrow the moon will be higher, and I shall more easily ride in the night, if it should be necessary. The roads have been much inferior to day, to those I had yesterday, and the dust has been much more inconvenient as the Wind drove it into the Carriage.

By what I can learn from the Postillons &c. I have been all day in the Province of Normandy: I am not sure of it however: for I have no map about me, and the Postillons, are some of the most ignorant, beings in the Creation: Real Yahoos: their horses have much more merit than they themselves.[5] I have seen no Vines on the whole Rout; but grain of diverse kinds, some grass, (which is not an inch high,) and a great number, of orchards, with all the Apple trees in blossom. This is I think, the only Province in France, which produces Cyder, a bottle of which I now have upon my Table, (I drink your health:) 'tis nothing but water Cyder, and this is I think, the worst house I ever was at in France. When I came in they ask'd me, if I meant to *faire maigre:*[6] as I had eat nothing all day except, from the Provision, I brought with me, I told them I would eat some meat. Well, they had du Veau frais and de la Sallade. But they were determined I should not transgress, and have brought, me, only a couple of ribs without any meat: so that I shall breakfast dine and sup to day upon some sallad.

I did not sleep above three hours last night, and am so fatigued that I must go to bed immediately. My Cabriolet, though it goes, too hard, holds out very well as yet. I have however been obliged, to have one of the wheels mended to day.

Rennes May 14th. 11. at night

Worse and worse! I think I never was at such a tavern in my life: there is a very good one in town, and I went to it, but there was not

145

one bed vacant.[7] They have nothing to give me here, and I have eat nothing since 9 in the morning; though I have swallowed dust enough, to take away all my appetite.

I have come only 13 and 1/2 posts to day. I came a different road from the ordinary, and thereby shortened my Journey, three posts; I have had most horrid roads, and trembled at the sight of every town: for they are all paved in such a manner, that one would think it had really been done, with a design to break Carriages all to pieces: never in my life was I so banded about: my poor Cabriolet too is dreadfully injured: what with the heat of the Sun, and the badness of the Roads, the pannels are split in a number of places; and I think I shall be very lucky if I get 15 guineas for it: I hope it will be taken for that.

I came several leagues more through Normandie, cross'd through the Province of *le Maine*, and about 7 Posts back, entered into *Bretagne*: but something very extraordinary, and unexpected, was that when I came on the frontiers of this Province, a custom-house officer appeared, and ask'd me whether I had nothing contrary, to the kings orders: and upon my answering, I had only, my baggage necessary, he replied it was well, without demanding to search my trunks; or a *sou* of money; he told my Postillion to proceed: so that I have nothing to fear for your silks nor for Esther's *Dols*.—The Country all along, looks dreadfully for want of Rain. Grain is the product of the fields in general, and there are a great number of orchards; much Cyder is made in this Province, as well as in Normandy and le Maine; though it has not so high a reputation.

I have eighteen posts from this to l'Orient, and shall not stop on the road, for I am determined, not to lodge again in such houses, as this and the one I was in last night.

L'Orient Monday morning 4 o'clock may 16th

Just arrived here, and have got again into a very indifferent house:[8] I will continue in the evening for I must now go to bed.

Tuesday Morning May 17th

At about 11. o'clock yesterday morning I went to see Mr. Barclay who has bean detained here several days, by illness: he is not yet well by any means, but proposes leaving this place for Paris to-morrow morning: (you will not let Mrs. Barclay know that he is unwell.) He will be at Paris, very near as soon as the Post, and I shall therefore send this by him: What think you was my astonishment when he told me, that all the packets have positive orders to sail on the 3d. Tuesday of every month: and that they never wait for the mail from Paris that arrives here, wednesday morning, unless they are detained by contrary winds. Is it not abominable that Monsr. le Couteulx the director of the Packets, should not know this: he told Mr. Chaumont that he would be here soon enough if he left Paris on Saturday: he depended upon this, and would have arrived here a day too late, had not the last packet been detained 24 hours by a bad wind. Unless the same happens now, (which is not probable, for the wind is quite fair) I shall lose all the Letters that will come by to-morrow's post; as the Captain has positive orders, to sail to day. When I went to Monsr. de Mazois; (the director of the Packets here) to pay for my Passage:[9] I told him how disagreeable it would be for me to lose the Letters that will come to me to-morrow: he was very polite, and said, that if he had the power of ordering the packet for a day, he would do it: but if he was to do this, and the wind should become contrary on wednesday, he should be responsable for the detention of the packet: so my only hope now is that the wind may stop us one day. I saw the Captain, who told me Mr. Williamos, had written him on my Subject: and that he had kept the round house for me:[10] Present my best Compliments to Mr. Williamos, and let him know how much I feel myself obliged to him for this and all past favours: tell him I have thought of nobody since I left Paris more than of him: my Imagination has very often represented to me how much more agreeably I should have ⟨*performed*⟩ gone thro' this Journey, had it bean with him: and on the voyage I shall have equal Reason to regret him.

I went yesterday to the man,[11] who sold the Cabriolet to Mr. Randall: he appeared very glad to find it so soon returned, and said he would give the 30 louis as he agreed: but when he saw it and found all the damage, that had happened to it, his face lengthened very considerably. Mr. Rucker and Mr. Grubb[12] were with me, and we prevailed upon him to give me 25 louis d'ors, for it, as it was: which upon the whole was very reasonable: besides the repairs I had done to it, and a trunk which I have bought to put the things the imperial contained, in, I am still a gainer, of about 3 louis d'or's in this bargain; so that my Speculation has turn'd out very well.

I have not yet been to see Mr. Thevenard, the commandant, but think of going to day. I shall write to your Pappa, if I can find any time, but I am much hurried by the Packet's sailing to day. You will present my respectful Compliments to all our friends in Paris; but especially to Mr. Jefferson and Coll. Humphreys. I regret exceedingly, the Letters of Introduction, that the Coll. was so kind, as to promise to send by the Post. I promised myself much entertainment, and instruction, from the acquaintances, they would have enabled me to form. Mr. Jarvis will I suppose be gone before this reaches you: if not, remember me to him: and present my hearty thanks to him, for his very obliging letters: I must not forget Mr. Randall, who will hear with Pleasure, that I have been so successful, with respect to the Cabriolet.

Your very affectionate brother.   J. Q. Adams

RC (Adams Papers). The text is written on eight small numbered pages. JQA continued using the same size leaves for his next ten numbered letters to AA2, extending through 1 Oct., and running to 104 sequentially numbered pages. All ten letters appear below, and all should be read with JQA's Diary entries (*Diary*, 1:266–346).

¹ Dreux is about forty-five miles west of Paris, on the border between Normandy and the Ile de France. JQA gives the correct date of his departure, Thursday, 12 May, at 12:30 p.m., in his Diary.

² The French post stations were about six miles apart.

³ Françoise d'Aubigné, Marquise de Maintenon, founded this school at Saint-Cyr, about two miles west of Versailles, in 1686, about the time that she was privately married to Louis XIV. For the remainder of Louis' reign, Madame de Maintenon showed an increasing preference for the daily life of her school over the court life at Versailles, and following the king's death in 1715, she spent her last four years at Saint-Cyr, in almost total seclusion from the outside world. Hoefer, *Nouv. biog. générale*.

⁴ This small town, now spelled Pré en Pail, was in Maine, about fifteen miles west of Alençon.

⁵ JQA makes this reference to Jonathan Swift's *Gulliver's Travels* especially apt by contrasting his postillions with their horses, just as Swift placed his Yahoos, beasts in the shape of men, below his rational horses, the Houyhnhnms.

⁶ That is, to abstain from meat.

⁷ The good inn was at "the sign of the sheep, (*au mouton*)"; the bad one was the Hôtel d'Artois (*Diary*, 1:268).

⁸ The Hôtel de la Marine (*Diary*, 1:269).

⁹ JQA paid Mazois "500 livres for a passage, on board the *Courier de l'Amérique*, Captain *Fournier*" (*Diary*, 1:270).

¹⁰ JQA felt fortunate to be in the "round house" because the rooms below deck were "so small that two persons cannot easily fit together in one of them. They have no windows in them, which makes them so dark that it is impossible to read without a candle and must render the air extremely unwholsome. But the roundhouse has a large window and two small ones that open and being upon the deck it is not subject to the bad air that reigns continually below" (*Diary*, 1:271–272; and see JQA to AA2, 17 May, below).

¹¹ In his Diary JQA calls him Soret (*Diary*, 1:270).

¹² James Grubb, whom JQA identified as "from Carolina" when he first met him on 16 May, was a young Virginian; thirty years later JQA would employ him as his private secretary in London (*Diary*, 1:233, note 2, 270, 271, note 2).

John Quincy Adams to Abigail Adams 2d

N:2

L'Orient Tuesday eve: May 17th. 1785

Our winds are now contrary, and as they changed with the moon they may be three weeks as they are; which would by no means be *mon compte.* I am not sorry however that they have come round, because, I shall not lose my Letters from Paris, which I should have regretted extremely, if I had been obliged to leave them. When I went to see Mr. Barclay yesterday, he told me to have my baggage carried to his house, and take a Room in it: but I thought it was not worth while to give him or myself the trouble of moving my things, for one or two days: but I have been with him continually since my arrival, except when my business called me away. I went this morning with Captain Fournier, to see Mr. Thevenard, but he was not at home: I saw him a minute in the Street, and spoke to him. I have been this afternoon on board with the Captain, and have taken possession of my birth, which is the airiest and best on all accounts, in the Ship, except those of the Officers: somewhat dirty, but that cannot be helped: you know very well how the french are, on Land; it is impossible for their Vessels to be supportable. By what I can learn, we are but few passengers; I have already seen one or two whose appearance I must own, does not prepossess me in their favour; but the first Rule of a person, who has any thing to do with the world, should adopt, should be never to judge from appearances: I wish that in this Case they may be as deceitful as they often are.

I have become acquainted with a Mr. Grubb, from Virginia, much a friend of Mr. Barclay: he appears to be very much a gentleman, and, has been very polite to me: (and you know that we all form opinions of persons according to their Conduct with respect to ourselves.)

Wednesday afternoon May 18th

At 6. this morning I went on board the Packet with my two trunks and shall now be ready at 1/4 of an hours warning. After I return'd I went immediately to the post office and enquired if the Post from Paris was arrived: it was: I ask'd if there were any Letters for me, there were none: I then went to Mr. de Mazois the director of the Packets, and ask'd if he had received any Letters or Packets for me. Not one. I will make no observations upon this disappointment: I am sure, you will conceive, what were my feelings. Only one thing can excuse you: which is that your Letters were sent too late to come by the Saturday's post, and will not arrive till friday morning. Mr. Barclay has been so unwell to day, that he has put off his Departure till to-morrow. He will be the bearer of my No. 1. to you; and also of a Letter to your Pappa.[1] I owe him obligations, in addition to those we all owe him, and of which you are as sensible, and as grateful, as I am: he offered to pay me the 21. louis d'or's I carried to his Lady; but as I had no necessity for the money, I neither wished, nor supposed myself authorised to receive it. I have desired him to tell you that I shall not forget, going to the Post Office without effect. You know my vanity is wounded at any appearance of neglect from any of my friends: how much must it then be mortified, when, the person is so dear to me.

Thursday May 19th

Our winds continue still directly contrary. I have been on board all the morning, and have arranged all my Linen &c. in my draws. Among our Passangers, we have one *Salvius* a Sweed: if you see Mr. Jarvis pray ask him, what he could make of him, and who or what he is. His looks are certainly not in his favour. Mr. Barclay, left l'Orient this morning. He was not so well as I wish he had been. I sincerely hope, the Journey will be of Service to him. Please to present my best Respects to him, and thank him, for his hospitality and all his kindnesses to me, since I have been here.

Friday eve: May 20th

I must begin by begging your pardon, for having accused you of neglecting me: the charming No. 1.[2] I received from you this day, has proved the injustice of my Suspicion: I received at the same time a Card from Mr. Williamos and one from Coll. Humphreys: with a number of letters of Introduction,[3] for which I pray you would present my grateful thanks. The Letters from Miss Nancy, and from her Parents,[4] gave me much pleasure: more especially, as they inform me of the receipt of the pin. You are pleased with the Letter you have received; and I think I can say, you will not be disappointed in the opinion you have form'd of Miss Nancy's accomplishments. Your Letter I kept for the Last: I will not attempt to express my Sensations in reading it. Was I to tell you that a tear involuntarily started from my Eye, you would think I carry sentiment too far, and that I am weak: That Circumstance I will therefore keep to myself. I also received this morning from M. Thevenard, a packet from the Marquis.[5] So that I have now nothing, to make me wish to remain here any longer. The wind is fair this evening: if it continues so to-morrow morning, we shall positively sail. I will therefore close this Letter; and am your affectionate brother.   J.Q.A.

RC (Adams Papers). The text is on four small pages, numbered 9 through 12. See the descriptive note to JQA to AA2, [12] May, above.

¹ JQA to AA2, [12] May, above; JQA to JA, 18 May, below.

² Not found.

³ Charles Williamos to JQA, 14 May, and David Humphreys to JQA, undated (filmed under [*May 1785*]) are in the Adams Papers. Williamos enclosed a letter to a "Col. Burr," which introduced JQA; this was probably Thaddeus Burr of Fairfield, Conn., to whom JQA delivered a letter on 17 August. The recipients of the four letters of introduction enclosed with David Humphreys' letter have not been identified, but Humphreys had already given JQA letters of introduction to Gov. George Clinton and Gen. Samuel Webb.

In addition, Thomas Jefferson to JQA, 12 May (Adams Papers) mentions the Virginia congressmen Samuel Hardy and James Monroe as recipients of Jefferson's letters whom JQA would find "very worthy gentlemen" to know. Jefferson recommended JQA in his 11 May letters to Elbridge Gerry, to Hardy, and to Monroe, and he entrusted to JQA letters to Francis Eppes and to John Jay (two letters), all of 11 May, and to Edward Burd, to the governor of Virginia (Patrick Henry), and to Phillip Mazzei, all of 12 May. See JQA, *Diary*, 1:273, and notes 1–3, 306, and note 1; Jefferson, *Papers*, 8:141–152.

⁴ The letters "from Miss Nancy, and from her Parents" have not been found, and these persons have not been identified.

⁵ Lafayette's letter of 14 May, in French, is in the Adams Papers; the Marquis enclosed with it several documents for delivery and a page of current news from the Leiden *Gazette*. See also JQA, *Diary*, 1:273, and notes 2 and 3.

Abigail Adams to Charles Storer

Dear Charles   Auteuil May 18th 1785

I received your Letter¹ this Day when I was in Paris—for the last time! I took my leave of it, but without tears. Yet the thought that I might never visit it again gave me some pain, for it is as we say a dieing leave when we quit a place with that Idea.

But now with regard to the appartments, I shall wish to be supplied with dinner. Supper, we eat none. Breakfast and tea in the afternoon we shall find ourselves. One of the Adelphia Buildings at which I lookd when in London and I think the next to that which I had, was of the kind I mentiond. It had all the appartments I wish for, but was not supplied with linnen. I shall only want table linnen perhaps for a week untill ours arrives and I should rather have appartments in which we could be wholy to ourselves and only supplied with our dinners from without. Bed linnen I have with me. I have lived here in so large a house and so good an air that I dread being pent up. We expect to set of the 20th. [I]² know not how long we shall be in reaching nor where we shall alight. I believe it shall be at my old Lodgings the Adelphi untill I can see or here from you. Congress *oblige us* to oconomize. We must do as well as we can, but upon this Score, Silence.³ Your Friend and my son left us the 12th. We have not since heard from him. Your Cloaths are pack'd and your Books will come with our things,⁴ for which we have a permit, and the Duke of Dorset has been so obliging as to write to Mr. Pitt to give orders to the custom houses that we be admitted without Search, and has himself written to Dover for us. His Grace is vastly obliging. You see my haste, a thousand things are upon my hands and mind. Adieu remember me to your Sister. Yours   A A

RC (Adams Papers); endorsed: "Mrs. A.A. to C.S. 18th. May. 1785." See also AA to Storer, 28 April 1783, descriptive note (above).

¹ Not found.
² A dense ink blot makes the letter illegible.
³ Storer responded to this request, and to another by JA (see Storer to JA, 13 May, Adams Papers), by engaging rooms for the

family at the Bath Hotel in Picadilly (see Storer to AA2, [24 *May*], and AA to Thomas Jefferson, 6 June, both below).
⁴ These items may have been stored in Paris since July 1783, when Storer ended his service to JA and left France for England.

John Quincy Adams to John Adams

Dear Sir   L'Orient May 18th: 1785

After a very warm and dusty Journey, setting out early, and riding late, I arrived here on Monday the 16th. instant at about 4. o'clock in the morning. As soon as I had taken a little rest, I enquired for Mr. Barclay; and immediately went for him. He would have been in Paris, before now, had he not been retained by illness: he is not yet well but seems determined to go for Paris to-morrow morning: as Auteuil will be in his way, I desired him to stop there before he goes into Paris, and he will do so, if he arrives in the day Time: he has been exceedingly kind and serviceable to me, and was even so obliging as to offer me a Chamber in his House here: but I thought it would be best to remain at the Inn, as it was very probable that we should sail yesterday: the wind is now directly contrary, which for me is a lucky Circumstance, as it will enable me to receive the Letters, which I expect from Paris, this morning. I have got an excellent, and very *airy* birth, which I owe to the kindness of Mr. Jarvis and Mr. Williamos, who were so ⟨kind⟩ good as to write to the Captain in my favour: I have this morning been on board with my trunks; and as soon as the wind changes, if it is only 3 points, we shall certainly sail.

With Respect to my Cabriolet, I have been much luckier than I expected: as the wood of which it is made was quite new, the heat of the Sun, had split the pannels in a number of places, and it was otherwise much damaged: yet the man who sold it to Mr. Randall agreed to take it back for 25 louis d'or's, which was much more reasonable than I had hoped: I have received the money, and the Carriage has been delivered. The Imperial was of vast Service to me, for the Linen that came in my Trunk, was very considerably rubb'd, while every thing, that was put in the Imperial, arrived here without any damage at all.

Please to present my best respects to Mr. Jefferson, Coll. Humphreys, and all our friends in Paris. If you see the Marquis, you will inform him, that his Dogs are on board,[1] and shall be well kept, if my attention to them has any Effect.

Believe me to be, your dutiful Son.   J. Q. Adams

RC (Adams Papers).

[1] Lafayette was sending seven hounds bred in Normandy to George Washington. In a letter of 18 May (Adams Papers), which JQA probably did not receive before sailing, Lafayette asked JQA to see that the dogs were properly fed, and to deliver them to Dr. John Cochran in New York, who would send them to Mt. Vernon. See Lafayette to George Washington, 13 May, in *Lafayette in the Age of the Amer. Rev.*, 5:324–327.

Charles Storer to Abigail Adams 2d

[*Woodford* 24 *May* 1785]

I wrote you this, Amelia, in answer to yours, No. 8,[1] received a day or two ago, for which accept my thanks. I had really begun to think our correspondence had, to use a common phrase, "seen its best days," as you had suffered so long a time to pass without improving it. Now I hope other things. The number of this I cannot give you, as, being in the country, I have not my memorandum book near. But 'tis time I had put some date to my letter, that you may know when and where I write. 'Tis the 24th of May, and I write you from *Woodford*, a mile or two beyond Epping-Forest, from town. Here I have been some time, but mean to return to London again tomorrow. The Spring in this country is delightful—that is, the months of May and June—and this is a most charming spot. Hill and dale, lawn and grove, are upon each side of us; and melody is there without end, from every tree. Here is the noble prospect, seats, temples, castles, the river, villages, &c.; and here, too, are scenes where

> "Nature wantons as in youthful prime,
> And plays at will her virgin fancies."

This is being quite romantic, you'll say. This is the season, Amelia, and here the place. But I quit these pretty scenes, to reply to your letter, and change as far as change can carry me: I mean from hence to a court drawing-room.

You ask my advice respecting the dress necessary at Court. I of myself know nought about it, but have made some little inquiry. They tell me that the queen appears always in silk, and very plain, except on the king's birth-day. The princesses, too, generally appear in silk. The nobility dress variously. The last year muslin was much wore, worked with gold sprigs, flowers, &c., and may be worn this year also; 'tis worn over pink, lilac, and blue silk. The laces that are used are what the French term spring and summer laces, as I believe *point* is only worn in winter. But all join in telling me that you had not only better provide yourself in *every* common dress, laces, silks, &c., before you come here; but had also better make up a fashionable court dress, such as is worn at *Versailles*, which will just be *the ton* here; as fashions here are most all borrowed. This going to court will be very expensive. You must go upon all public days, and cannot appear twice or above twice, in the same suit. So you see the worst is not the presenting. This, to be sure, will be disagreeable—not, however, on account of being before their Majesties. You have too much good sense to be afraid of a king and queen. But the court all have their eyes upon one, and are too apt to make their remarks, sometimes aloud. This is very unpleasant, especially where there are—and there will be many, I believe—ill-natured observers. I should like, however, to bear you company, was it only to see how the king would receive your father.

How a certain young man will bear his late change, I cannot say. It will require some philosophy, and he has much good sense. As to the Knight of Cincinnatus, I know but little; I wish, however, they were as coolly received in America as they will be here.[2]

And Mrs. Jaris[3] is at Paris? I had not an idea of her coming to Europe. Please to return her my best compliments, and assure her I shall be very happy to wait upon her, on her arrival here.

To your papa and mamma you will not fail to present my best respects. I wrote him a few posts ago respecting his lodgings, and hope to have his instructions by to-day's post. I shall do my best to get him good accommodations.[4] I hope you will inform me *dans quell endroit vous proposez descendre*, that I may be ready to receive you.

Adieu! mais sans adieu! Qu'il vous puisse arriver tout ce que vous pouvreiz desirer, avec un bon voyage! Yours,   Eugenio

MS not found. Printed from AA2, *Jour. and Corr.*, 2:35–37.

¹ Not found.
² If "Knight of Cincinnatus" was correctly transcribed as singular from the lost MS, Storer may refer to Col. William Stephens

Smith, the recently appointed secretary of the American legation in Britain whom neither Storer nor the Adamses had met, but whose membership in the Society of the Cincinnati was known to AA2's parents (AA to Mercy Warren, 10 May, and note 5, above), and probably to AA2 and Storer. Whether Storer wrote "Knight" or "Knights," however, he may simply be responding to a general question or remark about the Cincinnati in some lost let-ter from one of the Adamses. The "certain young man" at the beginning of the paragraph refers to JQA.

³ Probably Amelia Broome Jarvis; see AA to Lucy Cranch, [5] May, above.

⁴ See AA to Storer, 18 May, note 3, above.

John Quincy Adams to Abigail Adams 2d

N:3.

At Sea May 25th: 1785

You have doubtless received before this, my Letter by Mr. Barclay, and you will have my N:2 in a day or two.¹ I address'd it under cover to Mr. Jefferson, in case it should arrive after your departure.

The morning after the date of my last, our Captain, ordered me to go on board, and at about 10 o'clock we weigh'd our anchors and set sail, but before we could get clear of the Harbour, the wind changed, and we anchored before Port Louis: a small town opposite l'Orient, which in the time of Louis the 14th. before l'Orient existed was a very considerable place. Its Citadel was built by Vauban, one of the greatest engineers that France has produced: but it has much fallen into decay, since l'Orient was built for the East India Company. In the evening our wind came round again, and at about 7 o'clock, we finally set sail, and in the morning when we rose we had nothing but the Sea, and the azure vault bespangled with Stars, within our Sight. We have had very good weather ever since but my hopes of a short passage, are much diminished: for we have already had two days of calm weather and I fear much that we shall have many more. The Captain is determined to go for the trade winds, which lengthens the voyage more than 200 leagues: but it is said the passages are much more certain, than when we go to the North of the western Islands.

29th

Our agreement when we parted was, never to let a day pass without adding something to the Letter which we were to be continually writing. This arrangement is too favorable to me, for me to fail fulfilling it: but the time I am at Sea, will not, I hope be comprised. Sea sickness has already prevented me for several days from putting pen to paper. You have been at Sea: you know the Sterility of Events, on board ship. I ⟨will⟩ need not therefore tell you that I have not every day, something interesting to say to you. I will not however be lazy. We have had very little wind these several days. We have not yet got into the trade winds. When we sail'd I did not expect to be more than 40 days at Sea: I now fear we shall be at least 50, which will be a very disagreeable Circumstance to me: for in the number of officers and passengers on board, there are two or three disagreeable Characters: I shall speak of them some future day.

⟨*July*⟩ June 1st

Yesterday we had a great deal of wind; but it was contrary. To day we have little which is fair. We expect in a few days to be in the Latitude of the trade winds. This afternoon we saw a large ship at about half a league's distance, but the weather being foggy, we could not well distinguish, what Nation she belonged to.

By this time I suppose you are in London, and in a more agreeable situation than you was at Auteuil: for several days past I have often ⟨*calculated*⟩ imagined, where you was at different times. Now you was before the door of the post house, with half a dozen beggars around you, now stopping at a public house, and at sight of the floor, and of the furniture; making comparisons, not very advantageous to France; Now at Monsr. Dessein's[2] waiting for a wind: and now, arrived safe in London. There is a real pleasure in thinking of our friends when absent, and the greater the illusion is, the more satisfaction we enjoy. I have here half my time when I have nothing else to do: for the rolling of the Ship prevents me from reading or writing much at a time: and in the evening no body is suffered to have any light: although this order is troublesome to me I cannot help approving it, because it is very possible, that in the number of passengers that sail in these packets there may be some whose imprudence, might be cause of a misfortune; and nothing certainly is more dreadful than a fire at Sea.

4th

Calm weather still. We do not certainly run more than 15 or 20 leagues a day, which is but slow travelling. We have continually the same scene, before us, and have seldom the small satisfaction, of being in sight of another vessel, which would at least furnish a little variety. Our Captain Mr. le Fournier is an excellent Seaman, and a good man. He has been a Seaman these thirty years. He has not all the politeness of a courtier, but what is much better, he is open hearted and sincere.

The second in command, is also a very good Seaman, but a man without any Principles, and as such I have no esteem for him. He is the person who displeases me the most on board.[3]

The third is a young man of about 20. I should like him very well: if he was a little older, and had a little more experience: he is certainly too young to command a watch in a stormy weather, but in this Season he may do very well.[4]

The fourth, is a boy, just let loose from a College, full of his knowledge, which is not very deep; and as proud, as if he ⟨was⟩ descended from the Royal family of France: yet nobody knows who he is. He knows very little more of the Sea, than I do. Very luckily there is a good Seaman on board, who keeps the watch with him: if it was not so, I should not sleep very sound in bad weather.[5]

The surgeon, is a good man: who understands his profession very well, which is a very agreeable circumstance on board a ship: as nothing is more disagreeable at Sea, than to have a number of sick people on board, and the extreme hot weather which commonly reigns in summer, in these parts, is very unwholsome.[6] I will speak of the passengers, another day.

8th

Contrary winds, and calm weather seem to have conspired together against us. We suppose ourselves now not far from the Western Islands, which according to the course we have taken is not more than a quarter of the passage. If we continue at this rate we are to be 70 days at Sea. I hope however we shall be more fortunate in future. At about noon we saw a large brigg, which pass'd about 2 leagues from us, and hoisted an English flag.

14th

Was I to write something every day, I should have nothing to say, unless I was to repeat continually, calm weather. From 8 to 15 leagues a day, has been the utmost extent of our navigation, for a week, but last night the wind freshened considerably, and we now run between 6 and 7 knots an hour. We are now in the trade winds which will carry us as far as the Bermudas. We shall then have two hundred leagues more to run; and shall be more exposed to calm weather than we have been till now so that I have but very little hopes of a shorter passage, than 55 days; and think it very probable we may be 2 months.

We are five passengers on board. A French gentleman, who went to America early in the war, and is settled at Albany. He is very much of a gentleman and a person of much information. I wish all the other passengers and the officers were like him.[7] . . . A Merchant from Nantes who has established a house in Philadelphia, and is going there to settle his affairs. He is ⟨a⟩ great wit, and a connoisseur in french poetry.[8] But I am not so much disposed to talk upon this subject at Sea, as when I am on shore. A Dutch merchant, who has a commercial house in Charlestown: A true Dutch man, except in two capital points: one, is that he never smokes, and the other that he sleeps 12 or 14 hours in the 24. which makes him so absent that we tell him he is in Love. He is a great traveller, and yet he has not lost the Character attached to that people.[9] Every nation seems to have a peculiar Characteristic, which nothing can efface: whether it is owing to Education, or to the nature of the different climates, I cannot tell. I rather think to both.

But the most curious character on board is a Sweed who came from America in this Packet, when Mr. Jarvis cross'd; remained a month at l'Orient where, he says himself, he had nothing to do: and is now going back to New York. I never saw in one person such a mixture of good and ill nature, of folly, and of good Sense. He has receiv'd a liberal education, and will at times reason upon different subjects very pertinently. But at other times he is really out of his head. When the moon is full there is really no living with him.[10]

18th

Still the old Story over again. I don't know when it will end. I was in hopes, when I wrote last, that we should keep the fine breeze we had: but it departed the day before yesterday, after having pushed us about 150 leagues. This day at about noon we saw something about 1/2 a mile from us, an object which immediately became a subject of discussion. About half a dozen spyglasses, were fixed upon it, and some said it was a boat overset; others a rudder others a part of a mast, and others a mere huge piece of wood. It did not pass far from us, but the question after all was not decided. All this will appear very trivial to you, but at Sea, the least object, that can form a variety in the midst of the most insipid uniformity, becomes interesting. For that reason we are never happier on board than when we have a vessel in sight, because, it makes diversity, and causes among us a vast number of speculations. In war time the effect produced by the same cause is quite different. Whenever a sail is seen, the first question, is, can she take us? The second: can we take her? And according, as those questions are decided, one vessel flies and the other pursues.

23d

This morning, we were again favoured with a breeze, after a week of calm weather we are now as far Southward as we shall go. Our Latitude is 26 degrees 30 minutes. The weather is extremely warm, and would be intolerable, were it not for the Sea air, which makes it a little less disagreeable. We have now been 33 days out and are not more than half way. We can hardly hope to be less time performing the other half; for the worst part of the voyage, is from the Bermudas, to the Coast, about 250 leagues.

28th

Since I wrote last we have had very fine winds, and have run upon an average 45 leagues a day. We spoke this afternoon to an American brig, from New London to Santa Cruce,[11] loaded with horses. Her estimation agrees very well with ours and we suppose ourselves about 400 leagues from the american Coast.

July 8th

We have again had upwards of a week without any wind, and such extreme heat, that we can bear no cloaths. We have not since the first of this month, proceeded 100 leagues. We have been not at a great distance from the Bermudas, and consequently under skies continually subject to thunder storms and gusts of wind. We had seen a number pass at a small distance from us, and had often prepared to receive them in case they should come to us. But they had only threatened untill, last evening, when five or six thunderstorms burst about our heads, one after the other. We had in the course of the day more air, than we had been favoured with for near ten days, but at about 6 in the evening, the weather darkned on every side, and the lightened flash'd in many quarters at the same time, from the blackest Clouds, I ever saw. The storms were violent and the thunder fell at a short distance from our vessel. The weather remained the same almost all night but this morning it cleared up and has left us a noble breeze, which I heartily wish may continue: we are much in want of it: for our fresh provisions, begin to be very scarce, and we have still 250 leagues at least to run: I have now made up my mind to a passage of 2 months: and I wish it may not be longer.

9th

In the morning we spied a sail which did not pass more than 2 miles from us, and we might with great ease have spoken with her. I wishd it much in order to ascertain more positively where we are; but our Captain did not chuse to. There is among mariners a false point of honour, which induces them, never to trust any estimation but their own, and a Captain thinks it almost dishonourable to be obliged to ask the opinion of another. This is one of the most absurd punctilio's that exist, for it is utterly impossible to know the space you have run through at Sea, especially after being near 50 days out of sight of Land. Many causes may concur to lead them into considerable errors; yet such is the power of prejudice, they prefer being mistaken, to being right by the information of another. Such are the pitiful passions that possess the breast of man. Don't laugh at me for moralizing: it is excusable after having been 50 days at Sea, between Europe and America, and not near arriving, to be a little *misanthropic*.

11th

Our fine weather continues still: and at length the Captain has been so modest as to speak to a schooner, that we spied this morning. She had been 5 days out of New York, was bound to Jamaica, and supposed we were about 120 leagues from the nearest land. This makes an error of about 15 leagues in the best calculation on board, which is the Captain's. 15 leagues is but a small error in this case, but it is of considerable importance, when a vessel arrives on the coast. The wind increased all day, and in the evening we have it very high. The weather looks very threatning. The heat lightening is so frequent, that the heavens appear in a blaze. If we had a painter or a writer of Romances, he would make much of the scene now around us.

14th

Your birth day, and consequently a *jour de fête* for me.[12] I have thought of you still more to day than I do commonly. You will doubtless pass the day much more agreeably than I have, though it has not been unpleasant to me. At two this afternoon we spoke to the Packet from Charlestown S. Carolina, bound to New Port. She has been 7 days out and tells us we are 45 leagues from land. The weather has been fine all day.

15th

Sounded this morning at 4 o'clock and found bottom at about 35 fathom. Very little wind all day. In the afternoon a most tremendous thundergust appeared to arise. It mounted by degrees, until about 7 o'clock, when it attack'd us all on a sudden, with an amazing violence.

The thunder rumbled, and the tempest frown'd.

It lasted about an hour, after which the wind abated considerably, but it was still so high, that our Captain chose to lay to, all night, in order not to be driven too near the land, which was a very prudent precaution.

16th

At half after 7 in the morning, a sailor came from the head of the mast and gave information that he had discovered land. We went immediately up to ascertain the fact, and found it real. Before noon we fired a number of guns for a pilot to come on board. At about 1. o'clock, we had one on board, and at 4 the wind, and tide being both against us we anchored, about a league from the light house on Sandy Hook. In the night we again sailed. I was obliged to remain on deck all night in order to translate the Pilot's orders. Form to yourself an idea how I was puzzled to translate English Sea terms that I did not understand into french Sea terms, which I knew no better. However I did as well as I could; at about midnight we pass'd by the other french packet; which had sailed from N. York in the morning; and was then at anchor, waiting for a tide. They sent their boat on board our vessel, and I had just time to write three lines to inform you of our arrival,[13] but the boat did not stay long enough for me to compleat and seal up this Letter. Mrs. Macauley with her husband, goes passenger in this packet. I fancy she leaves the Country with a less exalted idea of our virtues, than she had when she came to it. Young Chaumont came in this packet and had only 37 days passage. May, is too late for short passages from Europe.

Sunday July 17th

At length we are at anchor before New York and we shall all go on shore to dine. I will here close this Letter, which contains the account of my voyage alone. One of the numerous reasons for which I am rejoyced at arriving, is that for the future I shall not be obliged incessantly to speak of myself. I shall immediately begin another Letter, and I hope it will not be so insipid as this.

Your ever affectionate brother J. Q Adams

RC (Adams Papers). The text is written on twelve small pages numbered, beginning with the second, 14 through 24. See JQA to AA2, [12] May, descriptive note, above.

[1] JQA to AA2, [12] May ("N:1."); and 17 May ("N:2"), both above.

[2] Pierre Quillacq, called M. Dessein, owned the Hôtel d'Angleterre at Calais, made famous in Laurence Sterne's *A Sentimental Journey* (JQA, *Diary*, 1:195, note 1).

[3] This was M. Le Bel, whom JQA characterizes as "a perfect egoist" in his Diary (1:276).

[4] In his Diary JQA describes this officer, M. Halley, as "the most agreeable of the 3 officers on board" (1:276).

[5] The "boy" was Well de Singler, age eighteen, and this was only his second voyage. In his Diary JQA noted that Singler "pretends to be of noble birth and affects to despise everybody who is not noble." The "good Seaman" who kept watch with Singler was M. Le Breton, a twenty-year veteran of the sea (1:277, 278).

[6] The surgeon was M. Bouchant (Diary, 1:279).

[7] This was probably Jean Baptiste Fontfreyde, who had established himself in Albany by 1781. JQA praises M. Fontfreyde's virtues in his Diary (1:281, and note 2). The following elipses are in MS.

[8] JQA says much more about M. Huron Du Rocher in his Diary. This man may have gone by the name Lawrence Huron in Philadelphia (1:282, and note 1).

[9] In his Diary JQA notes that Mr. Molich of Amsterdam, who established the firm of Schmidt & Molich in Charleston, S.C., "is the person on board with whom I am the most intimate, and whose Sentiments agree the most with my own" (1:280–281).

[10] The Swede was Mr. Salvius; if he had arrived at Lorient on the same packet with James Jarvis, he had been in France since April (same, 1:285, 254).

[11] Probably Saint Croix in the Virgin Islands (same, 1:281, note 1), or a port in Cuba or Costa Rica. Another possibility is either of two ports in the Canary Islands.

[12] AA2 turned twenty on this day, three days after JQA's eighteenth birthday.

[13] This must be JQA to AA, 17 July, below.

Richard Cranch to John Adams

Dear Brother   Boston June 3d 1785

This will be handed to you by a worthy young Gentleman Mr. Bulfinch[1] Son of Doctor Bulfinch; I doubt not but his Conduct will render him worthy of your Notice. I have not time to write you on publick Matters at present. The County have put me into the Senate this Year and we have very hard Service. I have enclosed the Speech of our new Governour[2] &c. He is a Man of System and Application, and I hope our publick matters will take a better Turn by his Assistance. Your Children are well, Master Tommy spent last Week at our House, he left his Brother and all well; Brother and Sister Shaw were here Yesterday. Your Honored Mother and your Brother and Family are well, and all the other Branches of our old Circle. I received your esteemed Favour of the 13th. of December,[3] and must assure you that, without denying my Senses, I cannot but conclude that you would have the Suffrages of the People for filling a certain Chair, notwithstanding you think "it is impossible that the Body of the People should think of you for their G[overno]r." I design to get you some Information on the Exports and Imports, Fisheries, Distilleries &c.

in this State, and send you as soon as possible. I wrote by the last Ship Capt. Lyde to your Son, in answer to several very obliging Letters[4] that I have received from him. As this Letter is a Miscellany I w[ill . . .] that the Corporation of Harvard Colledge have voted the degree of [Doctor] in Divinity to the President Willard, Mr. Stevens of Kittery and your old Class-Mate Hemmingway—To Doctor Cotton Tufts the Degree of M.D. and Doctor Welsh the Degree of Batchellor of Physick. Which Votes were laid before the Overseers this Week, and will probably be con[firmed?].[5]

Brother Shaw informs me that Master Charles will be well fitted to enter the University at the ensuing Commencement.

I have but just time to add that I am with the highest Esteem and Friendship your affectionate Brother   Richard Cranch

Mrs. Cranch is just come to Town and will send a few Lines which will be enclosed.[6] We desire our kindest Regards to our dear Sister and your amiable Children. You will excuse this incoherent Scrawl as I write it in the Lobby in the midst of noise and disturbance. Adieu.

I have wrote some time ago to Messrs. John van Heukelom and Son respecting the Goods in my Hands not yet disposed of.[7] Sales are not quite so dull this Spring as they were, so that I hope to do something better with his Cloths now than I could last Year when the Glut of Goods was excessive.

RC (Adams Papers). The single sheet of text has split and been repaired at a worn fold with some loss of text, and a worn corner has damaged another word.

[1] Charles Bulfinch the architect, not quite twenty-two, departed Boston in June, resided in London from July to Dec. 1785, and then traveled through France and Italy as far as Rome, returning to London in Aug. 1786, and to Boston in Jan. 1787 (*DAB*; Charles A. Place, *Charles Bulfinch, Architect and Citizen*, Boston, 1925, p. 6–11; Ellen Susan Bulfinch, *The Life and Letters of Charles Bulfinch, Architect*, Boston, 1896, p. 43–57).

[2] Enclosure not found. James Bowdoin gave his inaugural address to the General Court on 27 May; it appeared in the *Independent Chronicle*, 2 June, p. [3].

[3] Not found.

[4] Only one letter, that of 6 Sept. 1784 (MeHi), has been found.

[5] Receiving the S.T.D. degree were Joseph Willard, A.B. 1765, Benjamin Stevens, A.B. 1740, minister at Kittery Point, Maine, and Moses Hemmenway, A.B. 1755, minister at Wells, Maine. Harvard awarded an honorary M.D. in 1811 to Thomas Welsh, A.B., 1772, who had married one of AA's cousins (*Harvard Quinquennial Cat.*, p. 1150; 195); but there is no record of Harvard awarding Welsh the degree of "Batchellor of Physick" at any time. Harvard granted the bachelor of medicine degree from 1788 to 1810 (same, p. 851–852).

[6] Of 4 June, below.

[7] See AA to Mary Cranch, 7 Jan., and note 4, above.

Mary Smith Cranch to Abigail Adams

My dear Sister   Boston June 4th. 1785

I have just heard that Scot is to sail tomorrow. I cannot let a vessel go without a few Lines when I know of it. I have a letter began at home for you, but I cannot get it Soon enough to go by this conveyence. The children have Letters for you and their Cousin but they must all wait for the next vessel.[1] I have had so much company lately that it has been impossible to write as we would have done. Our dear Sister Shaw has made us a visit and is just return'd. She is in better Health than I have seen her some time. Her ride Mr. Shaw says has been of great Service to her. Cousin Tommy has made us a little visit also. He is a fine Boy and I hope will make a good man. Miss Peggy White and Miss Hazen have spent a few Days with us. Miss White is perfectly recover'd and is grown very fat. Miss Hazen is as thin and sprightly as ever. She is with us still. I have receiv'd your Letter of March 13th.[2] Mr. Tyler has also receiv'd a Pacquet containing Letters from Cousin N[abby] to her Friends:[3] which I hope he will deliver in Season. ⟨Miss⟩ Mrs. Guild receiv'd her Letters ⟨ from⟩ which came to Mr. T. the 24th. of May, and then only two. From some circumstances, she thinks more have been sent her. He receiv'd them the beginning of April and why he did not send them to her before is as hard accounting for as why he did not forward one he receiv'd last Fall for Miss Broomfield,[4] till this Spring. She must never wonder why She does not receive answers to her Letters till She is sure they are receiv'd. She will receive Petitions from many of her Friends to have their Letters not incloss'd in Mr. T's Pacquit. They may give various reasons but they all mean the Same thing. It is one of his whims not to deliver Letters for a long time after he has recev'd them. He would not like to be Serv'd so himself. You may read this to her or not, as you may think best. I wish you were in England. I could write with much more freedom than I dare too at present as I find Letters can be oppend in France as well as in *America*.

If there is any thing which you may wish to be inform'd of which I have not told you ask me, and I will endeavour to Satisfy you.

It is no Small job I assure you to keep the moths from devouring all your woolen cloaths in your House. We examin them once in three weeks and always find it necessary to do so during the Summer Season. We have ventur'd to take the best Suit of Mr. A's cloaths for Cousin Charles. They were too Short Skirted for his Papa and would not have done for Cousin Charles another Summer if the moths had spair'd them. I have taken all the cloth and Cloaths out of the Hair Trunk as the moths had got into the Hair, and put them into a sheet and into a ceder chest. You may depend upon the utmost care, that we can take to preserve them. The whole pieces of red cloth we have pin'd up in a Sheet So Securly that I think nothing can get to it.

As you are in a Land of cambrick, you had better Supply your Self well. There is not an article so dear here. You cannot get any fit to wear under three Dollars a yard. We have taken the piece of unglaz'd to make ruffles for your Sons. By cousin Nabbys Letters I think we may expect your Son Soon. Dear youth with how much Joy will he be receiv'd. We will do every thing in our Power to make him happy. Betsy is rather feeble this warm weather. How this town will Suit her I know not. Musick may Possibly amuse, it does not often Serve as a brace.

Mr. Cranch is well, but is so busy that I have Scarcly had time to speak to him. The Senate is very thin and they keep him fully imploy'd. I will write you further Soon. I wish I could see you. Do not fail of Sending by every vessel. I know not if Mr. T. has wrote. He knows of this chance. He is well but grown so fat that he cannot wear his wastcoats without inlarging them. Your mother Hall is well, Sends her Love and thanks you for the money you sent her.[5] My dear Sister let nobody see this letter but your Self. Tis bad written I know, but this will not be what you will first attend too. If the vesel Should not sail so soon as we expect I will endeavour to write again. Remember me in the tenderest manner to Mr. Adams and my cousin[6] and believe me affectionately yours   Mary Cranch

RC (Adams Papers); endorsed: "May 22 Mrs Cranchs Letter 1785." No reason for the date in the endorsement is known to the editors.

[1] See Mary Cranch to AA, 19 July, below. The next extant letters from Betsy and Lucy Cranch to AA were written in Sept. 1785; see below.

[2] That is, AA to Mary Cranch, 20 Feb. [- *13 March*], above.

[3] None of these letters from AA2 have been identified.

[4] Not found.

[5] See AA to Mary Cranch, 9 Dec. 1784, and note 21, and Mary Cranch to AA, 25 April, and note 8, both above.

[6] That is, AA2.

John Thaxter to Abigail Adams

Madam   Haverhill 4th. June 1785

I had a few days since the pleasure of your favor of the 20th. of March last. Your reproofs are always accompanied with so much delicacy, that the reproved forget the Censor in the Friend. I confess I have been strangely inattentive to my friends on your Side of the Atlantic, and that I am entitled to a large Share of *their Remembrance*. 'Tis but an indifferent Apology to say, that I seldom write unless upon business—yet it is nevertheless true. My Aversion to Letter writing has become almost invincible. My long Silence must be imputed to that Cause, not to premeditated design. My friends have the same Share of my Remembrance and affectionate Regards as ever, altho' they have had but few epistolary Testimonies of the same on my part for a long time.

Your Picture of the old World is an exact Resemblance, and just such an one as I expected from you, who must have seen and most sensibly felt the Difference between the two Countries in contrasting them. When a Nation has reduced to Cultivation the last Inch of its Soil, it has passed the Zenith of its Virtue. I contemplate with pleasure the vast Extent of our back Territory, and view it not only as a Mine of Wealth but a future Nursery of hardy and virtuous Citizens. Agriculture must be one of our Bulwarks. The more we cultivate our Lands, the more free and independent will be our Country. 'Tis an honorable Profession, and to him who reaps in peace the fruit of his Labor, an independent one, more exempt from dangerous Temptations and those fascinating Vices, which hold up in appearance a substantial good but in reality leave us a substantial Evil to combat with.

You tell me not to expect a detail of politicks from your Pen. I was very sorry to find that Clause in your Letter, as I expected much useful Information with a few Cabinet Secrets accompanied with your ingenious Observations upon them. Let me intreat you, Madam, not to deprive me of such a Source of Happiness. I am much obliged however by the short detail you sent me. Mr. A. has a knotty perplexed Negotiation to go through before a Commercial Treaty is formed with England. I can hope every thing from his diplomatic Talents and Experience in Negotiation, but from my knowledge of his past sufferings and difficulties, from a consideration of the present temper of the English Nation; ⟨*from*⟩ the false friends and disguised Enemies that he must detect and will detect in every stage of his progress, I say, from a consideration of these matters, I cannot but feel for him most sensibly. It must be a work of time. The golden opportunity for this business is past. The Year 1783 opened the best prospect of a liberal Treaty. The English are now possessed of an Idea that we cannot do without them, and I confess our own Conduct has too much favoured and confirm'd such a Sentiment. We have verified their predictions, that all the Trade of America would return to its antient Channel after the peace. Indeed they courted it back by their large and long Credits, and some of them will find that the poverty of their Debtors will last much longer than the Credit of their Creditors, and of Course meet with disappointments, that they did not expect from what they supposed to be a masterpiece of policy. But they have done with Credits to this Country. For one I rejoice, and believe it will produce the best effects eventually. It will be a long time before our Merchants pay day comes. Their present Debts will remain for a very considerable time unpaid, not from a want of disposition, but from inability. We have swallowed their Bait and left the Hook bare. They have sent us their Luxuries, and we can remit nothing but ardent wishes for more with complaints of poverty and inability to pay for what we have already recieved. Our Importations have been a peaceable kind of privateering upon them, and will prove so in the end, if they don't alter their System. They may laugh at and deride what they call our Miserable situation since our Seperation from them—but let them laugh that win. Time will shew whose Calamity is to be laughed at, and who are to mock when fear cometh.[1]

Whenever your Son returns, you may be assured, Madam, that Inclination and Duty will equally induce me to render him all that Assistance, and to furnish him with such Advice and Council, as may be in my power. His Genius and Application will ever secure the Attention and Advice of his Friends, and enable him to make a distinguish'd figure in whatever profession he engages in. I am per-suaded, it is Mr. A.s Ambition, that he should study the Law, after spending some time at our University. It is natural for Parents to wish to see their Children distinguishing themselves in a profession in which they have shone with a peculiar Lustre. Children become more endeared to their Parents. It ⟨often⟩ reminds me of what Thomson says of the smiling Offspring of the happy pair—"and every day Soft as it rolls along, shews some new charm, The Father's Lustre, and the Mother's Bloom," whenever I see a promising Youth.[2] Parents renew their Age, and go through life as it were a second time in that of their Children.

This is certainly the best Country for our own Youth to be educated in. I have no very exalted Opinion of foreign Schools, Acadamies, or Universities or whatever other name they are called, for the Educa-tion of American Youth. They advertise with great Pomposity, and promise to teach every thing, while few of their Scholars learn any thing of Consequence. Fidling, Dancing, Fencing and Horsemanship are the Accomplishments of a fine Gentleman, but are not the substantial benefits for which our Youth ought to be sent to Schools and Universities. They engross too much time, are too captivating and too consonant to the Volatility of Youth and the Warmth and Activity of that ⟨age⟩ period to be so much indulged in this Country as in the old World.

The Words, "I will go to Holland and see if I cannot make America less dependent upon France," I very well remember, as you suppose.[3] It is sound Doctrine, and has stood the Test in more Instances than one. It was founded in a most laudable Ambition and supported with as much Ability as Integrity. It was genuine Policy, as it is increased our Reputation at the same time that it divided a Dependence that one Power wished to engross. It demonstrated to all Europe, that altho' America might boast of one Philosopher who could guide the Thunder bolts and disarm the winged Lightning of their fatal shafts,[4] yet could She exult in another, who atchieved more noble exploits still, one who had softened and conquered the prejudices and guided the temper of a whole Nation, and counteracted the plots of ⟨a second⟩ two more. You will readily perceive, that I allude to the Treaty with Holland, and to the Opposition of two great Nations.[5] I shall ever reflect with pleasure upon the progress and close of that Negotiation, and that all the plots, difficulties, Objections, dissuasives and even threats that were conjured up by open and disguised enemies to thwart and obstruct it, were eventually counteracted in the formation of a liberal Treaty. I saw and felt so much, that I could not but rejoice at the disappointment of some Enemies.[6] And tho' we are forbid to rejoice when our Enemy falleth, yet there is no Law against it when his devices are confounded, or at least in acquiesing in the determinations of Providence.

You have forbid Courts, Writs and females to rival me in your Regards. You except a *Wife—a solemn Exception*. As it does not apply to me, nor never will I believe, there will be no necessity for *that* Exception. You tell me not to be alarmed at the Word, "Wife." The Idea makes me shudder. Courtship in this place is systematic. It begins with Attentions, then follows Addresses which is succeeded by Courtship and Matrimony. I am only in the first stage of this Labyrinth, and if all Accounts are true, I have made a rapid progress—but common fame is a common Liar. I am slow of belief in these matters. Confidence is of slow growth in a Batchelors bosom. I die daily unto the *Sin* of Courtship, and am more and more alive unto the righteousness of a single life. But still I am no Enemy to the fair Sex. I cannot live without a female friend—there however I must stop. I dare not "soothe the Ear with more than friendship." To mention "Love's suspected name" would "startle" me, if not one of the fair. I am so ignorant of the mode of proceeding in these matters, that I am persuaded I should faulter, stammer, stutter and never give Utterance to that dreadful Word *Love*. I don't think I am *faint hearted*, and yet there is something in the *popping* of the question so called, that strikes me with more terror, than addressing a large Assembly. What is the Reason of it? I wish I knew of a good Receipt to fortify the Heart. If I was sufficiently bold, I cannot say what would take place shortly. You will think by all this, that I would be serious if I could. Be not decieved. I am at a great remove from Matrimony, I assure you. But of this enough.

You will please to remember me very affectionately to Amelia. I esteem her sincerely, tho' She thinks I have forgotten her. She judges me too hard.

With unfeigned Respect, I am, Madam, your most humble Servt.

JT

RC (Adams Papers); endorsed: "Mr Thaxter june 4 1785."

[1] Proverbs 1:26.
[2] James Thomson, *The Seasons: Spring*, lines 1145–1147.
[3] See AA to Thaxter, 20 March, and note 4, and AA to Cotton Tufts, 3 Jan., and note 8, both above.

[4] For this image of Benjamin Franklin, see JA, *Papers*, 6:173, 174, and note 5; and Franklin, *Papers*, 27:frontispiece and p. xl.
[5] That is, Great Britain and France.
[6] Proverbs 24:17.

Abigail Adams to Thomas Jefferson

London Bath Hotel Westminster

Dear Sir[1]   June 6. 1785[2]

Mr. Adams has already written you that we arrived in London upon the 27 of May.[3] We journey'd slowly and sometimes silently. I think I have somewhere met with the observation that nobody ever leaves Paris but with a degree of tristeness. I own I was loth to leave my Garden because I did not expect to find its place supplied. I was still more Loth on account of the increasing pleasure, and intimacy which a longer acquaintance with a respected Friend promised, to leave behind me the only person with whom my Companion could associate; with perfect freedom, and unreserve: and whose place he had no reason to expect supplied in the Land to which he is destinied.

At leaving Auteuil our domesticks surrounded our Carriage and in tears took leave of us, which gave us that painfull kind of pleasure, which arises from a consciousness, that the good will of our dependants is not misplaced.

My little Bird I was obliged, after taking it into the Carriage to resign to my Parissian Chamber Maid, or the poor thing would have flutterd itself to death. I mourn'd its loss, but its place was happily supplied by a present of two others which were given me on Board the Dover pacquet, by a young Gentleman whom we had received on Board with us, and who being excessively sick I admitted into the Cabin, in gratitude for which he insisted upon my accepting a pair of his Birds. As they had been used to travelling, I brought them here in safety, for which they hourly repay me by their melodious Notes. When we arrived we went to our old Lodgings at the Adelphia,[4] but could not be received as it was full, and almost every other hotel in the city. From thence we came to the Bath hotel where we at present are, and where Mr. Storer had partly engaged Lodgings for us, tho he thought we should have objections upon account of the Noise, and the Constant assemblage of Carriages round it, but it was no time for choice, as the sitting of parliament, the Birth Day of the King, and the celebration of Handles Musick[5] had drawn together such a Number of people as allready to increase the price of Lodgings near double. We did not however[6] hesitate at keeping them tho the four rooms which we occupy costs a third more than our House and Garden Stables &c. did at Auteuil. I had lived so quietly in that Calm retreat, that the Noise and bustle of this proud city almost turnd my Brain for the first two or three Days. The figure which this city makes in respect to Equipages is vastly superiour to Paris, and gives one the Idea of superiour wealth and grandeur. I have seen few carriages in Paris and no horses superiour to what are used here for Hackneys. My time has been much taken up since my arrival in looking out for a House. I could find many which would suit in all respects but the price, but none realy fit to occupy under 240 £. 250, besides the taxes, which are serious matters here. At last I found one in Grovenor Square which we have engaged.[7]

Mr. Adams has written you an account of his reception at Court, which has been as gracious and as agreeable as the reception given to the Ministers of any other foreign powers. Tomorrow he is to be presented to the Queen.[8]

Mr. Smith appears to be a Modest worthy Man, if I may judge from so short an acquaintance. I think we shall have much pleasure in our connection with him.[9] All the Foreign Ministers and the Secrataries of Embassies have made their visits here, as well as some English Earls and Lords.[10] Nothing as yet[11] has discoverd any acrimony. Whilst the Coals are coverd the blaize will not burst, but the first wind which blows them into action will I expect envelop all in flames. If the actors pass the ordeal without being burnt they may be considerd in future of the Asbestos kind. Whilst I am writing the papers of this day are handed me. From the publick Advertiser I extract the following. "Yesterday morning a Messenger was sent from Mr. Pitt to Mr. Adams the American plenipotentiary with notice to suspend for the present their intended interview." (absolutely false.)[12] From the same paper.

"An Ambassador from America! Good heavens what a sound! The Gazette surely never announced anything so extraordinary before, nor once on a day so little expected. This will be such a phænomenon in the Corps Diplomatique that tis hard to say which can excite indignation most, the insolence of those who appoint the Character, or the meanness of those who receive it. Such a thing could never have happened in any former Administration, not even that of Lord North. It was reserved like some other Humiliating circumstances to take place

Sub Iove, sed Iove nondum
Barbato——"[13]

From the morning post and daily advertiser it is said that "Mr. Adams the Minister plenipotentiary from America is extremly desirious of visiting Lord North whom he Regards as one of the best Friends the Americans ever had."[14] Thus you see sir the begining Squibs.

I went last week to hear the Musick in Westminster Abbey. The Messiah was performd, it was Sublime beyond description. I most sincerely wisht for your presence as your favorite passion would have received the highest gratification. I should have sometimes fancied myself amongst a higher order of Beings; if it had not been for a very troublesome female, who was unfortunately seated behind me; and whose volubility not all the powers of Musick could still.[15]

I thank you sir for the information respecting my son from whom we received Letters.[16] He desires to be remembered to you to Col. Humphries and to Mr. Williamos. My Daughter also joins in the same request. We present our Love to Miss Jefferson and compliments to Mr. Short. I suppose Madam de la Fayettee is gone from Paris. If she is not be so good sir as to present my Respects to her. I design writing her very soon. I have to apoligize for thus freely scribling to you. I will not deny that there may be a little vanity in the hope of being honourd with a line from you. Having heard you upon some occasions express a desire to hear from your Friends, even the Minutia respecting their Situation, I have ventured to class myself in that number, and to Subscribe myself, Sir Your Friend and Humble Servant

A Adams

The publick Advertiser—

Yesterday Lord Gerge Gordon had the Honour of a long conference with his Excellency John Adams, (honest John Adams) the Ambassador of America, at the hotel of Mons. de Lynden Envoye extraodinaire de Leurs Hautes Puissances.[17]

This is true, and I suppose inserted by his Lordship who is as wild and as enthusiastic as when he headed the Mob. His Lordship came here but not finding Mr. Adams at home was determind to see him, and accordingly follow'd him to the Dutch Ministers. The conversation was curious, and pretty much in the Stile of Mrs. Wright[18] with whom his Lordship has frequent conferences.

An other paragraph from the same paper—"Amongst the various personages who drew the attention of the drawing-room on Saturday last, Mr. Adams, minister plenipotentiary from the States of America was not the least noticed. From this Gentleman the Eye of Majesty and the Court glanced on Lord——; to whose united Labours this Country stands indebted for the loss of a large territory and a divided and interrupted Commerce."[19]

RC (DLC:Jefferson Papers); endorsed on the back of the enclosure: "Adams Mrs"; and, also in Jefferson's hand in list form: "⟨Sanois⟩⟨Nightingale⟩⟨journal⟩55/ ⟨Pilatre⟩/Houserent/⟨Wealth⟩ of Lond./Squib." This was a list of topics that Jefferson discussed in his reply of 21 June, below (Jefferson, *Papers*, 8:181). Dft (Adams Papers). Material in the Dft that does not appear in the RC will be noted below.

[1] With this letter, AA begins a rich correspondence that extended, with long interruptions, to 1817. She and Jefferson eventually exchanged over fifty letters, over two thirds of which were written from 1785 to 1788.

[2] The Adamses resided in the Bath Hotel in Picadilly from 26 May until 2 July; see notes 3 and 7. Both the performance of Handel's *Messiah*, and JA's conference with Lord George Gordon mentioned in the enclosure to this letter, occurred on 8 June, indicating that part of the letter was written sev-

eral days subsequent to the dateline; see also note 8.

[3] JA wrote two letters to Jefferson on 27 May, both saying that the Adamses reached London on the 26th (Jefferson, *Papers*, 8:166–167). JA recounts the family's journey from Auteuil to Calais in his letters of 22 and 23 May to Jefferson (same, 8:159–161).

[4] AA and AA2 had stayed at Osbourne's Hotel in the Adelphi Buildings in the Strand when they first arrived in London in July 1784 (AA to Mary Cranch, 6 July 1784, and note 24, above).

[5] Parliament had been in session since 25 January. George III's birthday was on Saturday, 4 June, and occasioned a massive levee which JA attended, and which he described to Jefferson on 7 June (Jefferson, *Papers*, 8:183). Handel's *Messiah* was performed in Westminster Abbey on 8 June, with AA in attendance (see *The London Chronicle*, 4–7 June and 7–9 June; and AA to Elizabeth Cranch, 2 Sept., below).

[6] The draft has "therefore."

[7] On 9 June, JA signed a lease for this house for twenty-one months with its owner, John Byron of Purbright. The late eighteenth-century structure, standing at the northeast corner of Grosvenor Square, became the Adams' home, and the first American legation in Britain, when the family removed to it from the Bath Hotel on 2 July. See JA, *Diary and Autobiography*, 3:xii–xiii, 180–181, note 1, and illustration facing p. 288. A copy of the lease, dated 9 June, is in the Adams Papers.

[8] At this point in the draft AA adds: "after which I suppose I must pass through a similar ceremony." JA was received by George III on 1 June; he described that moving occasion quite briefly to Jefferson on 3 June (Jefferson, *Papers*, 8:176), and in detail to John Jay on 2 June (LbC, Adams Papers; PCC, No. 84, V, f. 469–484; *Dipl. Corr., 1783–1789*, 2:367–371; JA, *Works*, 8:255–259). JA was presented to Queen Charlotte on 9 June, thereby dating this section of the letter at 8 June (see JA to Jefferson, 7 June, Jefferson, *Papers*, 8:183). JA's remarks to George III, and his reply, are recorded in JA's hand in the Adams Papers (1 June), as are his remarks to Queen Charlotte, and her brief reply (9 June).

[9] AA noted the appointment of Col. William Stephens Smith as secretary of the American legation in her letter to Cotton Tufts of [26 April], above. Smith arrived in London on 25 May (JA to Jefferson, 27 May [2d letter], Jefferson, *Papers*, 8:167).

[10] See JA's list of visitors, [*June–July? 1785*], in his *Diary and Autobiography*, 3:178–180. This list of about three dozen names is certainly not a complete record of those who called on the new minister, but it does include envoys from Prussia, Sardinia, and Russia, the earls of Abingdon and Effingham, Lord Mahon and Lord Hood, two generals, several other prominent Englishmen who were well disposed to America, and a few of JA's old friends.

[11] The draft adds: "in the publick papers."

[12] The draft adds: "for as the forms of presentation are not yet past with her Majesty, no application has yet been made to any minister upon Buisness," and omits "From the same paper."

[13] "Under Jove, but Jove not yet barbaric."

[14] This exact passage appeared in the *Morning Post and Daily Advertiser*, 7 June 1785. The *Morning Post* was one of the most anti-American of London papers at this time.

[15] The draft adds: "for she had such a general acquaintance throughout the whole abbe that not a person enterd but what she knew and had some observation to make upon their dress or person which she utterd so loud as to disturb every person who sat near her."

[16] Jefferson sent word of JQA's arrival in Lorient in his letter of 25 May to JA (Adams Papers; printed in Jefferson, *Papers*, 8:163). From Lorient JQA had sent the letters of [12] May and 17 May to AA2, and of 18 May to JA, all above.

[17] An almost identical paragraph appears in *The Daily Universal Register* of 9 June, dating the conference at 8 June. Lord George Gordon first came to prominence when, as a member of Parliament and president of the Protestant Association, he had petitioned the Commons to reimpose certain disabilities recently lifted from Roman Catholics. This led quickly to London's massive "Gordon Riots" of June 1780, which were only quelled by twenty thousand troops. Gordon was imprisoned in the Tower for several months, and tried for high treason in Feb. 1781, but was acquitted. He remained a Protestant hero for several years, and by 1784 was at the center of national and international controversy involving the Dutch and Emperor Joseph II. By 1786 Gordon's polemical targets included the French court. About 1787 he converted to Ju-

daism. In 1788 he was convicted of two counts of libel, one against Marie Antoinette, and was sent to Newgate Prison, where he died in 1793. *DNB.* Dirk Wolter Lynden van Blitterswyck was the Netherland's minister to

Great Britain. JA, *Diary and Autobiography,* 3:180, note 1.

[18] See AA to Mary Cranch, 6 July 1784, above, under 25 July, and note 46.

[19] Lord North is probably intended here.

Elizabeth Smith Shaw to Abigail Adams

Haverhill June 12th. 1785

I have but just returned, my much loved Sister, from my Southern Excursion. You know how agreeable these always were to me. To see, and to visit my Friends constitutes a great part of my Happiness. To behold the Smile of Benevolence and Friendship, heightened by the Ties of Relationship is a rich ingredient in the Cup of Life. The pleasure it gives cannot be described, but we find, that indeed it "doth good like a Medicine."[1]

I will pass over what I suffered, for want of your charming Society in the dear rural Cottage, and only tell you that as necessity led me to go with Eliza, to look for some things you left there for your Sons, I felt strangely upon entering your Chamber—I steped back for a moment—the Chamber Stairs was the last place I saw you. It felt like hallowed Ground, and as if I was going to commit sacrilege.

Upon looking after something in a Trunk, we came across Brother Adams Green velvet Cap. Look Eliza said I, we have heard of a Fools Cap, but here is the Cap of Wisdom—for how much have I seen contained in this little Cavity—and how much ⟨are we⟩ is our Country indebted to its good and excellent Owner. We fell into as moralizing a strain as the Son of Henery the 4th., when he took up the Crown of his dying Parent.[2] I folded it at last with great veneration, and pressed it with an ardent petition to Heaven, that I might live to see *him* return, whom his Country "delighteth to Honour."[3] The Journals and the Letters I met with at Braintree, afforded me a most agreeable Repast.[4] Knowing Your Taste for Literature, I am not at all surprized that you should prefer Theatrical Amusements to any-other. To find the Soul alive to all the finer feelings, can be no unpleasing Sensation to the humane Breast, and the frequent Exercise must give them strength and greatly conduce to refine the moral Taste, and strengthen the virtuous Temper, for a very slight inspection into human Nature must convince us, that no Objects have so powerful an impresstion on us, as those which are immediately impressed on our Senses—and therefore those things which have not a tendency to mend the Heart, and improve the Genius, ought never to be exhibited.

> "To make Mankind in conscious Virtue bold,
> Live o'er each Scene, and be what they behold."

was the Purpose for which the Comic Muse first trod the Stage.

We have had a Cold Winter, and Spring. There was good passing over Merimac upon the Ice till the 14th. of April which is much longer than has been known for a great number of Years. Months after you told me of your going into your Garden, to give directions about your Flower-Pots, we in the Latitude of forty two were shivering by our fire sides.—But you can hardly conceive of a more rapid Vegetation, than we have had for these three Weeks past, or of a richer Verdure upon the Earth, "the Vallies are covered over with Grass, and the little Hills rejoice on every side."[5] Though I sometimes long to be with you in your beautiful Gardens, viewing the Curiosities and Embelishments of Art, yet I imagine the Mind may be as much delighted with the rough, and august strokes of Nature. Here, in her wild Scenes, the sight wanders up and down without confinement and is charmed with an infinite variety of Images, without limitation or controul.

Upon our Journey we called at General Warren's, found all well but poor Charles, he is still in a bad way. The Doctor thinks will not continue through the Summer. We kept Sabbath at Hingham, Mr. Shaw preached for Mr. Gay, our Fathers venerable old Friend. We drank Tea there with the Widow Derby. She seems as alert as ever. Some of the Company observed Ralph Inman had very lately buried his Wife, and he was expected in Town soon, to pay his Compliments to Madam. Upon which she simpering[6] told us that her Son in Law Derby advised her last Week, that if Mr. Inman, or any one else solicited her hand in Marriage, to crook her elbow, and swear by the living—that she would never enter into Wedlock again.

Uncle and Aunt Thaxter are well. Cousins are well, rather lean, as well as I. Cousin Lucy Thaxter was married to Mr. Cushing three Weeks before I was there,[7] and was going to housekeeping in about a fortnight. Cousin Nancy has made us a Visit, since my return, with one of Mr. Benjamin Thaxters Sons, who will be married to her next Fall I suppose.[8] Mrs. Lorring[9] is well. She has two Daughters. We returned a Sabbath Evening to our hospitable and kind-hearted Aunt Tufts's. Weymouth can never be to me what it once was. Yet dear is the place of my Nativity. Every Hill, and every Vally, and every Tree

I recognize as my former Friends. On the brow of this Hill, how often have I sat, encircled by the little social band, and talked down the Summers Sun. How have I set delighted beneath the Shade of yonder Tree, while every Grove was Melody, and every Gale was Peace. All, all speak of pleasures past. For my life I cannot look upon the Mansion which was once the beloved Habitation of our dear Parents without bursting into Tears. And there is nothing but a firm belief that they are gone to a House, not made with Hands, that calms and sooths my Mind.

I received your kind Letter dated March 30th.[10] at Braintree. Uncle and Aunt Smith came and made a friendly Visit, and handed me your Letter which gave us the agreeable intelligence of your Health and welfare. I do not wonder that you feel the greatest reluctance at parting with your Son. But it is their Children's good, and not merely their own pleasure, and satisfaction, that the wise Parent regards.

I pity Cousin Nabby the most, as it must deprive her of her most intimate Friend, and Companion. We at this distance cannot be competent judges of the Qualifications of your Son. But Mr. Shaw, Mr. Thaxter, Judge Dana and all his Friends here suppose it would be more advantageous for Mr. JQA to tarry at Colledge 2 years, On account of the phylosophical Lectures, and the excellent Library. But what his Fathers chuses must determine the Matter. Mr. Charles has been here so long and behaved so well, that it is with grief I think of parting with him, (and his Chum that is to be) Samuel Walker. They mean to live together at Colledge. They are very fond of each-other. Samuel Walker is determined to find knowledge, if it is to be acquired by hard Study. He is a steady virtuous Youth. His Father modestly objected against their living together, as Mr. Charles was one of the first Families, he supposed he would look higher for a companion. But we told him we knew his Parents did not wish for any such distinction, Merit alone, in your Minds was the Test of Rank.

The Trunk you mentioned[11] is not yet arrived. I have taken 2 yards of red Cloth, and that Camblet for Coats, for Cousin Charles. I purchased black Sattin for Waistcoat and small Cloaths, and I have got 2 good Taylors into the House, and have made him 2 Suits of Cloaths. But I cannot perswade him to honour us, with the wear of them, till after his return from Cambridge.

I find you are anxious about your American Friends, even in your Dreams. Indeed my Sister, when I went into Boston I was upon the point of beleiving that if he was there, it would be wholly verified. For I found Cousin B. Relations greatly incensed against Mr. ⟨. . .⟩[12]

Conduct. Cousin herself was troubled, and knew not what to make of all his speeches, though I thought she was much disposed to put the best constructions, upon every-thing he said. It was evident to me that *Love* covered a multitude of Faults. Nothing can be more emblematical than to portray the little Deity as blind. And they are certainly so, who are under his Dominion.

Both my Cousins are in good Health. Tommy is a nice Child. He went the week before we went our Journey to Braintree, because I thought it would be best for him to be absent at the same time we were. We got Mr. Williams who is School-master to stay here, and gave him his board for taking Care of the Others in Mr. Shaws absence. I must bid you adieu, assuring the best of Sisters, of the tenderest, and most affectionate Love of her   Eliza Shaw

Mr. Shaw presents his best regards, hopes soon to assure you of your sons acceptance at Cambridge.

Excuse the writing. I cannot Copy.[13]

RC (Adams Papers); endorsed by AA2: "Mrs Shaw june 12th 1785."

[1] Proverbs 17:22.

[2] Shakespeare, 2 *Henry IV*, IV, v, 20–47.

[3] Esther 6:6–11.

[4] Shaw refers to letters from AA to the Cranches, and to herself, mailed in March, particularly those to Mary Cranch, 20 Feb. [-13 March], and to Elizabeth Cranch, 8 March, both above.

[5] Psalms 65:12, 13 (quoted in reverse order).

[6] Shaw added "simpering" in the margin.

[7] Lucy Thaxter married John Cushing on 8 March (*History of Hingham*, 3:233).

[8] Anna Thaxter married her first cousin, Thomas Thaxter, on 27 Aug. 1786 (same).

[9] Undoubtedly Joanna Quincy Thaxter, who had married Thomas Loring Jr. in 1780, is meant (same; vol. 4:296, and note 11).

[10] Not found.

[11] JQA's trunk sent from The Hague to Boston; see the Inventory of JQA's Clothes and Books, 6 Nov. 1784 (Adams Papers), and

AA to Elizabeth Shaw, 14 Dec. 1784, and note 7, above.

[12] A character is struck out here. Shaw may refer to a passage in AA's lost letter of 30 March; AA does not record a dream expressing such anxiety in any extant letters written from France. The editors have not been able to identify "Cousin B." or her suitor, but on 6 June, in a letter to Mary Cranch, Elizabeth Shaw wrote: "When I got to Boston I imagined Sisters Dream, was near to be realized, for I found Cousins friends very much incensed against Mr. A—. Four years have elapsed since the Courtship commenced. From Spring to Fall, and from Fall to Spring has been the Line; Winter nor Summer, it seems, are no Friends to the hymenial Torch. However he talked to the Col. who called to see him a Saturday about keeping House— having a family &c. This looked well did it not?" (DLC:Shaw Family Papers).

[13] This line was written in the left margin.

Thomas Jefferson to Abigail Adams

Dear Madam   Paris June 21. 1785[1]

I have received duly the honor of your letter,[2] and am now to return you thanks for your condescension in having taken the first step for settling a correspondence which I so much desired; for I now consider it as *settled* and proceed accordingly. I have always found it best to remove obstacles first. I will do so therefore in the present case by telling you that I consider your boasts of the splendour of your city and of it's superb hackney coaches as a flout, and declaring that I would not give the polite, self-denying, feeling, hospitable, good humoured, *people* of this country and their amability in every point of view, (tho' it must be confessed our streets are somewhat dirty, and our fiacres rather indifferent,) for ten such races of rich, proud, hectoring, swearing, squibbing, carnivorous animals as those among whom you are; and that I do love this *people* with all my heart, and think that with a better religion a better form of government and their present governors their condition and country would be most enviable. I pray you to observe that I have used the term *people* and that this is a noun of the masculine as well as feminine gender. I must add too that we are about reforming our fiacres, and that I expect soon an Ordonance that all their drivers shall wear breeches unless any difficulty should arise whether this is a subject for the police or for the general legislation of the country, to take care of.

We have lately had an incident of some consequence, as it shews a spirit of treason, and audaciousness which was hardly thought to exist in this country. Some eight or ten years ago a Chevalr. ³ was sent on a message of state to ⟨*demand*⟩ the princess of—of—of (before I proceed an inch further I must confess my profound stupidity; for tho' I have heard this story told fifty times in all it's circumstances, I declare I am unable to recollect the name of the ambassador, the name of the princess, and the nation he was sent to; I must therefore proceed to tell you the naked story, shorn of all those precious circumstances). Some chevalier or other was sent on some business or other to some princess or other. Not succeeding in his negociation, he wrote on his return the following song.

Ennivré du brillant poste
Que j'occupe récemment
Dans une chaise de poste
Je me campe fierement:
Et je vais en ambassade
Au nom de mon souverain,
Dire que je suis malade,
Et que lui se porte bien.

Avec une joue enflée,
Je debarque tout honteux:
La princesse boursoufflée,
Au lieu d'une, en avoit deux;
Et son altesse sauvage
Sans doute a trouvé mauvais
Que j'eusse sur mon visage
La moitié de ses attraits.

Princesse, le roi mon maitre
M'a pris pour Ambassadeur;
Je viens vous faire connoitre
Quelle est pour vous son ardeur.
Quand vous seriez sous le chaume,
Il donneroit, m'a-t-il dit,
La moitié de son royaume
Pour celle de votre lit.

La princesse à son pupitre
Compose un remerciment:
Elle me donne une epitre
Que j'emporte lestement,
Et je m'en vais dans la rue
Fort satisfait d'ajouter
A l'honneur de l'avoir vue
Le plaisir de la quitter.[4]

This song ran thro all companies and was known to every body. A book was afterwards printed, with a regular license, called "Les quartres saisons litteraires" which being a collection of little things, contained this also, and all the world bought it or might buy it if they would, the government taking no notice of it. It being the office of the Journal de Paris to give an account and criticism of new publications, this book came in turn to be criticised by the redacteur, and he happened to select and print in his journal this song as a specimen of what the collection contained. He was seised in his bed that night and has been never since heard of. Our excellent journel de Paris then is suppressed and this bold traitor has been in jail now three weeks, and for ought any body knows will end his days there. Thus you see, madam, the value of energy in government; our feeble republic would in such a case have probably been wrapt in the flames of war and desolation for want of a power lodged in a single hand to punish summarily those who write songs.

The fate of poor Pilatre de Rosiere[5] will have reached you before this does, and with more certainty than we yet know it. This will damp for a while the ardor of the Phaetons of our race who are endeavoring to learn us the way to heaven on wings of our own.

I took a trip yesterday to Sannois and commenced an acquaintance with the old Countess d'Hocquetout.[6] I received much pleasure from it and hope it has opened a door of admission for me to the circle of literati with which she is environed. I heard there the Nightingale in all it's perfection: and I do not hesitate to pronounce that in America it would be deemed a bird of the third rank only, our mockingbird, and fox-coloured thrush being unquestionably superior to it.

The squibs against Mr. Adams are such as I expected from the polished, mild tempered, truth speaking people he is sent to. It would be ill policy to attempt to answer or refute them. But counter-squibs I think would be good policy. Be pleased to tell him that as I had before ordered his Madeira and Frontignac to be forwarded, and had asked his orders to Mr. Garvey[7] as to the residue, which I doubt not he has given, I was afraid to send another order about the Bourdeaux lest it should produce confusion. In stating my accounts with the United states, I am at a loss whether to charge house rent or not. It has always been allowed to Dr. Franklin. Does Mr. Adams mean to charge this for Auteuil and London? Because if he does, I certainly will, being convinced by experience that my expences here will otherwise exceed my allowance. I ask this information of you, Madam, because I think you know better than Mr. Adams what may be necessary and right for him to do in occasions of this class. I will beg the favor of you to present my respects to Miss Adams. I have no secrets to communicate to her in cypher at this moment,[8] what I write to Mr. Adams being mere commonplace stuff, not meriting a communication to the Secretary. I have the honour to be with the most perfect esteem Dear Madam

Your most obedient & most humble sert　　　　　　Th: Jefferson

RC (Adams Papers).

[1] This letter was sent with Jefferson to AA, 7 July, below.

[2] Of 6 June, above.

[3] Blank in MS. The editors of *The Papers of Thomas Jefferson* identify the envoy as the Chevalier de Boufflers, and the princess as Maria Christina of Saxony, sister of Joseph II of Austria, and of Marie Antoinette, and they argue persuasively that Jefferson's "inability to recollect the name of the ambassador and other circumstances was obviously feigned" (Jefferson, *Papers*, 8:242; *Cambridge Modern Hist.*, 13:genealogical table 33).

[4] *Journal de Paris*, 31 May 1785.

⁵ On 15 June, Jean François Pilâtre de Rozier and a companion, Pierre Ange Romain, plummeted over one thousand feet to their deaths near Boulogne when the double balloon in which they were attempting to cross the English Channel caught fire and partially collapsed. Pilâtre de Rozier and another companion had been the first men to achieve free flight in a balloon, in Nov. 1783. See Jefferson to Joseph Jones, 19 June, and to Charles Thomson, 21 June, *Papers,* 8:237, 245; *London Magazine Enlarged and Improved,* June 1785, p. 462–465; *Gentleman's Magazine,* July 1785, p. 565–566; and Hoefer, *Nouv. biog. générale.*

⁶ Elisabeth Françoise Sophie, the Comtesse de Houdetot, a poet, held a literary and philosophical salon at Sannois, about ten miles northwest of Paris (Hoefer, *Nouv. biog.*

générale).

⁷ On 27 May, JA had asked Jefferson to direct his wine merchant, Anthony Garvey, to stop the shipment of all of his wine "except one Case of Madeira and Frontenac together" because of the high duties he would have to pay to bring the wine into England. He repeated this request with even greater urgency on 7 June. Jefferson had reported his initial difficulty in executing this order in his letter of 2 June. Jefferson, *Papers,* 8:166, 172–173, 175, 183–184.

⁸ AA2 had decoded two paragraphs of Jefferson to JA, 2 June (Adams Papers), and in that letter Jefferson remarked that JA had "transferred to [AA2] the commission of Secretary" upon JQA's departure for America (Jefferson, *Papers,* 8:173).

Abigail Adams 2d to Mary Smith Cranch

N 1.

London June 22d. 1785

The flattering mark of attention which I yesterday received from my Dear Aunt¹ demands my earliest acknowledgments. Be assured Madam it has not arrisen from want of respect to you, or doubting your interest in my happiness that I have not long ere this addressed you, but from the fear of increasing the Number of my correspondents so far as to render my Letters uninteresting to those who flatter me with their attentions, and from being very sensible that a Person who writes a great deel must either be possessd of a great fund of knowledge to communicate or unavoidably expose themselvs the [to] the just observations of the judicious and sensible. I have never closed a packet of Letters but I have wished after they were gone that it was in my Power to recall and Burn them,² but my friends are partial enough to me to acknowledge some pleasure derived from my scribling and from it I am induced to continue. There are very few who can sufficiently Guard their minds upon every side against the influence *of flattery* especially when presented under the pleasing veil of commendations from those whose judgment we respect and whose good opinions we are happy to attain, upon this score I am influenced by my Dear Aunt to continue an account of myself and whatever I shall meet with worthy a relation.

My Brother who I hope will arrive before this Letter possibly can, will give you an account of us, till the Period of his Leaving us which was a Painfull event to me particularly having lost in him a good Brother an agreeable companion and friend. Since my arrival here I regret it more than ever and cannot sometimes avoid wishing that he had been induced to stay—but upon reflection every selfish principle is overballanced by the idea and assureance that it was an important event as it respects himself, being fully convinced that if he is to spend his Life in America it was time for him to go there, for by so long an absence and at so early a period of his life, he had never acquired or greatly lost just ideas of the Country, People, manners, and Customs. He will acquire a taste and disposition for them all I doubt not. Yet the difference in the manner of Life in Europe and America is so very great that one should not be too long accustomed to the one if they propose happiness to themselves from the other. For myself I have no fears. My early Education and the example of many Good friends had formed in my Mind such Principles sentiments dispositions and taste, as I think will never be shaken by dissipation Gaiety or the Glitter Pomp and Show of this or any other Country—in all of which this Place equals every other Perhaps in the World.

To say that I am greived and sorry for the unhappy State of our friends at Germantown[3] is only repeating what I have often said and long felt, as it can afford them no relief it seems as if it were not enough to say. I hope your kind attention to our friend Eliza will be the means of recovering her health. She and the Whole family have my sincere wishes for their Prosperity and happiness.

I have just heard of an opportunity to forward Letters to America and could not omit to make my earliest acknowledgments to you my Aunt for your kind favours. Mamma will write largely I suppose, if I have time I shall certainly write to my Cousins But I am told tho the Ship will sail a thursday.[4] If I should not you will be so good as to excuse me to them. I shall write frequently as opportunities Present often to Boston and shall hope for the continueance of your Letters. Be so good Madam as to Present my respects to my Uncle and regards to my Cousin Billy.   A Adams

RC (MWA:Abigail Adams Corr.); addressed: "Mrs Mary Cranch Braintree Massachusetts"; docketed: "Letter from Miss A Adams, London June 22d. 1785."

[1] Not found.

[2] See AA2 to Elizabeth Cranch, [9 Nov. 1782], above, and n.d. [1782], "Hingham," MHi:C. P. Cranch Papers.

[3] Gen. Joseph Palmer's family; "Eliza" in the following sentence is certainly Elizabeth Palmer.

[4] That is, the next day.

Abigail Adams 2d to Lucy Cranch

N 3

London June 23d. [1785]

Disappointment upon Disappointment, Mortification upon Mortification My Dear Lucy shall no longer be subjected to, if it is in my Power to sheild her from them. You will before this Letter reaches you I hope receive from my Brother a long Letter from me[1] which will dissipate every unfriendly idea of forgetfullness, neglect, &c &c. I have indeed so many correspondents that I must acquire a considerable Share of Vanity to suppose it is in my Power to gratify them all tho I were to address a Letter to each. I have it is true the best disposition in the World to please them—but I may fail of success. My Cousin may be assured I have none that I think more worthyly of than herself or who are entitled to my earlier attentions.

Your gentle spirit must have been wounded by so many scenes of unhappiness and distress as you have been witness to in the Good family at G[ermantown]. I Pitty them from my heart, but alas how unavailing is Pitty, it seems to mock Misfortunes like theirs. They are indeed an example from which one may derive many Lessons for future Life, and Learn to act with that resignation and Patience which distinguishes them. I am happy to hear that Eliza is better, they all have my sincerest wishes for Health and happiness.

Your list of adventures was as you intended agreeable[2] and your efforts to please will never fail of success with your Cousin.

You talk of comeing to see us in a Balloon. Why my Dear as Americans sometimes are capable of as imprudent and unadvised things as any other People perhaps, I think it but Prudent to advise you against it. There has lately [3] a most terible accident taken place by a Balloons taking fire in the Air in which were two Men. Both of them were killed by their fall, and there limbs exceedingly Broken. Indeed the account is dreadfull. I confess I have no partiallity for them in *any* way.

My Brother will not disappoint you. He is gone—alas to my sorrow—for I lost in him all the Companion that I had—and it is not *possible* his place should be supplyd. I doubt not but he will answer the expectation of his friends, and contribute to their happyness.

You wish to Visit the Theatres. I should be very happy if you could accompany me to them for I am sure you would be pleased. I think a good Tragedy well acted is a rational amusement. I never derived

6. "BOTH OF THEM WERE KILLED BY THEIR FALL, AND
THERE LIMBS EXCEEDINGLY BROKEN"
ABIGAIL ADAMS 2D TO LUCY CRANCH, 23 JUNE 1785
See page x

so much sattisfaction from any other. I have been twice to the Play since I have been in London. There is such a difference between French and English Theatres that one would scarce be led to suppose that they merited the same title. The first peice I saw here was the School for Scandal,[4] and *I fear* there never was a more just picture of real life. I think I have within my own knowledge some Persons of simular characters tho Perhaps they may not have arrived at so great a height of folly. The second time I went they gave a Tragedy of Thomsons Tancred and Siggismundi,[5] which you well remember I dare say. The characters were very well supported in general and Tancreds in particular. They gave a very Laughable peice after it, which is all ways the Case, but I was too much interested in the Tragedy to be pleased, with so oposite an entertainment. You know I was never fond of very Laughing characters. I dont know why it is for I am sure I prefer seeing People happy rather than otherwise.

I think the People, generally; do not discover so much judgment at the Theatres here as in Paris. In seeing a good Tragedy acted at the Comedy Francaise you will hear ever good sentiment applauded highly, even by the Partarre, but here it is the action rather than the sentiments which they applaud.

I considered myself a little unfortunate in not arriving soon enough to see the universally Celebrated Mrs. Siddens whose fame has extended to so many parts of the World, and of whom every Person without exception, I beleive, are equally delighted. She has lately appeard in Comedy and tho She is allowed Great Merit from the manner in which she acquitted herself, I think she was too eager after reputation not to be contented with the share She had acquired in Tragedy, but I have not yet seen her in either Character.[6] When I have my Cousin shall know my opinion, but she may be assured beforehand that I shall not dare to disent from all the World. My father whose Judgment we may depend upon says, She appears to have understood human Nature better than the Author whose peices She acts. A proof of this May be drawn, from the manner of her Leaving Bath [where] she had been first received as an actress, and the Managers objected to her going when she had acquired some reputation. She told the Company one Evening that She had three very powerfull reasons for Leaving them, to go to London. They were sufficient in her own Mind and she hoped they would sattisfy them all. If the Company would permit She would offer them the Night following. The Next Eve the House was much crouded when the Curtain was drawn up. Mrs. Siddens came upon the stage Leading in her three Children, made a Curtsey to the Audience and retired amid the general Applause of the Company who were so much pleased with this Compliment Paid to their sensibility and generossity that they made no objections to her Leaving them so much for her own advantage.

Adeiu my Dear Lucy. Remember me to all my friends, and write often to your affectionate Cousin   A Adams

RC (MWA:Abigail Adams Corr.); addressed: "Miss Lucy Cranch Braintree Massachusetts." Slight damage to the text where the seal was cut away.

[1] Of 6 May, above.

[2] AA2 refers here and below to a letter not found.

[3] Space in MS; on this disaster, see Thomas Jefferson to AA, 21 June, note 5, above.

[4] Richard Brinsley Sheridan's comedy, first produced in 1777.

[5] James Thomson published *Tancred and Sigismunda* in 1745.

[6] See AA2 to JQA, 24 Sept., and note 2, below.

Abigail Adams to Mary Smith Cranch

june 24. 1785[1]

My dear sister   London Bath hotel westminster

Captain Lyde is arrived and I have 3 Letters by him, one from Doctor Tufts one from Dr. Welch and one from Mrs. Storer.[2] I will not accuse my dear sister because I know she must have written to me tho I have not yet received it. I know so well how many accidents may prevent for a long time the reception of Letters, that whilst I ask candour for myself, I am willing to extend it to others.

I have been here a month without writing a single line to my American Friends. About the 28th. of May we reachd London and expected to have gone into our old quiet Lodgings at the Adelphia, but we found every hotel full, the Sitting of parliament, the Birth day of the King, and the famous Celebration of the Musick of Handle at Westminster Abbey, had drawn together such a concourse of people, that we were glad to get into Lodgings at the moderate price of a Guiney per day, for two Rooms and two Chambers, at the Bath hotel Westminster Picadily, where we yet are. This being the Court end of the city, it is the resort of a vast concourse of carriages, it is too publick and noisy for pleasure, but necessity is without Law. The Ceremony of presentation, upon one week, to the King and the Next to the Queen was to take place, after which I was to prepare for mine. It is customary upon presentation to receive visits from all the Foreign ministers, so that we could not exchange our Lodgings for more private ones, as we might and should; had we been only in a private character. The Foreign ministers and several english Lords and Earls have paid their compliments here and all heitherto is civil and polite. I was a fortnight all the time I could get looking of different Houses, but could not find any one fit to inhabit under 200. besides the taxes which mount up to 50 & 60 pounds. At last my good Genious carried me to one in Grovenor Square, which was not let because the person who had the care of it, could let it only for the remaining lease which was one Year and 3 quarters. The price which is not quite 200, the Situation and all together induced us to close the Bargain and I have prevaild upon the person who lets it; to paint two rooms which will put it into decent order so that as soon as our furniture comes I shall again commence house keeping. Living at a hotel is I think more expensive than house keeping in proportion to what one has for their money. We have never had more than two dishes at a time upon our table, and have not pretended to ask any company and yet we live at a greater expence than 25 Guineys per week. The Wages of servants horse hire house meat and provision are much dearer here than in France. Servants of various sorts and for different departments are to be procured, their Characters to be inquird into, and this I take upon me even to the Coachman; you can hardly form an Idea how much I miss my son on this as well as many other accounts. But I cannot bear to trouble Mr. Adams with any thing of a domestick kind, who from morning untill Evening has sufficient to occupy all his time. You can have no Idea of the petitions Letters and private applications for a pittance which crowd our doors. Every person represents his case as dismal, some may really be objects of compassion, and some we assist, but one must have an inexhaustable purse to supply them all. Besides there are so many gross impositions practised as we have found in more instances than one, that it would take the whole of a persons time to trace all their stories. Many pretend to have been American soldiers, some to have served as officers. A most glaring instance of falshood however Col. Smith detected in a man of these pretentions, who sent to Mr. Adams from the Kings bench prison and modestly desired 5 Guineys, a qualified cheet but evidently a man of Letters and abilities.[3] But if it is to continue in this way a Galley Slave would have an easier task.

The Tory venom has begun to spit itself forth in the publick papers as I expected, bursting with envy that an American Minister should be received here with the same marks of attention politeness and civility which is shewn to the Ministers of any other power. When a minister delivers his credentials to the king, it is always in his private closet attended only by the minister for Foreign affairs, which is called a private audience, and the Minister presented makes some little address to his Majesty, and the same ceremony to the Queen, whose replie was in these Words, "Sir I thank you for your civility to me and my family, and I am glad to see you in this Country," then very politely inquired whether he had got a house yet? The answer of his Majesty was much longer, but I am not at liberty to say more respecting it; than that it was civil and polite, and that his Majesty said he was glad the Choice of his Country had fallen upon him. The News Liars know nothing of the Matter, they represent it just to answer their purpose.[4] Last thursday Col. Smith was presented at Court, and tomorrow at the Queens circle my Ladyship and your Neice make our compliments. There is no other presentation in Europe in which I should feel so much as in this. Your own reflections will easily [suggest?] the reasons. I have received a very friendly and polite visit from the Countess of Effingham. She calld and not finding me at Home left a Card. I returnd her visit, but was obliged to do it by leaving my Card too: as she was gone out of Town. But when her Ladyship returnd she sent her compliments, and word that if agreeable she would take a Dish of tea with me; and named her Day. She accordingly came, and appeard a very polite sensible woman. She is about 40, a good person, tho a little masculine, elegant in her appearence, very easy and social. The Earl of Effingham is too well rememberd by America to need any particular recital of his Character.[5] His Mother is first Lady to the Queen. When Her Ladyship took leave, she desired I would let her know the day that I would favour her with a visit, as she should be loth to be absent. She resides in summer a little distance from town. The Earl is a Member of Parliament which obliges him now to be in town and she usually comes with him and resides at a hotel a little distance from this. I find a good many Ladies belonging to the Southern states here, many of whom have visited me. I have exchanged visits with several, yet neither of us have met.[6] The Custom is however here, much more agreeable than in France, for it is as with us, the Stranger is first visited. The ceremony of presentation here is considerd as indispensable. Their are four minister plenipotentiarys Ladies here, but one Ambassador and he has no Lady. In France the Ladys of Ambassadors only are presented there. One is obliged here to attend the circles of the Queen which are held in Summer one a fortnight, but once a week the rest of the year, and what renders it exceedingly expensive is, that you cannot go twice the same Season in the same dress, and a Court dress you cannot make use any where else. I directed my Mantua Maker to let my dress be elegant but plain as I could possibly appear with Decency, accordingly it is white Lutestring coverd and full trimd with white Crape festoond with lilick ribbon and mock point lace, over a hoop of enormus extent. There is only a narrow train of about 3 yard length to the gown waist, which is put into a ribbon upon the left side, the Queen only having her train borne, ruffel cuffs for married Ladies thrible lace ruffels a very dress cap with long lace lappets two white plumes and a blond lace handkerchief, this is my rigging. I should have mentiond two pearl pins in my hair earings and necklace of the same kind.

thursday morning

My Head is drest for St. James and in my opinion looks very tasty. Whilst Emelias is undergoing the same operation, I set myself down composedly to write you a few lines. Well methinks I hear Betsy and Lucy say, what is cousins dress, white my Dear Girls like your Aunts, only differently trimd, and ornamented, her train being wholy of white crape and trimd with white ribbon, the peticoat which is the most showy part of the dress coverd and drawn up in what is calld festoons, with light wreaths of Beautifull flowers. The Sleaves white crape drawn over the silk with a row of lace round the Sleave near the shoulder an other half way down the arm and a 3d. upon the top of the ruffel little flower[s] stuck between. A kind of hat Cap with 3 large feathers and a bunch of flowers a wreath of flowers upon the hair. Thus equipd we go in our own Carriage and Mr. A and Col. Smith in his. But I must quit my pen to put myself in order for the ceremony which begins at 2 oclock. When I return I will relate to you my reception, but do not let it circulate as there may be persons eager to Catch at every thing, and as much given to misrepresentation as here. I would gladly be excused the Ceremony.

fryday morning

Congratulate me my dear sister it is over. I was too much fatigued to write a line last evening. At two a clock we went to the circle which is in the drawing room of the Queen. We past through several appartments lined as usual with Spectatirs upon these occasions. Upon entering the antiChamber, the Baron de Linden the Dutch Minister who has been often here came and spoke with me. A Count Sarsfield a French nobleman with whom I was acquainted paid his compliments. As I passt into the drawing room Lord Carmathan and

Sir Clement Cotterel Dormer were presented to me.[7] Tho they had been several times here I had never seen them before. The sweedish the polish ministers[8] made their compliments and several other Gentleman, but not a single Lady did I know, untill the Countess of Effingham came who was very civil. There were 3 young Ladies daughters of the Marquiss of Lothan[9] who were to be presented at the same time and two Brides. We were placed in a circle round the drawing room which was very full, I believe 200 person present. Only think of the task the Royal family have, to go round to every person, and find small talk enough to speak to all of them. Tho they very prudently speak in a whisper, so that only the person who stands next you can hear what is said. The King enters the room and goes round to the right, the Queen and princesses to the left. The Lord in waiting presents you to the King and the Lady in waiting does the same to her Majesty. The King is a personable Man, but my dear sister he has a certain Countenance which you and I have often remarked, a red face and white eye brows, the Queen has a similar countanance and the numerous Royal family confirm the observation. Persons are not placed according to their rank in the drawing room, but tranciently, and when the King comes in he takes persons as they stand. When he came to me, Lord Onslow[10] said, Mrs. Adams, upon which I drew of my right hand Glove, and his Majesty saluted my left cheek, then asked me if I had taken a walk to day. I could have told his Majesty that I had been all the morning prepareing to wait upon him, but I replied, no Sire. Why dont you love walking says he? I answerd that I was rather indolent in that respect. He then Bow'd and past on. It was more than two hours after this before it came to my turn to be presented to the Queen. The circle was so large that the company were four hours standing. The Queen was evidently embarrased when I was presented to her. I had dissagreeable feelings too. She however said Mrs. Adams have you got into your house, pray how do you like the Situation of it? Whilst the princess Royal[11] looked compasionate, and asked me if I was not much fatigued, and observed that it was a very full drawing room. Her sister who came next princess Augusta, after having asked your neice if she was ever in England before, and her answering yes, inquird of me how long ago, and supposed it was when she was very young. And all this is said with much affability, and the ease and freedom of old acquaintance. The manner in which they make their tour round the room, is first the Queen, the Lady in waiting behind her holding up her train, next to her the princess royal after her princess Augusta and their Lady in waiting behind them.

7. PRINCESSES CHARLOTTE, AUGUSTA, AND ELIZABETH, ABOUT 1784,
BY THOMAS GAINSBOROUGH
See page xi

They are pretty rather than Beautifull, well shaped with fair complexions and a tincture of the kings countanance. The two sisters look much alike. They were both drest in lilack and silver silk with a silver netting upon the coat, and their heads full of diamond pins. The Queen was in purple and silver. She is not well shaped or handsome. As [to] the Ladies of the Court, Rank and title may compensate for want of personal Charms, but they are in general very plain ill shaped and ugly, but dont you tell any body that I say so. If one wants to see Beauty they must go to Ranaleigh,[12] there it is collected in one bright constelation. There were two Ladies very elegant at court Lady Salsbury and Lady Talbot,[13] but the observation did not in general hold good that fine feathers make fine Birds. I saw many who were vastly richer drest than your Friends, but I will venture to say that I saw none neater or more elegant, which praise I ascribe to the taste of Mrs. Temple and my Mantua Maker, for after having declared that I would not have any foil or tincel about me, they fixd upon the dress I have described. Mrs. Temple is my near Neighbour and has been very friendly to me. Mr. Temple you know is deaf so that I cannot hold much conversation with him.

The Tories are very free with their compliments. Scarcly a paper excapes without some scurrility. We bear it with silent Contempt, having met a polite reception from the Court. It bites them Like a serpent and stings them like an adder.[14] As to the success the negotiations may meet with time alone can disclose the result, but if this nation does not suffer itself to be again duped by the artifice of some and the malice of others, it will unite itself with America upon the most liberal principals and sentiments.

Captain Dashood came why I have not half done. I have not told your Aunt yet that whilst I was writing I received her thrice welcome Letters, and from my dear cousins too, Aunt Shaw and all,[15] nor how some times I laught and sometimes I cry'd, yet there was nothing sorrowfull in the Letters, only they were too tender for me. What not time to say I will write to all of them as soon as possible. Why I know they will all think I ought to write, but how is it possible? Let them think what I have to do, and what I have yet to accomplish as my furniture is come and will be landed tomorrow.[16] Eat the sweet meats[17] divide them amongst you, and the choisest sweet meat of all I shall have in thinking that you enjoy them.[18]

I hope you have got all my Letters by my son from whom I shall be anxious to hear.

Adieu adieu.

Esther is well, John poorly. Do not any of you think hard of me for not writing more, my pen is good for nothing. I went last Evening to Raneleigh, but I must reserve that story for the young folks. You see I am in haste, believe me most tenderly yours   A Adams

june 28[19]

Make the corrections, I have not time; Mr. Storer was well this morning when he left us, he was of the party last evening.

RC (MWA:Abigail Adams Corr.).

[1] AA completed most of the body of this letter on the 24th, but the last paragraphs date from the 28th (see notes 12 and 18), and she wrote the first sections on Wednesday and Thursday, 22 and 23 June.

[2] Cotton Tufts to AA, [*11*], and 19 April; and Hannah Storer to AA, 3 May, are all above. The letter from Dr. Thomas Welsh has not been found; AA replied to him on [25 Aug.], below. This opening paragraph is omitted from AA, *Letters*, ed. CFA.

[3] This may have been the prisoner who wrote to JA on 2 June (Adams Papers), introducing himself as W. R. Coleman, a Revolutionary War veteran from Virginia.

[4] The *Daily Universal Register* of 10 June includes a squib describing the "cool reception of the American Ambassador." One paragraph speculates: "The *closet-scene* on a late introduction at St. James's, must have been curious. It is thought on one side the *blush* was as deep as die, as the *flesh* on *Eve's* cheek when she first saw *Adam*." *The Morning Post and Daily Advertiser* of 13 June asserted that JA was so embarrassed at his first audience with George III that he could not "pronounce the compliment prescribed by etiquette." For JA's account of his reception by George III, see AA to Thomas Jefferson, 6 June, note 8, above.

[5] Thomas Howard, ninth baron Howard of Effingham and third earl of Effingham, married Catherine, daughter of Metcalfe Procter, in 1765. Effingham was a prominent opponent of Lord North's government and an outspoken supporter of American rights in the House of Lords from 1770 to 1782. He supported Pitt in 1783, became master of the mint in 1784, and was named a lord of trade and plantations in 1785 (James E. Doyle, *Official Baronage of England*, London, 1886, vol. 1; Vicary Gibbs and H. A. Doubleday, *The Complete Peerage*, London, 1921; Alan Valentine, *The British Establishment, 1760–1784*,

Norman, Okla., 1970).

[6] AA evidently means that she was out when her Southern visitors called, and they were out when she called on them.

[7] Francis Godolphin Osborne, son of the fourth duke of Leeds, sat briefly in the House of Commons as the Marquis of Carmarthen (1774–1775). He entered the House of Lords as Lord Osborne in 1776, but was commonly known as Carmarthen until he became the fifth duke of Leeds in 1789. A privy councilor from 1777, he served as secretary of state for foreign affairs from 1783 to 1791. He was a strong supporter of the North ministry until 1780, when he lost his post as lord lieutenant of the East Riding of Yorkshire for refusing to oppose the county association movement. Although he then joined the opposition, he always defended the justice of Britain's effort to keep her colonies. See Namier and Brooke, *House of Commons*, 3:236–237; JA, *Papers*, 8:370, and note 6.

Sir Clement Cotterell Dormer was knighted in 1779, and appointed Master of the Ceremonies at St. James's Palace, a position held by members of his family from 1641 to 1808 (William A. Shaw, *The Knights of England*, London, 1906, 2:296; *DNB*, under Cotterell). Dormer wrote to JA on 22 June (Adams Papers) to describe the proper manner of AA's presentation to the Queen.

[8] Gustaf Adam, Baron von Nolcken, was the Swedish envoy; Franciszek Bukaty was the Polish minister (*Repertorium der diplomatischen Vertreter aller Länder*, 3:409, 310).

[9] William John Kerr became the fifth marquis of Lothian in 1775. JA and JQA had met his son, William Kerr, earl of Ancram, in Paris in 1783. John Bernard Burke, *Peerage and Baronetage*, London, 1853; JQA, *Diary*, 1:185, and note 1.

[10] George Onslow, son of Arthur Onslow, speaker of the House of Commons under

George II, also sat in Commons, 1754–1776. In the latter year he became the fourth baron Onslow, and in 1780 he was appointed a lord of the royal bedchamber. *DNB*.

[11] Charlotte Augusta Matilda, George III and Queen Charlotte's eldest daughter, born in 1766; she married the prince of Würtemberg in 1797 (*DNB*). Her sister Augusta Sophia, mentioned below, was born in 1768 (*DNB*).

[12] The public entertainment rooms erected at Ranelagh Gardens in Chelsea in 1742 were the site of regular promenades of the British upper classes. Ranelagh closed in 1803, and was torn down soon thereafter (Wheatley, *London Past and Present*). AA's reference to Ranelagh here may indicate that the text from this point was written on 28 June, for she evidently attended Ranelagh on the 27th; see note 19.

[13] Mary Amelia, who married James Cecil, seventh earl of Salisbury, in 1773, and Charlotte, who married Earl Talbot in 1776, were sisters, the daughters of Wills Hill, the earl of Hillsborough, who so angered Massachusetts' patriot leaders when he served as secretary of state for the colonies, 1768–1772. Cecil became the first marquis of Salisbury, and Hill the first marquis of Downshire, in 1789. Burke, *Peerage and Baronetage*.

[14] Proverbs 23:32.

[15] "Your Aunt" has not been positively identified. Mary Cranch's (and AA's) aunt Elizabeth Storer Smith seems the most likely candidate; Lucy Quincy Tufts is another possibility. By "dear cousins" AA probably means her nieces Elizabeth and Lucy Cranch. Of the several letters that AA evidently refers to here, only Elizabeth Cranch to AA, and Elizabeth Shaw to AA, both 25 April, both above, have been found.

[16] This was JA's furniture from the American legation at The Hague. See AA to Cotton Tufts, 3 Jan., and note 4, above; and AA to JQA, 26 June and note 2, below.

[17] See Cotton Tufts to AA, [11] and 19 April, both above.

[18] The text from this point through "my pen is good for nothing" is omitted from AA, *Letters*, ed. CFA.

[19] This date certainly applies to all the text from "Captain Dashood came," and perhaps to the text at AA's first mention of "Ranaleigh." This dated postscript is omitted from AA, *Letters*, ed. CFA.

Abigail Adams to John Quincy Adams

London Bath hotel Westminster
My dear son   june 26 [1785]

I have not written you a single line since you left me. Your sisters punctuality I saw would render my pen unnecessary and I have resignd to her all the minutia, as her leisure is much greater and her cares fewer. Capt. Dashood is to sail in a few days for America, and tho as you may well imagine I have much upon my hands, and miss your assistance not a little, I have determined to write you a short Letter, and I know not but that it will turn out a very long one, for my pen will always run greater lengths than I am aware of when I address those who are particularly dear to me and to whom I can write with unreserve.

I hope you had an agreeable passage and that this will find you safe in your native Land, that you are now fix'd in persueing those studies which we have so often talkd over together in your Chamber at Auteuil. I doubt not that you met with as friendly a reception from our Friends as I ensured you: I shall be anxious to hear from you and every circumstance which respects you, tho you forgot even to mention me in your Letters to your sister.[1] I suppose she has written you every thing respecting our quitting Auteuil, our journey and our arrival here. We could not continue at Lodgings here as no such thing is practised ⟨here⟩, even by those Ministers who have no families. We have procured a house in Grovenor Square and we hourly expect our furniture. Lotter[2] comes with it, to see it safe here. The General Idea here is that the United States find a house and furnish it like other powers, but we know the contrary to our cost. The wages of servants house rent and every other article is much higher than in France. The constant Letters petitions and applications from every quarter is incredible, and the fees to the Court Servants the same as in France, only they come to your house here and demand them as the perquisites of their office. After presentation, and a new Years day you have the same to go over again. We have got through with the payment of 23 Guineys. Your sister I suppose has acquainted you with our being obliged to attend court here. We were presented last thursday at a very full drawing room, and stood more than four hours. You will easily conceive that we were suffcently fatigued. I own I[3] had some dissagreeable feelings upon the occasion. His Majesty had got over his worst, in the presentation of your Father whom however he received with much civility. He therefore look'd very jovial and good humourd when I was presented to him. Her Majesty was evidently embarassed and confused. She however spoke to me with politeness, and askd me if I had got into my House, and how I liked the situation. The two princesses, had something to say both to me and your sister, in an obliging familiar Stile. But their task is not to be Coveted, to attend these circles once a week, except in the summer, when they hold them only once a fortnight, and to have to go round to every person and find something to say to all, is paying dearly for their Rank. They do it however with great affability, and give general satisfaction, but I could not help reflecting with myself during the ceremony, what a fool do I look like to be thus accutored and stand here for 4 hours together, only for to be spoken too, by "royalty." The Ministers from all the Courts had visited your Father immediately after his presentation, and since mine they have several of them repeated the visit to me. The Baron de Linden whom you know I believe, is often here and is very civil. Count Sasfeild too often visits here. They were both at court, so was Lord Mount Mon's[4] whom we saw in Paris. They all paid their compliments to me there; which took of some of the dissagreeable feeling of being known by no one. Lord Carmathan was introduced to me there and Sir Coteral Dormer, who tho he had attended your Pappa, I had not seen before. A Sir John Hoart[5] and two or 3 others got themselves introduced and the Countess of Effingham I have found vastly obliging, so that I had my share of conversation and notice, and was not stuck up quite such an object to be gazed at as I feard. I found the Court like the rest of Mankind, mere Men and Women, and not of the most personable kind neither. I had vanity enough to come a way quite self satisfied, for tho I could not boast of making an appearence in point of person or richness of attire with many of them—the latter I carefully avoided the appearence of, yet I know I will not strike my coulours to many of them. We have no reason to complain of any want of politeness or attention at Court. The Newspapers Scriblers complement us with their notice, but we despise their ribaldary. No Tory so bitter that I hear of, as old treasurer Gray,[6] who I hear declares now, that he would hang your Father if it was in his power. As to success in negotiation time will disclose it, but more time may be necessary than perhaps our Country will immagine. There are many prejudices to remove, and every wheel is in motion to spin the threads stronger, but they must take care they do not make it into a Gordeon knot least it should like that, require the sword to cut it. Col. Smith from the acquaintance I have had with him fully answers the kind things the Marquis[7] said of him. He appears to be a man of an independant spirit, high and strict sentiments of honour, Much the Gentleman in his manners and address, no cincinatus advocate the badge of which he has never worn and I have ever reason to think from conversation with him that he wishes the order totally annihilated.[8]

This is Sunday, the forenoon of which we went to Hackney all of us to hear Dr. Price. This is the 3d Sunday we have attended his meeting, and I would willingly go much further to hear a Man so liberal so sensible so good as he is. He has a Charity which embrases all mankind and a benevolence which would do good to all of them. His subjects are instructive and edifying.[9]

Give my Love to your Brothers and tell them and the rest of my Friends that I will write to them as soon as I get a little setled. Write me my dear Son and write me with freedom your sentiments respecting a Friend of your sisters.[10] Cover those Letters which you wish *me only* to see to Col. Smith but do not address them, in your handwriting. I will some time or other take occasion to mention to him that if he should receive any letter addrest to me, to give it me alone.

june 27

Mr. Lotter is arrived with our things. I shall not have an other moments leisure. Poor Pelitir Rozier I dont know whether I spell the name right, is dead blown up by the ballon catching fire. You will read the account in the Papers. Adieu.

RC (Adams Papers); endorsed: "Mamma. June 26. 1785"; docketed twice by JQA: "Mrs. Adams. June 26. 1785," and "My Mother. 26. June 1785."

¹ Of [12] and 17 May, above.

² Christian Lotter served as a steward to JA at The Hague from 1784 or earlier; his correspondence with JA extends from Aug. 1784 to Oct. 1787. Lotter made the inventory of JQA's clothes and books of 6 Nov. 1784 (Adams Papers); and an F. Lotter checked the long inventory of the furnishings of the Hôtel des Etats-Unis at The Hague, prepared in two sections, by John Thaxter in May and October 1782, and by Marie Dumas in June 1784 (Adams Papers; second item filmed under 14 May 1782, Adams Papers, Microfilms, Reel No. 357). Christian Lotter brought the items listed on the inventory of furnishings to London in June 1785. The Adamses brought many of these furnishings home to Braintree, where they remain today in the Adams National Historic Site.

³ AA wrote "own I" above the line.

⁴ AA may intend Irish patriot Hervey Redmond Morres, viscount Mountmorres, whom JA met in France in 1782 (JA, *Diary and Autobiography*, 3:96; *DNB*).

⁵ Sir John Hort was appointed consul general at Lisbon in 1767, and made a baronet the same year; he served as chargé d'affaires at Lisbon, 1770–1772 (John Bernard Burke, *Peerage and Baronetage*, London, 1853; *Repertorium der diplomatischen Vertreter aller Länder*, 3:169).

⁶ Harrison Gray served as treasurer of Massachusetts until the Revolution, when he went into exile in England. He was the father-in-law of Samuel Allyne Otis, and grandfather of Harrison Gray Otis. See Samuel Eliot Morison, *The Life and Letters of Harrison Gray Otis, Federalist, 1765–1848*, Boston and N.Y., 1913, vol. 1, chap. 1; and JA, *Diary and Autobiography*, 1:270–271, for JA's early opinion of Gray.

⁷ Lafayette; see AA to Mercy Warren, 10

May, above.

⁸ This passage seems rather misleading, and William Stephens Smith may have been less than candid with the Adamses about his role in the Society of the Cincinnati. They knew before meeting him that he was a member of the order (JA to Elbridge Gerry, 28 April, LbC, Adams Papers; AA to Mercy Warren, 10 May, above), but AA evidently did not know how prominent a member he was, nor did she imagine how prominent he would become. Smith was a leader of the New York state branch of the Society as early as May 1784, when he played a key role in the national meeting that amended the first plan of the organization. In the 1790s he was elected vice-president, and then president, of the Society's New York branch, and served several terms. In the same decade he was painted by Gilbert Stuart wearing the badge of the order. See William Sturgis Thomas, *Members of the Society of the Cincinnati*, N.Y., 1929, p. 138; Minor Myers Jr., *Liberty without Anarchy: A History of the Society of the Cincinnati*, Charlottesville, 1983, p. 59, 61, 130, 192, 195; and Katharine Metcalf Roof, *Colonel William Smith and Lady*, Boston, 1929, p. 336, and illustration facing p. 332.

⁹ JA was familiar with Dr. Richard Price's economic and political writings at least from 1778 (JA, *Papers*, 7:361–362; JA to Price, 8 April 1785, LbC, Adams Papers), and AA quoted from his moral writings with approval in 1783 (to JA, 19 Oct., above), but they apparently first met him upon moving to England in 1785. They became good friends of the liberal dissenting preacher, and worshiped regularly at Hackney, much to AA's satisfaction, until their return to America in 1788 (JA, *Diary and Autobiography*, 3:188, 203, 215).

¹⁰ Royall Tyler.

John Adams to John Quincy Adams

Bath Hotel Westminster
My dear son   June 26. 1785

I hope, that before this day you are Safely arrived at New York, and that in another Month, I shall receive a Letter from you dated from that City. Before this reaches you I Suppose you will be at Boston or Cambridge, or Braintree or Haverill or Weymouth. Let me hear from you as often as you can.

We have taken a House in Grosvenor Square, at the Corner of Duke Street, and hope to get into it in a Week. We have gone through all the Ceremonies of Presentations and Visits, which are more tedious I think at St. James's than at the Hague or at Versailles. You will see by the Papers that the despicable Spight, of the old Boston Tories, Still bears an honourable Testimony to your Fathers Integrity and faithfull Perseverance in the Cause of his Country.[1] I have met, however with a very different Reception at Court.

Your Brother Charles I hope will enter Colledge this Year, and that you and he will be very happy together.

Let me know how Mr. Thaxter succeeds in Business, and whether he is a Speaker at the Bar,—the same of Mr. Tyler.

My Love & Duty where due. Your affectionate Father

John Adams

RC (Adams Papers).

[1] A squib in the *Daily Universal Register* of 14 June, which describes JA as "a quondam declared rebel," employs an ironic use of Proverbs 22:29, to attack him. "See'st thou a man diligent in business (said Solomon) and he shall stand before princes and great men, &c.–A-la-mode John Adams."

Charles Williamos to Abigail Adams

Dear Madam   Paris 27th. June 1785

I had the pleasure of writing to Mr. Adams four or five days after your departure[1] to acquaint you of your son's safe arrival at l'Orient, and as I did not know your proper adress, I enclosed my letter to Mr. Clarke at Counsellor Brown's, Chancery Lane, with very particular charge to wait on you immediately on your arrival. Mr. Clarke has not wrote to me since, and by Miss Adams's note[2] I am led to think my former letter has miscarried, be kind enough therefore to excuse my apparent neglect, a thing, far, very far indeed from my thoughts; I then mentioned that my letter from the Captain and officers of the Packet gave me every hope that your son would meet with every attention and find thereby his passage less Irksome.

I was very happy in seeing Mrs. Hay but should have been much more so if I could have rendered her stay here as agreable as possible. Mr. Carnes[3] Joined with me in every endeavour. But large towns are such a bore to the true pleasures of Society that I fear she did not relish Paris much; I was much surprised after parting with her the evening before, that when I called the next morning I was told of her departure; Your mantua maker behaved so very Ill that altho' I went to her, and to Mrs. Barclay's on purpose, and sent my man several times to her, she would not finish your things till many days after Mrs. Hay went away. I am looking every where for a safe opportunity to send them.

The June Packet sails from L'orient. I have sent Miss Adams's letter to a friend at New York[4] with particular directions to deliver, or forward it, the next packet, and some merchant vessels are certainly to go in the Course of next month from Havre. I shall sail in the very first, doctor Franklin proposes doing the same if possible;[5] we are all very well here but feeling every day more and more the loss of our most valuable Auteuill friends. How does, the Change of places, manners and things agree with them? but with such minds as they possess can they but be happy every where?

Mr. Jefferson has some letters ready many days since, which only wait for a *Safe Conveyance*. They are not *often* met with.[6]

The May packet is not arrived yet, all our american news which appear important are by the way of England.

Can I flatter myself Madam that if my feeble services can be of any use on this or the other side of the Atlantick you will Command them freely.

Nothing could render me more truly happy than opportunities of rendering agreable the unfeigned [respect?] and most sincere regard [. . .] which I have the honor to be [perfe]ctly

Madam your most obedient devoted servant   C: Williamos

My best respect ever truly attend Mr. and Miss Adams; I am very happy to hear Col. Smith is arrived Safe and well.

RC (Adams Papers); addressed: "Mrs. Adams Bath Hotel Westminster *London*"; stamped: "IU/30," and, in a red ink, an illegible word or words; endorsed: "Mr Williamos Letter 27 june." Some text has been lost where the seal was cut away.

.

[1] Not found; see AA to Williamos, 1 July, note 1, below.

[2] Not found.

[3] Burrill Carnes was an American merchant who was living in Lorient in Sept. 1785, and was appointed an American agent at Nantes by consul general Thomas Barclay in Feb. 1786 (Jefferson, *Papers*, 8:544; 9:303).

[4] Probably one of AA2's letters to JQA, written in May or early June, which have not been found. See AA2 to JQA, 4 July, note 1, below.

[5] Franklin's plan to sail directly home from Le Havre was frustrated by a lack of vessels leaving that port for America, and he sailed from England in late July. Williamos did not sail at all. See AA to Williamos, 1 July, note 2; Williamos to AA, 21 July, note 2, both below.

[6] Jefferson still retained his letter of 21 June to AA, above (see note 1 to that letter; Jefferson to AA, 7 July, below; and Jefferson to JA, 22 June and 7 July, both Adams Papers, printed in Jefferson, *Papers*, 8:246, 265).

Abigail Adams to Isaac Smith Sr.

London Bath hotel Westminster

Dear Sir   june 30th 1785

You obligeing favour[1] I received by Captain Lyde and thank you for its contents, which assured me of your kind remembrance of me, and your politeness at the same time: in being the first of our American Friends who crost the water to visit us in Stile. Many English Lords and Noblemen have visited us in the same way, but as it is not in our power to return the visit untill we happily reach the American Shore, you will in the mean time accept my thanks in this way. Be assured Dear Sir that I wrote you by my Son[2] and that I should have written to you oftner if I had thought I could have entertaind you, and that my omission has been neither oweing to want of Respect or affection.

The magnifying glass is still made use, of by Englishmen in looking at America, and every little commotion there, is represented as a high handed Roit, and it is roundly asserted that their is neither Authority or Government, there. I was in company the other day and heard these observations, but as they were not addrest to me, I did not think myself Authorised to enter into a political dispute.

When the shop tax past here the other day,[3] the shops throughout the city were shut up, some hung in black, and the statue of Gorge the 2d put into deep mourning. Upon the shops was written shops to be let, inquire of Mr. Pitt. Upon others no Pitt, no shop tax, damn Pitt. In Several places he was hung in Effigy. In the Evening every body was apprehensive of a Mob, as they threatned very much to assail the House of Commons, the Militia and city Gaurds were all under Arms, and had enough to do to keep the Mobility in order. If such an opposition to Authority had taken place in America, it would have been circulated in the highest coulouring as far as British Newspapers could carry it.

The disposition amongst the mercantile part of this Nation is not very favourable to America, and the Refugees are very desperate bitter and venomous, and none more so that I hear of than the former Treasurer of Boston.[4] Some of them I believe are wretched enough, but it does not work conviction in them, that they have erred and strayed like lost—not Sheep, but Wolves—for they would devour us yet if they could. Some Merchants say they can have our trade without any treaty, others what is a trade good for with a people who have nothing to give in return? Others that we are not united enough to take any resolutions which will be generally binding and that Congress has no Authority over the different states.

Time will discover whether this system is to opperate in the Cabinet. The civil and polite reception given to the American Minister and his family, from the Court, does not ensure to America justice in other respects, but so far as forms go; America has been treated in her Representitive with the same attention that is shewn to Ministers from other powers.

If you should have an opportunity to send us a Quintel of good salt fish we should be much obliged to you. It may be addrest to Mr. Rogers. Dr. Tufts will pay for it.

Be so good sir as to present my duty to my Aunt to whom I will write as soon as I get setled in my house to which we shall remove this week in Grovenor-Square. My Love to all my cousins. I visited Mr. Vassels family this week at Clapham,[5] they inquired after you, and Miss Hobart particularly desired her regards to you and my Aunt.

My daughter desires her duty and Love may be presented to all her Friends and relatives. Mr. Adams will write as soon as he can get time. Believe me Dear Sir most affectionately Your Neice

Abigail Adams

RC (MHi:Smith-Carter Papers); addressed: "Isaac Smith Esquire Merchant at Boston"; notations on address sheet, in other hands?: "sh.2.16"; and "Hond by Cap J Ingram"; docketed: "Mrs Adams London 1785."

[1] Not found.
[2] Of 8 May, above.
[3] 25 Geo. 3. c. 30.
[4] Harrison Gray.
[5] William Vassall, distressed by the disorders of the coming Revolution, but considering himself neutral in the conflict, fled Massachusetts for England in 1775, and died there in 1800. He had apparently been a client of JA's at some point (JA to Thomas Jefferson, 3 May 1816, in JA, *Works*, 10:214–215), but the nature of the case(s) is not known. Vassall had employed several lawyers in the 1750s, when he maintained interminable law suits against several fellow Bostonians. *Sibley's Harvard Graduates*, 9:349–359.

Abigail Adams to Charles Williamos

Dear sir   july 1 1785

I received your favour last evening which is the first line we have had from you; I shall send to this Mr. Clark and see if the other Letter is to be found.[1] We are at present in much confusion our furniture having just arrived at our house which we are aranging as fast as possible, so that I am between the Bath hotel and Grovesnor Square much occupied. I assure you it would be a great addition to our happiness if the intercourse between the Friends we had in Paris could be as easily mantaind here as at Auteuil. You know that I did not live long enough in Paris to become so great an Idolatar of it, as some of my fair countrywomen, and it is not to be wonderd at that the same Religion Language customs and some likeness of Manners should give me a Bias in favour of this Country. Heitherto I have had nothing to complain of, not even the compliments in the Gazzets which are beneath notice, and spring from the corrupted source of torry Malevolence, but nothing better can be expected from those who have been paricides to their Native Land. From the Court we have received every mark of politeness and attention which we had any reason to expect. Upon the last drawing room of the Queens I had the honour with my daughter of being presented to their Majesties the ceremony of which is very different from a presentation at Verssailes. When the Lord in waiting presents a Lady to the King, she draws of the Glove of her right hand and his Majesty salutes her right cheek. He then speaks to her and the Queen does the same. The princess Royal and her elder sister who are the only two that attend the drawing room go round in their turn and speak to all who have been presented. It is very tiresome however and one pays dear for the smiles of Royalty. I was four hours standing, for it was a crouded drawing room and the Royal family have a task of it to find small talk sufficient to speak in turn to the whole.

I thank you sir for all your Friendly attentions to me and mine whilst at Paris and since my arrival here. My Matua Makers word I never found much reliance upon, but her work is so much to be prefered to any thing I can get done here, that if it was not attended with so much difficulty I should send her all my Cloaths to make. If Mrs. Barclay had a commission to Execute for me as soon as it is accomplishd I would have the things all put together and I inclose you a letter unseald to Mr. Hales the ⟨*Duke of Dorsets*⟩ British

Secratary of Legation by which you see I have requested his care of them. I have been informd that the duke of Dorset has a trusty person who passes weekly in a carriage from Paris here. If you will be so kind as to take charge of this Letter and see Mr. Hale I dare say I shall be at no further trouble in looking out for a conveyance and Mr. Jefferson I fancy may trust his Letters safely in the same bundle with out even mentioning them as they will not be subject to Search. Mrs. Barclay had some lace to send me which if not already forwarded may be sent by the same way. Mrs. Hay speaks very highly of your particular attention to her as well as the rest of my Friends at Paris. Her situation required her embrasing the first opportunity of returning to England and she had only a few hours notice of the opportunity. She begg me to present her respects to Mr. Jefferson and the rest of the Gentleman who were so kind as to notice her. My Regards to Mr. Jefferson, Col. Humphries, Mr. Short and my good Friends the Abbes. Respectfull compliments to Dr. Franklin and Son.[2] The Marquis and Lady are I suppose gone into the Country. Whenever you embark for America I wish you a pleasent voyage. I shall always be happy to hear from you. Mr. Adams will write soon to Mr. Jefferson. Col. Smith and Col. Humphries seem to be standing upon points of punctilio who shall make the first advances towards renewing an old acquaintance. We are much pleased with Col. Smith I assure you.

⟨*My daughter joins me in sentiments of Regard accept*⟩
Believe me Sir with sentiments of Esteem your Friend and humble servant AA

Dft (Adams Papers); notations on the first page by CFA: in blue ink: "To Mr Barclay. London July 1. 1785"; and in pencil: "To Mr Barclay?" See note 1.

[1] Although a transmission of three days from Paris was quite rapid, the references in this sentence, and those in the following paragraph to AA's Paris mantua maker and to Mrs. Hay, are all to Charles Williamos' letter of 27 June, above. Williamos' other letter, sent to JA, ca. 25 May, in care of "Mr. Clarke at Counsellor Brown's, Chancery Lane" in London (Williamos to AA, 27 June), has not been found. The conjecture by CFA that the intended recipient of this letter was Thomas Barclay (see descriptive note) probably owed to AA's references to Mrs. Barclay, below. But no other letter by AA to Barclay, or from him to her, has been found, and only one letter is known from Mary Barclay to AA (5 Sept., below).

[2] AA certainly means Benjamin Franklin's elder grandson, William Temple Franklin; Franklin's younger grandson, Benjamin Franklin Bache, was also returning with him to America. The three departed from Passy on 12 July, and reached Southampton, England, on the 24th. There Franklin had one last, painful meeting with his son, the loyalist exile William Franklin, whom AA had probably never met. See Jefferson, *Papers*, 8:281, 308; Claude-Anne Lopez and Eugenia W. Herbert, *The Private Franklin: The Man and His Family*, N.Y., 1975, p. 279–281.

Mary McCann to John Adams and Abigail Adams

May it please your Excellency   2nd July 1785
Madam

Having humbly presumed to wait on you to solicit the honor of serving your Excellency's Family with Cream and Milk, and had the honor to give you at the Hotel last Fryday, a Recommendation from his Excellency the Spanish Ambassador's Steward, you was pleased to order me to wait at your House in Grosvenor Square Yesterday Morning with Cream and Milk, which I accordingly did; but may it please your Excellency, I am humbly to inform you, that a Woman in the Care of the House refused taking either from me, tho' I told her I came by your Excellency's Order: thus refused by her, I beg leave with all Humility to address your Excellency with these few lines, humbly to solicit the honor of serving your Family.

As I have Madam the honor of serving now His Excellency the Spanish Ambassador, and likewise had the same honor to serve Prince Caramanico, and Count Pignatelli[1] when here, I presume to hope my Conduct is always approved off; and if your Excellency will permit me to hope for the honor of receiving your Commands, it shall be my pride and Study to merit the honor of your Excellency's Countenance and protection, and in Duty I shall be bound to pray!

Mary McCann
No. 1 Great Quebec St.
Portman Square

RC (Adams Papers).

[1] The Spanish ambassador was Bernardo del Campo y Pérez de la Serna (made the marqués del Campo in Aug. 1786), who served in London from 1783 to 1795. Francesco d'Aquino, Principe di Caramanico, served as the Sicilian envoy to Britain from 1781 to June 1784, and then to France, Oct. 1784 to Jan. 1785. Michele, Conte Pignatelli, preceded d'Aquino as Sicilian envoy to Britain, 1771–1781, and to France, Aug. 1783 – June 1784. *Repertorium der diplomatischen Vertreter aller Länder*, 3:432–433, 424, 423.

Abigail Adams 2d to John Quincy Adams

N ⟨*1*⟩5[1]

London Grosvenor Square July 4th. 1785

Every day, hour, and minute, your absence *mon chere frere*, pains me more and more. We left last saturday[2] the Hotell and have got settled in peace and quiettness in our own House in this Place. The situation is pleasant. I would walk, my Brother is gone. I would ride, my Brother is gone. I would retire to my chaimber. Alas, I meet him not there. I would meet him in his appartment—but—where is it? I would set to my work, and he would read to me—but alas, this is Passed—and I am to draw the comparison between Auteuil and Grosvenor Square and sigh, and—and, wish to recall, the former. No. I do not wish to recall the former. I only wish for you and I should esteem myself happy. We shall live more as if we were a part of the World; than when in France. And we already find ourselvs, better pleased. But I have much to regret in thee. More than you can Judge—with *all your knowledge of yourself*. The C[olonel][3] has taken Lodgings. He is civil and your father is pleased with his Principles and sentiments as they respect His appointment with Him. You know what they must be.

Least you should tax me for want of particularity, I will give you a description of my appartment. A Bed, on one side, three chairs of Green velvet—you know them I dare say, a bureau, and dressing Glass, one of the secretaries of which the Covers Shut in, at which I am now *writing*. On the top of it there is placed, my *secret Box*. The Book cases which Contain Bells Edition of the British Poets[4] which my father has made me a Present of, with a few other Books. Over it I have hung a picture intended for yourself, of which you have here-tofore spoken to me.[5] I would not mortify you by saying I think it a likeness nor Pay so Poor a compliment to my own judgment. However as it was intended for you I shall look upon it for you, and derive some satisfaction from it, and at the same time wish it were better.

From this day my narative shall commence. We hope you by this time arrived at New York, if not in Boston, but many weeks must pass before we hear from you. Our family is not yet quite arranged. I dont know what will become of us. We are obliged to have more servants here than in Paris—and their wages, is much more. Instead of 11 Guineas to Petito we are obliged to give a Person in the capasity of a butler 30. Guineas, but out of Livery, to a foot man with a Livery 18, to a Cook 15. For Horses and Coachman we have engaged to give 110. Guineas a year, or 11 Guineas by the Month—which is less than we gave in Paris, a little. We have had our Coach fitted up, and it answers. The C— keeps a Carriage. There is not one expence Less-end here, but every one augmented.

Pappa and the C— dined to day with Mr. Bridgen, perhaps you may recollect him. He Married the Daughter of the celebrated Richardson but she is Dead lately.[6] He has been to see your father several times.

General Oglethorp who called upon Pappa when he was in London before, appointed a day to call upon him a week or two ago, and came accompanied by Mr. Paradise.[7] Your Pappa returnd His visit, and the Last week he died. A surprising Man he was an hundred and two years oald, and the oaldest General in the Kings service and also the oaldest in the Emperiors. Since I have heard of His Death I have regreted that I did not see him when he visitted my father. I have heard he was sprightly and chearfull, to a very surprising degree for His age, and was perfectly possessed of His reason and senses. He was the first Governor of Georgia and a friend to America.[8]

To day being the anniversary of the independence of America there was a Large Party dined together out of Town. Your father was invited but was engaged before. Mr. Storer came and dined with us, and after dinner went with your Mamma and myself to some Shops. By way of anecdote let me tell you that when we first arrived in London, it was necessary to take immediately a Carriage and Horses. For the former we sent to Mr. Foster of whom you purchased our Coach.[9] He furnished us with a handsome Chariot till he could repair our own Carriage, and your Pappa took Horses and Coach Man from another Person, who was recommended Perhaps not sufficiently—to discriminate is a dificult matter in these Countries where every one offers their services, and never lack sufficient recommendations from themselvs. However we soon found that we had a drunken Coach-man, but as he had been several days in our service, and your father many visits to return upon his first arrival, he thought it best not to Change till we should go to our own House and take a Coach Man into the family as is the Custom in this Country. One afternoon Pappa went out to return some visits, and while he was drinking tea with a Gentleman, the Coach Man being drunk got asleep upon His Box, fell down, broke the two front Glasses, and split the fore part of the Carriage. But as nought is never in danger he received no Hurt himself, by His fall. This is a matter of about six pounds—but we nevertheless, continued Him in service till we got to this House, where we have taken a fellow, who, except talking amaizingly fast, has every appearance of being what we shall want Him to.

Tuesday

Pappa dined with Mr. S. Hartly, Cousin of Mr. David H[artley], the latter has been to see us. Mr. Hammond has not.[10]

July 1785

Thursday[11]

Pappa went to the drawing room, and we had four American Gentlemen to dine with us. *Coln. Norton* who is again here, a Mr. [12] from New York, a Mr. Noise from Boston, and a Mr. Remington from Watertown. Tis true we were not in the best order imaginable to receive company, but Pappa thought not of that you know when he invited them. However we did very well, with the assistance of a servant of the *Coln.* for our own butler has not yet come. We have a foot Man besides John Brisler who is in very Poor Health, but he is a German and does not understand English perfectly and seems to be an honnest, quiet, stupid, kind, of a Creature. After we had dined Mamma and myself went to take a ride, intending to Call upon Mrs. Temple and take her with us. Just as we were in the Carriage *Coln.* Smith came up in his Carriage with a General Stewart from America, who is a very handsome Man. Mamma told the C— that She intended to have asked Him to accompany her, but he had company. He ordered the Door opened and in jumpt telling his Companion that he would find Pappa at Home. He went on and we rode off. Perhaps you will say the Coln sacrifised politeness to Gallantry. We proceeded on our way to Mrs. Temples, but soon overtook her with Mr. Trumble and a Mr. and Mrs. Wheelright going to walk in Kensington Gardens. We concluded to accompany them and joined them at the entrance of the Gardens where we walkd for some time and returned Home.

a Wedensday

The Baron de Linden called upon us at about eight oclock in the Evening and told us he had just come from *Breakfasting* with the Dutchess of Bedford, to which he was invited for four *oclock*. Ridiculous, beings these are. I was told the other day of an invitation which a Gentleman had to *dine* with the Duke and Dutchess of Devonshire at *Eleven oclock at Night*. In time it is to be hoped they will come to be reasonable in this matter of aranging their time. By such continued changes, they must inevitably sometimes come right, however they may indeavour to avoid it.

Pappa is not much pleased with the Foreign Ministers here. They have all visiitted him and are very sivil, but he thinks them much less respectable as individuals, than those in Holland or France. There is but one Court which is represented by an Ambassador here, which is France. He has arrived within a few days from Bath, and is said is going soon Home to His own Country upon account of His Health.

Fryday

We have received a third visit to day from Mrs. and Miss Paradise and an invitation to dine with them next thursday. They tell us that they had the pleasure to know you. Therefore any description or account of either of the Ladies is needless, and I am sure I should be at a Loss to know how to give you an idea of them. The only observation that I could make upon Mrs. P[aradise] when I first saw her was, that I had never seen any thing like her before. She appears to me to be a singular Character. But I will Leave her, to describe to you a young Lady who called upon us to day, with Her Uncle, a Mr. Hamlington[13] from Philadelphia. He has brought this his Neice over to this Country to give her an education, suitable to a fortune which he intends to give her. She is now at a boarding school, her Name is Miss Hamlinton. She is I should Judge 15 or 16 years oald, not very tall an agreeable size, good complexion not remarkably fair, brown Hair, good Eyes, and tolerable teeth, a good share of animation in her countenance, her Manners easy delicate and pleasing. I think you would have thought her pretty. Pray what think ye of Miss Hazen. Is she all your friend, W[inslow] W[arren] told you of Her.

Mr. Storer has called upon us, this afternoon and says that He shall Leave this Country and embark for America certainly this Month with His sister and Her family. I shall continue my narative till it is necessary for to seal my packet for Him. When you receive it you must not be unmindfull of your Prohibitions to me. Sentiment you could get from Books therefore I was to avoid them. You wanted only a Plain relation of facts as they should take place in the family, which I shall indeavour to fullfill to the best of my knowledge and ability. I could sincerely complain an Hour of your being absent, but this you do not want to be told again to beleive, I trust. The next packet I shall expect Letters from you and I am well assured that I shall not expect to be disappointed, if you arrive safe by that time and Heaven Grant you may is the sincere wish of your affectionate sister.

July 14th. thursday

Pappa Mamma and myself, went agreeable to the Letter of our invitation at four oclock to dine with Mr. and Mrs. Paradise but unfortunately were two hours too early. The company did not collect till near six, consequently we did not dine till that Hour. I will give you the circle at table. Mrs. Paradise your Mamma, Coln. Smith, your sister, Dr. Price, a French Gentleman Mr. Paradise another French

Gentleman Miss Paradise, Mr. de Freire, Charge des affairs from Portugal, my Lady Hawk and your Father, in this way we were seated. I had the pleasure and honour of being seated next to Dr. Price .. but Wise Men you know are allways silent in mixed companies. The Dr. I have heard seldom enters upon any important subject in company, he however paid attention enough to me in this way as to *sattisfy* me. But in truth I dont recollect one thing said at table worth relating. Our dinner was *a la Francaise* la tout, and every civility was paid to us, that we could wish or expect. When we returnd to the drawing room we found several Gentlemen, who had not been of our diner party, the company increased, and we were expected to spend the Eve. Several Gentlemen and Ladies were invited we *were* told, upon our account, but your Pappa and Mamma came away before tea, and did not see all the company, I feard at the risk of haveing offended the People we visitted, however you know that seven years hence, it will be all one.

Fryday 15th

We drank tea with Mrs. Temple where we met Mr. and Mrs. and Miss Vassall. We are upon very civil terms—that is, sufficiently distant. Mrs. T is a Lovely Woman, but we are to loose her soon, for they assert that their passages are taken to go out to America this Month.

Saturday 16th

Dined with Mr. and Mrs. Roggers, in company with Mr. and Mrs. Temple Mr. Granvile Temple, and Coln. Smith. I dont know a Man who can please more than this said Mr. T when he indeavours to be agreeable, and how ever one may be prejudiced against Him, his manner of behaviour, dispells it all.

Sunday 17th

We went to Hackney to Hear Dr. Price. He has been giveing his People his sistem of religion, in a Course of sermons. We have been to Hear them all. This day forghtnight he proposes to conclude. I think you would have been pleased to have been of our party. We have been treated with respect to seats with the utmost civility and politeness.

Monday, 18

Mamma and myself rose before six o clock, and went out to take an early Breakfast with Mrs. Atkinson. The rain we had yesterday had made the air sweet and has given or rather renewed in some measure the verdure, and our ride was cleaver, enough. Mr. Atkinson talks of going out in August. Charles will go with them and I expect this Letter will be handed you by this Mr. Charles Storer, if he should not conclude and *preconclude* the ensueing season in the same way as he did the last with respect to visitting France. He postpones his journey thence, for some time, but however I beleive, hopes it may arrive some time or other. Pappa and Coln. Smith dined with Mr. Vaugn,[14] for the 2d. time, to day, and the Spanish Minister came and drank tea with us. His Name is le Chevalier del Campo, he speaks English well, for a Foreigner. I see nothing in his favour, but that he is a very ugly Man. His eyes are squint very black, and *sharp* enough to be agreeable.

Wedensday 20th

Mrs. Hay came to town from Hampstead and spent the day with us. Pappa went to the Levee. His Majesty is very sociable, in general, and your father says, sometimes utters very good things. He disapproves the arangment of the day, and recommends, order and regularity, says he allways, rises at six oclock, and in winter is the first Person up in the Palace and generally makes his own fire, for he says a Man who is not capable of helping himself is a *Slave*. He shaves himself also, as he asserts, and sometimes wears his *scratch Wig* to the Levee, so much for His Majesty. All the World are gone into the Country. The Levees and drawing rooms are very thin at present and one may easily dispence with going to Court at this season. We have not yet been since we were presented. Perhaps her Majesty will think we were offended at her reception—*it was better suited to the Present season than to the Winter*, is very true, but it is not in the Power of the Smiles or Frowns of Her Majesty to affect me, either by confering pleasure or giveing Pain. I was wholy incapable of takeing the place She seemed to assign me when I was presented to Her. I suppose she assented to the assertion made by some Persons in this Country that there were no People who had so much *impudence* as the Americans, for there was not any People bred *even at Courts* who had so much confidence as the Americans. This was because they did not tremble, Cringe, and fear, in the Presence of Majesty.

Coln. Smith has not been to Court since he was presented. He says he does not Love them and he will see as little as possible of any belonging to them. His aversion is I beleive quite equal to Coln. H[umphrey]s. He does not express, so great a degree, however. He desired me to day to present his compliments to you when I should

210

write you and, to tell you that he *had* wished to become acquainted with you before he left America, from the account he had heard of you, and he now regrets your absence—in which I can sincerely join him, for I mourn at it—and yet think you acted right in going home. By this time we hope you are arrived in Boston.

Fryday 22d

To day Mr. Charles Bullfinch has called upon us. He arrived a day or two since in Scot, and has brought us, some Letters.[15] We dined by invitation this day with Mr. and Mrs. Copely, in company with Mr. and Mrs. Roggers, Mr. West Mr. Clark, and Mr. Whiteford.[16] The latter was seated next me at table, and after haveing lookd at me through his *spectacles*, which you know he all ways wears and haveing diverted the company with a few *puns*, for which you also know he is *famous*, if not in____,[17] he began by telling me how very disappointed he was by *your* not haveing come here with your father, and by enquiring whether you should return here soon. I told him that you had gone with the intention of setling in America. "What said he, then I suppose he is going to be married." I told him of your design of entering Colledge, and could sincerely join with him in whatever regret he might express on account of your absence. He talked about France, and said many things respecting the French which I could only reconcile, from his being an Englishman. I am not surprised when I hear People who have never been out of this Island, perhaps not out of the Town of London, expressing such iliberal sentiments upon other Nations, which one from charity would attribute to the score of ignorance. But when I hear a Man who has travelled, who has seen Mankind and had an opportunity of judging and whom one might suppose was not unreasonably prejudiced, express, a contempt for any particular Class of People, I only Pitty those principles which prevent him from discovering and doing justice to real merit wherever it is to be found in whatever Country or Climate. "One would scarce beleive it possible that a distance of seven Leagues, for its is absolutely no farther says Yorick,"[18] the character of the two People should be so strongly marked, and that so constant a communication, should not have worn off some of those illiberal prejudies, which discover themselfs in every mind on this side the Water. I have absolutely discoverd, disapprobation in the countenances of almost every person who has asked me, how I was pleased, with France, after I answered them that I found it agreeable, and that the General Manners of the People pleasd me much. They will be satisfied with nothing less than a studied preference in favour of their Country, which I cannot nor will not ever give them at the expence of my cincerity. Mrs. B[ingham] says she made many enemies by giving the preference to the French. If I have been truly informed she did it not in the most delicate manner or the most polite. She has been in London lately and they set of this day for Spar,[19] from thence propose going to Brusells, and spend the first Part of the Winter in Paris, come over here, in February perhaps *"before the Birth day,"*[20] and go to America in the Spring. I have been so fortunate as never to have seen Mr. B. but once.[21] Mrs. B. has made us three very agreeable visits.

Sunday July 24th

The weather is very warm, at present. It is said that a season like the present has not been known in Europe for many years, if ever. In France they have scarce had any rain since you left it and you know, well how much it was wanted when you was on the road. There has been but two or three rains since we arrived here, and none thought sufficient for the fruits of the Earth, by People of reason and Common sense. Yet such is the dispossition of the People that the papers often assert that rain is not wanted and that the season is very promising, on this Island.

Tuesday July 26th

I had like to have set down this Eve and to have complained of not having any thing to communicate to you, but recalling to mind your injunction *"be punctual and let no circumstance however trivial escape your Pen"*[22] I have tax'd myself with not having fullfilled it, in many respects and now determine to make up all Past deficiencies at least in this respect. Indoubtedly you well remember Grosvenor Square, as it is said to be the finest in[23] this *Capitall*. We have some respectable Neighbours, at least they inherit every title to which the World afix the Ideas of *respectability*, and ⟨many of them⟩ some are perhaps ⟨so⟩ entitled to the epithet from their own merit. Lord Carmarthen, lives about five houses from us, but not upon the same side of the Square. He is said to be a worthy Man. You know I suppose what [h]is title is. When we first came into this House, the Man of whom we hired and who furnished Mamma with some few articles of furniture, is a singular kind of a Body, very sivl, not intirely ignorant, and his business, leads him to some knowledge of these great Folks, it being what is here called upholster and undertaker. We made some few inquiries of him by whom we were surrounded and I must give it you as he told it us. Upon the right hand said he is Lady Tacher and on the left Lady Lucy Lincoln sister to the Famous Conway[24] and there is my Lord Norths and there a House formerly belongd to the Duke of Dorset, but he has sold it. Such a House belongs to the Dutchess of Bedford who ran over to France the last Winter—and in such a one, lives, Lady, *what do you call* her whose husband ran a Pen through her Nose the other day, &c. &c. &c.

You are sattisfied I suppose by this with an account of our Neighbours. Lady Lincolns Parlores Window makes one side of the square and, our drawing room windows the other thus, so you see we have a chance of looking at each other, an opportunity we each have already taken advantage of. She peeps at us, and we can not do less you know than return the compliment. The English may call the French starers but I never saw so little civility and politeness in a Stare in France as I have here. In short I beleive the French are the politeest People in the World and take them for all in all, I neer expect to Meet their like again.[25] Our house stand

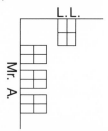

at the Corner of Duke Street. The situation is much in its favour. It is a descent House, a little out of repairs, but such a one as you would not blush to see, any of the Foreign Menisters in. The front doer is a little in the corner. At the entrance there is a large Hall, with a large Stair Case, all of Stone. On the left Hand, is the dining room, which will hold 15 Persons with ease, and, next to it is a littel room, more retired in which we usually dine, when we have no company, and from this you go into a long room of which Pappa has, made an office, for doing Publick business. The Kitching is blow Stairs. Above, over the dining room is the drawing room, as large as the room below and from it a little room of which Mamma has mad a Common setting Parlour, to breakfast and drink tea if we choose and out of it is another long room in which Pappa has put his Library, and in which he writes usually himself. This is a very descent suit of rooms, and we have another very small one which servs to breakfast and set in at this season. Our Chaimbers are upon the 3d. floor, of which there are four besides a dressing room. Mamma took one of the front Chaimbers to herself, the other she has appropriated for to Stand empty for a spare bed, to which you will be perfectly well come if you will come and spend the Night with us. I have a chaimber over the small setting room. It looks only into a little peice of a yard with which we are favour. It's so situated that the sun does not approach it any part of the year, and I have a most extensive prospect from it, of the tops of all the Houses which surround us, and I can count an hundred Chimneys from it—and see Norths et[c] et[c]. Dont you envy me the Prospect. The Chaimber is very tidy and cleaver. Over the Library is Esters room, out of mine, and above are chaimber for the servants. Now you know every room in the House, and were you set down blind fold at the Corner of Duke Street Grosvenor Square, you would be at no loss, where to find my chaimber I suppose.

To day, is the first time that we have pretended to see company to dine. We had a company of fifteen. Mr. and Mrs. Temple and their son Mr. Granvile Temple, Mr. and Mrs. Roggers, Mr. and Mrs. Atkinson, Mr. Storer, Dr. Price, Mr. Charles Bullfinch, Coln. Smith, and ourselvs. You know not how much ⟨we⟩ I missd you and how much I wished for you. The Customs of different Countries are different, and even when one knows how to Conduct in the one, you may be ignorant of the next you visit. You often meet here with an imitation of the French, customs, especially, at diner, and Courses are as Common allmost here as in France, but they do not arange matters so well. Were I to follow my will, I would Introduce the Whole Custom of dining in the French Stile here. In the first place, in this Country when your dinner is said to be on table, instead of the gentleman of the House Gallantly handing, the first Lady in company in to diner and every other Gentleman following his example, the Lady of the House rises and desires the Lady in company who happens to be the Greatest stranger or higest rank to walk to dinner, and every one follows accordingly, then the Gentlemen, like a flock of Sheep one by one, not ⟨yoked⟩ in Pairs. When you get to the table the Ladies must all sit in a cluster, and the Gentlemen by themselvs. And, now every one is thus seated why they must all set quietly with their hands before them till, the Gentleman or Lady of the House and [yore?] served a Whole [circle?] of 20 and said Pray Mam or Pray Sir will you be helpd so and so—and to be sure every Person in Company, will make choise of one dish, that one Person may have the extreme felicty of setting quite Starved till every one at table is helpd, then all must begin together, and when every one has their Plate changed and the cerimony is to perform over again, through every dish at table, nor will they eat if you leave it to themselvs to make a choise. *Ridiculous formality*. Then there must be, every two minutes, Mam will you do me the favour to drink a Glass of Wine with me, which obliges some to say, with pleasure, when in reallity they never drink any thing but Water and had rather be excused. And then the additional formality of drinking Health and toasts which above all things I detest, and will not now nor henceforward for ever more do it. In short one cannot consult their ease and pleasure but must be enslaved with fashion and customs. And another thing I dislike, that I mean of the Ladies rising from table and the Gentlemen, continueing seetting, but it is quite the fashion here to go from the dining table to the Card table. I am told, I have not dined any where yet where I have seen it done. By this time you will laught at me, I doubt not and tell me what you used to foretell has come to pass—of the preferance, I should have for France when I got here. True it is I give the preferance, to many customs amongst that People to what I find here, but it is such a priveledge, to be able to talk that it allmost over ballances every other consideration. But I am sure, you would find yourself much happier here than you were in France. Yet I hope you will be still more so where you are—and I will not doubt it.

Our company was large enough to be agreeable, and had every one consulted his own ease and that of his Neighbour, we should have been much pleased at least I shold. It is the department of the Butler to change the Course and put every thing upon table. We have a cleaver fellow in this capacity. He has more solemnity and not so much alertness as Petit,[26] and he is thought to be perfectly honnest. Our Cook, gave us a good [dinner?]. Pappa is not so pleased with the English Cookery as the French. He says Now we shall all soon be sick with eating raw meat and I confess, I am partial to the Country I have left—at least to its rationallities. And I veryly beleive there is less of what one may Call folly there than here, howe[ve]r the People here may affect to despise their Neighbers.

Oh one peice of News—Mamma had a Letter from Mr. Williamos,[27] who is Still in Paris and who still waits for an opportunity more eligable than by way of Lorient, that informed her that Dr. Frankling had arrived at Rouen, in Health on his way to the Isle of Whight from which he is to embark in a Ship commanded by Capt. Truxton for Philadelphia. The King of France sent the Dr. his picture set in diamonds of Greet vallue, and two letters from the Comte de Vergenes !!!!!!! Mrs. Williams has gone out with the Dr.[28]

By the way, I must not omit to tell you, what a rage for Painting has taken Possession of the Whole family. One of our rooms has been occupied by a Gentleman of this profession, for near a forghtnight, and we have the extreme felicity of looking at ourselvs upon Canvass.

The Paper yesterday had this paragraph "Sir J. Reynolds is employd in takeing a portrait of Lady Dungannon. Copely and Brown are exerting their skill upon their illustrious Country Man Mr. Adams the American Ambassador." *I expect it will be next that Mr. Brown is painter to the American Ambassadors family.* He was very sollicitous to have a likeness of Pappa, thinking it would be an advantage to him, and Pappa Consented. He has taken the best likeness I have yet seen of him, and you may suppose is very Proud, when so many have failed before him. Mamma has set for hers, and I, followed, the example. It is said he has taken an admirable likeness of my Ladyship, the Honble. Miss Adams you know. It is a very tasty picture I can assure you, whether a likeness or not. Pappa is much pleased with it, and says he has got my character, a Mixture of Drolery and Modesty. I wish we could have the other three, yourself and Charles and Thomas. I think we should make a *respectable Group.* He has a good likeness of Mamma, too.[29]

Sunday July 31st

This Morning Mamma and myself went out to hear Dr. Price, it being the last sermon, he is to Preach for some time, as he tells me he allways makes a practice of going into the Country in the Month of August. Dr. Jebb, who has visitted your father several times since we arrived, and who is of his opinions I beleive in Politicks, brought his Lady to see Mamma this Morning. She is also a great Politicianess, which consequently pleased Mamma.[30] The American War, Present dispute with Ireland, and the Propositions which have just passed, and which are now sent over to Ireland to be accepted or refused, furnished this Lady with subject of conversation. She was of opinion that the propositions would pass, the House of Commons, in Ireland, but that the People will not accept them. Your father thinks if they are accepted, that he shall have no chance of succeeding in his treaty of Commerce, with this Country, as the fourth proposition, is intended to bring the Irish to join this Country in all their Commercial arangments, so that *we* feel ourselvs much interested in the matter.[31]

Now do not Laugh at me, for, writing Politicks to you, and tell me I am a *dunce*, for I assure you that all I mean is to indeavour at giving you some little information respecting *us*. If I fail, you will not refuse me what is due for right intentions.—The Parliament were sitting till Tuesday the 2d. of August and then adjourned till october.[32] Mr. and Mrs. Temple invited us to go to the House, of Commons, if the King

8. ABIGAIL ADAMS 2D, JULY 1785, BY MATHER BROWN
See page xiii

came to make his speach, upon the adjournment of the House, but, he did not meet them, so we consequently did not go to see him in his robes of State and Crowned.

Wedensday—3d. of August

This Morning as I was setting at work in my room, Mamma came and told me there was a Gentleman below, who wished to see me. I not a little surprised at being inquired for, went down, and who should it be but Mr. Short just arrived from Paris. His comeing was not unexpected, neither, his business I dont know. I beleive however it was to bring some Papers of consequence safe.[33] We were very much pleased to see him, and he brings us accounts of the Health of all our friends there, which will give you pleasure to hear I know. Do you recollect Mr. Adams that this day, twelvemonths we went to Richmond, together, and walkd in Popes Gardens, &c.[34] We were then Strangers almost and we are nearly so again I fear. But we know, a little more of each other and by constant and unreserved communications I hope we shall not loose the Knowledge we mutually gained in the last twelvmonths of each others sentiments and dispositions. It is a very unpleasing Idea to me, that a Whole family, should grow up, Strangers to each other, as ours have done, yet it has been unavoidable, and will tis probable Still continue so.

Thursday 4th

This Morning Mr. Short came and Breakfasted with us, and before we had finished Mrs. Wright, came in, as Crazy as usual, "with such a Budget," was her term. You know her figure. Pappa introduced Mr. Short to her as an American and friend of Mr. Jeffersons. I expected she would have saluted him as usual, but she dispenced with this ceremony, and said, her Countryman did her great honour to be sure—by way of compliment. She visits Colln. Smith very often, and there is no such thing as getting rid of her. She came with a particular account to day, of the affront which has been offered to the English flag, by the French. The account in the papers, is as follows—Why now the Paper is lost, and I cant recollect the paragraff, so you must excuse me, for Leaving this space blank.[35]

August 11th

You will not surely complain of me for not having written enough, this time. I only fear that you will say you can find nothing in it all. Tell me if this is the Case and I'll abridge.
Adieu.[36]

Colln. Smith received a letter from his friend Colln. H[umphreys] who informs him that he is writing another Poem, which is to be much longer than the address to the Army,[37] and he assures him will have *equal merit*. He wishes to get some Person to Print it here and suggests that he thinks he may expect it will furnish [*him*] with the *means* of visiting this Country. An hundred and fifty Gunieas he proposs himself from it. We dont know what the subject is, and Mr. Short declares he cannot inform us. The King of France has accepted the dedication of the Vision of Columbus, and subscribed for a Number of Coppys, upon *this* Condition that the Count de Vergennes should be permitted to examing it to be assured there is nothing too severe against *this Nation* nor the Spainairds, in it. What think you of this *Condition*?

Before you receive this Letter, I suppose you will have arrived, in Boston, been received by all our Friends, visitted them as much as your time will permit, taken the opinion of some respecting the preparation necessary for your entering the university, and perhaps set yourself down for a few Months, in Mr. Shaws family, with application and diligence to accomplish your design. And now permit a sister who feels herself, greatly interested in every event in which you may be engaged, to inquire how you are pleased and gratified, whether contented and happy, from the idea of *intending right*, or from, the sattisfaction which you find resulting from your decisions. Tell me all that I am entitled to know, of what passes within your own Mind, from what scources you derive pleasure, and from what you receive Pain. No one can more sincerely rejoice in the one, regret the other and participate in Both than a sister, and a sister who is often influenced by them, herself. Tell me also, all that you wish to, respecting myself or others. Remind me of all my errors, mistakes, and foibles, and convince my judgment, Guide my opinions, and may you also approve of all past present and future decisions. If I ever take any important Step, contrary to your judgment, it will be because you are not present to give it.

Tell me also, if I am too particular in writing you, or whether I am not enough so—whether you find yourself informed by my scribling, of things which y[ou] wish to know. When I know what will gratify you, I shall indeavour as far as my ability will enable me to contribute to this Gratification. You will not say I am mistaken when I suppose it in my Power. If you should, you must suppose this error founded, upon a wrong judgment, which originated from anticipating the pleasure I shall receive from *your Communications*.

I want much to know, whether your disposition for rambling has left you. If it has, I beleive you bequeathed it to me, not as a blessing I fear. I have as much the wish, to wander, as a certain *American Lady*.[38] But necessity prevents its appearance. For my part I should like above all things to make one of a *Party to go* round the World. When this proposal, is put in execution we will, take you with us, provided you should be as, unreasonably inclined as, those who will undertake it. But to be serious, I cant see why People who have the *inclination* (and *ability*) which to be sure is the most essential of the two, should not gratify themselvs, by indulging it and seeing as many and curious parts of the World as it should Lead them to visit. If they are possessed of proper Principles, it will not injure them, but make them Wiser and better and happier. Pray dont you feel a great deel Wiser, than if you had never been outside the limits of the State of Massachusetts Bay, which tho a very respectable place, one may gain a little knowledge in other Parts. And then you know with a little Policy, one may be thought nearly more *Respectable*, for the People of our Country have a Wonderfull liking to those who can say, "I have been in St. Pauls Church. I have seen the Lions, Tigers, &c. in the Tower. I have seen the King, and what is more have had the extreme honour of being saluted by him. What the King? Yes by George the Third King of Great Britain France and Ireland, defender of the Faith &c. And I have seen the Dancing Dogs, Singing Duck, and little Hare which beats the Drum, and the Irish Infant,   [39] feet high, but not yet the Learned Pig." The Tumblers of Sadlers Wells, have made great objections that the Learned Pig, should be introduced upon the Stage and have I beleive left it.

Thursday August the 11th. 1785

Mr. Storer has just now informed me that there is an opportunity to convey Letters tomorow, to Boston. Altho I had intended to send this Letter by him, I will take advantage of this conveyance as it is a forghtnight sooner than, he will sail, and as I would not fail of punctuallity to you, or give you reason to suppose me capable of it. I have not the pleasure to hear yet of your arrival at New York, but the packet is expected dayly and I hope soon to have the pleasure of acknowledging the receipt of long Letters from you. Mamma has written you this Morning, and we are going this afternoon to Hampstead with Mrs. Roggers, to visit Mrs. Hay, and are to Leave the Letters at the New England Coffee House to go tomorrow. I must wish you Health happiness and peace and hasten to subscribe myself your affectionate sister   A Adams

Dft (Adams Papers); notation at the top of the first page: "My Brother JQA—sent by Capt Lyde." The letter is written on thirty-two numbered pages of small, irregular size.

[1] AA2's letters to JQA numbered 1 through 4 have not been found, but for No. 1, see JQA's letter of 17 May, above.

[2] 2 July.

[3] William Stephens Smith.

[4] *Bell's Edition: The Poets of Great Britain complete from Chaucer to Churchill*, appeared in 109 pocket-size, illustrated volumes between 1777 and 1782 (*DNB*).

[5] This is probably the Isaak Schmidt portrait of JQA, done in Holland in 1783, and given by JQA to AA2 (see Andrew Oliver, *Portraits of John Quincy Adams and His Wife*, Cambridge, 1970, p. 17–19). Long held by AA2's descendants, it was recently acquired by the National Portrait Gallery; see the Descriptive List of Illustrations, vol. 5.

[6] Edward Bridgen, a close friend of the Adamses, had married Martha, daughter of the novelist Samuel Richardson, in 1762 (*DNB* [Richardson]).

[7] John Paradise was an Englishman who had married Lucy Ludwell of Virginia, in London in 1769 (JA, *Diary and Autobiography*, 3:184).

[8] James Oglethorpe, the founder of Georgia, died on 1 July. Although he was only eighty-nine, he was described in two contemporary accounts as being over one hundred. Oglethorpe had begun his military service in England in 1710, and in Europe a few years thereafter (*DNB*).

[9] See JQA to JA, 30 July, and 6 Aug. 1784, both above.

[10] JA had met both David Hartley and William Hammond in 1778 at Passy, and had dealt with both in the peace negotiations in 1783 (JA, *Diary and Autobiography*, 2:303, and note 2; 4:65–66; John Thaxter to AA, 18 April 1783, above).

[11] AA2 appears to have confused her daily entries, probably beginning either here or at the next entry, "a Wednesday." To read her headings literally, in order, would give dates of Tuesday, 5 July; Thursday, 7 July; "a Wednesday," 13 July; "Fryday," 15 July; and then "July 14th. thursday." Thereafter her dating is clear and correct.

[12] Left blank in MS.

[13] AA2 probably intends Ann Hamilton and her uncle, William; Ann soon became a close friend of the Adamses (see JA, *Diary and Autobiography*, 3:184, and note 1).

[14] Probably Benjamin Vaughan, who had served Lord Shelburne as a confidential observer at the peace negotiations in 1782–1783 (JA to AA, 12 Oct. 1782, note 3, above; JA, *Diary and Autobiography*, 3:54, note 2).

[15] See Richard Cranch to JA, 3 June, above. Mary Cranch to AA, and probably John Thaxter to AA, both 4 June, above, were included in this set of letters.

[16] The dinner guests included the artist Benjamin West; Caleb Whitefoord; and Richard Clarke, John Singleton Copley's elderly father-in-law.

[17] Blank in MS.

[18] AA2 quotes roughly the opening passage of Laurence Sterne's *A Sentimental Journey through France and Italy, by Mr. Yorick*. Seven leagues (twenty miles in Sterne) is the distance from Dover to Calais.

[19] Spa, in eastern Belgium about twenty miles southeast of Liège, was one of the earliest resorts to become famous for the medicinal effects of its waters.

[20] Opening quotation mark supplied. Anne Bingham was presented at court in Feb. 1786. The occasion marked the celebration of the Queen's birthday (see AA to JQA, 16 Feb. 1786, and AA2 to JQA, 9–27 Feb. 1786, both Adams Papers).

[21] AA2's apparent negative opinion of William Bingham agrees with that of JQA, recorded earlier in the year (*Diary*, 1:222, 250–252).

[22] See JQA to AA2, 25 May, above.

[23] From this point to note 28, the text is written less carefully, on much coarser, irregularly-sized paper, and many passages are difficult to decipher.

[24] Gen. Henry Seymour Conway, a prominent commander on the Continent in the Seven Years' War, was a steady and outspoken opponent of Britain's treatment of America, from the 1760s to the 1780s (*DNB*).

²⁵ AA2 adapts Shakespeare, *Hamlet*, I, ii, 187–188. In her journal for 27 Aug., AA2 wrote that she "read Shakspeare after dinner. Papa purchased his works this morning, upon my saying I had never read them" (*Jour. and Corr.*, 1:ix).

²⁶ The Adams' servant at Auteuil.

²⁷ Of 21 July, below.

²⁸ The coarse paper and poorly written text end here. Marianne Alexander Williams was the wife of Benjamin Franklin's nephew, Jonathan Williams Jr. Mr. Williams was about to sail for America with his uncle, while his wife and her sisters were to go to London to live (Jefferson, *Papers*, 8:423).

²⁹ Mather Brown, born in Boston in 1761, had come to London in 1781 to study painting with Benjamin West. Of the three Adams portraits that he executed in 1785, that of JA and AA are lost. On 2 Sept., AA2 recorded JA's reaction to a portrait done of him, presumably that by Brown, in her journal: ". . . we had some conversation upon the pictures below. Papa said they were spoiled; he was not at all content with his own, yet thought it the best that had ever been taken of him. No one had yet caught his character. The ruling principles in his moral character were candour, probity, and decision. I think he discovered more knowledge of himself than usually falls to the lot of man" (*Jour. and Corr.*, 1:80). Brown painted JA again in 1788 for Thomas Jefferson, who owned this portrait until his death; it is now in the Boston Athenaeum. Brown's portrait of AA2 is at the Adams National Historic Site, Quincy, Mass. A "Portrait of a Lady," in the N. Y. State Historical Association, previously identified as that of AA by Mather Brown, is no longer considered to be by Brown. The identity of the sitter, as well, is now questioned. The painting is signed by Ralph Earl but no evidence exists that he painted AA at this or any other time. The eyes of the "Lady" are blue; those of AA in her other likenesses are brown. These reasons are enough for the editors to doubt, until further supporting evidence is found, that the "Lady" is AA (Dorinda Evans, *Mather Brown, Early American Artist in England*, Middletown, Conn., 1982, p. 195). See the Descriptive List of Illustrations in this volume.

³⁰ JA and JQA had met Dr. John Jebb in Nov. 1783. Jebb was a former cleric of radical theological views, and a physician, scholar, and strong supporter of the American cause whom JA warmly admired. His wife, Ann Tor-

kington Jebb, also wrote ably on radical issues. JQA, *Diary*, 1:202, note 1; JA, *Diary and Autobiography*, 3:197; *DNB*.

³¹ For the background to the twenty propositions approved by the British Parliament on 25 July for presentation to the Irish Parliament, see AA to Cotton Tufts, [26 April], note 10, above. The fourth proposition provided: "That it is highly important to the general interests of the British empire, that the laws for regulating trade and navigation should be the same in Great Britain and Ireland; and therefore that it is essential, towards carrying into effect the present settlement, that all laws which have been made, or shall be made, in Great Britain, for securing exclusive privileges to the ships and mariners of Great Britain, Ireland, and the British colonies and plantations, and for regulating and restraining the trade of the British colonies and plantations (such laws imposing the same restraints, and conferring the same benefits, on the subjects of both kingdoms), should be in force in Ireland, by laws to be passed in the parliament of that kingdom, for the same time, and in the same manner, as in Great Britain" (*Parliamentary Hist.*, 25:935). The full text of the proposals is in the same, cols. 934–942. In mid-August, the twenty propositions met such an angry reception in the Irish House of Commons that the British administration in Dublin tabled the matter, and it quietly died. Vincent T. Harlow, *The Founding of the Second British Empire*, London, 1952, vol. 1, ch. 11.

³² The only hints in the MS of the point where AA2 may have finished writing on 31 July, and began writing on 2 Aug., are a long dash before "Now do not Laugh at me . . .," here rendered as a paragraph break, and the shorter dash before "The Parliament were sitting . . ."

³³ These papers were one or more copies of the treaty of amity and commerce between Prussia and the United States, signed by Franklin at Passy on 9 July, by Jefferson in Paris on 28 July, by JA in London on 5 Aug., and by Baron von Thulemeyer, the Prussian envoy, at The Hague on 10 September. JA to Richard Cranch, 3 April 1784, note 4; JA, *Diary and Autobiography*, 3:182, note 1.

³⁴ See AA to Mary Cranch, 2 Aug. 1784, and note 3, above.

³⁵ The *Morning Post and Daily Advertiser* for 1 Aug. stated that the British warship *Wasp*, Capt. Hills, met a French lugger in the English Channel. The French vessel refused

to salute the British flag and its captain informed the officers of the British ship that he had specific orders from the French government not to do so.

[36] Following this farewell the text starts on a new page, although some space remained on the previous page. It is not clear if AA2 wrote the next four paragraphs, up to the dateline "Thursday August the 11th. 1785," below, on the 11th, or wrote it earlier, perhaps on the 4th, and then added the three sentences immediately before "Adieu" on 11 August.

[37] David Humphreys had published *A Poem Addressed to the Armies of the United States of America* in 1780. His *A Poem on the Happiness of America Addressed to the Citizens of the United States* was first published in London in 1786. Joel Barlow's *The Vision of*

Columbus, written over a period of eight years, was published in 1787, with a dedication to Louis XVI. *DAB*.

[38] Perhaps Anne Willing Bingham; see notes 19–20.

[39] Left blank in MS. The quotation mark after "Learned Pig" has been supplied. Most of the amazing animals in this passage—lions at the Tower of London, performing dogs and hares, and particularly "the Learned Pig," which made its London debut early in 1785, are discussed in Richard D. Altick, *The Shows of London*, Cambridge, 1978, see esp. chs. 3 and 7, and illustration 6 on p. 41. By 1812 both Sadler's Wells and Drury Lane had dropped their opposition to animal acts (same, p. 310–311; see also Wheatley, *London Past and Present*, [Sadler's Wells]).

Thomas Jefferson to Abigail Adams

Dear Madam   Paris July 7. 1785

I had the honour of writing you on the 21st. of June, but the letter being full of treason, has waited a private conveiance. Since that date there has been received for you at Auteuil a cask of about 60. gallons of wine. I would have examined it's quality and have ventured to decide on it's disposal, but it is in a cask within a cask, and therefore cannot be got at but by operations which would muddy it and disguise it's quality. As you probably know what it is, what it cost, &c. be so good as to give me your orders on the subject and they shall be complied with.

Since my last I can add another chapter to the history of the redacteur of the Journal de Paris.[1] After the paper had been discontinued about three weeks, it appeared again, but announcing in the first sentence a changement de domicile of the redacteur, the English of which is that the redaction of the paper had been taken from the imprisoned culprit, and given to another. Whether the imprisonment of the former has been made to cease, or what will be the last chapter of his history I cannot tell.—I love energy in government dearly.—It is evident it was become necessary on this occasion, and that a very daring spirit has lately appeared in this country, for notwithstanding the several examples lately made of suppressing the London papers, suppressing the Leyden gazette, imprisoning Beaumarchais,[2] and imprisoning the redacteur of the journal, the author of the Mercure of the last week has had the presumption, speaking of the German newspapers, to say "car les journaux de ce pays-la ne sont pas forcés de s'en tenir à juger des hemistiches, ou à annoncer des programes academiques." Probably he is now suffering in a jail the just punishments of his insolent sneer on this mild government, tho' as yet we do not know the fact.

The settlement of the affairs of the Abbé Mably is likely to detain his friends Arnoud and Chalut in Paris the greatest part of the summer. It is a fortunate circumstance for me, as I have much society with them.—What mischeif is this which is brewing anew between Faneuil hall and the nation of God-dem-mees?[3] Will that focus of sedition be never extinguished? I apprehend the fire will take thro' all the states and involve us again in the displeasure of our mother country.

I have the honour to be with the most perfect esteem Madam your most obedt. & most humble servt.   Th: Jefferson

RC (Adams Papers); docketed in an unknown hand: "Mr Jefferson 1795." The "9" is faint and may be an incomplete "8" rather than an error.

[1] See Jefferson to AA, 21 June, and notes 3 and 4, above, and Jefferson, *Papers*, 8:265. The *Journal* did not actually cease publication between 4 and 27 June, but it did announce a new editorial office, under the heading "Changement de Domicile," in its 27 June issue.

[2] Pierre Caron de Beaumarchais had been imprisoned at St. Lazare for a few days in March 1785, at the insistance of a member of the royal family who became offended at Beaumarchais' vigorous defense of his controversial and extraordinarily popular comedy, *Le mariage de Figaro* (JQA, *Diary*, 1:233–234, and note 3, 236).

[3] Between 10 April and 5 May, competing groups of merchants, mechanics, and manufacturers held several meetings in Boston's Faneuil Hall and filled the local press with polemic essays in an attempt to formulate an effective policy to counter the flood of imported British manufactures that was disrupting the city's economy. The protests led to the passage of a navigation act and a protective tariff by the Massachusetts legislature in June and July. Jensen, *The New Nation*, p. 290–293; Mass., *Acts and Laws*, 1784–1785, p. 439–443, 453–457; JQA to JA, 3 Aug., note 3, below. "God-dem-mees" (Goddems; Goddams) was a synonym for Englishmen in common use by the nineteenth century (*OED*).

John Quincy Adams to Abigail Adams

July 17th. 1785
1. o'clock in the morning

Dear Madam

We are now sailing up North River; and have met the french packet about 6 leagues from New York: she will sail to morrow morning; and has sent her boat on board, while we are at sail. I profit of the only ⟨*minute*⟩ instant I have to inform you, that after a tedious passage of 8 weeks, we expect [by] noon to be at New York. I have not even time to seal the Letter I have prepared for my Sister,[1] and must request she, and my Father, will excuse me if the peculiarity of the circumstance prevents me from writing to them.

Your ever affectionate Son.   J. Q. Adams

RC (Adams Papers); addressed: "Mrs. A. Adams. ⟨*to the care of Mr. J. Elworthy, Merchant N. 1 Broad Street.*⟩ London"; in another hand after the canceled material: "Corner of Brooke St. Grovesnor Sqr."; docketed by AA2: "JQA. July 17th 1785"; marked: "B" and "PP R T"; and stamped: "SE[. . .]" and "[. . . o]'clock." Slight damage to the text near the torn seal.

[1] That of 25 May, above.

John Quincy Adams to Abigail Adams 2d

N: 4.

New York July 17th. 1785

I went on shore upon Long Island with our Captain, and visited Monsr. de Marbois, who has taken a house there for the summer. He received me with politeness, invited me to dine with him, and enquired concerning my father in as friendly a manner, as he could have done had he wish'd him well. Madame de Marbois, may be called a pretty, little woman. She was a quaker, but appears not to have retained any of the rigid tenets of that sect.[1] As this is Sunday, I have not as yet delivered any of my Letters; and have done nothing but walk about the town.

18th

I have delivered a number of my Letters, and have acquired some information, but which you will doubtless know before this reaches, you. Messrs. Jackson and Tracey, arrived in Boston, the 18th. of last may, after a passage of only 20 days. Poor Temple took the small pox in Ireland, and died on the passage. Mr. Bowdoin is present governor of Massachusetts and increases, in popularity every day. Mr. Hancock, being too infirm, to act as Governor of Massachusetts, is chosen as Member of Congress for the next year, and will probably take his rest, in the President's seat, next November. This is escaping Scylla to fall into Charybdis; or is rather like a man I have read of; who being offered a glass of wine: answered, that he could not take a glass, but that he would take a bottle. The other delegates in Congress from Massachusetts for next year, are Mr. Sedgwick, Mr. King, Mr. Holten, and Mr. Dane.[2] (not Mr. Dana).

I waited upon the Massachusetts' delegates before I went any where else, except to Mr. Jay's. Mr. Gerry was glad to see me, on account of *his friend*,[3] and Mr. King was very polite. They went with me and introduced me to the president,[4] who enquired very particularly concerning my father. I also waited upon the Governor, and upon *Don Diego de Gardoqui*, who had about a fortnight since, his public audience of Congress,[5] and who shows away here to an high degree. He made a speech when he had his audience; and I believe, I may affirm confidently, that he tired none of his auditors. You will see the speech in the Papers.

19th

The President of Congress this morning, at breakfast at Mr. Gerry, invited me to take an apartment in his house. I endeavoured to excuse myself as well as I could: but at dinner at his house, he repeated his invitation. I again offered my excuses, but he press'd it on me, with so much politeness, that I did not know how to refuse. Such attentions, embarass me, yet they give me more, pleasure, than they would, if I was myself the object of them.

I met Mr. Church this morning: he sails the 4th. of next month in the british Packet, and has offered to take any Letters for me. You will receive my N:3.[6] and probably this by him.

20th

At tea, this afternoon, at Mr. Ramsay's, for whom Mrs. Rucker, was kind enough to give me Letters,[7] I met Mr. Gardoqui, and his secretary Mr. Randon, who, if common report says true, is soon to marry Miss Marshall (Mrs. Rucker's Sister.) Much good may do her, with the swarthy Don: his complexion and his looks: show sufficiently, from what country he is. How happens it, that revenge stares through the eyes of every Spaniard? Mr. Gardoqui was very polite, and enquired much after my father, as did also Mr. van Berkel the Dutch minister.[8] Governor Livingston was appointed some time ago minister for Holland, but did not accept. Mr. Rutledge, governor of S. Carolina, is now appointed: but will it is presumed also decline.

Doctor Mather, you will see by the Boston Papers, is dead. I have a Letter from your Pappa to him, and a small packet from his Son. I don't know who I shall give them to.[9]

Mr. Dana has been appointed a judge of the supreme Court in our State, and is now riding the Circuit.

I moved this morning to the President's house. I determined upon this with some reluctance, not knowing whether it would meet with your Pappa's approbation. But the President repeated his invitation with so much politeness, and Mr. Gerry and Mr. King whom I consulted on the subject, being of opinion I could accept of it without impropriety, I thought I could not do otherwise.

Hearing in the morning, that the british June Packet had arrived, last night, I immediately went to Mr. Jay, and enquired after you. He had received Letters from my father; and had sent them to Congress. I was certain, there were some for me: I then went and found out Mr. Curson, who inform'd me he had seen you, the last day of May: but he had not a line for me.[10] I was much surprised. I had supposed that your Pappa was so much engaged in business, that he had no time to write, but I could not conceive, why I had not one word from Mamma, nor from you. Perhaps you supposed I should have left New York before, the packet would arrive. I cannot account otherwise for your silence.

22d

Mr. van Berkel, with whom I dined to day, begins to expect his Daughter: he has certain information that she sail'd, from Amsterdam, the 2d. of May, in a *Dutch vessel*. She has now been nearly 12 weeks out, and consequently it is almost time for her to arrive. It is observed that there is here now a Dutch vessel, that sailed from Amsterdam 3 days before the ship that returned lately from China, sailed from Canton, and arrived here three days after her.[11] I Drank tea this afternoon with Mr. Secretary Thomson.

23d

We were a dozen or 14 to day, who dined at General Knox's. He lives about 4 miles out of the City.[12] The Virginia and Massachusetts delegations Mr. and Mrs. Smith, Lady Duer, a Daughter of Lord Stirling, Miss Sears, Mr. Church, Coll. Wadsworth and Mr. Osgood, form'd our Company. You know almost all these persons.[13] Lady Duer is not young, nor handsome. I saw but little of her: not enough to say any thing concerning her. Miss Sears has been ill, and looks pale, but is very pretty. She has the reputation of being witty, and sharp. I am sure she does not look *méchante*.

24th

I am very impatient to hear from you. The french packet for June will soon he expected. I hope you will not neglect that, as you did the English one: especially, if Mr. Williamos comes out, in her. The Day before yesterday, Mr. Gerry moved in Congress, that, Mr. Dana's expences for a private Secretary, while he was in Russia, be allow'd him, and Congress resolved that those Expences should be paid.[14]

25th

I have been strolling about the town, almost all day. The weather here, has been exceeding fine, all this Season: no extreme, heat; plenty of rain, and not too much. The Crops will be excellent, and if those in Europe, turn out as bad, as it was supposed they would when I came away, we may profit, very considerably, by ours. Fruit has not been so successful, as there has not been sufficient hot weather.

26th

I dined with the Delegates of the State of Virginia; Mr. Arthur Lee, left this Town in the afternoon. He was this day chosen, by Congress, to be one of the commissioners of the Treasury. Mr. Osgood is now in Town; and does not find it an easy matter to get clear, from the Confusion in which the late financier left the office.[15]

27th

I breakfasted with Mr. Söderström the Sweedish Consul,[16] at Mr. Gerry's house. He arrived in town only a day or two ago, from Boston: all your friends there were well, when he left it. Dined at Mr. Ramsay's with a large Company. General Howe,[17] Mr. Gardoqui, Mr. Randon, Miss Susan Livingston &c. Miss Livingston passes for very smart, sensible young Lady; she is very talkative, and a little superficial I think. I cannot say I admire her. Miss Marshall is very agreeable: I cannot help pitying her, when I am told she is about to marry, that swarthy Don.

At length after a passage of a little more than 12 weeks, Miss van Berkel, arrived two days ago at Philadelphia. Her father is gone to meet her. The young Ladies here are all very impatient to see her, and I dare say, that when she comes, remarks, and reflections, will not be spared on either side. The Beauties of this place, will triumph, but I hope with moderation.

28th

I have had a visit this morning from Dr. Crosby:[18] he tells me he has received lately a letter from uncle Quincy, who was ill, almost all last winter, and is now only recovering. All the rest of our friends are well. The weather is much warmer than I have for many years been accustomed to: yet I hear every body say that there has been no hot weather this year. There is almost every day a morning, and an evening breeze, that are very refreshing, and temper agreeably the heat of the day.

29th

I expect to stay here about a week longer: but I am not yet determined whether to go in a packet to Rhode Island, and from thence by Land; or to go all the way by land through Connecticut. In the heat of the Season, a Journey by land would be more disagreeable than a voyage by water, and it would certainly be longer: but I am very desirous to see the fine Country between this and Boston. And there are many persons that I wish to see too. Upon the whole I rather think I shall go, by Land. We are in a great dearth of news: nothing of any Consequence is going forward. The merchants complain very much that trade is continually dying away, and that no business is to be done.

30th

The President had a large Company to dine with him: all gentlemen; he entertains three times a week, but never has any Ladies because he has none himself. His health is not in a very good ⟨state⟩ way, and I believe the Duties of his place, weary him much. He is obliged in this weather to sit at Congress from eleven in the morning, till near 4 afternoon, which is just the hottest, and most disagreeable part of the day. It was expected that Congress would adjourn during the dog days at least: but there is at present little appearance of it: they have so much business before them, that a recess, however short would leave them behind hand.

31st

I went with Mr. Jarvis, a brother of the gentleman you know, to Jamaica, upon Long Island;[19] 12 miles from the town. We there had the pleasure of seeing Coll. Smith's mother and Sister's.[20] I spent the day very agreeably. Mrs. Smith, has had Letters from her Son, since

229

he arrived in London, in which he mentions having already seen you all. I am really very impatient to hear from you. *Your Brother*

J. Q. Adams

RC (Adams Papers). The text is on eight pages, numbered, beginning with the second, "26" to "32." See JQA to AA2, [12] May, descriptive note, above.

¹ JQA had met François Barbé-Marbois in 1779; see JQA to JA, 3 Aug., note 6, below. In 1784 Barbé-Marbois married Elizabeth Moore, daughter of William Moore, a Philadelphia merchant and member of the Supreme Executive Council of Pennsylvania from 1779 to 1782 (Hoefer, *Nouv. biog. générale*; *DAB*).

² Nathan Dane of Beverly, Mass., first elected to Congress in June 1785, served until 1788 (*Biog. Dir. Cong.*).

³ That is, JA.

⁴ Richard Henry Lee served as president of Congress from Nov. 1784 to Nov. 1785 (*Biog. Dir. Cong.*).

⁵ Gardoqui was the son of Joseph Gardoqui, the Bilbao merchant whom JA and JQA had met on their journey through Spain in Jan. 1780. He was received by Congress on 2 July, and served as the Spanish chargé d'affaires until 1789 (*JCC*, 29:494–496; JQA, *Diary*, 1:30–31, 289, and note 5).

⁶ That of 25 May, above. "Mr. Church" was the Englishman John Barker Church (see JQA, *Diary*, 1:310, and note 2).

⁷ JQA had met Mr. and Mrs. John Rucker in Paris in March (*Diary*, 1:233, and note 2). Ramsay was probably South Carolina congressman David Ramsay, one of the earliest historians of the American Revolution (*DAB*).

⁸ JQA first records meeting Pieter Johan van Berckel of Rotterdam in that city in May 1783, just before van Berckel sailed for America as the first Dutch minister to the United States. JQA next met van Berckel in New York on 18 July 1785 (*Diary*, 1:174, 289; JA, *Diary and Autobiography*, 3:135, note 1).

⁹ Rev. Samuel Mather, youngest son of Cotton Mather, his father's successor at the Second Church in Boston, and brother-in-law of Gov. Thomas Hutchinson, died on 27 June 1785, still estranged from his loyalist son Samuel, then a refugee in England (*Sibley's Harvard Graduates*, 7:216–238).

¹⁰ The letters sent after JQA left Auteuil were JA to John Jay, 13 May, 29 May, 30 May,

and 1 June (all PCC, No. 84, V, f. 413–420, 437–439, 461–464, 465–466); see Jay to JA, 3 Aug. 1785 (Adams Papers). All appear in *Dipl. Corr., 1783–1789*, 1:495–498; 2:345–346, 365–367, 373–376. The N.Y. merchant Samuel Curson, whom JA had met in Amsterdam in 1780, brought the letter of 29 May, and probably that of 30 May (JA, *Diary and Autobiography*, 2:450).

¹¹ The *Empress of China*, returning from the first voyage by an American merchant ship to China, sailed from Canton on 28 Dec. 1784 and arrived in New York on 11 May 1785 (Philip Chadwick Foster Smith, *The Empress of China*, Phila., 1984, p. 201, 206).

¹² In his Diary, JQA locates Knox's home "2 miles out of town" (*Diary*, 1:293).

¹³ The Virginia congressmen were William Grayson, Samuel Hardy, Richard Henry Lee, and James Monroe; the Massachusetts congressmen were Elbridge Gerry, Samuel Holten, and Rufus King. "Mr. and Mrs. Smith" were probably the N.Y. congressman Melancthon Smith (*Biog. Dir. Cong.*), and his wife. Catherine Alexander Duer, called "Lady Kitty," was the daughter of Maj. Gen. William Alexander, who claimed the ancestral title of Lord Sterling; she had married the N.Y. merchant, financier, and congressman William Duer in 1779. Rebecca Sears was the daughter of the N.Y. merchant and popular leader Isaac Sears. Jeremiah Wadsworth of Connecticut had served as commissary general of the Continental Army, and of Rochambeau's forces. The former Mass. congressman Samuel Osgood was a commissioner of the U.S. Treasury (Burnett, ed., *Letter of Members*, 8:lxxxvii–lxxxviii; xcviii; *DAB*). AA2 had probably met several of the Massachusetts delegates, and perhaps Rebecca Sears, whose family lived in Boston, 1777–1783; the others she knew only by reputation, if at all.

¹⁴ *JCC*, 29:569–570.

¹⁵ Samuel Osgood had been highly critical of Robert Morris, the superintendent of finance, 1781–1784. In January 1785 Osgood was

appointed to the three-man treasury commission that replaced Morris (*DAB*).

[16] Richard Söderström was the Swedish consul in Boston; JQA had met his brother Carl Söderström in Jan. 1783 in Göteborg, Sweden, on his return trip from Russia to Holland (*Diary*, 1:167, and note 1).

[17] Robert Howe, commander of the Southern Department of the Continental Army, 1777–1778 (JQA, *Diary*, 1:290, and note 2).

[18] Ebenezer Crosby, named professor of midwifery at Columbia College in 1785, was from Braintree (same, 1:295, and note 1).

[19] Both Benjamin and Charles Jarvis accompanied JQA to Jamaica, L.I.; AA2 had met their brother James Jarvis in France in April (same, 1:254, 296; AA to Lucy Cranch, 7 May, above).

[20] JQA met the recently widowed Margaret Stephens Smith and her many daughters, of whom he noted Sarah Smith as "handsome" in his Diary, and in his letter of 1 Aug., below. Sarah would marry CA in 1795. *Diary*, 1:296, and notes 1 and 2.

Mary Smith Cranch to Abigail Adams

My Dear Sister   Braintree July 19th 1785

I have been waiting till I am out of all patience to hear that you are returnd to England. One or two vessels have sail'd for London without taking Letters for you. I did not know they were going till it was too late to write. I sent you a hasty line by Mr. Charles Bulfinch[1] which I hope you receiv'd and to tell you the truth I have written you two letters Since, which I thought proper to commit to the Flames when I had done. There are many things which would do to be said, that it would not be prudent to commit to writing.[2] We have been expecting Cousin John every day above a week past: There is a vessel in from France the capt. of whom says he Saild four days before him. I hope soon to welcome him to his native country. Tomorrow is commencment: our children are all gone to Boston to day, to be ready for an earley ride in the morning. Cousin Charles's Heart beats thick I dare say. His trial comes on next Friday. Billy says, he is exceedingly well fitted and has no need of any fears. Billy will look him a good room, and will give him all the Brotherly advice that he may need. He will have enough to spring upon him if he does not stand firm in the begining. He or you will repent it, if he does not. He shall not need any Friendly counsel that I will not give him. I will gain his Love and confidence if *Possible*. I shall then be sure of influence.

Friday 22d

I have been very ill ever since I wrote the above, with a pain across my Breast. The Rhumtism the Doctor says. I am better but very weak. The children are returnd and a fine day they had. Mr. Shaw and Cousin Charles were there. He will return with his uncle and come next week if he is accepted, and there is no doubt but he will be.

Cousin John will be here I hope by that time. I am prepair'd to doat upon him. May nothing happen to interrupt the Harmony and happiness of our dear Boys. I am indeed happy at present in my children. From every thing that I can see and hear Billy behaves just as I could wish him too. Betsy is in Boston very attentive to her Harpsicord and is in better health than I have known her for many years. Lucy is at home affording her mama all the assistance she is able too, and if her Soul is not tuned to Harmony it is to Science. Had she been a Boy she would have been a Mathamatition. Billy plays prettily both upon the violin and Flute, and when he joins them to his Sisters instrument they form a Sound very agreable to the Ears of us who have not heard the finer musick of your opereas. Betsy wishes Cousin Nabby to learn the musick of France, that she may bring her home some new tunes.

Aunt Tufts is in a very poor way. Her Feet and ancles are much swell'd and turn purple and black and every dissagreable colour. You know she never could bear the Bark, and it seem now to be more than ever necessary for her. I am very much affraid of a mortification if She cannot take it.

Uncle Quincy was confin'd to his House from the 25th of November to the beginning of July With the Rhumatisim in his Hip. He is much better but not well. Our Germantown Friends are all of them in a poor weak State. The general himself very feeble. Cousin Betsy is better but her cough is still troublesome. Miss Paine is very spry, can dress and undress very well, has spent a week or two with me lately, is now at Germantown but next week goes to her Brothers for a home as she supposes.

As to Mr. Palmers Family Mr. Tyler must give you an account of them. He knows more about them than any one else.[3] Madam Quincy and Miss Nancy are well. Miss Nancys fortune has not yet procur'd her a Husband. Mrs. Quincy desires to [be] most affectionately remember'd to you. Mrs. Guild has spent a week with her little Boy at Braintree. She is not well by any means, but looks chearful and behaves exceeding well under her dissapointment. She has sold all the Furniture of her best room and chamber and remov'd into that end of a House which Miss H. Otis liv'd in. What a reverse of Fortune in one year! Mr. Guild looks as if he was going into the Grave soon. His pale Face is paler than ever. His countenance excites pity from every eye. No alteration has taken place in your Neighbourhood that I know of. Mr. Adams Family are well, your mother Hall is upon a visit at Abington. She was here a few days since and was well. Turtius

Bass and wife are parted. He has sold the House and land which his Sons liv'd in and divided his Estate into four parts, given his wife one fourth part, one half to his two Sons. The remainder he has taken to support himself and Nell Underwood in their Perigrinations to the Eastward whither he is going he says to settle. And as he is going into a new country, tis proper he should take a young person to help People it, and her abbillity to do it She has given ample proof off by presenting somebody (she swore them upon Leonard Clevverly) with a pair of Twins last winter. She liv'd in Mr. Bass's Family—but as they both dy'd she was at Liberty to pursue her Business as Housekeeper in some distant part of the State as well as at Braintree, and who would be Maid when they might be mistress? Mr. Bass was so generious to the Girl, that he keept her in his house to lay in, and gave Mr. Tyler a handsome Fee as Counsel for her in case Mr. Cleaverly should deny the charge which he did most solemnly. In this case the woman has the advantage in law. He was oblig'd to enter into Bonds, but the children dying, and Mr. Tyler not appearing, he took up his bonds and Mr. Bass was oblig'd to bear all the charges. Mrs. Bass is in great trouble. Seth is mov'd into the House with her, and the other Son with his wife and child are mov'd seventy mile into the country out of all the noise of it—so much for Scandle.

Capn. Baxter is married to Mrs. Arnold and is gone to live in her House. Mrs. Arnolds eldest Son is married to Deacon Adams eldest Daughter[4] and lives in the House that Mr. Bass sold. Our Parson visits us as usual, but forgot this year that it was Election day till it was half gone. He ought to have had his grandchildren about him beging for coppers to bye them an election cake.[5]

I once mention'd to you a clergemans Family who were in our House at Weymouth. He has a Son almost eighteen, who tho he is a portrait Painter has not sacrificed much to the Graces.[6] He made several attempts to take the Face of our cousin Lucy Jones, but could never acquire stediness enough in his hands to do it. In short her fine Form had made such an impression upon his mind and Lucy *all-together* had taken such possestion of his Soul, that when he endeavourd to describe a *single* feature he found it impossible. The tremor was communicated to his Tongue and his speech also fail'd him. Poor youth what would he have done if it had not been for the blessed invention of Letters, by which ⟨*medium*⟩ he could pour out all his soul and save his Blushes—but alass this was only to insure his dispair, for she treated them with such neglect and contempt that it almost depriv'd him of his reason. In the silent watches of the night, when the Moon in full orb'd Majisty had reach'd her nocturnal height, He left his Bed and upon the cold ground told her his tale of woe, in accents loud and wild as wind.——Forgive the Stile my dear sister. No common one would do to relate this extraordinary affair in. It has caused us much amusement. They are both so young they did not know how to manage the matter. He all Passion. She full of Coquettry and at present without any kind of attachment to him is playing round the Flame without any aprehension of danger. There are some symptoms however of either Vanity or Love that make their appearence. She dresses more than usual and parades before the windows opposite to those he sets at. The other day she dress'd herself in white and walk'd into Capn. Whitmans Coppes set herself upon a rock under a fine spreading oak and was excited by the melody of a variety of Birds that were perch'd upon almost every bough, to add her note to theirs. The sighing swain was raking Hay at a little distance. The pleasing sound soon reach'd his ears. He left his Rake and pursu'd it, and (she says) was close by her before she perciev'd him but she like a nimble-footed Dauphne was out of his sight in a moment and was as pale aunt says when she enter'd the House as if she had been pursu'd by a snake.

July 30th

I give you joy my dear sister. Cousin John I hear is arriv'd at New York after a Passage of 56 days. He will be with us soon I hope. Mr. Cranch sent me word of it last monday. The same day he found a Letter from you to me in the Post-office.[7] I find by it that a Mr. Chaumont brought it, but I cannot hear that he is in Boston. I am mortified that you are still in France. What is become of Mr. Adams commission for the court of London. I wish you were at home every soul of you. I fear your expences must have been greatly increas'd by the dryness of the season. Our news Papers say you have had almost a Famine in Europe occationd by it. Here we never saw a finer season. The best of English Hay has been sold in Boston for two shilling a hundred and some as low as one and four pence. Meat is high, but vegetables very plenty. We have fine crops of english grain, and the Indian looks finely. Your Gardens yeald plentifully. Your sable Tenants[8] almost maintain themselves by selling the produce of them. Betsy is return'd to spend the Dog-days with us. Will go again in the Fall to take a few more Lessons. Billy has tun'd the old Spinnet at home, by which means she will not loose any time.

Betsy and Lucy spent a forenoon this week over-looking the things at your House and picking out furniture for master Charles chamber, who is become a student at Harvard college.[9] He is hear and very well. Mr. Shaw offer'd another schooler, who is a very cleaver Fellow and is to be his chambermate.[10] I could have wish'd the two Brothers might have liv'd together. Upon some accounts it would be less expencive. Cousin John comes I dare say impress'd with a sense of the importance of eocomimy. I have been telling Cousin Charles He must begin right, and that his Papas Station in Life will subject him to many inconvenincs if he is not upon his Guard. I have consulted with Doctor Tufts in every thing that I have done with regard to the children and shall continue to do so. I have pursued that plan you mention with regard to money matters[11] already as I thought it would be the simplest, and be assur'd my dear Sister so far as I am capable I will do every thing in my Power to supply, the place of a mama to them. I hope to gain their confidence and esteem. They feel like my own children and if I can but gain as much of their Love as you have of my childrens I shall feel very happy.

As soon as Cousin John comes I will write more with regard to him. I hope to have many Letters by him. I do not suppose that our April Pacquet reach'd you before he imbark'd. I wish it might have done so for many reasons. The letters for him will not be half so acceptable to him here as if he had reciev'd them in France.[12]

Aunt Tufts remains very Ill. The Doctor seems quite discourag'd about her. Her Legs and Feet grow worse. She is in great pain and wasts fast. I fear she will not continue thro the Dog-days. Tis true she bears the Bark but she has such a constitution as I think cannot hold out long unless she is suddenly reliev'd.

Old Mrs. Tullur dy'd about six weeks ago very suddenly. Was well in the morning and dead before night, and this afternoon Fanny Nash is bury'd. She has been in a consumtion all winter.

August 1d

I have just heard of Mr. Adams presentment at the court of London. Mr. Cranch writes me that he has seen an account of your arrival in England. He saw it in a [*New*] York paper. Cousin John is not yet got to town. What is he doing with himself? He does not know that every moment seems an hour till he arrives. Charles and Billy are here waiting with impatience. I feel as if you were half way home at least. I shall now be able to write oftner and with greater Freedom.

England must I think be more agreable to you than France for many reasons. Your being able to converse will be a great addition to your Happiness and seeing so many of your old acquaintance and Friends will make you feel as if you was half an american at least, but are you not almost sick of Parade? To have been made happy by show and equipage your mind should have been less cultivated, and yet tis only to such, that these things can do no harm. A Scientific mind, will be pleas'd only with their novelty and the useful observations it helps them to make upon Men and Manners.——But this Embassa of three years—what shall I say to it? Will it be necessary that you should stay so long. Cannot the Business be compleated before that time. How does cousin Nabby like the Idea. She would not wish to come without you I dare say, unless every thing here was fit to receive her. Money is very hard to be got where it *is* due, and where there is the *greatest* attention and puntiallity in business what is procur'd by it, must be very prudently us'd or it Will not buy Farms and Houses, repair them Handsomely, and maintain a Family genteelly. You conclude your last Letter by saying that "you hope——is very busy and to great purpose."[13] I hope soo too, but I know very little about him for he is very seldom in Braintree and when he is, very little at home. He has attended the courts in Boston the last winter and this summer, and does not come home till the Sessions are over.

Mrs. Hunt is here and desirs I would give her most affectionate Love to you, and beg you to come home for she longs to see you and that she cannot bear to pass by your House. She visits us often and is better than for years back. She works forever, has spun and knit above eighty pair of stockings since you went away.

You mention Mr. Adams's having receiv'd a Letter from the Amsterdam merchants, complaining that they had receiv'd no accounts of the sales of their goods.[14] I forgot to write about it in my Spring Letters. Mr. Cranch wrote them last winter a state of their merchandize such as what goods remain'd unsold, and the custom of giving six months credit. The Difficulty of selling for ready money, and the danger of trusting The Bill of Sale he could not then send because Mr. Austen who you know had the care of dispossing of them had remov'd to Casco-Bay in the beginning of the winter, and by accident carried all the Papers with him, and the season was so severe that we never could get them till this spring, when he came up and brought them himself. Mr. Cranch has put what remain'd unsold into the Hands of Mr. Greenlief & Foster Vendae Master, to be dispos'd

236

of at private Sale in the best manner they can. Mr. Cranch has had a great deal of trouble with them. Most of them were very unsalable articles, and too high charg'd for the inundation of Goods that were soon roled in after the peace upon the country.

August 3d

Cousin John not come yet. I hear there is a vessel to Sale in ten days for London. If I keep writing I shall swell my Letter too a volume, for I am continually thinking of something which I want to communicate. I cannot bear to seal my Letter till I have seen my cousin, and yet I fear if I do not send it to town the vessel will slip away without it.

August 7th

It is just as I fear'd. I hear a vessel sal'd for England this morning, and I was told she would not go this week. Cousin John not yet come. Several People are come from [*New*] York who have seen him, and say he will be here in a few days. You may easily judge how impatient I am, but I am determin'd to wait no longer, but send this to be put into the Bag and write again if he should come before the next chance.

Aunt Tufts sinks fast. She has had a Dissentery, which tho it has abated has wasted her much. Her Feet and ancles are very bad, all manner of colours, much swelld and very painful. I have seen the last Week. You would scarcly know her. She appears calm and resign'd, has no expectation of Living. She will be a great gainer by the exchange for she is indeed a very good woman. The poor will loose a great benefactor. Her Family also will feel her loose for tho she could not do much she look'd well to her household. Lucy will a second time loose a mama,[15] and she seems very sensible of it. O my sister one more removal and Weymouth will loose all its charms. Every Freind departed makes me wish more for your return. Three years is a great while to look forward too. Many very many may be the changes that may take place before that period arrives. I dare not trust myself with the thought. Resignation to the will of Heaven is what I am constantly seeking after. I have been very unwell myself for above a month but I hope I am geting the better of my dissorder. I am weak yet the Feverishness has not left me, but salt of wormwood which I take every two or three days will I hope kill it.

Cousin Charles is in fine Health and spirits, and rejoices over and feasts as heartily upon a large Whorttle Berry Pudding as you can at any of your great entertainments. Would not a Dish of Green Corn relish &c. be acceptable to you? We are all Busy fixing your Son for college. The piece of Linnin which I got for them made seven shirts for Charls and four for Tom.

Miss Paine desires I would not forget her Love to you all.

I depend upon it that you will not expose my writing to any one not even to my dear Brother, to whom present my Love and best wishes and tell him tis a sad world we live in and that the more merit he has, the better mark he will be for Envy to shoot at—but she cannot sting him.

Charles Warren yet Lives, but look like death. He is planing a voyage to Lisbon, he thinks he cannot stand our cold winters. I do not beleive he will live to reach it. Mrs. Warren is much destress'd to know what to consent too.—Did you ever find her Letters which you thought you had lost. She thinks you have. Do not forget to tell me.

The distresses of our Germantown Friends will never have an end. Last week Tom Feild cut his Back and Shouldar in a dreadful manner with a scythe. The wound is two feet long and very deep in some places. The Doctor put fourteen stiches in it. He has lost a great deal of Blood, but is in a good way, and unless a Fever should set in, will tis thought do well.

Adieu my dear Sister and believe me your ever affectionate

M. Cranch

Love to cousin Nabby.

RC (Adams Papers).

[1] Mary Cranch to AA, 4 June, sent with Richard Cranch to JA, 3 June, both above.

[2] Cranch may refer to her growing concern about Royall Tyler. See below in this letter, her letter to AA of 4 June, above, and several of her letters of October-December, below; and AA to Mary Cranch, 15 Aug., below.

[3] By 1785, Royall Tyler had become a close friend of Gen. Joseph Palmer's son, Joseph Pearse Palmer, and his family, and lodged with them in Boston. By the late 1780s he was helping to support the financially ruined family, and in 1794 he married Palmer's daughter Mary. G. Thomas Tanselle, *Royall Tyler*, Cambridge, 1967, p. 19, 24–29.

[4] Mehitable Adams, eldest daughter of JA's double first cousin, Ebenezer Adams, married Joseph Neale Arnold on 16 June (A. N. Adams, *Geneal. Hist. of Henry Adams of Braintree*, p. 410).

[5] If by "Our Parson," Mary Cranch means Rev. Anthony Wibird, her image must be ironic, for Wibird never married (*Sibley's Harvard Graduates*, 12:226–230).

[6] The artist John Hazlitt was the eldest son of William Hazlitt. Lucy Jones, just shy of seventeen, was the daughter of Cotton Tufts' sister, Anna Tufts Jones. In 1787 John Hazlitt, unmarried, returned to England with his family. *The Journal of Margaret Hazlitt*, ed. Ernest J. Moyne, Lawrence, Kansas, 1967, p. 15–20; Mary Cranch to AA, 6 Nov. 1784, note 3, above.

[7] AA to Mary Cranch, 15 April, above.

[8] Phœbe and William Abdee.

[9] CA's printed admission form to Harvard College, dated 17 Aug., is in the Adams Papers.

[10] Samuel Walker.

[11] AA to Mary Cranch, 15 April, above; see the account in Cotton Tufts to JA, 10 Aug., below.

[12] Mary and Elizabeth Cranches' letters to AA of 25 April, both above, and presumably other letters of about the same date, did not reach the Adamses until late June (see AA to Mary Cranch, 24 June, above). No letters from America to JQA, written in the spring of 1785, have been found.

[13] AA to Mary Cranch, 15 April, above, referring to Royall Tyler.

[14] See Richard Cranch to JA, 3 June, and AA to Mary Cranch, 7 Jan., and note 4, both above.

[15] Probably Lucy Quincy Tufts' niece, Lucy Tufts Hall, daughter of Dr. Cotton Tufts' brother, Dr. Simon Tufts of Medford. Niece Lucy's mother, Lucy Dudley Tufts, had died in 1768. *Sibley's Harvard Graduates*, 11:478–481.

Charles Williamos to Abigail Adams

Paris 21st. July *1785*

It is with much pleasure my dear Madam that I hear of your safe arrival in London and that you are once more fixed in a house of your own, the situation of which altho' not quite so pleasant as Auteuill is not without much merit.

Whatever base rancour and malice may invent, I am very sure that you will on all occasions meet with every Mark of respect which are every ways your due.[1] Yet I do not suppose, that the Court Notwithstanding its politeness will be very often graced with your and Miss Adams's Company.

Paris is not the livelier I can assure you Madam since you left it. Passy is deserted also—and we have accounts of the doctor's very safe arrival at Rouen from whence he was to proceed immediately to Havre—the King sent him his Picture most elegantly set in diamonds of great value, with two very polite letters from Count de Vergennes.

The peculiar honor and satisfaction I had in opportunities of paying my very Sincere respects to Mr. Adams yourself and family will ever be recollected as one of the most agreable events of my life and I shall never think myself happier than in opportunities to renew it. I am very sorry to have failed hitherto in every attempt to send your things. I went to Mr. Hailes's who desired his best respects and assured me it was out of his power to forward any thing larger than a packet of letters as the messenger goes no further than Calais where the master of the British packet takes charge of the letters.

This I communicated to Mrs. Barclay who agreed in thinking it best to wait for Doctor Bancroft who is to go in 8 or ten days but if an opportunity offers sooner we [will?] not fail to improve it. Mr.

Harison t[akes? c]harge of the lace by which means there are only gowns. Mr. Storer has some books with a Mr. Graff but Mr. Barclay thinks that as he is going to America they had better be sent there to him than trouble any one with them.

Mr. Jefferson and the other Gentlemen are very well. Col. Humphreys has wrote to Col. Smith. The June Packet is arrived but not all the letters. I am still waiting for a better opportunity than by L'orient, but fear much that I shall be obliged to take that rout.[2] Whenever I go and where ever I am I shall allways retain sentiments of highest respect and ever be Madam your most obedient devoted servant   C. Williamos

Be Kind enough to present my best respects to Mr. and Miss Adams.[3]

RC (Adams Papers); addressed: "Mrs. Adams Grosvenor Square *London*"; docketed: "Mr Williamos Paris june 27 1785"; stamped: "[J]Y/25," "2 o'clock," and, in red ink, "A PAYE PAR." AA's erroneous docketing may have been an inadvertent repetition of her docketing of the 27 June letter from Williamos, above. This letter was filmed at 27 July, Adams Papers, Microfilms, Reel No. 365. Some loss of text where the seal was torn off.

[1] Williamos refers to AA's remark about "torry Malevolence" in the London press, in her letter of 1 July, above. He may have been particularly sympathetic to the Adams' plight at this time because of "the atrocious falshoods which have too Successfully been attempted by the lowest and most infernal Malice," which, he claimed, had suddenly turned Thomas Jefferson against him just two weeks before the date of this letter (Williamos to Jefferson, 8 July, in Jefferson, *Papers*, 8:275, and see p. 269–273, 276–277).

[2] Williamos had been planning to sail to America since February, but various complications, including his sudden falling out with Jefferson on 7 July, and eventually his ill health, delayed him, and he died in Paris in November (Jefferson to AA, 20 Nov., below; Claude-Anne Lopez and Eugenia W. Herbert, *The Private Franklin*, N.Y., 1975, p. 280).

[3] This sentence was written along the left margin of the last page of text.

Abigail Adams to Mary Smith Cranch?

My dear sister   [*ca. July–Aug. 1785*]

I wrote you by Captain Dashood just when I was about removeing from the Bath Hotel to Grovsnor Square,[1] since which I have had a buisy time getting my House in order and procuring a thousand little necessaries for different countries have different fashions and what suits in one will not answer in an other. For instanc my kitchen furniture was made for a hearth fire none of which could be used with grates and then the coars ware belonging to a family is never worth a remove so that I found I had many things to purchase.

Then the great and important article of servants was to be arranged. Of Ester I made what is here calld Ladies Maid, her Buisness is more imediately about my person. She always dresses my Hair and your neices and is a great proficient in that most *important* Buisness. She take care of all the Linnen, delivers it out and receives it in. The remainder of her time is employed at her needle. The person who works with her is the Buttler. His Buisness is to take care of the wine, to market for the family, to keep the weekly accounts, to see the table and side Board in order to attend as overseer of the table, to take care of the Plate and to have a general care of the lower servants. He is allways calld Mr. I hope we have been fortunate in the choise of ours. He appears a very civil well bred Man. The House maid is next. She makes beds cleans the house taking it from the top of the kitchen stairs and going up. The two footmen[2] go behind the carriage wait at table rub the table and chairs of the dining room and attend the door, for there is no entrance into a house in this Country but by wrapping or ringing a Bell which is with out side the door. No door is permitted one moment to be left open, you could have no security for any thing within, if it was. The cook is next in order who prepares the victuals and the kitchen maid takes the House from the kitchen stairs and goes down to the kitchen pantrys, housekeepers room, Buttlers room and servants Hall as it is calld. She washes dishes, cleans knives and candle sticks &c. &c. The coachmans buisness is to take care of his carriage and horses.

You will think I suppose that I have got a comfortable number, but with less I could not get the necessary buisness of the family done, not because there are not more than sufficient, but because none of them will do any thing but in their particular department. A House keeper a Laundry Maid and a Porter are 3 more which they would be very glad that I would add, but I am determined against it, as I cannot but think 3 Americans would do the whole work of the Eight and think they had no hard task. The work of the family here is by no means so much as Mrs. Newcomb has herself done in my family at Braintree for my washing is all put out, and we have no company to sup. But in a country crowded with inhabitant they get as many of their poor supported in this way as possible and every news paper is filld "with wants a place." Yet are the wages of those who are good for any thing very high. So far from feeling myself in a more desirable situation than when I moved in the small sphere of my ⟨lowly⟩ Braintree Cottage, I assure you I look to it as an envyable situation.

Fewer cares and less anxiety attended my rising up and sitting down, my Friends all smiled upon me and met a hearty welcome under the lowly roof.

My Habitation here is in one of the pleasentest squares of London. We are in the same Row if not in the same Box of most of the great people in this Country, *opposite* however to Lord North. A near Neighbour to Lord Thurlow and the Marquis of Carmarthan. Yet the street as well as city is quite deserted, for nobody lives here in the summer who can go into the country. In the middle of the square which is very spacious is a circuleer inclosure in which clumps of trees are planted which look like shubbery as the trees are small and close together. Round them is the hedge which when cut has a very rural appearence. In the middle is the King on horse back. The whole is laid out into walks and those who live in the square have a key to one of the gates which you may make use of for to walk.

Dft (Adams Papers). The text fills two pages of a folded leaf; it has little punctuation and no paragraph breaks. It is likely that Mary Cranch, not Elizabeth Shaw, was the intended recipient (see note 1). The editors have added paragraph breaks and some punctuation.

[1] AA to Mary Cranch, 24 June, above, is the only extant letter that fits this description.
[2] John Briesler was one of the footmen.

John Quincy Adams to Abigail Adams 2d

N:5.

Monday
New York August 1st. 1785

In my last[1] I just mentioned having been over upon Long Island, and paid a visit to Mrs. Smith, the Colls.s Mother: she was very polite to me, and appeared to miss her Son, much. All the family are in mourning for the old gentleman who died about 9 months ago. There is one Son here now, and if I mistake not, 6 daughters. *Sally* strikes most at first sight: she is tall; has a very fine shape, and a vast deal of vivacity in her eyes, which are of a light blue; she has the ease and elegance of a French Lady, without their loquacity. Her conversation I am told is as pleasing as her figure: but of that I only speak, from hearsay.—There is also on this island a celebrated beauty by the name of Miss Ogden: she looks I think, something like Mrs. Bingham: *she is not so tall, nor so red, although I believe she has more colour.*

2d

I have been writing a letter to your Pappa;[2] but it is full of politics. I don't know whether he will not think I meddle too much with them: but there are some things he may wish to be inform'd of, and at many places where I go into company I hear nothing else: so that I am obliged bongré, malgré, as the french say, still to dip a little in that subject: but I don't care how soon, I leave it off entirely. Mr. Church goes on Thursday.

I dined to day with Doctor Crosby, who came the other day, as soon as he knew I was in town, to see me. I imagine he thinks me a very cerimonious being: for, the day that he first saw me, he ask'd me to drink tea with him that afternoon. I promised I would: but I happened to dine in a Company where I was kept till it was too late, to wait upon the Doctor. The next day I went to his house to make an apology, but he was not at home: and yesterday I received a card containing a most formal invitation to dine to day. I find it a very nice matter here, to take a just medium between Ceremony and ease. If a person is formal he is laugh'd at, and if otherwise he often offends. It is exactly the fable of the miller and his Son.

3d

I have been spending the evening with Mr. Gerry and Mr. King. Mr. Gerry writes to your Pappa, by Mr. Church who is to sail to morrow morning, and to whom I have given 2 letters for you; and one for your Pappa.[3] I have not been able to find time for writing to Mamma. You will present my duty to her, and make an apology for me.

I was shown this evening a poem in manuscript, called a receipt for a wife: it is a catalogue of the celebrated beauties in this town, abusing some, and commending others. I would send you a Copy of it, but it is really such a pitiful performance, that it would not probably furnish you any entertainment. I am told of another piece in the same way; if I find it better I will give you some extracts from it, in case I can get a copy of it.

4th

Mr. Church sail'd in the Packet this morning with my letters: they will show you that I have not been forgetful of my promises. I dined[4] with a large Company at Mr. Osgood's. I was introduced this morning to a Miss Riché[5] lately arrived from Philadelphia; and was this evening in Company with her at Mr. Sears's. She is a great beauty, but if I mistake not has a good deal of Affectation. She sings, plays upon the harpsichord, and writes songs herself: consequently she must be witty; but she is affected.—The Miss Sears's, you know I believe. Polly was married last spring to Mr. Bordieu. Sally, some say, is soon to be married to a Mr. Gamble; but fame has not yet disposed of Becca, the prettiest of them all.

I have got a Copy of the poem I yesterday talk'd of. It speaks of Miss Becca as follows.

> If Becca would but learn to walk
> And not be so afraid to talk
> With greater lustre she would shine
> In other eyes as well as mine.
> Praise her for elegance of form
> Which would the coldest marble warm
> Praise her for sprightliness of wit,
> Her Character you'll justly hit.
> She's tender, virtuous and mild
> But walks, as if she was a child.

You know, that part of our agreement is to give each other our opinion upon Characters; but I trust you will allow me to quote from other People, especially, when it is in verse. I am told the author of this piece is partial, in favour of Miss Sears when he says she is witty: as she is not much celebrated as a wit. Of this I cannot decide, for although I have been several times in Company with her, I don't know that four words have ever pass'd between us.

5th

The President[6] has a large Company of 20, or 25 persons to dine with him, three times a week: but as he has no Lady himself, he entertains none but gentlemen. Once a week, he has a musical Entertainment, as it is here called, that is, he invites a number of persons among his Company, that sing songs after dinner, and, there was one to day. Among the singers the most curious was Genl. Howe, of whom you have often heard. *He is you know not less famous for cracking the bottle, than for singing a song.* Being requested to day to sing, he endeavoured once or twice to begin but found something wanting. At last he cried out, "give me that Madeira to revive me, for I have been flattening my voice by drinking Burgundy." And after drinking his glass he sung, "Once the gods of the greeks," very well.

I went this Evening, with the President to a Mr. Eccles's. Miss

Eccles, is the most perfect at the harpsichord, of any Lady in the City, or perhaps on the Continent. I must again quote from the same poem, which speaks of this Lady thus.

> Miss Eccles now my lay commands,
> Her mind harmonious as her hands.
> Six hours in every twenty four
> For nine revolving years or more
> (Some rigid moralist may say)
> Is too much time to spend at play.
> I own the observation true,
> But still admire the music too
> For he that hears her must forget
> The time she lost in learning it.

I am sure my Sister would never agree to purchase perfection in the art of music upon such conditions, and I should be very sorry if she would.

6th

Young Chaumont, who has been at Philadelphia, almost all the time since he arrived, return'd here a few days since, and is going shortly to Boston. Perhaps we shall go both at the same time. When he first arrived here he presented a memorial to Congress, requesting that, they would order all the paper money, which french merchants had received in the course of the war, or which now lies in their hands, to be paid in hard money, dollar for dollar.[7] This will surprise you probably as much as it did every body on this side the water. Yet Chaumont really presented his memorial with hopes of succeeding. Congress have not given any answer, and he begins to think that the plan will not take. He tells me he will show me his memorial, and says, I shall then own that his pretensions, are absolutely just, and equitable.

7th

I attended Church this morning at St. Paul's, for we have a St. Paul's here, as well as you in London, but it is something like Alexander the great, and Alexander the Copper smith.[8] This is however the largest and most frequented Church in [New] York, and is more consistent with the smallness of the City than it would be if it vied in grandeur and magnificence with its namesake in London. After Church I left a card at Miss van Berkel's; she arrived here two days ago, from Philadelphia. She had a passage of 13 weeks (in a Dutch vessel) and yet her brother, who had been informed of the time of her sailing, by the arrival of other vessels; told me, that she arrived before he expected her.—I paid a visit too this forenoon to Miss Alsop. Her father is acquainted with our's.[9] She is called a Coquet.

> Why is not Alsop often told
> That coquetry is grown quite old?
> That nothing is more out of date
> Than affectation, and conceit?
> The eye half shut, the dimpled cheek
> And languid look, are arts too weak,
> To win the heart of any youth,
> Who loves simplicity and truth.

These lines have not however cured her of her fault: for the 5th. and 6th. are an exact description of her appearance, as it was to day, and I am told she is always so. She is fair, and pretty, but injures her appearance much by those simpering airs.

I was at a party at tea this afternoon, and Miss van Berkel was present. There were only two or three persons in Company that could speak to her, so, I was obliged to converse with her, near two hours together. *And here I must tell you, that I believe more and more firmly, that what a certain* FRIEND *of mine said of her, is a most infamous falsehood. She behaves as well, as any young lady I know of, and I believe if her brother knew what that coxcomb said of her, he would make him repent it heartily.* She complains of not understanding the language, as bitterly, as you did when you first arrived in France. She says she had no idea, how awkward one appears in a large company, where one can neither hear what is said nor speak one's self. You have had sufficient proofs of the truth of this observation: tho' you was not often subjected to the inconvenience.

8th

I went out this morning with some Company to Content, a seat, about 3 miles out of town, where Lady Wheate lives. She is one of the most celebrated belles in the City. As for Sense, her conduct has shewn her not overstock'd with that. About two years ago she married Sir Jacob Wheate, a british officer between 60 and 70 years old; she herself was not 16. Sir Jacob before he had been married a week, went to the West Indies and there died. He left her an handsome fortune; and it is said she is now soon to marry a Captain Cochran, son to Lord Dundonald, a scotch Nobleman. The author of the aforesaid Satirical poem appears quite enraged in speaking of her.

> If Wheate should live till she be old
> She will not marry then for gold
> When Nature took such special care
> To form her so divinely fair
> She gave her not those matchless charms
> To bless a dotard's gouty arms.
> "A title, and a vast Estate
> May purchase love, and conquer hate."
> The person may be bought I own
> But barter'd love was never known.
> The girl that weds for money's sake
> A titled fool a batter'd rake
> Deserves as much a bad renown
> As any woman of the town.

This is carrying the matter too far: though I cant say I admire any person who makes fortune the only object in marriage. Miss S. Smith was with Lady Wheate, and has spent about a week at Content. I am vastly pleased with this Lady. The contrast between her manners and those of Lady Wheate is highly in her favour, and very striking.

I dined to day in Company with Genl. Greene, at the president's. He arrived in town only a few days since, and he will make but a short stay, here. He is going to settle I am told, in Georgia, where he has a very large landed Estate.

My Paper bids me close, but I take my leave of you only till to-morrow. Mean time I am as ever, your's.   J. Q. Adams

RC (Adams Papers). The text is written on eight small pages, numbered from "33" to "40"; see the descriptive note to JQA to AA2, [12] May, above.

¹ Of 17 July, above.

² Of 3 Aug., below.

³ Gerry's letter of 3 Aug. is in the Adams Papers. JQA's two letters to AA2 were of 25 May, and 17 July, both above; his letter to JA is identified in note 2.

⁴ The word is written over and illegible; JQA wrote "Dined" in his Diary (*Diary*, 1:297).

⁵ On Miss Riché, and on Miss Eccles (under 5 Aug., below), see same, 1:297–298, 299, 300.

⁶ Of Congress, Richard Henry Lee.

⁷ On 30 June, Congress appointed a committee to consider "the letter of June 30 from the Secretary for Foreign Affairs on the letter of June 14 from [*the French chargé*] Barbé Marbois and a memorial from James Le Ray de Chaumont acting for French creditors" (*JCC*, 28:489). This committee was discharged on 7 July, and the matter was referred to the Treasury Board. On 30 July, the Board completed a report on the general issue of financial obligations to French cred-

itors, in response to the memorials of Barbé-Marbois. Concerning Chaumont's memorial, the Board simply referred it to Congress' general decision on the issue of obligations. John Jay presented the Board's report to Congress on 2 August; Congress took no action on Chaumont's memorial. *JCC*, 29:517, 598–606.

[8] St. Paul's Church, on the west side of Broadway between Partition and Vesey streets, a few blocks south of the present City Hall, was built in 1764–1765 (I. N. Phelps Stokes, *The Iconography of Manhattan Island, 1498–1909*, 6 vols., N.Y., 1915–1928, repr. 1967,

1:331, 415–416, and plate 54b). Alexander the Coppersmith was an opponent of the Apostle Paul at Ephesis. He is mentioned in only two verses of Scripture, and nowhere else (2 Timothy 4:14–15, although 1 Timothy 1:19–20, and Acts 19:33, may refer to him).

[9] Mary Alsop was the daughter of the N.Y. merchant John Alsop, a member of the First Continental Congress whom JA had met in New York in Aug. 1774. Mary Alsop married Rufus King in 1786. JA, *Diary and Autobiography*, 2:98, 106; JQA, *Diary*, 1:297, note 2.

John Quincy Adams to John Adams

Dear Sir   New York August 3d. 1785

Mr. Church proposes to embark on board the british Packet, which is to sail to-morrow. He has offered to take my Letters, and I suppose, he will be the bearer of dispatches from Congress.—Our Passage, though it was not a stormy one, was very tedious. Of eight weeks, that we were at Sea, we had at least four of such calm weather as not to proceed more than 8 or 10 leagues a day. As we were coming up the River, we met the other Packet, which was sailing for France. I had only time to write a Line, and inform you of my arrival:[1] I hope she has by this time performed a large part of her voyage, and that three weeks hence, you will receive my Letter. I shall remain here some days longer than I expected, when I left you; as it was too late when I arrived here, for me to be at Boston before Commencement, I thought there was less necessity of my being in haste to go. The President has been polite to me, even beyond what I could have expected; he has given me an apartment in his House, where I have been these ten days. Mr. Jay was so kind before I came here to make me the same offer.

The Politicians here, wait with great impatience to hear from you. Matters seem to be at a Crisis. The British instead of delivering up the Posts, have lately sent there a reinforcement of troops. I have heard from merchants here, that the fur trade from which we are thus precluded, by an open breach of the Treaty of Peace, is worth annually 50,000 pounds Sterling.[2] This may be overrated; but the reluctance the British ⟨shew⟩ to leave the Posts, is sufficient proof that it is an important object. It is supposed that your next Letters, will give information on the Subject, and let us know what is to be depended upon.

The Duties laid on imported goods, by many of the States, and the prohibition of all English vessels in Massachusetts, are another subject of much Conversation. Merchants, who often adopt the proverb, that Charity begins at home, endeavour to demonstrate that the Country will suffer very much, by these regulations. They say that all foreign nations, will be discouraged from bringing us any goods while, they are encumbered with such heavy imposts; and if we go for them ourselves, they will sell them only for money, which we have not. Many of them are still very much afraid of Great Britain: they dread a war; and in case she be not able to carry one on, they tremble lest she should shut her ports upon us and stop our trade with her West India Islands. They ⟨say⟩ own that those Islands cannot subsist without us, but they think we could not hold out, if we had no market to carry our productions to, so long as they could without them. You will easily see that this is the reasoning of a merchant who fears present Losses, and does not consider future advantages. Fortunately the Spirit of the People is different, and I doubt not, in Case Great Britain should persist in her present Conduct, sufficient firmness will be shown, on this side the water. The State of Massachusetts have already prohibited all british vessels to come in their Ports. A frigate appeared since the act was pass'd, but was not suffered to enter.[3]— The States have not yet given to Congress the power of regulating their trade: but it is almost universally considered here, a necessary measure. The President of Congress is however much against it. He has written you by this opportunity, and perhaps he has given you his opinion upon the subject.[4]

You doubtless know before this, that Mr. Bowdoin, was elected governor of Massachusetts, at the last election, in the place of Mr. Hancock, who was chosen Member of Congress for the next Session. The parties shew some rancour and acrimony at the Time, but since the Election, every thing has subsided, and the present governor is very popular. It is generally supposed here; that Mr. Hancock, will next year be seated in the chair of Congress. I don't know however, whether he has accepted the appointment.[5]

Mr. Osgood, Mr. Walter Livingston, and Mr. Arthur Lee, are the Commissioners of the Treasury. Mr. Lee was chosen a few days since: and has accepted. The board could not be composed of persons more universally respected.

Mr. de Marbois it is said will in a short time leave America; and Mr. Otto, formerly, a secretary to the Chevalier de la Luzerne, is to succeed him: I believe he will not regret this Country: nor do I think he will be much regretted himself. The Chevalier is supposed to be much more friendly to the Country, and is much more respected here. Many persons wonder why a Minister is not sent from the Court of France.[6]

After reading this Letter, you will perhaps think I had better be at my Studies, and give you an account of their progress, than say so much upon politics. But while I am in this place I hear of nothing but politics. When I get home I shall trouble my head very little about them. I propose leaving this next monday the 8th. instant and shall certainly be in Boston by the 20th.

I am your dutiful Son.   J. Q. Adams

P.S. Please to present my duty to my dear Mamma: I will write if I can find time.[7]

RC (Adams Papers); docketed by AA2: "JQA August 3d 1785."

[1] JQA to AA, 17 July, above.

[2] The British were obligated to surrender several military posts in the northwest, on and near the Great Lakes, under arts. 2 and 7 of the Definitive Treaty of 3 Sept. 1783, but they continued to occupy them while controversies over the claims of British subjects in American courts (arts. 4 and 5) remained unresolved.

[3] "An Act for the Regulation of Navigation and Commerce," passed on 23 June, provided that as of 1 Aug., all exportation from Massachusetts in British vessels would be prohibited, and all importation in British vessels would be restricted to three ports—Boston, Falmouth (later Portland, Maine), and Dartmouth (including the port of New Bedford)—where such imports would pay higher duties than those on American ships. The ban on exporting on British ships could be lifted by the governor and council if they learned that the British government had rescinded its recent prohibition of American ships from several ports in the British Empire. Mass., *Acts and Laws, 1784–1785*, p. 439–443.

JQA may refer to the British frigate *Mercury*, Capt. Henry Stanhope, which conducted several transport ships from Nova Scotia to Boston to bring live stock back to the large Loyalist refugee populations at Shelburne and Halifax. Both the *Mercury* and the transports did enter the port of Boston in mid-July, but local newspapers sternly warned their readers to reject the British appeal for cargoes as long as they were to be carried away in British vessels. These warnings apparently prevented the loading of the transports. They may also have contributed to a bitter exchange of letters between Capt. Stanhope and Gov. James Bowdoin between 1 and 4 August. See the *Boston Gazette*, 11 and 18 July; the *Independent Ledger*, 11 July; and AA to Thomas Jefferson, 19 Oct., below.

[4] Richard Henry Lee to JA, 1 Aug. (Adams Papers); printed in *The Letters of Richard Henry Lee*, ed. James Curtis Ballagh, N.Y., 1911, 1914, 2:378–381.

[5] Hancock, elected to Congress in June, did accept his election, and he was chosen president of that body in Nov. 1785, but ill health kept him in Boston. In May 1786 he resigned the presidency and his seat in Congress. Burnett, ed., *Letters of Members*, 8:lxxxviii; *Biog. Dir. Cong.*

[6] JQA had met François Barbé-Marbois, then the official secretary to Chevalier Anne César de La Luzerne; Louis Guillaume Otto, La Luzerne's private secretary; and La Luzerne himself in June 1779, when he and JA accompanied the Frenchmen to America on *La Sensible*. La Luzerne served as French minister to the United States until 1783, when he returned to France. Barbé-Marbois continued, as chargé d'affaires, until 1785, when he was appointed intendant of Saint Domingue. JA, *Diary and Autobiography*, 2:380–400; Hoefer, *Nouv. biog. générale*.

[7] JQA next wrote to AA on 6 Oct., below, wherein he explains his tardiness as a correspondent.

John Quincy Adams to Abigail Adams 2d

N:6.

New York August 9th. 1785. Tuesday

Mr. Söderström, the Sweedish Consul, has been here about a fortnight. I went this morning about a mile out of town with him, and was introduced to a Mr. Bayard. He has two Daughters that are among the toasts; one of them I think very pretty. Mr. Bayard I hear was in the late war violent on the wrong side of the Question. It is the case with a great number, of the most reputable families in the place. But those differences are in a way to be forgot, and families of both parties are sociable together.[1]

Dr. Johnson, a delegate from ⟨*Rhode Island*⟩ Connecticut, went out of town a few days ago. Mr. Ellery from Rhode Island lately sprain'd his ancle, and cannot attend Congress, so that there are now only 8 States on the floor:[2] very little or no business can be done, when there are no more present: and therefore this day Congress adjourned till next Monday. It is expected, that before that time, Doctor Johnson will return, and Mr. Ellery will recover. And there is a delegate expected daily from North Carolina; this will make up eleven States. There has not been a fuller representation since the Confederation was form'd.

10th

I dined to day in company with Mr. Paine, the author of common Sense; with Dr. Witherspoon, and Dr. Gordon,[3] who arrived here a few days since.—Wherever I go I hear a repetition of the same questions, how you all do? How you like Europe? What Country you prefer? When you will return? and a hundred other such. I am almost wearied to Death with them, and I sometimes think of writing a list of the Questions with the answers, and whenever a person begins to make any Questions, I would give him the Paper, and so content him at once. I expect the evil will rather increase than diminish, when I get to Boston. But there will be an end to it.

Since my arrival here, Every moment of my time has been taken up, and yet I have had little or nothing to do. I had a great number of Letters, as you know, and have been wholly employ'd in paying visits and going into Company. I have been introduced at different times to almost all the Members of Congress, and to a great number of the Inhabitants of the City. I have every where been treated with a great deal of politeness and complaisance and it has been peculiarly pleasing, because upon many occasions I knew attentions were paid me, for my father's sake. I have spent more time than I expected to when I arrived; several circumstances have detained me, from day to day, but is now high time for me to think seriously of being gone: and of this you may be sure, that if I am in good health, I will not be in New York, after next Monday the 15th. instant.

11th

I have at length been over to Long-Island, and paid my visit to Madam de Marbois. I ought to have done it long before now: for I don't know any place where People are more attach'd to a certain etiquette, (that of visiting) than here. Madam, is a spruce, pretty, little woman; and speaks french very well. There was a very sumptuous entertainment to day at Genl. Knox's. Near thirty persons present.[4] I there saw the Baron de Steuben for the first time: he lives at a Country seat near the City, which he calls his *Louvre. What a name, for a Republican! Such a trifling incident sometimes discovers the real sentiments of a man, more than important actions.* However we must never form an opinion rashly upon any subject.

12th

I am much at a loss how to go from here. If I go by water, I shall lose an opportunity of seeing the Country; and probably another will not present itself for many years; if ever. If I go by the stage, it is so close, a carriage, and goes I am told so fast, that I shall have little opportunity of seeing any part of the Country I shall go through: and it is an expensive way of travelling.[5] I have been advised to buy an horse, and go in that manner: I am told that I may sell him when I get to Boston, near as much if not quite, what one will cost me here: and go in that way at least as cheap as I go in the Stage. But then I am exposed to twenty chances, and am not sure of selling him, if I should get safe home. I am quite in a dilemma: and much in want of advice: I have been looking at several horses: and have found only one, that would be proper: he belongs to the Dutch Minister: but he asks 50 £ this currency for him. This sum frightens me, and I believe I must after all go in the Stage, next Monday.

13th

Mr. Chaumont left Town this afternoon, and will wait for me to morrow, at a place 10 miles distant from the City, for I have at length determined, for the sake of going with him, to buy the horse as Mr. van Berkel has agreed to take 45 £ for him. Mr. Chaumont goes in a Chaise, with two horses. I shall ride, alternately in the Chaise with him and on my own horse, and I hope in ten days time to be at Boston.

The president is in a very ill state of health; and his present Situation, is certainly not the thing for recovering it. He intended to sail down to day to Sandy Hook, and try if the Sea air, would not be serviceable to him. But he found himself so unwell this morning that he could not go. Why is it the lot of great men to call with justice their lives a long disease? And why cannot one person be blest, with health of body, and strength of mind?

14th. Hall's tavern[6] 10 miles from New York

This afternoon I came here, and found Mr. Chaumont waiting for me; to-morrow we shall proceed on our journey. I am afraid our Parents will think this is an imprudent, headless scheme of mine, and I now almost wish I had either gone by water or by the Stage to Boston. But I chuse they should know every thing I have done. I may commit faults, but I will not add to them, by concealing them.

This is one of the most elegant tavern's I know of. I have never seen any in England superior to it. It is a very large house situated upon a small hill, and commands a most beautiful prospect. Parties of Company often come from the City, to spend a day here: and the master of the house owns the stage that goes to Boston. To morrow we are told we shall have bad roads: those from N. York here are very good.

15th. Rye

We have been able to come only 22 miles to day. The roads have been very bad, and this is the hottest day, we have had since I arrived. We are here but 5 miles distant from the rivulet which seperates the States of N. York and Connecticut. So that I shall be to morrow, in the midst of the yankee Country.—This State you know, formerly was settled by the Dutch. It seems as if that people, had a mortal aversion, to every piece of ground that was not a bog. Their settlements on the coast of Africa, are all low lands like their own Country. Their islands in the West Indies, lie almost all of them level with the water or very near it. And in this State, which belonged to them, the lands are very low. They are however in general very good, and their produce is for the most part, the same, with that in the New England States. The

253

crops this year are uncommonly fine; all, except those of indian corn, which has not had rain, enough. This may be of great advantage to us, if the drowth in Europe continued after I sail'd.

16th. Norwalk. Connecticut

We are now only 54 miles from New York. The Sun, has been still more powerful to day than it was yesterday, and we have rode only 21 miles. We are absolutely necessitated to lay by 5 or 6 hours, in the middle of the day, and can only ride mornings and evenings.—I can perceive a great alteration in the manners of the People already. There is a bluntness, and an assurance here, which does not exist in the State of New York. The manners of the People there are much more similar, to those of the Europeans. Their ancient form of government, was not so free as those of New England. Their extensive manors, which descended by law entirely to eldest sons, promoted an aristocratic spirit, which was very contrary to Liberty. The Legislature of the State are so fully sensible of this that they have pass'd laws, permitting the Proprietors of the manors, to dispose of them as they please, and divide them in as many parts as they please. This will probably have an excellent effect, but the People have not yet acquired that Republican Confidence, which wise Laws, and a longer enjoyment of their Liberty, may inspire them with, and which the inhabitants of N. England possess in an high degree.

18th. New-Haven

I could not write a word yesterday, because, in order to get here, we rode till almost midnight; for this is 38. miles from Norwalk, and that, with this weather, and these roads, and the same horses, is a very long days journey. This is one of the Capitals of Connecticut, and was about 18 months ago made a City: five towns, Hartford, New-Haven, New London, Norwich, and Middleton, were form'd into Corporations, so that this State has five Cities, while poor Massachusetts has not one, for there they could not form a corporation even at Boston.—I had a number of Letters for this place, and among the rest, those of Mr. Jarvis for his Lady, and for Mr. Broome.[7] I have deliver'd them, and Mr. Broome, has been polite beyond my expectation. But unfortunately I shall not be able to see Mrs. Jarvis, who is now at Huntington on Long Island, and will not be here in less than a month's time. Mr. Broome lives in a charming situation. His house is on an hill, directly opposite the harbour, and the tide comes up within 20 rods of it. Mr. Platt lives a few doors from him on the same hill, and with the same prospect. I have met with my friend Brush[8] here too. He sail'd from Marseilles a few days before I did from l'Orient, and had a much longer passage. He has been here about a fortnight. It is said he is an admirer of Miss Betsey Broome; I wonder at it much, if it is true, for their characters appear to me to be very dissimilar. He is full of vivacity, and life, and she seems to be as phlegmatic, and cool, as a Dutchman. He is quite sociable, and from her, it is with the utmost difficulty you can draw from her the assenting particles yes and no. But when she goes so far as to say "that is true," and "it is so," it is quite a miracle. Do not think this a precipitate judgment. I own I cannot be myself a competent judge, as I never saw her before to day: but this is her reputation every where: and Brush himself has given me nearly this Character of her. You know Mr. Broome has two twin sons. Yesterday, they were both of them taken ill together, and were so, all night: to day they are both much better: this is a very singular circumstance, and it has already happened once before. We dined at Mr. Broome's to day, and were going in the afternoon, about 2 miles out of town to view a Cave famous for having served as a shelter for two of Charles the 1sts. Judges.[9] But a thunder shower prevented our going. It was a most tremendous one, while it lasted, which was not more than half an hour. We had some as heavy claps as any I remember ever to have heard and the lightning fell once in the water about 30 rods from Mr. Broome's door.

19th

I this morning paid a visit to Mr. Stiles the President of the College here.[10] He was very civil, and shew me all the curiosities belonging to the University. The library is neither as large nor as elegant, as your Pappa's, and the natural curiosities, as well as artificial are but few. There are however a number of stones found in the Country, which would not disgrace an European Cabinet. They were more interesting to me, on account of their belonging, to the natural history of my own Country.

To morrow morning we shall again set out to proceed on our journey, and Mr. Broome and Mr. Brush will go with us as far as Hartford. I am very impatient to get home to Boston: both because I wish to see my friends there; and because I expect to find letters there from you. I shall continue my relation as I have done till now; although I very much fear it will look dull and insipid to you. Your Candour is all on which I depend. Your Brother.   J. Q. Adams

RC (Adams Papers). The text is written on eight small pages, numbered from "41" to "48"; see JQA to AA2, [12] May, descriptive note, above.

[1] Although JQA had not previously met William Bayard, he knew Bayard's brother-in-law and business partner, Herman Le Roy, from his stay in Holland in 1781 (vol. 4:148, note 1; JQA, *Diary*, 1:57, and note 5). In his Diary at this point JQA laments the fact that "the connections of almost all the finest girls in and about N. York, were of the british party during the late war" (*Diary*, 1:300).

[2] The states lacking two or more delegates in attendance in most of Aug. 1785 were Connecticut, Delaware, New Jersey, North Carolina, and Rhode Island (Burnett, ed., *Letters of Members*, 8:lxxxiii–xcviii, and table on p. xcix). Just under thirty congressmen attended sessions sometime in late July–early August, and JQA met most of them; see his Diary and references in this and previous letters to AA2.

[3] Both Thomas Paine and Rev. John Witherspoon, president of the College of New Jersey (Princeton) from 1768 to his death in 1794, and a congressman, 1776–1782, were new acquaintances for JQA. He had probably met Rev. William Gordon of Jamaica Plain, Mass., in Braintree in 1775 (JQA, *Diary*, 1:301; vol. 1:229, descriptive note; *DAB*; *DNB*).

[4] In his Diary, JQA records the presence of "a number of delegates, and the president of Congress, the Dutch, Spanish, and French Ministers &c." (*Diary*, 1:303).

[5] On 13 Aug., Rev. William Gordon wrote to JA (Adams Papers) that he had persuaded JQA to travel to Boston with him, by water to Newport and then Providence, R.I., but JQA's text immediately below suggests that he rejected the water route on 12 August.

[6] Probably either in northern Manhattan or in the Bronx, just across the Harlem River from Manhattan (see Stephen Jenkins, *Old Boston Post Road*, N.Y., 1913, chap. 5).

[7] Samuel Broome, father of Amelia Broome Jarvis (Mrs. James Jarvis), had been a business partner of Jeremiah Platt, and of Eliphalet Brush, both mentioned below (JQA, *Diary*, 1:307, notes 1 and 2).

[8] JQA had met the N.Y. merchant Eliphalet Brush on 10 June 1781, in Amsterdam (same, 1:76, and note 1).

[9] William Goffe and Edward Whalley, two signers of Charles I's death warrant, had fled to Boston at Charles II's restoration, and lived in a cave near New Haven in the summer of 1661, before settling in Hadley, Mass. (same, 1:307, note 3).

[10] Ezra Stiles, president of Yale College, 1778–1795. In his Diary for this day, JQA notes that Thomas Jefferson once told him that he thought Stiles "an uncommon instance of the deepest learning without a spark of genius" (same, 1:307–308).

Cotton Tufts to John Adams
With Enclosed Account

Dear Sir   Weymouth Aug. 10. 1785

The Want of a sufficient Power in Congress to regulate the national Concerns of the United States is now pretty generally seen and has been severely felt. In the opening of the last Session of the Gen Court, the Governor in his Address to both Houses among other Things laments that Congress had not been authorized to regulate their foreign Trade, and suggests the Necessity of further Powers being given to that Body. The Legislature took the Matter into Consideration and prepared Letters to the several States, to the President of Congress and to their own Delegates proposing a Convention for the purpose of revising the Confederation and of curing the Evils felt and apprehended. But untill that could be effected, Measures were adopted and Laws enacted to prevent the Excess of Importations and to counteract the operation of those Laws of Great Britain which more immediately affect our Commerce—as You will find by the enclosed Papers.[1]

I have enclosed an Account of the Transaction of your Affairs to the 21st. Ultimo which Mr. Cranch has examined.

Master Charles has entered College. Mr. John has arriv'd at New York. I expect him dayly. In a few Days I shall probably draw upon You for £50 or 100£ as I apprehend the encreasing Expence of the Education of Your Children will make it necessary. I wish You equal Success at London, as heretofore at the Hague, And Am with sincere Regard Yours   Cotton Tufts

P.S. I shall write more fully to Mrs. Adams upon Your domestic Concerns.[2]

ENCLOSURE

THE HONBLE. JOHN ADAMS ESQ. TO COTTON TUFTS AS HIS ATTORNEY

Dr.

1784.	June.	24. To Cash pd. Nath. Austin 19/6	
	July.	1. To Nath. Willis 30/9	.2.10. 3
	July.	21. To 1/2 m. Nails 4/	
	Aug.	11. To Cash pd. Jno. Gill 24/	
		1/2 qe Paper 9d	.1. 8. 9
	Sept.	29. To Thos. Russell Esq for 16 years	
		Rent of Verchilds Land	38. 8. 0
		To Elkh. Thayer for ditching 30/	
		pd for Glass & Putty 9/	.1.19. 0
	Octob.	6. To Saml. Eliot for Cloathing for	
		yr. children	.2. 6. 1
		To half a Day at Braintree in	
		adjusting Accounts &c	.0. 6. 0
		28. To Revd. Jno. Shaw 40/ To Sundry	
		Persons by ordr. of Mrs. Adams 72/	.5.12. 0
	Nov.	18. To Revd. Jno. Shaw 60/ To Jona.	
		Marsh for a pr. Boots to	
		Charles 27/	.4. 7. 0
		To 1/2 Day at Boston 7/6	

		28.	To	1/2 Day at Braintree 6/ 0.13. 6
Dec.	10.	To	Cash pd. for recordg. Will. Adams Deed
				2/6 for Searchg Records of 2 1/2 . . . 0. 3. 8 1/2
		14.	To	Do. paid David Bass for Salt Marsh
				bought of him 32.16. 3
			To	1 Day at Braintree settling the
				Survey Purchase &c 0.12. 0
		16.	To	Cash pd. for recordg Deed 3/ 0. 3. 0
1785	Jany.	8.	To	1 Day myself & Horse 12/ To Cash
				pd. James Thayer for Land £60 . . . 60.12. 0
		17.	To	Cash pd. for Cloathing for Mast.
				Charles & Thos. 4.11. 2
		27.	To	Revd. Jno. Shaw £6. To
				recordg James Thayers Deed 2/6 . . . 6. 2. 6
	March	3.	To	pd for a Singing Book 6/
				Wards Grammar 3/ for Thos 0. 9. 0
		17.	To	Revd. Jno. Shaw £10.16.0
		23.	To	1/2 Day at Braintree 6/ 11. 2. 0
			To	pd for 2 Crevats 8/2
		24.	To	1/2 Dy. at Boston 7/6 . . . . 0.15. 8
		29.	To	Gayus Thayer for Your own and
				Farm Rates 10.12. 4 1/2
	April	9.	To	Andw. Newell 8.3.0. To part of
				a Day at Boston 7/6 . . . . 8.10. 6
			To	Cash pd. Elias Burdett in Advance
				for Building 62. 0. 0
		11.	To	a Journey to Medford to give
				Lease for Medford Farm &c 0.12. 0
		21.	To	Revd. Jno. Shaw 90/
	May	13.	To	part Journey to Boston 6/ 4.16. 0
		26.	To	Cash for 1 pc. Linnen for
				Children 84/
		30.	To	Davd. Marsh's Bill for Shoes 57/4 . . 7. 1. 4
		30.	To	Revd. Jno. Shaw 71/10
	June	1 & 2d.	To	Mrs. Shaw to purchase
				Cloathg. 8.4.0 . . . . 11.15.10
		16.	To	Revd. Jno. Shaw Quarty
				Bill 14.8.0 To Register
				1/ 2 1/2 To Phoebe 8/ 14.17. 2 1/2
	July.	2.	To.	Ebenz. Burdett in full for
				Building as Pr. Agreement 62. 0. 0

5. To Thos. Russell Esq 1 Yrs. Rent
for Verchilds Land 48/ 2. 8. 0

6. To Willm. Homer for Repairs of
House at Boston 4.10. 6

19 & 20. To Cash for Charles a Hat and
Cravats 3. 1. 4 1/2

£367. 3. 0

1785. July 21. To Cash now on hand to Ballance   4.16.11 1/2

£371.19.11 1/2

Cr.

1784

June 16. By a Ballance of Cash left in
my Hands by Mrs. Adams 7.13. 4

28. By Cash recd. of Mrs. Smith left
in her Hands by Do. 1. 6. 8

By Do. recd. of the Executors of
Revd. Willm. Smiths Will 15. 0. 0

Sept. 16. By Do. recd. of Andw. Newall 1 qr.
Rent 15. 0. 0

Octob. 8. By Do. recd. of Matthew Pratt for
Yoke of Oxen 9. 0. 0

22. By Do. recd. of Phoebe 36/2

Nov. 18. Andw. Newall 1 qr. Rent 15£ 16.16. 2

23. By Do. recd. of Matthew Pratt for
Farm Produce 11. 0. 0

Dec. 15. By Do. recd. of Alexr. Hill on
Ballance of Acctts. 3. 0. 7

1785. Jany. 6. By Do. recd. of Benj. Guilds in
full of his Note 103. 5. 0

10. By do. recd. in part for Certificates
for Intt. on Continl Notes 8. 2. 0

14. By Do. recd. of Phoebe 12/10

March 24. By Thos. Pratt on Acct. 16/6 . . . . 1. 9. 4

Jany. 1. By my Bill of Exchange in favour
of James Elworthy for £50 stg.
5 P. Ct. above par is 52.10.0—
Lawful Money 70. 0. 0

March 24. By Cash recd. of Matthew Pratt.
Ballance of Farm Acctts. 22. 2. 9

By Do. recd. of Royall Tyler Esq
for Debts collected 29. 3. 9 1/2

259

April	9. By Do. recd. of Andw. Newall
	1 qr. Rent . . . . 15. o. o
May	Do. recd. of Mrs. Otis for Dorset
	Alley 1 Yr. . . . . 1.16. o
June	4. By my Order in favour of James
	Elworthy for £11. 12. o sterg
	Exchange 6 P. Ct.–in Law My. . . . 16. 8. o
	16. By Andw. Newall 1 qr Rent to
	the 30 Apr. last . . . . 15. o. o
July	1. By Cash recd. for Interest . . . . 1. 5. o
	4. By Do. recd. of Matthew Pratt
	on Farm Acct. 9.11. 4

371.19.11 1/2

Weymouth July 4. 1785
    Errors Excepted Per Cotton Tufts

Weym[outh]: July 21st. 1785. At the Request of the Honble. Cotton Tufts Esq. I have particularly gone over and examined the foregoing Account, and find it right cast and properly Vouched in all its Parts.
    Richard Cranch

RC (Adams Papers), with enclosed account. Letter endorsed: "Dr Tufts August"; account endorsed: "Dr Tufts's Account 1785."

[1] Gov. James Bowdoin's address, delivered on 31 May, was published in the *Independent Chronicle*, 2 June, in the *Boston Gazette*, 6 June, and in the *Continental Journal*, 9 June. A list of all laws passed in the May-July ses-

sion appeared in the *Independent Chronicle*, 7 July. See also JQA to JA, 3 Aug., note 3, above.
    [2] Cotton Tufts' next extant letters to AA are dated 12 and 14 Oct., both below.

Abigail Adams to John Quincy Adams

London
My dear son   August 11th. 1785 Grosvenor Square

I went from my own little writing room below stairs just now into your Pappas; where Mr. Storer was writing for him. Col. Smith having set of upon a Tour in order to see the Prussian Review which takes place upon the 20 of this Month,[1] Mr. Storer whilst he remains here; has offerd to supply his Place. Upon my going into the room he told me that a vessel would sail for Boston tomorrow, which is the first I knew of the Matter. Lyde is expected to sail in a few days and by him I design to forward Letters to my Friends, but tho as usual I have several partly written none are compleat. I however told Mr. Storer that I would take my pen and write you a few lines, just to tell you that we are all well and are now quite settled, that we wait with impatience to hear from you. Mr. Short came here last week from Paris upon Buisness, he sets of tomorrow for the Hague. Mr. Jefferson Col. Humphries Mr. Williamos &c. are all well. Mr. W is waiting as usual for the moveing of the waters.[2] If you get the English news papers you will think that the Father of Liars is turnd Printer. Not a paper which has not some venom. I hope the Scripture Benidiction will be fullfilld upon those who are falsly accused and persecuted.[3] They however do not often attack us personally, only as the Representitive of America &c. I was not displeased with one paragraph provided it would have a proper effect upon our Country. It was this "the American minister has not yet paid his Way, that is given a diaplomatick dinner to the Ministers, because Congress Paper will not pass here." If it was expensive living in France, it is much more so in London, but I trust our Country will either consider us, or permit us to return.

The King of France has publishd an Arret prohibiting British Manufactories under severe penalties, in concequence of which 8 thousand Gauze and Muslin looms have stoped working here.[4] I will inclose to you two or 3 News papers.

Captain Lyde will take Letters. The contents of *some of them*, you will be surprizd at, but, at the same time you will approve the wise conduct of the writer who has shewn a firmness of mind and prudence which do *her* honour. Be Silent! We are all rejoiced because it came of her own accord free and unsolicited from her, and was the result I believe of many Months anxiety as you were witness.[5]

Remember me to all my Friends your Brothers in particular. I have not time to add an other line. I do not know whether your sister writ[es] by this vessel to you.[6] Let me hear from you by every opport[unity.] I have given Mr. Storer a Letter from Mr. Murray for you.[7] M[r.] and Mrs. Temple sail next week for New York. Tis near four and I must dress for dinner. Once more adieu. Your sister and I miss you much. We want you to walk and ride with us, but we know and hope you are much more usefully employd. I am going with your sister this afternoon to Hamstead to drink tea with Mrs. Hay, who resides out there. I shall call and take Mrs. Rogers to accompany us. We all went last week to accompany Mr. Short to the Hay Market,[8] but who can realish the English after having been accustomed to the French Stage? A Siddons may reconcile me to it, but I believe nothing else will.

I never know when to leave of, once more adieu and beliee me most tenderly Yours.   A A

RC (Adams Papers); addressed by Charles Storer: "Mr. John Quincy Adams"; endorsed: "Mamma Augt. 11th. 1785"; docketed: "My Mother 11. Augt. 1785," and "Mrs. Adams. Augt. 11. 1785." Some loss of text where the seal was torn away.

¹ See AA to William Stephens Smith, 13 Aug., below.
² See Charles Williamos to AA, 21 July, note 2, above.
³ Matthew 5:10–12.
⁴ Louis XVI issued this edict in council on 10 July to pressure the British ministry to conclude a treaty of commerce, as provided for in the art. 18 of the Anglo-French Treaty of Versailles of 1783. The two countries did conclude a new commercial treaty in 1786. JA to John Jay, 10 Aug., PCC, No. 84, V, f. 601–604, printed in *Dipl. Corr., 1783–1789*, 2:428–430; *Cambridge Modern Hist.*, 8:284–286.

⁵ See AA2 to Royall Tyler, [*ca. 11 Aug.*]; AA to Mary Cranch, 15 Aug.; and AA to Cotton Tufts, 18 Aug., all below.
⁶ AA2 sent JQA her journal letter of 4 July, above, by this ship; see her last dated entry, of 11 Aug., in that letter.
⁷ William Vans Murray to JQA, 2 Aug. (Adams Papers).
⁸ The Haymarket Theatre, sometimes called "The Little Theatre in the Haymarket," was built on the east side of Haymarket Street, between Pall Mall and Coventry Street, in 1721 (Wheatley, *London Past and Present*).

Abigail Adams 2d to Royall Tyler

Sir   [*ca. 11 August 1785*]¹

Herewith you receive your letters and miniature with my desire that you would return mine to my Uncle Cranch, and my hopes that you are well satisfied with the affair as is   A. A.

MS not found. Printed from *Grandmother Tyler's Book*, p. 76. No other versions of the letter survive, nor is there any evidence to show whether the text is complete.

¹ The date is suggested by AA to JQA, 11 Aug., above. See also AA to Mary Cranch, 15 Aug., and notes 3–7, and AA to Cotton Tufts, 18 Aug., both below.

Abigail Adams to Thomas Jefferson

Grosvenor Square London
Dear sir   August 12 1785

I would not omit so good an opportunity as presents by Mr. Short,¹ of continuing the correspondence which you have done me the honour to Say you consider as settled.

Your obliging favours of june 21 and july 7th were punctually deliverd, and afforded me much pleasure.

Were you to come to this Country, as I sincerely hope you will, for the sake of your American Friends² who would rejoice to see you; as a Husbandman you would be delighted with the rich verdure of the field, and the high cultivation of the Lands. In the Manufactory of many articles, the Country can boast a superiority over their Galician Neighbours. But when you come to consider the Man, and the social affections; ease, civility, and politeness of Manners, this people suffer by the comparison. They are more contracted and narrow in their sentiments notwithstanding their boasted liberality and will not allow their Neighbours half the Merrit, they really deserve. They affect to despise the French, and to hate the Americans, of the latter they are very liberal in their proofs. So great is their pride that they cannot endure to view us as independant, and they fear our growing greatness.

The late Arrets of his most Christian Majesty[3] have given the allarm here. They term them Calamitous, and say they will essentially affect their trade. If Ireland refuses the propositions[4] with steadiness, and firmness, England may be led to think more justly of America. If a person was to indulge the feelings of a moment, the infamous falshoods, which are daily retailed here against America, would prompt one to curse and quit them, but a statesman would be ill qualified for his station, if he feared the sarcasm of the sarcastic, the envy of the envious, the insults of the insolent or the malice of the dissapointed, or sufferd private resentment to influence his publick Conduct. You will not I dare say envy a situation thus circumstanced, where success is very dubious, and surrounded with so many difficulties. It is rather mortifying too, that Congress appear so inattentive to the situation of their Ministers. Mr. A has not received any letters of any concequence since the arrival of Col. Smith, nor any answers to the lengthy Letters he has written. Mr. Short informs us that you are in the same situation. What can have become of the said Mr. Lamb mentiond by Mr. Jay? Is he gone with all his papers directly to the Barbary Powers? I suspect it, but Mr. A will not think so.[5]

I fear Mr. Short will not have a very favourable opinion of England. Unfortunately Col. Smith set off, upon a tour a few days after his arrival, and Mr. Short having but few acquaintance will not find himself highly gratified; we have accompanied him once to the Theater, but after having been accustomed to those of France, one can have little realish for the cold, heavy action, and uncouth appearence of the English stage.[6] This would be considerd as treason of a very black dye, but I speak as an American. I know not how a Siddons may reconcile me to English action, but as yet I have seen nothing that equals Parissian ease, and grace. I should like to visit France once a year during my residence in Europe.

The English papers asscribe the late disturbances in the provinces of France, to the example set by the Rebellious Americans, as well as every failure of their own Merchants and Manufact[urer]s[7] to the *Ruinous* American trade, tho prehaps two thirds of them never had any intercourse with America. O! for the energy of an absolute government, aya and for the power too. How many Letters de cachet have these abusive Beings deserved?[8]

The cask of wine you mentiond in your Letter, Mr. Adams request you to take if agreeable to you. He has written to Mr. Garvey with respect to that which is under his care.[9] As to the House rent which you mentiond, neither you or Mr. Adams can do yourselves justice unless you charge it, and Mr. A is fully determined to do it. There is an other heavy expence which I think he ought to Charge this Year.[10] These are the Court *taxes*. Being considerd as minister in Holland, the servants applied for their perquisites which was allowd them by Mr. Lotter, tho realy without Mr. Adams's knowledge or direction. At Versailles he went through the same ceremony, and when he came to this Court all the servants and attendants from St. James came very methodically with their Books, upon which both the Names of the Ministers and the sums given were Specified. Upon the New Years day this is again to be repeated: and the sum this year will amount to not less than a hundred pounds, which will be thought very extravagant I suppose; but how could it be avoided? Our Countrymen have no Idea of the expences of their Ministers, nor of the private applications which they are subject to, many of which cannot be dispenced with. All the prudence and oeconomy I have been able to exercise in the year past, has not enabled me to bring the year about; without falling behind hand. I have no objection to returning to America, but I have many, against living here at a greater expence than what our allowence is: because we have 3 children in America to Educate, whose expences must be, and have been borne by our private income which for 12 years past has been diminishing by Mr. Adams's continued application to publick buisness: these are considerations Sir which some times distress me. As I know you are a fellow sufferer you will excuse my mentioning them to you.

You were so kind sir as to tell me you would execute any little commission for me, and I now take the Liberty[11] of requesting you to let Petit[12] go to my Paris shoemaker and direct him to make me four pair of silk shoes, 2 pr sattin and two pr fall silk; I send by Mr. Short the money for them. I am not curious about the colour, only that they be fashonable.[13] I cannot get any made here to suit me, at least I have faild in several attempts. Col. Smith proposes visiting

Paris before he returns, and will be so good as to take Charge of them for me. An other article or two I have to add, a Glass for the middle of the table. I forget the French name for it. I think they are usually in 3 peices. If you will be so good as to procure it for me and have it put into a small Box well pack'd and addrest to Mr. Adams; Col. Smith will also have the goodness to take care of it for me; and to pay you for it: I do not know the cost, as we had one at Auteuil, which belongd to the House. I have to add four *Godships*,[14] these are so saleable in Paris that I think they are to be had for Six livres a peice, but should they be double that price it cannot be thought much of for deitys. Apollo I hold in the first rank as the Patron of Musick Poetry and the Sciencies. Hercules is the next in my favour on account of the numerous exploits and enterprizing Spirit. If he is not to be had, I will take Mercury as he is said to be the inventer of Letters, and God of eloquence. I have no aversion to Cupid, but as I mean to import them through the Hands of a Young Gentleman, one should be cautious of arming persons with powers: for the use of which they cannot be answerable; there cannot however be any objection to his accompanying Madam Minerva and Diana, Ladies whose company and example are much wanted in this city. If you have any command to execute here you will do ⟨*me*⟩ a favour by honouring with them Your obliged Humble Servant   A. Adams

RC (DLC:C. W. F. Dumas Papers). Dft (Adams Papers); the Dft is incomplete.

[1] Because William Short traveled to The Hague before returning to Paris, Jefferson did not receive this letter until 23 Sept. (Jefferson to AA, 25 Sept., below).

[2] The draft has "Friend."

[3] See AA to JQA, 11 Aug., note 4, above.

[4] See AA2 to JQA, 4 July, and note 31, above.

[5] On 11 March, John Jay had entrusted four commissions, directing JA, Franklin, and Jefferson to negotiate treaties with Algiers, Morocco, Tripoli, and Tunis, to Capt. John Lamb, a mariner and merchant from Norwich, Conn. Jay referred to these documents in his letter to the three commissioners of the same date, and suggested that they appoint Lamb, who had offered his services for this task in February, to negotiate with the Barbary powers, under their direction (Jefferson, *Papers*, 8:19–22). Jay also briefly mentioned Lamb in his letter of 13 April to JA (*Dipl. Corr., 1783–1789*, 1:480–483). All these documents are in the Adams Papers. On John Lamb and negotiations with the Barbary

states, see AA to Cotton Tufts, 18 Aug., below; JA, *Diary and Autobiography*, 3:182, note 2; and Burnett, ed., *Letters of Members*, 8:72–73, 250–251.

[6] The draft adds: "Indeed most of the Ammusments of this Metropolis are closed, for the Season."

[7] This word, barely legible, appears to have been corrected from "Manufactories." The draft has "Manufactory."

[8] Jefferson had given ironic praise to the energy of absolute government in his letters of 21 June and 7 July, above.

[9] See Jefferson to AA, 21 June, and note 7, above; and JA to Anthony Garvey, 16 July (LbC, Adams Papers).

[10] In her draft, AA adds here: "I wish you would give me your opinion of it." Also in the draft, AA calls these "Court *taxes*," "Etraines," as she had earlier in writing of them; see AA to Cotton Tufts, 3 Jan., and enclosure, above.

[11] The draft has "liberty to send by Mr. Short a Louis requesting . . ."

[12]Adrian Petit had served the Adamses at

Auteuil, and after their departure for London in May, he helped Jefferson handle the disposal of the wine JA had bought. At some point between May and September he entered Jefferson's service. See Jefferson, *Papers*.

¹³ The draft adds: "they are all for me, and the whole four pair will not cost me more than one pair here." In the draft, AA does not say anything about her failure to find shoes that suited her in London.

¹⁴ The draft ends here, at the bottom of a page; the remainder is missing. Jefferson discusses the "four *Godships*" in his reply of 25 Sept., below.

Abigail Adams to William Stephens Smith

London, Grosvenor Square,

Dear Sir   August 13, 1785

Your letter from Harwich, dated August 10,[1] reached us upon the 11th. We were very glad to hear of your arrival there, and continue to follow you with our good wishes.

When you tendered me your services, and asked my commands, I did not know you had any thoughts of returning by the way of Paris; otherwise I should have charged you with a few. I now write by Mr. Short, requesting your care of an article or two which Mr. Jefferson will be so good as to procure for me.[2]

Nothing new in the political world has taken place since you left us, but a fresh report by way of Minorca, that the Algerines had, upon the 13th[3] of July, declared war against America. This I suppose is circulated now, in order to raise the insurance upon the few American vessels ready to sail. The report says that twelve of their ships are ordered to cruise in the Mediteranean for ours;[4] but it will probably be so long before this letter will reach you, that what is news now, will not be so then.

I have taken the liberty, sir, of requesting Mr. Jefferson to introduce you to two gentlemen and ladies; the first of the gentlemen is much esteemed in the world, for his patronage of the sciences, and for his knowledge and skill in music and poetry; and the other for his notable exploits and heroism. One of the ladies is of a very ancient and noble family; she is eminent for her wisdom, and exceedingly fond of all those in whom she discovers a genius, and a taste for knowledge; the other is a single lady, remarkable for her delicacy and modesty.[5] As there is some talk of their coming to London, they may possibly accompany you here. There will be no difficulty on account of the language, as they speak one as perfectly as they do the other.

I had some idea of mentioning a young gentleman[6] of my acquaintance, whose manners are very insinuating, but as he does not always conduct himself with the prudence I could wish, and is very fond of becoming intimate, his company sometimes proves dangerous; but Mr. Jefferson, who knows them all, I presume, will use his judgment, and upon that you may safely rely.

I hope you will not travel so rapidly as to omit your journal, for I promise myself much entertainment from it upon your return. I presume that the family would join me in their regards to you, if they knew that I was writing; you will, from the knowledge you have of them, believe them your well wishers and friends, as well as your humble servant,[7] A. Adams

RC not found. Printed from AA2, *Jour. and Corr.*, 1:119–121. Dft (Adams Papers); notation on last page by AA2: "To Co Smith"; and by CFA on the first page: "To Col Smith." The editors have favored the printed text over the Dft here on the supposition that it is based on the RC, which passed from William Stephens Smith to his and AA2's daughter, Caroline de Windt, who published it along with various other letters by and to AA2. A few variants in the Dft are noted below.

[1] Not found. Col. Smith wrote to JA from his lodgings at Leicester Fields on 4 Aug. (Adams Papers), asking permission "to take a small tour on the Continent—a general Review of the Prussian Army takes place the latter end of this or the beginning of the next Month, I should like to see it." On 5 Aug., JA, imagining that Smith would make a fairly brief tour beginning in a month that was "so dull and so disgusting and unwholesome in London" with the city "so deserted by Men of Business as well as others," granted his request (PCC, No. 92, I, f. 19).

The colonel departed London on 9 Aug. for the North Sea port of Harwich to catch the boat for Holland, in company with Francisco Miranda, the South American soldier whom he had met in New York during the war (and whose 1806 abortive military expedition to free South America from Spanish rule Col. Smith would be charged with aiding). Smith carried letters of introduction from JA to C. W. F. Dumas at The Hague, and to Messrs. Willinck and Staphorst at Amsterdam (LbCs, Adams Papers).

Smith and Miranda reached the Netherlands on 11 Aug., and traveled through Rotterdam, The Hague, and Amsterdam into northern Germany, stopping at Minden, Hanover, Brunswick, and Potsdam before reaching Berlin on 31 August. They reviewed Prussian troops and visited garrisons and cultural sites in the Berlin-Potsdam area from 5 to 23 Sept., and then continued their tour through Leipzig, Dresden, and Prague to Vienna, staying in the Austrian capital from 14 to 26 Oct., when Col. Smith finally departed for Paris.

The expansion of his "small tour" delayed Smith's return to London to early December, long after JA expected him, and considerably annoyed the minister, who found himself coping with an extensive correspondence in the fall without a secretary. Col. Smith recorded the better part of his journey, from 11 Aug. to 26 Oct., in great detail; this diary is published, in English, in *Archivo Del General Miranda, Viajes Diaros 1750-1785*, Caracas, 1929, 1:354-434. See Hoefer, *Nouv. biog. générale* (Miranda); *DAB* (Smith).

[2] See AA to Jefferson, 12 Aug., above.

[3] The draft has: "The Eleventh of july."

[4] From this point, the draft reads: "Mr. Short will set out on tuesday, ⟨but as⟩ it is not probable that this Letter will reach you untill you arrive in Paris it will then be so old a date that I should not have written but to have askd your care of my things."

[5] AA refers to the four "*Godships*"—Apollo, Hercules, Minerva (Athena), and Diana (Artemis)—mentioned in her letter to Jefferson of 12 Aug., above.

[6] Cupid; see AA to Jefferson, 12 Aug., above.

[7] This paragraph is not in the draft, which has in its place: "Callihan is arrived from Boston this day, if any thing worth communicating should come to hand when I get my Letters which I am just going to seek it shall be communicated by Sir Your Friend and humble servant."

Mary Smith Cranch to Abigail Adams

My dear Sister   Braintree August 14th. 1785

I have just Sent away one Letter[1] and shall now begin another to be ready for the next ship. Cousin John is not yet arriv'd. I hear of him upon the road. He has not quite done his duty. He should have written to one of his uncles[2] at least as soon as he came on Shore, but I will not chide him without hearing his reasons, I feel inclin'd to be very partial to him.

I have just heard that cousin Charles is not like to have the chamber he petition'd for, nor any other. Half his class will be oblig'd to Board out in the Town. Mr. Cranch and I are going tomorrow to see how it is, and to procure him a place if necessary. The Doctor desires I would take the whole care of providing for him off his Hands, as he is so hurried with business of a publick nature.[3] I will most chearfully do it. You cannot think how sorrowful your son looks about the loss of his chamber, but I hope to make him happy yet. I have got all the Furniture ready, (this is the part he is to find). The Bed and Linnin is found by his chum a very worthy pretty youth, who study'd with him at Mr. Shaws. Walker is his name, he is from Bradford.

17th

Charles is happy he has got his chamber. I return'd last night. I found he had his petition'd granted. He is in the same college with Billy has a Room upon the lower Floor.[4] I have got him a pine Table made to stand under his looking glass. It doubles over like a card Table and is painted Marble colour and looks very well. He has the Square Tea Table to stand in his study. I got a few things for him in Boston as I came from Cambridge, and now I think he is equip'd and will go tomorrow with the best advice I can give him. You may assure your self my dear sister that I shall watch over him with the Parential Eye of tenderness. In sickness and in health He shall be my peculiar care.[5]

[*post 27 August*][6]

Cousin John is come, dear youth, and brought with him in his own Face such a resemblance of His Papa and Mama as I never before saw blended in one. And I am happy to perceive that it is not only in his Person that he bears such a likeness to his Parents. I have already discover'd a strength of mind, a memory, a soundness of judgment which I have seldom seen united in one so young. His modesty is not the least of his virtues. In the Eyes of his cousins, tis of great price. If his applycation is equal to his abilities he cannot fail of makeing a great Man. He will be destitute of his Fathers ambition if ⟨he⟩ it is not. His mothers animated countinance assures me I need not fear a dissapointment.

[ca. 4 September]⁷

Cousin came last week, spent some time in Boston and Cambridge consulting with his uncles and the President about his future studies. He does not understand Greek ⟨*enough*⟩ nor make Latten well enough to be admitted into Billys Class. They all advise him to go to Haverhill and study With his uncle Shaw till April, by which time if he applys himself very closly he may enter. Billy is to spend part of the winter vacancy with him by his uncles desire.

Haverhill Sep: 8th

Here we are my dear sister. Cousin and I arriv'd last night. I came with him that I might have the pleasure of introducing a Nephew I am proud enough off to all the good Folks on the road. I find he is quite a Stranger in his own country. We came thro Cambridge and call'd upon my Sons⁸ there. They were well and I trust very studious and good. We all drank Tea at Mr. Gannetts.⁹ My Fellow traveller and I Lodg'd there. They Would not suffer us to go further. He has given our children an invitation to visit him frequently. Billy is too diffident. He does not accept of the repeated invitations of the Gentleman of the Town to visit them. Tis true he does not need to accept them for the sake of seeing company so much as some others, but it will give him importanc to be notic'd by them. Cousin John has promis'd me he will dispel some of his diffidence when he is fixd there.

Mr. Shaw will take your son and give him all the instruction in his power. We shall return in a few days to prepair for cousins residence here, as soon as possible.

I find Sister Shaw in better health than I have seen her for several years. Little Betsy has had a bad Boil¹⁰ which has reduc'd her to skin and Bone. She is very pale and I think in a poor way. Thomas is ⟨very⟩ well and is a very good child his aunt says. He is made ⟨very⟩ happy by the return of his Brother, Whos living here will be a ⟨very⟩ great advantage to him. They are very fond of each-other.

I thank you my dear sister for your Letter by Cousin and for the present to Betsy and Lucy.[11] They wanted nothing to increase their Love to the best of aunts. Their gratitude must be express'd by all the assistance and every attention they can give their Cousins.

I came thro Boston in my way here and had the pleasure to find a large Pacquit from my dear sister, brought by Capn. Dashwood,[12] and very intertaining I find it. I cannot enough thank you for your kindness in writing so often and so largly to me, and have only to regret that ⟨I fear⟩ I cannot send you any thing that will afford you half the amusement. I have no new scenes to introduce you too nor new dress to inform you off but what your sisterly kindness has help'd me too, unless the disposition of your gauze cap and white Bonnet which we found at the bottom of a Trunk crowded down by half a dozen Blankits Would afford you any. The children brought them home pull'd them to peices and out of them Betsy made a cap for Lucy a Bonnet for me and a Hankercheif for herself. We thought we had better do so and repay you in something or other to the children, than let them lay, and turn yellow till they were useless.

Your account of your Presentation was curious. Mere men and women indeed. I observe but one wise Speech among all that were made you. One would suppose His Majestys Eyes were really open'd to the best interest of his own Nation if he was sincere when he told your Friend that "He was glad the choice of his country had fallen upon him," for sure I am that he has reason to be so. I Wish Mr. Adams may not have the least influence in his own country.[13] I verily think he has more to fear from the envious Spirit of some of us than from any other quarter. It is a mean vice. It will be very hard indeed if He who could so suddenly change the sentiments of a whole People, remarkably slow in their determinations and gain their interest in our Favour, while under the influence of two powerful Nations exerting themselves to the utmost to prevent it,[14] should not have the confidence and warmest gratitude of those who employ him. To me this has always appear'd one of the most wonderful and most important events in our History.

So long as human nature remains as it is you cannot be surpriz'd at the spight of the Torys, but they will not hurt you. I do not wonder you felt dissagreably when presented to a Person who had done all in his Power to humble in the dust the country and people you represent. Your benevolent hearts must have felt more for him than for your selves. There is not another court in Europe Where you could have had such a Triumph. The Countess of Effingham I am greatly pleass'd with, I want to know more of her character. Her Friendly politness to my sister has made me partial to her. Introduce to me all your acquaintance and acquaint me with their characters.

Mr. Thaxter is doing very well here. He is greatly respected by all denominations. He is very attentive to his Business and very puntual. Tis a good sign when a young Gentleman of his profession is almost always excepting while the courts are siting to be found in his office or near it.[15] *Forgive* this Blot.

The Merchants in our seaports are breaking all to peices, three in Salem last week.[16] Jo[seph] Otis last spring and his Brother about three weeks since to the supprize of almost every body. Miss Hannah I hear has secur'd her fortune. He has broke for a very large Sume, and what is dreadful is that he has ruin'd a Mr. Johnson who was bound for him for a large debt due to a Gentleman in England.[17] He has a large Family and is now absent upon a voyage and could secure nothing. Every thing he has in the world is attach'd. The Family are greatly distress'd. I pity Mr. Otis exceedingly. The attack upon him was so sudden that he had not time to Secure any body at any distance. Some people think he can pay every body some that he owes much more than he is worth. I have not seen any of the Family yet. He has much owing to him, but tis suppos'd he will never be able to collect it half, and as to the Estate he has in his hands we well know that when tis known that a man is oblig'd to Sell, the thing offer'd will not bring him half as much as if this circumstance was not known. Harry[18] is more mortified than I think he ought to be. He is in poor Health Spits Blood.

Cousin Johns Trunks are come from Holland. Many of the cloath will do for his Brothers. There are about eight or Ten Shirts some of them will do for himself, others for Charles. They all want a great deal of mending. Cousin Charles sends his Linnin to me to be done up. I chuse he should. I can now see that tis mended when it should be. I hire a Girl to help wash and Iron. I have not been able to do any thing about it this summer. Betsy has been in Boston, and I wish not to put too much upon Lucy. She has been my strength this summer. Betsy Cleaverly left us last spring and John the fall before. I have only Becca and a Boy of nine years old a Brother of Seths and Peters who us'd to live with us.[19]

We have had several Letters from Mr. Perkins since he arriv'd at Kentucka.[20] He had a most dangerous fatigueing Journey. He travelled alone part of the way in constant fear of the Indians who had cut of several Parties but a little before he sat out, and whos mangled Limbs he beheld as he pass'd along. He was one night alone in the woods, without any Shelter but a Blanket. He tied his Horse he says in a green Spot to feed, then wrap'd himself in his Blanket and with two Pistols in his hands sat him ⟨self⟩ down to guard himself and Horse from the wild Beast who were howling around and from the more Savage Indians who were thursting for his Blood. The roads were so deep by reason of great rains which had lately fallen that every Step he took for weeks was up to his Horses knees. He could go but one mile in an hour. For three weeks it thundred lighten'd and rain'd incessantly. In a few days after he set out, he overtook five hundred People in one company, who were going to Kentucka. A great number of them caught the Measles upon the road and tho the Weather was so bad they all did well. His Letter is a curiosity. I will get Betsy to copy it and send you. He is well and in good business.

Aunt Tufts is better but very low. She cannot bear her weight upon her Feet yet if you could see her you would not think She had much to bear neither.[21] I never saw any body much thiner. I wish you would write to her. She think hard of it that you do not.[22] Mr. Cranch is well and still in the Treasurys office, but he has almost got thro with the business, and what he will then do for imployment I know not. He begins to look anxious about it. He thinks of returning to watch work, but he has so long been imploy'd in Publick business that he feels dissagreably, when he thinks of it. Money is very scarce, it [at] present but I do not design to distress my self. Something unforeseen may turn up. We have more than half got thro with Billys college education. He has been a very prudent child has made us as little expence as he could possibly help.

Lincoln Sepr. 14th

We came here last night fatigued almost to death by coming a cross road from Haverhill. We find this Family all well and much grattifyed with their Letters and your kindness to your Neice.[23] She as well as the other children are surprizingly grown. She is a fine girl. Sister is comfortable Supported, and enjoys fine Health. I ask'd cousin John yesterday, whether his Friends answer'd his expectations. He says they have greatly exceeded them. I could not bear to have him dissapointed. If attention will please him he must be pleass'd. He receives it as he ought, it does not puff him up with vanity. He is admir'd every where he goes for his modest behaviour. I want to know what he thinks of us all. He enters into characters with a penetration that astonishes me. If I had anything in my disposition that I wish'd to hide I would not be acquainted with him. He is form'd for a Statesman. I shut him out of the room when I want to work. I can do none when he is in it. I can do nothing but look at him. Tis an expressable pleasure that I feel in tracing the countenance, the air, and manners of my dear Brother and Sister most agreable united in him. I do not wonder you were loth to part with him. I was very sorry he had not receiv'd our Letters[24] before he came. Do send them to him that he may see that we did not promise more than we mean to perform and that we were not unmindful of him when abroad.

Braintree [16] Sepr.[25]

We returnd last evening by the way of Boston. I stay'd but one night at Lincoln. I heard more of Fashons and new dresses while I was there than any where upon my Journey. I was make heartily sick of Folly and flurtation airs. I could learn nothing certain about a relation of ours.[26] She told me some dismal Storys about him. I believe he is strip'd of his Store and every thing he had in it, and for an infamous debt. Poor child I do not love to think of him.

I read part of your Letter to Mrs. Sam. Adams. She was much pleas'd with your descriptions, desir'd me to give her most affectionate regards to you. I thank you my Sister for the importance, you have given me. I find the knowledg of my having a Letter decriptive of your dress and reception at court will introduce me any where. I have been careful who I read it too. I Went to see Mr. and Mrs. Otis. I felt very dissagreably as I approach'd the House, the outside window Shutter of which were all shut up. They live up stairs. The knocker is taken of the Door for what I know not. Mrs. Otis and Betsy were gone out. He look'd out of the chamber window to see whether he might let me in or not. As I had no demands upon him but those of Friendship I was admitted. He looks very pale and dejected. He tells me General Warren, wants to sell his Farm at Milton, that he has offer'd it for Sale, but that he has refus'd two thousand pound which has been offer'd him by a Mr. Furgarson from the southward, and to be paid in Bills of Exchange. Mr. Otis thinks Such a price will never be offer'd him again. I am affraid they are embarress'd. He was sued at the spring court for an English debt of five hundred sterling. I have been talking with the Doctor about geting your debt. He says he knows nothing about it from you. She spoke to me about it the other day, Said she wish'd to pay it in Something or other. The money she could not pay. Doctor Tufts Says as he had no orders nor any papers about it, He does not chuse to take it in any thing but money: but that I may do as I please. I cannot help having fears. She offer'd Linnins but I found I could buy them cheaper else where. If I had not I believe I should have venturd to have taken them and turn'd them into money for you. I wish you would give the Doctor directions what to do about it. She told me they had enough to pay all their debts if they could but Sell any of their places to their minds. This speech alarm'd me.

I design to send this Letter to Boston tomorrow to be put on board the first Ship that Sails. There are several almost ready. Thank you my Sister for my Share of the Sweetmeats.[27] There is one Pot of citron. I shall keep some of that to put into cake for our children at college. I shall take some of your cinnamen to put into cakes for Cousin Charles. They have been so use'd to eat Something between their stated meals that they want a little bit yet. Charles says, you will make me Some, wont you aunt? Yes my dear Boy you shall have your quarter cake as well as your cousin. I have taken Some of the Sugar you left for the purpose. He took Some of it with him for his coffee. They like coffee better than Tea. I gave him a pound ready ground. [John was?][28] last thursday with his cousin at Mr. Fosters. We have got Mr. Foster to let your children dine there, whenever they are not invited else where. Tis the only time our children can see their Papa and uncles.

I hope my last Letter[29] has reach'd you. Remember me most affectionatly to Mr. Adams and be assur'd of the Sincere Love of your Sister   Mary Cranch

You wont complain of short Letters from me I hope.

RC (Adams Papers); endorsed: "Mrs Cranch August 14th. 1785." Dft (MHi:C. P. Cranch Papers); notation in an unknown hand: "Mrs. Cranch to Mrs. Adams Aug. 14. 1785." The Dft is incomplete. Major differences are noted below.

[1] Mary Cranch to AA, 19 July, above.

[2] The draft has "to His uncle Tufts or Mr. Cranch as he was consign'd to them."

[3] Cotton Tufts served as both a state senator and a justice of the peace throughout the 1780s, and he was active in the Massachusetts Medical Society and several other organizations (*Sibley's Harvard Graduates*, 12:497–498).

[4] CA roomed in Hollis Hall, where his cousin William Cranch also had a room. CA's room was in the northeast corner on the ground floor (JQA, *Diary*, 1:316, note 3; Richard Cranch to JA, 13 Oct., Adams Papers).

[5] The draft adds here: "He is much of a gallant I assure you. Not too much so neither—only pleasingly attentive to every Body."

[6] JQA arrived at the Cranches on the evening of 27 Aug. (JQA to AA2, 20 Aug., below; JQA, *Diary*, 1:313–314). The following paragraph could have been written between his arrival and his return to Boston, on 29 Aug.,

or as late as the next paragraph (see note 7).

[7] In the draft the following paragraph begins with the more specific "Cousin came last Saturday week," which roughly dates the passage. JQA conferred with Harvard's president, Joseph Willard, on 31 Aug., and returned to Braintree on 3 Sept. (Saturday). He and Mary Cranch departed for Haverhill on 6 Sept. (JQA to AA2, 29 Aug., below; JQA, *Diary*, 1:317–319).

[8] Mary Cranch evidently refers to CA as well as to her own son, William. In the draft she writes "our Sons."

[9] Caleb Gannet, steward of Harvard College from 1779 to 1818 (see JQA, *Diary*, 2:xi, and index).

[10] The draft has "bad Sore upon her thigh." Elizabeth Quincy Shaw was five.

[11] AA to Mary Cranch, 8 May; to Lucy Cranch, 7 May; and to Elizabeth Cranch, 8 May, and 12 May, all above. The postscript to AA to Lucy Cranch mentions AA's present for the sisters, a large piece of silk.

[12] AA to Mary Cranch, 24 June, above.

[13] AA's account of the Adams' presentation at St. James's Palace is in her 24 June letter to Mary Cranch, above. The closing quotation mark in the previous sentence is supplied from the draft of this letter. Cranch's ambiguous remark about JA's "influence in his own country," is probably a reference to AA's quotation of Scripture (Mark 6:4) in her letter to Elizabeth Cranch, 12 May, above.

[14] Mary Cranch evidently refers here to JA's triumph in persuading the Dutch to recognize the United States in 1782. The "two powerful Nations" pressuring the Dutch were presumably Great Britain and either France, or possibly Prussia.

[15] At this point Mary Cranch heavily crossed out an entire line, making it illegible.

[16] The draft does not have "three in Salem last week," but adds: "Ned Green I suppose you know broke last spring. He is execrated by every Body. Mrs. Leveret put all her Business of settling her Husbands Estate in His Hands. He has collected above one thousand pound of it and [*has*] been living away as if he own'd it all, and tho repeatedly call'd upon would not be accountable to Mrs. Leverett for any thing. He is now shut up in an uper Chamber in his Brother Greens House. He has had a small shock of the Palsy since. I pity his poor wife from my Heart. Uncle Smith and aunt meet with trouble in their connections, as well as others. Tis the lot of mortals."

[17] The draft arranges essentially the same material on the Otises somewhat differently, adding that Joseph Otis was "of Barnstable," and that the large debt due to a creditor in England was for "sixteen thousand pound." Joseph Otis, Samuel Allyne Otis, and Hannah Otis were younger siblings of the late James Otis Jr., and of Mercy Otis Warren. Samuel's marriage to AA's and Mary Cranch's cousin, Mary Smith, made his bankruptcy a family tragedy.

[18] Harrison Gray Otis, son of Samuel Allyne Otis. In the draft, Mary Cranch also mentions Harry after his father's misfortune, and then adds: "I cannot think what is the matter with all the young Fellows. One quarter of them at least are spiting Blood."

[19] The draft continues: "We have let our Farm to the Halves, to Shalhouse. His wife makes a good dairy woman."

[20] Thomas Perkins' letter to Elizabeth Cranch, dated "Danville, Kentucky, March 1st 1785," which Mary Cranch summarizes in this paragraph, was published anonymously in *The Boston Magazine*, Sept. 1785, p. 342–345.

[21] The draft ends at this point.

[22] See AA to Lucy Tufts, 3 Sept., and note 1, below.

[23] Louisa Catharine Smith.

[24] No letters from the Cranches to JQA in 1785 have been found. Those to which Cranch refers may have been written around 25 April, when both Mary and Elizabeth wrote to AA, both above.

[25] Mary Cranch arrived in Braintree on 15 Sept., after an overnight stay in Boston; JQA stayed two nights in Boston, reaching Braintree on the 16th (JQA, *Diary*, 1:324–325).

[26] Their brother, William Smith Jr.; see Mary Cranch to AA, 25 April, above; and Catharine Smith to AA, 27 April, above, and 26 Oct., below.

[27] See AA to Mary Cranch, 24 June, above.

[28] The text is lost in a tear; see JQA, *Diary*, 1:325 (15 September). JQA's cousin in this sentence could have been either Billy Cranch, visiting from Cambridge with CA, or Betsy Cranch, who apparently was living in the home of Boston merchant William Foster, as was her father, Richard (same, 1:318).

[29] Of 19 July, above.

Abigail Adams to Mary Smith Cranch

London Grosvenor Square

My dear sister   August 15 1785

When I wrote you by Captain Dashood,[1] I was obliged for want of time to break of before I had noticed certain parts of your Letter,[2] some of which gave me anxiety, particularly that which related to a certain Gentleman, of whose present affairs, or future intentions we know nothing of. I had written to you upon this Subject but not having time to transcribe more than half my Letter, that part was omitted. I am not now sorry that it was, as neither he or his affairs in future will be of any material importance to us, for when this reaches you it will accompany a *final* dismission of him.[3] I have for sometime observed a more than common anxiety in the appeerence of your Neice, which I sometimes attributed to the absence of her Brother, but several times she had dropt hints as if returning to America soon, was not an object near her Heart and I knew that nothing had taken place here to attach her.[4] A few days since, something arose which led her in conversation to ask me, if I did not think a Gentleman of her acquaintance a Man of Honour? I replied yes a Man of strict honour, and I wisht I could say that of all her acquaintance. As she could not mistake my meaning, instead of being affected as I apprehended she said, a breach of honour in one party would not justify a want of it in the other. I thought this the very time to speak. I said if she was conscious of any want of honour on the part of the Gentleman, I and every Friend she had in the world, would rejoice if she could liberate herself.

Here ended the conversation, she retired to her Chamber and I to mine. About two hours after she sent me a Billet, with the copy of two Letters,[5] which she desired me to communicate if I thought proper. In the Billet she asks if her Father was included in the Friends I mentioned. If he was, she should be deliverd from a state of anxiety she had long known. She adds that she dreads his displeasure, and will not in future take a step unapproved by him. Thanks Heaven that her mind is not in so weak a state as to feel a partiality which is not returnd. That no state of mind is so painfull as that which admits, of fear, suspicion, doubt, dread and apprehension. "I have too long" says she "known them all—and I am determined to know them no longer." You may be sure I did not fail of communicating the whole to her Father, the result of which was a conversation with her. He told her that it was a serious matter, and that he hoped it was upon mature deliberation she acted, that he was a perfect stranger to the Gentleman, that his Character had been such as to induce him to give his consent not so freely as he could wish: but because he conceived her affections engaged. But if she had reason to question the strictest honour of the Gentleman, or supposed him capable of telling her that he had written Letters when he had not, he had rather follow her to her Grave, than see her united with him. She has not received but one Letter since last December, and that a short one, and by what I can learn only four since she left America.[6] In that by Lyde[7] he says that he had written to her and to her parents by way of Amsterdam. I doubted it when she told me, tho I kept silence, but I find now she is of the same opinion. She request that neither the Name or subject may ever be mentiond to her, and I hope none of her Friends will be so unwise as to solicit for him. The Palmers will be the most likely, but the die is cast.

It is not worth his while to make a Bustle. I dont think it will kill him. He would have been more solicitious to have kept his prize, if he had known the value of it. It is a maxim in a favorite Author of his, that a woman may forgive the man she loves an indiscretion, but never a neglect. But it is not merely a want of proper attention you well know my Dear sister which has been the source of anxiety to me, or to her either. I have always told him, that he was his own greatest enemy. Such he has proved. She appears much more cheerfull since she has unburthend her mind. There is however a degree of delicacy necessary to be preserved, between persons who have thought favourably of each other, even in their seperation. I do not wish that a syllable more may be said upon the subject, than just to vindicate her, and I believe very little will do that, in the Eye of the world.

We are agreeably enough situated here in a fine open square, in the middle of which is a circle inclosed with a neat grated fence; around which are lighted every night about sixty Lamps. The border next the fence is grass, the circle is divided into five grass plots. One in the middle is a square upon which is a statue of Gorge 2d. on horse back. Between each of the plots are gravel walks and the plots are filld with clumps of low trees thick together which is calld Shrubbery, and these are surrounded with a low Hedge, all together a pretty effect. I have got a set of servants which I hope are good, but time must prove them. I shall lose a very agreeable companion in Mrs. Temple. She goes out this week. I have had more intimacy with her than with any other American, as she has been situated near to me, and has been very sociable. Mrs. Rogers is benevolence itself, it is impossible to know her without feeling a sisterly regard for her. I regret that she is 3 miles distant from me. Mrs. Atkinson too is agoing out in a few days, as well as Mr. Storer whom we shall greatly miss. Mrs. Hay resides at Hamstead about 4 miles out. Mrs. Copely is an agreeable woman whom I visit. Mrs. West also; wife to Mr. West the celebrated painter, is a friendly sensible Lady in whose company I expect a good deal of pleasure. Mr. Vassels family who reside at Clapham I have both visited, and received visits from. There is a Mrs. Johnson Lady to a Gentleman from Philadelphia who is setled here in Buisness that I have some acquaintance with. There are several others who have visited me, but almost everybody is out of Town. I am not however so solitary as at Auteuil. They tell me I shall get attached to England by and by, but I do not believe it—the people must Love my country and its inhabitants better first. They must discover a more amicable temper towards us. Yet there are worthy good individuals here whom I Esteem.

What you wrote with respect to my Mother gave me uneasiness.[8] I am sorry she had not spoken her mind before I went away. I know Mr. Adams has written to her[9] desireing her to call upon the dr for what she may want. As to Mr. Adams's having every thing which belong'd to her in his Hands, I know not the meaning of it. The estate which was left him by his Father which did not amount to more than 30 acres of land; I know she had her thirds in, and it was never divided; but the income of it could not amount to much deducting taxes. I will send by Mr. Storer 2 Guineys to be given to you for her, which you will take a receit for, and I will take some opportunity to mention it to Mr. Adams and take his orders about it. I should have done it before now, but he has been so engaged with publick buisness and private applications that I hated to worry him as I knew this would. And then there were at the time, other things in the Letter, that I did not wish to trouble him with.

I hope my son has arrived before now, tho the French Consul who calld yesterday upon us with Letters from some of Mr. Adams friends in Boston brought no news of the May pacquet tho he left Boston the fourth of july. I have not yet got a line by Capt. Callihan. I cannot but think I must have some letters from some of you.

I have been to Mr. Elworthys in hopes to find Letters but not one can I hear of. From thence to the post office. Mr. Storer got his on Saturday, this is tuesday and I hear nothing of any. The servant came yesterday to me for two Guineys and half to pay the postage of a packet of Letters from America. Well now thought I we have got a fine Bugget. I ran and got the money, and down I went in full expectation, and when I came, behold it was a pacquet from New York for Col. Smith, who being gone a journey had orderd all his letters to be left here. One of the Bundles contains the New York papers up to 6 of july, but alass no mention of the arrival of the May pacquet, which makes me not a little anxious: for supposing all well it must have been at sea for more than six weeks.

I have sent by Captain Lyde a few Books amongst the children which you will see distributed as directed. What letters I cannot get ready to send by him Mr. Storer will take. Continue my dear sister to write me particularly tell me all, and every thing about my Friends my Neighbours, &c.

If an opportunity should offer I wish you to send me a doz. of Chocolate, it must be put in some captains chest.

Esther is well now tho she has been very sick since she came to England. I keep her intirely about my person so that she has no hard work of any kind to do. She sews and dresses my hair and Nabbys. She has not even to sweep a chamber, as that falls into the department of the House maid, and is considerd as beneath a Ladies Maid. I do not say this because she is not willing to do it, or any thing else, but as there was one person whom I must have in that capacity; I chose it should be she. They are more particular here I think than in France.[10]

Remember me to every body who inquires after me. Mrs. Temple is to visit me to day for the last time before she goes out.

I shall endeavour to write by every opportunity. Love to Mr. Cranch and my dear Neices to whom I shall write if I have time. Let me know how Charles succeeded! Adieu. We have company to dine to day, and I must quit my pen to dress.

Believe me most tenderly & affectionately Yours   A Adams

Mr. Bulfinch was well a few days since when he calld here. He has been here several time[s]. I met Master George Apthorp in Kensington Gardens the other day, he was so grown that I did not know him at first. My compliment to his Mamma and sisters.[11]

RC (MWA:Abigail Adams Corr.).

¹ On 24 June, above.

² Of 25 April, above.

³ Neither any rough draft of AA to Mary Cranch, 24 June, containing AA's remarks about Royall Tyler, nor any MS version of AA2's "*final* dismission" of Tyler has been found. The only text of AA2's letter to Tyler appears, undated, in *Grandmother Tyler's Book*, p. 76, and is printed above, at [*ca. 11 August*].

⁴ This remark ignores William Stephens Smith's recent interest in AA2, which may not yet have been reciprocated by her. AA's purpose here is to declare to her American friends that AA2 broke off her engagement with Tyler only because he did not correspond regularly with her, and because she believed that he was not being truthful with her. Whatever AA2 thought of Smith in August, however, AA was most aware that he was attracted to AA2. AA later wrote to JQA that when she saw Smith's interest in AA2, she told him that AA2 was still "under engagements" with Royall Tyler. Smith then thought it prudent to take his trip to Prussia. See notes 6 and 7; William Stephens Smith to AA, 5 Sept., below; and AA to JQA, 16 Feb. 1786 (Adams Papers).

⁵ Neither the billet nor "the copy of two Letters," probably AA2 to Tyler, and perhaps AA2 to Cotton Tufts (see AA to Tufts, 18

Aug., below), or possibly to Richard Cranch, have been found.

⁶ AA2 returned these letters to Tyler about this time (see AA2 to Tyler, [*ca. 11 Aug.*], above); none have been found.

⁷ This letter, not found, was probably written in late April, the date of several other letters sent from Braintree and Boston to the Adamses by Capt. Lyde that are printed above. Tyler's reference to his writing the Adamses by way of Amsterdam may be to Col. Beriah Norton, who carried Cotton Tufts' 11 April letter to AA, above. See Mary Cranch to AA, 25 April, above.

⁸ See Mary Cranch to AA, 25 April, and notes 7–9.

⁹ No letters from JA to his mother have been found.

¹⁰ That is, AA's English servants were even more particular than her French servants in performing only those duties traditionally associated with their positions. See AA to Mary Cranch, 5 Sept. 1784, above.

¹¹ Probably George Henry Apthorp, son of James Apthorp, one of nine Braintree loyalists who were declared "Inimical to the United States" on 9 June 1777 (John Wentworth, *The Wentworth Genealogy*, 1870, 1:300–301, 305; *Braintree Town Records*, p. 481–482). On the Apthorps of Braintree, see JQA to AA2, 19 Sept., below.

Abigail Adams to Elizabeth Smith Shaw

My dear sister   [*ca. 15 Aug. 1785*]¹

I have been situated here for near six weeks. It is one of the finest squares in London. The air is as pure as it can be so near a Great city. It is but a small distance from Hide Park, round which I sometimes walk, but oftner ride. It resembles Boston Common, much larger and more beautified with Trees. On one side of it is a fine river. St. James Park and Kensington Gardens are two other fashonable walks which I am very sensible I ought to improve oftner than I do. One wants society in these places. Mrs. Temple is the only person near me with whom I can use the freedom of calling upon to ride or walk with me, and she to my no small regret I am going to lose. Mrs. Rogers is an American and one of the most Benevolent women in the world: but is 3 miles distant from me. A sister of hers is like to be setled near you I hear. Visit her my sister, she is the counterpart of the amiable Mrs. Rogers. I have some acquaintance with her, she is the Friend and correspondent of your Neice. Mrs. Rogers and she too, have too much of "the tremblingly alive all over"[2] to be calculated for the rough Scenes of Life. Mrs. Hay resides out at Hamstead about 4 miles from London. We visit, but they have such a paltry custom of dinning here at night, that it ruins that true American Sociability which *only* I delight in. Polite circles are much alike throughout Europe. Swift's journal of a modern fine Lady[3] tho written 60 years ago is perfectly applicable to the present day, and tho noted as the changeable sex; in this Scene of dissapation they have been steady.

I shall never have much society with these kind of people, for they would not like me, any more than I do them. They think much more of their titles here than in France. It is not unusual [to find people of the highest rank there, the] best bred and the politest people. [If they have an equal share of pride, they kn]ow better how to hide it. [Until I came here, I had no idea what a] National and illiberal inveteracy the English have against their better behaved Neighbours, and I feel a much greater partiality for them than I did whilst I resided amongst them. I would recommend to this Nation a little more liberality and discernment. Their contracted sentiments leads them to despise all other Nations: perhaps I should be chargable with the same narrow sentiments if I give America the preference over these old European Nations. In the cultivation of the arts and improvement in manufactories they greatly excell us, but we have native Genious capacity and ingenuity equal to all their improvements, and much more general knowledge diffused amongst us. You can scarcly form an Idea how much superiour our common people as they are termd, are to those of the same rank in this country. Neither have we that servility of Manners which the distinction between nobility and citizens gives to the people of this Country. We tremble not, neither at the sight or Name of Majesty. I own that I never felt myself in a more contemptable situation than when I stood four hours together for a gracious smile from Majesty. Witness to the anxious solicitude of those around me for the same mighty *Boon*. I however had a more dignified honour as his Majesty *deigned to salute me.*[4]

I have not been since to the drawing room, but propose going to the next. As the company are chiefly out of Town the ceremony will not be so tedious.

As to politicks, the English continue to publish the most abusive bare faced falshoods against America that you can conceive of. Yet glaring as they are, they gain credit here, and shut their Eyes against a friendly and liberal intercourse. Yet their very existence depends upon a friendly union with us. How the pulse of the Ministry beat, time will unfold, but I do not [promise or] wish to myself a long continuance here. [Such is the temper of] the two Nations towards each other, that [if we have not peace] we must have war. We cannot resign the intercourse and quit each other. I hope however that it will not come to that alternative.[5]

Captain Callihan arrived last week from Boston which place he left 4 of july. I was not a little mortified in not receiving a single Letter by him. I sought for them in every place where I thought it probable they might be. I am not without hope that the Captain himself may yet have some in his private care as the letters in the bag generally are landed at Dover and sent by land several days before the ship gets up, but as Captain Lyde sails directly I must finish my Letters and send them this afternoon.

I am not a little anxious for my son, as we have the News papers from New York up to july 6th and he was not then arrived. He sailed the 21 of May, and must have a very tedious passage. I shall wait very impatiently for the next packet. I had hoped that he was in Boston by that time.

How did Charles succeed, I want very much to know? And how Tommy comes on. I have sent him a Book and one to each of my neices and Nephews. I wish it was in my power to do more for my Friends, but thus it is. We did not bring the last year about upon our anual allowence, and very far were we from being extravagent.

Remember me kindly to Mr. Shaw, Mr. Thaxter and all our Friends and believe me most affectionately   Your sister

RC (DLC:Shaw Family Papers); notation on the first sheet: "London 15 August 1785." Printed: AA, *Letters*, ed. CFA, 1840, p. 304–306. Some of the MS has been obscured by opaque tape, and is supplied from the printed edition, in brackets.

[1] The "near six weeks" in AA's opening sentence, counting from the date of the Adamses moving to Grosvenor Square on 4 July, supplies the dateline.

[2] The editors have supplied the closing quotation mark. Abigail Bromfield Rogers and Daniel Denison Rogers left Boston for Europe in 1782, and returned in 1786. Abigail Rogers' sister Sarah married Eliphalet Pearson, who spent part of his career in Andover, near Haverhill. JQA came to know this cou-ple well at Harvard in 1786. See vol. 4:343, and note 1; JQA, *Diary*, 2:96, and note 1. This paragraph, from "Mrs. Rogers is an American" to "rough Scenes of Life," is omitted from AA, *Letters*, ed. CFA.

[3] Jonathan Swift's "Journal of a Modern Lady" was published in 1729.

[4] See AA to Mary Cranch, 24 June, above.

[5] All the text from this point to the signature in omitted from AA, *Letters*, ed. CFA.

Abigail Adams to Cotton Tufts

August 18th 1785

My dear sir   London Grosvenor Square

Captain Lyde is to Sail this week. I will not let him go without a few lines to you, tho Captain Callihan has arrived without a Single Letter from my Friends. Mr. Adams received 3 by Monssieur Le Tomb, from his Boston Friend's.[1] If my son had been lucky enough to have had such a passage as I hoped he would, I should have heard of his arrival by Captain Callihan or the New York packet which saild the 7 of july. He left Lorient the 21 of May, and must have a very tedious passage. I am not yet without hopes that the French packet which does not leave New York untill the 20th may, will[2] bring intelligence from him.

I find that our reception here had not reachd Boston when Captain Callihan left it. Tho treated by the Court with as much civility as could have been expected, it has not Screened us, or our Country from the base falshoods, and bilingsgate of hireling Scriblers or the envenomd pen of Refugees. Their evident design has been to get Mr. A. to notice them, and to replie to their peices. They have tried every string. Sometimes they will not even allow him the Rank of Minister, then they will represent the title in a ridiculous light, calling him commercial Agent, proscribed Rebel, snearing at him for having taken Dr. Price as Father confessor, because we have usually attended the Drs. meeting. Sometimes they have asserted that the king treated him with the utmost disdain, at others that Lord Carmathan and the American plenipo, were at the utmost varience, that the foreign ministers would not associate with him, that he could not give a publick dinner because Congress paper would not pass, and tradesmen would not credit, that the Secratary to the Legation could neither read or write, but that his principal had sent him to an evening school to qualfy him, that Hearing the Honble. Mrs. Adams's Carriage call'd was a little better than going in an old chaise to market with a little fresh butter; in short the publication which they have daily publishd have been a disgrace to the Nation.[3] Now and then a peice would appear lashing them for their Scurility, but they are callous, and refuse to publish in favour of America, as I have been told or rather demand such a price for publishing as to amount to a prohibition. Mr. A has never noticed them.

The Massachusetts Navigation act has struck them dumb, for tho

3 days publishd not a syllable of abuse has appeard; by a vessel which arrived yesterday from Virgina it is said, that assembly has passt similar acts and prohibited any tobaco being exported in British vessels,[4] which will essentially affect the revenu, by the British navigation act. No vessels but British and American have been permitted to bring tobaco. The duty paid here last year upon tobaco, amounted to four hundred and Eighty two thousand pounds. It is supposed that 3 hundred thousand pounds worth was smuggled. The severity of the Laws against Smuggling has led them to suppose they should collect seven hundred thousand pounds this year. Three Virgina vessels which went not long since to the West India Islands being sent away without permission of unloading have raised the old Spirit amongst them. Thus is this Nation driving us into greatness, obliging us to become frugal, to retrench our Luxeries, to build a Navy to have a great Number of Seamen, and by and by to become a terrour to evil doers.[5] The very measures they are taking to prevent it, will hasten it. Mr. A. soon after his arrival communicated to the Marquiss of Carmarthan the various subjects of his mission agreeable to his instructions. He had some conferences with him, in all of which the Marquis discoverd a liberality of sentiment and a mind open to conviction. Through him these matters pass to the minister of State.[6] Yet not a syllable of replie to any one thing proposed has been returnd. It is thought they mean to wait, and see what effects the propositions[7] are like to have in Ireland. If they can oblige the Irish to swallow them without much struggle, they will then be ready for America. But by the present appeerence Ireland determines not to be triffled with, and it is thought best not to push these matters at present. If the States empower Congress to regulate their commerce it will have happy concequences for at present, there are those who have the ear of the ministry and persuade them that there is not union sufficient in the States to accomplish any thing jointly. Every little petty disturbance is represented as a dissolution of all government.

It is hoped here by the Friends of America, and there are many such yet, that the measures which are taken there, will be well weighed and matured, that the legislators will not suffer any narrow contracted sentiments and principals to operate, but that they will view objects upon a large Scale looking forward to concequences, rearing the Edifice upon a rock that will not be shaken.[8]

You will consider some parts of my politicks as confidential Sir and excuse my being so buisy in them, but I am so connected with them, that I cannot avoid being much interested.

With regard to our private affairs sir I wrote you by my son[9] and nothing new occurs at present to my mind. Mr. Elworthy presented your Bill which was paid upon Sight, and Mr. Storer who is soon to sail for America will receive 12 Guineys at New York from Dr. Crosby, being money paid upon the dr account here, which money he will deliver to you.[10] We do not find living here, less expensive than in Paris I assure you sir, but there is one comfort that we cannot go to Kings bench[11] untill our commission is vacated. But we should soon be in a condition for that place if we were disposed to take the credit which is offerd us. Notwithstanding all the abuse in the papers we receive none from any other quarter, tradesmen are as civil and as obliging as in any country, and there are constant solicitations from them to Supply us. But I chuse no credit, so long as we have money we shall pay it, and when we cannot live here we will come home. Go *to Market* again with *fresh Butter*.

I suppose sir you will receive by this vessel, two Letters which may supprize you.[12] Mrs. Cranch will communicate to you what I have written to her. It is a matter I believe concluded upon after long deliberation and mature reflection. The former assent of her Father seems to have sometime hindred her from taking this step, and tho perfectly agreable to our wishes, we had never expresst them, nor scarcly ever mentiond the name of the person. Being once free, I believe she will in future proceed with a caution purchased by experience. You will not be very well pleasd with the commission,[13] yet as it was her own act and the choise she has made is so wise, I hope you will comply. I have scarcly room upon my paper to present my duty to my dear Aunt or to Assure you how affectionately I am Yours

A A

Since I finishd my Letter Mr. A has received Letters from France from Mr. Jefferson,[14] inclosing the two Arrets of the King of France, prohibiting english Manufactories, which make them grumble here very much, but it will all work for good to us. It has been publishd here in the papers that our "good and *Great Ally*" had shut us out of the French West Indias, whereas Mr. Jefferson writes no such thing had taken place, but that more of our vessels were now at the French West Indias than ever was known before, and that he is not without hopes of obtaining particular priviledges for us. What an impolitick

Nations this, it has been hinted that this Court are striving to set the Algerines to war with us. Congress sent important papers by a Mr. Lambe to the minister more than 3 months ago. No such man has arrived and their Hands are tied for want of this intelligence. Nobody can tell what is become of him or his papers. He had been tendering his Services to congress to go there as consul.[15] They sent him to the ministers to do as they thought best—but no Papers or Man has come. Thus you see sir how the most salutary measures may be obstructed and parties blamed when they have done what was their duty and exerted themselves to the utmost for the publick benefit. Col. Smith has taken a tour to Berlin to see the Grand Review which commences the 21 of the month, he appears a Gentleman solid sedate tho warm and active when occasion requires. He is sensible and judicious, dignified sentiments of his own Country and a high sense of honour appear to govern his actions. Mr. A is very happy in him.

RC (Adams Papers); endorsed: "Mrs. Adams London Aug 1785 recd Sept." The postscript is written on a separate fragment of a full sheet of paper.

[1] On 14 Aug., Philippe André Joseph de Létombe, the French consul in Boston, called on JA at Grosvenor Square with letters from Samuel Adams, 2 July, and Thomas Cushing, 3 July (both in Adams Papers; see AA2 to JQA, 26 Aug., below).

[2] Thus in MS; "will" is written above the line. AA perhaps intended to write "untill the 20th [*July*] may bring," and then, in reading over the letter, mistook "may" for "May" and added "will."

[3] JA was identified as "the same person who was proscribed as a REBEL," in the *Daily Universal Register* of 9 June. On 10 June the same newspaper stated that his reception at Court had been "cool," and on 14 June it reported: "It is whispered the celebrated Dr. Price is political father confessor to the new Plenipo, and has already given him absolution." Similar attacks and attempts to discredit JA appear in the *Daily Universal Register* of 6, 21 and 22 July.

[4] Virginia levied a 5 shilling per ton duty on all goods imported in English ships; this act went into effect in October (William Waller Hening, ed., *The Statutes at Large; being a Collection of all the Laws of Virginia*, Richmond and Philadelphia, 1809–1823, 13 vols., 12:32; Jensen, *The New Nation*, p. 299).

[5] AA appears to paraphrase Scripture here, perhaps Romans 13:3, or 1 Peter 2:14. Several verses in Isaiah, Jeremiah, and Psalms also speak of "evil-doers."

[6] AA probably intends the prime minister, William Pitt. On 6 Aug., JA wrote Pitt to request a conference. Pitt replied on the 16th, agreeing to meet the following day, but that meeting was evidently postponed to 24 Aug., when JA had his first meeting with the prime minister (JA to Pitt, 6 Aug. [LbC], Pitt to JA, 16 Aug., both Adams Papers; JA to John Jay, 25 Aug., PCC, No. 84, V, f. 605–619, printed in *Dipl. Corr., 1783–1789*, 2:455–462).

[7] See AA2 to JQA, 4 July, note 31, above.

[8] Luke 6:48; Matthew 7:24–25.

[9] On 2 May, above.

[10] On 5 March, JA accepted Tufts' bill of £50, and directed Richard & Charles Puller, bankers in London, to pay that amount to James Elworthy, and charge the sum to his Amsterdam bankers, on his account with the United States (JA to Elworthy, 5 March, to Richard & Charles Puller, 5 March, both LbCs, Adams Papers). On 1 Jan., Tufts had received £70 lawful Massachusetts currency for his £50 bill of exchange, drawn "in favour of James Elworthy" (account entry in Tufts to John Adams, 10 Aug., above). Dr. Ebenezer Crosby owed the twelve guineas to JA for a medical instrument that JA had recently purchased for him (Crosby to JA, 14 April, Adams Papers).

[11] King's Bench Prison in Southwark, where debtors as well as criminals were held (Wheatley, *London Past and Present*).

[12] The identity of these letters, concerning

Royall Tyler, is not certain, but see AA2 to Royall Tyler, [*ca. 11 Aug.*], and AA to Mary Cranch, 15 Aug., both above.
¹³ Probably to recover a miniature of AA2, her letters, and certain other items, from Royall Tyler. See Tufts to AA, 13 April 1786, and AA to Tufts, 22 July 1786 (both Adams Papers).

¹⁴ Jefferson to JA, 10 Aug., and perhaps also 6 Aug. (Jefferson, *Papers*, 8:361–362, 347–353).
¹⁵ The *JCC* says nothing about Lamb's seeking the position of consul to the Barbary States; see AA to Jefferson, 12 Aug., and note 5, above.

John Quincy Adams to Abigail Adams 2d

N:7.

Middleton¹ August 20th: 1785

This morning we left ⟨Hartford⟩ New Haven, accompanied by Mr. Broome, and Mr. Brush, who wishing to take a ride to Hartford, took this opportunity, which is a very agreeable Circumstance to us. We at first intended to have gone directly to Hartford this day. But as I had a Letter for Genl. Parsons,² one of the aldermen of this City, and as we were told it was worth ou[r while to us]e this road, which is only 2 miles longer than the other, we [determined t]o go no further than this, to-day: it is only 28 miles from New Haven. This is a much smaller place than that, but I think full as agreeably situated. It stands upon the side, of an hill on the banks of the Connecticut River, which deserves the poet's lays as much as ever the Rhine, the Danube, or the Tiber did. Many parts of the Country through which we have past, and especially the banks of this River, are highly cultivated, and I was never so much delighted with the appearance of any Country, probably because, I never felt so much interested, in any of those I have travell'd through. Genl. Parsons spent the Evening with us. I feel a peculiar veneration for him, because he told me, he was three years at Harvard College, with my father, and was at that time intimate with him. We proceed to-morrow, for Hartford.

Hartford Augt. 21st

It is only 14 miles from hence to Middleton, so that we got here, before 9 o'clock this morning. Part of the road, is along by the side of the River, but some times you leave it, to ascend an hill from whence there are some of the most beautiful Prospects I ever beheld. There are several such on this Road. Three miles before this we came through, the town of Weathersfield, which is greatly celebrated for the Singers, it produces. Indeed all over Connecticut, they pay great attention to their singing at meeting. Mr. Chaumont went with us this afternoon; and as soon as the Service was over, he told me he had been struck with the singing. I own I was very agreeably, although I had already been told, of the fact. Here I have seen Coll. Wadsworth, with whom I suppose you are not acquainted, and Mr. Trumbull,[3] with whom I had a great deal of Conversation this afternoon. I wish I could have an opportunity of forming a nearer acquaintance; but cannot be gratified, as we propose leaving Hartford to-morrow.

22d

We have rode 16 miles this afternoon: for we did not leave Hartford till 4 o'clock. Mr. Broome, and Mr. Brush, left us in the morning, and return'd to New Haven. We went in the forenoon out with Coll. Wadsworth, to his farm, 2 or 3 miles out of the City. He there shew us a number of the largest oxen we ever saw: they really appeared monstrous to us, yet, Cattle of this size, are not uncommon, we are told in this State. What such an amazing difference, in the same kind of animals, is owing to I cannot conceive. We dined with Coll. Wadsworth, and were not able to ride further this afternoon, on account of the weather which is very warm.

23d

Thirty six miles nearer home, than yesterday, and at length arrived into the State itself. At about 9 this morning, we cross'd Connecticut River, near Springfield, where it serves as a barrier between the two States.[4] Two days more will carry us I hope to the town [*Boston*]. The roads in this State, are much rougher, and more disagreeable than the greatest part of those in Connecticut. I have been known at two or three taverns, by my resemblance to my father, who has travelled these roads more than once.[5]

24th

We have proceeded, only 31 miles to-day owing to several circumstances; we shall have 42 to-morrow, an hard days work, but I hope we shall perform it, if the weather is good. The roads as we are told, and as we may naturally suppose, grow better as we come nearer to the Capital. We came through Worcester this afternoon, and a[re] now but 6 miles from it.[6] This I think is where your Pappa studied Law, and the appearance of the town pleased me very much; I wished to stop there this Night, but it would have made our Journey of to-morrow, too long.

August 1785

The heart of the most loyal frenchmen, has not felt this day, so great, and so real a pleasure as mine has. Our motives are certainly very different. Their's because it is the *jour de fête, de Son bon Roi*; (all kings of France you know are bons Rois)[7] mine, the idea, of being after a seven years absence, return'd to my own dear home, and amidst the friends of my Infancy, and those who are dear to me by the ties of blood. My Satisfaction cannot be now complete. The absence, of two of the best Parents in the World, and of a Sister on whose happiness my own depends, can certainly be compensated by nothing; but I will think as Little of this as possible, and turn all my ideas to pleasing Subjects. I have not yet told you how I got here. This morning, before 4 o'clock, we got under way, and by riding till about 9 this evening, we got to Bracket's tavern. There was no lodging to be had there: the house, was full, as there are now a great number of foreigners in town. We then came down, to a Mrs. Kilby's in State Street, where we have obtained one Room between us both. It is now eleven o'clock, and I am much fatigued: so I must lay down my pen for the present.

26th

The first thing I did this morning, was to go to Uncle Smith's. Betsey[8] came to the door, and as you may well suppose I knew her immediately: but she did not know me. Your uncle was at his Store; and Mr. William set out this morning, on a journey to the Eastward.[9] Your Aunt ask'd abundance of Questions about you. I went down to Uncle Smith's store. He knew me as soon as he saw me, and immediately enquired when I arrived. Upon my telling him, last night, I suppose, said he, you could not find the way to our house. I found here all my trunks, both those that were sent from Holland, and those I embark'd at New-York. But I enquired in vain for Letters from you: none were to be found, so I am now obliged to set out on fresh hopes; and though I have received but four short pages from you, since I left Auteuil,[10] yet I have no doubt but you have been as punctual as myself; and I am sure, if all I have written, affords you half the pleasure, one of your Letters does to me, I shall never regret my time. I Dined with Uncle Cranch, Lucy and Betsey were both in town. We sat, and look'd at one another; I could not speak, and they could only ask now and then a Question concerning you. How much more expressive this Silence, than any thing we could have said. I am glad to see you, will do for a Stranger, and a person quite indifferent to us; but may I always find a silent reception from my real friends. Don't think I am grown too sentimental; I felt so impatient to see my brother that I would not wait till to-morrow, and went in the afternoon with Mr. Smith and your Cousins, to Cambridge. Charles and your Cousin, are both well; but I spoilt Charles for Conversation by giving him your Letters;[11] he was so eager to read them, that he was employ'd a great part of the time we were there. He comes on well in his Studies, and, what is of great advantage, to a Student, has for his Chambermate, a youth, whose thirst for knowledge is insatiable. His name is Walker. He ⟨*studied*⟩ was about six months in Mr. Shaw's family, and it will be sufficient to say that all our friends, are much pleased with their being together at College. And I am perswaded it will afford peculiar Satisfaction to our Parents, who well know how much benifit is derived from the Spur of Emulation. I hope I shall be as fortunate as my Cousin, and brother have been, when I enter College, myself. To-morrow we go to Braintree.

Augt. 27th. Braintree

At length all the ideas, which have been for so long a time been playing upon my imagination, are realized, and now I may truly say,

A tous les coeurs bien nés que la patrie est chere!
Qu'avec ravissement, je revois ce séjour![12]

I left Boston early in the afternoon, but stopp'd on the road at several places; so that it was eight before I got here. Mr. Toscan, (the Vice, as you used to call him)[13] and Mr. Chaumont came 4 or 5 miles out of town with me. You remember your Pappa gave Mr. Chaumont a Letter for the former governor,[14] Who has occupied, Mr. Swan's house in Roxbury, all this Summer. He deliver'd it this afternoon. And I thought this might be a proper time to pay him my visit too. He is at this time troubled with the gout, but not enough to prevent his seeing Company. From thence we went and drank tea at Mr. Hichborne's, Summer Seat, (for Summer Seats are high in vogue now). He was not at home himself, so that I saw only his Lady. There was considerable Company.[15] There I left the gentlemen, and proceeded to Genl. Warren's. There I was cordially received. Poor Charles, is going again to try if he can recover any portion of Health. He went last Winter to the West Indies, and found himself much better, but has pined away again since he return'd, and intends now to sail in the Course of the Week for Europe: he proposes spending the Winter at Lisbon. My wishes for him are much greater than my hopes. My last Stage, was at Uncle Adams's, there I saw our aged honour'd Grandmamma, and I am perswaded, I have been more heartily welcomed by no person. The Question, which is so often repeated to me, When will they return? was one, of the first she ask'd me. I could only answer with a sigh, which she understood as well, as if I had spoken. May she live to see the joyful day! It will be an happy one to her, and then may she never wish for your return again! When I arrived here,[16] I perceived that I had left your Packet for Mr. Tyler, and the letters for your aunt, at Boston in my trunk. I was sorry it happened so; but the Circumstance was to my own Advantage, for it made them all more sociable, than they would have been; for as one of our Cousins told me, they have now time enough to talk with me, but your Letters will not last so long, and therefore when they have them, they must make as much of them as they can. Miss Eunice Paine, has spent some weeks here, and Cousin Betsey has spent a great part of the Summer in Boston; where she is learning to play upon the harpsichord.

28th

I have attended the meeting twice to-day. I could not have supposed that the parson's[17] voice, and looks and manner, would seem so familiar to me. I thought while he was preaching, that I had heard him every week ever since I left Braintree. As I look'd round the meeting house every face, above 30, I knew; scarcely one, under 20. This did not at all surprize me, as I had already made the same observations with Respect to persons of our own family. As for Billy Cranch: I might have been an hundred times in Company with him, without having the most distant suspicion who he was, though I should at first sight, have known his father and mother, wherever I might have seen them. This afternoon I went down, and view'd the well known habitation. My Sensations on this occasion cannot be described, but they were such that I did not stay two minutes in the House, nor would it give me the least pain, was I forbidden to enter it again, before your return. I went to the Library, and look'd over the books, which are in good Condition; only somewhat musty and dusty, which shows that their owner is not with them.

My Paper bids me close, but it shall not be for long. Compliments, are useless to those we love. Your's.   J. Q. Adams

RC (Adams Papers). The text is written on eight small pages numbered "49" to "56"; see the descriptive note to JQA to AA2, [12] May, above. Small fragments of the text have been lost at folds and edges, and through the tearing away of the seal. The MS was water damaged in the wreck of the ship *Ceres*, which brought its courier, Nathaniel Barrett of Boston, to France. See AA2 to JQA, 5 Dec., below.

[1] Middletown, Conn.

[2] The letter was from Connecticut congressman William Samuel Johnson, whom JQA had met in Fairfield on 17 Aug. (JQA, *Diary*, 1:306, 308–309). Samuel Holden Parsons, Harvard 1756, had served in the Continental army throughout the war, reaching the rank of major general. JA wrote to Parsons at least once a few years after college; in 1776 they became regular correspondents. See *Sibley's Harvard Graduates*, 14:50–73; JQA, *Diary*, 1:309, note 2; and JA, *Papers*, 1:46–47; 4:index.

[3] John Trumbull, the Connecticut poet and lawyer, had studied law with JA in 1773–1774, had written the epic poem *McFingal* in 1775, and was regarded, in 1785, as the leader of the Connecticut Wits (JQA, *Diary*, 1:310, note 1; *DAB*).

[4] JQA also makes this curious statement in his Diary (*Diary*, 1:311), perhaps because the river nearly coincided with the point where his particular route crossed the state border.

[5] JQA's Diary suggests Scott's Tavern in Palmer, Mass., fifteen miles east of Springfield, as one location where he was recognized as JA's son. JQA and Chaumont probably reached either Western (now Warren) or Brookfield, Mass., this evening (same, 1:311, note 3).

[6] The travelers probably lodged in Shrewsbury, Mass., this evening (same, 1:312, note 1).

[7] In his Diary, JQA notes this as the festi-val day of St. Louis, France's "good king" Louis IX, the pious crusader monarch of the thirteenth century (same, 1:312).

[8] Elizabeth Smith, youngest daughter of AA's aunt and uncle, Elizabeth Storer Smith and Isaac Smith Sr., was fifteen; she would not have seen JQA since he was twelve or younger, and she only nine.

[9] In his Diary, JQA records that he did see Isaac Smith's son William before William's departure (same, 1:312).

[10] Not found. This was probably AA2's "No. 1," which JQA received on 20 May, in Lorient; it was probably written about five or six days earlier, at Auteuil (JQA to AA2, 17 May, above, under "Friday eve: May 20th").

[11] Not found.

[12] Voltaire, *Tancrède*, III, i (JQA, *Diary*, 1:313, note 1).

[13] Jean Joseph Marie Toscan was currently the French vice-consul in Boston (Abraham P. Nasatir and Gary Elwyn Monell, *French Consuls in the United States*, Washington, 1967, p. 567–568).

[14] JA's letter to John Hancock, dated 14 April, merely recommended Chaumont to Hancock (LbC, Adams Papers).

[15] Included in the party at the home of Boston lawyer Benjamin Hichborn was Lt. Gov. Thomas Cushing (JQA, *Diary*, 1:313, and note 4).

[16] The Cranch's home in Braintree.

[17] Rev. Anthony Wibird.

Abigail Adams to Thomas Jefferson

London Grosvenor square

Dear sir   August 21 1785

The Gentleman who is so kind as to convey this to you is from Carolina, his Name is Smith.[1] He is a distant relation of mine, tho I have not the pleasure of much acquaintance with him. He has resided in England some time, and bears a Good Character here. Give me leave sir to introduce him to your notice.

Mr. Short left us last twesday for the Hague, I did myself the honour of writing to you by him.[2]

I find by the last papers from New York that Mr. Rutledge is appointed Minister at the Hague; in the room of Mr. Levingstone who declined the embassy.[3] There is no mention made of a Secretary.

You will probably see our Massachusetts Navigation act before this reaches you; it has struck the hireling scriblers dumb. There has been less abuse against the Americans in the papers since the publication of it; than for a long time before.

Ireland has exerted herself,[4] and Pharoah and his host are overthrown. The Courier of Europe will doubtless give you the debates. The july packet arrived last week. Tho she left New York the seventh of july, she brought not a line of publick dispatch. A private Letter or two for Col. Smith, the contents of which we cannot know; as he is absent upon a Tour to Berlin.

I was much dissapointed to find that my son had not arrived when the packet saild. As the French packet sails sometime after the English, I am not without hopes that I may hear by that, and I will thank you sir to give me the earliest intelligence if she brings any account of the May packet.

Be so good as to present my Regards to Col. Humphries. Mr. Short gives us some encouragement to expect him here this winter. My Love to Miss Jefferson, to whom also my daughter desires to be rememberd. Our[5] good old Friends the Abbes, I would tender my Regards. If I could write French; I would have Scribled a line to the Abbe Arnou.

I think Madam Helvitius must be very melancholy now Franklin as she used to call him is gone. It is said here by a Gentleman lately from Philadelphia, that they determine to elect the doctor president upon his arrival, as Mr. Dickinsons office expires in october.[6]

In my Letter by Mr. Short I had taken the Liberty to request you to procure for me two or 3 articles, and to convey them by Col. Smith who talks of returning by way of Paris. But if he should not visit you, Mr. Smith when he returns will be so good as to take charge of them for me. But this I shall know in the course of a few weeks, and will take measures accordingly.[7]

I am sir with Sentiments of Esteem Your Humble Servant

Abigail Adams

RC (DLC:Jefferson Papers). Dft (DSI:Hull Coll.).

[1] James Smith of South Carolina (JA to Thomas Jefferson, 18 Aug., in Jefferson, *Papers*, 8:400).

[2] On 12 Aug., above.

[3] The draft has "the 7 of july" after "New York." On 23 June, Congress elected Gov. Wil-

liam Livingston of New Jersey to replace JA as minister plenipotentiary to the Netherlands, but Livingston promptly declined. Congress next turned to John Rutledge of South Carolina on 5 July, but on 1 Aug., he too declined the service. Congress never did replace JA, who continued as minister to the Netherlands until his resignation, and return to America, in 1788. *JCC*, 28:474, 481; 29:497, 654–655.

[4] See AA2 to JQA, 4 July, and note 31, above.

[5] The draft has "My"; the "Abbes" were Arnoux and Chalut.

[6] The office was president of the Supreme Executive Council of Pennsylvania, that commonwealth's equivalent of governor. Franklin was elected to this post in October, and held it until Nov. 1788 (*Colonial Records of Pennsylvania, Minutes of the Supreme Executive Council*, Harrisburg, 1852–1853, 16 vols., 14:557, 565; 15:584).

[7] This paragraph is not in the draft.

John Adams to Richard Cranch

Grosvenor Square Westminster

My dear Brother   Aug. 22. 1785

I have received your kind Letter of June 3. and rejoice to hear of the Health and Welfare of our Friends.

The County did themselves Justice, when they put you into the Senate, and the State did itself Honour when it placed Mr. Bowdoin in the Chair. I think you must be happy and prosper under his Administration.

The Massachusetts, wise as it often has been, never Struck a more masterly Stroke, than by their Navigation Act. I hope they will persevere in it, with inflexible Firmness. This is playing a sure Game.[1] It will compell all the other States to imitate it. If they do not, the Massachusetts will soon get so much of their carrying Trade as will richly compensate her, for any present Inconvenience. But I hope You will not Stop. Go on. Lay on heavy Duties upon all foreign Luxuries especially British and give ample Bounties to your own Manufactures. You will of course, continue to do all these Things upon the condition to continue in force only untill they Shall be altered by a Treaty of Commerce, or by an Ordinance of Congress.

My oldest son is with you, I hope, the Second is at Colledge and the third in good Health at Haverhill. Mrs. A. and Miss are with me, in Grosvenor Square in the Neighbourhood of Lord North.

We have a very good House, in as good an Air as this fat greasy Metropolis, can afford: But neither the House nor its furniture nor the manner of living in it, are Sufficiently Showy for the Honour and Interest of that Country, which is represented by it. If I ever do any Thing or carry any Point it will not be by imposing upon any Body by the Splendor of my Appearance. An American Minister should be able to keep a Table, to entertain his Countrymen, to return the

Civilities of his Friends, to entertain People whose Aid is necessary to his political Purposes, and to entertain the foreign Ambassadors: But as the People of America, choose to place their Pride in having their Ambassadors abroad despized, or rather as they choose to be despized themselves, let them have their Choice. It is their Affair. I wish I was out of it.

Your affectionate Brother   John Adams

RC (NhHi:Hibbard Coll.).

[1] An "x" appears at the beginning of this paragraph, and at the end of this sentence. Cranch may have excerpted this passage to show members of the Massachusetts legislature and other political leaders (see Cranch to JA, 10 Nov., Adams Papers).

Abigail Adams to John Quincy Adams

My dear son   London August 23 1785

I hope this will find you upon terra firma, tho in vain I searcht the New York papers of july 7th. to find you, since which I have been very anxious. Your passage I hope has been safe tho long and tedious.

I have written to you twice before since you left me[1] and I believe you have a steady and faithfull correspondent in your sister, who having substituded you as her correspondent in lieu of her L[ove]r[2] hopes to find more punctuality in the return, than it seems she has met with else where. But this between ourselves.

I know you will be anxious to hear how the treaty is like to Succeed. You know the progress of courts, and that during a whole twelve-month only one has concluded a treaty.[3] The propositions are before the m[inistr]y. I have reason to think a conference will be held upon them this week.[4] What will be the result time must unfold, the temper and disposition of the people does not look very favourable.

You will hear the fate of the Irish propositions, labourd with so much Zeal here as to keep the Parliament setting untill this month. The Irish however have made short work of them. You will also see the Arrets of his most Christian Majesty[5] prohibiting the use of British Manufactories, which has turnd out of employ the english Newspapers say twenty thousand hands already. They are vastly angry with that seditious state of Massachusetts for their late navigation act. Mischief always begins there, they say, but they deceive them-selves with the hopes that the states will be divided. Talk of prohib-iting any American vessel from comeing here, that is the mercantile threaten, but they look very serious and I dare say the act will operate greatly for our Benifit.

Pray what do you think is become of that Said Captain Lambe who was sent out 3 months ago, with papers &c. You know upon what buisness. He has not arrived neither here nor in France. Mr. Jefferson and your Father are very anxious. Neither of them have yet had any acknowledgement of a single Letter writen for a whole twelvemonth past, nor has any packet brought them any publick dispatches except the commission to this court.

I do not know what C[ongre]ss mean by such proceedings, or rather by no proceedings. Did you hear any talk of supporting us here. I should be glad they would recall us, or put us in such a situation that we need not, nor our Country be squib'd at for not being able to give a dinner now and then to the Ministers. And it is most certain if we do that we must live very meager all the rest of the Year, and my poor Lads at home suffer for it. I suppose such a system of occonomy will now get into their Heads, that they will rather think of curtailing more. Let them use at Home occonomy where it is a virtue, but do not let them disgrace themselves abroad by narrowness. Mr. Temples Sallery as consul I am informd is equal to what our country allow their ministers. Besides fitting him out, he has taken out 5 different Sorts of carriages with him. Yet of a consul it is not expected that they live in splendour—but enough of this.

Write me very particularly, if you want any thing in my *power*, let me know, you know how limited they are, so your wants will be in proportion. Remember me to your Brothers and be assured that I am at all times Your ever affectionate Mother   A A

Your Friend Murry dined here last week. West I believe is in the Country. I have not seen him a long time. Appleton[6] was here a few days since. Why does not he go home? Captain Lyde says he shall be here in the winter again. Be sure you write largely by him.

RC (Adams Papers); addressed by JA: "To Mr John Quincy Adams Boston"; notation by AA: "pr favour Capt Lyde"; endorsed: "Mamma. August 23d. 1785"; docketed: "My Mother. 23. Augt. 1785," and "Mrs. Adams. Augt. 23. 1785."

[1] 26 June and 11 Aug., both above.

[2] Royall Tyler.

[3] The completed treaty was that with Prussia; see AA2 to JQA, 4 July, note 33, above.

[4] JA had his first conference with William Pitt the following day, when he presented his proposals for settling the issues that remained outstanding between the United States and Great Britain: the British army's occupation of the forts in the Northwest, British trade restrictions, compensation for slaves carried off by the British army during the war, and American debts due to British creditors. But he made no more progress with the prime minister in August than he had in June and July with the foreign secretary, Lord Carmarthen, and these issues remained unresolved until the Jay Treaty of 1794 (see JA to John Jay, 25 Aug., PCC, No. 84, V, f. 605–619, printed in *Dipl. Corr., 1783–1789*, 2:455–462; JA, *Diary and Autobiography*, 3:181–182, note 1).

⁵ Louis XVI of France; see AA to JQA, 11 Aug., and note 4, above.
⁶ Perhaps John Appleton, son of Nathaniel Appleton of Boston, whom JA and JQA had met in Europe in 1780, and whom JQA last recorded seeing in Paris in Jan. 1785 (JQA, *Diary*, 1:35, and note 2, 52–54, 216).

Abigail Adams to Thomas Welsh

My dear sir   [25 *August* 1785]¹

Your obliging favour of April 25² came to hand by Captain Lyde just after my arrival here. The important affairs of Court Etiquette and prepareations for shewing myself at St. James occupied my time so fully that I could not write you as I wished by Captain Dashood who saild soon after. When this great epocha of my Life was past, I had to seek a habitation and to see it put in order for ⟨my⟩ the reception of the family. After much inspection and serching not for the Grandure of the Building but for an airy situation, I very fortunately lit of one in the most reputable and prettyest Squares in London. If I could feel myself elated by my vicinity to Nobility I might boast the greatest share of it, of my square in London, but I am too much of a republican to be charmd with titles alone. ⟨*We are however still opposite to Lord North.*⟩ We have not taken *a side with* Lord North but are still *opposite* to him.³

The sedition of Massachusetts is much the topick of conversation at present, and your late Navigation act is termed a ruining of yourselves. So tender are these good people of their *Dear American Friends* that they tremble at your rash passion, for say they the⁴ other states will never come into it, and Massachusetts will be intirely shut from our ports. But those who see beyond the present moment view the Massachusetts in concequence of it, rising into power and greatness should this nation be mad enough to continue on its present System. It will soon make the American states a formidable Naval power. It will force upon them frugality, oconomy, industery and give a spring to manufactorys which would otherways lag on for years without any considerable improvements. ⟨*A few temporary inconveniencies will be felt at first which will creat some discontents.*⟩ Excellence is never granted to man but as the Reward of Labour, but those who persevere in habits of industry however slow their advances will meet a sure ⟨*reward in*⟩ recompence in the end. A few temporary inconveniencies will be felt at first, which will create disgust in some, but they are the only measures which can be persued to bring this country to reasonable terms with ours. And should those fail we shall certainly reap the benifit, for we shall be improveing and advancing our National prosperity whilst Britain is diminishing hers. Mr. A. had yesterday a conference with Mr. P.⁵ and he appears to see much further than the avoued dispisers of America, but he is under the weight of Irish resentment and British Bilingsgate. His Friends tremble for him, least the opposition should tumble him from his seat, but his private Character is so good, and his application and assiduity so constant that however unpopular the Irish propositions have made him, I rather think they will not be able to Shake him. But whether he will have courage to encounter British prejudices against America time only can determine.

It was a saying of king Richards "that God helps those who help themselves."⁶ I should think our Countrymen have too often experienced this doctrine not to see their path plain before them.

Having set before you my dish of politicks I will inquire a little respecting domestick fare. Pray how does Mrs. Welch and the Young Brood? Tell her I desire to have so much respect for my Name if she will not for her own as to Name the next daughter for me.⁷ Is cousin William like to be married yet?⁸ Tell him to wait a little longer and who knows but that I may have the Honour of calling him son yet?!

When you write tell me all about your good Towns folks, whose married whose born and whose dead? There is not a cat if it is American, but what I have a value for.

This is a delightfull country and with cash enough one may enjoy every comfort and conveniency of Life aya and misery too. I wish it was in my power ⟨to see more of it. The load of taxes is so enormous that it destroys much of the Beauty and Harmony of the Whole.⟩ to make the tour of it. All the vilages round London are like so many gardens, but the people groan and justly under the loads of taxes which are enormous. ⟨Two⟩ ⟨3⟩ 5 additional taxes have taken place since my comeing here, one upon shops one upon pedlars and one upon gloves—in short you can scarcely name an article but what is taxed. They may talk of the lawless Americans and the disturbances which they magnify here into annihilation of Government, but there is ⟨more⟩ twice the real discontent in this Nation which subsists in any part of America.

But I am running on in great length yet have many others to write to. My best regards to Mrs. Welch and the children, Love to cousin Betsy.⁹ Tell her I often reflect upon the many pleasant hours we have spent together with much delight. Mr. Adams joins me in affectionate remembrance to all our worthy Friends. We hope our son is with you before now. Let me recommend him to you as a Youth not altogether

Ignorant of Men or Books who I hope will deserve the good will and esteem of Gentleman of Learning and abilities and the Friendship of those particularly allied to Sir your Friend and Humble Servant

A Adams

Dft (Adams Papers); notation by CFA: "1785." Filmed under date of July? 1785 (Adams Papers, Microfilms, Reel No. 365).

[1] On the date, see note 5.

[2] Not found.

[3] That is, Lord North lived on the opposite side of Grosvenor Square (see AA2 to JQA, 4 July, above, under "Tuesday July 26th"; AA to Mary Cranch, [*ca. July-Aug.*], above).

[4] Above the line AA inserts "ye," an extremely rare case of her using the thorn.

[5] For the substance of JA's 24 Aug. meeting with William Pitt, see AA to JQA, 23 Aug., note 4, above.

[6] For an earlier usage of this same quotation, see AA to Royall Tyler?, [*post 4 June* 1783], above.

[7] Abigail Kent Welsh was Rev. William Smith's niece; she married Dr. Thomas Welsh of Boston in 1777. In 1785 she was raising Dr. Welsh's two daughters by his first marriage, Charlotte and Harriet, as well as her son, Thomas Jr., and the *Records of the Church in Brattle Square, Boston*, p. 191, show the baptism of "William, son of Thomas and Welch" in Oct. 1784. Abigail Welsh evidently had no daughters, but the Welshes would name their last son John Adams Welsh in 1792. AA had known Dr. Welsh since at least 1775 (vol. 1:219, and note 8), but his lost letter to her of 25 April, and this reply, begin a correspondence that lasted to 1798. Dr. Welsh, his wife, and his daughter Harriet were among the closest friends of the Adams family from the late 1780s through the 1820s.

[8] Isaac Smith's son William.

[9] Probably Isaac Smith's daughter Elizabeth.

Abigail Adams 2d to John Quincy Adams

N 6

Grosvenor Square August 26th. 1785

Lyde sailed the 24th. with a long Letter for you from me,[1] and I have now commenced N 6, which I propose giving to the Care of Mr. Storer he talks of going next week. If so, this will be but short. But alas my Brother 14 weeks have elapsd since you left us, and we not yet any account of your arrival. Hopes and fears alternately possess my mind, and I can not banish anxiety upon your account. May you be safe, and happyly settled with your friends ere this. I think of you continually—our days are dull, and our Evenings very lonesome. Tis then I miss you most. You know not what a Winter I have in anticipation, the weather horrible, little society, no associates, no Brother, to enliven the scenes. Ah, I wish you were here. But I must indeavour to recollect the few event which have taken place since I closed my last. For this I must turn to my journal.[2] It tells me that a fryday the 11th.[3] your Mamma and myself and Mr. Storer called upon Mrs. Roggers and took her with us, to make a visit to Mrs. Hay at Hamsted, but there was not any thing took place worthy a relation.

Fryday, 12

Early in the Morning I heard a strange Noise about the House like the ringing on a warming Pan. Upon inquiry when I went down to Breakfast found from the servants that it was a set of People who Stile themselves Marro bone and cleavers,[4] belonging to the Prince of Wales, who had assaulted the House because it was his Highnesses Birth day,[5] and demanded mony as due to them from all the Foreign Ambassadors. However as Pappa had been deceived by the same People when he first arrived who called themselvs His Majestys Marro bone and cleavers—to whom he gave a gunia, and afterward found that they were not in the list of those who had a right to demand any thing—he did not give them any thing. When we first arrived we were applied to dayly, allmost Hourly by the People of the Kings Household, with their Books, with the Names of all the Foreign Ministers with sums given by each. These were Porters footmen Bell ringers under Porters, and the duce knows wholl all. Some demanded one Gunia and others 2, the whole sum which Pappa was obliged to give was not less than 25 or 30 Gunieas. This is a Custom of Courts, and you know one might as easily attempt to alter the course of the flowing of the sea, as to refuse them. Pappa has had a thrille fortior[6] this year. He gave Etrennes to you know what amount in France. Mr. ⟨Lotter⟩ Dumas was applyd to at the Hague, and Paid the usual sum, on your father account, and here he has Paid it upon being Presented, and at Cristmass, it will be demanded again. The whole will not amount to less I suppose than an hundred Guineas. Congress think not of these kind of demands. Perhaps some of them would rather think they ought to be refused—let them try.

Saturday 13th

Mr. Storer came to town from Hampstead and told us of the arrival of Calliham. He had received Letters we have none yet.

Sunday, 14

In the Morning Monsieur le Tombe called upon us just arrived from Boston, in Calliham. He brought Letters for Pappa but Mamma nor myself have received a single line.

We dined to day by invitation with Dr. Jebb and Lady. The company was not large. No Ladies except ourselvs. Dr. Jebb is an Irishman for which reason he is so greatly interested in the Present Commercial arangements with that Country. There were 4 Gentleman of the Party. Dr. Brocelsby, is an Englishman, the redness of whose face and the blackness of his habit did not form that pleasing contrast which sometimes pleases us. He is Said however to be a very sensible Man and Great in his Profession. He was moderate. There was one flaming son of St. Partrick. He had got his dinner some where else, and when we went to table had nothing to do but talk, and so improved his faculty of speach that he stund the rest of the company. Such Prejudices against the French Nation, I never heard. The Country its Government Laws, manners, customs &c. were atacked by him without reason Prudence or good sense. He was very voilent upon the American War also. He approved the independance of Ame[rica] because it could not be avoided by this Country but attributed to the fault of their Generals that we were not conquered. He would have granted the independance at first, and then have attacked the French. He could bear to see America independant but he could not support it, that France should be at peace. Every Englishman and Irish Man too I suppose thinks he has a right to Condemn or oppose the measures adopted by the rulers, as they seem fit in his Eyes. My Lord North Mr. Fox, &c. were condemd without Jury. In fine there was nothing that did not receive his disapprobation in the line of Politicks. When your father was speaking or appeard as if going to speak, he was all attention. I feard he would sometimes make Poppa warm, by his ignorance of our Country, and at the same time giving his Wise opinions respecting the War. There was another Irish Gentleman Present who seemd more reasonable. He did not say much.

The 4th. Gentleman was an Englishman, a Mr. Remain. He was young, and appeard to be possessd of a degree of Modesty bordering upon diffidence. He said but little. What he did discovered good sense but not unprejudicd [opinions?]. He was Silent while diner but at the desert found his tongue. I was seated next him at table, and he began by inquiring how long I was in France. He had been there, but viewed every thing I found with an Eye of prejudice. Paris was not so fine a City as London, the French Ladies he was sure could not be agreeable in the Eyes of the English, and in all he found a preference to this Country. I had like to have been in the sittuation of the Chevelier, who thought Mrs. Bingham belonged to Boston when he gave the preference to that part of the Continent to any other,[7] for before I sat down to table I had conceived an opinion that this gentleman was a Native of France but had been long in this Country. From his Name, complexion, and manners I was led to Judge thus, and I thought myself perfectly safe in the preference I shold give to that Country. But I soon found that I had a rong idea, for he was veryly English. Both the Dr. and Mrs. Jebb, spoke highly ⟨*in his*⟩ Praise of his abilities good sense Judgment &c., and I was willing to beleive them. Thus you have some account of the company. Were I to attempt a description of Mrs. Jebb, I should find myself unequal to the business. Perhaps you never saw just such a looking Woman. If you have seen Miss Polly Palmer[8] you have seen good Nature, softness, and sweetness of Countenance when compared to this Lady, but dont show Miss P— P— this. The Dr. is said to be a very Wise sensible Man, that he is an agreeable one, I can assure you. He says he wants to go to America and does not think it impossible that he may make the tour of America. Poor Man looks as if he was not intended long as an ornament to Learning, or Science: his Health is very Poor.[9]

Monday 15

My journal says, thus. Alas how frequently have we cause to observe upon what slender foundations we have raised our hopes of happiness and yet no sooner than the Ilusion of one prospect vanishes than we are building upon their ruin our future hopes, and this from a full confiction that it is necessary to cheat ourselvs thus. For three Months past I have been looking forward to the arrival of the July packet in hopes that it would bring the pleasing account of the arrival of my Brother. For three weeks past the anticipation of this and the hopes of receiving Letters from him have employd most of my thoughts wishes and expectations—but the packet has arrived without any account of my Brother. Thus at one moment all my pleasing prospect vanishes, and I have now to build other hopes and anticipate from other scources this pleasure.

Mortifying reflection that we are not permitted to look forward with any degree of certainty even to the next hour. Blind unthinking ignorant beings we are, yet Proud Vain selfsufficient arrogant and presuming. What is happiness? what is misery? How Poor a title have we to the former, and yet how little do we think of the latter.

⟨*Monday*⟩ Tuesday 16

We had a company of Gentlemen only to dine with us. Mr. David Hartly, dressed as usual.[10] Pappa asked him what he thought of the Massachusetts Navigation act. He said if the two Countries wished to be at variance he thought it very well. He would venture to Prophesy, that it would be the means of destroying ⟨*every*⟩ all Navigations acts whatever. He would not venture to say it would be done either one two or three years, but he firmly beleived that it would eventually be the effect of it. Pappa proposed to him in a banter that they shold undertake to repeal them, as his Commision for making a treaty of Commerce still existed. But he said that depended upon the higher Powers. He was willing however.

Mr. B[arthelemy] the Charge des affaires, from France,[11] was one of the company. Tho he has been in this Country a year and an half he does not pretend to speak English. His appearance has nothing very striking in it. His dress and Manners are Englasied. There is nothing very pleasing in them. Dr. Jeb, and Dr. Brocelsby dined with us, and your friend Mr. Murry. He seems to be in Poor Health and his spirits appear affected I think by it. He does not talk so much, nor discover so great a portion of vivacity as when I saw him last year. We talked about you, hoped you had arrived, yet wished you were here. Mrs. Temple and her Daughter drank tea with us. Mrs. T— is not gratified with the prospect of going out to America at all. They sail, the next week. I do not wonder at her reluctance ⟨*at all*⟩.

Monday 22d

There is a new Play lately given at the Hay Market called (*Ill tell you what*).[12] Much has been said in its Praise. It was written by a Lady two which you may be sure, in the Eyes of all Persons of discernment, is in its favour. Mr. Short said he should have returnd to France with a Poo opinion of the English Stage if he had not seen this Peice. Mis Farren Play as Principle character in it and Mr. S— observed she was the only Woman he had seen in England who knew she had Eyes. He was much pleased with her. I think she is the best actress I have seen upon the ⟨*Theatre*⟩ stage. They are in General, terrible. I often think of Mrs. Binghams comparing the Actors and Actresses upon the English stage to the stormitans—and must acknowledge that when compared with the French they appear nearer to resemble the former. Pappa went this Evening to see the New Commedy. It is rather what the French call a *drame*, some scens are said very affecting and others very comic. A Gentleman who had seen it told me that if one went to see it with an intention of becomeing critick they mingt find many faults, for [he] said, only think it was written by a Poor *Woman*, but if one went to see it and be pleased, he had found no peace which had given him so much pleasure.

A Letter from Mr. Jefferson, came by the Post to day.[13] He writes in sypher, and when there is nobody elce to desyper I have the agreable task. I am paid perhaps for my trouble by knowing what is written. *"He say the Cardinal Prince of Roan is confined to his Chamber under Guard for reflection on the Queen, who was present in Council herself on his examination the first time She was ever there—and the first instance of so high an eclesiastical character under acted force."*[14]

They are propagating reports here that American Ships are capturd by the Algerines, but whether true ⟨*or false is not known*⟩ or whether to raise the insureance is not known. Your father thinks the latter is the Plan. He has no accounts of any.[15] Mr. Lamb, who was sent by Congress to go to Algiers has never been herd of, this side the Water. Your father and Mr. Jefferson think it so necessary that something should be done that they think of sending some other Person. Mr. Barcley offers to go, but whether he is accepted I dont know.

Tuesday 23d

To day we had a large company to dine of Gentlemen and Ladies. The Baron de Linden, an old Womanish kind of a Man this, ⟨*and a Dutchman.*⟩ I have often heard that every thing was clean in a Dutchmans house but his Wife. Were I to form a judgment from this Man, I should think that the Husband ought also to be accepted for I never saw him decent in my Life. He goes to Court with a beard that looks as if it had not felt a razor for a week—and his ruffles look as if he did not often pay for their washing. I think one may easily discover strong traits of the character attributed to his Country Men in General perhaps universally for one may easily discover by little things the ruling Principles of the Mind and those which influence the Conduct ⟨*of People*⟩. Mr. Mrs. and Miss Paradise, were a part of our company. Mrs. P— discovered as many traits of singularity as ever. I beleive the Womans head is a little turnd. She has a Wondrous knowledge of Great Folks. Charles [*Storer*] was quite diverted with her. She had a great deel of conversation with him, and her manners were so particular that he says, he dreampt of her all Night. She inquired of him who was comeing as Ambassador from France in the place of Count D'adamar whose health will not permit his return. He told her the papers mentiond Monsieur la Baron de Bretuil.[16] Bretuil, Bretuil—Breteuil, remember Bretuil said She to her Daughter who sat next her, and turning to him again and said, I am going to ask you a very impertinent question and hope you will not be affronted. Pray what was the Name of that Gentleman who is said to be comeing Ambassader from France? The Baron de Bretuil, answer he again,

304

and She repeated it as many times. But her manners and actions are so singular that you must see her to have any idea of them.

Mr. and Mrs. Copely, Mrs. Church, and a Mr. James Smith, from Carolina, a distant relation of Mammas who is going to France to pass a twelvemonth, Mr. Trumble[17] and Dr. Bancroft made the company. The Dr. has just arrived from Paris, where he has been ever since we arrived here. Tis not the Custom in this Country for the Company to Leave you as soon as diner is over as it is in France. For sociability I prefer the Custom here, for ceremony I shuld choose the French Custom. But you know one must give in to all these kind of fashions, in every Country, for you can neither invite them to stay longer in France nor desire them to go sooner here. They parted about ten oclock. There are a kind of assemblys here called routs, were the name changed I should not dislike them. A Lady sets apart a particular day in a week when She is to be found at home and her acquaintance who wish to see her, call upon her that Evening, or She sends invitations to whatever Gentlemen or Ladies She pleases. Cards are usualy introduced after tea and those Play who choose. Others who do not, let it alone. And at ten or Eleven the company Leaves her. The Lady of the House never Plays herself, and it is a kind of rule that if you Play at one House, you must at every one, at which you visit in this Way. This Mrs. Paradise has a Musical [Part?] every sunday Eve. Miss P— Plays, and she has a Number of Gentlemen and Ladies of her acquaintance who sing and Play, who visit her that Evening. She has no Cards. She has often told Mamma and myself that she is allways at home of a sunday Eve, but we have not yet ever visitted her, nor I dont suppos ever Shall.

Fryday 26th

A Monday last Count Sarsfeild called upon Pappa. He has lately returnd from the Country, where he has been with some of his friends. Pappa asked him to dine with him a tuesday, but he was engaged but proposed dining with us this day, upon which Pappa invited the Baron de Linden and Mr. B[arthelemy] to dine with him. We received afterwards a Card to dine with a Mr. and Mrs. Smith who Live at Clapham. He is a Member of Parliament, and Married a Miss Capes.[18] A Brother and two sisters of this Lady Live also at Clapham. They have all visitted us, and seem to wish for an acquaintance. This is the second invitation to dine which we have had and been obliged to refuse. I was sorry, that it so happened to day, because

I shuld like to visit every Person who invited me, but it was unavoidable. The Baron de Linden did not come. Count Sarsfeild and Mr. B dined with us, quite in a sociable way. A Mr. Crew from Virgina[19] and Mr. Charles Bullfinch were all the company. The Count is allways in good spirits and very entertaining you know. He was more so to day than I ever saw him, for he was not under any restraint from Company. Mr. B— felt quite at home too, and was very clever. The other and the enclosed Letter is from a friend of yours we suppose.[20] It was sent us by Mr. Roggers. Pappa has inquird of Mr. Bartlemey and Count Sarsfeild, if they know the French Minister at Naples, but they did not seem to feel themselvs authorised to give any Letters. If you wish to write him I will put your Letters, into the Care of Mrs. Roggers.

Fryday september ⟨1st⟩ 2nd

This Morning Mrs. Wright came and breakfasted with us. I never heard her converse so rationally in my Life. She asked if we had heard of your arrival and sayd to Mamma do you know that I predict great things of your son—and spoke much in your praise. I shall like her better for the future, I need not tell you what, but save your vanity. The Mrs. Smith, from whom we had an invitation to dine, called upon your Mamma, but she being dressing I went down. There was with her a Mis Brailsford—and they provoked me by their ignorance of us. Which Country, said Miss B— do you like best France or this. I told her I preferd some things in each—but surely said She you prefer this Country to America. Indeed Miss answerd I, I do not. You must think this the finest Country, the Cultivation is greater and every thing superior. That may be, but I have friends and Connections in America that will ever make it dear to me. Tis not merely the place which I regard, tis what friends and acquaintancees I find.[21]

september 5th. Monday Morning

Last Night I wrote you thus far, but had not spirit to proceed. This Morning just as I went down to breakfast one of the servants came up with a huge packet, with Mr. Churchs Compliments. I was so rejoiced as I cannot tell you how. Your hand writing was first sought for, and as soon as found the seal broke, where I found your two Letters N 3, and 4,[22] and such a feast as it was, no one thought of tea toast or bread and butter, for an hour, quite sattisfied with the food for the mind. And now I have perused, them and ⟨*gained a little*⟩ and got a little over the agreeable flutterations and heart beetings I am prepared to acknowledge their receipt to thank you for your punctuallity to chide you for not having been more particular to excuse you for this time, and to give you a little sisterly advice, and many more things which Shall follow. 1st. Monday Morning sep. 5th. 1785. Nine oclock, received from Mr. Church your Letters, after a passage of only 1 Month, which heightend their vallue, much. 2d. Your punctuallity in writing on Ship Board, leads me to hope you will never forget your promises, and that I shall know something of you every day, and thus encourage me to pursue my diary, which sometimes I fear is too minute, but you shall determine its continuance. 3dly. to Chide you for not having told me more about the folks you became acquainted, than their Names. I wanted to hear your comparisons, and your remarks, upon every one, in Short I wished you only to have thought aloud, to me. I was a little surprised to hear Miss Sears termed a *Wit*. She was not called so in Boston I beleive. My idea of her was that she possessed a simplicity, more amiable than smartness. I wished to have heard your remarks upon Mr. R–.[23] I have seen him but have not the slightes personal acquaintance with. I have heard his character, perhaps not justly described, but I can excuse you because I know when one first arrives, in a strange place, we feel, puzled, hurried. The attentions we receive demand much of our time and attention. Now for my advice. As I feel myself so much interested in your following it I hope you will excuse it. You are a young Man, with a warmpth of temper which you leads you to judge rather prematurely and to condemn without sufficiently considering the for and against. Think this not a harsh accusation. You supposed I had neglected you when you found Mr. Cursen had no letter for you[24]–the Gentleman had seen me, and it was quite unpardonable that I did not write. Now, you must have given place in your mind to an Idea disadvantageous to me, and as it was not just I must feel myself injured by it. Appearances were in your favour I'll allow, but as I wish you to avoid the painfull idea of my inattention to you, I must beg in future that you would weigh possibilities in future, and Ill tell you ⟨*what*⟩ [how?] it happend that Mr. C. Carred you no Letter. The unsettled situation we were in the Continued visits made us, and the Whole suit of adventures enough to puzzle the Brain of a Philosopher, did not prevent me from writing. I had finished my Letter and seald it for Mr. Cursen, but Colln. Smith who had promised to deliver it to him happend to forget it, and he [*Curson*] left town, without it. Now, ⟨*please to retract*⟩ as I know it is not plasing to retract, I will excuse you provided you will consider the next time before you condemn. The letter I forwarded immediately to Mr. Williamos to go in the June packet and he informs me that he inclosed it to a friend, who would deliver it if you were at N. York when the packet should arrive and if you were gone on, would forward it to you.[25] In a few days I wrote you again and Colln. Smith inclosed my Letter to Mr. King, since which I have written too long letters besides this—which is N 6.[26]

I fear your Passage was long and disagreeable, your passengers not the most agreeable, neither. I know well how painfull a Life on Ship board is, even where every one indeavours to make it tolerable. The insipid sameness, which must forever reign, must be tiresome, and an impatient disposition must suffer more than I can have an idea of. But you are safe landed, Heaven be praised, and in health. Take care to preserve it. Great attention will be necessary, for you. I am happy that you found so many friends, and were shewn so much attention, for nothing is so pleasing, whether it arrises from our own merit or our connection with People of merit. I have sometimes thought that we are better pleased with those attention which we receive upon account of our friends than those paid merely to our-selvs. In *some* cases, I have been assertaind of the preference, and beleive it will allmost pass for a general rule. Why is it that our American Ladies, are so fond of connections with foreignors?[27] I confess it does not strike me in an agreeable point of view. There are no People, easier deceived than we are, I beleive nor, none more easily [daizled?] by Glitter and Show. But they should remember that

> Not all that tempts your wandring Eyes
> And heedless hearts, is lawfull prise,
> Not all that Glissters Gold.[28]

The National Characters are very strongly impressed upon most People, yet I would not venture to pass upon any without exception, for there a[re] Men from every Nation untinctured by the Character-istick vices, or foibles of it. Tho ninety Nine in an hundred, Dutch-men May be Misers, avaricious, and, mean spiritted, and the same proportion of Englishmen, surly Ill Natured, prejudiced ⟨and self⟩ Drunkards, the Spain[ish] Jealous and revengefull, the French, flighty inconstant and insincere, yet I would not venture to affirm that either of these Characters were universal in their Different Countries, for the *one* in an hundred may posess the virtues of each, and be exempt from any real vices.

Your Father wishes that some person would except the embassey to Holland, for something or other is continually presenting to teise him, which an Minister there would releive him from. Tis hard that he should be tormented with so many perplexities which the attention of Congress might releive him from.

You will hear accounts of the season from the Papers. The drought has been excessive, especially in France. They endeavourd to furnish themselvs with fodder from this Country, but, it was obliged to be prohibitted here. Count Sarsfeild said the other day, that he knew not what to do, the ensueing Winter. If he stayd in Paris, he should [*be*] put to it to keep his horses, and if he went into the Country it would be worse, and added that a great Number of Cattle must be killed, for want of provender. Every thing here is dearer than usual, on account of the drought. Tho the late, plentifull rains have been of vast service, fruit here is Scarce and dear as well as far from being Good. We have given, sometimes half a Guniea for a Mellon, and sixpence a peice for every peach. This must sound very surprising with you [Now?].

Miss Van Berkel, must have had a disagreeable time I think. The Ladies, make remarks, and perhaps triumpth, if there is opportunity. They had better appear conspicuoes for their Candour, for their is not a more amiable ⟨*principle*⟩ trait in the Character of a Lady, and, prove themselvs superior, by their behavour towards her, than a greater degree of beauty could render them.

Tuesday september 13th

Charles [*Storer*] procastinate from day to day his departure. He now says he shall go tomorrow certainly but it may be the latter part of the week. I am very glad that I set my last by Lyde. I am sure he may make half his passage before, this young Man sails. The last week nothing took place to tell you of, except what Mamma has writen you,[29] that Mr. Barcley and Mr. Franks, are going to Algiers, and that the latter is here at present, waiting for his instructions from your father. Very unfortunately the day after his arrival, your father was seized with a [violent?] inflamation in his Eyes,[30] that rendered writing all most impracticable. And Mr. Smith has not yet returnd from his tour. But perhaps I have never yet told you where he has gone, and I now inform you, to Berlin to be present at the King of Prussias reveiw. We expect him soon.

We fear that you will not have so frequent opportunities to write us from Boston as we shall wish to hear from you, therefore request that you will write by the Packet send your Letters to some Member of Congress, and desire them to be forwarded by the English packet. Dont fail. You know how very sollicitous we shall be to hear frequently from you, and, you also know how apt People who get to America are to be inattentive. Let us not suppose it universall.

I have sent you by Mr. Storer a box containing a pd of sealing Wax. I think it is good. You will see from whence it came, and think it a Modest way of begging. When we first arrived we had continual applications of this kind. They are at present less frequent. Your Books and watch Chain I have also put into the Care of Mr. Storer. If there is any thing which you want and it is in my Power to send it you, write for it. In return I request, a lock of your hair, which I forgot to have before you left us. I dont mean, Sampsons locks, nor, a lock from your Eye brows, and hope you will not demand mine in return.

I do not recollect at present any news, or any thing interesting to communicae. And as my Letter I fear is already so long as will tire your patience I shall haste to subscribe myself your affectionate sister

A Adams

[I?]³¹ thank fortune we are not dependant upon the favours nor Smiles of Majesty, nor think ourselvs servilely dependant upon their customs, so we will act as we like, and bid them defiance not fearing Mob or any thing else. Your father says he observes a fear in every one of the Foreign Ministers of being known to have any intimacy with him least they should be mob'd. One would not like to be in danger to be sure. I should as willingly put myself at the Mercy of so many savages as to the Mobility in this Country. But all this is high treason so keep it to yourself.

Dft (Adams Papers); the text is written on twenty-one small pages, several of them numbered. The MS is in good condition; it is AA2's occasionally poor hand and her incomplete expressions that call for the bracketed material.

¹ Of 4 July, above.

² The MS of AA2's journal has not been found; all that survives in journal form appears in AA2, *Jour. and Corr.*, vols. 1 and [3]. The printed journal from 7 Aug. 1784 though 4 June 1785 (*Jour. and Corr.*, 1:viii, and 7–79) gives some idea of how regular and full AA2's complete diary probably was. Fragments of her journal from 26 Aug. through 18 Dec. 1785 are in *Jour. and Corr.*, 1:viii–xi, 79–84, and [3]:185–205. Large sections of all six extant AA2 letters to JQA in 1785, however, were probably copied with little alteration from AA2's journal, including much of the present letter. AA2's journal entries for 28 Sept. through 18 Dec. 1785, printed in *Jour. and Corr.*, [3]:185–205, were also incorporated in a letter to JQA, which has not been found.

³ The 11th fell on Thursday.

⁴ "Marrowbones and cleavers" was an eighteenth-century term for ancient British instruments of "rough music" (*OED*).

⁵ The Prince of Wales, later George IV, was twenty-three.

⁶ This Anglo-French compound phrase, written as though entirely French, appears to be AA2's coinage, apparently meaning a "strong shock."

⁷ The exchange between Maurice Riquet de Caraman, who had traveled to America

with the Marquis de Lafayette, and Anne Willing Bingham, a native of Philadelphia, occurred at Lafayette's home on 7 March (*JQA, Diary*, 1:230).

[8] Mary Palmer, a daughter of Gen. Joseph Palmer, had been an invalid since her youth, when a gun discharged near her head caused a permanent nervous condition (*Grandmother Tyler's Book*, p. 23–25).

[9] Jebb died "of decline" the following March at age fifty (*DNB*).

[10] Perhaps dressed quite plainly, as he appears in Romney's portrait of him (Namier and Brooke, *House of Commons*, 2:592).

[11] François Barthélemy had served as chargé d'affaires, with one brief break, from July 1784 (*Repertorium der diplomatischen Vertreter aller Länder*, 3:118).

[12] Elizabeth Inchbald's well-received comedy, *I'll Tell You What*, was first performed on 4 August. Elizabeth Farren's role was the "Lady" (*Some Account of the English Stage from the Restoration in 1660 to 1830*, 10 vols., Bath, England, 1832, 6:368–369).

[13] To JA, 17 Aug., with a decoding of the encoded passages, in AA2's hand, on the blank third sheet of the letter (Adams Papers).

[14] The underscored passage, beginning at "the Cardinal Prince," quotes AA2's decoding of Jefferson's letter, but introduces a few errors: the decoding has "Rohan" for "Roan," and "reflections," it places "herself" before "in Council", and it has "actual force" rather than "acted force." AA2's decoding agrees almost exactly with Jefferson's uncoded draft text; see Jefferson, *Papers*, 8:394–395. On Cardinal Rohan and the Diamond Necklace Affair, see Jefferson to AA, 4 Sept., note 3, below.

[15] Presumably meaning "of any captures." See AA to William Stephens Smith, 13 Aug., and note 4, above.

[16] Jean Balthazar, Comte d'Adhémar, the French ambassador to Great Britain since May 1783, had been minister plenipotentiary to the Austrian Netherlands, 1774–1781. He was not replaced in London at this time, although he took several leaves from his post, and he served until Jan. 1787. Louis Auguste Le Tonnelier, Baron de Breteuil, a French envoy to several countries over two decades, held no posts after 1783. *Repertorium der diplomatischen Vertreter aller Länder*, 3:118, 128 (Adhémar); 113, 122, 125, 136, 139 (Le Tonnelier).

[17] John Trumbull, the painter, had been in London for over a year, studying with Benja-

min West (*DAB*).

[18] William Smith, the son of a merchant of Clapham Common, entered the House of Commons for Sudbury in 1784, and sat almost continuously, for various districts, until 1830. He was a supporter of Pitt's parliamentary reform effort of April 1785, and was later a dissenter and an opponent of all religious tests for office, as well as of the slave trade. Smith married Frances Coape in 1781. Namier and Brooke, *House of Commons*, 3:452–453.

[19] Robert Crew was a London tobacco merchant from Virginia (Jefferson, *Papers*, 7:434; 18:309).

[20] AA2 does not set this and the following sentences off from the preceding text despite the sudden and obscure change in subject matter. The editors have not identified "the other" or "the enclosed Letter." In Aug. 1785, Dominique Vivant Dénon, the French chargé d'affaires in Naples, had just departed for France; his replacement, Louis Marie Anne, Baron de Talleyrand-Périgord, a relative of the famous diplomat of the Napoleonic era, had just arrived (*Repertorium der diplomatischen Vertreter aller Länder*, 3:139).

[21] AA2, *Jour. and Corr.*, 1:79–80, gives a longer account of the exchange with Miss Brailsford, in which AA2 expressed her views with less reservation, and compared both the United States and France favorably to England in several respects. Her opinions there are quite similar to those of AA in her letter to Elizabeth Storer Smith, 29 Aug., below.

[22] Of 25 May, and 17 July, both above.

[23] The editors have not identified "Mr. R—." In his letter of 17 July, JQA mentions meeting Dr. David Ramsay and John Rutledge, both of South Carolina, and Francisco Rendon, the secretary to the Spanish envoy, Diego de Gardoqui. It is not known whether AA2 ever met any of these three men.

[24] See JQA to AA2, 17 July, and note 10, above.

[25] This letter, probably marked N. 2 and written about 1 June, has not been found.

[26] AA2's letter to JQA, marked N. 3, dated 13 June, and sent with a William Stephens Smith letter to Mr. King [Rufus King?], presumably by a vessel sailing for New York, was received by JQA at Boston on 31 Aug. (JQA to AA2, 29 Aug., below), but has not been found; nor has another letter, probably marked N. 4, and perhaps written toward the end of June. The second of AA2's "too long letters besides this" is N. 5, of 4 July, above.

[27] AA2 is probably responding to JQA's critical remarks, in his letter of 17 July, above, on the impending marriage between Miss Marshall of New York and Francisco Rendon.

[28] Thomas Gray, *Ode on the Death of a Favourite Cat.* The last line reads: "Nor all, that glisters, gold."

[29] AA wrote JQA on 6 and 12 Sept., both below.

[30] Lt. Col. David Salisbury Franks arrived from Paris on 10 Sept. (AA to JQA, 12 Sept., below), placing the onset of JA's malady on the 11th. Col. Franks served in the war from 1775 to 1780, then as a diplomatic courier, and briefly as vice-consul at Marseilles. On 4 Sept., Jefferson proposed to JA that Franks be named secretary to Thomas Barclay, whom they were sending to Morocco to negotiate a commercial treaty (Jefferson, *Papers*, 8:473). Franks carried Jefferson's letter to JA, and another from Jefferson to AA, of the same date, below, to London, where JA approved the mission on 15 Sept. (same, 8:521–522). Franks served in the Morocco mission until Dec. 1786. Hersch L. Zitt, "David Salisbury Franks, Revolutionary Patriot (c. 1740–1793)," *Pennsylvania History*, 16 (1949):77–95; Morris, *Papers*, 1:255–256.

[31] This character appears to be written on the edge of the page.

Abigail Adams to Lucy Cranch

London, (Grosvenor Square,)

My dear Lucy   27 August, 1785

I have not yet noticed your obliging favor of April 26th,[1] which reached me by Captain Lyde, whilst I was at the Bath Hotel. I had then so much upon my hands, that I did not get time to write but to your mamma and cousin, who I hope is with you before now. By him I wrote many letters, and amongst the number of my friends, my dear Lucy was not omitted.[2]

If I did not believe my friends were partial to all I write, I should sometimes feel discouraged when I take my pen; for, amongst so large a number of correspondents, I feel at a loss how to supply them all.

It is usual at a large entertainment, to bring the solid food in the first course. The second consists of lighter diet, kickshaws, trifles, whip syllabub, &c.; the third is the dessert, consisting of the fruits of the season, and sometimes foreign sweetmeats. If it would not be paying my letters too great a compliment to compare any of them to solid food, I should feel no reluctance at keeping up the metaphor with respect to the rest. Yet it is not the studied sentence, nor the elaborate period, which pleases, but the genuine sentiments of the heart expressed with simplicity. All the specimens, which have been handed down to us as models for letter-writing, teach us that natural ease is the greatest beauty of it. It is that native simplicity too, which gives to the Scotch songs a merit superior to all others. My favorite[3] Scotch song, "There's na luck about the house," will naturally occur to your mind.

I believe Richardson has done more towards embellishing the present age, and teaching them the talent of letter-writing, than any other modern I can name. You know I am passionately fond of all his works, even to his "Pamela." In the simplicity of our manners, we judge that many of his descriptions and some of his characters are beyond real life; but those, who have been conversant in these old corrupted countries, will be soon convinced that Richardson painted only the truth in his abandoned characters; and nothing beyond what human nature is capable of attaining, and frequently has risen to, in his amiable portraits. Richardson was master of the human heart; he studied and copied nature; he has shown the odiousness of vice, and the fatal consequences which result from the practice of it; he has painted virtue in all her amiable attitudes; he never loses sight of religion, but points his characters to a future state of restitution as the sure ground of safety to the virtuous, and excludes not hope from the wretched penitent. The oftener I have read his books, and the more I reflect upon his great variety of characters, perfectly well supported, the more I am led to love and admire the author. He must have an abandoned, wicked, and depraved heart, who can be tempted to vice by the perusal of Richardson's works. Indeed, I know not how a person can read them without being made better by them, as they dispose the mind to receive and relish every good and benevolent principle. He may have faults, but they are so few, that they ought not to be named in the brilliant clusters of beauties which ornament his works. The human mind is an active principle, always in search of some gratification; and those writings which tend to elevate it to the contemplation of truth and virtue, and to teach it that it is capable of rising to higher degrees of excellence than the mere gratification of sensual appetites and passions, contribute to promote its mental pleasures, and to advance the dignity of our natures. Sir Joshua Reynolds's observations[4] with respect to painting may be applied to all those works which tend to refine the taste, "which, if it does not lead directly to purity of manners, obviates, at least, their greatest depravation, by disentangling the mind from appetite, and conducting the thoughts through successive stages of excellence, till that contemplation of universal rectitude and harmony, which began by taste, may, as it is exalted and refined, conclude in virtue."

Why may we not suppose, that, the higher our attainments in knowledge and virtue are here on earth, the more nearly we assimilate ourselves to that order of beings who now rank above us in the world of spirits? We are told in scripture,[5] that there are different kinds of glory, and that one star differeth from another. Why should not those who have distinguished themselves by superior excellence over their fellow-mortals continue to preserve their rank when admitted to the kingdom of the just? Though the estimation of worth may be very different in the view of the righteous Judge of the world from that which vain man esteems such on earth, yet we may rest assured that justice will be strictly administered to us.

But whither has my imagination wandered? Very distant from my thoughts when I first took my pen.

We have a large company to dine with us to-day, and I have some few arrangements to make before dinner, which obliges me to hasten to a conclusion; among the persons invited, is a gentleman who married the only daughter of Richardson.[6] She died about six months ago. This gentleman has in his possession the only portrait of her father which was ever taken. He has several times invited me to go to his house and see it. I design it, though I have not yet accepted his invitation.

Write to me, my dear Lucy, and be assured I speak the words of truth and soberness when I tell you that your letters give real pleasure to Your affectionate aunt, A.A.

MS not found. Printed from AA, *Letters*, ed. CFA, 1848, p. 261–263; 1841, 2:109–112; 1840, p. 306–310.

[1] Not found.
[2] To Lucy Cranch, 6 May, above.
[3] The 1840 edition lacks "favorite."
[4] The 1840 edition has "observation."
[5] "Scripture" is capitalized in the 1840 edi-

tion. The scriptural verse is 1 Corinthians 15:41.
[6] Edward Bridgen had married Martha Richardson (see AA2 to JQA, 4 July, above).

Abigail Adams to Elizabeth Storer Smith

My dear Madam   August 29 1785 London

Mr. Storer your worthy Nephew will be the Bearer of this Letter. I congratulate his Friends upon his return to them, after several Years absence, tho we shall essentially feel his loss, being as much attached to him as if he was our own. The appointment of a secretary of Legation prevents Mr. Adams from taking any other, which he realy stands in need of. If he had been allowed one, Mr. Storer would have had the preference, and we should have had much pleasure in keeping him in our family. I hope by returning to America he will be able to do better. A Young Gentleman at his time of Life, ought to be establishing himself in some profession, whereby he may serve himself and his generation. It was a thorough conviction of this truth, that induced us to part with our Son, who I hope is safe arrived before this time in his Native Country, where by application and industry he may be sure of obtaining his Bread.

The more my dear Madam that I see of Europe the more I am attached to the method of Education persued in the state of Massachusets. If our Youth have not all those opportunities for improvement in some branches of Literature, and the fine Arts, which these old countries can boast, they have sufficient to qualify them for any departments they may be called to fill. An acquaintance with foreign Countries, is no doubt a benifit when properly improved, as it tends to ⟨improve⟩ remove prejudices, and enlarge the mind. But I question much whether out of the many Youth who come Anually from all parts of America, more of them do not return with corrupted morals, and a distaste to the purer manners of our own Country, than with improved understandings or wiser Heads. As to civility of behaviour, politeness of Manners, true Hospitality and Benevolence, this Country have much more need of going to America to learn them, than our Country has of any embelishment this can bestow. I have seen and heard more narrow prejudice, more Illiberality of Sentiment, not merely with regard to America, but every other Country and its inhabitants; since my residence here, than I ever Saw or heard in America in my whole Life. And all the contracted Sentiments which we ever possesst with respect to other Countries, we imbibed from this, when we Reverenced her and her sentiments as our parent. But as soon as we came to think and act for ourselves, we broke the shackles.

I have never been in company since my return from France without being immediately ask'd which Country I prefer? This I should esteem as mere words of Course if I did not see how quick it touches them to have the least preference in any respect given to France; tho on many accounts I like this Country best, and have in my heart a greater fondness for it, I have been often tempted to shew the Contrary, on purpose to mortify the pride of this people, who realy in point of civility to strangers, and good Breeding, are not to be compared with their Neighbours whom they so contemptably despise. You will think I fear that I am desplaying those very prejudicies which I condemn; but I will appeal to the judgment of all my Countrymen who have visited the two Countries.

Dr. Price has the most liberal sentiments of any Gentleman I have heard converse since my residence here, he is indeed one of the best of Men, but the dessenting Clergy in this Country appear a very different set of Men from those which inhabit ours. They are

315

cramped contemned and degraded, they have not that independant appearence, and that consciousness of their own worth which gives an Air of dignity to the whole deportment. Dr. Price notwithstanding his literary fame, and his great abilities, appears like a Man who has been brow beaten. In America he would be revered and caresed, as his merit deserves.

We had a visit the other day from Mr. Tom. Boylstone. He appears to have an affection for Boston and his old Friends, tho he will not allow that there are any honest folks there, my good uncle excepted. He appears to wish for an amicable settlement between the two Countries, tho he says he shall not live to enjoy it.[1] He has had a severe fever which he says has left him weak as a Child in Body and Mind. His Nerves are much affected. You will easily believe he is allarmed when I tell you that he keeps a Pheaton and pair,[2] and rides every day. He talks of going to the South of France for the winter.

I have been once to see Mrs. Hollowell since I returnd,[3] she seems much broke since last I saw her. If I was not here in a publick Character, I should visit her more, and cultivate our old family Friendship, but there are persons who will belie one, and say things which were never meant or thought of, so that there is no safety but in keeping quite clear. Many of the Refugees appear to have lost all Idea of truth, and even those who are well disposed too readily credit their assertions.

I visit Mr. Vassels family, and have seen there, a Mrs. Hobart, who always kindly inquires after you.

I shall miss Mrs. Atkinson and am very sorry to part with her. Mrs. Hay and She are to dine with me to day. You will be so good as to remember me kindly to Mr. Otis and Lady to all my cousins and be assured Dear Madam that I am most affectionately Yours   A A

Nabby desires her duty and Love to all her Friends.

RC (MHi:Smith-Carter Papers); addressed: "Mrs. Elizabeth Smith Boston"; notation in pencil: "Mrs. Adam[s] London—1785." A mend at a fold obscures the notation. Dft (Adams Papers).

[1] The draft concludes the sentence: "but looks to me as if he would not live long to enjoy it."

[2] AA likely refers to Boylston's notorious stinginess; see vol. 2:295, and note 2; 4:342, note 2.

[3] The draft continues: "she is much broken I think since I saw her last year. I should be fond of keeping up an acquaintance and Friendship with the family for her sake, but it is so difficult to visit any of these people without being belied by those with whom one cannot have any connection and who are full of resentment, that I know not any safety in their company." Despite her caution, AA did become a close friend of Mary Boylston Hallowell, who was JA's mother's first cousin.

John Quincy Adams to Abigail Adams 2d

N:8

August 29th. 1785 Boston

I came into Boston this morning, and shall probably spend the week here, in order to pay all my visits, and see all those persons, that it will be necessary to show myself to. Stopping at Milton, I was very much surprized, when Mrs. Warren inform'd me, that Mr. Otis[1] shut up last Saturday Evening: had the news come from any other Person, I should not at that time have believ'd it, for I was introduced to him, Saturday on the exchange, and dined at Uncle Smith's, in Company with him and his family. But it was as I have been told to day in town, a Circumstance, which happened in the afternoon, that obliged him finally to Close. Uncle, and Aunt Smith, and their family, are as you may well suppose, very much affected by this Event, which I imagine, was unexpected, even to them. There is a visible dejection in their Countenances, and I heartily sympathize with them. I saw Harry pass in the Street to day. Nobody I believe feels the misfortune, more than he does. I Dined to day at Mr. Breck's, in Company with Mr. Toscan, Mr. Tom Appleton, the brother of the gentleman now in England, Mr. Chaumont, Mr. L. Austin, and his brother, and two other french gentleman; and a Mrs. Shepherd, an English Lady; (I must beg her pardon, and your's for not introducing her first.)[2] She is about twenty five I imagine, very fair, well shaped, *and the only objection I have to her, is that she has what I call Italian eyes*. I don't know whether you will understand me, without an explanation. I mean no defect, but something very piercing, and rather harsh, that I have most commonly observed in the eyes of the Italians I have been acquainted with, there is something disagreeable to me, in it, and if I am whimsical, I must claim indulgence. Mr. Appleton I suppose you know at least as much of as I do: so I say nothing of him. It Rain'd in the afternoon, so that most of the Company stayd. The sight of cards drove me off early in the evening, for of late I have a great aversion for them, and should be perfectly contented never to touch another: pack. I spent the Evening at Dr. Welch's. Uncle Smith and his family were there; all in very low spirits, which you will easily account for.

August 30th. Tuesday

The Supreme Judicial Court, met to day: I went and heard the

317

Chief Justice, deliver the Charge to the grand Jury. I never heard either Lord Mansfield, Lord Thurlow, or Lord Loughborough (and I have heard them all,) speak with more dignity: they never spoke upon a more important subject; for it was almost entirely upon the Education of youth. I was very sorry to hear him Complain, that many towns in the State have neglected to maintain the public Schools: and I sincerely hope, what he said may be productive of good effects. Mr. Thatcher afterwards was called upon for a prayer, and made, one, extempore, very well adapted to the occasion. Mr. Dana for the first time fill'd one of the judge's Seats.[3]

Cambridge 9 at night

I came here this afternoon, and shall return to morrow. You have heard doubtless of the Bridge, they are building over Charlestown ferry: it was a great undertaking; and is carried on with a vast deal of Spirit. It was not begun till the latter end of May, and will be about half finished before the Winter comes on. If the Ice does not destroy it, (and I am told every possible Caution has been used to protect it) by the middle of next Summer it will be compleated; and if it stands, it will be a great saving in the End to the public, and will turn out, vastly to the advantage of the undertakers.[4] Charles is very much pleased with his situation here: and comes on well with his Studies. His Class is one of the most numerous of any that have entered.[5]

Boston August 31. Wednesday

Mr. Chaumont went to Cambridge this morning, and saw the Library and the museum, belonging to the University. I waited upon President Willard and deliver'd your Father's Letter.[6] Upon the account I gave him of myself, ⟨he s⟩ and upon my telling him I intended to wait till the next Commencement, he advised me rather to enter in the spring, so that I might have the benifit of two lectures upon natural Philosophy. So it is now decided that I am to go and spend some months at Mr. Shaws, though I do not expect to get there finally before the beginning of October. I return'd here with Mr. Chaumont, and as I was standing in the Street before the door of the Post Office with Mr. Tyler, a letter was handed to me from it; my hopes were immediately raised, I broke the seal, and found a very polite Letter from Mr. King, enclosing your N:3. June 13th. from the Bath Hôtel.[7] I never received but one Letter that gave me more Pleasure, and that was about 14 months ago from my friend Murray.[8] You begin with a

Caution which I am sorry to have given Cause for, but for which I sincerely thank you. It is a great Consolation, when we are Sensible of having failed, to have friends, who can kindly reprove us. Let me request you my Sister, that you will continue to be my monitor when I may fall into other errors, and I am sure that will correct me if any thing can. Your N:2 I wait impatiently for.[9] I hear not a word of Mr. Williamos, though you was ⟨*mistaken?*⟩ misinform'd as to there being no packet to sail in June from France, for she is arrived at New York after a passage of 52 days *from l'Orient*. What this second change, in the place of departure, is owing to I cannot imagine. Not to the influence of Mr. W. I believe.—I am very sorry to find you are not more pleased with your present Situation, than you was when at Auteuil: but I hope, you will, be more pleased after a Residence of some time: the first months are most commonly disagreeable, in a new place; because a person has not had time to form a society sufficient to pass pleasantly the leisure hours: but a number of Circumstances combine, to make your acquaintance more extensive than it was in France, and I dare say, by this time you relish your Situation much better, than you did the former. I am sufficiently sensible of your partiality for me, readily to believe, that you in some measure miss me. Had I consulted my present feelings, I certainly could not have been induced to leave you; but there is no necessity for me to inform you, of my motives; you know them and approved of the measure, as being the most advantageous for myself, that I could take. Was I now placed in the Situation I was in six months ago; although I might be still more sensible than I was, then, how much I should suffer, by a seperation from the best of Parents, and of Sisters, yet should I again follow the same course that I have pursued. My preferring to return home, has surprized a number of my young acquaintance here; much more than it would probably, if they had seen as much of Europe as I have. As for the diversions, and the splendor of those Countries, I have not bestow'd so much as one regret upon them: and if I ever do it will be because I shall be at a loss, what to do, and I am not afraid of that ever being the Case.—Do not think my Sister, that any thing coming from you, can ever be by me considered as ridiculous or trifling; I have been in my former Letters often so minute, that I was afraid it would be tiresome; but I now hope otherwise, and am certain it cannot be so, if I judge of your feelings from my own.—I have seen in the London Papers some Specimens of british (or rather refugee) politeness; but all

319

those paragraphs are like certain fowling pieces, which instead of wounding the game they are pointed as [*at*], as Mc:Fingal says,

> Bear wide, and kick their owners over.

I am not afraid of seeing any thing of the kind, directed against any of you, that will give me a minutes pain. The most ineffable contempt is the only Sentiment, they will ever raise in my breast. I want very much to hear how you went through the Ceremony of the presentation; with proper dignity and assurance, I dare say: but what I want are the minutiae. What will the King say, what the Queen &c., &c., &c. I suppose some trite, common place, things, which will be ennobled by coming from those who are the fountains of honour and dignity. The mighty of the Earth, seem to be conscious of their inferiority to the rest of the world; and therefore they chuse to envelope themselves in all the majesty of obscurity. Perhaps had I gone with you, I might also have enjoy'd the felicity of a presentation to his Majesty; but it cannot be and I must endeavour to bear my misfortune as firmly as possible.—I am glad to find you have engaged an house in so fine a Situation as Grosvenor Square, and I hope, that before now you are finally settled in it. And I am very glad to hear, that you will have the Dutch furniture. By the bye; perhaps Madam Dumas, will send my watch by that opportunity to you; if she does you can send it by Charles Storer to me, for the one I have does not go so well as I wish. If it should not be sent to you before this reaches, I wish you would send for it by the first good opportunity, and you will, I suppose find some body, that will take charge of it, for me; I little thought of such a seperation from it, when I left it at the Hague.—I have read in several of the London Papers that the Earl of Effingham, was to come here as Minister from that Court: you do not mention any thing upon that Subject in your Letter; but by the visit you had from the Countess I suppose the Intentions of the Court are really in that Case, as the Papers represent them.[10] Mr. Temple has been expected as Consul, at New York, these four months. I expected to have found him there on my arrival; Many Persons have enquired of me, whether he had sailed, and many here seem to doubt of his appointment: I have not been able to give any information on the Subject; and your Letter does not say a word concerning him. His Daughter, the great Toast of this town, is generally supposed to be about preparing a Treaty of alliance with Mr. Tom Winthrop:[11] and it is said the Preliminaries are agreed on by all the parties interested.

I have waited on the Governor, but have not yet had the good fortune of seeing Miss Temple.—There is a passage in your Letter which puzzles me very much: I cannot imagine what Character it is you allude to, and whose baseness has drawn a few misanthropic reflections from your pen. I read the passage of your Letter to Mr. Tyler, and ask'd him if he could explain it in any manner; *he thinks you must mean the husband of a Lady who is said to resemble you so much; he that was at Auteuil the day I left you:*[12] he tells me there is a story, very much to his disadvantage, and supposes you was inform'd of it after I came away: I was exceedingly surprised at this, and I cannot believe there is any truth in it. In one of my former Letters you will see an account of my reception in Consequence of a Letter from that person; but I did not tell you that he was enquired after by all the family, with as much apparent affection, as if he had been an own son, and Brother. And is it reasonable to suppose, that the parents and the Sister of an injured Lady, would show such a degree of fondness for the person who is supposed to have done her the harm: from the time I left you to this day I have never had Reason, to form one Suspicion against his Character, and I have often consider'd myself under obligations to him, as the Letters he gave me, have made me acquainted with a number of agreeable persons; and if he is the person you mean to speak of, I sincerely hope, you are mistaken as to his Character. I ask'd Mr. Tyler if he had written you this anecdote he told me of, and he says no: perhaps after all you was speaking of some other Character. I wish you would in your first Letter to me, after the reception of this, write me, how the matter is.—— I think with you, it was paying you but a poor Compliment, to find so great a Resemblance between you and me. But there are certain features, which I suppose every family have peculiar to themselves, and consequently a person of Mr. West's profession, who is obliged to study physiognomy, may perceive a likeness, which a man in any other, would not think of.—I perceive, that I have run on these six pages[13] in replying to your Letter, and I am very glad you have at length furnished me with subjects to write on; for I was quite ashamed to have nothing to say but what related to myself. But now I will again proceed in my narrative. I dined to day at Mr. Storer's in Company with Uncle Smith's family and Mr. Green's.[14] There was nobody present, that you are not acquainted with, so that there is no necessity of my giving you my Opinion, concerning any person there. This afternoon I paid a visit to Mr. Cushing the lieutenant Governor, but he was not, *chéz lui*. Drank tea at Mr. Appleton's, though I did not see him. Charlotte, has been for a long time in ill health, and is supposed to be in a Consumption. She is pretty, but I think not equal at present to her Sister Betsey;[15] I am thought here, some what peculiar in my taste: Ideas of Beauty are often local; and it is probable I have in Europe, corrupted mine. This Lady is not considered as extraordinary here; and I have been much less struck by several, whose Reputations, for personal Charms, are much higher. Her shape has been form'd by Nature such as the Ladies in Europe, [take?] so much pains to acquire; like a Wasp, as your Mamma used to say. Her manners are very easy, and she is properly sociable. I have seen very few young Ladies since my arrival, whose first sight has been so pleasing to me: and now my dear Sister, I must bid you good night, for I have written so much to day, that I have fairly tired myself out, and I am afraid you too. But I will make no apology lest it should induce you to shorten your Letters.

Thursday September 1st

We went to the forenoon ball at Concert hall.[16] There were very few Gentlemen there, but I should have supposed, every young Lady, in the town. At any rate there was more than an hundred, high and low, short and tall, plain and pretty, all in a jumble. Dined at Mr. Cushing's. The Company was not large. There were two young Ladies present, but I had no Conversation with them, and I do not know their names, though I believe they are nieces to Mr. Cushing. I have been paying as many visits as I possibly could all this week, for visits, I am obliged to pay; and not a few, I hope however by Saturday, to have nearly finished with Boston.

Friday 2d

Mr. Chaumont, was obliged to leave town to day, having made but a very short stay here.[17] He went in the afternoon, and I went as far as Roxbury with him. He is pleased with his Reception in Boston, as every foreigner must be, and proposes returning and spending some weeks here in the Course of the Winter or of the next Spring. The forenoon was very rainy so that I have not been into any Company to day. I spent the Evening with Dr. Tufts and Uncle Cranch. Aunt Tufts has been very ill, of late, and her life was despaired of; but she is now in a fair way of Recovering: her Son, I have not yet seen, though he has been in Boston all this week: this will not surprise you.[18]

Saturday 3d. Braintree

I left Town this morning at about 11 o'clock, and dined at Genl. Warren's. Mrs. Warren, went to Boston This forenoon, with Charles, who sails in the beginning of the Week, for Cadiz, from whence he proposes to go and join his brother at Lisbon. But I fear greatly he will never get there: I have but little hopes of ever seeing him again: though I sincerely wish I may be mistaken. The Genl. with the three other Sons, dined at home. He talks of selling that place, and returning to Plymouth. I have been told he has lately been offered 2000£ for the house, and farm, at Milton, but he will not take less than 2500. But the Price of Lands has fallen of late, and will it is supposed fall still more, so that it is doubted whether any body, will come to his price. I drank tea at Uncle Adams's, and found them all well. I did not get here till near 7 o'clock. It took me the whole day to Come from Boston here.

Tuesday 6th. Cambridge

Sunday, and yesterday I spent at Braintree. This morning, aunt Cranch and I set out together for Haverhill. We dined in Boston, and as the Wind was pretty high, aunt was not fond of crossing the ferry, so we took the round about way, and made it so late before we got here, that we thought best not to proceed any further, this Evening, and we are now at Mr. Gannett's, whom I suppose you know. I found in Boston to day, Letters from you, and our dear Parents.[19] I miss very much your N.2. without which I cannot but lose entirely the thread of your Relation; I wonder Mr. W[illiamos] to whom you say you sent it, did not forward it by the last french Packet, if as I shrewdly suspect, he did not come himself. But I will wait with patience, and in the mean time reply to your N.4.—I am not at all surprised at your preferring the French Stage to the English; Every person of taste and delicacy, cannot I think avoid it, unless blinded by national prejudice, and I have met with English men, and there are Writers, who are sufficiently candid to acknowledge the Superiority of their neighbours in that respect. Tancred is a very tragical Story. I admired the original tale, when I read it, in Gil Blas, from whence Thomson took it.[20] But I know not for what Reason, I never admired this authors Dramatic pieces; the Representation may give them more interest, than we should suppose they have, when we only

323

read them. As they inculcate Virtue and Morality they have great merit, and it must be remembered they are the productions of an Author who never wrote

> One line which dying he might wish to blot.[21]

Wednesday the 22d [*June*] say you, Pappa went to dine with Mr.——. Perhaps you intended I should fill up the name; but it is not a matter of very great importance. Your account of the presentation, was exactly such as I wish'd for; it is sufficiently minute to make me attend you in my imagination, through every step, from the morning till the joyful instant when you went into your Coach, to return home; for if I am not mistaken that was the most pleasing Circumstance that you met with in the Course of the day. That the whole Ceremony, as all those of Courts are, was beyond measure Ridiculous, is as true, as that it was absolutely ⟨*Ridiculous*⟩ Necessary for you to go through it. Was Heraclitus himself present at such assemblies, he could not, I believe, refrain from laughing. I think that since they are obliged to go through this Drudgery so often, they might make the matter still more Systematical, and never say but one thing which they might repeat upon every occasion, and to every body. But mankind can be brought by constant use, to relish almost every thing, and perhaps these very levees to which we should consider it as a misfortune to be subjected, are an enjoyment to those, who have been bred to them. The different speeches of the R[oya]l personages, were such as I expected. Why her M[ajest]y should be confused I cannot imagine, but there seems to be some meaning, in what she said, though by the Way, you seem in your answer to have hit exactly the Court Style; a Compliment, though at the expence of your real opinion. And I own you could not with propriety have given the preference to your own Country upon that Occasion.[22] You will I suppose often attend the drawing Room, and although I suppose it will never be agreeable, to you, yet I imagine, it will never give you so much uneasiness again, as it did the first Time.

It was certainly very impolite in the Gentleman, whoever he was, that suffered a Servant to say he was at home: and I think the apology very proper. ⟨*I think*⟩ That custom of being absent when you please, is the best invention possible, both to avoid importunate visits, and to dispatch those that are necessary; and I think it a pity the King, cannot have the priviledge, of being out too.

They have been very civil with Respect to your furniture; but you have not said any thing about the Wine, which you mentioned in your last: I want to know, how that matter ended. Your next I suppose will be from Grosvenor Square, and I hope you will be then finally settled. I shall expect quite a minute detail of matters, and conceive great hopes for the future from your former punctuality. Charles Storer is shortly expected, and I shall doubtless have a fine packet by him. Aunt Cranch had from Mamma a particular account of your presentation; so that we do not want for information on that Subject.

Haverhill Wednesday 7th

We intended when we left Braintree, to lodge at Lincoln, last Night, and come here to day. But as We did not come further than Cambridge, yesterday, we determined, to wait till we return'd before we went to Lincoln. We came by the shortest Road; dined at Andover at Mr. French's. He was not at home.[23] We got here some time before Sunset; and found all our Friends well. Tommy was at his Studies, when we got here. So my Uncle took me, to the Chamber, where he was, and said, Here's somebody wants to see you; we stood two or three minutes without saying a word, either of us. At last Mr. Shaw ask'd Tommy, don't you know this person. I believe I do says Tom, I guess tis brother John: so you see I could not remain long incog. Mr. Thaxter of Course knew me; You know it is said he is courting. Fame seems now pretty obstinate, and rather increases than otherwise. He is there every day, and was proceeding that way, when we met him in the Street. A propos, since I am talking of courting; you know Cousin B.K. is or is not going to be married near here; the problem is as great as ever.[24]–Miss Hazen is still here. Her person answers all the expectations, which had been raised by the descriptions of yourself, and my friend at Lisbon.[25] I will wait till I be more acquainted with her, before I give you my opinion of her Character. Yours as ever

J. Q. Adams

RC (Adams Papers). The text is written on small pages numbered "57" to "72," and also "1" to "16"; see JQA to AA2, [12] May, descriptive note, above.

[1] Samuel Allyne Otis; "Harry," mentioned below, is his son Harrison Gray Otis (see Mary Cranch to AA, 14 Aug., and notes 17 and 18, above; and JQA, *Diary*, 1:315).

[2] Samuel Breck Sr. was a Boston merchant and maritime agent for Louis XVI; JQA had delivered a letter to Breck from Lafayette on the 26th (JQA, *Diary*, 1:312–313, and note 5). The Austins at dinner were probably Jonathan Loring, whom JQA had met in Europe, and Benjamin; the two were merchants, and usually business partners (JA, *Diary and Autobi-*

ography, 2:299, and note 2; 4:49; JQA, *Diary*, 1:36, note 1; *Sibley's Harvard Graduates*, 16:306). The two Frenchmen were probably a Mr. Issotier and a Mr. Serano (or Serane) (JQA, *Diary*, 1:316, 318).

[3] William Cushing had served as chief justice of the Superior Court of Judicature from 1777, and in the same post when the court was renamed the Supreme Judicial Court under the Constitution of 1780 (*Sibley's Harvard Graduates*, 13:30). JQA had heard Lord Thurlow, and presumably Mansfield and

Loughborough, in June 1784 (JQA to JA, 15 June 1784, above). William Murray, first earl of Mansfield, was lord chief justice of England from 1756 to 1788; Alexander Wedderburn, first baron Loughborough, was chief justice of the Court of Common Pleas, 1780–1793 (*DNB*). Francis Dana was appointed a justice of the Supreme Judicial Court in Feb. 1785 by Gov. Hancock, and began serving, riding the western circuit, in April (Dana to JA, 30 Jan., p.s. 19 Feb.; and 10 April, both Adams Papers).

⁴ The Charles River Bridge, the first bridge to connect Boston and Charlestown, opened with great festivities on 17 June 1786, the anniversary of the Battle of Bunker Hill (see JQA, *Diary*, 2:50–51).

⁵ CA's class was by far the largest of the decade, with 53 students, at its formation in 1785. By commencement in 1789, however, it was little larger than the classes that graduated in 1784 and 1786, and somewhat smaller than the class of 1787, of which JQA would become a member. Harvard University Faculty Records, vols. 5 and 6 (microfilm); *Harvard Quinquenial Cat.*, p. 195–204.

⁶ JA to Joseph Willard, 22 April (Col. Soc. Mass., *Pubns.*, 13:115–116 [Feb. 1910]).

⁷ See AA2 to JQA, 26 Aug., note 26, above.

⁸ This, the earliest known letter from William Vans Murray to JQA, dated 23 July 1784 (Adams Papers), announced to JQA that *"Your dear mother and lovely sister are arrived"* in London.

⁹ See AA2 to JQA, 26 Aug., note 25, above.

¹⁰ The London *Daily Universal Register* reported on 9 June, "It is said, the Earl of Effingham is to go to America, in capacity of Ambassador." The countess of Effingham visited the Adamses sometime before 22 June (AA to Mary Cranch, 24 June, and note 4, above).

¹¹ Elizabeth Bowdoin Temple would marry Thomas Lindall Winthrop in July 1786 (Temple Prime, *Some Account of the Temple Family*, N.Y., 1896, p. 52).

¹² The character whom AA2 intended in her lost N. 3 cannot be identified, but in this paragraph JQA appears to be defending the character of James Jarvis, a New York merchant whom the Adamses had met in Auteuil in April. JQA notes Jarvis' presence at Auteuil on 12 May, the day JQA departed for America, and records the hospitable reception he received from Jarvis' father-in-law, Samuel Broome, and Jarvis' siblings and in-laws, to whom he had carried letters from Jarvis. See

JQA, *Diary*, 1:254, 266, 294, 296, 306–307.

¹³ That is, since beginning the entry for this day, at *"Boston August 31. Wednesday,"* above.

¹⁴ Probably Joshua Green Sr., his wife Hannah Storer Green, a close friend of AA, and perhaps their son, Joshua Greene Jr. (same, 1:22).

¹⁵ Charlotte, daughter of Nathaniel Appleton and Rachael Henderson Appleton, and sister of JQA's European acquaintance, John Appleton, was just turning nineteen; despite her apparent illness, she lived until 1798. Elizabeth was seventeen. W. S. Appleton, *A Genealogy of the Appleton Family*, Boston, 1874, p. 14.

¹⁶ This was the fortnightly ball of William Turner's dancing class (see JQA, *Diary*, 1:317, and note 1).

¹⁷ Chaumont was departing for Albany (same, 1:318).

¹⁸ JQA may be implying that Cotton Tufts Jr. had little family feeling, and that AA2 knew of this feature of young Tufts' personality. JQA would sharply criticize Tufts on the occasion of his mother's death in October (same, 1:352).

¹⁹ AA2's letter N. 4, to which JQA begins to reply in the next paragraph, has not been found, but it must have been dated near those to JQA from AA, and from JA, both 26 June, both above (see same, 1:319–320).

²⁰ AA2 had seen both Sheridan's *School for Scandal*, and James Thomson's *Tancred and Sigismunda* in London in June (AA2 to Lucy Tufts, 23 June, above), and had evidently discussed the second play in her lost letter N. 4 to JQA. Thomson's *Tancred* was based on a tale in Alain René Le Sage's *Histoire de Gil Blas*. JA gave JQA a four-volume edition of the later work in 1780; it is now in MQA.

²¹ From Lord Lyttleton's prologue to Thomson's posthumously produced *Coriolanus*.

²² The only known accounts of the 23 June interchange between Queen Charlotte and her daughters Charlotte and Augusta, on the one side, and AA and AA2 on the other, appear in AA to Mary Cranch, 24 June, and in abbreviated form in AA to JQA, 26 June, both above. AA's remarks there do not make clear what AA2 said.

²³ Rev. Jonathan French of the South Church in Andover was a native of Braintree whom JA had known since the 1770s or earlier; his wife, Abigail Richards, was a native of

Weymouth (*Sibley's Harvard Graduates,* 17:514–520; JA, *Diary and Autobiography,* 2:45).

[24] JQA probably intends Elizabeth (Betsy) Kent, daughter of AA's aunt, Anna Smith Kent, who would marry Rev. Jonathan Allen

of Bradford, Mass. in December (see Mary Cranch to AA, 10 Dec., and JQA to AA, 28 Dec., both below).

[25] Winslow Warren; see AA2 to JQA, 4 July, above.

John Adams to John Quincy Adams

Grosvenor Square Westminster
Corner House between Duke Street
My dear Son   and Brook Street. Aug. 31. 1785

I hope Mr. Storer, when he delivers this Letter, will find you a Student in the University, or upon the Point of becoming So.

We have as yet no News of your Arrival in America, but We hope to learn it by the first ship.

We are comfortably Situated here, and have all enjoyed very good Health hitherto in England. But Home is Home. You are Surrounded by People who neither hate you nor fear you.

I have no other Idea of an happy Life: Than Health and Competence, with a clear Conscience and among People who esteem and love you. All these you may and will have, I hope. The Conscience Health and Competence I may have here. I may even be esteemed: but never can be beloved, as you may easily suppose.

Write me as often as you can: let me know how you like your Situation: and if you want any Books from hence. Charles I take it for granted is at Colledge, and Thomas is I hope well.

I wish he was with me, but this cannot be. I dont know how to do, without one of my sons at least with me. But am obliged to deny myself this Pleasure.

My Respects wherever they are due. Your affectionate Father

John Adams

RC (Adams Papers).

Abigail Adams to Elizabeth Cranch

No 8

London Sepbr 2 1785
My dear Betsy   Grosvenor Square

At the Bath hotel I received my dear Neices Letter of April.[1] I have told your Sister and other Friends why I did not write then, but I should have no excuse to give if I omitted so good an opportunity as now offers by Mr. Storer.

This day two months ago we removed here, where I should be much delighted if I could have my Sisters my Cousins and connections round me, but for want of them every Country I reside in, lacks a principal ingredient in the composition of my happiness.

London in the Summer season is a mere desert, no body of concequence resides in it, unless necessitated too, by their Buisness. I think the Gentry qui[te right?][2] in every view to retire to their Country seats, residing upon them is generally a great benefit to the propriater. Many noble Men expend vast sums anually in improveing and Beautifying their estates. I am told that one must visit some of these Manors and Lordships to form a just estimate of British Grandeur and Magnificence.

All the Villages which I have seen round London are mere Gardens, and shew what may be effected by Culture, but we must not expect for many Years to see America thus improved. Our numbers are few in comparison with our acres, and property is more equally distributed which is one great reason of our happiness; Industery there, is sure to meet with its recompence and to preserve the Labourer from famine from Nakedness and from want. The Liberal reward which Labour meets with in America is an other Source of our National prosperity, population and increasing wealth result from it. The condition of our Labouring poor is preferable to that of any other Country, comparatively speaking. We have no poor except those who are publickly supported. America is in her early vigor, in that progressive state, which in reality is the Cheerful and flourishing state to all the different orders of Society. It is so to the humane constitution, for when once it has reachd the meridian it declines towards the Setting Sun. But America has much to do e'er she arrives at her Zenith. She possesses every requisite to render her the happiest Country upon the Globe. She has the knowledge and experience of past ages before her. She was not planted like most other Countries with a Lawless Banditti, or an Ignorant savage Race who cannot even trace their origon, but by an enlightned a Religious and polished people. The Numerous improvement which they have made during a Century and half, in what was then but a howling Wilderness, proves their state of civilisation. Let me recommend to you my dear Girl to make yourself perfect mistress of the History of your own Country if you are not so allready; no one can be sufficiently thankfull for the Blessings they enjoy, unless they know the value of them.

Were you to be a witness to the Spectacles of wretchedness and misiry which these old Countries exhibit, crouded with inhabitants; loaded with taxes, you would shuder at the sight. I never set my foot out, without encountering many objects whose tatterd party coulourd garments, hide not half their Nakedness, and speak as Otway expresses it "Variety of Wretchedness,"[3] coverd with disease and starving with hunger; they beg with horrour in their countanances; besides these, what can be said of the wretched victims who are weekly Sacrificed upon the Gallows, in numbers Sufficient to astonish a civilized people? I have been credibly informd that hundreds of Children from 4 years and upwards, sleep under the trees fences and Bushes of Hide Park nightly, having no where else to lay their heads, and subsist by day; upon the Charity of the passenger. Yet has this Country as many publick institutions for charitable support of the infirm, as any country can Boast. But there must be some essential defect in the Government and Morals of a people when punishments lose their efficacy and crimes abound.

But I shall make you sick with my picture of wretchedness. Let it excite us to thankfulness my Dear Girl that our lives have fallen to us in a happier Land, a Land of Liberty and virtue, comparatively speaking. And let every one so far as there Sphere of action extends, and none so contracted as to be without Some influence, Let every one consider it as a duty which they owe to themselves to their Country and to posterity to practise virtue, to cultivate knowledge and to Revere the deity as the only means, by which not only individuals, but a people or a Nation can be prosperous and happy. You will think I have turnd preacher. I know I am not writing to a thoughtless, but to a reflecting Solid young Lady, and that shall be my excuse.

How have you advanced in your musick. The practise of Musick to those who have a taste and ear for it, must be one of the most agreeable of Amusements. It tends to soften and harmonize the passions, to elevate the mind, to raise it from earth to Heaven. The most powerfull effects of Musick which I ever experienced, was at Westminister Abbey. The place itself is well calculated to excite solemnity, not only from its ancient and venerable appearence, but from the dignified Dust, Marble and Monuments it contains. Last year it was fitted up with seats and an organ loft sufficiently large to contain six hundred Musicians, which were collected from this and other Countries. This Year the Musick was repeated. It is call'd the celebration of Handles Musick. The sums collected are deposited, and the income is appropriated to the support of decayed Musicians. There were 5 days set apart for the different performances. I was at the peice call'd the Messiah,[4] and tho a Guinea a ticket, I am sure I never spent one with more satisfaction. It is impossible to describe to you the Solemnity and dignity of the Scene. When it came to that part, the Hallelujah, the whole assembly rose and all the Musicians, every person uncoverd. Only conceive six hundred voices and instruments perfectly chording in one word and one sound! I could scarcly believe myself an inhabitant of Earth. I was one continued shudder from the begining to the end of the performance. Nine thousand pounds was collected, by which you may judge of the rage which prevaild for the entertainment.

How do all my good Friends and old Neighbours. Let me hear as often as possible from you. Never conceive that your Letters are trifling, nothing which relates to those I Love appears so to me. This Letter is to go by Mr. Storer, as I told you in the begining; a smart youth for some of you; and what is better a virtuous and good Young Man. We are sorry to part with him, for he is quite Domesticated with us, but we hope he will be benifited by the exchange. It is time for him to be some way fixed in a profession for Life. He thinks of Divinity, and now I am talking of Divinity I will inquire after my Friend Mr. Wibird and chide you all for never mentioning him—for I have seen him twenty times Since my absence come up your yard, and enter the house, and inquire (after having thrown aside his cloak) "Well, have you heard from your Aunt? What does She say, and how do they all?"

I hope you have seen your cousin before this time and in your next you must tell me how you like him. You must cure him of some foibles which he has. He will take it kindly of you, for he is a good youth only a little too possitive. My paper only allows me to say that I am Yours   AA

RC (MHi:Jacob Norton Papers); docketed: "Letter from Mrs A Adams to Miss Eliz. Cranch London Septr. 2d. 1785. (No. 8)."

[1] Of 25 April, above. AA probably received this letter about 21–22 June, when she and AA2 received several letters from Boston (AA to Mary Cranch, 24 June; AA2 to Mary Cranch, 22 June, both above).

[2] Text partly lost in a worn fold.

[3] Closing quotation mark supplied. The phrase has not been located in the works of Thomas Otway, a Restoration poet and dramatist (*DNB*).

[4] AA attended this performance on 8 June; see AA to Thomas Jefferson, 6 June, above.

Abigail Adams to Lucy Quincy Tufts

My Dear Aunt[1]   London Sepbr 3d. 1785

And why my dear Madam have you not written a few lines, and tuckt into a corner of my good uncles Letters when he has favour me with one? Perhaps you think I ought first to have adrest you. I knew I was writing to both, whenever I scribled to my honourd Friend, and that my sisters and Neices would communicate to you their Letters whenever there was any thing worthy your notice.

I know Madam that you Live a Life so retired and are now so frequently seperated from your worthy companion that I flatter myself a few lines from me will not be unacceptable to you: tho I were to amuse you with what is the Ton of London, The learned pig, dancing dogs, and the little Hare that Beats the Drum.[2] It is incredible what sums of Money are nightly lavishd upon these kinds of Amusements, many of them fit only to please children. The Tumbling and rope Dancing is worth seeing once or twice, because it gives you an Idea of what skill agility and dexterity the Humane frame is capable of, and of which no person can form an Idea without having seen it. The House where these wonderfull feats are exhibited is calld Sadlers Wells and is accomodated with Boxes and a Stage in the manner of a play House. Upon the Stage two machines are fixed upon which a rope is extended about 15 foot from the floor. Upon this the Dancers mount drest very neat with a Jocky and feathers and a silk Jacket and Breaches, the Jacket very tight to the waist and a sash tied round the Jacket. He bows to the company; upon which a person who stands near him gives him a long pole made thick at each end. With this pole which serves to Balance him, he commences his dance to the Musick which he keeps time with. He will run backwards and forwards poise himself upon one foot, kneel jump across the rope, spring upon it again, and finally throws down the pole and jumps 6 foot into the air repeatedly, every time returning upon the rope with the same steadiness as if it was the floor, and with so much ease, that the spectator is ready to believe he can perform, the same himself. There is one man who is stilled the little devil, who dances with wooden shoes, and I have seen him stand upon his head with his feet perpendicular in the air. All this is wonderfull for a Man, but what will you say, when I assure you I have seen a most Beautifull Girl perform the same feats! Both in Paris and England. Why say you what could she do with her peticoats? It is true that she had a short silk skirt, but she was well clad under that, with draws, and so are all the female Dancers upon the stage, and there is even a law in France that no woman Shall dance upon the stage without them; But I can never look upon a woman in such situations, without conceiving all that adorns and Beautifies the female Character, delicacy modesty and diffidence, as wholy laid asside, and nothing of the woman but the Sex left.

In Europe all the lower class of women perform the most servile Labour, and work as hard with out door as the Men. In France you see them making hay, reaping sowing plowing and driveing their carts alone. It would astonish you to see how Labourious they are, and that all their gain is coars Bread and a little ordinary wine, not half so good as our cider. The Land is all owned by Marquisses Counts and Dukes, for whom these poor wretches toil and sweat. Their houses through all the villages of France consist of thatched roof Huts, without one single pane of glass. When they have any buisness which requires light, they set out of Door, and this they usually do through the whole season, for Heaven has blesst them with an admirable Climate, and a soil productive of every necessary and delicacy that Luxery can pant for. But there Religion and Government Mar all heavens Bounty. In Spain I have been told that it is much worse.[3] I believe in England the common people live more comfortably, but there is wretchedness and oppression enough here, to make a wise Man mad.

If I was not attached to America by a Naturel regard, as my native Country, when I compare the condition of its inhabitants, with that of the Europeans, I am bound to it by every feeling of phylanthropy, and pray that the Blessings of civil and Religious Liberty, knowledge and virtue may increase and shine upon us, in proportion as they are clouded and obstructed in the rest of the Globe, and that we may possess wisdom enough to estimate aright our peculiar felicity.

I will not close untill I have inquired after your Health and that of your Son and Neice[4] to whom present my Love. Mr. Adams and your Neice also tender you their regards. As I esteem a good domestick I would not forget them in the number of your family, or any of my Towns f[ol]ks who may think it worth while to inqure after Your affectionate Friend and Neice   Abigail Adams

RC (Adams Papers); addressed by Charles Storer: "Mrs. Lucy Tufts Weymouth"; docketed in an unknown hand: "1785 AA." Slight damage to the text at the seal.

¹ This is the only extant letter from AA to Lucy Quincy Tufts; it probably went to America with Charles Storer (see AA to Cotton Tufts, 16 Sept., descriptive note, below), and therefore did not reach her before her death on 30 October.

² See AA2 to JQA, 4 July, and note 39, above.

³ Sources for this view of Spain may have been JA and JQA. Their journey through northern Spain, Dec. 1779 – Jan. 1780, is fully recounted in vol. 3:243–272; and in JA, *Diary and Autobiography*, vols. 2 and 4; JQA, *Diary*, vol. 1; and JA, *Papers*, vol. 8.

⁴ Probably Lucy Tufts Hall; see Mary Cranch to AA, 19 July, and note 15, above.

Thomas Jefferson to Abigail Adams

Dear Madam   Paris Sep. 4. 1785

I was honoured with your letter of Aug. 21. by Mr. Smith who arrived here on the 29th. I am sorry you did not repeat the commission you had favoured me with by Mr. Short as the present would have been an excellent opportunity of sending the articles you wished for. As Mr. Short's return may yet be delayed, will you be so good as to write me by post what articles you desired, lest I should not otherwise know in time to send them by either of the Mr. Smiths.[1] The French packet brought me letters from Mr. Jay and Dr. Ramsay only. They were dated July 13.[2] They do not mention the arrival of your son. Dr. Ramsay's letter was on a particular subject, and Mr. Jay's letter was official. He may have arrived therefore tho these letters do not mention it. However as he did not sail till June, and Westernly winds prevail in the summer I think the 13th. of July was too early to expect him to have arrived. I will certainly transmit you information of his arrival the moment I know it.

We have little new and interesting here. The Queen has determined to wear none but French gauzes hereafter. How many English looms will this put down? You will have seen the affair of the Cardinal de Rohan so well detailed in the Leyden gazette that I need add nothing on that head.[3] The Cardinal is still in the Bastille. It is certain that the Queen has been compromitted without the smallest authority from her: and the probability is that the Cardinal has been duped into it by his mistress Madme. de la Motte. There results from this two consequences not to his honour, that he is a debauchee, and a booby. The Abbés[4] are well. They have been kept in town this summer by the affairs of the Abbé Mably. I have at length procured a house in a situation much more pleasing to me than my present. It is at the grille des Champs Elysees, but within the city. It suits me in every circumstance but the price, being dearer than the one I am now in.[5] It has a clever garden to it.

I will pray you to present my best respects to Miss Adams and to be assured of the respect and esteem with which I have the honour to be Dear Madam Your most obedient & most humble servt.

Th: Jefferson

RC (Adams Papers); docketed by AA2: "Mr Jefferson Sep 4th."

[1] That is, James Smith, who carried AA's 21 Aug. letter to Jefferson (above), and Col. William Stephens Smith.

[2] These letters appear in Jefferson, *Papers*, 8:292–294.

[3] For a highly-detailed account of the scandalous Diamond Necklace Affair involving Louis René Edouard, Prince and Cardinal de Rohan, his mistress, Madame de La Motte-Valois, and Queen Marie Antoinette, see Simon Schama, *Citizens, A Chronicle of the French Revolution*, N.Y., 1989, p. 203–210.

[4] The abbés Arnoux and Chalut.

[5] On 17 Oct., Jefferson would move from his house on the Cul-de-sac Taitbout (now the Rue du Helder), just off the present Boulevard Haussmann, which he had leased in Oct. 1784, to the second floor of the Hôtel de Langeac, at the corner of the Rue Neuve de Berry (now the Rue de Berri) and the Avenue des Champs-Elysées, abutting the elaborate city gate, called the Grille de Chaillot, that stretched across the avenue. This passage is evidently the first surviving record of Jefferson's intention to move. The lease was drawn on 5 Sept., and signed on the 8th; his yearly rent increased from 6,000 livres, at his former address, to 7,500. See Jefferson, *Papers*, 7:xxviii, 442–443, illustration facing 452; 8:xxviii–xxix, illustration facing 247, 485–492.

Mary Barclay to Abigail Adams

My Dear Madam   Paris September 5–1785

I did not know till this moment that Coln. Franks would set out this evening, who has just Call'd on me for my Commands. I dare not detain him long, and cannot let him depart without a few lines to assure you of my attachment and best wishes.

I am glad to find you are agreeably fixed[1] and that you enjoy a good society which is certainly much superior to all the fashionable amusements of, this, or any other place, tho' you are so happy in your own family that you must feel the want of it much less than any one I know.

When Dr. Bancroft left this I thought of settling at L'Orient during Mr. Barclay's absence[2] but on maturer reflection it is not a place proper for the Education of our Children, therefore have determined to remain some where in or near Paris where those advantages may be procured that I would wish to have for them. Catharine stay'd with me till the 10 of August, and as I then expected to leave Paris in a few days she engaged with the Family which came into the house at Mont Parnasse which we were obliged to quit at that time, and removed to Hotel D'Aligre rue d'Orleans St. Honoré.

Pauline I believe to have too good Principles as well as too great a love for this life, to put an end to it in the maner you mention.[3] She

334

was happily placed about three weeks after you left this with a Lady who gives her three hundred livres a year besides Profites which are considerable, yet she seems to regret much your service.

I pray you remember me respectfully to Mr. and Miss Adams & believe me with the greatest sincerity your Friend & humble Servant

Mary Barclay

RC (Adams Papers).

[1] Mary Barclay refers, here and below, to a missing letter from AA, presumably written in July or August.

[2] On or just before 4 Sept., with JA's prior agreement, Jefferson instructed Thomas Barclay to negotiate a commercial treaty with the Barbary States. Barclay intended to depart soon thereafter for Morocco but was delayed until Jan. 1786 by the need to settle Caron de Beaumarchais' accounts. See Jefferson, *Papers*, 8:394, 424, 473; 9:91, 214.

[3] Pauline had served the Adamses at Auteuil.

Elizabeth Cranch to Abigail Adams

My dear Aunt   Boston September 5th. 1785

My Papa came in this evening and brought a great Letter directed to Mama, superscrib'd by my Uncle Adams.[1] Mama is at Braintree, *we* had no Letters to satisfy *us*. The Pacquet was laid upon the table. I took it up, examined the seal, and wanted much to get at the contents, then took the stocking, (which I was lining the Heel of for your Charles), and work'd upon it a little, all the time immagination busy in anticipating what might be in the Letter before me. My *impatience* shewd itself and was a *kind* of *apology* for Papa's *curiosoty*, who after a serious Pipe, sedately laid it down, took out his spectacles, wip'd them, and I very *dextrously* cut round the Seal, and gave it to Him to read. Imediatly, from the humble scenes around me; my immagination was borne away to the circles of Kings, Queens Earls and Countesses, to brilliant rooms, to birth nights, and to Balls. My head is even now full of them, and I certainly shall dream, and feel as great as any lady to night. I have to thank you for a great degree of entertainment which your account has afforded me. I was in Love with your dresses. I would have given (I dont know *what*) to have peepd in upon you, but tis almost as good to heare your discriptions.

The week before last we had the pleasure of recieving and welcoming our dear Cousin John to his native Land. I do not wonder that you regret the loss of him. I am sure I shall Love him tenderly. I am pleased when I look at him, to trace the features of both his parents so plainly in his face and more of *yours* my dear Aunt than either of your other Children can show. I have not yet seen him half eno'; he

335

has been engagd, visiting, the Boston gentry, for a whole week, tho he has calld upon me a little while every day. The day he arrivd (or rather the day after)[2] which was the first of my seeing him, he dined with my Papa and me at our present Lodgings. Lucy had come to town with a design of going up to Cambridge to see our *Brothers* there, and drink tea with them. So we took our Cousin John, and Isaac Smith with us and went. The meeting was joyful indeed between the Brothers and Cousins. We intended to have surprizd Charles with an unexpected interview. We arrivd first, and kept him up in Billys Chamber, but [he] would go below, and was looking out, when he saw Cousin John alight at a distance he call'd John! John!, and made the Colledges echo. Cousin J heard, but did not know from whom or from whence, for he did not expect to hear the *voice* of a *man* when his Brother spoke. But he repeated his calls, till he drew his attention, and before we thought of it Mr. Charles, came and introduced his Brother to *us*, and we did have a sweet, charming time of it. I am sure my good Aunt could you have lookd in upon us, sitting around our tea table, looking so much chearful *happiness*, you would have felt a glow of pleasure, unequalled perhaps, by *any* the drawing-room ever afforded you! It was pleasure, even to a degree of pain, for tears, and smils, alternately had there dominion. We wanted our Tommy to compleat our happiness. We left, the *Colledge Lads*, and returnd to Boston and spent the eve at Uncle Smith. After I got to my own Lodgings, I retired and to compleet the pleasure of the day, read yours and Cousin Nabby's Letters.[3] Never will it be in my power my dear dear Aunt to make you any returns for your unequalld attention and kindness to me, so many excellent Letters as you have favourd me with. How shall I express my thanks. I know not how you will be repay'd, but by the reflection of that happiness which you bestow. Tis past midnight. I must not write more at present tho I feel much inclind to.

Sepr 6

This morning my Mama came to town with Cousin John. They dined here, and have this afternoon sat out to make a journey to Haverhill. Tis most delightful weather, and I could with pleasure have accompanid them, had it been in my power; Mama has been much out of health this Summer. I am hoping that this ride may be of service to her; especially as she has so agreable a companion. My dear Aunt, we all look with pleasing wonder, upon your Son. When we *hear* him converse; we think tis the Language of *experiencd age*—so *wise*, so *firm*, so *solid*; tis almost impossible to concieve these to be the qualities of *eighteen*. Did we not behold sprightliness, ardor, softness, benevolence, and all the youthful Virtues, as conspicuous in his countenance, we should be apt to doubt that there was some mistake in reckoning years. What is there peculiar in the Climate of Europe, that can thus surprizinly mature the mind? I hope he will not find that of America less favourable, to its cultivation.

You say you are to live in *Grosvenor Square*. Do you not sometimes think, that Lady Grandison Lady G— and L— and all the good Folks in the *book*[4] are around you, and your neigbours? The name always brings them to my mind; I should sit my immagination to work to form resemblances of them, and in Idea enjoy the pleasure of seeing them.

One thing I have to request, although I dare say your own curiosity will prompt you to it. It is, that you will visit all those beautiful enchanting, Seats and places that we read about, and are so much charmed with in discription—Lord Coltanes Gardens, Windsor, Bleinham, and *Hagley* and the *Leasomes*, above all. O that I could go with you! Methink I should be *perfectly happy*. My desire to see England is as ardent as ever. I think encreasing. I am a good mind to run aboard a ship, and say nothing about it to any body. Would you recieve such a vargrant? Why Ma'am, it would not be worse, than some *better folks* than I have done, but it wont do to reason upon the *matter*. Ships Sail frequently, and here am I at Boston. Tis a good Season. I can stay the winter and spring with you, and return in Summer. The winter I can pass, in the *West*, with my good Cousins and Uncles, and [*in*][5] the spring, visit all these fine Seats, and Paridises with you. I dont want to go to *Court*—and then just take a sail back again. Was there ever a better Scheme? I am sure tis good! But heigh ho!

In The last Letter I wrote you my dear Aunt,[6] I believe I mentioned *my hopes*, that when I got to *Boston* I should find something, to amuse and entertain you with; but alas I am dissapointed. I see nor hear any thing entertaining. I think my greatest *pleasures*, *amusements* and *gratifications* are all derivd from you and my Cousin. Your Letters, make all, the variety of my Life. A little news I have to tell, but probably it will not be so to you ere this reaches you. Mr. *Otis, has shut up*!—and this is an event at which we are all grievd and surprizd. Mrs. O possesses a remarkable uniformity of Temper, and is not so much depressd by it as one might expect. Hary looks—very sad. Tomorrow my Aunt the amiable and good Charles Warren, embarks for Lisbon! But I am much afraid his passage is for another Port, from which no traveller returns. His health is much worse than when you left us. He looks like death. I saw him pass to day, with his Mama in Mrs. Kiessels Carriage. I believe twas the last look I er'e shall have. Mrs. W[arren]s countenance wore the most expresive anxiety. Poor Lady, my heart aked for her. I think her task must be hard indeed.

Braintree septemr. 18th

This sheet of Paper has lain by so long that I know not what I was going to write on the remainder of it. I have changed my habitations and plans, since I wrote the above. You have heard by former Letters[7] that I was going to spend the Summer in Boston, to have a little instruction in musick. Mr. Selbys price was so exceedingly high, that I could not have the advantage, of a great number of Lessons, a dollar a Leson, he chargd. Miss Peggy White has got a new *Forte Piano*, carried it to Haverhill, and has a Master there who teaches for *one Shilling* per Lesson. He has instructd a great many Ladies in Portsmouth, and other places. Mama and Cousin John, have been to make a visit to Aunt Shaw. They returnd last week, and Mrs. White and Miss Peggy, have given me a most pressing invitation to spend a month or two with them, and Learn upon her instrument and of her Master. Tis much for *my* advantage, and Miss White has been so good as to say, it will be a great pleasure to her to have me a fellow Pupil. I believe we shall both learn much better for having, a companion. So instead of tarying 2 months longer in Boston, as I had designd, I quit it, for H, and shall next week go up with Cousin John in the Stage.

I had hoped to have returnd to Braintree, but my interest leads me from it. I shall have the pleasure of more of Cousin Johns company, than at home. This is one strong additional inducement. I have not yet said half a thousandth part of what I thought I had to say to him, tis not yet my turn. I rode up from Boston the day before yesterday with him,[8] and I believe tired the poor young Man with my interogataries, but he was patient. He is in fine Spirits. I thought sometimes People would immagine I had a crazy creature with me. He sang some curious songs, in which he thought *action* necessary, and a Chaise was not a very conveniet Stage, to display His theatrical abilities upon, especially when he was driving. I do not know when I have laugh'd so immoderately.

I believe we felt a little like strangers to him at first, by this time [I] hope he feels and reallizes, that we are most affectionate Friends.

Since your [abse]nce I have felt an unusual tenderness for ⟨*you*⟩ my Cousins, who you [lef]t behind, a tenderness, bordering upon (if not really, a weakness) fills my heart, whenever I look upon them, and I feel as if they were more than ever dear to me. One Clause in my Uncles Letter to Papa,[9] affected me more than I have been in reading a deep tragedy. I know not why, but I instantly burst into tears, as I read it, nor can I reccollect it without feeling the same emotions. ⟨*twas not*⟩ "Take care of my Boys in their Orphan state, advise counsel and direct them!" I cannot tell you *why*, it had this effect, but it touched the tenderest string in my heart. Whenever *I* can be useful to them either by contributing to their good, pleasure, or happiness, I shall [exert?][10] the extent of my power to do it. My heart cannot know a greater satisfaction! I am much, obligd for the present, recievd by Cousin John. I have no claim, to such kindness, my dear Aunt, but I know that every oppertunity of exerting your benevolence is an encrease of your happiness. Continue Madam, if you can find the time, still to write me as particularly as you have done. By the last Vessel Capt. *Solmes*[11] I had not one Letter from you or my Cousin Nabby. Tis the first time, and I must not complain.

Numbers of your Friends and accquaintance in Boston desird me to present their compliments. I cannot name them all. Mr. and Mrs. Foster where I have kept this Summer, present their most respectful compliments, not from personal knowledge, do they presume to offer them, but from a respect they feel for the Characters of my Uncle and Aunt and from an interest they have naturally taken, in your concerns, from hearing and knowing so much of you from us. I must write to Cousin Nabby, and fear I shall have nothing to say, unless I conclude, soon, this long Letter to you.

I am my dear Aunt, with the liveliest sentiments of Love, respect, & gratitude your ever affectionate Neice,   Eliza: Cranch

If my respected Uncle, thinks, the sincere and hearty good wishes, of, one so little important, worthy his acceptance, please to offer them always to him.

RC (Adams Papers); addressed: "Madam Abigail Adams London"; endorsed: "E Cranch Septr 5 1785"; docketed by AA2: "Elisa Cranch sep 5." Some loss of text where the seal was cut away.

[1] AA to Mary Cranch, 24 June, above.
[2] 26 August.
[3] The latest letters from AA and AA2 that Elizabeth could have read on the evening of 26 Aug. date from 6, 8, and 12 May, at Auteuil, all above; the Adams' first letters from Lon-

don did not reach Boston until 5 September.
[4] All these are characters in Samuel Richardson's *Sir Charles Grandison*.
[5] Here a caret appears above the line, but no word.
[6] Of 25 April, above.

⁷ See Elizabeth Cranch to AA, 25 April, above.

⁸ On 16 September.

⁹ JA to Richard Cranch, 27 April, above.

¹⁰ Written over an illegible deletion.

¹¹ The arrival of the ship *Olive Branch*, Capt. Somes, from London was reported in the *Boston Gazette* of 12 September.

William Stephens Smith to Abigail Adams

My dear Madam   Berlin 5th. September 1785

Your benevolence I know will excuse the particularity of this address, when you confide in the assurance of its proceeding from a sincere heart nourishing the most exalted sentiments of the virtue and sensibility of yours. Accept of my thanks for the reply to my note,[1] I feel myself complimented by your confidence and beleive I am not capable of abusing it. I hope for an advocate in you, should Mr. Adams think my absence long. Tell him, that—what will you tell him? Can you say with Stern[2] that it is a quiet Journey of the heart in pursuit of those affections, which make us love each other, and the world better than we do ⟨?⟩, or will you say he is flying from—? Hush, madam, not a lisp—but I will not dictate, say what you please. Whatever you say and whatever you do (confiding in the spring of your actions) I will subscribe to it.

Mr. A, I hope, received my Letters from Harwich and Amsterdam.[3] I dare not permit my pen to enter upon my journal, least I should tire you. I'll reserve the tales for winter Evenings, when I dare say I shall at least receive your thanks for sharpening your appetite for your pillow, that you may form an Idea of the channel thro' which they'll run. I shall only hint, that I have visited the Cabinets of the Curious both natural and artificial, Palaces, Libraries, Arsenals, fields of Battle, Monuments on those fields, Cathedrals, and have descended with a taper into the sepulchre's, of monarchs—"I took a turn amongst their tombs—to see where to all Glory comes"—and find Royalty cuts but a poor figure here.[4] And from the humble Cottage of the impovrished Peasant where he shared with me his peas and his beans, I have crept silently up to the throne of Majesty. Crept Did I say? No Madam. I walked firmly up to it, marking the stages to the last Step of the ascent, from whence with an Eye of compassion, I reviewd the vale thro' which I had passed and with the aforementioned favourite author I asked heaven only for health and the fair Goddess of Liberty as my Companion and all beyond let wild ambition grapel for, and gain. I shall not envy it. Pretty tolerable rant this, you'll say. Well I'll check a Little.

We have been favoured with seven day's steady rain, but this did not stop us. But now I'll tell you what did. In the Centre of a Plain in the dominions of His Prussian Majesty, exactly two Sabbath day's Journey from a house either way, the perch of our carriage broke, exactly one inch and a half from the centre.[5] You would have laughed at the solemnity with which we got out of it, and gaped at each other, but the worst is yet to be told. The Postilion could speak nothing but German. Miranda, my Servant and *your* most humble Servant, colectively, could boast of English, French, Italian, Spanish and of cracking Joak's with monks in Latin, but all this Madam would not do, for the Postilion knew nothing but *German*, and perhaps this was the case for a Circuit of 10 Miles. Now I know you pity me. I cannot expect you will form any right conjectures how we extricated ourselves from this difficulty, and if I were to Attempt to tell you now, I might spoil a good story by endeavouring to bring it within the compass of this sheet. For the present you must therefore only know we were relieved by two Ladies, who by a Kind Stroke of smiling chance were Journeying the same way. Their conduct on this occasion has heightned (if possible) the favourable opinion I have alway's nourish'd relative to the sex, and convinces me we should cut but a silly figure on this stage without them. Notwithstanding great exertion, it was two in the morning before we got in motion again. It is well that those actions which proceed from generosity and benevolence, carry their reward with them. As soon as I was seated, the carriage moved and the Ladies bid us adieu. I could not help exclaiming—Peace, happiness and pleasantry attend your steps ye tender productions of your makers works. May no rough Line, ever cross your path—nor interrupting Obsticle check your passage down the stream of Life. May benevolence alway's greet you with a welcome, and hospitality extend her Arms to receive you. After this, the obligation Sat easier. It was the only return I could make.

The badness of the roads and the delay occasioned by the fracture—(for the assistance we had recieved only enabled us to move with sobriety to a neighbouring Village) put it out of our power to reach Bresleau within the destined Period.[6] And Philosophers may as well hope that the transit of Venus will be postponed untill they are prepared to make their observations, as that Frederic will on account of wind or weather delay an hour in the execution of a Military Order. By the Letter to Mr. Adams which this accompanies you will see he is not a man of words, whatever he may be of deeds.[7]

I this morning entered the field—as [*at*?] a Military school. I shall be a constant attendant from 6 to 12 every day untill the business is over when I shall haste to pay my respects to you. I hope both as a young Politician and as a Soldier (casting a veil upon every thing else as much as possible) to be richly repaid for this excurtion. May I hope, that a Letter will be deposited, with my Versifying Friend *David*[8] at Paris, acknowledging the receipt of this, and informing me how you all do in Grosvenor Square, by the time I arrive there? Yes I will expect it—and as I find I am drawing insensibly to the last page of the sheet, I shall make this period comprehend my best wishes for the uninterrupted happiness of every branch of your family and expressive of the sincerity with which I shall alway's acknowledge myself—Your most obliged Friend and Humble servt.   W. S. Smith

RC (Adams Papers); docketed in JA's late, trembling hand: "Col Smith 5. Sep. 1785 Berlin."

[1] AA replied on 13 Aug., above, to Smith's note from Harwich, of the 10th, not found.

[2] Laurence Sterne, author of *A Sentimental Journey*. AA's reply to Smith of 18 Sept., below, makes it clear that Smith is referring to his strong interest in AA2, and his feeling that it was best for him to leave London for a time because AA2 was still involved with Royall Tyler.

[3] Smith's letters to JA from Harwich, 10 Aug., and from Amsterdam, ca. 15 Aug., have not been found (for the dates at these locations, see Francisco Miranda's and Col. Smith's diaries, in *Archivo del General Miranda, Viajes Diaros 1750–1785*, vol. 1, Caracas, 1929, p. 353, 358–361).

[4] Smith records his tour of the Potsdam-Berlin area, from 30 Aug. to 5 Sept., in considerable detail in his Diary (same, p. 374–378).

[5] This mishap occurred on 26 Aug., near a village which Smith calls "Barnstadt," be-tween Helmstedt and Magdeburg. Smith describes the day in detail in his Diary, using much the same language to express his gratitude to the women who, with their servants, came to his assistance (same, p. 370–371).

[6] Smith never did travel to Breslau, which he had planned to visit from the outset of his journey (see JA to Wilhelm & Jan Willink, and to Nicolaas & Jacob van Staphorst, 9 Aug., LbCs, Adams Papers; Smith, Diary, p. 360).

[7] In his letter of 5 Sept. to JA (Adams Papers), Smith copied his brief letter of 3 Sept. to Frederick II, requesting permission to view Prussia's military exercises, and Frederick's very brief but polite consent, in French, dated 4 September.

[8] David Humphreys, secretary of the American legation in Paris, to whom AA's reply of 18 Sept. to Smith, below, was carried by Col. Franks.

Abigail Adams to John Quincy Adams

No 4.

London Sepbr 6. 1785

My Dear Son   Grosvenor Square

Yesterday being Sunday I went with your papa to the Foundling Church,[1] Dr. Price whom we usually attend being absent a few weeks in the Country. When I returnd from Church I went into my closet and took up my pen with an intention of writing to you; but I really felt so *trist* at not having heard of your arrival that I could not compose myself sufficently to write to you, so I scribled to your Brothers.[2] By the time I had finishd my Letters, I was call'd to tea. Mr. Brown the painter came in and spent part of the Evening. I read a sermon in Barrow[3] upon the Government of the Tongue, and went to Bed with one of my old impressions that Letters were near at Hand. This Morning went below to Breakfast, the Urn was brought up Boiling, the Chocolate ready upon the table, Enter Mr. Spiller the Butler, who by the way is a very spruce Body, and after very respect-fully bowing with his Hands full "Mr. Churchs compliments to you Sir, and has brought you this pacquet, but could not wait upon you to day as he was obliged to go out of Town." Up we all jumpt, your Sister seized hold of a Letter,[4] and cry'd my Brother, my Brother. We were not long opening and perusing, and I am so glad, and I am so glad, was repeated from one to an other. Mamma did not fail remark-ing her old impression. The Chocolate grew cold, the top of the tea pot was forgotton, and the Bread and Butter went down uneaten, yet nobody felt the loss of Breakfast, so near akin is joy and grief that the effect is often similar.

Your Pappa had a prodigious quantity of writing to do before, and his packets from Congress just received has increased it much. I know not what he would have done if Mr. Storer had not lent him a hand, and copied his Letters for him. Yet it is a little hard upon him, as he is very buisy in preparing for his voyage. The Prussian Review which was to commence upon the 20th of last Month, was drawing together all the great Military Characters in Europe. It was like to prove an object of vast importance as it was to consist not only of the best troops, but of the greatest number, and to be reviewd by the most celebrated military Sovereign now living. Col. Smith considerd it as an object which merited his attention, and requested leave of absence for a few weeks. Your Pappa readily granted his request, as at that time there was little prospect of Buisness, but it has so happend that from Holland from France, America and here, there has been much to do, and much yet remains undone. Dispatches must be got ready for Mr. Storer who is to sail in a few days. The Col. has been gone a month, we have received two Letters from him[5] and may I think look for his return daily. He does not live with us, he has appartments in Leiscester Fields, he always dines with us. I like him much, but I do not rely wholy upon my own opinion. I will quote your pappas words writing of him to the President of Congress. "Col. Smith has been very active and attentive to Buisness, and is much respected. He has as much honour and spirit as any Man I ever knew. His principals are those of his Country, and his abilities are worthy of them. He has not the poetical Genius of Humphries, but he has much superiour talants, and a more independant temper as a politician. In short you could not have given me a Man more to my taste."[6] I may further add that he is sedate, not too much given to amusement, and a mind above every little mean thought or action. He appears formed for a Military Life, and will figure at the Head of an Army should we have occasion for him. I assure you I am not without apprehensions that such an event is not so far distant as I once hoped: the temper and disposition of this People is as hostile towards us, as it was in the midst of the War. Pride envy and Revenge rankles in their Hearts and they study every method in their power to injure us, in the Eyes of all Europe by representing us as Lawless, divided amongst ourselves, as Bankrupts. Every hireling Scribler is set to work to vilify us in the most reproachfull terms, and they refuse to publish any thing of a contrary tenor unless you will bribe them to. Much of this bilingsgate is circulated in order to prevent Emigrations from Ireland. If your Pappa had attended to the Letters he has received, and would have given any encouragement, he might have settled whole States, but he has always refused to do any thing upon the Subject. There is scarcly a day passes without applications.[7]

Our Countrymen have most essentially injured themselves by running here in Shoals after the Peace, and obtaining a credit which they cannot Support. They have so shackld and hamperd themselves that they cannot now extricate themselves; merchants who have given credit, are now Suffering, and that naturally creates ill will, and hard words. His Majesty and the Ministry shew every personal respect and civility which we have any right to expect. "The Marquiss de la Fayette, writes that he had always heard his Majesty was a great dissembler but he never was so throughly convinced of it, as by the reception given to the American Minister."[8] I wish there conduct with regard to our Country was of a Peice with that which they have shewn to its representitive. The Marquis of Carmathan and Mr. Pitt, appear to possess the most liberal Ideas with respect to us, of any part of the Ministry. With regard to the Negroes they are full and clear that they ought to be payd for,[9] but as to the posts; they say, the relinquishment of them, must depend upon certain other matters, which you know they were not at liberty to explain in private conversation. But it is no doubt they mean to keep them, as a security for the payment of the Debts, and as a rod over our Heads. They think we are as little able to go to war, as they are. The Bugget has not yet been offically opend. A Generous Treaty has been tenderd them, upon which they are now pondering and brewing. The fate of the Irish propositions has thrown weight into the American Scale, but there are so many Bones of contention between us, that snarling spirits will foment into rage, and cool ones kindle by repeated Irritation. It is astonishing that this Nation Catch at every straw which swims, and delude themselves with the Buble that we are weary of our independance, and wish to return under their Government again.[10] They are more actuated by these Ideas in their whole System towards us, than any generous plans which would become them as able statesmen and a Great Nation. They think to Effect their plans by prohibitary acts and heavy duties. A late act has past prohibiting the exportation of any tools of any kind.[11] They say they can injure us; much more than we can them, and they seem determined to try the experiment. Those who look beyond the present moment foresee the concequences, that this Nation will never leave us untill they drive us into Power, and Greatness that will finally shake this kingdom. We must struggle hard first, and find many difficulties to encounter, but we may be a Great and a powerfull Nation if we will; industery and frugality, wisdom, and virtue must make us so. I think America is taking Steps towards a reform, and I know her Capable of whatever she undertakes. I hope you will never lose sight of her interests, but make her welfare your study, and spend those hours which others devote to Cards and folly in investigating the Great principals by which nations have risen to Glory and eminence, for your Country will one day call for your services, either in the Cabinet or Feild. Qualify yourself to do honour to her.

You will probably hear before this reaches you of the extrodanary affair respecting the Cardinal Rohan. It is said that his confinement is in concequence of his making use of the Queens name to get a diamond Neclace of immence value into his Hands. Others say it is in concequence of some reflections cast upon the Character of the Queen. Others suppose that the real fact is not known. I send you one Newspaper account of the matter,[12] and have not room to add more than that I am your affectionate   A A

Please to remember I have not a single Line from you.[13]

RC (Adams Papers); endorsed on the last page: "Mamma London Septr. 6: 1785," "My Mother. 6. Septr. 1785," and "Mrs. Adams. Septr. 6: 1785."

[1] Sunday fell on 4 Sept.; AA probably began this letter on 5 September. London's Foundling Hospital was on Guildford Street; its chapel, erected in 1747, was the site of several performances of Handel's *Messiah*, initially led by the composer, and it remained

famous for its choir, drawn from the hospital's children. After 1760 the hospital did not house foundlings, but illegitimate children whose mothers were known. See Wheatley, *London Past and Present*.

[2] No letters from AA to CA or TBA for this period have been found.

[3] The eminent seventeenth-century mathematician and divine, Isaac Barrow, was master of Trinity College, Cambridge, and a teacher of Isaac Newton; his sermons were widely popular in the eighteenth century. JA's library contains several volumes of his mathematical and theological works (*DNB*; *Catalogue of JA's Library*).

[4] JQA to AA2, 17 July, above.

[5] See William Stephens Smith to AA, 5 Sept., note 3, above.

[6] To Richard Henry Lee, 26 Aug. (LbC, Adams Papers). AA quotes JA accurately, but omits JA's third sentence, following ". . . any man I ever knew." That sentence reads: "I suspect, however, that a dull diplomatic life, especially in a department so subordinate, will not long fulfill all the wishes of his generous heart." In explaining his granting of Col. Smith's request for leave to review the Prussian army's maneuvers, JA adds to the information supplied by AA that Smith "had been attacked with a slight fever, which I know by horrid experience to be a dangerous thing in these great Cities in Summer."

[7] See John Woddrop (of Glasgow) to JA, 22 July and 15 Aug., both Adams Papers; and William Wenman Seward (an Irishman living in London) to JA, 1 Sept., Adams Papers, JA to Seward, 2 Sept., LbC, Adams Papers, and Seward to JA, 4 Sept., with enclosure, Adams Papers. This long paragraph is omitted in AA, *Letters*, ed. CFA.

[8] AA is paraphrasing from Lafayette to JA, 13 July (Adams Papers; printed in *Lafayette in the Age of the Amer. Rev.*, 5:333–335). JA's account of his audience with George III in his letter of 3 June to Lafayette (LbC, Adams Papers) is too spare to have elicited this reply, but Lafayette may have heard a fuller account from Jefferson, with whom he dined in Paris on 4 July.

[9] AA refers to slaves taken by the British army from American plantations during the war; art. 7 of the Peace Treaty provided that "his Britannic Majesty shall . . . without causing any Destruction, or carrying away any Negroes or other Property of the American Inhabitants, withdraw all his Armies, Garrisons & Fleets from the said United States." Below, AA refers to Great Britain's refusal to surrender several forts on the Great Lakes to the United States, as provided in art. 2 of the Treaty, until Congress and the several states effectively pressured American debtors to pay their English creditors, as provided in arts. 4 and 5 of the Treaty (Miller, ed., *Treaties*, 2:155, 154).

[10] An example of this delusion appeared in the *London Packet or New Lloyd's Evening Post* of 26–29 Aug.: "Loaded with taxes, oppressed by poverty, and groaning under the yoke of a junto of arbitrary despots . . . [Americans] now look back with regret to those happy times, when, under the wings of Great Britain, they enjoyed peace, plenty, and real freedom."

[11] 25 Geo. 3. c. 67. See JA to John Jay, 28 Aug. 1785 (LbC, Adams Papers; PCC, No. 84, V, f. 621–624, printed in *Dipl. Corr.*, 1783–1789, 2:462–463), which summarizes the act in considerable detail.

[12] Not found.

[13] This sentence appears in the left margin of the first page, but was probably written as a postscript. There is no mark in the text of the first page to indicate its insertion. JQA's brief letter to AA of 17 July, above, went from New York by the French packet, and arrived much later than JQA's letter of 17 July to AA2, and of 3 Aug. to JA, both above. This sentence is omitted in AA, *Letters*, ed. CFA.

Abigail Adams to Thomas Jefferson

Dear sir   London Sepbr 6 1785

I cannot omit by this opportunity acquainting you that on sunday the August packet arrived in which came Mr. Church and brought us Letters from our Son[1] to our no Small joy. He arrived the 17 of july after a very tedious passage. He was however in good Health and spirits. Mr. Adams has at Length received Some Letters from the President from Mr. Jay and a private Letter from Mr. Gerry, together with some Newspapers and journals of Congress.[2] The papers contain nothing very material. Mr. Osgood Mr. Walter Levingston and Mr. Arthur Lee are the commissioners of the Treasury.[3] Mr. Lee was chosen a few days before the Sailing of the packet and was just gone from New York. It is said that the commissioners will have a difficult task to bring order out of the confusion in which the late financierer[4] left the office. Mr. Rutledge had not accepted his appointment when the gentlemen wrote. Mr. Jay writes that about the 29 of May Lambe sent for the papers from Congress that they were sent, and that he saild soon after.

They are very anxious in America with respect to the Posts especially since a reinforcement of troops have been sent out. The Merchants say that the trade is worth Annually 50,000 pounds sterling.[5]

From the present movements here, there is no great prospect of obtaining them by fair means. *The prospect here*, is not the pleasentest in the World. But I must recollect this is to go by the post. Mr. A. is very buisy writing to New York as Mr. Storer is going out in a few days. He desires me to inform you that he would take any dispatches you may have, provided you could trust them here. Mr. Storer was formerly private Secretary to Mr. Adams. I will tuck this in one corner of Mr. A.s Letter.[6] Yours, &c.

RC (DLC:Jefferson Papers).

[1] JQA to AA2, 17 July; JQA to JA, 3 Aug., both above.

[2] Richard Henry Lee to JA, 1 Aug., printed in *The Letters of Richard Henry Lee*, ed. James C. Ballagh, N.Y., 1914, 2 vols., 2:378–381; John Jay to JA, 3 Aug., printed in *Dipl. Corr., 1783–1789*, 2:418; and Elbridge Gerry to JA, 3 August. All are in Adams Papers.

[3] The Board of Treasury (Samuel Osgood and Walter Livingston) wrote to JA on 1 Aug.; Arthur Lee had written on 27 July (both Adams Papers).

[4] Robert Morris.

[5] That is, American merchants placed this value on the fur trade that centered on the Northwest forts at Detroit, Michilimackinac, Niagara, and Oswego, which the British army still occupied, contrary to the Peace Treaty, to pressure Americans to pay their debts to British creditors. See AA to JQA, 6 Sept., and note 9, above.

[6] Presumably JA to Jefferson, 4 Sept., Jefferson, *Papers*, 8:476–477.

Elizabeth Smith Shaw to Abigail Adams

My Dear Sister   Haverhill ⟨*August*⟩ September 7th. 1785

The long looked for, the modest, the manly, the well accomplished Youth, is come at last. And had he needed any thing to have made him doubly welcome to our House, but his own agreeable Behaviour, the evident Credentials he bears in his Eyes, about his Mouth, and in the Shape of his Face of being the *Son* of my excellent, and much loved Brother and Sister, would alone have gained him a most hearty Reception.

I must beg your pardon Mr. Adams, for looking at you so much.

Indeed my Aunt said he, I must ask the same Favour for myself.

Never was a youth that bore a greater resemblance to both Parents. "The Father's lustre and the Mothers bloom." His looks, and some particular Actions, strongly recall to my mind the happy Days I spent with you, when you first kept House.[1] Before my Brother had assumed the Austerity, and dignity of the Statesman, and the Republican.

I hope my Cousin Charles has informed you himself of his favourable, and gracious acceptance at the University. He promised me he would write to you the first Opportunity. As he was now conscious he should obtain his parents favour, he thought he should write with a better grace, and with greater ease, than he could while a matter of so much importance to his Happiness was depending. When Mr. Shaw and my Cousin Charles, returned from Cambridge, they put on long Faces, and attempted to look very *trist* when they rode into the yard, but I could easily discern by the⟨ir?⟩ Countenance⟨s⟩, (which seldom fails of being the medium of Truth) that Joy, and satisfaction, played sweetly at their Heart. Samuel Walker thinks Mr. Shaw his best Friend, for paying so much attention to him, as to gain him honorable admitance, and he is now the Classmate and the Chum of your Son. They have obtained the Chamber they pettioned for, and I hear are very happy together. They are both at present pleasant and lovely in their Lives, and I hope, will be kept pure, and unspotted from the guilty World. I miss them both exceedingly. Tommy dear Boy, I know must be lonly. But he is of such a pleasant Temper, and happy turn of Mind, that he is loth to own it. He is really an exceeding good Child, and we all love him and [*his*] obliging Temper, will forever gain the esteem, and good wishes of every-body.

Mr. JQA has been soliciting Mr. Shaw to undertake the direction of his Studies. However pleasing it may be to have so amiable a Youth as he appears to be in his Family, yet he feels fearful, how he may acquit himself of the Charge. To qualify a young Gentleman to enter the University as Junior Sophister, is not what is commonly practiced in the Schools, and must needs peculiar application, and attention, both in the Pupil, and in the Preceptor. By my Cousin Billy's[2] diligence he was advanced half a year, and so escaped Six months freshmanship. The Books ⟨he was?⟩ Mr. Shaw was then obliged to look into, will make it much less dificult for him now to teach my Cousin John. And should he engage in it, I believe I may venture to say, that no one would with greater fidelity, and pleasure discharge their Office.

As to me, I feel no Qualms of Conscience, that I have not done for your Children, what in an exchange of Circumstances, I could have wished for mine. Indeed I take a particular pleasure in serving them, as I consider it, as a medium, through which I am happy to convey my Love, and Gratitude.

I have now my Dear Sister to acknowledge the Receipt of yours dated May the 8th. and 10th. handed me by your Son Yesterday. My Sister and he, are both here, and intend spending a Week with us, and I have stolen from their Loved company to write a few Lines to you, by a Vessel which was built in our River, and is to sail very soon. I will wish it good speed, as it will convey to you an account of your Children, and will bear a testimonial of my Love. What though I cannot give you a Discription of Kings, Queens, Counts, and Count-esses, which afford *me* so much entertainment, yet I can inform you, of that, which is of ten-fold more importance to your Happiness—the Health, and good Behaviour of your Children.

I think Mr. Adams has conffered great Honour upon the University at Cambridge, by chusing his Son should complete his Education there. I wish that all his Sons by their application to their Studies, their amiable, and virtuous Deportment, may follow the Example of their Father, and do likewise.

My Cousin says he will go back with his Aunt, and visit a few of his Friends, and return here as soon as possible. We have a very easy, and fine Conveyance in our Haverhill Post Coach, for him, or for any baggage he may chuse to bring. He need not fear any black Dust, nor the woeful Consumption of an elegant band Box—which to a mind a little less improved than yours, might have produced a fatal Catastrophe.[3]

My paper is so bad, and the Time is so short that I have to write, that I hope you will excuse its ill Look. I shall send this Letter by James Wilson, who was brought up in Master Whites Store, whom if you see, you will treat as an American, I dare say. If I can possibly get time before Mr. Whites's Vessel sails I shall write to my Cousin. Mr. Shaws and my kindest wishes ever attend you all.   Eliza Shaw

349

The Lace you was so kind as to procure, is a very nice one, and much cheaper than I could get in Boston—8 Dollars is given credit for.[4]

RC (Adams Papers); endorsed: "Mrs Shaw Septer 7 1786."

[1] AA records that Elizabeth Smith (Shaw) spent considerable time with the Adamses in the summer and fall of 1766, and paid them a brief visit in Jan. 1767, all before JQA's birth. She also helped them move to Boston in April 1768 (vol. 1:54, 55, 57, 61, 65).

[2] Elizabeth Shaw's nephew, William Cranch, had studied with Rev. John Shaw from April 1783 to February or March 1784, when he entered Harvard (AA to JA, 7 April 1783; CA to William Cranch, 14 March 1784,

both above).

[3] In her letter to Elizabeth Shaw of 8 May, above, AA had described the destruction of a her bonnet, caps, and handkerchiefs and their box by a bag of coins that she had placed in her baggage near them, on her journey from London to Paris in August 1784.

[4] This sentence was written in the margin of the first page, but clearly as a postscript; AA mentions the lace at the end of her letter of 8 May, above.

John Quincy Adams to Abigail Adams 2d

N: 9:

Haverhill September 8th. 1785

All this day has been employ'd in answering Questions respecting you, and all is not over yet. I must mention one Circumstance, although it may appear too trifling. You may Remember, that in your Letters by me, you gave an Account of the Ceremony at Nôtre Dame.[1] All the family, were very much entertained, by your Relation, but there was a Question arose to day, what, *the Ring* was. One supposed the Ring, was a technical term, meaning the Court; another, that it was a band of music, and another, that it was some great personage, present at the time. While the debate lasted I could not conceive what the Subject of Conversation was. At length I was applied to, to inform what *the Ring* you mentioned was. When I came to see the letter I found it was only a mistake of the R. instead of the K. but had I not been used to your hand writing, I should certainly have read it Ring too. It needed no further explanation to perceive what was meant, by the *Ring's* being dressed so and so, walking, somewhat, carelessly &c. Mr. Thaxter has been with us a great part of the day. Business and so forth, has dried up all his epistolary ink.

9th

I went in the forenoon with Mr. Thaxter, and was by him introduced to Mr. White, and his family. We can seldom, at first sight form an opinion of any thing more, than the outward appearance of a Person: You have seen more of this family, than I have as yet; so that

I can only say what my thoughts are, after such a transitory glance. Mr. White appears a very hospitable man; and has much more of the reality, than the show. Benevolence, and Politeness are written too plainly in the Countenance of Mrs. White, to leave any doubt, of their being a Characteristic of her. Peggy did not answer my expectations, as a Beauty. She is uncommonly fair, and has a good set of features, but there is something harsh, if I mistake not in her Countenance. She has grown very fat of late, and is perfectly recovered, of the melancholy disorder she was afflicted with last Summer, and now enjoys it is said, a fine flow of Spirits. A number of young Ladies, were here at tea, and part of the Evening. Among the rest Miss Duncan, Mr. Thaxter's reputed belle.[2] She is celebrated for her personal and mental accomplishments. But I shall wait before I give you my opinion of any of the Ladies here, till I have a better acquaintance with them.

10th

We dined at Mr. White's, in Company with Mr. Smith the Minister, of the Baptist Congregation here, and Mr. Bartlett.[3] We propose leaving this place in the beginning of the Week, and I hope to be here again by the first of next Month.

12th. Monday

This forenoon I was invited and went to an Entertainment, which was quite a Novelty to me, and I know not by what name to call it. Dr. Woodbury of this town, was yesterday publish'd, to Miss Hannah Appleton, (I suppose you know neither of the persons,) and in Consequence of this, was given this breakfast, or dinner, or whatever it is. There were a great number of People, there, all men, but I knew only two or three persons present: I was out a great part of the ⟨Evening⟩ Afternoon, when I return'd, I found Mr. Thaxter, the two Miss Duncan's, and *Mr. Allen*, here.[4] They were engaged in curious Conversation. Mr. Collins the Minister of a neighbouring Town, with his wife, have been here all the Afternoon; it seems one of the young Ladies, thought he had not paid sufficient attention to his wife;[5] he had been the whole afternoon with her, and had not said a single word to her, nor so much as look'd at her. Mr. Thaxter thought he had with great propriety taken no Notice of her; there were many things said on both sides, concerning the proper attentions due to a wife; but it was observed that Mr. Allen, suddenly rose, in the midst of the Conversation and took his leave. Mr. Collins soon after

351

return'd, and will lodge here to Night. He appears to me, to be at least of a very phlegmatic, cold, dutchman like disposition, incapable of feeling the pleasures that are derived by persons of sensibility from those minute attentions, which it seems he makes but little use of.

13th. Tuesday. Lincoln

Your aunt and I, left Haverhill, this morning between 8 and 9. About 7 miles this side the River we stopp'd a few minutes at Mr. Symmes's, one of the ministers of Andover.[6] You have perhaps been at the house. His wife is one of the sprucest, nicest tidiest persons I have seen this long while. I almost thought myself in Holland, when I went into the house. A little further forward we stopp'd at Mr. French's, and there was a contrast. Mr. French as soon as I was introduced to him asked me, how the *Doctor* did; I knew not what he meant, and was going to ask him, what Doctor; but he repeated his question immediately *how does Doctor Adams*. He is very solicitous that the title should be given him, for the honour of our University, and never calls him otherwise himself, than Doctor Adams.

After riding, till near 6 this evening, through, very tedious disagreeable roads, we at length arrived at Aunt Smiths where we now are. They are all well; but what think you were my feelings, when I saw those five charming Children, and reflected upon the Prospects before them. I must not dwell upon this subject; it would only raise useless sighs, upon Circumstances, which have too often already pained you.

14th. Wednesday. Boston.

We dined to day at Lincoln and soon after, continued our Journey, drank tea at Cambridge with our brother and Cousin, and got in Town just at Dusk. You know on this Road, you pass through Lexington and Concord. These places will be looked upon with great veneration by Posterity; and if ever the Spirit of Pilgrimage seizes our Country men, I hope, these ⟨will⟩ may be the places, they will resort to. Si l'apothéose est dû à l'homme, (says the Abbé Raynal, who has often noble thoughts) c'est à celui qui ⟨combat pour⟩ defend sa patrie.

Charles and our Cousin are both well, and happy in their Situation. I intended to visit Mr. Dana, but he is not at home now. Your Cousin Betsey has been very unwell since, we went from here but is now recovering. Uncle and aunt Smith went yesterday, with the Governor, Lieutt. Governor, and their Ladies, to Mr. Gill's seat at Princeton, about 50 miles from town. I have been with Mr. Isaac Smith this Evening to a Club; there were present, Dr. Welch, Dr. Dexter, Dr. Appleton, and Mr. Brewster. It was at Mr. Clarke's; the Colleague of Dr. Chauncy.[7] This gentleman, has a reputation as a speaker in the Pulpit, and is called a man of genius and learning: you know him perhaps; he holds his head I think about 3 inches too high. Dr. Appleton, is not so handsome a man, as either of his brothers, but has something in his Countenance, and in his Conversation very pleasing; Dr. Dexter you are acquainted with, and used to like him *hugeously* I am told. The *old gentleman* does not appear to have such designs as you supposed, or at least if he has does not pursue them with great ardour. I shall not have that rival to fear, I believe. You will perhaps be surprized to see I have found out who *the old Gentleman* is: but such things will happen now and then. So you see my Prospect of success is much better than you would have thought; strange things may happen yet, and you must be prepared for such.[8] The other gentlemen that were present, you know.

15th. Boston Thursday

I intended to have return'd this day to Braintree; but it threatened to rain, and I was advised to stay. Charles and William, have been in town all day, but we did not dine together. We spent the afternoon at Dr. Welch's. Mrs. W. has not said a word to me, about french fashions, or indeed any other fashions, so I have not yet had an opportunity to display my learning on that subject. The fondness for show, and dress, here, is carried to a greater pitch, than I had an Idea of, but I imagine it will decrease, for although the will is by no means wanting, the power is, and that is a Capital point: Not a few persons have been like the silk worm, first a mean insect, then a tawdry butterfly, and at length again, a worm of the dust. I hope a reform will take place, but absolute Necessity alone can bring it about.

16th. Braintree. Friday

Cousin Betsey came up from Boston with me to day. The air of a City does not agree with her, and she has been very unwell for several days. She is much better now, and I doubt not but the clear unpolluted element, that is breathed here will soon entirely recover her health. She has spent most of the Summer in Boston, to take Lessons at the harpsichord. We found Cousin Lucy all alone; she had been so the whole week.

17th. Saturday

I have been all day reading, and writing, without stirring out of the house; Uncle and Aunt return'd from Boston this Evening, as did also Mr. Tyler. I have been looking over all the books that were sent from the Hague. They were very carefully put up, and none of them are damaged at all. I perceive there is one wanting, or perhaps I forgot to send for it. It is a *Plautus*.[9] If I mistake not there is only one, in your Pappa's Library in Europe, and there is none, in the one here.

18th. Sunday

After attending Mr. Wibird twice to day, I went down with Mr. Tyler to pay my devoirs to Madam Quincy, and afterwards, at Mr. Alleyne's, we found Mr. and Mrs. Guild, with the former: they both look very much out of health. They have been very unfortunate; but I know of no persons in the same situation, that are so universally well spoken of. Mrs. Guild, has behaved upon the occasion, admirably, and what commonly greatly injures persons, in the opinion of the world seems to have been attended with effects directly contrary, with regard to her. Mrs. Quincy inquired particularly concerning Mamma and you: and Miss Nancy often smiled with all imaginable sweetness. At Mr. Alleyne's we found Mr. Boyce, the admirer of Miss Hannah Clarke, and an old gentleman, by the name of Hutchinson; but that is all I know of him.[10] I was ask'd, as I often am what part of Europe, I prefer'd to the rest. I think this Question is not fair, in a mixed Company. It has several times embarassed me; for fear I might offend some person present; you remember, how the *Chevr. de Caraman*, looked, when after he had declared his partiality for Boston, Mrs. B. told him she had never been there.[11] I am often exposed to the same danger, but I generally either give an evasory answer, or own my fondness for France, observing, that as it is the part of Europe, which I have seen the most of, my partiality may be owing to that. As yet I hope I have offended no body, and I wish I may always have the same success. Adieu my Sister, Adieu,   J. Q. Adams

RC (Adams Papers); written on small pages numbered 73 through 80, and 1 through 8; see JQA to AA2, [12] May, descriptive note, above.

[1] AA2's letter describing this event, presumably written either to one of the Cranches or to Elizabeth Shaw, has not been found. It probably dated from about 6 May, when AA2 wrote to both Elizabeth and Lucy Cranch (both above). The event was probably the Te Deum of 1 April, which AA2 describes in *Jour. and Corr.*, 1:65–68; and JQA in *Diary*, 1:242–244.

[2] Elizabeth Duncan, daughter of James Duncan Sr. and his first wife, Elizabeth Bell Duncan, would marry John Thaxter in 1787 (JQA, *Diary*, 1:321, note 1).

[3] For Rev. Hezekiah Smith, and Bailey

Bartlett, who would marry Peggy White in 1786, see same, 1:322.

[4] Elizabeth and Margaret Duncan; and probably Rev. Jonathan Allen of neighboring Bradford, Mass. Allen was a native of Braintree. See JQA, *Diary*, 1:336, 350; William B. Sprague, *Annals of the American Pulpit*, N.Y., 1857, 2:483, note; *Braintree Town Records*, p. 795.

[5] JQA's Diary suggests Nancy Hazen as Collins' critic; the Rev. Samuel Collins of nearby Sandown, N.H., is probably meant here (*Diary*, 1:322).

[6] This was William Symmes, Harvard 1750; he married his second wife, Susannah Powell of Boston, in 1774 (*Sibley's Harvard Graduates*, 12:582–587).

[7] This was apparently the Wednesday Evening Club, founded in 1777, a small gathering of clergymen, lawyers, physicians, and merchants. JQA was a member of the club from 1791 to 1809. Here he names three of the four physicians who are listed in club records as members at this date. Neither "Mr. Brewster," nor Isaac Smith Jr. is recorded as a member, but a "William Smith," probably Isaac's brother, is listed. With the exception of Brewster, each of these men is identified in JQA, *Diary*. See same, 1:324, and notes 2–5; and *The Centennial Celebration of the Wednesday Evening Club: Instituted June 21, 1777*, Boston, 1878, p. 48–49, 51–52, 142–145.

[8] Neither the "old gentleman" nor the woman whom AA2 evidently thought was the object of his and JQA's interest has been identified.

[9] MQA eventually contained nine editions of the comedies of the 3d-2d century B.C. dramatist Plautus, in Latin, French, and English, and one Latin edition of Plautus' "Lectiones," all published before 1785, in France, Holland, Germany, or England. Six of these editions show some mark of JQA's ownership.

[10] Mr. Hutchinson has not been identified. "Mr. Boyce" was Jeremiah Smith Boies of Milton, who in September announced his intention to marry Sarah [Hannah?] Clark. See *Braintree Town Records*, p. 887; Pattee, *Old Braintree and Quincy*, p. 59.

[11] See AA2 to JQA, 26 Aug., note 7, above.

John Adams to John Quincy Adams

Grosvenor Square Westminster

My dear Son   Septr. 9. 1785

I have received your Letter by Mr. Church,[1] and am very happy to hear of your Safe Arrival, and kind Reception at New York. You have a good Opportunity, to See the Place and principal Characters, and from the hints you give your Sister[2] I Suppose and indeed I hope, you went home by Land, and Saw the Country and Persons you wanted to See.

I want to hear from you at Boston, and to learn what is become of your Samples of Oil and your Proposals for a trafick in that Commodity. Send me the Name of the Gentleman who has the Contract for enlightening thirty Cities in France and his Address if you have it.[3]

We are comfortably Settled, in this Place, but See no present Prospect of doing much material Service for the Publick. There are Prejudices in the Way, too Strong to be easily overcome. I hope our Countrymen will learn Wisdom, be frugal, encourage their own Navigation and Manufactures and Search the whole Globe for a Substitute for British Commerce.

But why am I entertaining you, with publick Affairs? At your Age, and with your Prospects, Justinians Institutes or Theophilus's Commentary, would be more proper.[4] I would not advise you, to be wholly inattentive or insensible to the Prosperity or Adversity of your Country, but on the other hand I hope you will not Sour your temper or diminish the natural Chearfulness of your Disposition by dwelling too much upon the gloomy Complaints of the times. Letters and Science demand all your Time, and you must prepare yourself to get your Bread. Instead of being able to provide for you, I think it very probable that in a very little time, I shall find it very difficult to provide for myself. I have no longer youth and strength on my Side, and cannot labour as you can and as I could five and twenty Years ago. You must sett an Example of Frugality, Modesty and Sobriety among your young Friends.

I would warn you against the danger of keeping much Company. It consumes ones time insensibly, and young as you are, you will have none to Spare. Choose your Friends with caution and Reflection. There is nothing in which a young Man shews his Judgment more than in this. Have an Eye to the moral Character, and the Virtues and fine Feelings of the Heart in this Choice, as well as to Talents, Genius and Studies.

I See with Pleasure, that your Style is improving and begins to run very easy. It is well worth your while to be attentive to this. You have Time and means to make your Self a Master of your native Language.

My affectionate Regards to your Brothers, and to all our Friends. Your affectionate Father   John Adams

RC (Adams Papers); endorsed: "My Father. 9. Septr. 1785," and "Mr. Adams. Septr. 9. 1785."

[1] Of 3 Aug., above.

[2] In his letter of 17 July, above, under 29 July.

[3] See JQA to AA2, 29 Aug., and note 2, above; and JQA, *Diary*, 1:319–320, for JQA's delivery of a proposal to establish a commerce in whale oil with France to Samuel Breck Sr. The name JA sought was Tourtille de Sangrain (Jefferson, *Papers*, 8:144–145).

[4] Theophilus was a member of the commission of jurists appointed by the Emperor Justinian to compile his code of Roman law (Hoefer, *Nouv. biog. générale*). JA recounts his own discovery of Justinian in the *Earliest Diary* and *Diary and Autobiography*; his interest in Roman law, unusual among his common law-trained contemporaries, is the subject of Daniel R. Coquillette's "Justinian in Braintree: John Adams, Civilian Learning, and Legal Elitism, 1758–1775," in *Law in Colonial Massachusetts 1630–1800*, ed. Daniel R. Coquillette and others, Boston, 1984, p. 359–418. JQA would first refer to studying Justinian's *Institutes* in his Diary in 1788 (*Diary*, 2:461), during his own preparation to practice law. He would eventually acquire editions of Justinian in Latin, Italian, and French (MQA).

Abigail Adams to Mary Smith Cranch

My dear sister   London Septr 11th. 1785

I have enjoyed very good Health ever since I came to London, untill ten days past. I had about a week since a small attack of the Fall disorder which I hoped I had got the better of. The next seizure was such a swiming in my Head when I laid down in the Bed, as to throw me almost into convulsions. It finally produced a violent puking which relieved me of that, tho I cannot say I feel well. You know I am accustomed to ill turns in the Fall,[1] and I fear this damp climate will not be any service to me. The great distance of time which we pass in this country between meals, is unfavourable to Health. I have got wholy out of the Habit of more than two meals a day. We generally Breakfast at Nine, or before, and dine at four when we have no company, otherways not till Six. You must expect to receive visits and pay them from one till four or 5. I have however set a part one day, which is every tuesday to be at Home for company, by which means I know who and who wishes to find me at Home, by their visiting upon that day.

I wrote you by Captain Lyde[2] who saild a fortnight ago. Since that we have been made very happy by hearing of the safe arrival of our son! He is with you I dare say before now, and very happy to find himself in his Native Country. I hope he will be cautious with respect to His Health as he has not experienced so hot a climate for many years.

Charles I presume has commenced student at Harvered College, where I hope he will never give pain to his Friends by any misconduct. How little do Children know the solicitude and anxiety of a Parents Heart, or how tenderly their conduct affects them. Our poor unhappy connexion,[3] whose Life has been one continued Error, gives me pain. How difficult to recover the right path when the feet have once wandered from it. How much resolution is necessary to overcome evil propencities? More particularly a habit of intemperence. I never can think of the closing scene of our dear venerable Fathers Life but with an anguish I cannot express; breathing out his last breath and Labouring in the agonies of Death for the reformation and salvation of the prodigal.

> "The sweet remembrance of the just"
> "Shall flourish when they sleep in dust"[4]

How dear to me is the remembrance of my Parents how sweet the recollection of their virtues, how forcible their example? There is a pleasure arising from a connexion with virtuous Friends and relatives, which neither power wealth or titles can bestow without it. This month my mind is always particularly impressd with the recollection of my dear parents.[5]

How carefull ought young people to be, when they are about entering into connections for Life, to look to the Heart of those to whom they bind themselves. If that is false and deceifull towards the Deity, they can have little hopes of fidelity towards themselves. In short their is nothing binding upon the Humane mind, but Religion.

I hope our sister S-h [*Smith*] conducts with prudence and discretion becomeing her critical situation and that the Children will prove comforts to her and their Friends. I felt most dissagreeaby the other Day at a circumstance which took place. Col. Smith came in and told me that he had received a very extrodanary Letter from a person whom he never saw or heard of before. He took it from his pocket and began to read it. The purport of it was, that he, the writer had heard of his late arrival in this Country, and of his appointment. Conceiving him to be in an Eligible Situation, he had taken the liberty to request the payment of a debt which he must remember he owed him in such a year, at the time he faild in buisness and fell into misfortunes. As he had never given him any trouble about it, he would consider him so much of a Gentleman as to suppose he would make no difficulty of answering the inclosed order to the House of Champion & Dickenson. He concluded by signing his Name Gorge Erving. The Col. had not gone half through his Letter before I was sensible who was meant, and he would have seen my agitation if he had look up; I did not know what to say, whether to let him know his mistake, or suffer him to marvel at the matter. He had pend his answer and went on reading to me his replie which exprest his surprize at receiving a Letter of that kind from a person wholy unknown to him. That he was quite insensible to the misfortunes he alluded to, as well as to the Debt, for that he was conscious he never owed any person a quarter the Sum mentiond in his Life. That so far from being in Buisness the year mentiond, he was a student at College. But that if Mr. Erving wish'd any further explanation, he was to be spoken with at his Lodgings in Leister feilds any hour after ten in the morning.[6] When I had a little recoverd myself, I told him I could explain the matter to him; upon which he was not less surprized than before, never hearing a Brother mentiond ⟨before⟩. He was a good deal embaressed at having read the Letters, and giving me pain as he saw he had, but there was no fault on either side. I only wish there had never been occasion for such a demand.

Captain Lyde expects to return here in the winter. You will not fail writing me very particularly by him. You know there are certain Matters which I shall be very anxious to know the event of.[7] I mentiond to you sending two Guineys by Mr. Storer for my Mother [*Susanna Boylston Adams Hall*], but upon second thought, I will write to Dr. Tufts to pay her Anually 20 dollars which will be more independent. There is also a black russel peticoat which I never wore but once or twice. I would have you take it and give it to her. If the Dr. has advanced any thing let that go as a part of the 20 dollars. I wish however that she might be benifitted by it. Sister Shaw wrote me that she had carried some things of Tommys to Boylstone. I would not have any thing given there, but what is pretty good. There is (between you and I) more pride than she may be aware of. But if any thing can be of service without the Idea of there being old Cloaths, I wish he may have them.[8] I know between all S[9] they must have many things which will serve somebody. Let them be disposed of where they cannot give offence. And an other thing I wish which is that any little matter I may send to my Sisters or Neices may be silently received, that I do not want them to say Aunt or sister sent it to me. I wish it was in my power to send them any thing worth notice, but they know the will is good. I should be loth the Moths should devour what I left behind, yet I feel unwilling to have the things disposed of. I hope to come home and use them ere long.

My Love to Mr. Cranch and duty to uncle Quincy, with remembrance to all my old Neighbours who I flatter myself remember me with the same affection which I do them.

How does Pheby. Does her income make her comfortable. If it does not, I would willingly contribute towards her support. Advise my dear sister and believe me most tenderly yours   Abigail Adams

I must quit my pen to dress. Captain Callihan dines here to day and Col. Franks. Mr. Storer will tarry with us till he sails which he expect in a few days.

RC (MWA:Abigail Adams Corr.).

[1] AA first connects some of her illnesses with the fall season in a letter to JA, 8 Oct. 1780 (vol. 4:3). On AA's health, see the indexes in vols. 2 and 4, above.

[2] Of 15 Aug., above.

[3] Their brother, William Smith Jr.; see note 6.

[4] AA quotes from Nahum Tate and Nicholas Brady, *A New Version of the Psalms of David, Fitted to Tunes used in Churches*, Lon-

don, 1696. These lines render Psalm 112:6; AA substitutes "they" for "he" in the second line.

⁵ AA inserted this sentence in the space that she left for a paragraph break. Her mother, Elizabeth Quincy Smith, died on 1 Oct. 1775; her father, Rev. William Smith, on 17 Sept. 1783.

⁶ Col. Smith's correspondent was probably the Boston merchant George Erving, brother-in-law of James Bowdoin, and a reluctant loyalist émigré with strong sympathies for the American cause who lived in England from 1776 until his death in 1806. The account in Erving's letter to Col. Smith given here places

the contracting of William Smith Jr.'s debt to Erving as occurring in the early 1770s, when Col. Smith was still a student at Princeton. See *Sibley's Harvard Graduates*, 14:151–157.

⁷ Most likely Royall Tyler's reaction to AA2's decision to end her connection with him.

⁸ In addition to the matter of pride, AA and JA's nephew Boylston Adams was nearly eighteen months older than TBA, whose clothes he was receiving.

⁹ AA probably intends the whole Shaw household, including her sons.

Abigail Adams to John Quincy Adams

My dear son   Sepbr 12th. 1785

Mr. Storers departure is delayed from day to day so that I fear he will have a dissagreeable time upon our Coast. It gives me an opportunity of adding a few more lines to you. Col. Franks arrived here on Saturday with dispatches from Mr. Jefferson. The Ministers not hearing a Syllable of Lamb, and reports growing every day more serious, tho many of them are really false, yet they have the effect of raising ensurence and greatly obstructing trade. In concequence of which it is determined to send Mr. Barclay without further delay and Col. Franks goes Secretary upon the Buisness which Lambe was Charged with. It is of importance that this matter be kept from this Court, and that occasiond Col. Franks comeing with the dispatches.

Your old acquaintance Stockdale is bought up by the M[inistr]y and receives a pension of 4 hundred per Year.¹ It is said he is quite a different Man from what he was when you knew him. Not a single paragraph can be publishd in favour of America, suppose it only six lines under 3 or 4 Guineys. They have offerd a Bounty here of 500 to the British whale man who shall take the largest Quantity this Season, 400 to the next, 300 to the 3d, 2 to the fourth and one to the 5th. In concequence of this a Number of vessels have saild from hence. They take the Mates of the American vessels here and give them the command of a good Ship for this purpose. They have pickd up all the Negroes who were stragling about and starving, and engaged them in this buisness. The M[inistr]y secretly allow any American vessel which comes here to go out in the whale fishery and bring their oil in here free of duty. This is done in order to intice our Whale Men here. At the same time they are prohibiting under the severest penaltys any artificer from going to America and prohibiting all hard-ware tools. The Court Scriblers publishd last week that ⟨*your*⟩ the American minister had been closeted with the king in a long confer-ence. The concequence was an Immediate rise of stocks. This Manuver was on purpose to try what Effect it was probable might be produced by a treaty.

Mr. Jefferson writes me[2] that the Queen of France has agreed in future to wear only French Gauze, that Cardinal Rohan is Still in the Bastile, and that it appears he was the dupe of his Mistress Madam la Mote.

I have nothing further to add but that I found two or 3 stocks Night caps &c which I have sent by Mr. Storer and a pair of Buckles which I have had mended for you. Adieu. Yours &c.   A A

RC (Adams Papers); endorsed: "Momma. Septr. 12th. 1785"; docketed: "My Mother 12. Septr. 1785," and "Mrs. Adams. Septr. 12. 1785."

[1] If the Pitt ministry did try to buy Stockdale's support in 1785, the arrangement did not endure. In 1789 the government tried Stockdale for publishing John Logan's *Review of the Charges against Warren Hastings* (1788), which the ministry considered a libel against the House of Commons. The court, in a major decision affecting British libel law, acquitted him. See JQA to JA, 20 May 1784, and note 2, above; *DNB*.

[2] On 4 Sept., above.

Abigail Adams to Elizabeth Smith Shaw

My Dear Sister   London Septr 15 1785

Mr. Storer says the ship in which he is to embark will go down to day and that he shall go on Board tomorrow. I cannot let him depart without a few lines to you tho I wrote you so lately by Captain Lyde[1] that I have nothing New to add. I have not been lately either to Court or the Play. I have made some visits into the Country to a couple of families who have been very polite to us. When we first came they got introduced to us, and have twice invited us to dine. Both times we were unfortunatly preengaged. The Gentleman Name is Smith he is a Member of Parliament, and he married into the other family whose Name is Copes. They are very agreeable people and live about 4 mils from Town at a very pretty village call'd Clapham. Next week I propose going to Court as it is the aniverssary of his Majestys Coronation.[2] I may probably find some entertainment for you from that quarter.

This week the Theatre at Covent Garden opens and Mrs. Siddons appears in the Tradigy of Othello in the Character of Desdamony. We have sent a Week before to engage places. I promise myself high entertainment from this admired and celebrated actress, but heitherto I have seen nothing that I can realish since my comeing from Paris. Of the Theatrical kind I should say.

If I had come to this Country with high expectation I should have been dissapointed, but as I have no taste and passion for Routes, and gameing, tables, &c. I cannot string over to you such a Night at my Lady H's Ball and such a night at the Countess C—s Route or the Dutchess ofs, Card party. I am so little Qualified for my station and so old fashiond as to prefer the Society of Dr. Price, Dr. Jebb, and a few others like them to the midnight Gamblers, and the titled Gamesters, and I am so impudent, impudent the English call it, as to take a pride in acknowledging my Country despightfully as this people treat it. I am neither ashamed of it, or the great actions which dismemberd it from this empire. Some of our Countrymen who mix much with this people, have confessd to me; that they secreat their Country, and pass themselves for Natives to avoid being insulted—but I am loth to part with the Scripture Benidiction, "blessed are Ye when Men persecute and revile you falsly."[3]

I know they abuse America because they fear her, and every effort to render her unpopular is a proof of it. They go on deceiving themselves, thinking they can keep us low and poor, but all the time they are making us industerous, frugal wise and Great I hope.

I have sent to Mr. Shaw a little Treatise upon Education which was presented to Mr. Adams by the Author, tho unknown to him.[4] Mr. Adams thought it might be more usefull to Mr. Shaw than it could be to him, as it lay more in his particular department and accordingly directed me to send it to him.

I hope all your little family are well, and that you have only exchanged one Nephew for an other.

My best regards attend all my good Friends at Haverhill, to Madam Marsh in particular if the Good Saint is not yet gone to Heaven. Dr. Johnson used to make a practise of praying for his departed Friends. This is rather singular for a Protestant, who universally believe that Death excludes their friends both from the good or evil of those who survive.

But I must bid you adieu as I am going to take a little ride. I have been very unwell for several Days. I am very sensible I want excercise. O that I could go and see my sisters, my Aunts, my cousins.

Once more adieu. Most tenderly yours

RC (DLC:Shaw Family Papers); addressed by Charles Storer: "Mrs. Elizabeth Shaw, Haverhill"; endorsed: "Sep. 15 1785."

[1] Of [*ca. 15 Aug.*], above.

[2] George III and his queen, Charlotte Sophia, were crowned on 22 Sept. 1761, nearly a year after he ascended the throne.

[3] Matthew 5:11, altered and condensed; opening quotation mark supplied.

[4] The author and treatise have not been identified.

Abigail Adams to Cotton Tufts

Dear sir   London Sepbr 16th. 1785

I believe that Mr. Storer is going to leave Us in good earnest. He has so long and so many months been delay'd that I knew not when to give him my latest Letters tho I have so little to communicate that it is not of much importance whether my Letter was written a month ago or now. The talk of Captures by the Algerine is renewed again and I fear with two much foundation. Mr. Adams received a Letter yesterday from Spain from Mr. Carmichael[1] who informs him that he has vague reports concerning the Capture of two American vessels, and that it was said, the vessels Cargoes and prisoners were imediately advertized for sale. Mr. Storer can acquaint you fully of the measures taking by Mr. Adams and Jefferson, and the persons who are immediately going upon the buisness of a treaty with them, as well as the reasons which have so long delay'd it, the person[2] who was sent in May last from Congress respecting this buisness; never having been heard of since. If a measure fails, it is not going right to Court and receiving new orders, but you must cross and recross the ocean before any thing can be accomplishd, which never can take Less time than half a Year.

As to Buisness here, we presume it is hatching. The papers have become more civil and matters more serious. I can only tell you that no answers have yet been received from the Court and Ministry to all the bugget before them. I believe it will take them some time to ponder and digest. Those Houses connected with America are very anxious and I wonder not at it, as our Country my dear sir are most deeply indebted here. They complain most; of want of remittances from Virgina and New York. As to their permitting no more goods to go out, I believe it is a very fortunate circumstance for our Country. Time will shew. But sir can nothing be accomplishd with respect to our foreign Debt; that being still unfunded you may be sure does not increase our Credit, and the forgeries which are circulated throughout Europe respecting the unsettled State of our Government, and

the confusions and discontent which prevails amongst our people &c;
all these falshoods gain some credit with those who are not better
informd; and do us injury, especially whilst no method is persued to
establish our credit and Sink our National Debt. Mr. A has written
to Congress repeatedly and presst this matter with all the energy and
reasoning he is master of;[3] but heitherto it has accomplishd nothing.
The reluctance to the impost in some of the states has I suppose
retarded the measures of Congress. But what will be the concequence? The money we have in Holland must most of it be applied to
the treatys with these Barbarians.[4] The interest of the Debt in Holland has heitherto been pay'd, but how? Why by retaining sufficient
of the Capital. This can succeed no longer, nor shall we possibly have
credit for a New Loan tho to save us from Perdition at this rate.
France is continually dunning for her Interest. In short Sir the
embassys abroad, are one continued Scene of perplexity and anxiety.
I think I have been told that the Massachusetts have establishd a
committe to correspond with the members of Congress. I hope they
will think of the importance of these objects. The Board of Com-
misoners consists of able Men and I hope they will bring order out
of confusion, tho I fear they will find the publick money making
voyages to China.[5] I have been informd that the late Financerer[6] lived
at an expence of 5000 sterling a year.

But how I run on, excuse my politicks. I feel that I ought to be a
help Mate, for really my Friend has sometimes so much upon his
Hands from various quarters that I fear it will be too much for him.
The Quantity of writing is incredible, for you must reason in writing
and every thing must be laid before *certain persons*[7] in writing. Copies
of that must go to congress and you must reserve originals for
yourself. Communications must be made often to the American
Minister in France, all of which must be put into cypher, unless a
special Messenger is Sent. The preperations for the present treaty
are obliged to pass from France here and then from hence back again.
Writing for a long time together affects Mr. Adams's Eyes very much.

But to quit politicks, I hope Lyde by whom I wrote[8] is safe arrived.
My son too has visited you before this day. My other I hope is in
colledge. Mr. Storer will pay you 17 Guineys which you will credit us
for. I believe I mentiond that we payd the Bill of Mr. Elworthy upon
sight. Mrs. Cranch wrote me respectting my Mother. I wish sir you
would pay her 20 dollors per An. Quarterly, taking her receipt for the
same. Excuse this hasty Scrawl and believe me at all times most
affectionately Yours   A A

RC (Adams Papers); addressed by Charles Storer: "The Honourable Cotton Tufts Esquire Member of Senate Boston"; endorsed: "Mrs. Adams London Sepr. 16 1785 Pr Mr Storer recd Nov."

¹ Of 2 Sept., Adams Papers.

² Col. John Lamb.

³ See, for example, JA to the president of Congress, 10 Jan. (PCC, No. 84, V, f. 367–370; LbC, Adams Papers), printed in *Dipl. Corr.*, *1783–1789*, 1:472–473.

⁴ The Barbary States.

⁵ The "Board of Commissioners" was presumably Congress' three-man Treasury Board. AA apparently refers to news found in several letters, and probably in some newspapers, recently received by JA. On 28 May, the president of Congress, Richard Henry Lee, reported from New York (*The Letters of Richard Henry Lee*, ed. James C. Ballagh, N.Y., 1911–1914, 2 vols., 2:362–364) that America's first merchant vessel sent to China had returned from Canton with a valuable cargo

(see JQA to AA2, 17 July, note 11, above). And on 7 June, James Sullivan wrote from New York (Adams Papers) concerning the trade crisis and the need for a stronger national government to deal with it. In addition, the 10 Aug. letter from Cotton Tufts, above, which JA had probably not received by 16 Sept. (see AA to Cotton Tufts, 5 Oct., below), briefly refers to the state legislature's recent issue of letters to state governors, to the president of Congress, and to its own congressional delegation, all urging revision of the Articles of Confederation to meet the nation's fiscal and commercial crisis.

⁶ Robert Morris.

⁷ Presumably members of the British ministry.

⁸ On 18 Aug., above.

Abigail Adams to William Stephens Smith

Dear sir   [18 September 1785]¹

Col. Franks being detained to day by an accident gives me the opportunity of replieing to your kind Letter² last evening received; Col. Forrest had inclosed them to Mr. Adams and we were not a little rejoiced to hear from you after an interval of 4 weeks in which we had spent many conjectures where you was at one time, and where you ⟨was⟩ were at an other. Mr. Adams received your Letter from Amsterdam³ but knew not where to address to you, and we began now to look every day for your return.

Mr. Adams has not been impatient tho he has sometimes wished for you, for as luck would have it, he has been obliged to write twice as much since you left him, as for any Space of time since he came here before. But Mr. Storer has been very good and helpfull to him, or I know not what he would have done, as writing only one evening about a week ago brought on an inflamation in his Eyes for several which obliged him almost to lay aside his pen. But his dispatches are now all finish for New York, and for the Barbarians. Do not mistake me Sir, I mean the Algerines and not the English. He will be more at leisure than for some weeks past. Mr. Storer left us on thursday morning⁴ to our no small regreet. He lamented that he had not Letters and dispatches from you as he Saild directly for New York, but I have the pleasure of assureing you that your Mamma and

365

Friends were well in july. My son after a tedious passage of 55 days was arrived. He mentions visiting your family upon Long Island, and that your Mamma had received Letters from you since your arrival in England.[5] I have here a Number of Letters and bundles of Newspapers for you and if I was sure Col. Franks would find you in Paris I would send them on to you. But if he should not it would accumulate a weight of postage all ready too heavy. You must write to your News paper correspondents never to seal them up for then they are sent and paid for as Letters. What do you think of having to pay for 60 or 70 News Papers as Letters?

You have found a Letter from me if you have reachd Paris. I wrote by Mr. Short.[6] Prudence dictates silence to me, take a draught of Lethe[7] and all will be as it ought. There are entanglingment as Lady G. terms them from which Time the great solacer of Humane woe only can relieve us. And Time I dare say will extricate those I Love from any unapproved Step, into which inexperience and youth may have involved them. But untill that period may arrive Honour, Honour, is at Stake—a word to the wise is sufficient.

I depend much upon the cherefull Social converse during the long winter evening which are now fast approaching, many of which we have already spent quite alone wishing for a Friend to enliven the Scene. You know we are not those kind of people who delight in Gambling and Routes and go seldom to the Theater. I was last Evening however at Drury Lane and Saw for the first time Mrs. Siddons.

> Grace was in all her steps heaven in her Eye
> And every Gesture dignity and Love.[8]

She appeard in the tradegy of Othello, and acted the part of Desdemona. Othello was represented blacker than any affrican. Whether it arises from the prejudices of Education or from a real natural antipathy I cannot determine, but my whole soul shuderd when ever I saw the sooty ⟨*heretik?*⟩ More touch the fair Desdemona. I wonder not that Brabantio thought Othello must have used Spells and magick to have won her affections. ⟨*The Character of Othello*⟩ Through the whole play ⟨*is that of a Noble Generous open Manly*⟩ the Character of Othello is Manly open generous and noble, betrayed by a most artfull villan and a combination of circumstances into an action that his Soul abhored. ⟨*but I So powerfull was prejudice that I could not seperate the coulour from the Man and by which means*⟩

366

9. SARAH KEMBLE SIDDONS AS DESDEMONA
See page xiv

That most incomparable Speach of Othellos lost half its force and Beauty, because I could not Seperate the coulour from the Man.[9] Yet it was admirably well spoken.

> O now, for ever
>   Fare well the tranquil Mind! fare well content
> Fare well the plumed troop, and the big warss
> That make ambition virtue! O fare well
> Fare well the Neighing steed, and the shrill trump,
> The spirit stiring Drum, the ear piercing fife
> The Royal banner; and all quality,
> Pride pomp and circumstance of glorious War!
> And O you mortal engines, whose rude throats
> The immortal Jove's dread clamours counterfeit,
> Fare well! Othello's occupation gone.[10]

You will no doubt visit all the theatres in Paris during your Stay. I think you will be pleased with them. I have been told that your companion is quite an antigallican.[11] I however do not regard these Speaches. A Gentleman of understanding such as I esteem him to be, who has travelld merly to remark Men and Manners, will never be indiscriminate either in Praising or Blameing Countries or people collectively. There is something I dare say esteemable in all, and the liberal mind regards not what Nation or climate it spring up in, nor what *coulour* or *complexion* the Man is of.

It is Sunday and I have just returnd from Hackney. The good Dr. [*Price*] inquired kindly after you. When I hear from you in Paris, I shall suppose you be soon returning. Daniel is vastly impatient, and a few days ago sent by my maid to inquire if I had heard from you. I believe he behaves very well during your absence. He is very often here. I have had occasion to send for him sometimes and Daniel is always to be found at home. Col. Franks will tell you that he has been very serviceabl to him since he has been in London. I shall have an ⟨aditional⟩ article or two which Mrs. Barclay will deliver you or send to Mr. Jeffersons for me, in addition to those I have already named, and of which I request your care. As to politicks Col. Franks can tell you all and I am not enough in Love with them to mix them here. Mr. Adams I suppose will write you.[12] I have only room to add my compliments and regards to all my Paris Friends and to assure you you have the good wishes of the family for your prosperity and happiness.

Dft (Adams Papers, filmed at [*Sept. 1785*], Microfilms, Reel No. 365); notation in CFA's hand: "To Col Smith. London September 1785."

[1] The date is established by AA2 to JQA, 24 Sept., below, which states that the Adamses visited the Drury Lane Theater on 17 Sept. to see *Othello*; in the present letter AA mentions this event as occurring "last Evening."

[2] Of 5 Sept., above.

[3] Dated ca. 15 Aug., but not found; see Smith to AA, 5 Sept., note 3.

[4] 15 September. But on 16 Sept., AA wrote to Cotton Tufts, above, that Storer was "going to leave"; on 24 Sept., AA2 wrote JQA, below, that Storer had left on Monday, 19 September.

[5] JQA to AA2, 17 July, above, under 31 July.

[6] On 13 Aug., above.

[7] Lethe was one of the rivers of Hades in Greek cosmology, its name meaning "oblivion." A drink of its waters caused the spirits of the dead to forget their past lives. In the following passage, AA refers to AA2's relationship with Royall Tyler.

[8] Milton, *Paradise Lost*, viii, 488–489; Milton wrote "In every Gesture . . ."

[9] For a similar expression by an Adams of the difficulty in admiring *Othello*, and particularly the character of Desdemona, see JQA's remarks upon the play and its heroine, expressed in conversation with the actress Fanny Kemble in 1833, recorded in 1835, and published in 1835 and 1836 (CFA, *Diary*, 5:84–86).

[10] III, iii, 347–357.

[11] The source of AA's information that Don Francisco Miranda harbored anti-French feelings is not known.

[12] No letter or other reference to a letter from JA to Col. Smith has been found.

John Quincy Adams to Abigail Adams 2d

N: 10

Braintree September 19th. 1785

I have been in a manner cheated out of this day by the library; for in looking over the books, and sometimes dipping into one, the fleeting hours (as the poets say) have disappeared; and night in her sable chariot, has performed a considerable part of her course. Your Uncle, went this morning to Boston, as he regularly does, and Mr. Tyler, has been very closely engaged all day.

Tuesday 20th

In the afternoon I went over, with both our Cousins, to pay a visit to aunt Tufts, who has been dangerously ill, but is now in a fair way of recovering. She ask'd abundance of Questions about you, and I felt no small pleasure in answering them. By the way, do you know that Lucy Jones, has an admirer, whose passion seems to outstrip every thing, that Romance can produce; absolutely an *Orlando furiosos*.[1] The son of Mr. Haslet, was suddenly (and to be sure violently) smitten with her charms: he did not, sit like patience, on a marble monument: smiling at grief. But called the Earth; the Sun, moon, Stars, and every other planet, to witness, that she was the fairest, noblest, sweetest, most beauteous damsel, that was ever beheld by mortal eyes. In short he was nearly raving. And it has been thought necessary, to keep him, out of her sight, that he might not have a relapse, which would be very disagreeable. While we were gone, Mr. Nash, and Miss Lucy Apthorp, were at your Aunts. And who is Mr. Nash, perhaps you will say. He is the 2d. lieutenant on board his Majesty's ship, Mercury, and was bearer, of some infamous letters to the governor, which you will see in the Papers, (this however is nothing to his disadvantage). While the ship was in Boston harbour, he formed an Acquaintance with Mr. Apthorp's family, and is now returned here on Purpose, to take the Lady. Her father is highly gratified with the honour of such a Son in Law, and I am told, Miss Lucy said it ⟨was⟩ should be just as Pappa pleased. So you see, she has at least been taught the obedience, with regard to marriage; which her illustrious birth requires. In all this transaction, there appears only one favourable Circumstance for her in the Eyes of the world; the gentleman, bears a respectable, and an amiable Character. I am sure she will need such an one, for I fear many trying scenes await her. They are to be married next Saturday.[2]

Thursday 22d. Boston

I was all day yesterday, packing up my trunk, and preparing every thing to send to Haverhill. This morning I forwarded them here, and wish'd to come myself, to see them put into the stage, that goes to-morrow. But we had an Invitation from Madam Quincy, to dine with her to day, and after a long deliberation upon the matter, I concluded to wait on her. Your Cousins went in a Chaise. Mr. Tyler and I march'd it. We were too late, and as is usual, excuses were made on both sides, though there was no necessity for them on either. Parson Wibird was there: this was the first time, I had seen him, out of the meeting house. Well! you have been in Russia; how do you like the Ladies there? As soon as I had answered he enquired about the French, Spanish, and Dutch and in short of the Ladies in every part of Europe I had seen. At length I said to him, You seem, Sir, to enquire of nothing, any where but the Ladies. Why; to be sure says he, I always make it a Rule, to enquire for the best things, first: and then laugh'd heartily. He was very merry, and now and then paid a Compliment, but as often let fall a Sarcasm, on the fair sex, which is always the way with an old batchelor. Soon after dinner we left them, (I mean Mr. Tyler and myself) and, proceeded this way. We stopped in at Genl. Warren's. Mrs. Otis[3] was there: looked solemn; but you know she has a vast deal of aequinimity. Mrs. Warren has not enjoy'd for a considerable time past, good health, and looks quite unwell now. When I got here between 6 and 7 this Evening (for it commonly takes me, an whole day, to get from Braintree, to Boston) I was told the post would not go to-morrow, as Mr. Peabody, has broke his Carriage. So I have concluded to send them by a Vessel, which is to sail in the beginning of next week; and I shall go with him next week.

I have been playing Cards, this Evening for the first Time since I arrived: it is not the most agreeable way of spending time, to me: you may remember I was not so fond of it before I left you, as in the beginning of the Winter; and my aversion has rather increased than otherwise. I shall not lose much time, very soon I imagine with them.

23d

I was introduced this forenoon, to three gentlemen in the Profession of the Law. Mr. Lincoln, Mr. Gardiner, and Mr. Hughes.[4] The second of these gentlemen pronounced the Oration, upon Independence day. You may have seen the performance. It is one of the most curious thing of the Kind, that I have seen, for a long Time. He has a particular attachment to blank verse, for the whole work if divided into ten syllable lines, would form quite a swelling Poem. Mr. H you are perhaps acquainted with. He is said to be a little Sarcastic, and in a miserable farce, called *Sans-souci*,[5] from a Club, who made last winter a great deal of noise, and that went by that name, he is represented under the Character, of *Jemmy Satirist*.

I dined with Mr. Toscan, and after dinner went with him to pay my Respects to the Governor, but he was engaged in business; I then paid a visit to Mr. Russel, and saw there, Mr. Seaver, who arrived yesterday, from Russia. Quite a smart young man; and I fancy *a traveller*. Mrs. Russel desired I would present you her Compliments; and said she had been disappointed, in not receiving, any Letters from you, since you left America. I told her I had always thought, you had written her twice at least, but she said she had not received a line.[6] Mrs. Vaughan, and her daughters were there,[7] but I did not know who they were, untill after we came away Mr. Toscan told me. From thence we went and drank tea with Mr. Tudor. There was a large Company, but of persons I was not acquainted with. Mr. and Mrs. T, were very Polite, as usual you know. He desired I would make his house, as much my home, as he had formerly my father's. How much that was I do not recollect;[8] we had a sort of a Concert, a young french Gentleman was present, who is exceeding fond of music; and

371

quite a *virtuose*.[9] He sung and play'd on several instruments. From thence I went and pass'd the evening and supp'd, at Mr. B. Austin's: who was married in the Summer; his Lady's name I don't know. Mr. Ben: Cutler Mr. James Lovel, Mr. Hughes, Mr. L. Austin, and Mr. Tyler, form'd the Company.[10] Mr. Cutler, is a very handsome man, and is fully Sensible of it. Somewhat affected; which is not uncommon, in a person celebrated for personal advantages, especially a Man. Mr. Lovel, is perhaps somewhat in the same predicament, though with less Reason. Mr. Hughes told us a few stories, and discovered a little of the disposition, I have already mentioned. He is short sighted: and when he looks steadily at anything, there is always a contraction about the eyes, that is quite laughable. Mrs. Austin, is not handsome, rather otherwise, genteel, talks but Little. The evening was agreeably spent except, that we play'd Cards: we must endeavour in matters of little Consequence, to conform, to the customs of the world, enough to preserve us from the reproach of singularity.

24th. Saturday

Mr. Nash, and Miss Apthorp were married in the morning, at the Chapel.[11] There was a large Crowd present; for you know marriages in a Church, are a great Rarity here. I never saw upon any stage, more strikingly express'd, the different passions that are excited in different breasts by the same Event. Here indeed it was real, and the expression was consequently not so deep, but more affecting. The old man, held up his head; look'd as happy, and as exalted, as he could if he was created peer of G. Britain: very differently from what he did upon a former occasion of the same kind; and in the general opinion he was equally wrong, both times. The mother was exceedingly dejected; I feared she would faint.[12] She leaned against a pew, and hung down her head. I pity'd her, very much. The bridegroom was dress'd plainly in his uniform, and his Countenance display'd a proper mixture of joy, and solemnity. The bride was in a dark colour'd lutestring, her hair very elegantly dress'd: she looked like a victim led to the altar, and trembled, like one in an ague fit. And now the matter is over, and there is no going back: but indeed I have great doubts as to the happiness of this match. Can an acquaintance of less than three months, give any two persons sufficient insight, into each others Characters, to assure them, that they may trust to each other their happiness for life? Can a lieutenant of a Man of War, with little, or no private fortune, (as the case is here I am told) maintain a family as handsomely, as this Lady expects? Can a young Lady, who leaves every friend and every Connection she has in the world, never to see them more, and goes into a Country, where every body will be a stranger to her, be happy? If these three Questions can be affirmitively answered, Mrs. Nash bids as fair for happiness, as any body I know. Excuse me my Sister, if I thus run on in the Sentimental way, which was in some measure excluded from our agreement, but it comes upon me sometimes unawares, and I often write on a long time before I remember the engagements.

I intended to have gone this evening as far as Milton, and spent the day there to-morrow, but it began to storm about noon, and rained so hard in the Evening, that I was obliged to stay in Town; I went with Mr. Tyler, and spent the Evening at Mr. Gore's. Mrs. Gore is a very sociable little woman, comely; not handsome.[13] Mr. Gore told us some anecdotes concerning a Mr. *le Washington*, who arrived in one of the last Vessels from England. This man, is either a very great knave, or is wanting in Common Sense. With a settled serious Countenance, he tells the most extravagant Stories I ever heard of; People here stare at him, and wonder at his Proficiency in the art of fiction. But if he supposes he excites their Admiration, he is exceedingly mistaken. For I know of no People, disposed more to doubt a traveller's Veracity, than my Countrymen, and I am sometimes afraid to tell real facts, lest I should, gain the Reputation of dealing in fiction too.

Sunday 25th. Braintree

As the storm continued as violent as ever, in the morning, I staid in Boston; and went to Church at the Chapel. Parson Freeman, preach'd a very short Sermon, as he always does. He has adopted the anti trinitarian System, and makes use of a new form of Prayer. Many People have followed this new innovation, and I don't see, but there are as many Contests upon religious Points, as in any other-part of the world, although it is not carried to so great lengths. Mankind, will forever dispute whether the egg shall be broke, at the great or at the small end.

After Church, as the Storm had in a great measure abated, I left town and came here. It was about meeting time; when I got to the meeting house so I stopp'd in, and heard our Parson, whose manner of speaking is as familiar to me, as if I had heard him every Sunday since I went from America.

Genl. Palmer and his Lady where here, about an hour, after meeting was over.

Monday 26th

Your Aunt and I, are quite alone, as Uncle went this morning to Boston. Mr. Tyler is there too, and our two Cousins who went last week to see Lucy Apthorp married, and will remain in Boston till Betsey goes to Haverhill, which is to be next Friday, with me. She is going to spend two or three months there, with Peggy White, and to learn to play on the harpsichord.

This afternoon I went down to our house, and stay'd there two or three hours. There is something to me, awful in the look of it now. All within is gloomy, and sad, and when it will look more pleasant—oh! I must not think of that. I very much fear, it will be yet a long, long time before, I shall see you again. I dare not tell our friends here, my real thoughts on the Subject.[14]

Tuesday 27th

Mr. Apthorp, came this morning from Boston: but return'd in the afternoon; all the family are there, and will spend all this week there. He had invited me, and I had promised to go and see him, so I took this forenoon. He was very glad to see me; ask'd me what passage, I had &c, and soon came, to the Question, of which I complained in my last Letter to you; what part of Europe, did I like best? I told him, I had been most in France, and that might be the Reason, that I was most pleased with it.—Why yes; he believed that France, and the French, were really better than they had been represented. They were certainly a great Nation; and had many good Qualities: but they were not sincere: they would make great Professions; without any meaning. Don't you think now said he, that the genuine English plain heartedness, and real Benevolence, though not accompanied with so many exteriors of Complaisance, are much more noble and manly. I could not answer in a negative way decently, and I could not, with propriety in the affirmative so I turn'd it off as I could.[15] But what is your Opinion of England. Do you not admire that Country very much? I thought the best would be, to let him have his own Way, and I agreed with him, as far as I could. Upon other subjects I thought he spoke sensibly, but whenever he came upon the Topic of England; his gratitude, and fondness absorbed every other sentiment.

In the afternoon, I took a walk down with Mr. Tyler, and drank tea at uncle Quincy's: I have every day Reason to say more and more, it is not good, that the man, should be alone. A single life in this Country, cannot I think be an happy life. But do not you be afraid my Sister, that I shall be so fond of a connected life, as to have too soon any desire, to enter, in it myself. I well know that Study for years and years to come, is to be my only mistress, and my only Courtship that of the Muses. These sentiments, which my Parents, and dearest friends, have always, inculcated in me, and which my own Reason, and Inclination confirm, will, I have no doubt be lasting. To-morrow I leave Braintree finally for this Winter: and indeed probably I shall not come here again, before next Commencement; for I suppose I shall go directly from Haverhill to Cambridge, in the Spring.

Wednesday 28th. Cambridge

I left Braintree between 9 and 10 o'clock this morning, and got to Boston a little before one. I met on the exchange, Dr. Waterhouse, who has been at Providence these 6 weeks, delivering lectures upon natural Philosophy. He did not know me at first, and I was obliged to introduce myself to him. As soon as he found me out, he was as sociable as ever. I spent part of the afternoon with him. This Evening, I came here, and shall stay here till to-morrow afternoon, with our brother, Who is well contented, with his Situation here, and behaves in such a manner as has gained him the friendship of his Classmates, and given Satisfaction to his Tutor.

Thursday 29th. Boston

In the morning I went and paid a Visit to Mr. Tracey, but he was not at home. Mr. Dana, (or to speak more properly, Judge Dana) is riding the Circuit, so that I could not visit him. At about noon I had a billet from Miss Eliza. Cranch, to inform me, that I must certainly be in town before dinner in order to go with Mr. Peabody to Haverhill. I was to go in a Chaise, and she could not go, because, another Lady, had engaged the remaining place. Off I posted immediately, and when I got here, I found the plan alter'd again. We are to go to-morrow morning at 7. o'clock. I have had nothing to do this afternoon but stroll about the Streets. Spent the Evening at Dr. Welch's. Mr. W. Smith return'd from a Journey, last Evening. He has been gone ever since, I first arrived: I don't hear much said about his being married. Perhaps *his time is not yet come.*

Friday 30th. Haverhill

Here I am at length and am now at my Journey's end. At about ⟨6?⟩ 8 this morning, I was placed by the side of a Mrs. ⟨*Brewster?*⟩ Webster, in a Chaise; I am not over froward in beginning Conversation, with a person, I am not acquainted with. We rode two or three miles without saying a word. At length I made some common place Observation, upon the weather: Yes Sir, No Sir, I think so, was every thing I could draw from her, so upon the whole, I thought I had as good be silent too, and we jogged on from 8 in the morning till 5 afternoon, without saying six words, on either side. I often regretted the Company of our Cousin, with whom I should have been all sociability.

I found all our friends here well; send abundance of Compliments: and Aunt will write I suppose from Boston; where she is going, next Week. And now having brought you to Haverhill, and to the end of the month; I must for the present bid you adieu. Your affectionate brother   J. Q. Adams

RC (Adams Papers). The text is written on small pages, numbered 81 to 92, and 1 to 12; see JQA to AA2, [12] May, descriptive note, above.

[1] Lodovico Ariosto's *Orlando Furioso* (1532) tells the story of Charlemagne's perfect knight, Orlando (Roland), who forgets his military duty in his passionate pursuit of the princess Angelica. When Orlando discovers that she has married a Moor, he goes on a destructive rampage. MQA has a 1771 Italian edition and a 1780 French translation, both with JQA's bookplate, and a 1785 English translation by John Hoole.

[2] On Lt. Richard Nash bearing "infamous letters" to Gov. Bowdoin, see AA to Thomas Jefferson, 19 Oct. and note 5, below.

[3] Probably JQA's cousin, Elizabeth Smith Otis.

[4] Mr. Lincoln was presumably Levi Lincoln Sr. (not Gen. Benjamin Lincoln, as given in JQA, *Diary*, 2:index); his colleagues were John Gardiner, author of *An Oration, Delivered July 4, 1785*, Boston [1785], Evans, No. 19017, and James Hughes (*Harvard Quinquennial Cat.*, p. 195, 1151, 198).

[5] *Sans Souci, Alias Free and Easy:—Or, an Evening's Peep into a Polite Circle. An Entire New Entertainment in Three Acts*, Boston, 1785 (Evans, Nos. 19234, 19235). See Charles Warren, "Samuel Adams and the Sans Souci Club in 1785," MHS, *Procs.*, 60 (1926–1927):318–344, esp. 335, note, which cites marginalia to a copy of the play at MBAt, identifying another character, "Mr. Bon Ton," as "Cutler," possibly the Benjamin Cutler mentioned at note 10. Other marginalia, in the MBAt and the MWA copies, connect certain roles with Perez Morton and his wife, Sarah Apthorp Morton (see note 12), Harrison Gray Otis, Mercy Otis Warren, and other figures who were well known to JQA and his family.

[6] Mrs. Russell was Sarah Sever, daughter of William Sever of Kingston, Mass., and Sarah Warren Sever, James Warren's sister; she had married Thomas Russell of Boston in 1784. Her younger brother James was the traveler returned from Russia. See vol. 4:153, notes 1 and 3.

[7] Perhaps Sarah Hallowell Vaughan, wife of Samuel Vaughan, a merchant of Jamaica and London, and mother of Benjamin Vaughan, and of William Vaughan, whom JQA had met in London in 1783. Her daughters were Ann, Sarah, Barbara, and Rebecca. See JQA, *Diary*, 1:198–200, 204; 2:456; MHS, *Procs.*, 2d Ser., 17 (1903):406–409; *NEHGR*, 19:343, 355 (Oct. 1865).

[8] William Tudor had clerked and read law at JA's Boston home and law office from 1769 to 1772.

[9] This was Mr. Serane (or Serano), whom JQA had met in late August.

[10] Benjamin Austin Jr., a merchant and political figure, had married Jane Ivers (*DAB*). Of his guests, "Ben: Cutler" may have been the merchant, Benjamin Clarke Cutler (Thwing Catalogue, MHi). James Lovell was presumably the eldest son of the Adams' old friend, James Lovell. James Hughes is already mentioned (note 4). L. Austin was probably the host's elder brother and business partner, Jonathan Loring Austin. Royall Tyler was a Harvard classmate (1776) of young Lovell's (*Harvard Quinquennial Cat.*, p. 191, 196, 197; *Sibley's Harvard Graduates*, 16:303–308).

[11] King's Chapel.

[12] Lucy Apthorp's parents were James Apthorp and Sarah Wentworth Apthorp. The

"former occasion of the same kind" was probably the marriage of their daughter Sarah to the Boston lawyer Perez Morton in 1781. James Apthorp was an outspoken loyalist, while Morton was a prominent patriot (*Sibley's Harvard Graduates*, 17:555–557).

[13] Christopher Gore, Tyler's classmate, and later governor of Massachusetts, had married Rebecca, daughter of Edward Payne of Boston, in 1783 (MHS, *Colls.*, 3d ser., 3:206).

[14] In his Diary, JQA elaborates: "In the afternoon I went down to our house, and looked over many of the things. I can never feel gay in this house, while its owners are absent, and this evening my aunt accused me of being melancholy; a reproach I am very seldom loaded with. I had a disagreeable headache, and really felt very dull" (*Diary*, 1:331).

[15] JQA recounts this discussion differently in his Diary, principally by writing there that "as I had heard of [*Apthorp's*] Character before I saw him, I purposely spoke in the highest terms, of the french Nation and their Country" (same, 1:331).

Lucy Cranch to Abigail Adams

Braintree Sep. 19. 85

Indeed my ever honoured Aunt I should have been much disapointed if my Cousin had not brought me a letter from you.[1] Your pen Madam is never so far exhausted that every sentence that falls from it does not yeild pleasure or instruction. In your letters indeed those qualities are so happily blended that we cannot take from the one without distroying the other.

I hope before this you have heard the pleasing news of the safe arival of your son at Newyork. Many must have been the anxieties of the parents and the sister for the safety of a son and a Brother so deservedly loved. We heard of my Cousin at Newyork six weeks before he arived here. We waited with impatience for him during the vacation which my Brother and Cousin Charles spent here. We heard of him every week. Charles grew so impatient at last that he said if he did not come within a week he would not be glade to see him: I told him he would have a hard task to help it.

I wonder not my dear Aunt that you was unwilling to part with your son. The attachments of nature must be hieghtened on both sides where the Virtues which draw each to the other are so great. He is indeed worthy of *his* parents, and an honour to them.

Your *Orphan* Children as my Uncle calls them[2] will recieve every attention that is in the power of their friends to render them and as far as is in their power they will supply the place of their parents.

What ever little services it is in *my* power to do them will ever add to my happiness. It is by those alone that I shall ever be able to show my gratitude to you.

Mama will write and give you all the information you wish for with regard to Charles, who is now commenced Collegian.

Your last letters[3] gave us great entertainment. Your descriptions of Ranelaugh and several other places you reserve for the young folks. Then Madam I hope your neice may come in for a share. The pleasure which I always recieved in reading your Letters, makes me ever feel sorry when a pacquet comes without one for me. Though I see *all*, yet it does not feel so good, as to have one paticularly for myself. But hush presuming ⟨*me thinks*⟩ girl you will say, do you expect to be favoured, so much more highly than those that are in every respect so much your superiors. I own the rebuke is just, and will be silent.

Except my muched Loved Aunt my sincerest thanks for *the silk*. My obligations to you are more than I shall ever be able to cancel. A greatful heart is all the return I can make for your many favours: from your *own* heart you will recieve your reward.

Be assured Madam of my warmest wishes for your happiness and of my Uncles. And believe me to be with every sentiment of Love and Gratitude your Niece.   L Cranch

RC (Adams Papers); addressed in an unidentified hand: "Madam Adams—London"; endorsed by AA2: "Lucy Cranch sep 19 1785."

[1] Of [5] May, above.
[2] JA to Richard Cranch, 27 April, above.
[3] The text is uncertain; Lucy Cranch may have corrected "letters" to "letter" here. Only

AA to Mary Cranch, 24 June, above, with its mention of Ranelagh, and AA's intention to "reserve that story for the young folks," fits this reference.

Abigail Adams 2d to John Quincy Adams

[*No.*] 7

Saturday Septr. 24th. 1785

Last fryday I closed my Last to you[1] and Mr. Storer sailed on Monday from Graves End so that it is now on its way to Greet you with health peace and Contentment I hope. A saturday the 17th. we went to see Mrs. Siddons, in the Character of Desdemona. Altho I saw her under many disadvantages, the part not being such as I shold have chosen, and her present situation[2] renders it impossible for her to Play so well, as formerly, yet I think She answered my expectations. I did not go into fits, nor swoon, but I never was so much pleased with any person I ever saw upon any theatre. Her Countenance is certainly expressive of every thing it ought to be and She has the most perfect command of it. Her voice is inexpressibly Swet and harmonious. In Short she approaches nearer to perfection than any Woman I ever saw. Colln. Franks had stayed allmost on purpose to see her and was, much Gratified. This is a Curious Genious, I assure you. We saw him in Paris you know, and I recollect you did not approve him.[3] He has a great portion of vivacity and appearant good nature, which amused us very much. At breakfast and dinner he kept us all upon the Laugh. Even Pappas Gravity was often amused.

Sunday 18th

In the Morning we went out to hear Dr. Price, at Hackney, the first time since his return from the Country, where he has been for a few weeks. We had four Gentlemen to dine with us, all Americans. A Mr. Beverly from Virgina resembles a little Mr. Short. Mr. Chew, you know his sons in Paris. He is a very great Man in his own opinion and very affectd. I dont like him much. Mr. Waring you know. He took his Leave of us, and sails soon for Carolina. And Mr. Randal who you also know.[4] He is quite a favourite with me. I assure you there is something in his manners and behaviour that pleases me. I dont mean that he is *sans pareil*. He proposes going out to New York early in the Spring. He says he thought he shold be the cleaverest fellow in the World, by comeing to Europe but he is monstrously disappointed for he finds no alteration in him self at all, and all he wishes for is to get home.

Monday 19th

Colln. Franks set off for Paris. I had forgot to tell you that a Saturday Eve Pappa received a Letter from Colln. Smith dated at Berlin. He sends your father a Coppy of his Letter to the King of Prussia, and His Majestys answer.[5] His Letter was to ask permission to be present at the reveiw, every officer being obliged to have Leave from the King. The King, tells him he shall be very happy to see Monsieur la Colln. Smith at his reveiw, and that the permission he has requested is Granted, that he will ⟨*Pray the Boon Deiu*⟩ Prier le Bon Dieu for the health of Monsieur la Colln. Smith, and, that is his answer. The reveiw was to be finished the 20th. We do not expect Monsieur la Colln. Smith home, till the begining of next Month as he is going by way of Paris to Pay his respects to his friend Monsieur le Colln. Humph[reys].

Wedensday

Your father dined with the Baron de Lynden, after the Levee, and Mr. Trumble and Copely Spent the Evening with us. Mr. West has lately Gained a Great Prise at a sail of old Pictures, which had lain

379

a long time in a picture cleaners Garret. He purchased a picture
which to every appearance was a ruind painting, being totally disguised by dirt paint &c. The picture had been ordered to be sold for
thirty Gunieas, and if it could not fetch that for fifteen. Mr. West
observed some parts of it were well painted and, Gave twenty Guneas,
for it but upon having it cleaned it proves to be a Painting of the
famous *Titian*. The subject is the Death [*of*] Actaeon, and he has
been offered a thosan Gunias for it already. It was formerly in the
Collection of King Charles, and it appears very evident that it was
purposely disguisd for it is now said to be as perfect as, ever.[6]

Thursday

Being the Anniversary of his Majestys Coronation we all went to
Court. There was a full drawing room at least I thought it so, for I
was excessively fatigued. The King and Quen Prince of Wales, Princess Royal Augusta and Elisabeth were Present. This is such a ridiculous ceremony that I allways feel provoked when I am Present, to
see so many, People, waiting in expectation to be spokent to by the
Royal Family, and eagerly sollicitous for their Smiles. Ill tell you
what—I like the King better than the Queen. At Least he dissembls
better. She is a haughty Proud imperious Dame—and I beleive feel
excessivly Mortified to see our family at her drawing room, for which
reason, I shold choose to go [often and once atten?] for pleasure no
one can ever attend, unless it is such a spighfull pleasure as I shold
enjoy. Her Countenance is as hard and unfeeling as if Carved out of
an oak knot. It nevertheless expresses her sentiments with respect to
us, and we may easily see, that She does not forgive us. Peace be
with her. I thank Heaven, that I am not dependant upon her frowns
or smiles. The Princess Royal is the handsomest of any of the family
that I have yet seen. When she smils She is really pretty, but there
seems a great vacancy, in her Countenance, and in all the rest of
them. The Prince was very well dressed. He is called in general
handsome, but it is a tribute that is payd to fashion I am inclined to
beleive rather than spoken from sincerity. He is very fat and looks
flushd, report says, it is not ⟨with all honourable virtues⟩.

Pappa dined with Lord Carmarthen and in the Eve Mrs. and Miss
Paradise made us a visit.

Fryday, 23d

⟨To-day⟩ We have been waiting in expectation of receiving Letters
from our friends in Boston by Capt. Folgier, who has just arrived. He

called upon us this afternoon ⟨*but*⟩ and brought me one Letter. I received another from Betsy Palmer from Mr. Elworthy and these are all that have yet come to hand.[7] ⟨*Tis as*⟩ We find our very [*family?*] had heard of your arrival at New York, and were anxiously expecting to see you hourly. They thought I suppose that the instant you arrived you wold post of to Boston, and they seem as sollicitous for your arrival as if the fate of the Continent depended upon it. Their expectations forerun all reason. I beleive they were tyred a looking for we supposed you not to arrive in Boston before the begining of September, after we heard from you.[8]

Your reception at New York was such as, I am sure must have been extremely pleasing to *you*, in particular, "for you know that we all form opinions of Persons according to their Conduct with respect to ourselvs," is a maxim of yours my Brother and *has been* a favourite one of mine, also, but I must confess to you that I begin to suspect the Justice of this sentiment. Was the World Honnest, and every one sincere in their proffers of civility Politeness and Friendship, we might have no cause to fear or to arm oursells with such sheilds as suspicion and distrust. But alas it is far other wise.

But I beleive there are many really Honest People remaining. I will not yet turn misanthrop.

Saturday Eve, 24th

This Morning I had set down and given you a detail of matters thus far, intending to send my Letter by Capt. Davis, but your Mamma came in and told me that some body from the City had just told her that Davis had sailed. The Morning was really fine and she proposed going to ride. We dressed and rode to Clapham. The sun shone very pleasant and the Country was beautiful. That rich verdure which I so much admire appeard in full perfection. We first made a visit to Mrs. Smith and Miss Copes, and then to Mrs. Vassall, where we spent an hour. Mrs. V is a little Lofty, but she put on more affability than usual. She is one of those kind of Folks that I should not wish to be mine enemy. The young Ladies, are agreeable enough. There is but one that has any title to beauty and ⟨*she*⟩ Miss Margret is really Pretty, but a little *possitive*. They were all very pleasing this Morning.[9]

Before we went out Count Sarsfield called on your Pappa and they went together to visit Dr. Price. The Count is generally in the Country but comes occasionally to town. Whenever he is here for a few days, he asks Papa which day it is that he is to be his Guest. You know the friendship he professes banishes all kind of ceremony, as it certainly ought. I dont know any Person whose Life is more agreeable than this mans. A fortune sufficient to follow the dictates of his inclination which Leads him to travell, to spend one summer in England a second in Holland a third in Spain if he pleases, and known to all Persons of Rank and Character wherever he goes, and universally respected and beloved.

We returnd home about three oclock. Mr. Tom Boilstone dined with us: would you beleive that he intends going soon to France and proposes spending the Winter there. He says he is very much out of health and he looks so, I think. He only wants to Live ten or fifteen years longer and then he thinks he shall die Content but you may be sure that interest is at the Bottom of this excursion. And he seems as sollicitous to affect his plans of trade as if he was not worth a hundred pounds.[10]

Pappa received a Packet from Mr. Jay to day, from N York, so late as the 26th of august.[11] Now how well may I retalliate complaints that you did not write one line. But I learn from the Papers that the French June Packet[12] had a fifty two days passage, and a Vessell from this place eight weeks, both of which I suppose had Letters for you. I fear you did not receive them before you set off for Boston. ⟨We⟩ Mamma received one day this week your Letter by the French July packet,[13] which informs us of your arrival. It would have given us great pleasure if we had not have known it three weeks agone.

To day as we were setting at Dinner. We received a Card from Capt. Hay, who has just arrived from the West Indies, and a Present of a Turtle weighing about an hundred weight.[14] This came very opportunely as, your father had invited all the Foreign Ministers and my Lord Carmarthen to dine with him next fryday, and such a Dish as this will not be improper, upon such an occasion. I shall not be able to give you any account of the Folks, as your Mamma nor myself shall not be *at home* upon the occasion. We have a most admirable friend in Exeter. The week before last we received a Basket containing two fine large salmon, directed to Pappa, and the Porter who brought it told us that it came in the stage from Exeter which was all we could find about it, there being no Letter nor any thing but a simple direction to Pappa.

And the Last week a Porter brought a Box, from the same Place under the same direction which upon opening we found to Contain a Dozen Partriges, but no Letter. We have been upon the round of Conjecture and have concluded they must come from Mr. Jack

Cranch. He does not intend to be known, to be sure. These kind of attentions are very flattering, but the obligation one feels under for them is not very light, especially when one knows of no good way to return them.

The day we had the salmon Colln. Franks dined with us. He drunk the Health of the Doner in a Bumper, and entitled him Fish Monger to the United States of America. It was the finest I ever tasted, and the Partriges were very fine. They are called Game here you know, and the laws are very strict against those persons that buy it. Indeed a Person who purchases Game is subject to a penalty. It often happens that People of whom it is purchased will give information of the purchasers, and the penalty is severe, so that those People who have not Parks, are obliged to receive it throught the Courtesy of their friends, if they have it at all. Pappa says he intends to rally Mr. Jefferson upon the civilities he receives here, but says I must not let Congress know it for they will asseredly Leessen my salary, and to be sure they have no reason to do that.

By the Way I have forgot to tell you that Mr. Jefferson has, changed his Hotell for one, just out of the Barrier at Challiot, near the *Champs Elysées*, not far from the Spanish Ambassadors. He found his first Hotell too small, and too far from the ⟨Pub⟩ Walks, of which he is very fond. Petit lives with him and he likes him very much, but Petit would willingly come to London to us, if we would but give Leave. Paulina, soon got into service, and advantageously for herself. The Lady she is with gives her   15 a year. She says however that she should prefer Living with us.

Lamb has at last arrived, but as Mr. Barclay was engaged to go to Moroco, he agrees to go to Algiers, as ⟨two⟩ a person to each is necessary. Mr. Barclay will I suppose set off soon. Poor Mrs. Barclay, will have another tedious Winter. They have given up their House at Mount Parnassus, and are at Present in an Hotel. Mrs. B. talks of a Convent while Mr. B. is absent. Mrs. Montgomery and her son Bob, have arrived in Paris. Mrs. M. I hear from those who have long known her is as Sprightly as ever but it is thought that she will only be talking of the Education of her son, till he is too oald for to receive an Education. At Present he is under the Care of Mr. *Noris* who you have not forgot I dare say.[16]

Colln. Franks says he was at Renelagh[17] in the Bois de Bologne, where you may recollect you were with me last summer, the week before he left Paris, and the Queen with Madam Elisabeth and Madame de [Paliniach?], honourd it with their Presence. Her Majesty has determined to wear none but French Gauze. If you see the English Papers you will see a great deal respecting the Cardinl de Roan, and Madame de la Motte, and some Diamond. That he has been taken up, and Confined is true. It has made much Noise in Paris, but what has been the reall cause, does not appear certain. I wrote you about this in a late Letter.[18]

Paul Jones, is undertaking a voyage to Kamskatta. The English News Papers say that he is fitting out two Vessels at his own Expence, and that he is enabled to do this by the Prise Money he has lately received. That he has such a project Dr. Bancroft says, who is his friend you know, and he is Enterprising and resolute.[19]

⟨*Thursday septr. 29th*⟩ sunday septr. 25th

We went out to meeting at Hackney, and had a violent storm to come home in, which continued all day and night.

Monday

Mr. Paradise came and spent the Evening. You would be pleased with this Man as a visitor. He is a Member of the royal society, and proposes, to present your father, provided he is first sure of his reception, and he says he has no doubt of it.[20] The form of receiving a Member is this. At a meeting of the society, two members offer, ⟨*any*⟩ A person they wish to become one, and his Name is hung up, for twelve weeks. At the thirghteenth week they choose [. . .] by Ballot. All Persons except Crownd heads, Princes and Ambassadors are received in the above manner. The latter may be chosen without *hanging* twelve weeks. Mr. Paradise, seems to have been acquainted with all the Litterati of his age. He told us this Evening some curious anecdotes of Dr. Johnson. But in the midst of his Conversation Mrs. Wright came in with such a Budget, and wanted so much private confab, which nobody was to hear except your father, not Wives to be admitted She said, that she kept Pappa an hour hearing her Story.

Wedensday

Now what a Chance for making your fortune have you lost young Man. How say you? Is it not to be retreived? No never. Why I'll tell you. Mr. Boilstone is going to France about his Cargo of oil, that he has just received, and by which he hopes to get an admittance into France in future. Now if you was here, from the *Natural benevolence of his Character* it is easy to suppose that he wold not object to making you a present of half of it, to go with him and assist him by your knowledge of the Language, to persuade the Ministers there to receive it in future. But do not distress yourself at having lost this opportunity—because you might not have found him even so genrous as to propose it.

Your Mamma and myself went this Morning to make some visits. 1st. we called upon Madame de Pinto Lady to the Minister from Portugal but according to the fashion she was not at home. We left our Cards and called upon Mrs. Smith a Carolin Lady lately arrived here. She came for her health, is sister to Mr. Rutledge, and her husband Brother to Mr. James Smith, lately gone to France.[21] She is not handsome but there is something agreeable in her manners. She is to dine with us next Tuesday. We called upon Mrs. Church and upon Miss Hamilton of whom I spoke to you in a late Letter. She is to dine with us also a tuesday and I will tell you more about her. Mr. Short fell in Love with a picture taken of her, in Philadelphia tho he had never seen the original, and says this was the Love affair that used to trouble him so much last Winter and made him so Melancholy.

Thursday

You know not how much I wish you were here. We are so inanimate and stupid without you, that I expect you will hear of me from Bedlam next, as a Melancholy Mad one. I declare I wish you had not gone home. Here you have been gone allm[o]st five months and I have not heard from you but once.[22] As soon as I find you negligent I promise you I will write no more, and perhaps you may rejoice at my determination. You taxed yourself with my Correspondence upon such terms as I cannot avoid fullfilling. If I tire your patience tell me so, and I shall not continue to. I am really in earnest, for I really fear that you will be sick of my Letters. I have not been more entertained a long time. Count Sarsfeild came an dined with us sans ceremony and he was perfectly unreserved in the afternoon very sociable and entertaining.

Fryday 30th

To day is the important day. I can only give you the names of the Gentlemen expected.[23] Mamma and myself are going to spend the day with Mrs. Roggers.

Fryday Eve

We went and found Mrs. Roggers in trouble having lately heard of the account of her Mammas death. She is an excellent little Woman.

Her kindness and sollicitude to send in all the assistance to her friends that is in her Power must ensure to her the esteem of all who are acquainted with her.

We returned about Nine oclock. The Gentlemen were not all gone. However we did not see them. My Lord Carmarthen told your father he should have been very happy to have dined with the Ladies. Every thing was conducted with propriety and order. Our butler on whom every thing you know depends on such an occasion, is very well acquainted with his business, and gives general sattisfaction. Indeed we at present seem to be well suited with servants. They are all Steady prudent People, which is very essential, you well know, and there is as much harmony as one can expect amongst them. There never will be a perfect agreement unless they are all in one Box.

Saturday october 1st 1785

You have not I dont beleive a finer sun Shine clearer air or more delightfully clear Sky than we have had this day. It has been quite an American day. I have been sitting at my Desk Writing all day, and getting my letters ready for Calliham who dines with us tomorrow, and is to sail the begining of the week. I shall give this and two or three other Letters to his Care.[24]

About 3 o clock Colln. Franks arrived from Paris again. It was found necessary to make some alteration in the Commissions instructions &c. after Lamb arrived. From Colln. Franks, and other People accounts, he does not appear very well adapted to the business he is going upon they say. He can Speak no Language, for he does not speak even his own English with any degree of propriety, that he seems to have neither knowledge Judgment or Prudence, all of which are very essential for if it should be made Public, it is supposed that the influence of this Country will be made use of to obstruct the making a treaty on any accomodations with those Barbarians. Mr. Jefferson thinks it very necessary that some person should go with Lamb, who can be perfectly confided in and, who possesses what he lacks of qualities for the business. Charles Storer, if he was here would be a likely person, it is thought, as he was willing to go, but this is now impossible. Several persons have been mentiond but no Person applied to as yet. I dont know how it will be determined. Congress seem [*not*] to have made a Wise choise in sending him. Your father receivd a Letter under the signature of a Capt. of an American Vessell from Philadelphia from Algiers who had been taken sometimes in July. He at first thought it a forgery but Mr. Jefferson has another which he knows comes directly from Algiers, and he thinks that it is without doubt that some Ships have been taken by them.[25] The week before last there was a Letter in the News Paper signed by Capt. Truxton, which said that he was taken on the 22d. of July and Carried into Algiers, and that the next day after the date of his Letter they were to be sent to slavery, that Dr. Frankling bore it surprisingly. This Letters in a day or two was proved to be a fogery,[26] and indeed there are so many and various means made use of here to deceive and mislead People that we know not what to beleive or when to credid what they had asserted.

Madam de Pinto called upon us just now. She was going to the Play, and could not make us a very long visit. She had never seen Mrs. Siddons. This Eve She appears in the Character a Lady Mackbeth. It is said she appears well in this Character. I wish very much to see her in a Character where she will appear to most advantage.

I requested in my last Letter that you would write us by way of New York, and I must again sollicit you to, for I am sure we shall hear very seldom from Boston, from prese[n]t appearances at Least. I suppose the Trade will become less and less, while the present measures are held. Your father has laid every thing necessary before Mr. Pit and has had a conference with him. But he has not received a single answer of any kind or notice of them. The King is advised by People of his Party from America to retain his Navigation act, in its full rigeur tho he has been so effectually deceived by following the opinions of this kind of People heretofore. Yet he does not seem to be any more inclined to disbeleive them than ever. What it will all end in we know not. Your Pappa does not expect they will give him any answer till the Parliament set again which is not to be till February, so that nothing can be done till Spring, Should they be disposed to. The American Merchants will be impatient, before that time, but it is not to be avoided they must know if they know any thing. Many will Judge and condemn without proper reflection it is to be expected.

Not knowing when I might meet with so safe a conveyance for your Watch as by Mr. Short, I wrote to him after he went to Holland, and desired him to take it and send it to me from France. I wrote to Miss Dumas, requesting her Mamma to deliver it which She did, but Insisted of having a receipt of Mr. Short.[27] Colln. Franks, has brought it to me and I shall wait your orders respecting it. I thought it had as well be in my possession as in Madame Dumas.

Poor Lotter who I beleive is as honnest a fellow as ever Lived, has by the intrigues of this Woman your Dear friend been turned out of the House. By Willinks he had requested to have His Livery in [some part?] of it for taking care of it, and keeping it clean, and your father had given his Consent but this Woman used her influence to get [him?] turnd out, after the Poor fellow had ⟨ *given up his* ⟩ sold some of his things, and had no place to go to.[28]

Dft (Adams Papers). The text is written on seventeen small pages; the second through the ninth, and the twelfth, are numbered.

[1] Of 26 Aug., above.

[2] AA2 refers to Siddons' pregnancy; see AA2 to JQA, 22 Jan. 1786 (Adams Papers), under "Wednesday" [*8 Feb. 1786*]. Sarah Kemble Siddons, who married William Siddons in 1773 at age eighteen, had five children (*DNB*).

[3] Nothing further is known about JQA's disapproval of Col. David Franks.

[4] Of these four men, nothing further is known of Mr. Beverly. JQA records seeing Mr. Chew, perhaps Benjamin Chew Jr., and Paul R. Randall, on 11 May, the day before his departure from Auteuil for America. The Benjamin Chew to whom AA2 refers may have been the pre-Revolutionary chief justice of Pennsylvania and loyalist sympathizer, who was sixty-two in 1785. His son Benjamin Chew Jr., age twenty-seven, had been studying law in London for several years, and returned to Philadelphia in 1786. JQA had met Mr. Waring, perhaps Dr. Thomas Waring of South Carolina, in Paris in January (JQA, *Diary*, 1:265, 216; Thompson Westcott, *The Historic Mansions and Buildings of Philadelphia*, Phila., 1877, p. 232–235, 248).

[5] See William Stephens Smith to AA, 5 Sept., above.

[6] See Robert C. Alberts, *Benjamin West, A Biography*, Boston, 1978, p. 185, and notes, p. 444.

[7] The letter delivered by Capt. Folgier has not been identified; the letter from Elizabeth Palmer has not been found. In a letter to AA dated 23 Sept. (Adams Papers), Elizabeth Palmer mentions having been given a letter from AA2 (also not found, but presumably written in late April or early May) by JQA when he visited Braintree.

[8] By JQA to AA2, 25 May, and 17 July, both above.

[9] Margaret Hubbard Vassall was the second wife of Boston's well-known loyalist emigré, William Vassall; her daughters were Margaret, age 24, and twins Ann and Charlotte, age 23 (Edward Doubleday Harris, "The Vassalls of New England," *NEHGR*, 17:115–116 [April 1863]; *Sibley's Harvard Graduates*, 9:349–359).

[10] Boylston was going to France to negotiate a contract to supply American whale oil. On Boylston's sale of oil to the French, see JA to James Bowdoin, 24 March 1786 (MHi:Bowdoin-Temple Papers, now in Winthrop Papers; printed in MHS, *Colls.*, 7th ser., 6 [1907]:92–93).

[11] John Jay's brief letter of 26 Aug. (Adams Papers; also printed in *Dipl. Corr., 1783–1789*, 2:383), acknowledged the receipt of JA's letters of 2, 6, and 17 June, which recounted his reception at the British Court.

[12] AA2 inserted "June" above the line; she apparently sent her second, third, and fourth numbered letters to JQA, not found, by the French and English June packet boats to New York.

[13] JQA to AA, 17 July, above.

[14] This small card, in the Adams Papers, reads: "Mr. and Mrs. Hay, present their Compliments to Mr. and Mrs. Adams, and Beg their acceptance of a Turtle. London Street No. 19 Sept. 24." Someone wrote "Dove" immediately after "Turtle," in a different shade of ink.

[15] Left blank in MS. Mary Barclay to AA, 5 Sept., above, gives Paulina's wages as 300 livres a year.

[16] Dorcas Armitage Montgomery was a widow from Philadelphia and a friend of the Bache family; her son Robert was about fifteen (Jefferson, *Papers*, 10:282–283; 13:164–166). JQA met Isaac Norris, an American Quaker who converted to Roman Catholicism, on 17 March, in Paris (*Diary*, 1:236).

[17] Ranelagh was a hall for public balls, founded in 1774 on the model of its London namesake. It was located on the west edge of Passy, near the Port de la Muette, a chief

entrance to the Bois de Boulogne (Larousse, *Grand dictionnaire universel*). Madam Elisabeth was the sister of Louis XVI.

[18] AA2 to JQA, 26 Aug., under "Monday 22d [*Aug.*]," above.

[19] John Paul Jones had joined with the Connecticut-born adventurer John Ledyard to mount an expedition in two French ships, with French crews, to open up the fur trade on the northwest coast of North America. Dr. Edward Bancroft was a financial backer of the venture. Determined opposition from Spain, which regarded the area as its domain, and respect for that claim by France, frustrated the effort, which came to nothing (Samuel Eliot Morison, *John Paul Jones, A Sailor's Biography*, Boston, 1959, p. 341–343).

Jones' proposed expedition did not involve the Kamchatka Peninsula on Russia's Pacific coast, but both Jones and Ledyard would be involved in Russia, quite independently, in the next four years, and Kamchatka was a possible supply point for a European expedition heading into the northern Pacific by way of the Indian Ocean. See Morison; Jefferson, *Papers*, vols. 8 (Jones), 11 and 13 (Ledyard); and *DAB*.

[20] JQA, and presumably JA, had first visited the Royal Society of London for the Advancement of Natural Science, then quartered in the new Somerset House in the Strand, on 13 Nov. 1783 (JQA, *Diary*, 1:203, 205). JA was not elected to membership in the Royal Society.

[21] Mary Rutledge Smith's brothers were John and Edward, both of whom JA had met when he first served in Congress in 1774 (JA, *Diary and Autobiography*, 2:114, 116, 119). Her husband was Roger Moore Smith, older brother of James Smith (*South Carolina Historical and Genealogical Magazine*, 4:41 [Jan. 1903]). In her journal entry for his date, after recording the social calls on Madam de Pinto and Mary Rutledge Smith, AA2 criticized, at some length, the European custom of persons not being at home to unexpected callers (*Jour. and Corr.*, [3]:185–186).

[22] AA2 had received JQA's letters of 25 May, and 17 July from John Barker Church on 5 Sept. (AA2 to JQA, 26 Aug., above, under "september 5th. Monday Morning").

[23] In her journal AA2 gives several names, saying: "The gentlemen who came were the Baron de Nalken, from Sweden; Baron de Lynden, Holland; Baron de H., a German nobleman; the Count de K., Germany; Count de L., Prussia; Conde de L., Venice; Count de

W., engaged; Baron de K., engaged; Chavelier del Campo, Spain; Chevalier de Pinto, Portugal; Chavalier de Pollen, disappointed, by hearing of the death of his mistress, the Queen of Sardinia; [*and*] several other gentlemen" (*Jour. and Corr.*, [3]:186).

[24] No other AA2 letters from this period have survived. All of AA's letters to Boston correspondents, from 15 Sept. to 1 Oct., and possibly to 5 Oct., probably went in Capt. Callahan's vessel.

[25] Capt. Richard O'Bryen gave JA and Jefferson the details of two captures by the Algerines, his *Daupin* of Philadelphia, seized off Portugal on 30 July, and the schooner *Maria* of Boston, also seized off Portugal, on 24 July. See Richard O'Bryen and others (at "Algir") to JA, 27 Aug. (Adams Papers); Richard O'Bryen to Thomas Jefferson, 24 Aug., in Jefferson, *Papers*, 8:440–441; Jefferson to JA, 24 Sept. (first letter), same, 8:542–544; and Jefferson to Richard O'Bryen, 29 Sept., same, 8:567–568.

[26] The *Daily Universal Register* of 13 Sept. briefly mentioned "the death of . . . Doctor Benjamin Franklin, on his way to America." On 19 Sept. this same paper stated that "the ship London Packet, Capt. Truxon . . . on board of which Dr. Franklin embarked as a passenger, had been boarded and taken by an Algerine pirate on the 22d of July." On 21 Sept. the story was retracted: "The fabricated letter [*from Capt. Truxton*] respecting the capture of Dr. Franklin was a forgery pregnant with the most cruel consequences . . . ." See also the *Daily Universal Register*, 13 and 14 October.

The Adamses would not likely have been taken in by this report because its fraudulent character was evident in the text itself. On 22 July, the day on which it stated that Capt. Thomas Truxon's vessel was captured, Franklin was just crossing the Channel from Le Havre to Southampton, and Truxton had yet to bring his ship to Southampton from London. Franklin boarded this ship at Southampton on 27 July, and Truxton set sail on the 28th, arriving in Philadelphia on 14 September. *The Complete Works of Benjamin Franklin*, ed. John Bigelow, N.Y., 1888, 10 vols., 9:261–262; *The Writings of Benjamin Franklin*, ed. Albert Henry Smyth, N.Y., 1907, 9:365–366, 372, 410–412, 463; Jefferson, *Papers*, 8:585–586.

[27] No letter from AA2 to William Short or to Nancy Dumas has been found.

[28] The dispute between Christian Lotter

on one side, and Marie Dumas and the banking firm of Wilhem & Jan Willink & Nicolaas & Jacob van Staphorst on the other, may have begun in the spring of 1785 in an argument over which services were being provided by Lotter, and which by Dumas, in caring for the Hôtel des Etats-Unis at The Hague, of which Lotter was steward and in which he lived with his family. JA remained personally satisfied with Lotter, who in June-July brought to London all JA's belongings remaining at the Hôtel, and through July JA favored allowing Lotter stay at the Hôtel rent free indefinitely, and intended to recommend him to whomever should succeed JA as minister to the

Netherlands. But Dumas somehow won this argument, and in September JA, who no longer had need of Lotter's services, and who felt he could not justify continuing to pay Lotter a salary when there was no minister resident at the Hôtel, allowed Willink & van Staphorst to settle all wages due to his steward, and to evict him. Lotter was evicted on 26 October. AA2 must have met Lotter when he came to London in early July. See the correspondence between Lotter and JA, and between Willink & van Staphorst and JA, extending from April to Dec. 1785, in the Adams Papers.

Thomas Jefferson to Abigail Adams

Dear Madam   Paris Sep. 25. 1785

Mr. Short's return the night before last availed me of your favour of Aug. 12. I immediately ordered the shoes you desired which will be ready tomorrow. I am not certain whether this will be in time for the departure of Mr. Barclay or of Colo. Franks, for it is not yet decided which of them goes to London. I have also procured for you three plateaux de dessert with a silvered ballustrade round them, and four figures of Biscuit. The former cost 192₶, the latter 12₶ each, making together 240, livres or 10. Louis. The merchant undertakes to send them by the way of Rouen through the hands of Mr. Garvey and to have them delivered in London.[1] There will be some additional expences of packing, transportation and duties here. Those in England I imagine you can save. When I know the amount I will inform you of it, but there will be no occasion to remit it here. With respect to the figures I could only find three of those you named, matched in size. These were Minerva, Diana, and Apollo. I was obliged to add a fourth, unguided by your choice. They offered me a fine Venus; but I thought it out of taste to have two at table at the same time. Paris and Helen were presented. I conceived it would be cruel to remove them from their peculiar shrine. When they shall pass the Atlantic, it will be to sing a requiem over our freedom and happiness. At length a fine Mars was offered, calm, bold, his faulchion not drawn, but ready to be drawn. This will do, thinks I, for the table of the American Minister in London, where those whom it may concern may look and learn that though Wisdom is our guide, and the Song and Chase our supreme delight, yet we offer adoration to that tutelar god also who rocked the cradle of our birth, who has accepted our infant offerings, and has shewn himself the patron of our rights and avenger of our wrongs. The groupe then was closed, and your party formed. Envy and malice will never be quiet. I hear it already whispered to you that in admitting Minerva to your table I have departed from the principle which made me reject Venus: in plain English that I have paid a just respect to the daughter but failed to the mother. No Madam, my respect to both is sincere. Wisdom, I know, is social. She seeks her fellows. But Beauty is jealous, and illy bears the presence of a rival.

But, Allons; let us turn over another leaf, and begin the next chapter. I receive by Mr. Short a budget of London papers. They teem with every horror of which ⟨nature⟩ human nature is capable. Assassinations, suicides, thefts, robberies, and, what is worse than assassination, theft, suicide, or robbery, the blackest slanders! Indeed the man must be of rock, who can stand all this; to Mr. Adams it will be but one victory the more. It would have illy suited me. I do not love difficulties. I am fond of quiet, willing to do my duty, but irritable by slander and apt to be forced by it to abandon my post. These are weaknesses from which reason and your counsels will preserve Mr. Adams. I fancy it must be the quantity of animal food eaten by the English which renders their character insusceptible of civilisation. I suspect it is in their kitchens and not in their churches that their reformation must be worked, and that Missionaries of that description from hence would avail more than those who should endeavor to tame them by precepts of religion or philosophy. But what do the foolish printers of America mean by retailing all this stuff in our papers?[2] As if it was not enough to be slandered by one's enemies without circulating the slanders among his friends also.

To shew you how willingly I shall ever receive and execute your commissions, I venture to impose one on you. From what I recollect of the diaper and damask we used to import from England I think they were better and cheaper than here. You are well acquainted with those of both countries. If you are of the same opinion I would trouble you to send me two sets of table cloths and napkins for 20 covers each, by Colo. Franks or Mr. Barclay who will bring them to me. But if you think they can be better got here I would rather avoid the trouble this commission will give. I inclose you a specimen of what is offered me at 100. livres for the table cloth and 12 napkins. I suppose that, of the same quality, a table cloth 2. aunes[3] wide and 4. aunes long, and 20 napkins of 1. aune each, would cost 7. guineas.

I shall certainly charge the publick my houserent and court taxes. I shall do more. I shall charge my outfit. Without this I can never get out of debt. I think it will be allowed. Congress is too reasonable to expect, where no imprudent expences are incurred, none but those which are required by a decent respect to the mantle with which they cover the public servants, that such expences should be left as a burthen on our private fortunes.

But when writing to you, I fancy myself at Auteuil, and chatter on till the last page of my paper awakes me from my reverie, and tells me it is time to assure you of the sincere respect and esteem with which I have the honour to be Dear Madam Your most obedient & most humble servt.   Th: Jefferson

P.S. The cask of wine at Auteuil, I take chearfully. I suppose the seller will apply to me for the price. Otherwise, as I do not know who he is, I shall not be able to find him out.

RC (Adams Papers); endorsed: "Mr Jefferson Sep 25 1785."

[1] The Jefferson Papers (DLC) contains a receipted invoice from: "Bazin Md. Rue des fossés St. Germain L'auxerois à Paris," dated 27 September. The invoice includes "1. Service de 3 plateaux a Balustrade et perles de Cuivre argenté garnis de glaces," at 192 livres, and "4. figures divinites de porcelaine en Biscuit," at 48 livres. The invoice totaled 264₶

17s. 6d; the receipt was dated 5 Jan. 1786 (Jefferson, *Papers*, 8:549, where the location of the receipt is mistakenly given as MHi).

[2] Squibs against JA and the United States from London papers were reprinted in Boston's *Continental Journal* of 4 August.

[3] The French equivalent of an ell; actual measurement varied from place to place.

Abigail Adams to Mary Smith Cranch

My dear sister   London septr 30th. 1785

Your kind Letters of july and August are before me.[1] I thank you most sincerely for the particular manner in which you write; I go along with you, and take an interest in every transaction which concerns those I love. And I enjoy more pleasure from those imaginary Scenes, than I do from the drawing room at St. James's. In one I feel my self your Friend and equal, in the other I know I am looked down upon with a sovereign pride, and the Smile of Royalty is bestowed as a mighty Boon. As such however I cannot receive it. I know it is due to my Country, and I consider myself as complimenting the Power before which I appear, as much as I am complimented by being noticed by it. With these Ideas you may be sure my countanance will never wear that suppliant appearence which begs for notice. Consequently I never expect to be a Court favourite, nor would I ever again set my foot there, if the Etiquette of my Country did not require it. But whilst I am in a publick Character I must submit to the penalty, for such I shall ever esteem it.[2] You will naturally suppose that I have lately been much fatigued. This is very true. I attended the Drawing room last week upon the Aniversary of the Coronation of their Majesties. The Company were very Brilliant, and her Majesty was stiff with Diamonds. The three eldest Princesses and the Prince of Wales were present.[3] His Highness lookt much better than when I saw him before. He is a stout well made Man, and would look very well; if he had not sacrificed so much to Bacchus. The Princess Elizabeth I never saw before, she is about 15, a short clumsy Miss, and would not be thought Handsome if she was not a Princess. The whole family have one complexion; and all inclined to corpulent, I should know them in any part of the world.

Not with standing the English boast so much of their Beauties, I do not think they have really so much of it, as you will find amongst the same proportion of people in America. It is true that their complexions are undoubtedly fairer than the French, and in general their figure is good. Of this they make the best. But I have not seen a Lady in England who can bear a comparison with Mrs. Bingham Mrs. Platt[4] and a Miss Hamilton who is a Philadelphia young Lady. Amongst the most celebrated of their Beauties stands the Dutchess of Devonshire,[5] who is Masculine in her appearence. Lady Salsbury is small and geenteel, but her complexion is bad, and Lady Talbot is not a Mrs. Bingham, who taken all together is the finest woman I ever saw. The intelligence of her countanance, or rather I ought to say animation, the Elegance of her form, and the affability of her Manners, converts you into admiration, and one has only to lament too much dissapation and frivolity of amusement, which has weand her from her Native Country; and given her a passion and thirst after all the Luxeries of Europe.

The finest English woman I have seen is the eldest daughter of Mr. Dana, Brother to our Mr. Dana. He resides in the Country, but was in London with two of his daughters when I first came here.[6] I saw her first at Raneleigh. I was struck with her appearence and endeavourd to find who she was, for she appeard like Calipso amongst her Nymphs, delicate and modest. She was easily known from the crowd as a stranger. I had not long admired her; before she was brought by her Father and introduced to me, after which she made me a visit, with her sister, who was much out of Health, at the same time that she has the best title of any English woman I have seen to the rank of Divinity. I would not have it forgotten that her Father is an American, and as he was remarkably handsome no doubt she owes a large share of her Beauty to him.

Since I took my pen I have received from Mrs. Rogers acquainting me with the death of her Mamma. I feard as much from what Mrs. Copely told me the week before.[7]

I dread to hear from my dear Aunt least the same melancholy tidings should reach me with respect to her. She is at the same critical period of life which proved fatal to Mrs. Broomfeild.[8] I will however hope that she may yet be spaired to her Friends. Tho her Health would never permit her to engage in the active buisness of her family, she was attentive to the interest and welfare of every individual of it. Like Sarah she was always to be found in her tent.[9] A more benevolent Heart never inhabited a Humane Breast. It was well matched and seconded in a partner equally Benevolent and humane, who has shared with us our former Griefs and will find us equally sympathetick towards himself should so great a misfortune attend him as I fear. Indeed I know not how to take my pen to write to him. I do not wonder that your Heart was affected or your spirits low under the apprehension of losing one so deservedly dear to us all. Should this ornament be broken from the original building it will be an other memento to us of the frailty of the whole, and that duration depends not upon age. Yet who would desire to stand the last naked Pillar of the whole? I believe our social affections strengthen by age. As those objects and amusement which gratified our Youthfull Years lose their relish, the social converse and society of Friends becomes more necessary.

> Needfull auxiliars are our Friends to give
> To social Man true realish of himself.

But I must close, as I am going to day to dine with my Friend Mrs. Rogers, where I have given myself an invitation, the occasion of which I will reserve for the Subject of an other Letter and subscribe affectionately Yours   A A

RC (MWA:Abigail Adams Corr.); addressed in an unknown hand: "Mrs. Mary Cranch Braintree Massachusetts."

[1] The only extant letter that fits this description is Mary Cranch to AA, 19 July, above, which she finished on 7 August.

[2] A caret appears in the MS immediately following this sentence, but no text that might be inserted appears in the letter.

[3] Charlotte Augusta Matilda, Augusta Sophia, and Elizabeth, and George, Prince of Wales, later George IV.

[4] Probably Abigail Pyncheon Platt of New York City and New Haven, Conn., who had spent some time in Europe with her husband (*NEHGR*, 38:47 [Jan. 1884]; JA, *Diary and Autobiography*, 2:302; JQA, *Diary*, 1:306, and note 1).

[5] Georgiana Spencer Cavendish, daughter of John Spencer, first earl Spencer, and wife of the fifth duke of Devonshire, was twenty-eight in 1785. She made a great impression on English society more by the force of her per-

sonality and her broad cultural and political interests than by her beauty, which several observers praised rather modestly. See *DNB*.

[6] Francis Dana's elder brother Edmund had sailed to England shortly after his graduation from Harvard in 1759, married Helen, daughter of Charles Kinnaird, sixth baron Kinnaird, in 1765, and taken holy orders in 1769. After 1774 he was vicar at Wroxeter, near Shrewsbury in Shropshire. His eldest daughter, Elizabeth Caroline, was eighteen, and his second daughter, Frances Johnstone, nearly seventeen when AA met them. *Sibley's Harvard Graduates*, 14:414–418; Elizabeth Ell-

ery Dana, *The Dana Family in America*, Cambridge, 1956, p. 484–485.

[7] This paragraph is omitted in AA, *Letters*, ed. CFA. Hannah Clarke Bromfield of Boston and Harvard, Mass., step-mother of AA's dear friend Abigail Bromfield Rogers, died on 17 August (Daniel Denison Slade, "Bromfield Family," *NEHGR*, 26:38–42 [Jan. 1872]).

[8] Lucy Quincy Tufts would die at fifty-five in October; Hannah Clarke Bromfield was sixty-one at her death. See AA2 to JQA, 24 Sept., under "Fryday Eve," above; vol. 4:348, note 1.

[9] See Genesis 18:9.

Abigail Adams to Mary Smith Cranch

My dear sister   October 1. 1785 London

I told you in my last, that I was going to dine with my Friend Mrs. Rogers. You must know that yesterday the whole Diplomatick Choir dinned here, that is his Lordship the Marquiss of Carmarthan and all the Foreign Ministers 15 in all,[1] and to day the Newspapers proclaim it. I believe they have as many Spies here as the Police of France. Upon these occasions no Ladies are admitted, so I wrote a card and beg'd a dinner for myself and Daughter of Mrs. Rogers where I know I am always welcome.

It is customary to send out cards of invitation ten days before hand. Our cards were gone out, and as good luck would have it, Captain Hay returnd from the West Indies and presented us with a noble Turtle weighing a hundred and 14 pounds which was drest upon this occasion. Tho it gave us a good deal of pain to receive so valuable a present from them; yet we could not refuse it without affronting them, and it certainly happend at a most fortunate time. On tuesday they and a Number of our American Friends and some of our *English Friends*, for I assure you we have a chosen few of that number, are to dine with us.

This afternoon I have had a visit from Madam Pinto, the Lady of the Portugal Minister. They have all visited now, and I have returnd their visits, but this is the only Lady that I have seen. She speaks english tolerably and appears an agreeable woman. She has lately returnd to this Country from whence she has been 5 years absent. The Chevelier de Pinto has been Minister here for many years.[2] Some years hence it may be a pleasure to reside here in the Character of American Minister, but with the present sallery and the present temper of the English no one need to envy the embassy. There would soon be fine work if any notice was taken of their Bilingsgate and abuse, but all their arrows rebound and fall Harmless to the ground. Amidst all their falshoods, they have never insinuated a Lisp against the private Character of the American Minister, nor in his publick Line charged him with either want of abilities honour or integrity. The whole venom has been leveld against poor America, and every effort to make her appear ridiculous in the Eyes of the Nation. How would they exult if they could lay hold of any circumstance in Either of our Characters to make us appear ridiculous.

I received a Letter to day from Mr. Jefferson who writes me; that he had just received a parcel of English Newspapers. They "teem says he with every horrour of which nature is capable; assassination Suicide thefts robberies, and what is worse than thefts Murder and robbery, the blackest Slanders! Indeed the Man must be of rock who can stand all this. To Mr. Adams it will be but one victory the more. It would [*have*] illy suited me. I do not love difficulties, I am fond of quiet, willing to do my duty, but irritable by slander and apt to be forced by it to abandon my post. I fancy says he it must be the quantity of Animal food eaten by the English which renders their Character unsusceptible of civilisation. I suspect that it is in their kitchens and not in their Churches, that their reformation must be worked, and that missionaries from hence would avail more than those who should Endevour to tame them by precepts of Religion or Philosophy."3

But he adds, what do the foolish Printers of America mean by retailing all this Stuff in our Papers, as if it was not enough to be slandered by ones Enemies without circulating the Slanders amongst ones Friends too?

I could tell Mr. Jefferson that I doubt not that there are persons in America equally gratified with them as the english, and that from a spirit of envy. But these open attacks are nothing to the secret and subtle Enemies Mr. A. has had heretofore to encounter. In Mr. Jefferson he has a firm and faithfull Friend, with whom he can consult and advise, and as each of them have no object but the good of their Country in view, they have an unlimited confidence in each other, and they have only to lament that the Channel divides their more frequent intercourse.

You ask me whether I must tarry out three years?4 Heaven only knows what may be the result of one if any probality appears of accomplishing any thing. Tis likely we may tarry. I am sure that it will be a Labour if not of Love yet of much perplexity, and difficulty. The immense debt due from the Mercantile part of America to this Country, sours this people beyond measure and greatly distresses thousands who never were or ever will be Polititians. The Manufactures who supplied the Merchants, and depend upon them for remittances, indeed I pitty their situation. At the same time I think our Countrymen greatly to blame for getting a credit, that many of them have taken no Pains to preserve, but who have thoughtlessly rioted upon the Property of others.

And this amongst other things makes our Situation dissagreeable and the Path very difficult for negotiation.[5]

You make an other inquiry too, how your Neice will like to tarry. I can assure you, and all those whom it *ever* concernd that I have not seen her half so happy and contented since she left America, as she has been for six weeks past,[6] and I am persuaded she has no particular attachment there more than we all have in common. The last vessels brought her no Letters but from a female Friend or two. A few lines only have found their way across the vast ocean since last December, and them through the utmost hazard of Barbarians Algerines &c. Who would dare to trust a Letter? But enough I will say nothing, as she wishes every delicacy may be used with respect to a Person whom once we thought better of. But you cannot wonder that she rather wishes to remain some time in Europe than for a speedy return.

Your Nephew you have had with you before now. As he did not arrive soon enough for commencment, he wished to see many Person in New York to whom he had Letters, and as he received much civility there, he did not leave it so suddenly as his Nothern Friends expected. He had permission to remain there a fortnight or more as he found it proper and convenient. I believe he is fully sensible of the necessity of oconomy. I never saw any inclination in him to unnecessary expence. He was my Book keeper all the time I resided at Auteuil and perfectly knows what our expences were; he will be very sensible they are not lessned by our residence in London, where we are more exposed to Company, and obliged to an attendance at Court. It mortifies me that I have it not in my Power to send amongst my Friends many things which I should rejoice to, as there are now so many articles restricted. If any particular thing is wanted by you or yours which I can put into the private trunk of a Captain, let me know it, and you shall have it.

I would have you write me by way of New York during the winter. Cover your Letters either to Mr. King or Gerry; which address will

Frank them to New York and they will forward them to me. I shall take the same method; as it is not likely any other opportunitys but by the Pacquet will offer. My Paper calls upon me to subscribe your affectionate Sister   A A

RC (MWA:Abigail Adams Corr.).

¹ See the list of guests in AA2 to JQA, 24 Sept., note 23, above.

² Luiz Pinto de Balsamão had represented Portugal since 1774 (*Repertorium der diplomatischen Vertreter aller Länder*, 3:317).

³ In this and the following paragraph AA quotes from Jefferson's letter of 25 Sept., above.

⁴ See Mary Cranch to AA, 19 July, above, under "August 1d."

⁵ All the text from this point to the signature is omitted from AA, *Letters*, ed. CFA.

⁶ That is, since she had written a note to Royall Tyler, [*ca. 11 Aug.*], above, terminating their relationship.

John Quincy Adams to Abigail Adams 2d

N:II

Haverhill October 1st. 1785. Saturday

I am now settled down for the Winter, and shall be obliged to pay an unremitting attention to my Studies. I am told I have much more to do, than I had any Idea of; in order to gain an admittance with honour, next Spring in the junior Class at the University. In the Greek I have to go from the beginning to learn the Grammar, which is by no means an agreeable task; to study the new Testament nearly or quite through; between 3 and 4 books in Xenophon's Cyropaedia, and 5 or 6 books in Homer's Iliad. In Latin I have little else to go thro' but Horace, part of which I have already done. In English, I have to Study Watts's Logic, Locke, on the human understanding, and something in Astronomy.¹ But what good is it to me, to know all this? perhaps you will say. Not much I grant; but it is only the preface, to a request, which I am obliged to make, much against my Inclination; it is, that you would relax from the Strictness of our Engagement untill I get to Cambridge. I shall go into very little Company here, there will probably be a Continual sameness, in every Event that will happen, so that I shall have little to write you that may be very interesting.² However, two days Every week I will set apart half an hour, to write something to you. If you claim the same indulgence I own I cannot in justice refuse it; and if you have the same Reason, I would not desire to. It would be a mortification to me, to hear from you less frequently, than I do, and I sincerely hope, you will continue to write as fully as you have done; but from the Impossibility I am in of fulfilling entirely my Engagement with you, I must now leave it entirely at your own option how often you will write. When I get to Cambridge, I shall not be obliged to study so much as I shall while here, and then I shall probably be able to renew the rule of writing something every day.

Wednesday 5th

Mr. and Mrs. Shaw, the day before yesterday set out, on a journey to visit their friends at Braintree, Bridgwater &c. They are to be absent near three weeks. I suppose you will be curious to know my opinion of the young Lady, that boards here.[3] She is in stature Rather short, but exceedingly well proportioned; a fine shape; a most expressive Eye, and very fair complexion: she is not a beauty but has in her Countenance, something, uncommonly interesting. As to her Character, I have not seen enough of it to give it you, exactly: you shall have what I have collected from other Persons, and the little I have observed; and when I become more acquainted with it, I will write you my Sentiments again. She lost her father when she was very young, which has been her great misfortune. She boarded for a considerable time at Mrs. Sheaffe's in Boston, and was drawn very young into the stream of dissipation. I have been griev'd since I return'd home, to see the Education, given to numbers of the young Ladies in Boston. We talk of the follies and fopperies of Europe; but I think we go much further, than they do; we have no Theatres, nor Masquerades I own; but there are assemblies, and Concerts, and Balls, and visits which appear to me, the most ridiculous method of killing time, that was ever Invented. In Europe, you commonly see that Even young Ladies of fortune, have an excellent Education given them, before they are introduced into the world; and they may afterwards make what use of it they please: But here, young Ladies, without fortunes to support show, without titles the dignity of which they are bound to maintain, think it beneath them, to know any thing but to dance, and talk scandal. In this last particular they have attained great perfection. They are carried into Company, while they are by far too young, and are taught, that if they can talk nonsense very fluently, and sit very straight and upright, five hours together in one Chair, they will be most accomplished women; you will think I am too severe; but it is certainly too often the case with our young women educated in the Capital. It has been an essential injury to Miss H[azen]: she has a fine natural genius; but it has been so long employ'd upon trifles, that they have almost become natural to it. Had she always been taught that prudence, and oeconomy, were qualities absolutely necessary for young People in this Country; that some knowledge in Literature, and especially in history, was a much greater ornament than a pretty face, and a fine shape; I doubt not but she would be much more universally admired than she is: she has been too much celebrated, by a parcel of fops, and if I am not much mistaken, Vanity is her ruling passion. This however must be said that Nature has been liberal to her in mind, and person, but that her foibles are probably owing to Education. She has worn off many, I have been told since, she came here, and I hope the rest will gradually disappear. Do not mention my opinions concerning Characters, any where out of the family. When I write to you; I endeavour to give you the Sentiments of my heart as they rise. To any body else, I should give a much more advantageous Character of this Lady, and yet speak nothing, but what I believe. But to you, I mean to speak not the truth only, but all the Truth.

8th

I have not as yet paid any visits. My trunks, which were sent by water, did not arrive till this Evening. Our Cousin Eliza, arrived the day before yesterday, and stays at Mrs. White's, where she will have an opportunity of continuing to learn, music, with Miss Peggy. She will spend some months here, which will be a great addition to my happiness.

I have seen here since my arrival a number of young People; you shall have my Sentiments concerning them, one by one; it was if you remember, part of our agreement. *Miss Debby Perkins*, is about 17. an Orphan, and niece to a Mr. Blodget, you may have seen in London, whose father lives in this Town.[4] She is of a middling Stature, a charming shape, a beautiful complexion, and if not the first beauty in Haverhill, at least the second. Had her eye, more expression in it, she would undoubtedly bear the bell; but amazingly wild. When she, and Nancy get together, it would make Heraclitus laugh, to see them. Yet it is enough to make any one weep to see natures gifts so abused: they both require the severe eye of a Parent to make them completely amiable.

Wednesday 12th

On Monday I went and paid a visit to Judge Sargeant, and spent the last Evening there. Our Company was composed of the Miss Sargeant's, Miss Perkins, Miss Hazen, Mr. W. Osgood, W. and Ben.

Blodget, and your brother. Miss Sukey Sargeant I take to be about 21, tall, not handsome, but looks as if her Countenance was lasting: that is that 15 years hence she will look very much as she does now, behaves with propriety; and has none of the wildness, conspicuous, in the two last Characters I have drawn. Mr. H. Porter, the minister of a neighbouring town in N. Hampshire, is paying his addresses to her, and it is said that all the parties are agreed, upon the match. Her sister Tabitha, (a patriarchical name) is about 18, tall, and large, but an agreeable countenance; there is a propriety, in her behaviour which all young Ladies do not possess;[5] I have lately conceived a great aversion to romping, and it is very pleasing to me, to see young Ladies, that do not pride in it.

I have spent part of this Evening, at Mr. White's, very agreeably. This family has paid more attentions to my brothers, and since my arrival, to me, than any other in town, and if our old maxim be true that it is according to the Treatment we receive from persons, that we form our opinions of them, I ought to have a very high opinion of them; and so indeed it is. Mrs. White is, I believe, an excellent woman. Peggy is very agreeable, and has more reading, than many of our divinities in this Town.

Saturday 15th

Thursday, we dined with Mr. Dodge. There was only Mr. Thaxter, Miss Nancy, and brother Tommy. Mr. Dodge, has not had what is called a Classical Education, but has always been very fond of reading, and is a man of extensive knowledge, in his own Language. He is very fond of enquiring, which flatters the Vanity of a traveller, more, than perhaps you know. It is as agreeable to give Information, as to receive it, and is more pleasing to our amour propre.

Yesterday, I dined at judge Sargeant's. There was besides his family, only Mr. Thaxter, Mr. Payson, and your brothers. Mr. Payson married last Spring, a daughter of Mrs. Sargeants. She, is in some measure the arbiter of Taste here, and is said to be very severe in her remarks, upon Persons whose dress does not meet with her approbation, or who has the misfortune of making a faux-pas in a Dance. She coquetted it for a long time, before she married this gentleman, and now it is certainly her own fault if she is not happy with him.

I pass'd the Evening, in a large Company at Major Bartlett's. This is a family, which I suppose you never visited. They have always been upon very indifferent terms with Mr. Shaw, whose settling here, they opposed violently. I have notwithstanding had an Invitation to visit them. Among the Company was a Mr. Stoughton, an Englishman, who has lately settled in this Town, and expects, his Lady here soon, from England. A Man of easy and agreeable manners, though an Englishman, but it must be observed that he has been a great traveller.

We had this day a Phenomenon, something, like that of the dark day, which you doubtless remember.[6] It was not to so great a degree; but at 3 o'clock this afternoon, I could not read a common print without a Candle; the clouds were thin, and of a yellowish colour, and they were driven along very fast. At four o'clock it was quite light, again.[7]

19th. Wednesday

Drank tea, and pass'd the Evening, on Monday at Mr. White's. Mrs. and Miss Williams, the Lady and Daughter of the Professor, of natural Philosophy, and Mathematics, at Cambridge, were there, on a Visit; the latter is a very intimate friend of Miss Hazen's; tall, rather large, but genteel and very pretty. But since I came home, I am grown more indifferent still to beauty, than I ever was. It is so common a thing, here, that, it loses half its value. Oh! that our young Ladies, were as distinguish'd, for the beauty of their minds, as they are for the charms, of their Persons! But alas! too many of them, are like, a beautiful apple, that is insipid, or disgusting to the taste. Stop, stop, young man, methinks I hear you say. It ill becomes you, at your age, to set up, as censor of the conduct of the Ladies: rather attend to your own. True my Sister, I will own I am wrong, and had I not made a resolution, to give you, my most secret thoughts, I would restrain the Indignation, which I cannot prevent from rising in my breast, when I see, the best gifts of Nature neglected or abused. But all this is a digression, and has nothing to do with Miss Williams, whose accomplishments may be very great, and whose foibles, if she has any, are entirely unknown to me. There were two Mr. Osgood's there. Perhaps you have seen them: though their family, and this, are very cool with one another. The youngest, Bil: bears a very good Character, and is said to be a great admirer of Miss H[azen]. This was the third or fourth time, I have seen them in Company together, and I think I have at least perceivd that she loves to teize him. They called to my mind Mr. Hickman, and Miss Howe;[8] but I dont know that Miss Howe, is any where represented as a Coquet. The gentleman has a great deal of softness, and Modesty in his behaviour; but some unreasonable ill natured creatures have said, that these are not the Qualities requisite for gaining a Lady's heart. (but no general rule without Exceptions.)

Yesterday I dined at Mr. White's; and immediately after dinner, Mr. James Duncan, Leonard White, Peggy, our Eliza, and myself, set out for Newbury.[9] We arrived there just at Dusk, and all went immediately to Mr. Dalton's. He was not at home, but came in soon after the rest of the family were there, and your friend Ruth (who is fatter than ever)[10] inquired after you. We spent the evening agreeably as Cards, will permit, and all lodg'd there. This day there was a regimental muster for training, about 900 men, were under arms, from about 9 in the morning till 2 in the afternoon, I was following their motions: They did not it is true perform their Evolutions, as the King of Prussia's troops do, but would not in Time of war, I believe, be less formidable.

We dined at Mr. Dalton's, in Company with Mr. Symmes, a young Gentleman, who is studying law, very agreeable, and pleasing in his manners. This afternoon we all return'd again, and I spent a very sociable evening at Mr. White's. I believe you never was at Newbury, though *Pappa's carriage*, was often so politely offer'd.[11] I assure you, I have not met with a more agreeable family, any where. Mr. Dalton, is much of a gentleman. He has a great deal, of that easy Politeness, which serves so much To make men happy, and to keep them so.[12] A talent, which most men cannot acquire, whatever pains they may take, but which some possess, naturally, and will show it, in whatever station of Life they may be placed. It has been observed that Mrs. Dalton resembled your Mamma. This is a sufficient elogium of her, and nothing, more is necessary to be said in her favour. Ruth, is a picture of Satisfaction and Content: her uncommon bulk, does not appear to give her, any anxiety, and her mind seems to be in a continual Calm: the Children, have all been brought up to do something in the Course of their Lives, and not to consider, that Idleness is the dignity of human Nature.

Saturday 22d

Thursday Evening, our Uncle, and Aunt returned from their Journey, and brought me, two Letters from Mamma, and one from, my friend Murray,[13] but not a line from you. I will not complain, even, if I finally receive none; because you have taught me, patience: but

I still hope, there is a letter from you somewhere in Boston. I will write to Murray, if I can possibly find time,[14] for I am so press'd for want of it, that, I have been obliged to neglect answering many Letters.

I was in great hopes, of receiving a letter from you, by the Post, which came from Boston yesterday, but none appeared. *Patience!* *Patience!* as an old french Officer, on board the Boston,[15] used to say. The weather yesterday, and today, has been exceeding stormy; it was a very lucky Circumstance, for Mr. and Mrs. Shaw, that they got home, on Thursday, for they could not have travelled, in this terrible weather.

Mamma's Letters mention that you had not when they were written, (their dates are Augt. 11th. and 23d.) heard of my arrival. I imagine, she must have received soon after that a line which I wrote before I landed, by the french Packet,[16] which sailed, the day I arrived at New-York. And you have I hope, long ere this my Letters by Mr. Church.[17]

Eliza, has been here, yesterday and this day. What an amiable disposition! She in some measure supplies your place, as a Sister, and if any body could make me forget your being absent, it were she. But that is impossible. I believe that absence, always has a tendency of rivetting the ties of friendship, more closely, as we cannot properly conceive the value, of any good thing untill we are deprived of it. When I shall see you, and my ever dear and honoured Parents again; alas! I know not. The Ocean is again between us! The Interests of a Nation keep, you on that side, and the Duty of an Individual keeps me, on this. But the hope, that some day will come, when we shall all meet again together, still cheers and encourages me, though it is like trees in the dusk, which seem lengthening as you go.

It is most probable, that none of us, will ever again see our Aunt Tufts. She has, as I believe I have mentioned in a former Letter, been ill, during the greatest part of the Summer. When I arrived in Boston, she was supposed to be recovering; and was at one time, well enough to see Company; but she soon relapsed, and has since that been continually growing weaker. It is the Opinion, of Mr. and Mrs. Shaw, who saw her but a few days agone, and of the Doctor himself, that she will continue in this World, but a short Time. She is one of the few, who can, look back with pleasure, on a life well Spent, and can submit cheerfully to the will of Providence, whatever it may be.

Good Night; my dear Sister! Or rather good morning for the Clock has struck one. Present my dutiful regards to our Parents. I wrote, about a fortnight since to Mamma.[18] The vessel sailed a few days since, and has also two or three Letters for you.[19]

Your ever affectionate Brother. J. Q. Adams

RC (Adams Papers). The text is written on twelve small pages numbered 93 through 104, and from the third page, 3 through 12; see JQA to AA2, [12] May, descriptive note, above.

[1] With the exception of "something in Astronomy," JQA details his reading in each of these authors and works in his Diary entries for Oct. 1785 – Feb. 1786 (*Diary*, 1:343–413). In addition to studying the works mentioned here, JQA began to translate Virgil's *Eclogues* in October (same, 1:335).

[2] In his Diary entry for this day JQA also worried that the period of study he was beginning would allow for so little social life that he would lack the necessary raw material to justify continuing his daily entries. Upon reflection, he concluded that he could make interesting observations upon local subjects and characters. And indeed, JQA's Diary for the five months that he spent in Haverhill does not show him avoiding company, as he anticipates here. He socialized frequently in a relatively small but lively circle of friends at Haverhill, and occasionally in neighboring towns, and gave himself ample opportunity for "sketching Characters," for his Diary. JQA held to his plan to reduce his correspondence with AA2 while at Haverhill. With the exception of his letter of [26] Oct., below, he did not write again until 15 March 1786 (Adams Papers), from Cambridge.

[3] Nancy Hazen.

[4] Mr. Blodgett was probably one of the five sons of Judge Samuel Blodgett of Haverhill; and was perhaps the Nathan Blodgett whom the Adamses had met or had some dealings with in 1778 and 1779 (JQA, *Diary*, 1:335, 338; vol. 3:140, and note 1; and JA, *Diary and Autobiography*, 2:370, 372, and note 2).

[5] Although JQA describes Tabitha Sargeant in roughly the same terms in his Diary, on 6 Oct., he there says that she "pleases me mightily" (*Diary*, 1:336).

[6] This was 19 May 1780. AA briefly described this day to James Lovell in May 1780; Cotton Tufts gave JA a quite full description in July of that year (vol. 3:355–356, 386–388).

[7] JQA wrote "again" with a pen point and ink that differ from the preceding text, and match the text of the next entry.

[8] Hickman and Howe are characters in Samuel Richardson's novel, *Clarissa Harlowe*.

[9] JQA may intend Newburyport, where JA's college classmate and old friend, Tristram Dalton, had his winter residence on State Street. In his Diary for 19 Oct., JQA remarks that Dalton had caught a cold "at New town, a seat which he owns, about half way between this and Haverhill" (*Diary*, 1:343). This description fits the Daltons' summer residence, Spring Hill, in Newbury, later West Newbury, about five miles west of Newburyport. See *Sibley's Harvard Graduates*, 13:569–578.

[10] In his Diary, JQA is even more graphic about Ruth Dalton's figure (*Diary*, 1:342).

[11] In 1783 the Daltons had invited AA2 to visit them at Spring Hill in Newbury, but it appears that AA2 did not go (AA to JA, 21 July, and AA2 to Elizabeth Cranch, 20 Aug. 1783, both above).

[12] The line is from Horace, *Epistles*, Bk. I, Epis. vi, line 2: "quae possit facere et servare beatum." In his Diary for this date, however, JQA applies Horace's maxim not to Dalton, but to a Mr. Herriman, the adjutant of the local militia exercises that he had just witnessed. "Some men," he observes, "whatever their Station in Life may be, have a natural grace and elegance, which never leave them; others though possess'd of the highest advantages, and train'd from their Infancy to the Science of politeness, can never acquire that easy agreeable manner which has so great a tendency: To make men happy and to keep them so." JQA's compliment to the adjutant sets the sentence in the letter immediately following the quotation from Horace in a fuller context, because while Dalton was the son of a wealthy Newburyport merchant, Mr. Herriman, JQA was informed, was "a joiner by trade" evidently without fortune (*Diary*, 1:343).

[13] AA to JQA, 11 and 23 Aug., both above; William Vans Murray to JQA, 2 Aug. (Adams Papers).

[14] No further correspondence between JQA and Murray is known until 1797.

[15] The frigate *Boston*, on which JA and JQA sailed for France in 1778.

[16] JQA to AA, 17 July, above.
[17] JQA to AA2, 25 May, and 17 July, both above.

[18] JQA to AA, 6 Oct., below.
[19] JQA to AA2, 8 and 19 Sept., both above.

Abigail Adams to John Quincy Adams

My dear son   London October 5th 1785

I began a Letter to you yesterday which I designd to have finishd last evening, but as we had a great deal of company, many of them Ladies who staid the evening, I could not command my time, and Captain Callihan wrote us a card last evening that he should go by nine this morning, so that I have only time to write you a few lines, to tell you about a fortnight after the arrival of Mr. Church, your first Letter by the French pacquet came to hand. Col. Franks is here again as express from France. That strange Creature Lambe is arrived at last in France. He is going to Algiers and Mr. Barclay and Col. Franks to Moroco. No time is now to be lost as we are now certain that there are two or 3 vessels taken. Had Lamb come in season probably this would not have happend. If Mr. Storer had not saild just as he did, he would have been sent as he wisht, for upon Lamb arrival, they were much put to it to find a proper person to accompany him. He wants somebody of *abilities and Education* to supply. Franks gives a curious account of him. As they chuse to keep this matter silent as possible, some trust worthy person was necessary. After much consultation with respect to the Americans here, Mr. Randle is fixd upon, the Gentleman from Newyork who visited us often at Paris. He has finally consented, tho it seem he is under a matrimonial engagement, and was soon to have been married to a Miss White from Philadelphia. He has negotiated the matter with her, by this time, tho he was under much embaressment what to do, whether to go without or entrust the Secreet to her. He applied for my advise. I was by all means for his telling her; and your Pappa, gave the same.[1] Col. Franks and he will set of for France on fryday. How they will succeed time must determine. The insurence here is very high.

At Length the Peace is signd between the Emperor and the Dutch.[2] The particulars you will see in the papers. Mr. Dumas inquires after you in his last Letters.[3]

Mr. Williamos has been very sick of a fever and is just recovering. I wrote a few lines in your Aunt Shaws Letter to you. I will repeat one injunction, which is for you to write to Mr. Jefferson, as he has no correspondent in the Massachusets.[4] I know your information from time to time would be agreeable to him, and you know his great Literary merit, and that you may avail yourself of much knowledge from him.

Your Pappa is overwhelmd with writing. I know not what he would do if it was not for Your sister who copies for him. So much writing and to so little purpose, is very mortifying. Col. Smith has not yet returnd.

Write me by way of New York this winter. Cover your Letters either to Mr. Gerry or King who will forward them. Remember me to your Brothers & believe me most tenderly yours   A A

You see my haste I cannot copy. I hope the Algerines will not take this. Storer saild a fortnight ago.

RC (Adams Papers).

¹ A fuller account of Randall's decision is in AA2, *Jour. and Corr.*, [3]:187–189.

² The Treaty of Fontainebleau, between Joseph II, emperor of Austria, and the United Provinces of the Netherlands, was not concluded until 8 November (*Cambridge Modern Hist.*, 6:643–646).

³ See C. W. F. Dumas to JA, 27 Sept.

(Adams Papers).

⁴ This was probably an enclosure, not found, in either AA to Elizabeth Shaw, [*ca. 15 Aug.*], or 15 Sept., both above. No correspondence between JQA and Thomas Jefferson has been found, between 12 May 1785 (Jefferson to JQA, Adams Papers), and 1794.

Abigail Adams to Cotton Tufts

Dear sir   London October 5th 1785

Captain Callihan sails sooner than we expected so that we have not time to write to several of our Friends, and indeed we have all written so lately by Mr. Storer, that nothing worth communicating has since occurd. Mr. Adams has written to Mr. Higinson¹ which letter I dare say he will communicate to you and that will give you a detail of politicks here, as well as inform you of the troubles which delays have brought us in; with respect to the Algerines.

Ever since last March Lamb has been intrusted with Papers which ought to have been here in May at furthest. But suppose our funds in Holland exhausted as they soon will be, can our Country expect to continue to Borrow money with their debt still unfunded? With their credit sinking, where will they get presents to Bribe these Barbarians? Or forces to encounter them. How difficult does our country render their foreign embassies by difficulties which uninimnity and virtue publick Spirit and some proper confidence might releive them from?

But I must quit politicks as I have only a moment. Mr. Adams received a few lines from you by Captain Folger inclosing an account,[2] which meet our approbation at the same time we heartily thank you for your kind care and attention.

My dear Aunt how does she? I am grived at the account I have received respecting her,[3] and almost dread to receive a Letter from my Friends. I pray heaven still to spair her Life and to restore her to health and to her Friends.

Believe me Dear sir most affectionately yours   A A

A Barrel of shag Barks[4] would be very pleasing to us if they could be procured.

I forgot to mention that by Mr. Storer we sent you Mr. Neckers works[5] of which we request your acceptance.

RC (Adams Papers).

[1] JA to Stephen Higginson, 4 Oct. (LbC, Adams Papers).

[2] Cotton Tufts to JA, 10 Aug., above.

[3] See Mary Cranch to AA, 19 July, above, under "August 7th."

[4] Shagbark hickory nuts (*Dict. of Americanisms*).

[5] In his letter of 21 Dec. to JA, Tufts acknowledged the receipt of this item and connected it with the receipt of JA to Tufts, 9 Sept. (both Adams Papers); but Tufts does not identify the work and JA does not mention it. Necker published half a dozen works in France between 1769 and 1785 (Hoefer, *Nouv. biog. générale*). His *Œuvres de M. Necker, contenant Compte rendu au roi. Mémoire sur l'établissement des administrations provinciales. De l'administration des finances de la France*, was published in London in 1785.

John Quincy Adams to Abigail Adams

Dear Madam   Haverhill Octr. 6th. 1785

I am afraid my dear Mamma, will accuse me again of neglect for not having written to her, since I left her, before now; several Circumstances have concurred to prevent me; and among the rest, the want of an opportunity to convey any Letters; the stagnation of commerce, has of late been so great; that no vessel since my arrival, at Boston has sailed from thence to any port in Great Britain, and that by which I hope you will receive this, was advertised to sail by the 10th. of last month. It has been waiting ever since that time, without freight; nor do I think it probable she will sail less than ten days or a fort'night.

I now have the Satisfaction of informing you that I am at length settled here, for some months, and shall be able to pursue my studies with more steadiness, than I ever could before. I hope to be able by the next spring to enter College, in the class where my Cousin Cranch is. I have been advised to enter then, rather than wait till

Commencement, in order to have the benefit of two Courses of lectures on natural Philosophy, which are delivered by Professor Williams.[1] If I do not mistake, it is the same Course repeated annually, but upon so important a subject, it is certainly advantageous to hear the same things twice. I feel very happy, that I have now nothing to draw my attention from my studies: and I could not have found a more agreeable place to follow them in. I shall at present particularly attend to the greek Language, the point in which I am the most deficient: though I hope, by the time I enter the University to be able to stand the test also, on that score: of the rest I am not so anxious.

I arrived here this day week, and last Monday, My uncle, and aunt, left us for about a fortnight, to pay a visit to their friends in Boston, Braintree and so on. Your house too they would wish to visit; but it is now deprived of all its attractions. While I was at Braintree, I went there two or three times, and at the first time, I felt the strangest sensations, of pleasure and pain mingled together, that I ever knew of. The first sight of it, brought to my mind the years I had past in it, and many little circumstances which I had entirely forgot but which then were peculiarly pleasing. When I entered in it, my feelings were very different. Bereft of its former inhabitants, it appeared to me, in a gloomy, unpleasant light. Every time I go into it, the involuntary sigh, rises in my breast, and ever must untill the return of those, who will renew its attractions. I believe I have heard you say, you don't want Sentiment in your Letters from America, but surely on this occasion it is excusable in me. And I know not that I am apt to be over-Sentimental.

We receiv'd about 3 weeks ago, your favours by Captn. Dashwood;[2] and the account of your presentation,[3] you will find acknowledged in My aunt Cranch's Letters. My Sister will receive my thanks for hers by this or the next vessel. I have not as yet had reason to complain of her punctuality; nor she I hope of mine.

Braintree has lately lost another of its Belles. Last Saturday Se'ennight, Miss Lucy Apthorp, was married in the Chapel at Boston, to Mr. Nash, the 1st. or 2d. Lieutenant on board the Mercury, whose Captain[4] wrote some very impudent Letters to the governor of this State. The vessel arrived if I mistake not, sometime in last July. While the frigate was in Boston Harbour; Mr. Nash became acquainted with Mr. Apthorp's family. And was so expiditious that he proposed himself before, he sailed: he had a conditional promise of the parents Consent: and return'd to Hallifax, proposing to be at Boston, next Winter; but having obtained from Charles Apthorp,[5] who had served several years in the same ship with him, a proper Letter of recommendation, he immediately came back, and is in a few days going with his bride again to Hallifax. It was observed that the father was much better pleased with the present match, than with a former one:[6] I am sure in that case his opinion is different from that of all the rest of the world; for this young Gentleman, has neither a fortune nor a prospect for one; as I am inform'd. His father is purser on board one of the king of G.B.'s ships. So that not even the favourite *idea* of *family*, could be much gratified. This family pride is surely much more ridiculous here than in any part of Europe. I heard an anecdote the other day, which made me laugh; Miss B. de Blois, has refused several very handsome offers, because the gentlemen were not of families sufficiently respectable; to mix with hers. But when her brother sometime since, paid his addresses to another Miss Apthorp, grand Daughter to Sheriff Greenleaf, and his consent was requested, for the marriage, he said, "he knew nothing against the gentleman personally; but he could not think of a connection, between that family and his own:" so that we have our ladder from the mud, to the skies, as well as all the European Nations.[7]

I do not know of any news to tell you. The Papers, which you probably see frequently in London; will give you every thing of a public Nature. Of the private kind, your Letters from your other friends, and mine to my Sister, will I hope give you sufficient accounts. I have not yet form'd many acquaintances in this place. I do not feel inclined to go much into Company, and my studies will take up so much of my time that I shall have but little to spare. Judge Serjeant, is riding the Circuits, so that I have not seen him yet. I have been several times to Mr. White's House: Mrs. White enquired much about you: Miss Peggy is perfectly recovered from her illness, and is as gay, as any young Lady I have seen here (and this is saying a great deal.)

Tommy, is very well. I have been endeavouring to perswade him to write you, but cannot prevail on him. He says he knows not what to write, except that he is well, and that I can as well do for him. Cousin Betsey Smith,[8] and the Children, are also pretty well.

Your Dutiful Son.   J. Q. Adams

P.S.[9] Will you please to present my Duty to my dear father. I will write to him if I can by this opportunity. I have already put into the bag two Letters to my Sister.[10]

RC (Adams Papers); endorsed: "J Q Adams oc 12 1786." The reason for AA's docketing error is not known.

[1] JQA describes Prof. Samuel Williams and his lectures in frequent detail in his Diary after his admission to Harvard in March 1786 (*Diary*, 2:1–232 passim).

[2] AA2 to Mary Cranch, 22 June, and to Lucy Cranch, 23 June; AA to Mary Cranch, 24 June; AA to JQA, 26 June; JA to JQA, 26 June; and probably AA to Isaac Smith Sr., 30 June, all above.

[3] At Court, on 24 June; see AA to Mary Cranch, 24 June, above.

[4] Capt. Henry Edwin Stanhope. On his troubles with a Boston mob and his subsequent angry exchange of letters with Gov. James Bowdoin, see AA to Thomas Jefferson, 19 Oct., and note 5, below.

[5] Charles Ward Apthorp, Lucy Apthorp Nash's brother, was a captain in the British Navy (John Wentworth, *The Wentworth Genealogy*, 2 vols., Boston, 1870, 1:300, 305, 306).

[6] See JQA to AA2, 19 Sept., and note 12, above.

[7] Miss De Blois was probably Elizabeth (Betsey) De Blois, daughter of the loyalist merchant Gilbert De Blois and Ann Coffin De Blois. She was briefly courted by Gen. Benedict Arnold in 1777, and her mother prevented her from marrying Martin Brimmer in the same year. She never married. Elizabeth had several brothers, both older and younger, who could have courted a Miss Apthorp, who was almost certainly Hannah, age seventeen, the eldest daughter of John Apthorp and Hannah Greenleaf Apthorp. Orphaned at an early age, Hannah lived with her aged grandfather, Stephen Greenleaf of Boston, the last sheriff of Suffolk County under the British Crown. Greenleaf, like both the Apthorps and most of the De Bloises, was a loyalist. Hannah Apthorp married her cousin, the architect Charles Bulfinch, in 1788. Her sister Frances, too young to fit this anecdote, married Charles Vaughan a few years later. See *NEHGR*, 67:11 (Jan. 1913); *Sibley's Harvard Graduates*, 7:182–190; James E. Greenleaf, *Genealogy of the Greenleaf Family*, Boston, 1896, p. 209; Ellen S. Bulfinch, *The Life and Letters of Charles Bulfinch*, Boston, 1896, p. 69–72, 80.

[8] This was Elizabeth Smith, eldest daughter of AA's brother, William; JQA's other cousin Betsy Smith, the youngest daughter of AA's uncle, Isaac Smith Sr., lived in Boston (Elizabeth Shaw to AA, 25 April, note 2, above). Elizabeth Shaw's young children were William Smith Shaw and Elizabeth Quincy Shaw.

[9] Here JQA struck out an entire sentence so thoroughly that it cannot be read.

[10] The next extant letter from JQA to JA is that of 2 April 1786 (Adams Papers). His two letters to AA2 were those of 8 and 19 Sept., both above.

Cotton Tufts to John Adams

No. 1

My Dear Sr   Weymouth Octobr. 6. 1785

On the 6th. Ultimo I drew on You for £100 sterling in Favour of Mr. Samuel Eliot, payable at 30 Days Sight of whom I received 5 Per Cent above Par. The Exchange has been somewhat higher, up to 7 Per Cent, but has fallen, and it is thought will be still lower. Part of the Money received I have let out for a few Months on private Security that I may if Occasion should call, have wherewith to answer any particular Demands that may arise. The Remainder I have vested in Government Securities to the amount of £300 Nominal Value.

Yours of March the 5th. and April 17.[1] I have received, the latter by your Son, who is now with Mr. Shaw. The President[2] advised Him to pursue his Studies especially in Latin and Greek untill April next and then to offer himself. We thought it would be best for your Son to be well skilled in the Languages, previous to his Admission (in other Respects he is fully qualified) and We have taken our Measures accordingly. I am exceedingly pleased with his Modest Behaviour, not less with his Judgment and Learning which I think are such as to afford You a most pleasing Prospect. The Trust You have committed to me I feel the Weight and Importance of, it shall however be my Endeavour to execute it with Fidelity.

Master Charles is now at the University, and conducts with Propriety. On his Entrance, I informed him of the Necessity of Diligence, a wise Choice of Company and of Oeconomy—that with respect to his running Expences, He must from Time to Time advise with his Uncle Cranch as to the Sum wanted, that I should in general make it a Rule not to advance Money without his first approving of the Quantum &c. As Mr. Cranch has a Son now at College and is more immediately acquainted with the necessary Charges, I conceived that he must be a better Judge than myself, that such a Rule might be useful, and hope it will meet with your Approbation.

I wrote to You June 4th.[3] and Aug. 10, in the Latter I enclosed my Accountt to July the 21. last and some News Papers. Since then We are assured of Your appearing at the Court of Gt. Britain. I know not the present Temper of that Court but I cannot conceive that the British Ministry can long persue any System, apprehending that the Nation is become a Prey to Parties and Party Men and that this in some Degree unavoidable while a System of Venality and Corruption prevails and a continued Load of Debt subsists, giving Occasion to all to complain and being such as to leave no Ray of Hope for the Discharge of it. Such a Scituation will afford ample Matter for Fermentation and there will not be wanting active Spirits to set it in motion. Their Passion for Commerce is great. They may feel the Effects of their injudicious Restrictions on American Produce and Commerce. As soon as these are felt, the Tide will turn, and I flatter myself that You will succeed. But a want of Vigor, Union, and a fained Adherence to National Faith on our Side will perhaps embarrass You. I much disrelish our meddling with ⟨sundry⟩ some matters and our Negligence in taking up some others. But I have not Time to dwell on this Subject now; and shall only add that the Sentiments disclosed in your last with respect to the 4th. Article of Treaty[4] will remain with me as all others that You may communicate that You would not be willing should be known. The same Caution I wish some others had observed. A Letter You wrote to Dr. G——n[5] a Year or two past, was communicated to one and another at a Time, when a popular Rage against the Tories prevailed and Your Authority quoted in favour of Indulgence to them, about the same Time yours and Dr. Franklins to Congress on the same Subject were published. Congress refuted this and I presume have taken Care to prevent the like for the future. The Bona fide Debts I think ought to be punctually paid. I have no Idea of severing the Interest from the Principal, and if the Treaty made the Debt valid and demandable, it must make the Interest also unless specially excepted. I forgot whether I informed You that by an Act or Resolve of the General Court Judgment may be recovered for the Principal, and Execution go out accordingly, but not for the Interest untill Congress shall have signified their ⟨Explan⟩ Sense of the 4th. Article (for which Application has been made to them). Our General Court will meet again the   [6] of this Month and will be chiefly taken up in settling the Valuation. I expect not to attend but a small part of the Sessions. The low state in which Mrs. Tufts has lain for some Months past has detained me much at home and will at least for some Time to come. Brother Cranch will inform You of what goes on at Court. Adieu My Dear Friend my best Wishes attend You & Mrs. Adams & Daughter to whom I beg to be remembered and Am Yours   Cotton Tufts

RC (Adams Papers).

[1] Evidently an error for JA to Tufts, 24 April, above, which JQA delivered to Tufts in August.

[2] Of Harvard, Joseph Willard.

[3] Not found.

[4] See JA to Tufts, 24 April, above.

[5] This is the letter containing quite candid criticisms of Benjamin Franklin that JA wrote to Dr. William Gordon, 10 Sept. 1783. No Letterbook copy exists and the recipient's copy has not been found, but the text survives, evidently quoted in full, in Gordon to Elbridge Gerry, 24 Dec. 1783 (MHS, *Procs.*, 63 [1929–1930]:501–502). "Yours and Dr. Franklins [*letter*] to Congress," below, is JA, Benjamin Franklin, and John Jay to the pres-ident of Congress, 10 Sept. 1783 (in Wharton, ed., *Dipl. Corr. Amer. Rev.*, 6:687–691). In an 8 April 1785 letter to JA (Adams Papers; printed in MHS, *Procs.*, 63:512–514), Dr. Gordon, commenting on the long period in which he had not heard from JA, wrote: "You best know, whether there is any truth in my suspi-cion, that the free use I made of your liberal sentiments respecting the Tories to counter-act the narrow and pernicious politics of some individuals, has induced them to cau-tion you against corresponding with me, espe-cially in that free and open manner."

[6] Left blank in MS. The Massachusetts legislature reconvened on 19 October (Mass., *Acts and Laws*, 1784–1785, p. 725).

Abigail Adams to Thomas Jefferson

Dear sir   London October 7th. 1785

Your very polite favour[1] was handed me by Col. Franks. I am much
obliged to you for the execution of the several commissions I troubled
you with. Be assured sir that I felt myself Honourd by your commands, tho I have only in part executed them, for I could not find at
any store table Cloths of the dimensions you directed. The width is
as you wisht, but they assure me that four yds and three quarters are
the largest size ever used here, which will cover a table for 18 persons.
To these Cloths there are only 18 Napkins, and to the smaller size
only twelve. I was the more ready to credit what they said, knowing
that I had been obliged to have a set of tables made on purpose for
me, in order to dine 16 or 18 persons. These rooms in general are not
calculated to hold more and it is only upon extraordinary occasions
that you meet with that number at the tables here. The Marquis of
Carmarthan who occasionally dines the Foreign Ministers, and has
a House found him by his Majesty, cannot entertain more than 15 at
once, and upon their Majesties Birth days, he is obliged to dine his
company at his Fathers the Duke of Leeds. The person where I
bought the Cloth offerd to have any size made, that I wisht for, and
agreed to take eight pounds ten shillings for 20 Napkins and a cloth
5 yds long. I gave seven for this which I send, and shall wait your
further directions. I took the precaution of having them made and
marked to secure them against the custom House, and hope they will
meet your approbation. I think them finer than the pattern, but it is
difficult judging by so small a scrap.[2] I have also bought you two pair
of Nut crackers for which I gave four shillings, we [find them so?]
convenient that I thought they would be equally so to [you. The]re
is the article of Irish linen[3] which is much superiour here to any that
is to be had in France, and cheeper I think. If you have occasion for
any you will be so good as to let me know. It cannot easily pass
without being made, but that could be easily done, only by sending
a measure. At the rate of 3 shilling & six pence pr yd by the peice,
the best is to be had. As we are still in your debt, the remainder of
the money shall be remitted you or expended here as you direct. Mr.
Adams supposed there might be something of a balance due to him
in the settlement of a private account with Mr. Barclay, which he has
orderd paid to you. He will also pay the money here for the insurence

of Mr. Hudons Life,[4] by which means what ever remains due to you can be easily settled.

Haveing finishd the article of Buisness, I am totally foild at that of Compliment. Sure the air of France, conspired with the Native politeness and Complasan[ce] of the writer to usher into the World such an assemblage of fine things. I shall value the warrior Deity the more for having been your choise, and he cannot fail being in taste in a Nation which has given us such proofs of their Hostility; forgiveness of injuries is no part of their Character, and scarcly a day passes without a Boxing match; even in this square which is calld the polite and Court end of the city. My feeling have been repeatedly shock'd to see Lads not more than ten years old striped and fighting untill the Blood flow'd from every part, enclosed by a circle who were claping and applauding the conquerer, stimulating them to continue the fight, and forceing every person from the circle who attempted to prevent it. Bred up with such tempers and principals, who can wonder at the licentiousness of their Manners, and the abuse of their pens. Their arrows do not wound, they rebound and fall harmless [to the ground?]. But amidst their boasted freedom of the press, one must bribe [Newspapers?] to get a paragraph inserted in favour of America, or her Friends. Our Country has no money to spair for such purposes; and must rest upon her own virtue and magninimity. [So we?] may too late convince this Nation that the treasure which they knew not how to value, has irrecoverably past into the possession of those who were possesst of more policy and wisdom.

I wish I might flatter myself with the hope of seeing you here this winter. You would find a most cordial welcome from your American Friends, as well as from some very distinguished literary Characters of this Nation.

My best regards to Miss Jefferson to Col. Humphries to Mr. Short, or any other Friends or acquaintance who may inquire after Your Friend and humble servant   A Adams

My daughter presents her respectfull regards to you and compliments to the rest of the Gentleman.

RC (DLC:Jefferson Papers); addressed in an unknown hand: "His Excellency Thomas Jefferson Esquire Paris." The upper right corners of both leaves are torn off, resulting in the loss of several words, and a worn fold and worn edge have destroyed a few characters.

[1] Of 25 Sept., above.
[2] The sample that Jefferson enclosed in his letter of 25 Sept., above. AA2 records AA's purchase for Jefferson on 4 Oct., as "a table-

cloth five yards long, two and a half wide, with eighteen napkins, seven pounds sterling" (*Jour. and Corr.*, [3]:189).

³ That is, shirt linen; see Jefferson to AA, 11 Oct., below.

⁴ In July, Jefferson had asked JA to arrange for a life insurance policy on Jean Antoine Houdon, who was about to depart for Virginia to execute a statue of George Washington.

After several inquiries in England and frequent correspondence with Jefferson on the subject, JA finally arranged this policy for £670, paying a premium of £32 11s. on 12 Oct., a few days after Houdon actually arrived at Mt. Vernon. See AA to Jefferson, 19 Oct., below, and Jefferson, *Papers*, 8:illustration facing 87, 283, 302, 340, 577, 663–664.

Royall Tyler to Abigail Adams

Madam   [*post 7 Oct. 1785*]¹

I am equally pleased with your Letter of the Ninth of May² and the very Delicate Friendly Motives which Induced you to Write it. Whilst I Continue to regard your Amiable Daughter, the Esteem of her Parents, independent of their Merit, will be ever dear to me: and whilst the human Mind is ever most Anxious for what it holds most Dear, I shall have my "*Apprehensions*" and feel gratefull toward those who are kind enou to quiet them.

You Prophecied truly respecting the British Newspaper Scurrilities: I do not know how they may affect you, whether you either [Despair?] or Disregard them. But for myself I think I should be but little moved by the Aspersions of a People, whose Characteristick, is, [. . .] the most Billinsgate Latitude with the most Respectable Ch[aracters]: whose National Representatives, in the same Publications, are Peculators, whose Ministers are Boys or Knaves, and whose King is an obstinate Numskull—Oh! Faugh—it is a very Vile Bird.

You mention some where in your Letters, that you prefer News to Sentiment, and that when you recieve Packets from America you always hury over the Sentimental and hasten to the Narrative.³ Now this is very Unfortunate For me, who am very apt to obtrude my Sentiments upon my Friends, who write unpremeditately and with the same unreserve as I Talk to those who share my highest Confidence. I will Confine myself to mere News in this Letter, and I Assure you that it is the only Restraint I ever Subjected myself to when writing to a Lady I so highly Respect and Esteem.

The Praises of your Son you Undoubtedly hear bruited from all your Correspondents. I have not been long enough Acquainted with him to Delineate his Character, and can only say, that the First impressions he made upon me were much in his Favour. He was present with me at the opening of the Supreme Judicial Court at Boston. As he was the only person, who set within the Bar, beside the Gentlemen of the Profession; he was naturally conspicuous. I dined in Company the same day with the Bench and Bar and was Inquired of by most of the Older Gentleman, whether the Young Person who was with me at Court was not a Son of Mr. Adams? as those Gentleman who had practiced with his Father declard they immediately concluded from his Countenance.

Mr. Pearsen, Precepter of Philipses Academy, is married to Miss Sally Bromfield; and was a few days since chosen by the Corporation of Harvard College, "Hollisian Professor of the Oriental Languages &c."4 He will accordingly be presented to the Overseers, who will doubtless Confirm the Election. This appointment is Acceptable to the People at large, very pleasing to the Bromfield Family, and peculiarly so to Mrs. Pearson, as she very much Disliked Andover.

The Salary will be two hundred pounds pr: An: with some Perquisites.

I am but very Superficially acquainted with Commerce or Financiering, But from the little Insight I can obtain, I scarce think it prudent to Communicate the particular State of either in this Country, to you in Europe.

The Land Tax &c. is Collected with great Difficulty, whilst the Impost has driven many Vessels, with the most valuable Cargoes; from the Entrance of our Ports, to the other States. The Failure of the Merchants Traders &c. is so common at B[oston] that it has Ceased in great Measure to be Disreputable. Scarce a Week passes without one or more persons shutting their Doors against their Creditors; and no man will venture to Scandalize that Situation, which may be his own or his most Intimate Friends on the morrow. I could add to these assertions and observations, and prove them just by the most Incontestable Examples. But I may have err'd in Writing even thus generally upon Subjects of this Nature.

I shall however particularize Two persons of your Acquaintance who have lately faild.

The one is Mr. S: B[arre]t commonly called Bishop B—. This happen'd upon the Seventh of this month. I have not obtained the particulars, only that his principal Creditors are English Merchants.

The other is Mr. S: A: O[tis] Father to Harry O: who studies the Law under Mr. L[owell]. He failed about Six Weeks past to the great suprize of his Friends and the Publick. His Debts are owed chiefly in England, and it is said amount to Forty Thousand pounds Sterling. I have seen a List which may be depended upon that carries them, to Thirty Thousand pounds Lawfull money. This List only included the Large Demands. It is said, however, that he has charged upon his Books to the amount of Ten Thousand pounds Lawfull money more than sufficient to Discharge his Debts. He will, I dare say, think that he does well if he can Ballance his Accompts even with the World and begin anew. The United States are Indebted to him Eight Thousand Pounds being the Ballance of his C——s Accompts. Your Uncle has not sufferd by him as I can learn. His Brother at B[arnsta]ble, has Failed in Consequence of his Failure. But his Sister has secured herself, by attaching His Property in her possession. Her Patrimony was in his hands and it was by great good Fortune that she was not Involved in his Ruin. She shut her Shop for a few Weeks, But by a legal transfer of the Property attached, she is enabled to prosecute her Bussiness as Usual.[5]

Mr. Nash, who the Newspaper will Announce to you, is married to Miss Lucy Apthorp, is the same Gentleman who was the Bearer of Capt. Stanhopes Letters to his Excellency, our Govenour. The Young Couple sailed on the third of this month for Shelburn where they Intend spending the Winter.

Miss Betsey Apthorp it is said, is to be married with Mr. Pearse, son to a Mr. Pearse of Cape Ann, a person who has Accumulated a large Estate during the War.

The original of the Letter from Kentucky, in the Boston Magazine for September, is by Mr. Perkins and was wrote to your Cousin Betsey C[ranch].

You will perceive in the Newspapers, I send Mr. Adams, an Extract of a Letter from London, giving an Account of Mr. Adams's Private Audience and Introduction to the King of G: Britain. This Extract was communicated by Governour Bowdoin at his Table and declared to be written by Mrs. Temple to himself, or her Mother, I could not determine which as I set at some Distance.

The match it is said is settled between Miss Temple and Mr. Winthrope, the Gentleman who Formerly courted Miss Derby.[6]

Mr. Adams's private Audience is a matter of much speculation. Congress have not Published an official Account, and the Members are not very Communicative as to this Event. I do not mean that they are peculiarly reserved in this Instance. But it is held Indelicate to Inquire of a member of Congress concerning any official Communications which they do not Chuse to Insert in the Publick Papers.

The People are some what Anxious to have Mr. Adams's Relation as they do not seem to Relish the British Insinuations, That he was put into a Deadly Freight by the Awfull Presence of the Royal Personage.

Boston Octr. 13. 1785

I wrote the above a few days since and endeavourd to Imagine myself in your Parlour at the Foot of Pens Hill, and all those questions which in a Cursory Chit Chat I supposed you might ask me I have answerd. I can not say it looks altogether pleasing on paper. I never subject my Correspondents to restrictions, but you will readily concieve what I mean. I Received a letter from your Son Yesterday.[7] He is well-pleased with his Situation and Expects to make Great Progress in his Studies. Your Sister Shaw is now at Bridgwater and will be at Braintree on Sunday next. Mr. Barret's Confinement was only Temporary and his affairs are Retrevable. Congress have made a Requisition for a large Sum of money from the States. The People are daily more Convinced of the Necessity of Extending the Powers of Congress and every day more averse to the measure. The Family at Ger[mantow]n, are as healthy as Usual, as to pecuniary affairs, Involved and Deploraple. Easters[8] Family is well. Fanny Nash, daughter to the Boatman, Dead. Young Mr. Palmer, is upon a Tour of Bussiness at the Eastward. I reside with them when in Boston. Our Family Consist at Present of Mrs. Clark and Son, Mr. Frazier and the Celebrated Dr. Moyes,[9] who is now delivering a Course of Lectures upon Natural History. You are Sensible I Trust Madam that notwithstanding haste and Inaccuracy I am with Respect your Friend

R Tyler

RC (Adams Papers); docketed on the first page: "1795 Tyler." Originally dated and filmed [*ante 13 Oct.*] (Adams Papers, Microfilms, Reel No. 366). Some damage on the right-hand margin of the first page, with slight loss of text.

[1] The supplied date is derived from Tyler's mention of the business failure of "S: B[arre]t. . . . upon the Seventh of this month."

[2] Not found.

[3] AA may have written this in her letter to Tyler of 9 May (not found); she apparently said much the same thing to JQA (see his letter to AA of 6 Oct., above).

[4] Eliphalet Pearson, Harvard 1773, was the master of Phillips Academy in Andover from its founding in 1778. He married his second wife, Sarah Bromfield, on 29 Sept., and succeeded Stephen Sewall to the Hancock (not Hollis) Professorship of Hebrew and other Oriental Languages in 1786. See Claude M. Fuess, *Andover: Symbol of New England, The Evolution of a Town*, Andover, Mass., 1959, p. 211–219; *Vital Records of Andover, Massachusetts*, Topsfield, Mass., 1912, vol. 2, p. 265; *Harvard Quinquennial Cat.*, p. 23, 195.

[5] Harrison Gray Otis read law with John Lowell from 1783 to 1786 (Samuel Eliot Morison, *Harrison Gray Otis, 1765–1848, The Urbane Federalist*, Boston, 1969, p. 39–42). Samuel Allyne Otis had been appointed a collector of clothing for the Continental Army in 1777 (same, p. 31). "Your uncle [*who*] has not sufferd" was AA's uncle Isaac Smith Sr., S. A. Otis' father-in-law. Joseph Otis was

419

S. A. Otis' "Brother at B[arnsta]ble"; Hannah Otis was his sister (Mary Cranch to AA, 14 Aug., and notes 17 and 18, above; *NEHGR*, 2:291–292 [July 1848]).

[6] Thomas Lindall Winthrop had probably courted Miss Derby in Salem, where he spent time in 1782–1783. See Lawrence Shaw Mayo, *The Winthrop Family in America*, Boston, 1948, p. 209, 212.

[7] Not found.

[8] Esther Field.

[9] Dr. Henry Moyes, a blind "philosopher of Natural History" on a lecture tour from Great Britain, announced a course of lectures in Boston, to begin in mid-October. At this same time, Moyes and Dr. Benjamin Waterhouse organized the Massachusetts Humane Society, devoted to saving victims of shipwrecks and other drowning accidents. *Mass. Centinel*, 3 Sept., 12 Oct.; Brooke Hindle, *The Pursuit of Science in Revolutionary America, 1735–1789*, Chapel Hill, 1956, p. 284–286.

John Quincy Adams to Mary Smith Cranch

My Dear Aunt   Haverhill. Octr. 8th. 1785

Mr. Thaxter will want a horse in a short time, to go a journey, and I should be glad, if mine is not wanted, that Charles should come with him; as he desires to. He will then be of some service and of no expense; if Uncle Tufts thinks proper, Charles can ride the horse here, when he comes. But if he does not think it for the best, will you favour me with a Line that I may inform Mr. Thaxter.

Cousin Betsy arrived here on Thursday evening, but Miss White will not let her come to keep house for us; but when Aunt returns she will spend some time here. Her being here affords me great pleasure. For I feel every day my aversion for forming new acquaintances, increase, and my affection for my old ones, take deeper root. I have seen no body since my arrival, and have been no where out of this house, excepting once at Mr. Thaxter's Office. Whenever I get settled in to my Studies, I feel as if I could live Hermit like: and I hope I may always preserve such Disposition to a degree.

All here, are well: Miss Hazen has as much gaiety, sociability and good nature as ever, Cousin B. Smith, as much solidity, prudence, and complaisance. Do you not think that these two Characters, which are both of them very amiable, form a striking contrast? It has often amused me to observe it.

Tommy does not study quite so hard as probably he would, *was his uncle at* home, and perhaps he may retort the charge, upon me. He attends however the writing school, very punctually.

Will you be so kind as to present my Respects and Compliments wherever they may be due, and especially to remember me to my uncle.

I am, my dear Madam, with every Sentiment of Respect, your Nephew   J. Q. Adams

RC (Private owner, New York, 1985); addressed: "Mrs. Mary Cranch Braintree"; docketed by Lucy Cranch: "J. Q. Adams. Haverhill 8. Octr. 1785. to my mother."

Elizabeth Cranch to Abigail Adams

My dear Aunt   Haverhill October 9th. 1785

You will percieve by the date of this that I am at H–: last thursday I arrived here. My Visit is to *Miss White*. She has spent the Summer in Boston, and has been attempting to learn Musick, like myself. She has brought her instrument to H– and sent me an invitation to come and pass a few months with her, and learn of her Master, who is a Man acquaintd with Musick, but not with much beside. He is poor, and thinks our employing him a *favour*. He is not so perfect a Master as Mr. Selby, but is so much more reasonable in his demands, that, we rather chose to make trial, for a little time.

Uncle and Aunt Shaw, are gone upon their *Annual* Visit, to Braintree &c &c. A young Man, belonging to Mr. Whites family, who was brought up in it, and is a very worthy member of it, will hand you this. His name is *James Wilson*. He came from England, *a* child. His father upon his return thither was unfortunately drowned. He has some relations there. In consequence of the death *of one of them*, who has left him a Legacy, he now makes this voyage, in a Ship belonging to Mr. William White of Boston. He sails in the course of this week. He is publishd to a worthy young Woman of this town, and will return in the Spring. Mr. White desired me to write by him. You will find a number of Letters from me in the same Ship, wrote a month since,[1] so that I can not say much at this time. We form a sweet agreable society here. Mr. Thaxter and My Cousin John, make to *me* a pleasing part of it, tho, I rather say this by *anticipation*, than from real enjoyment. Cousin J A, has been in town a fortnight, and has not yet made *one* Visit in it. *I* have been to see *him*. His Trunks did not arrive till yesterday, from Boston, and he was rather in a *Dishabille* for want of them. He will be very studious I doubt not. I wonder if his heart is *invulnerable* to the charms of the fair and beautiful, my dear Aunt? Not that I think it has *yet* recieved any impressions, but living in the house with a charming Girl,[2] *sprightly witty* and handsome, might have some effect upon *one less firm*, than my Cousin. Will you insure *him*? I think *you* would. But tis rather a dangerous situation I believe. He tells *me* his heart is wonderfully *Suceptible*, that he falls in Love one moment and is over the next. If so, I'll venture him—but I do not know him yet.

421

The matter is actually settled between Mr. Thaxter and Miss Duncan, at present, untill his bussiness is better, he will not be married. She is a fine Girl, and I believe he will never repent of his choice.

Our good Aunt Tufts has relapsed again into her late disagreable complaints, and we fear that she will not, cannot, struggle thro' them. I am sure that you will feel, with us, the breach such a loss would make in our connexions. But a change for her I doubt not would be happy.

Charles, Billy and Lucy, are coming to see us in the course of the *vacation* which begins next week. If Cousin Nabby was here she would compleat the company. All *your* Children and Mama's excepting *her*, will be here together. O how happy should we feel with that addition! I long to have more Letters from you, my dear Aunt. I am never satisfied, as soon as one Pacquett is read I am impatient for another. Continue to gratify me Madam by your kindness and attention in sending me those charming discriptions which from your Pen, have power to please almost equally, with the sight of them. You have another House, Gardens &c. to make me acquainted with, and I have an unbounded curiosity, to gratify.

Cousin Tommy *is* well and *does* well. I sent to know of them if they would not write by this opportunity, but they have already written. I thought, the later the Letters were the better, upon some accounts.

Please to remember most respectfully, & affectiona[te]ly to my Uncle & Cousin, & accept this triffling scrawl, only as a proof of the most dutiful affection of your ever obligd & grateful   E Cranch

RC (Adams Papers); addressed: "Madam Adams—Grosvenor Square. London"; with the notation: "favd by Mr James Wilson."

[1] Only that of 5 Sept. to AA, above, is known to the editors.
[2] Nancy Hazen.

Thomas Jefferson to Abigail Adams

Dear Madam   Paris Oct. 11. 1785

Your favor of the 7th. was put into my hands the last night and as I received at the same time dispatches from Mr. Adams[1] which occasion a great deal to be done for Congress to be sent by the Mr. Fitzhughs who set out tomorrow morning for Philadelphia as Mr. Preston the bearer of this does for London,[2] I have only time to thank you for your kind attention to my commission and your offer of new service. Your information as to the shirt linen draws a new scene of trouble on you. You had better have held your tongue about it: but as it is, you must submit to what cannot now be prevented and take better care hereafter. You will think it some apology for my asking you to order me a dozen shirts of the quality of the one sent, when I assure you they made me pay for it here 10 livres & a half the aune, which is at the rate of 6/6 sterl. the yard. I will pray you to chuse me linen as nearly as possible of the same quality because it will enable me to judge of the comparative prices of the two countries. There will probably be Americans coming over from London here in the course of the winter who will be so kind as to bring the shirts to me, which being ready made will escape the custom houses. I will not add to your trouble that of a long apology. You shall find it in the readiness and zeal with which I shall always serve you. But I find that with your friends you are a very bad accountant, for after purchasing the table linen, and mentioning the insurance money on Houdon's life, you talk of what will still remain due to me. The truth is that without this new commission I should have been enormously in your debt. My present hurry does not permit me to state the particulars, but I will prove it to you by the first opportunity. And as to the balance which will be due from me to Mr. Adams should he have no occasion of laying it out here immediately I will transmit it by some safe hand. I have not yet seen the table linen you were so kind as to buy for me, but I am sure it is good. The merchant here promises to shew me some of a new supply he has, which will enable me to judge somewhat of the two manufactures and prices. The difference must be considerable tho' to induce me to trouble you. Be so good as to present my respects to Miss Adams & to accept assurances of the esteem & respect with which I have the honour to be Dear Madam your most obedient & most humble sert.   Th: Jefferson

RC (Adams Papers); endorsed: "Mr Jefferson octr 11 1786."

[1] These were JA to Jefferson, 2 and 3 Oct., and the several items introduced and printed in Jefferson, *Papers*, 8:610–624, under the title "Documents Pertaining to the Mission of Barclay and Lamb to the Barbary States." JA signed these documents in London between 1 and 6 Oct.; Jefferson signed them in Paris on 11 October.

[2] Robert Preston reached London on 22 Oct., but told JA that he had unaccountably lost the letters that he was bringing to London from Jefferson. Preston did not accurately remember to whom these letters were addressed, but soon thereafter he found them. They included this letter, and Jefferson to JA, also 11 Oct. (Adams Papers). See JA to Jefferson, 24 Oct., and 4 Nov. (DLC:Jefferson Papers; printed in Jefferson, *Papers*, 8:663–664, 9:10–11), and AA to Jefferson, 25 Oct., and 24 Nov., both below.

Cotton Tufts to Abigail Adams

My Dear Madam   Octobr. 12. 1785

The anxious Sentiments of a Parent which You have manifested in the close of Your last Letter,[1] I have read with a sympathetic Feeling. It would give me singular Pleasure to have it in my Power to give you such Information as would entirely set your Mind at Ease.

I had hopes that Time would have produced such Evidence, as would have removed Doubt. I scarcely know what to say. If the Character in Question was a clearly desided one, I should not be at a Loss. If the Marks in favour of it are not such as to establish a full Confidence those against it are not such as to exclude all Hope. The Subject is delicate and I wish You to burn this as soon as You have read it, that it may not be open to the View of any other Person and should You wish for further Explanation, let me [be] assured of the Security of Your receiving it and its being confined to your own Breast. Whatever Friendship demands, I will tho' painful, at least attempt—and shall agreable to Your Desire, when I can find an Opportunity (which indeed but seldom occurs) and a Prospect of doing good, give the Advice requested.[2]

The Gold sent by Y[our] Son amounted to £51.7.10[3] lawf[ul] m[one]y. The greater part of it I have vested in State Notes. The remainder I propose to lay out in Pierce's. The former I bought @ 6/ 8 Per £ for the principal, the Interest on them are reckon'd at par. Pierces Notes are sold @ 3/ Per £.[4]

Yours   C. Tufts

RC (Adams Papers).

[1] Of [26 April], above; see Tufts to AA, 14 Oct., and note 1, below. AA briefly and rather obliquely discusses her concern about Royall Tyler in her May letter.

[2] See AA to Tufts, [26 April], above.

[3] An illegible symbol follows the number.

[4] Pierce's notes were the final settlement certificates issued to troops of the Continental Army after Congress assumed their claims in 1783. They bear the signature of Paymaster General John Pierce, and earned 6% interest. Soldiers frequently sold them at a discount for cash. See E. James Ferguson, *The Power of the Purse*, Chapel Hill, 1961, p. 179–180; William G. Anderson, *The Price of Liberty*, Charlottesville, 1983, p. 96–97.

Cotton Tufts to Abigail Adams

No. 1

My Dear Cousin   Weymouth Octobr. 14. 1785

Your agreable Letter of May. 10.[1] from Auteuil I received by your Son. His Absence You will feel and I do not wonder that you parted with him with Regret as his Ability to relieve his Parents from many Cares and Burdens must have been great. He is now pursuing his Studies with his Uncle Shaw, more especially in the Latin and Greek Languages. In other Respects he was qualified to have entered in the Third Year. With submission to Providence We propose agreable to the Advice of the President to offer him next April. He will then have a Year and a Quarter before taking a Degree. Master Charles is now at the University. He has a Chamber there, and I flatter myself from his good Dispositions, that I shall be able to give you much Pleasure in my future Communications.

As You are now in London I please myself with the Hopes, that my Letters will reach you with more Certainty and Security, than heretofore.

We have had a luxuriant Crop of Hay this Summer, but a [dr]ought succeeded and our Corn and latter Feed are very short. This, your Farm will feel. Pratt[2] has been unfortunate in the Loss of Two Horn Cattle and one Hog, the first by the horn Distemper, the second a young Hefer of some Disease unknown, the Hog died of a Distemper which has prevailed in Braintree among Swine. Phoebe tells me some of her Poultry have had the same Disorder. Some Horses have also died with it. It is said to be begin with a Swelling on the external Part of the Throat, increases till it prevents swallowing, even reaches to the Head and the Beast dies strangled. Diseases formerly unknown amongst our Cattle and Swine have latterly become frequent in one Part of the Country and another. If there is any Modern Treatise (that Mr. Adams can recommend and is not too bulky) wrote in England, I wish him to purchase for me and forward it. The Preservation of our Beasts is a Matter of great Consequence to us, there is scarcely a Farmer but what annually loses one or more.[3]

The Work on your House at Boston is compleated. Rents have fallen greatly and will be still lower, owing to the Scarcity of Money and frequent Bankrupcies. I am doubtful whether I shall be able to raise the Rent, notwithstanding the valuable Addition to the House.

I think it will be best to purchase the half of the House and Land which Elijah Belcher improves now claimed by the Heirs of ⁴ Apthorp. Mr. Morton their Attorney tells me as soon as he has got Possession, he shall dispose of it. This Purchase I should prefer to any others that have been proposed, as that half which Mr. Belcher lives in is tumbling to Pieces and greatly injures your half, and the land which belongs to it would make a valuable Addition to yours. Veazies is too poor to be purchased whilst Taxes are so high. Indeed our Farms are but of little Profit. Taxes and Labour consume it. Allen wishes to sell his Farm, and has solicited me to confer with him upon the Subject of Sale, but I have not had an Opportunity to visit him.

Sometime since Application was made to Mr. Isaiah Doane for the Payment of a Ballance of Accountt with which his late Father stood chargd on Mr. Adams's Books. Mr. Doane told Mr. Tyler, that he was confident that the Ballance was paid Mr. Adams on his Return from Portsmouth (or about that Time,)⁵ but he is not able to produce any Receipt. He however says if Mr. Adams will say that it has not been paid, He will instantly pay it, and desired that Mr. Adams might be wrote to on the Subject. I desired Mr. Tyler to draw out the Account which he has done and it is now enclosed⁶ and should be [issued?] as soon as may be to receive an Answer. I find that we are not to expect much from old Debts. I have received some Money collected from them as you will see by my Account transmitted to Mr. Adams.⁷

A wooden Bridge is now building from Charlestown to Boston. In the Spring Sessions of the General Court License was granted, a Company incorporated to enjoy the Toll for 40 Years—after which it is to enure to the Commonwealth—the Company to pay the University £200 per an. in lieu of the Ferrage. The Business is pursued with great Vigour and will be compleated in the Course of next Summer.

Mrs. Tufts has been confined to her Room for near Three M[onths] past and much of the Time to her Bed. Her Health has been failin[g for a?] Year or two past. Last Spring after her usual Cough, her Di[sease . . .?] on her Limbs and at length on her Ancles with excruciat[ing pain, with?] parts discoloured with a purple Hue terminating in a green and yellow Hue resembling the Dispersion of a Bruise. In the latter End of July she was seized with a Dysentery and for a considerable Time I viewed her Case as desperate. Of this she so far recovered as with help to walk across the Room. A Ten Days agone a Laxness came on and held with violence for some Days, has reduced her to extreme Weakness and I am apprehensive that I must ere long have to lament the Loss of my Bosom Friend.

Be pleased to remember me to Mr. Adams & Miss Nabby. I wish

for the Return of You all. May God preserve You in Health, crown my Friend's Labours with Success and believe me to be Your Affectionate Friend

Cotton Tufts

RC (Adams Papers). The MS is torn at one edge with some loss of text.

[1] AA to Cotton Tufts, [26 *April*], above, which she finished on 10 May. JQA probably delivered this letter to Tufts in Boston on 2 Sept. (*Diary*, 1:318).

[2] The Adams' tenant Matthew Pratt; see his payments in Tufts to JA, 10 Aug., enclosed accounts, above.

[3] See Cotton Tufts, "An Account of the Horn-Distemper in Cattle, with Observations on that Disease," in *Memoirs of the American Academy of Arts and Sciences*, 1 (1785):529–536.

[4] Left blank in MS. Tufts letter to AA of 13 April 1786 (Adams Papers) says that Morton, as attorney "to C. W. Apthorp, Esq.," offered Belcher's place for sale.

[5] Isaiah Doane was the son and heir of Elisha Doane, JA's client in the admiralty

case of Penhallow v. The *Lusanna*, first tried in Portsmouth, N.H., in Dec. 1777. See JA, *Legal Papers*, 2:352–395.

[6] Not found.

[7] See Tufts to JA, 10 Aug., above. Tufts' accounts show that £29 3s. 9 1/2d. in debts owed JA for his legal services were collected by Royall Tyler and paid to Tufts on 24 March. The sum of £3 7d. paid on 15 Dec. 1784 to Tufts by Alexander Hill, perhaps the Boston merchant and father of JA's 1774 law clerk Edward Hill, may also have been for JA's legal services (JA, *Papers*, 2:111; JA, *Legal Papers*, 1:ci). Together these sums amount to less than a tenth of the Adams' Massachusetts revenues for the fourteen months covered by Tufts' accounts.

Royall Tyler to John Adams

Sir
Braintree Octr. 15. 1785

It has not been without Anxiety, that I have refrained from addressing a Letter to you for some months past. But not having the Advantage of a Femiliar, or even the Honour of a Personal Acquaintance: There was but one Subject upon which I could write to you liberally: and I intended to have Desisted from that, Until the Completion of my Arrangements should enable me to Discuss it to our mutual Satisfaction. But as I am Apprehensive, that you may impute to some less pleasing motive, what really Originated in Respect: I Reassume my Pen.

I will observe generally, that although from the Unprecedented Scarcity of Current Coin in this Country; I have been impeded in the Collecting of my Dues, and Consequently retarded in the execution of my plans; I have at length brought them to such an Issue; That by the next Conveyence from this Port, I shall Candidly, and I think with great Propriety, Exhibit to you, the outlines of my Pecuniary Circumstances; and if you shall judge my Situation such, as to Countenance a Speedy Connection with your Daughter; I will hope your Consent and advice in the effecting of it. I shall with Pleasure resign this Task to your Judgment. As you are deeply Interested in it,

427

and I Fear that if it was left to me to determine; I should never suppose myself sufficiently prosperous or affluent, to render her Life Comfortable and Happy.

I need not Desire you, at that Time, to Recollect, that the Happiness of an only Daughter, depends not entirely upon the Character and Disposition, but in great measure upon the Prospects of the man, with whom she may be Connected: But I can Solicit you to Suffer no impulse of Delicacy to prevent your Delivering your opinion upon that Subject, with the Greatest Freedom.

The Preference you have given to your own Country by sending your Son home to compleat his Education, is spoken of here by Men of the First Character, as highly Gratefull to your Fellow Citizens. "This Conduct, say the People, if we could doubt Mr. Adamses Patriotism, affords an Unequivocal and Conclusive Evidence, that a Long and Extensive Intercourse with Foreigners, has not weakened his Attachment to his Native Land."

I am happy, that I can inform you, that your Son meets with general, Universal Respect and approbation: That he is remarked as having brought home no Tincture of what we Style, "European Frivolity of Manners," of which the Traveled Youth of our Country, Usually import so large a Quantity. He is Pleasing to The Old, as he is Respectfull in his Deportment; to The Young: as he affects no Superiority over the Youth of his Country, and Discovers none, except that which in his Conversation, is manifestly the Result of an Industrious improvement of Superior Advantages.

I Desire your Acceptance of a Bundle of American Pampletts &tc.[1] In Collecting them I have not Confined myself merely to what is Valuable, Excellent, or worthy your Acceptance; but have sent you indiscriminately whatsoever I can find that is New.

Amongst them you will percieve a Pamphlet, entitled "an Appeal to the Impartial Public &tc." This Production, I am Authorized to say, is by Mr. Sullivan, late Judge of the Supreme Judicial Court. It is Considerd here, as a pretty Exposition upon the Third Article of our Decleration of Rights. Mr. Parsons of Newbury Port, from some hints he lately gave, it is supposed, is preparing a Reply to it.[2] In that Case Mr. Sullivan assures me he shall rejoin. As I Esteem the Question of importance I wish to see it fairly Discuss'd.

The Liturgy published by the Society worshiping at the Stone Chapel in Boston,[3] is the present Topick of Conversation. They Declare themselves, as to Articles of Creed, to be Unitarian Christians: Mr. Freeman their Clergyman and the Bulk of the Society are of the Arrian Division of Anti-trinitarians. They Profess, however, to have calculated this Compilation, so as to offend no Class of Christians who can surmount the Objection of Using any set Form of Prayers.

They retain a remnant of the Episcopalian Leaven, as they are Desirous, that, Mr. Freeman should recieve ordination from the hands of some Bishop, and have made some kind of Private Application to Mr. Seabury, the Titular Bishop of Connecticut, for that Purpose; who it is said, will not Consent, Unless Mr. F. will previously Subscribe the Thirty Nine Articles of The English Church. If he should decline, they will apply to some European Bishop, and as their last Resort, they will Submit, if it can be effected, to the laying on of the hands of the Dissenting Pastors.[4]

I Rather hope they will not succeed in the Two former, as I Concieve, Independent Religious Societies are Conformable to the Genius of a Republican Government; and 'tho' I am for preserving the Rights of Consience in their most extensive Latitude, and am duly sensible, of the wide Difference there is between Civil and Ecclesiastical Powers, as they relate to our Government; Yet I humbly Concieve, that it is at least Desirable, that we should have no Authority confered upon our Citizens, whether Civil or Ecclesiastical, that shall be mediately or immediately Derived from any Foreign Power.

The Old Episcopalians affect to hold this Society in Contempt, for their innovating Spirit: but notwithstanding this, and although, *they* Refused to attend the General Convocation of the Episcopal Clergy, held at Philedelphia,[5] upon pretence of its being too expensive to send a Deligate, In a late meeting of the Episcopal Clergy of this State, held in Boston; they have materially alterd the Liturgy of the Church of England. This, I suppose they were obliged to do, in order to satisfy their Parishoners, who in this Enlightened Age and Country, would no longer be affronted with its monstrous Tenets and Glaring Absurdities. They yet, however, suffer themselves to be Styled, the Church of England, Forgeting that they have Assumed a Power, which by the Fundamental Canons of that Church, is vested in the Two houses of Convocation, and virtually in the British Parlement: and, that, in doing this, whether singly or Conjunctively; they are become, as to Church Constitution, as Real Independents, as any of our Forefathers, who Fled from Hierarchical Persecution.

The People of Connecticutt, notwithstanding their Hereditary Prejudices against the very name of Bishop, appear to Treat Mr.

Seabury with Respect and those of his persuasion with Liberality. The Congregational Clergy of that State, 'Tho' they must know his power to be extremely Circumscribed, and in its nature and pretensions merely Ecclesiastical, appear to be envious or jelous of this New Church Dignitary, and as they cannot deprive the Right Reverand Father of his Title, They attempt to merge its Dignity, in its general Use, Styling each other Indiscriminately, "Bishops of the Church of Christ." The Greek Terms, Εωίσκοπος and Πρεσβύτερος,[6] being applied Synonymously in Scripture, as they say, to the same Officer of the Church. President Stiles lately wrote a Letter to a Friend of mine, and addressed it *"To the Revd. John Clark Bishop of the First Church of Christ in Boston,"*[7] and the Graduates in the Dedication of their Thesis at the late Publick Commencement at Yale College, in the address to The Clergy, have Alterd The Usual Form of, "Ecclesiarum *Pastoribus* &tc," for, "Omnibus Ecclesiarum Nostrarum *Episcopis* Venerandis."[8]

At the late Commencment, Application was made to the President, that some Convenient Place might be Asigned for the Bishop and his Clergy in the Meeting-house. The President's Reply to the Gentleman who applied to him on behalf of the Bishop, I am Informed was, "Sir. There are one hundred and Seventy Six Bishops in this State; it is Customary for them to seat themselves promiscuously, as they enter the Building upon the Commencment day; and as President of this College, I do not Esteem myself Authorized to break through Established Customs and make any Invidious Distinctions among them."

Some workmen, removing a large Stone at the Corner of an Old Wall in Mystick, discoverd about Three months ago, near Three hundred small Brass Coins. I inclose you one of them. If you Think it of sufficient Consequence, you will oblige me by shewing of it to some Antiquarian of your Acquaintance. Our Literati Conjecture, that the impression bears some Considerable Resemblence to the Characters upon the *Taunton* Rock, a Transcript of which you may probably recollect to have seen in the Museum of Harvard College.[9]

There are Two Pampletts which I wish to peruse. As they are not known here, except by Report, I shall, venture to take the Liberty of Desiring you to present them to your Daughter, who will inclose them to me. The one is, the Translation, with the Translators Preface, of the Abbe Mably's "Observations sur le Gouvernement et les loix des etats unis d'Amerique." The other is, Wattsons, I Believe Bishop Wattsons, "Observations upon Gibbons's Roman Empire."[10]

Your Son went from Boston to Haverhill, The Twenty ninth day of September. He proposes to tarry the ensuing Winter at his Uncle's, and offer himself as a Candidate for the Senior Class immediately after the next Commencement.

Your Mother enjoys as much health, as is usual for person's of her Age. She has Desired me to give her Love to you, Mrs. A. and your Daughter, and hopes to live to see you once more at Braintree.

Capt. Young it is supposed will sail for England the Begining of the next month, but this is Uncertain from the almost Insuperable Difficulties the Merchants find in procuring Remittances.

The French Propositions, respecting the purchase of our Whale Oil,[11] are generally Acceptable. Our Politicians applaud the French Conduct, in this Instance; as the most Politick Commercial Manœuvre they have ever Displayed, and the most Adequate to the purpose of Detaching us from our British Commercial Connections.

There will be no Mercantile Company formed in this State, in consequence of their proffers, but our Merchants propose sending Mr. Nathanil Barret,[12] son to Deacon Barret, to France, to Negotiate Privileges for the People at large, similar, to what they have offerd to a Commercial Association.

Sir I am with the Greatest Respect Your Most Obliged   R: Tyler

RC (Adams Papers); endorsed: "Royal Tyler Esqrs Letter. 15. Oct. 1785 ansd 12. Decr."; and notation: "Dr Hunter."

[1] This bundle of pamphlets has not been found, but see the items that Tyler names, below.

[2] *An Appeal to the Impartial Public by the Society of Christian Independents*, Boston, 1785 (Evans, No. 19028), was James Sullivan's defense of the Universalists of Gloucester in their refusal to pay taxes for the support of the town minister; see also *Sibley's Harvard Graduates*, 15:307. Article 3 of "A Decleration of Rights," governing the establishment of religion in Massachusetts, was one of the few sections of the Massachusetts Constitution of 1780 that JA did not write (JA, *Papers*, 8:238, and note 12). No record of a reply to Sullivan by Theophilus Parsons has been found.

[3] On 19 June, the congregation of King's Chapel (the Stone Chapel) approved *A Liturgy, Collected Principally from the Book of Common Prayer, for the Use of the First Episcopal Church in Boston*, Boston, 1785 (Evans, No. 18938), which their Unitarian pastor, James Freeman, prepared by removing Trinitarian passages from the Book of Common Prayer, following the reformed liturgy made by Dr. Samuel Clarke of London (*DNB*).

[4] After both Bishop Samuel Seabury, in 1785, and Bishop Samuel Provoost of New York, in 1787, declined to ordain Freeman, he was ordained in Nov. 1787 by the senior warden of King's Chapel, Dr. Thomas Bulfinch (same; F. W. P. Greenwood, *A History of King's Chapel*, Boston, 1833, p. 135–142, 185–198).

[5] See the *Journal of a Convention of the Protestant Episcopal Church . . . Held . . . in the City of Philadelphia, from September 27th to October 7th*, Phila., 1785.

[6] Tyler erroneously wrote ω for π in ἐπίσκοπος. In the King James Bible these New Testament words are translated, respectively, as "overseer" (Acts 20:28); and "elder" (1 Timothy 5:17; Titus 1:5; Hebrews 11:2; and elsewhere).

[7] John Clarke was ordained in 1778 as a pastor of the First Church (Congregational) of Boston, assisting the aged Rev. Charles Chauncy, and became chief pastor at

Chauncy's death in 1787 (*The Commemoration by the First Church in Boston of the Completion of Two Hundred and Fifty Years*, Boston, 1881, p. 202).

[8] The second phrase is a part of the long title of Yale College's commencement proceedings, *Illustrissimo Matthaeo Griswold, . . . Hasce Theses, Quas in Comitiis Publicis Collegii-Yalensis*, New Haven, 1785 (Evans, No. 19393).

[9] Taunton Rock, an exposed ledge on the bank of the Taunton River, was and is better known as Dighton Rock. The prominent inscription on its face attracted the attention of New Englanders from the seventeenth century and several transcriptions of the curious characters were made, beginning in 1680. Speculation on the identity of the engravers ranged from Phoenicians to Norse. See Edward Everett, "The Discovery of America by the Northmen," *North American Review*, 98:188–189 (Jan. 1838); James Phinney Baxter, "Early Voyages to America," *Collections of the Old Colony Historical Society*, 4 (1889):15–17, 48–49. For JA's reception of the coins found at Mystic, see JA to Tyler, 12 Dec., below.

[10] On Gabriel Bonnet, Abbé de Mably's *Observations sur le gouvernement et les loix des Etats-Unis d'Amérique*, see AA to Mary Cranch, 5 Sept. 1784, note 1, above. In 1776, Richard Watson, who was consecrated bishop of Llandaff in 1782, had published his *Apology for Christianity . . . Letters . . . to Edward Gibbon*, a popular critique of the view of Christianity expressed in Gibbon's *Decline and Fall of the Roman Empire* (*DNB*).

[11] See JQA to AA2, 29 Aug., and note 2, above; Jefferson, *Papers*, 10:293–294, and note.

[12] Nathaniel Barrett did soon travel to France for this purpose. See the letters introducing him to Thomas Jefferson by Gov. James Bowdoin, 23 Oct., by Lt. Gov. Thomas Cushing, 25 Oct., and by JA, 2 Dec., in Jefferson, *Papers*, 8:662–663, 670–671; 9:73–75.

Abigail Adams 2d to John Quincy Adams

N 8.

Grosvenor Sqr. october 1⟨4⟩8th [1785][1]

Mr. James Jarvis called upon us yesterday but we were not at home. To day he wrote to Pappa[2] to let him know that he should sail next week for New York, and would take any Letters from this family. Altho I wrote Last week by Capt. Calliham[3] I will not permit this opportunity to escape me. Mamma tells me She is sure I cannot find anything to say, as I have written so largly so lately, but Calliham who has lain at Deal since Wedensday, waiting for a Wind, may continue there these three weeks and my Letter may be very old before it reaches you. I have not yet the pleasure to acknowledge the receipt of Letters from you since your arrival in Boston but we are eagerly expecting this happiness soon, two Vessells are expected one dayly. And if you do not write wo be to you.——I shall in future write by the English packet to New York. They have in general very fine passages, the september packet arrived last week in 28 days, and the august had less than thirty. Opportunities do not often present to Boston and besides, I have no inclination to have my Letters taken by those Barbarians,[4] as we fear there is danger. I wrote you in my Last by

Calliham, No. 7, that it was thought absolutely necessary that some Person should be procured to go with Lamb, to Algiers and a Person in whom the most perfect Confidence could be placed, some body who would have an eye over him and if he should go astray inform your Father. Mr. Lamb being an utter stranger to Both your father and Mr. Jefferson ⟨and⟩ his appearance not being much in his favour, and the delay he had made was so much against his judgment or penetration. If Charles[5] had not have sailed by a week so soon as he did, he would have been the proper Person for he was desirious of going with Mr. Barclay, and whether fortunately or unfortunately I know not, but he had sailed two days before your father heard of Lambs arrival. All the young Americans in Paris an London were thought of, and the choice fixd upon Mr. Randall our friend. He was applied to, and upon consideration agreed to go. He had first one matter to adjust—what think you was it—it seems his visit to this Country was to renew an attachment early formed with a young Lady Miss M. White whose family Left America during the War. He was soon to have been Married to her, and to have gone out to America, but the cause of humanity the Interest of his Country and the happiness of very many indivi[duals?] being engaged and under these particular circumstances depending in some measure upon him he hessitated not to go, and on fryday the 7th. of october sett of with Colln. Franks for Paris. The Whole matter is kept secret here, for the pres[ent], because it is thought that their success will in some measure depend upon its not being made known here, as the interst or influence of *this* Country may be employed to frustrate their designs. They have such a strong affection for America here, that their good offices would be employed I suppose to do us as much ill as possible.[6]

Tuesday August [*October*] the 4th

We had a large company to dine. Mr. and Mrs. Johnson, Mr. Ridley Mr. and Mrs. Hay Mr. and Mrs. Jebb, Dr. Bancroft Mr. Joy. Mrs. Joy was invited but was prevented comeing by indisposition. Mrs. Smith from Carrolina and Mr. Hamilton and his pretty neice, who is really a sweet Girl. I intend to be better acquainted with her, her manners are delicate sprightly affable and agreeable. She is yet very young only fifteen. Her Uncle appears to have for her the affection of a Parent and treats her in every respect as his own Daughter. Most of the Company you know, and you may know that there is very little to say about them.[7]

Wedensday 5th

We went to the Play, through the Courtesy of Mr. Hamilton who had taken a Box, and gave us an opportunity to have seats. The Play was the West Indian[8] by their Majestys Command, and who were present with the Princess Royal[9] and Augusta. The Celebrated Mrs. Abington played the part of Mis Rusport and it was to be sure most wretchedly performed. Stiff aukord insensible and unfeeling, void of that engaging delicacy which the character merited, was this Paragon of Perfection. She is fifty years oold and no one would have thought her more than twenty from her appearance.[10]

Fryday 7th

Mr. Randall set off with Colln. F— for Paris. Mr. Jennings dined with us—you know him.

Anecdote. A Member of Parliament meeting at Stockdales and conversing about American affairs which Led him to speak of your father said I hear Mr. Adams gives good dinners. I dare say he does answerd Stockdale and would willingly give you a dinner if you will visit him. Ah said the Gentleman I am glad to hear it for I thought they were starving like the rest of his Country men.

Query. Would it not be for the reputation of America were Congress to give their Ministers a salary sufficient to support himself and family, with[out] putting it in the Power of these People [to] make such assertions, as these[11]—"Mr. Adams lives away now but he is distressed to know what he shall do next year." Dont you think they are very kind to interest themselvs to much in our behalf.

Sunday 9th

Mr. Duker secretary of Legation to the Baron de Lynden dined with us en famile. He has been in America as secretary to Mr. Van Berkell and speaks English very well. I asked him about Miss Van Berkel who is in America. He has [hears?] She speaks French and is a very worthy agreeable young Lady—this to confute the assertion of a certain Gentleman.[12]

Monday 10th

Your father received Letters this Morning from New York.[13] I was disappointed in not hearing from you. I think you should have left Letters to have been forwarded. Pappa decides *as usual* that our continuance in Europe will be no longer than the Spring. *Je suis Content.* If I had not heard him say so ever since we have been here

I should think more of it, tho perhaps he had never before the same reasons to found his opinion upon. We know that it depends upon the measures adopted by this Country. Politicians say that it is their interest to act such a part towards America as should make us mutual friends. Should their conduct be such as to induce Pappa to return in the Spring I confess I should fear the consequences as distructive to our Present tranquility, tho I do not pretend to understand Politicks.

Tuesday 11th

Your Fathers friends the Abbées Arnoux and Challut introduced to us a Mr. Pointsa,[14] a French sculptor who has resided five and twenty years in Italy. He dined with us to day, and appeard un homme a d'Esprit, and possessed of a great share of knowledge which rendered his conversation very interesting and agreeable. There is so strong a Principle in the Mind of addapting itself to whatever situation in which it may be placed by ⟨*Chance*⟩ necessity or choice as to produce a strong partiallity to whatever spot ⟨*it may*⟩ we may have chanced to reside for a long time. This Gentleman was one instance more to confirm me in this sentiment. From having lived 25 years in Italy he thought it superior to every other Country in the World. Perhaps it may be.

I inquired after Mademoisell Lucilla, and this Gentleman tells me she is going to be Married, to the Young Gentleman who lived with the Farmer General, and who dined with us there.[15] I dont recollect his Name. He has neither family nor Fortune, but merit. And the Farmer General will it is probable Leave all his fortune or the greatest part of it to this young Lady who proves to be instead of an *Enfant trouva* his own Natural Daughter. This Gentleman told us he knew her Mother. He added that she might have married ⟨*a Man of Fortune*⟩ un [grand?] seigneur but preferd this gentleman. I hope if affection is the Motive of choice She will not follow the example of many of her Countrymen, nor he of his.

Saturday october 15

The affair of Capt. Stanhope has been received here the Last week, and has been related in the papers ⟨*with as much falshood as*⟩ in a very false point of veiw. It is represented that Capt. Stanhope was insulted from appearing in the Streets with his uniform.[16] Pappa has a ⟨*full*⟩ true account of the matter from Boston and orders from Congress, to represent it to the Ministry here. It is rather unfortunate as it will unavoidably create parties. He is son to a Gentle[man] who is Usher to the Queen, but his Character is ⟨that of a⟩ not very fair. He applied for some promotion not long since and was refused. General How said he did not know why a young mans indiscretion should plead in his favour. The Papers said to Day that He treated American Prisners in a cruel manner during the War. Every one who hears Jesse Dunbars story seem to regret that he did not have an opportunity to give Capt. S— one blow.

Dft (Adams Papers). The text is written on nine small pages; the first eight are numbered.

¹ AA2 probably first intended to close this letter after completing the text under "Tuesday 11th," below, and wrote "october 14" in the dateline; then, after deciding to add the material under "Saturday october 15," below, she altered the dateline to its present form.

² Not found.

³ AA2 to JQA, 24 Sept., above, completed on 1 Oct., a Saturday.

⁴ The Barbary pirates.

⁵ Charles Storer.

⁶ A fuller account of Paul Randall's decision to accept JA's request that he accompany Capt. John Lamb on the mission to Algiers is in AA2, *Jour. and Corr.*, [3]:187–189, 191, which says that Col. Franks suggested Randall. See also AA to JQA, 5 Oct., above; and Jefferson, *Papers*, vols. 8–10.

⁷ AA2, *Jour. and Corr.*, [3]:190, adds Col. Franks to this dinner party.

⁸ *The West Indian*, a comedy by Richard Cumberland, was first performed in 1771.

⁹ Princess Charlotte.

¹⁰ Frances Abington was a prominent actress at Covent Garden in the early 1780s. The role in *The West Indian* was "Lady," not "Mis," Rusport (*DNB*; *The Oxford Companion to English Literature*, ed. Sir Paul Harvey, Oxford, 1932). In her journal, AA2 adds: "The entertainment was the Rehearsal, a very stupid piece. Their majesties showed their taste, as it was the result of their command" (*Jour. and Corr.*, [3]:191).

¹¹ The bracketed material is added from the nearly identical sentence, ending "as these," in AA2, *Jour. and Corr.*, [3]:192–193.

¹² AA2 probably wrote this brief endorsement of Miss van Berckel, daughter of the Dutch minister to the United States, in response to JQA's reference to an attack upon her character by an unidentified critic in his letter of 1 August, above. Mr. Duker may have been P. G. Duker who served as the Netherlands' chargé d'affaires at Stockholm, 1781–1782 (*Repertorium der diplomatischen Vertreter aller Länder*, 3:269).

¹³ These probably included letters from Samuel Tucker (at Trenton), 29 Aug., Walter Livingston, 5 Sept., and John Jay, 6 Sept. (all Adams Papers). JA acknowledged receiving the last in his 15 Oct. letter to Jay (PCC, No. 84, V, f. 661). Jay's letter is in *Dipl. Corr.*, *1783–1789*, 2:387–389; JA's is in same, 2:478–479. See also AA2 to JQA, 24 Sept., note 11, above.

¹⁴ The reading of AA2's difficult hand, particularly the first two characters, is uncertain here, and the editors have not identified the artist. AA2, *Jour. and Corr.*, [3]:194, has "Mr. Pointea."

¹⁵ On 28 Oct. 1784, the Adamses dined at the home of Chalut de Vérin, one of the Farmers General of France, and a brother of the Abbé Chalut. On that occasion they met a young lady who called Chalut "mon père," and whom he called "mon fille." JA then told AA2 that the young lady had been chosen out of a foundling hospital by Mme. Chalut, and raised as her own daughter. Mme. Chalut had died a few years before AA2 met Chalut. On 31 Dec., AA2 met the young lady again, at the abbés Arnoux and Chalut, and there named her, "Mademoiselle Lucelle." AA2, *Jour. and Corr.*, 1:29–30, 37. By Jan. 1786 she was married to Monsieur Deville (Jefferson, *Papers*, 9:152; and see 16:306).

¹⁶ The London *Daily Universal Register* of 14 Oct. reported that Capt. Stanhope of the *Mercury* and his officers, "were insulted and stoned by the populace, who desired them to leave off their uniforms, d——d the K—g their master, and nearly killed Captain Stanhope

and two of his crew with stones." The article also summarized the correspondence between Stanhope and Gov. Bowdoin, related the publishing of "low and scurrilous abuse" in Boston newspapers (for examples of which see the *Massachusetts Centinel*, 3 and 6 Aug.), and concluded with Stanhope's threat, "that if any further insult was offered to the King's flag or his officers, he would lay part of [*Boston*] about his ears." A brief paragraph in the same newspaper of 17 Oct. mentioned that, "to the great satisfaction of every friend of peace and good order," the *Mercury* had

sailed from Boston.

Under a covering letter of 7 Dec., Lord Carmarthen sent to JA the Admiralty's report on the incident. In their report, also dated 7 Dec., the Lords of the Admiralty declared that, despite some extenuating circumstances, Capt. Stanhope's conduct had been unduly provocative and contrary to his orders (*Dipl. Corr., 1783–1789*, 2:545–548).

AA relates another version of these events in her letter to Thomas Jefferson of 19 Oct., immediately below.

Abigail Adams to Thomas Jefferson

Dear sir   London October 19 1785

Mr. Fox a young Gentleman from Philadelphia who came recommended by Dr. Rush to Mr. Adams,[1] will have the Honour of delivering you this Letter. We requested him to call upon Mr. Stockdale for your papers &c. Mr. Adams is unwell,[2] and will not be able to write you by this opportunity. I am to acquaint you Sir that Dr. Price has transacted the buisness respecting Mr. Hudon. The Money is paid, but the policy is not quite ready but the Dr. has promised that it shall be sent in a few days, when it will be forwarded to you.

In your English papers you will find an extract of a Letter from Nova Scotia, representing the abuse said to be received by a Captain Stanhope at Boston, the Commander of the Mercury. The account is as false—if it was not too rough a term for a Lady to use, I would say false as Hell, but I will substitute, one not less expressive and say, false as the English.

The real fact is this. One Jesse Dumbar a native of Massachusetts, and an inhabitant of a Town near Boston and one Isaac Lorthrope were during the War taken Prisoners, and from one ship to an other were finally turnd over to this Captain Stanhope Commander of the Mercury, who abused him and the rest of the Prisoners, frequently whiping them, and calling them Rebels. The ship going to Antigua to refit, he put all the prisoners into Jail and orderd poor Jesse 2 dozen lashes for refusing duty on Board his ship. This Mr. Dumbar felt as an indignity and contrary to the Law of Nations. Peace soon taking place Jesse returnd Home, but when Stanhope came to Boston, it quickened Jesses remembrance and he with his fellow sufferer went to Boston, and according to his deposition, hearing that Captain

Stanhope was walking in the Mall, he went theither at noon day and going up to the Captain asked him if he knew him, and rememberd whiping him on Board his Ship.[3] Having no weapon in his hand, he struck at him with his fist, upon which Captain Stanhope, stept back and drew his sword. The people immediately interposed and gaurded Stanhope to Mr. Morten Door. Dumbar and his comrade following him, and at Mr. Mortens door he again attempted to seize him. But then the high sheriff interposed and prevented further mischief, after which they all went to their several homes. This Mr. Stanhope calls assassination and complains that the *News papers* abuse him. He wrote a Letter to the Govenour demanding protection. The Govenour replied by telling him that if he had been injured the Law was open to him and would redress him, upon which he wrote a very impudent abusive Letter to Mr. Bowdoin, so much so that Mr. Bowdoin thought proper to lay the whole correspondence before Congress. And Congress past some resolves in concequence and have transmitted them with Copies of the Letters to be laid before Mr. Stanhopes Master.[4]

Dumbars Deposition was comunicated in a private Letter by Mr. Bowdoin himself to Mr. Adams, so that no publick use can be made of it, but the Govenour was sensible that without it the truth would not be known.[5]

Is Col. Smith in Paris? Or have we lost him? Or is he so mortified at the King of Prussias refusing him admittance to his Reviews, that he cannot shew himself here again? This is an other English Truth, which they are industriously Circulating. I have had however, the pleasure of contradicting the Story in the most positive terms, as Col. Smith had enclosed us the Copy of his own Letter and the answer of his Majesty, which was written with his own hand.[6] How mean and contemptable does this Nation render itself?

Col. Franks I hope had the good fortune to carry your things safely to you, and that they will prove so agreeable as to induce you to honour again with your Commands your Friend & Humble Servant

Abigail Adams

Compliments to the Gentlemen of your family and Love to Miss Jefferson. Mr. Rutledge has refused going to Holland. I fancy foreign embassies upon the present terms are no very tempting objects.

RC (DLC:Jefferson Papers); addressed by AA2: "His Excellency Thomas Jefferson Esqr Minister Plenipotentiary from the United states of America Paris favour by Mr Fox"; endorsed: "Mrs Adams." Dft (Adams Papers); notation by CFA: "1786." The

RC is longer with more detail, but the Dft contains some important variants and additional passages that are noted below.

[1] Samuel Fox, of a well-known Quaker family in Philadelphia, was introduced in Benjamin Rush to JA, 16 June (Adams Papers). Rush introduced Fox to Jefferson in a letter of the same date (Jefferson, *Papers*, 8:220).

[2] The draft finishes this sentence: "and I know not whether he will be able to write You as Mr. Fox set[s] of early tomorrow morning."

[3] The draft has "the Mercury", but Dunbar's deposition names the ship on which he was whipped as the *Russell*. AA may have re-read the deposition before preparing the recipient's copy; see note 5, below.

[4] The draft has "his Majesty" in place of "Mr. Stanhopes Master."

[5] In the draft this passage reads: "Dumbars deposition was sent by Mr. Bowdoin himself to Mr. Adams and is not amongst the papers forwarded by Congress. The abuse of Stanhope to Mr. Bowdoin is however evident enough without knowing the real cause. He has powerfull connections here and is of a respectable family, but his own Character is said to be that of a profligate. The Marquis of Carmarthan has been absent which has prevented his yet receiving the communications. Tomorrow they will be presented."

Gov. James Bowdoin wrote JA on 10 Aug. (Adams Papers), to state his side of the affair so that Adams could defend the honor of Massachusetts and the United States in this controversy. With his letter Bowdoin enclosed both a copy of the deposition of Jesse Dunbar (not Dumbar) of Hingham, Mass., dated 10 Aug. (Adams Papers), and copies of the five letters that he exchanged with Stanhope between 1 and 4 Aug. (all Adams Papers), which Bowdoin had sent to Congress. Dunbar's deposition, which AA's account here follows almost verbatim, gives the rough dates of his captivity, from 1780 until the peace, but not the date of his whipping aboard the 74-gun ship *Russell* at Antigua. It also names his companion, both on the *Russell* and in the Mall in Boston on 31 July, as William (not Isaac) Lathrop of Sandwich, Mass. (although "William" is inserted above the line).

In his letter of 10 Aug., Gov. Bowdoin told JA that until Congress decided what action to take the enclosed letters were only for his information. On 18 Aug., Congress voted to accept Secretary for Foreign Affairs John Jay's report, based on the five letters, which strongly protested Stanhope's behavior to the British government. Jay wrote JA on 6 Sept., forwarding this protest and directing him to present it, with the letters, to the British secretary of state (Adams Papers; *Dipl. Corr., 1783–1789*, 2:387–296). The Bowdoin-Stanhope correspondence appeared in the London *Daily Universal Register* on 21 October.

Dunbar's deposition, however, was neither sent to Congress nor presented to Lord Carmarthen, and therefore was not part of the official account of this incident. Capt. Stanhope, in his letters to Bowdoin, had not mentioned Dunbar by name, but said only that he had "been pursued and my Life as well as that of one of my Officers [*had*] been endanger'd by the violent Rage of a Mob Yesterday Evening without Provocation of any sort." He then urged Bowdoin "to adopt such Measures as may discover the Ringleaders of the Party that *Assassinated* me, and bring them to Public Justice" (Stanhope to Bowdoin, 1 Aug., copy in Adams Papers). While Bowdoin disapproved of Dunbar's assault, he felt that Stanhope had overreacted, particularly considering the orderly behavior of the crowd and the prompt action of the sheriff to protect Stanhope. And because Stanhope had not named Dunbar, Bowdoin saw no need to refer to him, but answered: "If you have been insulted, and your Life has been endangered, in manner as you have represented to me, I must inform you, that our Laws afford you ample satisfaction" (Bowdoin to Stanhope, 1 Aug., copy in Adams Papers). This reply incited Stanhope to stronger protests, prompting Bowdoin to send the correspondence to Massachusetts' delegates for presentation to Congress.

Jefferson became deeply interested in this incident, and sometime in November he wrote a brief account of the affair, to which he added a legal defense of Gov. Bowdoin's position, probably with an eye to publishing it in the Continental press to counter versions of the story that had just appeared in English newspapers which AA had forwarded to him (AA to Jefferson, 25 Oct., below; see AA2 to JQA, 18 Oct., note 16, above). Jefferson's principal source, in addition to the Bowdoin-Stanhope letters that had already appeared in print, was Dunbar's deposition, in the form in which AA summarized it in this letter. See Jefferson to AA, 20 Nov., below, and "Jefferson's Account of the Stanhope Affair," undated, in Jefferson, *Papers*, 9:4–7. Congress' handling of the affair is in *JCC*, 29:637–647 [18 Aug. 1785].

[6] In the draft AA ends this paragraph: "How feeble must that cause be which ⟨only⟩ has baseness meanness and falshood for its support. How contemptable does this Nation render itself?" See William Stephens Smith to AA, 5 Sept., and note 7, above.

Mary Smith Cranch to Abigail Adams

My dear Sister   Braintree [*ca.* 23] october 1785[1]

I hope my dear Sister you have receiv'd the Letter You was looking for in Callahan.[2] I think I did not send it till the next Ship Saild. I have put a very long letter aboard this Ship a month since,[3] supposing she would sail in a few days. Last night I receiv'd your Letter of the 16th of august[4] and am not a little surpriz'd at the contents.

My dear Niece has acted with a Spirit worthy of her Parents. We have been for a long time very anxious for her Happiness. I have been so affraid of making mischief that I know not if I have done my duty towards her. As it has turn'd out I am thankful I have said no more, but dear girl what a time she has had of it ever since she has been in Europe. I hope she will now enjoy herself, and that you my Sister will have more tranquil moments than I am sure you have had for these three years. She may assure herself of the approbation of every Friend she has. You need not fear any thing from *general* Palmer's Family: she will have nothing else there. I will give you the reason some other time, at present the least that is said will be best. I have not seen him, for a month. He boards at Mrs. Palmers at Boston.

Aunt Tufts my dear Sister has almost exchang'd this world for a better. She discovers great fortitude patience and resignation. She cannot continue many days I think. She has been like a Parent to us. Tis hard parting with such dear Freinds.

Mr. Shaw and Sister went from here last week. She looks better than I have seen her some time. Your Sons were well. I had a charming Letter from Cousin John.[5] Betsy he says has made him very happy by making her visit at Haverhil while he is there. He is very studious. Cousin Charles is here, 'tis their Fall vacancy.[6] He behaves well at college, loves his Tutor exceedingly. This is a very good Sign; He Loves his Aunt too, I believe, and that is another good sign. You know not my dear Sister how attach'd I feel myself to these children.

Your mother Hall is well and I believe contented. I have heard nothing since. I shall deliver her the money when it arrives.

Esters Friends are all well, all your Neighbours are so except Eben.

Belchers wife who I believe has almost kill'd herself with Rum. She is very sick and poor not a shift to her Back nor a Blanket to cover her.

Mr. Cranch deliver'd your compliments to Mr. and Mrs. Apthorp, soon after they sent in, the inclos'd Billit.[7] I send it as I could not express their Sentiments so well.

Cousin Betsy Kent is here and desires me to give her Love to you all. I have the same request from so many (uncle Quincy and Mr. Wibird in particular) that my paper will not hold their names. Miss Hannah Clark is publish'd. That Family are among the number who remember you with affection. Huldy Kent, Hannah and Sally Austin are thinking about matrimony.[8]

Lucy has already written you[9] but desires her Duty. Billy is at home and sends his. Mr. Cranch will send you some chocolate if he can find any that is good, and can get the capn. to take it in his chest. He desires his Love to you. He has sent a Long Letter to Mr. Adams[10] and all the news papers since the first seting of the Court to this day.

My most affectionate regards to him if you please & believe me your affectionate Sister

RC (Adams Papers); filmed under the date Oct. 1785 (Adams Papers, Microfilms, Reel No. 366).

[1] Two visits mentioned in the letter suggest that Mary Cranch wrote on either 23 or 24 October. Sunday was the 23d, the first day of the new week since the departure of Rev. John and Elizabeth Shaw from Braintree "last week"; they arrived in Haverhill on 20 Oct. (JQA, *Diary*, 1:344). CA's visit to Braintree during Harvard's fall vacation, ended with his departure for Haverhill on 24 or 25 Oct. (same, 1:347).

[2] Mary Cranch to AA, 19 July, above; see AA's letter to Cotton Tufts, 18 Aug., above, for her disappointment upon not receiving any letters from America by Capt. Callahan.

[3] That of 14 Aug., above, finished on 16 September.

[4] Dated 15 Aug., above, but finished on the 16th.

[5] Of 8 Oct., above.

[6] The fall vacation break at Harvard extended for two weeks, ending on 2 Nov. (JQA, *Diary*, 1:347, 350).

[7] Not found.

[8] Huldah Kent, apparently a granddaughter of AA's paternal aunt, Anna Smith Kent, married Rev. Israel Evans in 1786 (Cotton Tufts to AA, 14 Oct. 1786, Adams Papers). Hannah and Sally Austin were probably granddaughters of AA's paternal aunt, Mary Smith Austin (Thomas B. Wyman, *The Genealogies and Estates of Charlestown*, Boston, 1879, 1:29; 2:874).

[9] On 19 Sept., above.

[10] Richard Cranch to JA, 13 Oct. (Adams Papers).

Abigail Adams to Thomas Jefferson

Sir   London october 25 1785

I should not so soon have ventured to interrupt your more important avocations by an other Scrible, having writen you a few Days since, if it was not to inform you of the loss of your Letters by Mr. Preston.[1] He says that when he landed at Dover, he was very sick, and that he could not accompany his trunk to the Custom House, into which for *security* he had put his Letters, but upon his arrival here he found he had lost them; so that unless your Letter should contain any thing for the English News papers I fear I shall never know its contents. The Gentleman deliverd me a little bundle, by the contents of which I conjecture What you design,[2] but must request you to repeat your orders by the first opportunity, that I may have the pleasure of punctually fulfilling them.

A Dr. Rogers from America will convey this to you with the News papers, in which you will see the Letters I mentiond in my last, between Govenour Bowdoin and Captain Stanhope. Lord Gorge Gordon appears to interest himself in behalf of his American Friends, as he stiles them, but neither his Lordships Friendship or enmity are to be coveted.

Mr. Adams writes you by this opportunity.[3] I have directed a Letter to Mr. Williamos[4] to be left in your care, am very sorry to hear of his ill state of Health.

We hear nothing yet of Col. Smith, know not where he is, as we find by the Gentlemen last arrived[5] that he is not at Paris. I am sir with sentiments of Respect & Esteem Your &c.   A A

RC (DLC:Jefferson Papers).

[1] See Jefferson to AA, 11 Oct., and note 2, above.

[2] AA refers to Jefferson's request that she order some shirts to be made up for him; see AA to Jefferson, 7 Oct., and Jefferson to AA, 11 Oct., both above.

[3] On 24 Oct.; in Jefferson, *Papers*, 8:663–664.

[4] Not found.

[5] Presumably Preston, if "Gentlemen" here is meant to be singular, as it often is with AA.

John Quincy Adams to Abigail Adams 2d

Haverhill, October 16th [26], 1785[1]

We have had the most considerable freshet in the river that has ever been known. I mentioned in my last that it had rained for two days without intermission.[2] The storm lasted longer up in the country, and the river being the final receptacle of all, has been continually swelling till last night. The main street has been full of water, so that at some places boats have been necessary to go from house to house. A blacksmith's shop on the banks seems to have taken a fancy for a sailing party, and on its way knocked a vessel off the stocks. The damage done has been considerable.

Last eve, William and Lucy Cranch and Charles arrived here. The fall vacation began last week, but was only for a fortnight. I expected a letter from you by them, but was disappointed. I fear I shall have none, which shall not, however, prevent my writing, but if my letters are, henceforth, still more insipid than those I have already written, you must excuse me, for I have very little subject, and very little time. Now do not think that I am fishing for a compliment. I request you would not reply to this passage. If your affection and candor are such that you can receive any entertainment from such scrawls as I can afford, I have abundantly fulfilled my purpose.

Thursday 27th.

Our three cousins, two brothers, with Mr. Thaxter and Leonard White, (a youth of an exceedingly agreeable disposition and manners,) dined here to-day. The three brothers had not been together before for seven years.[3] I felt in such spirits, as you have sometimes seen me in, when you thought I was half mad; and yet, every now and then, the rising sigh would betray, that something yet was wanting; and I assure you I was not the only person present who recollected you, with painful pleasing sensations. Our cousins[4] leave us to-morrow to return to Braintree. Charles remains here till the end of the vacation. Lucy and Nancy are very intimate together, not, however, from any similarity of character—you know how serious, how prudent, how thinking your cousin is. Nancy is as gay, as flighty, and as happy, as you could wish to see a person; both their natural dispositions are very good, and that, I suppose, is enough to establish real friendship, though in many points there may be an essential difference.

Saturday 29th.

At length I have got your fine packet,[5] which was more agreeable, if possible, as I had given over all hopes of receiving any by this opportunity. Indeed, you do not know how much I was gratified; such parts as I thought might be communicated I read here, and afforded much entertainment to persons that you love and esteem. As I shall have probably nothing of great consequence to say of myself, I will draw my future subjects from your letters.

I am very glad to perceive you are so well pleased with your situation. Speaking the language, and being in the city, are circumstances that must contribute greatly to your satisfaction, and so large a library of books that you can read,[6] will serve to pass over the leisure hours more agreeably than when you were in France.

I remember the Mr. Bridgen you mention; he told me once, that all eldest sons ought to be hanged, it was not levelled at me, but against the accumulation of estates, for he is a very high republican. The breakfasts at 6 in the eve and dinners at midnight, are ridiculous enough, but of no great consequence. Nature demands food at some time of the day, but how much that may be varied, as well as the name given to the meal, is, I fancy, quite indifferent.

I am not a little pleased to find your judgment of persons conformable with what I thought of them, when I saw them. Mrs. P. has a Grecian for her husband;[7] he has studied his countryman, Plato, and perhaps has now and then to practise some of the precepts of Socrates. Miss H[azen] I have mentioned before; her form is very pretty, her wit agreeable, her ruling passion vanity.

[4 Nov.][8]

By the papers of yesterday, I was informed of the death of Mr. Hardy, a friend of Mr. Jefferson, to whom I had letters. Also the death of our aunt Tufts; these two events coming to me together, have made me quite sober; reflections upon mortality have been so often made, and are so often introduced into the mind of every one, that it could be no entertainment to you to give you my thoughts at present.

The fact is, a man of great knowledge cannot talk upon interesting subjects in mixed companies, without being styled a pedant; many people, and those perhaps the most fond of hearing themselves talk, would be excluded from conversation, and would call nonsense what they themselves could not understand. His majesty, to be sure, says very good things, and this I can say, he is not the only king I have heard of that could talk well and act ill; the sentiments he professes, I think, confirm what has been said of him, that as a private man, he would have acted his part much better than as sovereign of an empire.

I was very much gratified with the kind notice of Col. Smith. Attentions from persons whose character we respect, although not personally acquainted with them, are very pleasing; be kind enough to present my respects to him. My duty to our parents, and compliments where they will be acceptable.

Yours,   J. Q. A.

444

MS not found. Printed from AA2, *Jour. and Corr.*, [3]:89–93.

¹ The date is probably a transcription error; the arrival of the young Cranches and CA, which JQA's Diary records on 25 Oct. (*Diary*, 1:347), establishes the correct date.

² JQA to AA2, 1 Oct., above, under "*Saturday 22d.*" The collision of the sailing blacksmith shop with the vessel under construction occurred on 24 Oct. (JQA, *Diary*, 1:347).

³ In his Diary, JQA correctly says "six years," that is, since his and CA's departure for Europe in Nov. 1779 (same).

⁴ Lucy and William Cranch; Elizabeth remained at the Whites to continue her musical studies (same, p. 348).

⁵ AA2's long letter of 4 July, above.

⁶ Probably a reference to JA's library, which was brought, along with his furniture, from The Hague to London in early July (see AA to JQA, 26 June, above).

⁷ Lucy Ludwell Paradise and John Paradise, an Englishman partly of Greek descent.

⁸ In his Diary, JQA records learning of the deaths of Samuel Hardy and Lucy Quincy Tufts on 4 Nov., the first through reading a Salem newspaper of the previous day, the second from John Thaxter, who had just returned from Salem (*Diary*, 1:351; see also JQA to William Cranch, 6 Nov., below). Hardy, a member of Congress since 1783, was only in his late twenties at his death.

Catharine Louisa Salmon Smith to Abigail Adams

Dear Sister   Lincoln Octobr. 26th 1785

My heart has dictated many Letters to you since the recept of yours,¹ but my time has been so wholy taken up in my famely, (haveing no Schoole to send my little tribe to) that not a moment could be spared even for so necessary and incumbant a Duty.

Your kind letter was handed me by your Son, who I had long been most ardently wishing to see. He is indeed ten times welcome to this Section of the Globe again. I should feel myself happy if it were in the power of me or mine to render him any service and suply in any way the place of a Mama and Sister to him. But alas! my power is circumscribed within a narrow compass, and I fear I must set myself down contented with only wishing that I could be useful to my Friends. If you will point out any way wherein I can be serviceable to you, or yours, be assured that my utmost abilities shall be exerted for that purpose. My little Girls are tolerably notable with their Needles, and if you will oblige them with any commands of that sort they will execute them with pleasure, and you will confer an additional obligation on them and on their Mamma.

Young Mr. Adams is both in person and mind just what the fond heart of a Parent could wish, and were I not writeing to his Mamma I would say, he is the most ameable, and accompleshed young Gentleman I have ever seen. Your other sons I have not seen since I came from Weymouth, but I had the pleasure of hearing from them last Evening,² and they were well.

It is now almost two years since I have seen you. Had I been told when I parted with you at your Gate in Braintree that we should not meet again for such a length of time I should have been truely unhappy. Heaven for very wise purposes keeps the Book of fate fast locked that we may not unfold its leaves and see what is in the Bosom of futurity. What a scene of Misery would this World be to many of its inhabitants were it permitted that we should know but the one half of the ills we must suffer as we pass down the Stream of Life! In every Calamity the hopes of something better which we have in prospect keeps the Spirit from sinking, I speak experimentally for I have lived upon hope for many years past. I set and please myself with illusions, with dreams—and if it were not for treading so much on this enchanted ground I should dispair—but I will not suffer this enemy to happiness to approach me. I cultivate all in my power a Chearful dispossition. Tis a duty I owe my Children for how could I otherwise inspire them with a chearful gratitude to him whose sentence governs eternity and whose goodness is over all his Creatures, were they to see anxiety painted on my brows.

Judge Russel's famely are removed to Charlestown. The Judge has built a very elegant House on the same Spot where his other stood. There are a number of handsome buildings erected in Charlestown, and a Bridge is almost compleated across the ferry, which will be of great advantage to that formerly poor place. It begins already to make quite a smartish appearance. I'll assure you it gives me pleasure to see so great a number of the inhabitants again settled in their own peaceful habitations. May no enemy molest them and may they have nothing to make them affraid.

I feel the loss of Mr. Russel's famely very sensibly, it is like looseing a kind parents House. I have ever received the same friendly treatment from all the famely as if I had been a member of the same. Mr. Chambers R—l has purchased the Estate in Lincoln and lives upon it.[3] He wishes me to come to the House with the same freedom as when his father and Sisters were there, but he has no Lady nor is there a probability that he will have one soon. So I have never been to visit him. Their might be an impropriety in it in the Worlds Eye, and I have ever made it a fixed rule never to do a thing if I have the least shadow of a doubt concerning the propriety of it, and flatter myself that I find my account in being thus circumspect, in preferring my Reputation unsullied by the wicked breath of Malice, or the censor of an ill Judgeing world, who cannot always know our motives for doing a thing however laudable they may be, but must Judge by the appearance untill the Event justifies or condemns the Action.

446

Louisa is all Joy, and gratitude for your kind letter[4] and other testimonies of your kindness, and you will permit me to join my thanks with hers, for I feel myself as highly obliged. She is grown quite a great girl as tall as her mamma, and begins to look a little plumper not so *gauky* and holds up her head like a Miss in her teen's.

Mr. S[mit]h has not been in this part of the Country for almost two years. I seldom hear from him and when I do the intelegence is not what I could wish. Poor unhappy man! He has my prayers for his reformation and restoration to virtue and to his famely, and I hope they will reach him. With what a heart felt Satisfaction would I take the unhappy wanderer by the hand and lead him back into the path of rectitude and to a reconcileation with his God. It is yet in his power to add much to the happiness of his famely, and ensure to himself a comfortable evening of Life.

I hope before this time you have received a letter from me and one from Louisa which were wrote last Spring[5] I forget the date. If you have not you surely think me very negligent.

My little folks all send their duty. My most affectionate regards attend Mr. Adams and Miss Nabby. I will write to her as soon as I can get time.[6]

Adieu my dear Sister. I ought to apologize for the length of this. I am with the liveliest sentiments of Gratitude your affectionate Sister

Catharine L Smith

RC (Adams Papers).

[1] Not found, but probably dated in early May, when AA wrote letters to other relations and friends in America for JQA to deliver; JQA delivered the letter on 13–14 Sept. (see JQA to AA2, 8 Sept., above).

[2] No letters from CA or TBA to Catharine Smith have been found.

[3] The estate, now known as the Codman House, west of the center of Lincoln, had been inherited by Chambers Russell about 1743, who in turn left it to his nephew, Charles Russell. The Commonwealth of Massachusetts confiscated the property after Charles fled to Antigua as a loyalist refugee in 1775, but it was occupied during and briefly after the war by Charles' father, Judge James Russell, who had been burned out of his Charlestown, Mass., home by the fire accompanying the Battle of Bunker Hill. Charles' younger brother Chambers bought the estate in 1784 by paying a pre-Revolutionary lien on it, and lived in it until his early death in 1790, when it passed to his brother-in-law, John Codman Jr. Codman considerably remodeled and enlarged the house before his death in 1803. Catharine Smith first mentions Judge James Russell's friendship for her in her letter to AA of 27 April, above. See *Sibley's Harvard Graduates*, 9:81–87; 14:202–204; *An Account of the Celebration of the Town of Lincoln, Mass., 1754–1904*, Lincoln, Mass., 1905, p. 136, 142–146, and illustration at p. 66.

[4] Not found.

[5] Catharine Smith's letter of 27 April is above; young Louisa Catharine Smith's letter has not been found.

[6] No letter from Catharine Smith to AA2 has been found.

John Quincy Adams to William Cranch

Haverhill Novr. 1st. 1785

My two Brothers, Leonard and Charles,[1] will leave us to-morrow for Cambridge, and you would perhaps strike me from your books, was I to let them go without writing something: and as my inclination and my interest, are in this case, both on one side of the Question, I will say some thing, though it may not be worth your reading.

You know not how often I have thought of you, and wish'd for you, since you left us;[2] and now I am about to be entirely forsaken; Leonard and Charles, who have been since they arrived two sources of great pleasure, and amusement to me, will be gone to morrow and I shall have for my Consolation little else, but my studies; one or two families I can visit in the only manner which can give me any pleasure; I mean without form or Ceremony: and with their kindness and that of the family I am in, I shall spend the Winter as agreeably, as the impatient State of my mind, will permit.

How do you come on with the hymn of Cleanthes?[3] I shall insist upon it, that you send me your translation, as soon as it is finish'd, and you shall have mine at the same time; you will remember, to give ⟨it⟩ the book to Johonnot[4] with my Love when you have done with it. I wish to see his skill try'd too, on the same Subject.

I have had a most noble feast since you left us: a Letter from my Sister of 32 pages; I am sorry it did not come before you went, that you might have read it. The latest of the dates is August 15th.[5]

You will not forget my request concerning a Chum[6]—a sober, studious youth, of a good moral and literary Character, is what I wish for, and I hope, you may find such a one.

Your affectionate Cousin.   J. Q. Adams

A Very different Letter this, from that, I wrote you last;[7] I endeavoured before I began, to write; ⟨but my?⟩ be merry, but I cannot; put content in my face, or on my Paper, when I have it not at heart. My next perhaps, will be like the last. Adieu.

RC (MH); addressed: "Mr. William Cranch. Cambridge"; endorsed: "J. Q. A. Haverhill Novr. 1st. 1785."

[1] JQA's use of "My two Brothers" for Leonard White and CA suggests how quickly he had become a close friend of White. His younger brother TBA stayed in Haverhill.

[2] On 28 Oct., accompanying his sister Lucy Cranch to Braintree before returning to Cambridge (JQA, *Diary*, 1:348).

[3] The hymn to Zeus by the 3d-century B.C.

Stoic philosopher Cleanthes.
⁴ Samuel Cooper Johonnot accompanied JA and JQA to Europe in 1779, and studied in Paris with JQA in 1780. JQA's last reference to Johonnot was in Aug. 1783, shortly before Johonnot's return to America (same, 1:181; JQA to Johonnot, 31 Aug. 1783, CtY).

⁵ AA2 to JQA, 4 July, above. The letter's last entry is dated 11 Aug., but it may be a draft for a recipient's copy that ended on the 15th.
⁶ That is, college roommate.
⁷ No letter to Cranch has been found since that of 14 Dec. 1784, above.

John Quincy Adams to William Cranch

Haverhill Novr. 6. 1785.

I received on Saturday evening your kind favour of the day preceding,[1] and although I was then far, very far from being in a pleasant State of mind: yet I could not help smiling at your geometrical proof that if you shared my sorrows with me, they would not be so great. I had been much affected the day before, when Mr. Thaxter returning from Salem inform'd us of our aunt's[2] Death. I had read the same day in the Salem Paper, an account from New York of the funeral of Mr. Hardy, a gentleman I was well acquainted with and for whom I had the Sincerest esteem and Respect. Your own Sensibility will make you readily believe, that either of these Events was sufficient, to make any person very pensive, but coming both together, the Effect must be greater. But excepting these Circumstances I have regain'd entirely my peace of mind, which was for a few days a little ruffled; Few Persons I believe enjoy a greater share of happiness, than I do; and indeed I know few persons who have more Reason to be happy. Health, and the *mens conscia recte*,[3] two inestimable blessings, I as yet enjoy; and a person cannot be very unhappy I believe, with them.

I admire with you the conduct of our Uncle, upon so trying an Occasion. It called to my mind a beautiful passage in Hamlet who speaking of mourning cloaths says.

> These indeed seem,
> For they are what a man may put upon.
> But I have that within, which passeth show.
> These but the trappings and the suits of woe.[4]

Novr. 11th

Was I now to tell you my heart is at ease, you would with justice think me criminal. Oh! my friend! I have been witness to a scene of distress, which would call sympathy from a colder heart than your's or mine. Not all the comparisons that wits or Poets have ever made, can give a sufficient idea of the frailty of human life, and happiness. Experience alone, can shew it us. Wednesday evening, I was down at Mr. White's, the only house in Town, which I visit often and one, in which it is impossible to pass time disagreeably. At about 7 o'clock Mr. J. Duncan, came in and enquired for his mother. She had disappeared, about a quarter of an hour before. You will probably, before this reaches you, have seen a particular Account of the Event, with all the Circumstances, attending it.[5] It will therefore be enough for me to say, that after a fruitless search all night, she was found early yesterday morning, never to be lost again. This afternoon we followed her to the grave. The affliction of the different branches of that amiable family, is easily conceived; not expressed. But they bear it with that fortitude, and resignation, so becoming to Christians. They have only to grieve for themselves: the God who pleased in that manner to take her from the world, imputes not the evil to her, and we have no Reason to doubt but she is completely happy.

Adieu, my friend, let me hear from you as soon as possible: remember me, affectionately to Leonard. I fear this Event will affect him deeply, but I am perswaded his good Sense, will inspire him with proper firmness. My Love to Charles, and compliments to his Chum.[6] I wonder Charles has not written a word since he left us. I would write to him, but have not a minute of time to spare.

Your's

J. Q. Adams

P.S. Novr. 15th. This will go by Peabody, I have not found any body going to Boston, since I wrote it. I intend to go to see Mr. White's family and your Sister this Evening. They are all well and their affliction begins to lose its sharpest edge. We have had a dull time here, for a week, and countenances have not yet wholly lost the melancholy that was cast over them. Reason is troublesome, when the Passions are violently moved, but must inevitably resume after a short interval, its sway, over the human Breast.

Let me know your Progress in the noble Hymn of Cleanthes: don't wait till you have finish'd it, but communicate the Verses as you write them: be persuaded that I have friendship enough for you, to criticise freely, whatever I shall think, lends to criticism, and I only request you would serve me with the same candour.

Remember me again to your Chum.[7] I look forward with great Pleasure, to the five weeks, he will be here in the Winter, and wish, I could form the same hopes with Respect to you.

I dont know how long I should run on in this manner, had I time;

but I think I have already sufficiently exercised your Patience, and ⟨can⟩ will only ⟨say⟩ add I am your's   J. Q. A.

RC (Private owner, New York, 1957); endorsed: "JQA Nov 15th. 1785 Haverhill Death of Mrs. Duncan (felo de se.)" The Latin means "a felon against herself," that is, a suicide; see note 5.

¹ Cranch's letter of 4 Nov. has not been found.

² Lucy Quincy Tufts.

³ A mind conscious of rectitude.

⁴ *Hamlet*, I, ii, 83–86. JQA misquotes line 84, which reads: "For they are actions that a man might play." In his *Diary*, 1:353, JQA quotes line 86 as an approving comment on Dr. Tufts' decision not to wear mourning clothes.

⁵ In his Diary, JQA gives a full and quite moving description of the suicide of Elizabeth Leonard Duncan, second wife of James Duncan, Sr., sister of Sarah Leonard LeBaron White, and aunt of Leonard and Peggy White. Mrs. Duncan, "deprived of her Reason" for several months, had twice tried to commit suicide before drowning herself in the Merrimack River on the night of 9 November. JQA had seen her at the Whites' less than an hour before she disappeared (*Diary*, 1:354–355).

⁶ Samuel Walker.

⁷ Leonard White.

Elizabeth Smith Shaw to Abigail Adams

Haverhill Novemr. 6th. 1785

Your Son, My Dear Sister has been a Member of our Family for these five Weeks, almost three of those I suppose he will tell You, Mr. Shaw and I were absent upon our southern Journey. He came a Friday¹ in Peabody's Coach, and we began our Rout the next Monday. His Uncle spent Saturday in giving him Directions about his Studies, and what he could wish him to pursue till his Return. Greek seemed to be the grand Object which ought to claim his greatest Attention, he was therefore desired to learn the Grammer. Upon our Return We found he had not been idle, but like a truly ambitious Youth, endeavoured to do more than was required. He was as steady to his Studies as a Philosopher. He was out but three or four times while we were gone, and then only by an Invitation to dine, at Judge Seargants, Master Whites, and Mr. Dodges. Indeed he searches out Knowledge as if it was his Meat, and Drink, and considered it as more precious than choice Gold. When I was at Braintree, I drank Tea with Mr. Wibird. You know he was always very inquisitive. In the course of Conversation Your Son became the Subject. I asked him if he did not think Mr. Adams exceedingly like his Father.——Yes—² walking across the Room, but at my Question, took his stand before me, his Head inclined on his left Shoulder, one Eye half shut, and his right Hand in his Breeches Pocket. I could not said he, when I saw him, for my life, help thinking of what Addison puts in the Mouth of Syphax. "Curse on the Stripling how he Apes *his Sire*."³

There is not a Day passes but what I think of it, but not without wishing the imprecation transformed into a thousand—thousand Blessings.

We had a very pleasant and agreeable visit to Bridgwater, Plimouth, Marshfield, and Hingham, for we found all our Friends well there. But alas! when I came to Weymouth, what bitter ingredients were thrown into my Cup of Pleasure. Our dear amiable Aunt Tufts was laid upon the Bed of Sickness, unable hardly to lift her languid Head—fixed, and piercing were those Eyes which used to beam Benevolence on all. Almost closed were those Lips, upon which forever dwelt the Law of Kindness. Cold, and deathful were those liberal Hands that scattered Blessings, and delighted in seeking out, and relieving the Wants of the Poor, and necessitous. Indeed my Sister the Scene was too—too distressing. I could not speak a word, my Heart felt as if it would have burst it[s] bounds, and would no longer submit to its inclosure. But She is now no longer lingering, trembling, hoping, dying. This painful Scene has closed, and I trust Heaven has opened to her view. When I left her, I thought she could continue but a few Days. And Yesterdays Post has brought us intelligence of her Death. Her emancipation rather. Yes we may—we ought to drop a Tear over our Aunt—for she loved us next to her own Child, and we repayed it with equal tenderness and affection, for she was to us, but one remove from our excellent and much revered Mother. Sweet is the Memory of the just. May their Virtues live in us. May we catch the Mantle, and imbibe a double Portion of their Graces.[4]

The good Dr behaves like a true Christian. He neither despises the chastening, nor faint[s] under the afflictive Dispensations of Providence. His most sincere and devoted Friend, and Lover is indeed put far away. But Love cemented by Religion ends not here.

> "Nor with the narrow bounds of Time,
> The beauteous Prospect ends,
> But lengthened thro' the Vale of Death,
> To Paradise extends."

The Day I came out of Boston,[5] Capt. Lyde arrived. Mr. Shaw went eagerly to the Post Office for Letters, but could find none, only for JQA.[6] Mr. Gardner said he had a number in his Trunk, but could not get it on Shore. So we were obliged to Trudg home to Haverhill, without any particular Information of your Welfare. Your Sons both looked so happy to see us return, that I shall always love them the better for it. I knew I had insured a hearty welcome by the Letters I had brought.

Curiosity if directed in a right Line, and fixed upon proper Objects may lead to great Acquisitions. But such a curiosity as some People are possessed of—Pray did you never discover that your Sons was almost unbounded.

I never saw Mr. T[yler] in the whole course of my Journey, which to me was a matter of Speculation. For I supposed *we* were upon good Terms. I know not of anything that should have made it otherway[s] unless it was because I gave him in the gentlest manner the greatest Proof of my Friendship. Such *neglects* to *such affection* and to *such a Person*, was what I could not silently nor patiently see. It was too much for Sensibility to bear. —And now I have nothing to do but admire, at the Wisdom, the Fortitude and the Magnimity of that Lady, who would not suffer the voilence of Passion to blind her Judgment, and misguide her Reason,[7] and I must place, certain Decissions among the misterious Revolutions of an all wise Providence.

Your kind Letter[8] accompanied with presents to the Children, came safe to hand the 29th. of October. Accept my dear Sister of mine, and their Thanks. Betsy Q. [*says*] she has told all the Misses in the School that Aunt Adams lives in London, and sent her a beauty Book and Gown. Billy and Betsy Quincy speak very plain, and read very well. Billy was up in the Morning before it was light, got a candle, and set down to read his Book which he had received the night before from his Aunt Adams.

I brought home from Braintree a Suit of Cinnamon couloured Cloathe for Cousin Thomas which came from Holland,[9] and last Week we devoted to turning the Coat, and fixing the little Gentleman up, and I assure you he looked quite smart to Day.

Cousin Betsy Cranch is in Town, keeps at Mr. Whites, and learns Musick upon Miss Peggys Forte Piano. I wish we owned one, and then we should not lose the pleasure of her company. Story informs us of the Force, and power of Musick. Orpheous with his Lyre put inanmate nature in Motion, and brought Euridice even from the Realms below. But the power of Melody is now so lessoned, that should this lovely Maid strike the softest, sweetest Notes in nature, I fear they would not ⟨charm?⟩ bring you back to your native Land. Duty with you has a more powerful Charm.

Adieu my ever dear Sister, and believe me to be with the tenderest Love, Your affectionate Sister   Eliza. Shaw

RC (Adams Papers). Dft (DLC:Shaw Family Papers).

[1] 30 September.

[2] In the draft, "⟨*said he*⟩" appears after the dash.

[3] Joseph Addison, *Cato*, I, ii. The speaker was not Syphax, the Numidian ally and then traitor to Cato the Younger, but Sempronius, a Roman senator. Sempronius speaks of Porcius, one of Cato's sons, whom he sees as "ambitiously sententious," like his father.

[4] See Proverbs 10:7; 2 Kings 2:1–15, esp. verses 8, 9, and 13.

[5] 20 Oct. (JQA, *Diary*, 1:344).

[6] AA to JQA, 11, 23 Aug., both above; William Vans Murray to JQA, 2 Aug., Adams Papers (see JQA to AA2, 1 Oct., above, under "*Saturday 22d*").

[7] Both Mary Cranch and Cotton Tufts

were informed of AA2's dismissal of Royall Tyler in letters from AA (15 Aug., and 18 Aug., both above) carried by Capt. Lyde, who arrived in Boston on 20 October. The news evidently reached Shaw after her return from Boston, on the same day, although AA's letter to her of [*ca. 15 Aug.*], above, also carried by Lyde, does not mention the subject.

[8] Of [*ca. 15 Aug.*], above; there AA mentions sending books to each of Elizabeth Shaw's children, and to TBA.

[9] Perhaps the suit of "Chocolate coloured Cloaths" mentioned at the end of the 6 Nov. 1784 inventory (Adams Papers) of JQA's possessions that were sent from Holland to Boston; the last section lists clothes sent from The Hague to JQA at Auteuil.

Mary Smith Cranch to Abigail Adams

My dear Sister   Braintree November 8th [1785]

Although I have written so largly to you by the last vessels that Saild[1] I cannot bear to let another go without a few Lines. I have not yet receiv'd your Letters by Charles Storer. He is not come to Boston. I am anxious to receive them. I want to know what it is, whether any thing in particular has happen'd to make my Neice take such a determin'd part with regard to a certain Gentleman.[2] He is very jealous that I have acquainted you with some of his conduct which he knows I cannot approve. He is mistaken. I have been too much affraid of making mischief to do it, and I plainly perceiv'd that he would do his own Business for himself, without the assistance of any body else. You have not told me whether you receiv'd a Letter from me by Mr. Bulfinsh,[3] that is the only one in which I ever mention'd his ditaining cousins Letters for a long time from her Friends. I know not whether Mrs. Guild would have ever got hers[4] if I had not accidintly Seen them and told her that he had Some for her. She Sent for them often but he would neither Send them, nor go to see her although he was in Boston three weeks of the time out of the month he detain'd them. At last She talk'd to Mr. Wibird about it, and got him to ask him what he meant. Betsey was present when he did. He first ask'd him whether he had a Letter for Mrs. Guild. He colour'd up to his ears, but after Some time, in a mumbling manner he Said yes. "And why do you not give it to her?" "I have a particular reason for not doing it." "It must be a very particular one indeed or it will not excuse you from a charge of breach of trust."[5] The next day He sent two to her by Cousin Tommy. The first which I saw had the Seal broke, that She never receiv'd, so She told me the other day. He would have serv'd Cousin Betsy Palmer in the same manner If Betsy Cranch had not insisted upon his telling her whether he had one or not.[6] He open'd his Pacquit in the room with us. This was the first he receiv'd in the Spring. Cousin Betsy was present. We Saw five or Six Letters. He said there was but one of them for him. He gave Betsy Cranch one.[7] We ask'd him if there was not one for Cousin Betsy. He would not answer, but carried them all into his chamber. I thought there was one for her and told my Betsy to make him Say whether there was or not. "He did not know but there was." He look'd a little vex'd but went up and got it.[8] You cannot wonder if after this we could not place any confidences in him. He has conduct'd Strangly towards the Germantown Family ever Since last winter, has not been there above there [*three*?] times since, and he may have Spoken to Cousin Betsy Six times but not more, and all this for nobody know[s] what that I can find out. I could tell you more but as you are not like to be any further connected with him, I will let him alone: I have not Seen him Since his chagrine. His officce has been shut up and he in Boston for five weeks. The court has sat two of them. I know no more about his business than you do. If cousin knew how he had show'd her Letters about she would be very angry. He has I hear been reprov'd for it by some of the young Fellows he show'd them too. His answer was "He was so proud of Miss A's Letters that he could not help it." Did he mean (when he told cousin that he had written by the way of Amsterdam)[9] that he had written to her before the first october Letters? He told me and others that he never had written her one before, and that he had reciev'd Six from her before she could have had one from him. I ask'd him what excuse he had made for himself. He Said none, and that he would not let her know that he had reciev'd one of hers if he did not think other people would tell her. How he does delight to plague Those he thinks he can?

The Doctor has written you upon the subject[10] but he poor man has had his Hands and Heart full ever Since he reciev'd your Letters. Our good Aunt Tufts after a most distressing Sickness which She bore with a patience and fortitude which would have Surpriz'd you has exchang'd this troublesome World for one where all Tears will be wip'd from her Eyes. She so earnestly long'd for her release that her dearest connections could not wish for her staying longer here. She dy'd last Lords day evening about half after six o clock. I follow'd her to the Grave and saw her deposited by the side of our dear Parents. It Was a solemn scene to me. The Doctor behaves like a saint. His son is so softend[11] that he made us a visit the day after, and has promiss'd to repeat them. The poor have lost a Friend indeed but no one has met with so great a Loss as Lucy Jones. She is much affected.

Your Mother Hall is well. We have had several Sudden Deaths within a week in this Parish. Hannah Whits Husband, The widdow Crane and Sally Brackit a Daughter of James Brackit. She was sick but three days of a Putred Fever, you may remember her Blooming countinance.[12] Your Neighbours are well. Esters mother spent an afternoon with me a few days sinc. Cousin Charles Billy and Lucy have been to Haverhill to see their Friends: Betsy is there yet. They are all well. Cousin John very Studious, and is a mere recluse. He however went with Miss Peggy and Betsy to Newburry and Spent two days at Mr. Daultons, and pleass'd enough they were. Betsy will write you all about it.

Do not read any more of this Letter to any body than you find necessary. I do not wish to prejudice any body, but you know not how uneasey all of us have been, for the Happiness of your Family, and yet every Body was affraid to Speak. Before he receiv'd her last Letter he had written her a very long one. I wonder if he has Sent it. I wish you could see it if he has.[13] He is so suspicious of me that I believe I am not very favourably mention'd in it. I must repeat He has no reason for it. I have been his Friend as far as he would let me be so, but Surely I owe more to you than to him.—Mr. Cranch will send you Some chocalate by Capt. Young if he can get him to take it.

Cousin Charles behaves well at college. I have got a surtout of cousin Johns[14] alter'd for him and Tommy has taken his. I am going to get Some worsted stocking for them. Do you know that Cousin John has Sixty five pair of Stockings Thread cotton and Silk and not one pair of them have the Heels lin'd or run? We have been fixing a reasonable number for him and have put by the others till they are worn out. I am asham'd to send you this without copying it but my pen is so bad and my time So short that I cannot do it.

I do not know of another vessel to Sail for England this fall. If there Should be one I shall write again. I believe you have reciev'd more from me than from any one else. I feel as if I wanted to be always Scribling to you. Give my Love to Mr. Adams and my dear Niece and believe me at all times your affectionate Sister

M. Cranch

RC (Adams Papers); endorsed: "1785 Mrs Cranch 8 November."

[1] Mary Cranch to AA, 14 Aug., and [ca. 23] Oct., both above.

[2] Royall Tyler, whom AA2 dismissed on [ca. 11 Aug.], above; see AA to Mary Cranch, 15 Aug., to which Cranch responded on [ca. 23] Oct., both above.

[3] Of 4 June, above; see Richard Cranch to JA, 3 June, above.

[4] No letter from AA2 to Elizabeth Quincy Guild has been found.

[5] All closing quotation marks inserted by the editors.

[6] No letter from AA2 to Elizabeth Palmer has been found.

[7] This letter has not been identified.

[8] No letter from AA2 to Elizabeth Palmer has been found.

[9] See AA to Mary Cranch, 15 Aug., and note 7, above. Closing quotation mark supplied in the previous sentence.

[10] Perhaps Cotton Tufts to AA, 12 Oct., above, although that letter was a response to AA's concern about Tyler in May; no letter from Tufts to AA in late October or early November is known to the editors.

[11] See JQA to AA2, 29 Aug., note 18, above.

[12] Sarah, daughter of James and Mary Brackett, died on 31 Oct., at age 18 (Pattee, *Old Braintree and Quincy*, p. 123).

[13] No letters from Royall Tyler to AA2 have been found.

[14] Perhaps the "blue great Coat," listed in the inventory of 6 Nov. 1784 (Adams Papers), as being sent to Boston from Holland; or the "green Surtout" listed in the same inventory as sent from Holland to JQA in France.

Cotton Tufts to Abigail Adams

Dear Cousn   Boston Nov. 16. 1785

When I wrote to You by Capt. Cushing[1] I informed You of my Fears with respect to Mrs. Tufts's Illness. The Event which I then feared, has since taken Place. Heaven has executed its Will. The Partner of my Life is gone to Rest, She expired a[bout?] 7 oClock on the 30th. of Octob. in the Evening, after a long and painful Sickness.

Amidst the various Tryalls of Life, it is sometimes a Consolation that they will one Day terminate. It may be such when the Prospect is near, but when distant and the Suffering great, it is but a feeble Support, especially if the Idea of a future Existence be excluded, but when We Can look through present Sufferings to a future State of Ease and Tranquillity accompanied with [real?][2] Joy that will not only exceed our Wishes in Degree, but our Conceptions in Duration, it affords some solid Support, alleviates our Distresses and spreads over the Wound an healing Balm. Though of all Tryalls of Life that of the Loss of so near a Connection is perhaps one of the greatest, yet I am not without Consolation when I reflect upon that Patience Christian Fortitude and happy Temper of Mind which She discovered through the whole of her sickness and that Readiness which she manifested to obey the Call of Heaven and close the Scene. She has Weathered the Storm and is I trust arrived safe in the Haven of Felicity where May We my Dear Friend one Day meet and associate with those of our departed Friends and Relations. With Love to Mr. Adams and Cousin Nabby.

I am Yr. affectionate Friend & Uncle   Cotton Tufts

RC (Adams Papers); addressed: "Madm. Abigail Adams Grovesner Square Westminster"; endorsed: "Dr Tufts November 26. 1785." Some damage to the text at a tear.

¹ On 14 Oct., above.
² Written over another word.

Richard Cranch to John Adams

Dear Bror.   Boston Novr. 19th. 1785

I have just received the within Letters, and as I hear Capt. Young is to sail tomorrow I take the liberty of inclosing them to you.¹ By Capt. Cushing who sailed a few Weeks ago I sent you the News-Papers from last May,² and by Capt. Young I have sent the Papers since and a Register for 1786. I have also sent a little Bundle for Sister Adams.³

I wrote you largely by Capt. Cushing, and have wrote you again a few days ago by Capt. Young, who will wait upon you. He is related to ⟨your⟩ Mr. Tudor's Wife. I hope this will meet you under agreeable Circumstances, and that your Dear Lady and Daughter are well. Master Charles was with me to day and dined with Mrs. Cranch at Uncle Smith's; he is very well and behaves well at Colledge: your Sons at Haverhill were well this Week, as were also Brother Shaw and Family, and Mr. Thaxter. Your Honoured Mother, and your Brother were well last Sunday. I have recommended your Brother to the Governor for a Justice of the Peace, and the Governor has promised me that he shall be appointed. The movement of mine is yet wholly unknown to your Brother, and I intend it shall be so untill I carry him his Commission.⁴ I am with the highest Esteem, your affectionate Brother   Richard Cranch

Please to give my kindest Regards to your dear Wife and amiable Daughter.

Many Friends will write to you and Sister by this Conveyance. We have just heard of the arrival of Mr. Chs. Storer and his Sister⁵ &c. at N: York on the 8th. Instant all well. The Letters by him are not yet arrived.

RC (Adams Papers).

¹ The enclosed letters cannot be identified, but any of the following, written in Massachusetts between 18 and 24 Oct., directed to JA in London, and lacking an ad-

dress, could have been included with Richard Cranch's letters of 10 Nov. (Adams Papers, with elaborate address), and 19 Nov. (without address): Tristram Dalton to JA, 18 Oct., James Sullivan to JA, 23, and 24 Oct., and Jonathan Jackson, 24 Oct. (all Adams Papers).

[2] With Richard Cranch to JA, 13 Oct. (Adams Papers).

[3] Richard Cranch to JA, 10 Nov. (Adams Papers), states that Cranch is sending along "a little Bundle containing something that Mrs. Cranch sent to her Sister," probably the chocolate mentioned in Mary Cranch to AA, 8 Nov., above, and recent newspapers and "A Register for the Commonwealth of Massachusetts," in *A Pocket Almanack . . . 1786*, T. & J. Fleet, Boston.

[4] Cranch had nominated Peter Boylston Adams to Gov. Bowdoin on 5 Sept. (MHi:C. P. Cranch Papers). It was Mary Cranch who actually presented the commission to P. B. Adams, presumably in December (Mary Cranch to AA, 18 Dec., below).

[5] Elizabeth Storer Atkinson.

Elizabeth Smith Shaw to Abigail Adams 2d

Haverhill November 19th. 1785

Tuesday the first of November, I received from you, my ever dear Neice, a Letter dated the 3d. of August.[1] Were I to describe to you the Ideas I have, of the merit of its Author, it might perhaps, flatter your Vanity. For some I suppose you are possessed of, in common with the rest of your Sex, however you may modify and direct it. Roseau says, it is inherent, and constitutes a part of our very Nature. For he asserts that all Women are naturally Coqqettes[2]—which if allowed I conclude therefore that all Women must have a considerable share of Vanity and Presumtion. But quiting Roseau and all his odd Chimerical Ideas and Schemes, I will tell you plainly that your Letter throwed me into a very pensive and musing state of mind. It gave me both pleasure, and pain—pleased with the Manner, but pained at the thought of having given real uneasiness, to a Heart, which if it had need, I would have chose rather to have soothed—to have poured balm, and softened with my latest Breath.

I cannot recur to the Letter you mention,[3] because I have no copy. But as near as I remember, the Observations arose from the Idea, that we were *all*, but in *Youth* more especially, too apt to form wrong Judgment of persons and of things, for want of time, and critical Examination, for instance—put a strait stick into a Tub of water and when the Sun Shines upon it, you believe it broke or bent, and cannot suppose it otherways, only by repeated trials—just so we may be mistaken as to the merit, or real Character of Persons. Objects ought to be viewed in different points of light. We Judge by the exterior, and it is Time, the most accurat Observation, and experience alone, that can convince us, it is possible for our Judgement to err.

"O lovly Source
"Of generous Foibles, *Youth*! When opening a Mind
"Are honest as the light, lucid as air,
"As softening breezes kind, as Linnets Gay
"Tender as Buds, and lavish as the Spring!"

How often in the earlier part of my Life, have I thought it unkind, unjust, and the height of *cruelty* to suspect there was the least Ill, "where no Ill *seemed*." How dear thought I, must we pay for our knowledge of the World if the more we know, the less we must Love—and in proportion as that is extended, our Charity, and Benevolence must decrease.—But why do I run on thus. I meant to ask, *why*, so general Observations should give pain, and so much alarm my dear Niece. Believe me my Friend when I say, they were not made, because I thought you materially deficient in any part of your Conduct. No. Though I knew you, as human, *liable to Errors*, yet I have ever viewed you in a variety of Instances, as rising above your Sex, superior to the weakness, and the Foibles that more generally attend Us, as acting in a strict conformity to the highest notions, of virtuous affection; honour, and filial Duty. Few I beleive, of your age have more assiduously sought the *right way*, and undeviatingly [. . .] the Path—and such a Person cannot form an Opinion to Day, vary it tomorrow, and change it a week hence. Errors we find may result from a wrong Judgement, But when that is convinced, we may alter our Opinion, while the same *principles* are operating in our Breasts, without being charged I think with fickleness and inconstancy.

You ask, what more can be done, than endeavour to do right? I answer, that nothing more ought to be done. This is the only source from whence we can derive comfort. This is the Path which if pursued, will lead you on to Happiness—will lead you to a chearful Resignation to the various vissisetudes of Fortune. It will smooth your Pillow, and make your repose sweet and peaceful.[4]

I find by your Mamma's, and your Letters that an atachment to the French was daily increasing.[5] Moore in his Travels[6] says they are the most civil and polite to strangers of any people in the World, the most obliging in endeavouring to make them understand their Language, and the least apt to laugh, when errors are made in speaking it—and that Gentleman of Fortune from every part of Europe, resorted thither to spend them,[7] where they could enjoy the agreeable Society of the Parisians.

The account you gave of your presentation to their Majesties, and

460

of your Dress and Reception,[8] was a matter we felt ourselves interested in. Painful preheminence! I envied neither Royalty nor you.
Alas! that my Neices Taste should be so depraved as not to be
delighted with the Salutations, Ceremonies, and Honours of a Court.
You talk of the Mortification of your Pride, and of your being taught
to pay respect and defference to nothing but superior Virtue and
Merit. Why Child, one would think you lived in Queen Besses Days.

Your Remarks pleased me, upon the equality of the human Species.
If Titles, Rank, and Fortune could shield us from any one Misfortune,
and Evil to which Humanity is incident, they might be worth such
mighty contests as have disturbed the World. But on the contrary we
find, that exalted Stations, are often the very Cause which involves
them in Misery and though by their Office they are "stiled Gods, yet
they must die like Men."

In our late Journey to Braintree, Mr. Shaw had some Buisiness
which led him to visit, one of your Skadenmite Families.[9] Pray who
did you marry, said the good Woman? Upon being informed, Why
you was a *desperate* lucky Man and then went on to enquires about
your Family. We hear they have seen the King and Queen of England,
and that they kept them standing four Hours. I should have thought
they would have had more manners. I don't call myself desperate
mannerly and yet I am sure I would have given them Chairs to sit in.
I assure you I have been diverted to hear the different speeches, and
opinions of people upon this ocasion.

I have had a sweet Visit from Cousin Billy and Lucy Cranch, and
your Brother Charles in the October Vacancy. I felt gratified, and I
loved him the better for his looking so happy at being here again.
Here he recieved your affectionate Letter,[10] and token of Love. You
can hardly conceive how rich I felt, when I looked round our Table,
and could count eight own Cousins.[11] Such likely ones too, and those
that loved me so well. Some of my best spirits played round my Heart,
at that Moment.

It was in vain to wish *you* here—it could not be.

And now my dear Neice let me beg you to write to me as often as
you can freely, every thing that can affect your Happiness is of
importance to me. Mr. Allen is not yet married, but I suppose means
to be, if *ever* this Winter.

Mr. Thaxter according to his diffinition of Courtship is now on the
third stage. He is now quite seriously engaged,[12] and is considered
as a relative in the Family. Walked last week as a near mourner to
poor Mrs. Duncan's Grave—For she is gone. The Family disorder

seized her Brain. She was missing in the Evening, and found next Morning floating, a little way off one of the Wharffs. What consternation such an Event must occasin the Family, and her connections you can better conceive than I describe. She was a person of an excellent Temper, a kind Friend of a meek disposition, and I believe a very good Woman, and was grieved almost to Death when her Brother acted the like Part. Your Brother JQA in his Journal, I suppose will give you a particular account of the affair.[13]

Adieu my Dear Neice, may [*you*] enjoy all that satisfaction, & happiness which is insured to *Right Intentions*, is at all times the fervent Wish of your most Affectionate Aunt   E Shaw

Dft (DLC:Shaw Family Papers); addressed: "To Miss A Adams Grosvenor Square London."

[1] Not found.

[2] From Rousseau, *Emile, Sophie ou La Femme*, Book V.

[3] Evidently a letter from Elizabeth Shaw to AA2 that has not been found.

[4] The preceding paragraphs may be a discreet discussion of AA2's relationship with Royall Tyler. Elizabeth Shaw had learned of AA2's dismissal of Tyler by 6 Nov. (Shaw to AA, 6 Nov., and note 7, above). There is no direct evidence, however, that AA2 ever informed Shaw of her decision to dismiss Tyler, and it is far from certain that her letter to Shaw of 3 Aug. (not found), ever referred to Tyler.

[5] This probably refers to AA's favorable comparison of the French to the English in her letter to Elizabeth Shaw of [*ca. 15 Aug.*], above, and to some remarks in AA2's letter to Shaw of 3 Aug. (not found).

[6] Dr. John Moore, *A View of Society and Manners in France, Switzerland, and Germany*, London, 1779, letter IV.

[7] Shaw deleted "who have Fortunes, and wish to spend them," after "Europe," added "of Fortune" after "Gentleman," and left her now vague "them" reference unchanged.

[8] The description of the Adamses' presentation at court on 23 June was probably contained in AA2's letter to Elizabeth Shaw of 3 Aug. (not found); see AA to Mary Cranch, 24 June, above.

[9] That is, a family that lived in Scadding, the South Precinct of Braintree, later incorporated as Randolph (JA, *Diary and Autobiography*, 1:118, and note 22). For another account of this story, see Mary Cranch to AA, 23 Dec., below.

[10] No letters exchanged between AA2 and CA have been found.

[11] The eight cousins, all grandchildren of the late Rev. William Smith and Elizabeth Quincy Smith, who were at the Shaws' on 25–27 Oct., during Harvard College's fall vacation, were JQA, CA, TBA, Elizabeth Cranch, Lucy Cranch, William Cranch, William Smith Shaw, and Elizabeth Quincy Shaw (JQA, *Diary*, 1:347–348).

[12] To Elizabeth Duncan, whom he married in 1787.

[13] No extant letter from JQA to AA2 descibes the Duncan tragedy.

Thomas Jefferson to Abigail Adams

Dear Madam   Paris Nov. 20. 1785

I have been honoured with your two letters of Octob. 19. and 25. by Mr. Fox and Doctor Rodgers since the date of my last.[1] I am to thank you for your state of Stanhope's case. It has enabled me to speak of that transaction with a confidence of which I should otherwise have been deprived by the different state of it in the public papers and the want of information from America. I have even endeavored to get it printed in a public paper to counteract the impressions of the London papers and Mercure de France. I do not yet know however whether it will be admitted.[2]–Your letter to Mr. Williamos[3] I immediately sent to him. The illness which had long confined him, proved in the end to be mortal. He died about ten days ago.

Mr. Adams's letter of the 4th. instant[4] informs me that Mr. Preston had at length found my letter to him. I hope he has also found, or that he will in time find that which I took the liberty of writing to you. It was to pray you to order me a dozen shirts, of exactly the quality of the one sent, to be made in London. I gave for that 10₶ 10s. the aune, and wished to be able to judge of the comparative prices in the two countries. The several commissions you have been so good as to execute for me, with what Mr. Adams has paid for insuring Houdon's life leave me considerably in your debt. As I shall not get so good an opportunity of making a remittance, as by Colo. Smith, I trouble him with thirty two Louis for you. This I expect may place us in the neighborhood of a balance. What it is exactly I do not know. I will trouble you to give me notice when you receive your plateaux de dessert, because I told the marchand I would not pay him till you had received them; he having undertaken to send them. I give you so much trouble that unless you find some means of employing me for yourself in return I shall retain an unpleasant load on my mind. Indeed I am sensible this balance will always be against me, as I want more from London than you will do from Paris. True generosity therefore will induce you to give me opportunities of returning your obligations.

Business being now got through I congratulate you on the return of Colo. Smith.[5] I congratulate you still more however on the extreme worth of his character, which was so interesting an object in a person connected in office so nearly with your family. I had never before had an opportunity of being acquainted with him. Your knowlege of him will enable you to judge of the advantageous impressions which his head, his heart, and his manners will have made on me.

I begin to feel very sensibly the effect of the derangement of the French packets. My intelligence from America lately has become more defective than it formerly was. The proceedings of Congress and of the assemblies there this winter will be very interesting.

The death of the Duc d'Orleans has darkened much the court and city. All is sable. No doubt this is a perfect representation of their feelings, and particularly of those of the D. de Chartres to whom an additional revenue of four millions will be a paultry solace for his loss.[6] News from Madrid give much to fear for the life of the only son of the Prince of Asturias.[7]

Colo. Humphries comes to take a view of London. I should be gratified also with such a trip, of which the pleasure of seeing your family would make a great part. But I foresee no circumstances which could justify, much less call for, such an excursion. Be so good as to present my respects to Miss Adams and to be assured yourself of the sincerity of the esteem with which I have the honour to be Dear Madam.

Your most obedient & most humble servt.   Th: Jefferson

RC (Adams Papers); endorsed: "Mr Jefferson Nov 20. 1785."

[1] Of 11 Oct., above.

[2] See AA2 to JQA, 18 Oct., note 16, and AA to Jefferson, 19 Oct., and note 5, above.

[3] Not found; AA mentions it in her letter to Jefferson of 25 Oct., above.

[4] Jefferson, *Papers*, 9:10–11.

[5] The date of Smith's arrival in Paris is not known; he had departed from Vienna on his return journey on 26 Oct. (AA to William Stephens Smith, 13 Aug., note 1, above).

[6] Louis Philippe, Duc d'Orléans, died on 18 Nov., and was succeeded to the title by his son Louis Philippe Joseph, Duc de Chartres.

The successor was guillotined in 1793, but his son survived to become King Louis Philippe in 1830. Hoefer, *Nouv. biog. générale*.

[7] The source of Jefferson's information was William Carmichael's letter of 6 Nov., which he received on the 20th (Jefferson, *Papers*, 9:23–24). Ferdinand, son of Charles, Prince of Asturias, an infant just past his first birthday, survived. His father became King Charles IV of Spain in 1788, and young Ferdinand succeeded to the title Prince of Asturias the next year. Hoefer, *Nouv. biog. générale*.

Charles Storer to Abigail Adams 2d

New-York, November 21st, 1785

My word I mean always to keep, Amelia, so I write you from this place, though my letter may be barren of subjects to entertain or interest you. One thing, however, there is, which I hope, and am willing to be sure, is not indifferent to you, and that is the information of our safe arrival here. It is a matter of no little joy and satisfaction to me, be assured; your participation, as it will prove your friendship, will be no small addition to it.

Seven long weeks were we upon the ocean, during all which time the winds seemed to have conspired against us, yet one week ashore quite effaced the past trouble; so soon are our griefs forgot when their object ceases to be present; not so with our friends, Amelia. The sweetest ingredient of happiness is the esteem we bear them. This is a sentiment we can reflect ever upon with pleasure: nor can absence, or distance, pain, or sorrow, deprive us of it. The first part of my voyage, I felt forcibly the attraction of Europe, and many a thought centered there. In the mid-ocean, view me, on a balance, duty and affection in equipoise; still a little further and home preponderated. That moment gave birth to feelings exquisitely pleasing, and every thought came crowded with satisfaction. The nearer I approach, my impatience (as gravity increases the rapidity of a body the nearer it comes to the earth, in falling) increases. Yet, Amelia, great as my pleasure is on this occasion, I am not unmindful of those friends in Europe, who in their turns now are absent. I feel my heart dilated; my feelings expand, so as to embrace you all. Peace and happiness be with you. Remember Eugenio, and be assured in so doing you add much to his happiness in return.

Perhaps you little think, that you are much the subject of conversation here. There are many ladies who envy you your present situation. "Is not Miss A. very handsome?" says one. Yes, madame, she is called the American beauty. "She must be very accomplished; she has every opportunity she could wish to improve herself; the best of masters; the best of every thing." Ah! Amelia, I could not say much on the score of masters; but such qualifications of the mind and heart, as I knew you possessed, and which, seriously considered, are the best accomplishments; these I assured the many inquirers Miss A. was eminent for. You will not be angry with me for this; for what I said was only what I could say with justice. Going abroad, I find, gives one some consequence. When you return you must, therefore, prepare to be looked up to as a pattern for every thing. I advise you now, then, to learn a little assurance; that reliance on yourself that can only make you independant of others. But I beg pardon for dictating to you thus.

A Preliminary, Amelia, though here at the close of my letter. There is a certain gentleman[1] in your family, who I imagine, may be inquisitive in regard to our correspondence; my request is—but without telling him so—that he be not permitted to know what I write.

Adieu! Yours,
                                                                    Eugenio

MS not found. Printed from AA2, *Jour. and Corr.*, 2:38–40.

[1] This would appear to be a reference to William Stephens Smith.

Abigail Adams to Thomas Jefferson

Sir   Grosvenor Square Novr. 24th. 1785

I hope if the Marquiss de la Fayette is returned to Paris he may be able to give us some account of Colln. Smith for whom we are not a little anxious, having no intelligence from him since the begining of September when he wrote[1] that he should tarry at Berlin till the reviews were over which would be by the 20th. of that month and then should make the utmost expedition to Paris where his stay would be six days or six Hours according to the intelligence he should meet with there from Mr. Adams. Ten weeks have since elapsed and not a Line or Syllable respecting him has come to hand, in all that time we have been daily and hourly expecting his return. We should have been still more anxious, if the Spanish Minister[2] had not informed us that by a Letter which he received from Colln. Miranda[3] early in Septemr. he wrote him that he had some thoughts of going to Vienna. Colln. Miranda's friends are allarmed about him and have been here to inquire if we could give any account of him. We are now daily more and more anxious because we cannot account for Coll. Smiths long absence but by sickness or some disaster, and even then we ought to have heard from him or of him. You will be so good Sir as to give us every information in your Power as soon as may be.

We suppose you have made an excursion to Fontainbleau[4] by our not having heard from you for a long time. Mr. Preston found the Letters he supposed to have been taken out of his Trunk, amongst his Linnen ten days after his arrival. Your orders shall be executed to the best of my abilities.

Inclosed is a Letter which I found a few days ago respecting the Wine which you was so kind as to take.[5] Mr. Adams is uncertain whether he requested you to Pay to Mr. Bonfeild on his order 319 Livres for a Cask of Wine which he procured for him and of which he never received any account untill his arrival here. If Mr. Barclay has not done it Mr. Adams would be obliged to you to pay it for him.

A Vessell arrived this week from New York and brings papers to the 16 [15?] of Octr.[6] They contain nothing material. A Letter from Mr. Jay informs us that no Minister was yet appointed to the Hague, but that Mr. Izard and Mr. Madison were in Nomination, that the rage for New states was very prevalent, which he apprehended would have no good affect. He wished the Ministers abroad to bear testimony against it in their Letters to Congress.[7]

In this Country there is a great want of many French comodities. Good sense, Good Nature, Political Wisdom and benevolence. His Christian Majesty would render essential service to His Britanick Majesty if he would permit Cargoes of this Kind to be exported into this Kingdom against the next meeting of Parliament.

The Treaty lately concluded between France and Holland and the Conduct of England with respect to America proves Her absolute deficiency in each Article.

Compliments to the Gentlemen of your Family from Sir your Humble Servant   A Adams

RC in AA2's hand (DLC: Jefferson Papers); addressed: "His Excellency Thomas Jefferson Esqr. Minister Plenipotentiary from the United States of America residing at Paris"; stamped: "Angleterre," and "[2]5 NO"; endorsed: "Mrs Adams." Dft (Adams Papers).

[1] On 5 Sept., above.

[2] Bernardo del Campo y Pérez de la Serna.

[3] In the draft, here and below, AA spells this "Mirandy."

[4] The sixteenth-century royal palace forty miles southeast of Paris, where the French court resided each fall for the hunting season. Not wanting to pay for additional lodging, Jefferson made brief visits to Fontainebleau as duty required. He was there from 26 Oct. to 1 November. Jefferson, *Papers*, 8:362, 681; 9:51.

[5] This letter has not been identified. In the draft after this sentence AA struck out: "It will inform you who the person is of whom we had it and the price."

[6] The draft reads "the 15 of october." AA2's 5's and 6's are quite similar.

[7] AA refers to John Jay's letter to JA of 14 Oct. (Adams Papers), printed in *Dipl. Corr.*, *1783–1789*, 2:419–421. The proceedings of

Congress do not record a nomination of James Madison to be minister to the United Netherlands in 1785, but Jacob Read of South Carolina did nominate Ralph Izard for this post on 24 Aug. (*JCC*, 29:655). The "New states" being espoused by many local leaders in 1785, with the support of some congressmen, were the trans-Appalachian districts of Kentucky, then a part of Virginia, and Franklin, the western portion of North Carolina, which had not fully relinquished its claim to the region. Congress, however, did not record receiving any petitions for statehood for either district during the year. The passage in Jay's letter concerning this movement reads: "The Rage for Separations and new States is mischevious—it will unless checked scatter our Resources and in every View enfeeble the Union. Your Testimony against such licentious anarchical Proceedings would I am persuaded have great Weight."

Abigail Adams 2d to John Quincy Adams

N 9

November 27th. [1785]

Never was there a young Man who deserved more a severe punishment than yourself. I am so out of patience with you, that I am quite at a loss in what way to revenge myself. In short I know of no method that I think would be adequate to your deserts. Month after month has elapsd, ship after ship has arrived, from New York, and six months have passed since you left us, and I have as yet received

November 27th

N 9— never was there a young Man who deserved
more a severe punishment than yourself— I am so out
of patience with you— that I am quite at a loss in what
way to revenge myself— in short I know of no method
that I think would be adequate to your deserts——
Month after month has elapsed— ship after ship has arrived
—from New York— and six months have passed since
you left us— and I have as yet received but one Letter from
you in America— we are and have been looking for Vessells
from Boston till all our patience is exhausted. it is said
here that so long a time has not passed since the peace
without hearing from thence— my last went by Mr
James Jarvis— to New York— a few weeks have elapsed
since— without my writing a word to you— but you have
not any shadow of complaint to make— and I do not
even think it proper to make any apology to you—
So I shall pass over all that has passed— and you don't know
what interesting matters you may have lost— and
begin from yesterday when we dined at Mr B Vaughn
where I met a Lady who inquired after you— now if
I were to serve you right I should leave the matter here
and you to indulge your curiosity— but according to
my natural character and indulgence— I will tell
you a little more. it was a Lady who knew you in
Stockholm— now what think you young Man—
does not your heart go pit a pat— now bounce—
as if it would break your rib——

10. "NEVER WAS THERE A YOUNG MAN WHO DESERVED MORE
A SEVERE PUNISHMENT THAN YOURSELF"
ABIGAIL ADAMS 2D TO JOHN QUINCY ADAMS, 27 NOVEMBER 1785
See page xv

but one Letter from you in America.[1] We are and have been looking for Vessells from Bostons till all our patience is exhausted. It is said here that so long a time has not passed since the peace without hearing from thence. My last went by Mr. James Jarvis, to New York,[2] a few weeks have elapsd since, without my writing a word, to you, but you have not any shawdow of complaint to make, and I do not even think it proper to make any apology to you. So I shall pass over all that has passed, and you dont know what interesting matters you may have lost, and begin from yesterday when we dined at Mr. B. Vaughn where I met a Lady who inquired after you. Now if I were to serve you right I should leave the matter here and you to indulge your curiossity, but according to my *natureal* character and indulgence, I will tell you a little more. It was a Lady who knew you in Stockholm. Now what think you young Man. Does not your heart go pitepat, now bounce, as if it would break your rib. Nor do you know how many of yours adventures She confided to me. No matter what they were, I well remembered with how much pleasure you used to speak of Sweeden, and how many encomioums you passed upon *some* Ladies there. How Languishingly you used to look, about *the one* &c &c. I have a good memory of these things. *The Lady* has visitted us, and we shall return the visit. An acquaintance may ensue, of what degree, I will not yet venture to say. No Wonder you was a little caught, so young, so beautifull, so affable so easy, so accomplished, in short so—incomparable—a—. But I think you was not quite in your Politicks when *the* Gentleman offerd to get you presented at Court, to refuse.[3]

There was yesterday a Mr. de Wint and his Daughter. The young Lady is very pretty and very agreeable, they have Lived in Amsterdam many years. The young Lady speaks English a little. They are to pass the Winter here and the next year in Paris. There was another West India Gentleman and Lady and I think it was observed that there was but one Person at table who was not either Americans septentionial[4] or Islanders, and that was a French Lady.

Last week Governor Pownall called upon us, just returnd from the south of France,[5] where he says he has found a fine Country, and with a better religion and Government, he acknowledged he should think it one of the finest Countries in the World. We stay at home here sayd he, and vainly imagine there is no Country but this. I am convinced to the Contrary. Well said he addressing himself to me, I hope you like this Country better than France. I told him I liked this Country *very well*. You ought to like it answered he, for I have been inquiring and I find they like you very well. Mrs. Pownal, called but we were *really* not at home. They are gone to Bath for a few weeks where you know every body repairs at this season, not knowing in what other way to spend their time, and nothing can more surprise them than to find persons, who are not reduced to such means to exist. This People cannot live like the rest of the World. From my own knowledge I cannot Judge, but I am told by all Foreigners, and some who are of rank and importance and who have lived in this Country as many years as fourteen and fifteen, that there is no such thing here as society, even among People of equal Rank, and importance, in their own opinions. They say that all the intercource there is, is by formal cerimonious visits, and that you will never find an English Lady at home, if you visit ever so often unless it is by particular invitation, and when they do meet them the heighth of sociability is, yes and No. I do not give this as my opinion for I have not acquaintance enough to form any adequate judgment. Those English Ladies who I am acquainted with are, neither superior or Inferior to those of our own Country. The English Women affect a Masculine air and manner which to me is horrid beyond description, and they generally acquire it. The handsomest Woman I have seen in England was my Lady Stormont. She is really beautifull, for she has in her Countenance and manners a Modesty and a dignity, which must forever please.

Sunday Eve, the 27

We went to visit Mrs. Paradise who I have heretofore described to you. She sees company every sunday Eve, and there is generally a Number of sensible Folks there. Mr. P. seems to be sollicitous to cultivate an acquaintance with all the Foreign ministers and many of them visit at his House. There were no Ladies this Eve. But several Gentlemen.[6] As we had not a particular invitation the company was not chosen, tho not the less agreeable. We have never yet been able to persuade Pappa to go, altho Mr. P. visits us as often as 2 or 3 evenings in the week.

Tuesday 29th, of November

Capt. Cushing arived and brought Letters so late as the 25 of October but to my total astonishment neither Pappa nor Mamma have a line from you, and the 2 letters which I have received are neither of them later than from New Haven.[7] We are yet hopeing that the Capt. may have Letters for us.

Thersday [*1 Dec.*]

Pappa received a Letter from Mr. Nathaniel Barret from some port in France. The ship he was in had like to have been lost, and in indeavouring to save the money Letters and &c, the boat sank, and every thing which was in it was lost. Fortunately there was but one person drownd. We hope your Letters were not on board this ship.[8] I am particularly anxious to receive Letters from you from Boston, and I think you unpardonable if you have not written. But this I think all most impossible. Our Letters speak in the highest terms of you. We fear they will spoil you by the [. . . .][9] young Men, till they make them perfectly ridiculous. I know of no such characters in Boston and I hope they may never exist there, but at the same time there may be some danger in too much attention and praise. It will require much firmness and fortitude not to be injured by it. I learn from Letters received[10] that you are at Haverhill with Mr. Shaw, and proposed, entering Colledge in April. I hope it is true. Our accounts from my other two Dear Brothers are as favourable as we could wish, that Charles, is steady and studious and enjoys the good will of his Class and the Affection of his Tutor, but we are not told who he was. I hope you will be more particular—if you are not I will scold you.

Oh, how often do I wish myself with you, but when that will be Heaven only knows. My Brother [. . . .][11]

Your Letters from New York, and so far on your journey as I have received have given me much pleasure, and sattisfaction. I wish they had been later dates, or that I could yet acknowledge the receipt of Later Dates. I have written you often and largely but I fear my Letters will be to you tedious. Yet it is against my principles almost to make appologies for I allways think them the dullest part of a Dull Letter.

Lately I have had a good deal of writing to do for your father, for, Mr. Smith, has been absent near 4 months and tis near three since Pappa has heard a Word from him. In short we are tottally at a loss to account for his ⟨absence⟩ Conduct. It is quite a matter of specu-lation amongst his Brethren in Commission.[12] One of them told me yesterday he had not been in his own Country for ten years, that he wished ardently to go only for six weeks. If he could do as Coll. S— [. . . .][13] He[14] has lately finished a peice which has done him great Honour, and Mr. West said of him here the other day, that he knew of no young Man, who promised so much as he. He has just begun the battle of Bunkers Hill, and it is thought will have a very good picture. If he succeeds in this I am told he proposes to go on, with many of the important events in our own Country.

Count Sarsfeild came in to tell us that he could not pass our House without calling. He has made us many friendly visits lately, but goes to Paris next week. Before we had finished drinking tea Mr. Barthelemy Chargé des affaires du France, and Mr. d'Aragon, private secretary to Compt D'Adamah [*Adhémar*], came in. The former I have mentiond to you before I believe. He is an agreeable Man, and has less, of the Frivolity of a French man, than they generally possess. Mr. Daragon is a very opposite character, he has vivacity enough. We all agree that he resembles you very much. Mr. B. told him one day at table when we were remarking the resemblance, that he had a compliment to make him. "Vous avez l'Honneur a resembler le frere de Mademoiselle Adams." It is rather in his person, and his eyes than for I dont think him so well looking a young Man as mon frere. He has served in America as private secretary to Count Rochambeau, and speaks english very well. He is solliciting of His Court to be sent Consul to Boston, it not however very probable he will succeed.

Pray did you ever hear of the famouss Mademoiselle d'eon, who served as Chargé des affaires du France and afterwards as ambassador from that Court to this—who obtained le croix de St. Louis, and was in several engagements who fought two Duels on the part of some Ladies, and many more extrordinary matters—whose works, make thirteen vollumes &c. She has lately arrived in this City, and these Gentleman had dined with her and were speaking of her. She has resumed la habit des dames, but Mr. D. told me he was sure, She might go dressd in l'habit d'Homme and not be noticed, but she could not as a Lady. She wears her croix de St. Louis and as one may well suppose a singular figure, as well as an extrordinary Character.[15]

Saturday 3d

Mr. Paradise and Mr. Freime[16] secretary to the Portuguese Minister, calld and spent an hour or two. The Chavelier de Pinto has lately made proposals, or rather taken up, those which Pappa made to the Ambassador from Portugal in France, and he has written to his Court for full powers to form a commercial Treaty with America.[17] They seem sollicitous for it, and are desirios to send and receive ministers and Consuls to and from America. Pappa has written to Mr. Jay in favour of your friend W—[18] for Consul. This Mr. F. seems to be a steady sober young Man. He has been many years in this Country and speaks english well for a foreigner. They had finished their visit, and Mamma was gone up stairs to go to bed, it was about ten oclock when a foot mans rap, roused us, and who should it be but Madame de Pinto, to make a visit more gracious than is customary She came in and sat half an hour. Her visit was particularly to tell us, that She saw company every sunday Evening and should be happy to see us. She seems to be a friendly agreeable Woman, speaks english a little. Her manners are more French than English, par consequence plus agreable.

This Evening Mr. Joy sent my father Word that his Brother would go for NY in the Packet which would sail on Wedensday and he would take Letters for us. I intend giveing this and one other to his Care,[19] for there is not ship to sail from hence for a long time. I hope you will mind what I have said about writing by the 〈French〉 English packet from NY. We think it very extrordinary that there was no Letters from you after your arrival in Boston, and not a line to Pappa or Mamma.

The Ceres we fear is lost, the Passengers and People were all saved but the mony and Letters all lost. I hope yours were not on board, of her tho I fear it.[20]

Dft (Adams Papers). The text is written on 11 small, unnumbered pages. The bottom of page 6 and the top of page 7 have been cut out of the letter, resulting in the loss of text at three places (see notes 9, 11, and 13). The editors give their reasons for thinking this is a draft in notes 11 and 20.

[1] That of 17 July, above, carried by John Barker Church, who sailed from New York on 4 Aug., on the British packet (JQA, *Diary*, 1:297). AA2 received this letter, with JQA to AA2, 25 May, above, also carried by Church, on 5 Sept. (AA2 to JQA, 26 Aug., above).

[2] AA2 to JQA, 18 Oct., above.

[3] Neither JQA's letters written during his return journey from Russia in the winter of 1783, above, nor his Diary entries for that period, identify any of the Swedish ladies whom he met, or mention the offer of any gentlemen to introduce him at the Swedish court.

[4] That is, North American. AA2 met the persons mentioned in this paragraph at Benjamin Vaughan's on 26 Nov. (AA2, *Jour. and Corr.*, [3]:199–200).

[5] Thomas Pownall made this visit on 18 Nov. (AA2, *Jour. and Corr.*, [3]:199). Pownall was governor of Massachusetts, 1757-1760, a member of the House of Commons, 1767-

1780, and the author of several important treatises on Anglo-American relations, as well as on antiquarian, economic, and scientific subjects. Pownall and his second wife had been touring through southern France since the fall of 1784 (*DNB*). JA and JQA had visited Pownall at his home at Richmond Hill on 29 Nov. 1783 (JA, *Diary and Autobiography*, 3:151; JQA, *Diary*, 1:206).

[6] In her long journal entry for this day, AA2 particularly mentioned a "Mr. Horne Tooke," with whose manners and benevolent sentiments she was much impressed (*Jour. and Corr.*, [3]:200–201). See John Horne Tooke's entry in *DNB*.

[7] The two letters are JQA to AA2, 9 Aug., above, begun in New York and completed on 19 Aug., in New Haven; and probably JQA to AA2, 1 Aug., above. AA2's journal places the receipt of these letters on 28 Nov. (*Jour. and Corr.*,[3]:201–202).

[8] Nathaniel Barrett wrote to JA on 29 Nov.

(letter not found), and enclosed an earlier, undated letter, written "At sea Nov. 1785" (Adams Papers). Barrett's letter of 29 Nov. gave details of the shipwreck of the *Ceres* (JA to Barrett, 2 Dec., LbC, Adams Papers), which sailed from Boston in late October (see James Bowdoin to Thomas Jefferson, 23 Oct., and Thomas Cushing to Jefferson, 25 Oct., Jefferson, *Papers*, 8:662–663, 670–671), and which AA2 mentions at the end of this letter. JQA's letter to AA2 of 20 Aug., above, was on the *Ceres*.

[9] About eight full lines of text have been cut away here. See note 11.

[10] See Mary Cranch to AA, 14 Aug.; Cotton Tufts to JA, 6 Oct.; Cotton Tufts to AA, 14 Oct.; and Mary Cranch to AA, [*ca.* 23] Oct., all above.

[11] A comparison of the content of the text surrounding the three deleted passages (see notes 9 and 13), and the layout of this passage on two MS pages, point to this passage, of about fourteen lines, as the object of a deliberate deletion, uncommon in an Adams MS, with the shorter ones, above and below, being merely the reverse sides of this text.

If this letter is a draft, as seems virtually certain (see immediately below, and note 20), AA2 may have removed this passage herself. Because there is no other extant version of this letter, or any summary of one by JQA or others, the missing text cannot be reconstructed, but a possible topic of the passage is AA2's dismissal of Royall Tyler or some comment upon him. No such remarks appear elsewhere in AA2's letters to JQA. AA2 evidently did send a copy of this letter to JQA that has not been found (see AA2 to JQA, 5 Dec., below, the beginning of which refers to a longer version of the letter).

[12] That is, the diplomatic corps in London.

[13] Here again, about seven MS lines of text have been removed (see note 11).

[14] The artist John Trumbull. The piece that he had "lately finished" has not been identified. AA2 would describe Trumbull's *The Battle of Bunker Hill*, completed in March 1786, after seeing the work in progress in January (AA2 to JQA, 22 Jan. 1786, Adams Papers, filmed with AA2 to JQA, 5 Dec. 1785). See Theodore Sizer, *The Works of John Trumbull, Artist of the American Revolution*, New

Haven, 1967, figs. 145–151, and accompanying text.

[15] Chevalier Charles de Beaumont d'Eon (1728–1810) served as a French diplomat in Russia, and briefly in Austria, in the 1750s, and as secretary to the Duc de Nivernais, the French ambassador to Great Britain, in 1762–1763. For his efforts in concluding the Peace of Paris of 1763, and his earlier work in St. Petersburg, he received the Cross of St. Louis. He wrote extensively on the history, commerce, and government, and the fiscal and social problems, of Russia, France, and Great Britain. D'Eon often dressed in women's clothes, and genuine confusion as to his sex was widespread in his lifetime, but his death certificate, and the report of an autopsy performed before three witnesses in London by a surgeon to the exiled Louis XVIII, reported that he was male (Hoefer, *Nouv. biog. générale*).

[16] Cipriäo Ribeiro de Freire later served as Portugal's chargé d'affaires in London, 1790–1792, as Portugal's first minister to the United States, 1794–1799, and as minister to Spain in 1801 (*Repertorium der diplomatischen Vertreter aller Länder*, 3:317, 321, 320).

[17] See JA to John Jay, 5 Nov. (PCC, No. 84, V, f. 717–728; printed in *Dipl. Corr., 1783–1789*, 2:527–533); and JA to Thomas Jefferson, 5 Nov. (Jefferson, *Papers*, 9:18–22). Both letters report on JA's conference with Pinto on 4 November.

[18] JA wrote to John Jay on 3 Dec. (LbC, Adams Papers), to recommend Winslow Warren for U.S. consul to Portugal. Warren, however, returned to Boston unexpectedly in mid-December (Mary Cranch to AA, 18 Dec., below), and was not appointed consul.

[19] AA2's other letter sent to New York has not been identified; see AA2 to JQA, 5 Dec., below, under "Wedensday 7th."

[20] On this last page, written crosswise, and apparently partly under the end of AA2's text, is a sentence in AA's hand: "Mrs. Adams compliments to Mr. Brown request him to get the extract of the Letter from Boston inserted." Nothing is known about this sentence, but it does not appear to relate to AA2's letter. Its appearance, however, is yet another indication that AA2's letter is a draft, written here on a sheet of paper that AA had already used.

Mary Smith Cranch to Abigail Adams

My dear Sister   Braintree November 29th 1785

How provoking it is to be told that a vessel is to sail next week with our Letters and then have it stay in the Harbour six Weeks. I thought till yesterday that Capn. Young was half way to London at least, and behold he will not leave Boston this week. The Letters will be so old, that they will lose much of their value, but tis no fault of mine.[1]

I have been waiting some time without writing for those Letters you promiss'd me by Mr. Storer. He is not yet come from New York. I have very unexpectadly receiv'd two by Capn. Callahan for which I thank you most sincerly.[2] I am so gratified that mine give you any pleasure, that I feel determin'd to keep you well supplyd. If you have reciev'd all I have sent, you will think I have done my part as to quantity pretty well, especially if you knew how little time I can get from my Family affairs to write, and how unable I was last summer to write at all. I did not then Love to tell you how sick I was, nor how much it hurt me to write. I had a Rhumatick complaint across my stomack such as I used to have in my neck and shoulders. It is much better but I have enough of it yet to be troublesome.

I am glad to find you so well prepair'd to receive the account of our dear aunt Tufts' death. In my September Letter I wrote you that she was better, but alass! it was only a revival. We flatter'd ourselves for a little while that she would get through the winter, but the last attack was too voilent for her feeble Frame. The last month of her Life was a very distressd one, but she bore all her sufferings without a murmer or complaint and was only affraid that she should be too desirous to depart.

When I stood at her grave and saw her deposited by the sides of my dear Parents, surrounded by the multitude of weeping Friends and acquaintance which her benevolenc had gain'd her, O my sister! whither did my thoughts carry me. Far far beyond this vale of Tears to those blest abodes where I trust the souls of our dear departed Friends are receiving the rewards of their well spent Lives, and exedling to their utmost wishes those benevolent dispositions, for which they were so remarkable while here. May they not be minis-tering spirits to those who are most deserving the care of Heaven?

When I think of the closing Scene of our dear Fathers Life, Labouring with such ardour as he did for the salvation of a soul very dear to him:[3] that he seem'd almost insensible to the pains and

475

agonies of Death although they were as severe as Flesh could bear, I feel an anguish which is only exceeded, when I reflect how little the unhappy Prodigal has profited by it. I have not mention'd him in any of my Letters because I could not tell you any good of him, and I do not love to give you pain.

This winter is likely to be as lonely to me as the last and more so upon many accounts. Weymouth is become more melancholy to me than ever. Betsy is yet at Haverhill and will not return till Spring if the wishes of her Friends there can prevent it. The unhappy end of Mrs. Duncan the circumstances of which Betsy will I suppose tell you, has (sister Shaw says) made her company almost necessary to the happiness of Mrs. White and Peggy.[4] Their greif occation'd by this melancholy event has been excessive, especially Mrs. Whites. She had been very sick some time before and was less able to bear such a shock than she would have been at some other time. Betsy writes me[5] that she has been full of fears that their reasons would have been again affected but they had not been a moment depriv'd of it. I have been anxious least such distressing Scenes should hurt her health, but she says she was never better, in her life. Her uncle and aunt would have had her with them, but Peggy would not let her stir from her side. Although greatly shocked she was not so nearly connected but she could reason and Sooth and you know her gentle spirit is just fitted for such an imployment. I know not how to spare her and yet I cannot take her away while Mrs. White so earnesly petitions me "not to take from her one of the greatest comforts she has untill time shall have a little softend their affliction."

It is not the dissapated gay Companion which we wish for my dear sister in such an Hour as theirs. It is the chearful Freind who by gentle Soothings can calm the ruffled Passions and point us to those comforts and consolations which Religion only can afford.

Sister Shaw and your sons will write for themselves[6] so that I need not say any thing more about them than that Sister is as well as usual and your [*sons*] are very good and behave well. Betsy says in one of her Letters to me[7] "It forms a very great part of my happiness that I have my Cousin John Adams with me here. He spends much of his time when absent from his Studies at Mrs. Whites, and we are all fond of having him do it. I take more pleasure in conversing one hour with him, than in whole days spent with any other youth of his age. May nothing deprive us of him nor him of his shining Talents." Tommy is a good child and Cousin Charles behaves well, and is very prudent as to expences. I take the same care to provide for him, as

I do of my own son. His washing and mending is done as regularly as Billys. His cloths will last longer than if they were put out at Cambrige. They might be as well wash'd, but they would suffer for want of a stich in time. I have taken the Sugar you left in your Seller to make cake for Charles. It had contracted such a dampness, by being so long there, that it is as dark as the brownest of sugar.

I rejoice to find you have so many good Friends around you. As to the abuse of the refugees it cannot hurt you, but I think with Mr. Jefferson that it is very silly in our printers to publish it,[8] and your Freinds will do what they can to prevent it.

We do every thing in our Power to keep the moths from eating your things and I believe nothing will be much hurt. Mr. Adams has a number of old Black coats wastcoats &c that I am sure he will never wear again nor any of your children will they fit. They may make cousin Tommy some wastcoats, may we take them for this up. I often long to take your advice, but hope I shall meet with your approbation.

Adieu for the present. I shall write more. Yours affectionately

M. Cranch

RC (Adams Papers).

[1] The letters sent by Captain Young could have included all of those written to the Adamses in London by their Massachusetts relatives since the departure of the *Ceres* about 25 October. Long delayed in Boston, these letters were again delayed in England, where Young had to put in to Plymouth for repairs to his vessel. Arriving in the Channel in Jan. 1786, he did not come up to London with the last of the letters in his care until mid-March (AA to Cotton Tufts, 10 Jan., Adams Papers; to Mary Cranch, 26 Jan., MWA:Abigail Adams Corr.; to JQA, 16 Feb., Adams Papers; to Mary Cranch, 26 Feb., and 21 March 1786, both MWA:Abigail Adams Corr.).

[2] Charles Storer carried the letter by AA to Mary Cranch, 11 Sept.; AA's "two by Capn. Callahan" were of 30 Sept., and 1 Oct. (all above).

[3] That of his son, William Smith Jr.

[4] Elizabeth Cranch next wrote to AA on 20 May 1786 (Adams Papers); she said nothing about the suicide of Sarah Leonard LeBaron White's sister, Elizabeth Leonard Duncan.

[5] Letter not found; it probably dates from about 10 November. Mary Cranch promptly replied to it (letter not found), and Elizabeth Cranch in turn replied on 28 Nov. (MHi:Jacob Norton Papers).

[6] Elizabeth Shaw's next extant letter to AA is that of 2 Jan. 1786 (Adams Papers). No letters from CA to AA, and none from TBA to AA before 1796, have been found; but AA acknowledged the receipt of letters from JQA, CA, and TBA in her reply to JQA of 16 Feb. 1786 (Adams Papers). JQA's letter was that of 28 Dec., below; those by CA and TBA were probably from the same period.

[7] Not identified; perhaps the letter of ca. 10 Nov., not found, mentioned above (see note 5).

[8] See AA to Mary Cranch, 1 Oct.; and Jefferson to AA, 25 Sept., both above.

Abigail Adams 2d to John Quincy Adams

N *10*

London Monday Eve December
5th. *1785*

This Morning I wrote you[1] that we were going to the play with Mrs. Church. At six oclock we called upon her, and went to the Theatre of Drury Lane, where was performed the Confedrecy,[2] a Comedy, which I took to be as great a satire upon the manners, of high Life, as could have been written. It was not however any thing new. The entertainment was the Jubilee of Shakespear,[3] which is well worth seeing onc, the scenery is magnificent, and there is a procession of the Principles characters and a representation of the Principle scenes of every one of his Plays, which is very well-done, and at the close, they all appear upon the stage at one time. The Whole is very cleaver. But the Length of the amusements here render them allmost tiresome, to be kept five hours to any one particular thing is too much. Was it ever so good one would get tired of it. Miss Farren playd a principle part in the first peice, and She is my favourite Comic actress. They speak much of Mrs. Abington Mrs. Crouch, and Mrs. Jordon, but of the 3 first I prefer Miss F. Mrs. Jordon I have not yet seen.[4] We got home just at Eleven, and had scarce set down before Colln. Smith puts his Head into the room, and exclaimd—dare I see you Sir—to Pappa—and well he might have some fears of his reception for his Long absence, but who should present himself with him but Colln. H[umphreys]. We wellcomed them to London, and we sat down. Colln. S. told Pappa he had brought His friend as a peace offering. He was too well grown to stille him a Lamb. They informed us all our friends in Paris were well. Poor Williamos, died about three weeks ago. His dissorder was the Gout in his stomach. Many have lost a friend, for he was certainly of a benevolent disposition and as far as his ability enabled him he rendered every one assistance. Mr. Jefferson I think I have allready told you in a former Letter had moved. They say he has a very fine situation—*but exclaim mos teribly about his salery, declared he is 2 thousand in debt, and that He shall be ruind.*[5] This you know is entre Nous. Lamb and Randall have been sett off some time for Algiers. Mr. Barclay and Franks are not yet gone. Pettit has got the Place of Maitre D'Hotell, to one of the first Bankers in Paris Mr. C. The Baron de Stearl [Staël] is soon to be married or is allready, to Mademoise Neckar, Daughter to the Famous

478

Mr. Necker,[6] and it is said to His [Milrenary?] Daughter it seems the Baron is not rich, nor was he Nobly Born, but by beeing a favourite of the Ladies was, given the Tittle of Baron, and the embassy of Ambassador, out of the usual forms of Etiquette. It is said he is a favrite of the Queen of France, and I am sure he must be of every body. This I have given you some account of our Parisian Friends. I have not perhaps assended in just degrees. It might be dificult to determine them, but one thing more of them. Mademoiselle Lucille is to be married to Monsieur Deville first secretary to the Comt de Vergennes. The King has given him le place of Farmer General. Monsieur Challut lent his House at St. Cloud, to the King this summer for the accomodation of the Dauphin when he had the small Pox. The Court has been lately to Fointainbleau, but have returnd.

Tuesday the 6th

We had a large Company to dine both Gentlemen and Ladies. Mr. and Mrs. Chaning, from Carolina, they have been in England many years, but have allways been of the right side as it is called. Mrs. Channing is a Worthy sensible Woman, but Poor Lady, is Griveing to Death for the Loss of an only Daughter, who I have heard was as fine a Girl as any in the World. Mrs. C. had taken great Care in her education, and She was according to the English frase perfectly accomplished. Your Pappa was much pleased with Mr. C. Mr. Blake another Carolinian, his Lady was indisposed, and prevented comeing. He was in Boston he tells me the september after we left it, and is vastly pleased with it. He prefers N Y and Boston to any other part of the Contiment.[7] Mr. and Mrs. Vaughan you know as well as Mr. W. Vaugan[8] who has without exception a head the most like a fish, and an Haddock too, of any human being I ever beheld. I dont mean in the shape or outward appearance except his eyes. Mr. and Mrs. Smith, who if I recollect aright I have mentiond before to you. Mr. S— is a Member of Parliament, and Mrs. S— is a Cleaver agreeable Little Woman. Her Brother Mr. Copes [*Coape*], was in Boston last fall, and has now gone out to settle in Carolina. They have I may with justice say, payd us more attention than any other Family, that we have become acquainted with since our residence here. They Live at Clapham. We have had several invitations to dine there, but it has so happend that we have never had it in our Power to accept of but one. Mrs. Smith was very polite and gave me an invitation to go with her to the Assembly which they have monthly, during the Winter. Tho I was obliged by her attention I could not accept it, for I have ever avoided and ever shall during my residence here, such parties. Indeed I was never attached to them in America and in our own circle where every one is known to each other, and you cannot wonder that I do not wish to go into them here. If I had been blest with a sister who would have joind me in such amusements I beleive I should have been more pleased with them. But whenever I go into company I feel a kind of sollitude and lonesomeness, which has ever been painfull, and I am convinced my happiness lies not in that path. I had rather spend 3 hours in writing to you than in any Ball assembly Pat [Party?] or what ever name is or may be given to Twenty [Forty?] People meeting together for their own amusement. I used to like the Assemblys at Boston very well, because I had many friends and acquaintances amongst the circle. But I had like to have forgot the rest of our Company. Mr. Mrs. and Miss Paradise. Mr. Copes Brother to Mrs. Smith. Colln. H[umphreys] and Coln. Smith compleated our Party. The formers, is amaizingly alterd, there seems to be a Gloom upon his Countenance, and a sedateness of manners that I dont remember in Paris. Perhaps tis the loss of his knight Hood, his friend has prevailed upon him to leave off the badge,[9] while he resides here, and Ill venture to say he is lessened in his own estimation by quitting it. The Marquis[10] indeaverd to persuade C[olonel] S[mith] to wear his at Berlin but without affect. The King of Prussia rallyd the Marquis about his order, and asked him if his eagle had two Heads. All the French officers appeard with it. Duke of York[11] was there and many other English officers. The Duke, disliked the American Uniform and expressd his disapprobation to some of his Friends ⟨who⟩. His Character does not appear more worthy than His Brothers the Prince of Whales, it is said. Our company to day, were seventeen, seven Ladies and ten gentlemen and every one were dressd in Black. Indeed all London, I may say all England are in Mourning for the Queens youngest Brother, who died lately and there has not been known so General a Mourning for a Long time. It is a compliment every one seems to feel due to her Majesty, and must to her be very pleasing proff of the affection of her subjects.[12]

Wedensdy 7th

Mr. Joy and Mr. Bulfinch called upon us in the Morning, the former to inform your Father that he should not go in the Packet but in the Ship Morton which will sail next week. I have seald my, Letter N 9,[13] I shall give it to him, and convey this to Boston.

This Morning or this day about 3 o clock we received our Letters from Mr. Barret which we feard were lost. They were to be sure as Wet as they could be, but very fortunately not so damaged as to injure the writing. I have now the happiness to acknowledge the receipt of a Letter from you from Boston[14] but I am not sattisfied. No sooner had I finishd my two sheets, but I wanted to follow you farther, and to hear your observation upon folks and things. In short I dont feel content when an ⟨hour⟩ day has pasd after the date of your Last to the Departure of the Ship. I might complain of the Shotness of your letters when compared to the Prolixity of mine but I [seem?] to be enough sensible that your ⟨4?⟩ 2 Sheats contain as much as my 12 or more. Therefore I must only regret that my stile and manner is not so Laconic. I shall submit it to your correction, nevertheless craving your Mercy. Continue your Letters my Dear Brother. Do not led one opportunity of conveyance escape you. If you could know how pleasing and sattisfactory they are to me, you would not deny me this scource of happiness. I shall wish for April, and hope then you will come to Cambridge, for I shall then seem nearer. You will receive my Letters as soon as they arrive, and I fear you will not where you are.

Thursday 8th

Your Pappa went to Court, where there was a full drawing room, but there was I suppose nothing extrordinary. Colln. S[mith] dined with us, and read to your Mother some Letters from his family. In one of them you are mentiond as visitting them, which you told me of long ago.[15] I shall show your encomiuns upon Miss Sally to Her Brother. Belinda seems to be the favorite with him I think. Count Sarsfeild called and took one cup of tea if I wuld make it very weak. You know him, he is allways pleasant. Mamma told him that when she came from the [Play?] on Monday Pappa told her that he had been Quarrelling with Count Sarsfeild. Oh yes, we had a quarell, saide he. I dont Love to expose this Man to his Family, but he is sometimes a little week—dans la tette. I love his pleassantry very much. He was going to an Assembly, and on Monday setts off for France. Next May twelve months says he, the second dinner I eat in this Town shall be in this House. Pappa told him he did not know who he would find Living here.

Fryday 9th

Mamma and myself went out this Morning a shopping, that business you used to Love so well in Paris, but we are so indipendant here having the free use of our Tongues, that we are not under obligation to any body for talking for us. A happiness indeed. We stopped at the N England Coffe House to Leave a Card inviting Capt. Cushing to dine with us on sunday, and then we heard that a Ship is to sail for Boston on sunday. I shall indeavor to get this Letter on Board, some how or some how. Tomorrow we are to have a large company to dine, all Americans, and an Americain Dinner salt Fish. I tell you who they are. Mr. and Mrs. Hay, Mr. and Mrs. Rucker Miss R. Mr. and Mrs. Roggers. Mr. Trumble Mr. Parker Mr. Ward Boylstone Mr. Molsby an Englisman, Dr. Bancroft Colln. H and Mr. Smith.[16] It is now half after twelve the Watchman have just called. I am going to drink some Lemonade, as we used to do at Auteul. I wish you could sip with me now. I shall give my Letter to some body tomorrow to put into the Bag for me, so I shall not have time to add any thing more. Present my Love to Aunt Shaw, and my Brothers. Yours affectionately   A Adams

I was going to complain to you of the weakness of my Character but my time has all been taken up in narative.

Dft (Adams Papers); written on nine small pages. The Dft of AA2's No. 11 (22 Jan. 1786) continues on the back of the last page of No. 10.

[1] This evidently refers to the last entry in the recipient's copy of AA2 to JQA, 27 Nov. (not found), the draft of which, printed above, ends on 3 December.

[2] An advertisement for the Drury Lane Theater in *The Morning Chronicle and London Advertiser* for 5 Dec., publicized the appearance of Elizabeth Farren portraying Clarissa in Vanbrugh's *The Confederacy*. She acted in London from 1777 to 1797.

[3] *The Jubilee* of Shakespeare was "a Dramatic Entertainment of Dancing, Singing, and Dialogue, in Honour of Shakespeare" (*The Morning Chronicle and London Advertiser*, 6 Dec. 1785).

[4] AA2 had seen Frances Abington as Lady Rusport on 5 Oct. (AA2 to JQA, 18 Oct. and note 10, above). Anna Maria Phillips, a young singer and actress generally at Drury Lane, married a Lt. Crouch of the Royal Navy in 1785. Mrs. Jordan (born Dorothea or Dorothy Bland) began her career in Dublin in 1777; 1785 was her first London season. *DNB*.

[5] Jefferson's move in October is mentioned in AA2's letter to JQA of 24 Sept., above; see Jefferson to AA, 4 Sept., note 5, above. Jefferson gaves vivid expression to his financial worries in 1785 in letters to David Franks, 17 June, and to Samuel Osgood, 5 Oct. (Jefferson, *Papers*, 8:225, 588–591).

[6] Anne Louise Germaine Necker married the Baron de Staël Holstein in 1786, near the beginning of her literary career, and would be known thereafter as Madame de Staël (Hoefer, *Nouv. biog. générale*).

[7] John Channing and his wife moved from South Carolina to England in 1769 (*South Carolina Historical and Genealogical Magazine*, 21:14 [Jan. 1920], 27:111 [July 1926]; JA, *Papers*, 7:125). William Blake and his wife, Ann Izard Blake, had also lived in England for several years (JA, *Diary and Autobiography*, 3:182, note 1).

[8] That is, Benjamin Vaughan, Sarah Manning Vaughan, and Benjamin's brother William Vaughan (same, 3:53, and note 2).

[9] Of the Society of the Cincinnati. Col. Humphreys' friend was, of course, William Stephens Smith, who had learned of the Adams' strong feelings about the order during the summer (see AA to JQA, 26 June, note 8, above).

[10] Lafayette, head of the French chapter of the Society of the Cincinnati.

[11] Frederick Augustus, second son of George III, who had been studying French, German, and the military arts in Germany since 1781 (*DNB*). Among the other English

officers attending the review was Lord Corn-wallis, who was on a diplomatic mission to Prussia (*Lafayette in the Age of the Amer. Rev.*, 5:345–347, 349 note).

[12] *The Morning Chronicle and London Advertiser* for 7 Dec. announced that "their Majesties will not go to the Theatre till after the publick mourning for her Majesty's brother the late prince of Mecklinburgh Strelitz." This was George Augustus, prince of Mecklinburgh-Strelitz, a major general in the service of Austria. He died on 9 Nov. at Trynau, Hungary; his funeral was held on 12 Nov. at Pösing, Hungary (*Gazette de Leyde*, 2 and 6 Dec.).

[13] Of 27 Nov., above; but the recipient's copy of that letter, not found, was longer than the extant draft (see note 1).

[14] This was JQA's No. 7, dated 20 Aug., above. Begun in Middletown, Conn., it was completed in Boston on 28 August. The MS shows clear signs of water damage.

[15] JQA to AA2, 17 July, above, under "31st" July, and note 20; and JQA to AA2, 1 Aug., above.

[16] Of the guests in this party who have not previously been identified, "Miss R." was probably either a Miss Rucker, or Miss Ramsay, whom JQA met in Paris in March, at a gathering that included the Ruckers. The Adamses definitely saw Miss Ramsay in Jan. 1786; she may have been related to a Mr. Ramsay of New York, whom JQA met in July (AA2 to JQA, 22 Jan. 1786, filed with AA2 to JQA, 5 Dec., Adams Papers; JQA, *Diary*, 1:235, 290, 295). The Adamses had met a Mr. Parker of South Carolina in Paris in Jan. 1785 (JQA, *Diary*, 1:216, and note 1). Mr. Molsby, who was evidently the only Englishman present, has not been identified.

William Stephens Smith to Abigail Adams

Tuesday Morn'g. 10 oClock
[*6 December 1785*][1]

The three Letters which Mrs. Adams honoured me with were received at Paris,[2] and should have been answered, had an oppertunity offered. Permit me to pass an encomium on that prudence which dictates silence on painful Subjects, and to assure her while honour guides my actions and is my ruling star thro' Life—I shall alway's endeavour to appear as if I had taken the deepest draught from the stream recommended.[3] Indeed I am now a little surprized at myself for seeking it at such a distance—when reflection would soon have pointed it out as flowing from the mount of honour, any deviation from which can never give me satisfaction or lay a proper foundation for me to risk my happiness upon—for I should alway's doubt the purity of that mind, which could sacrifice the smallest particle of it on any shrine whatever. With these sentiments my friends must feel themselves shelt'red from a troublesome assiduity which is sometimes connected with similar Circumstances.

Give me your friendship and believe——W. S. Smith—capable of gratitude.

Dr. Madam

I intended to ask for my small trunk when I begun this note, but found it full sooner than I expected. I shall be obliged if Mr. Spiller will send it by the bearer. I shall soon pay my respects to Mr. A—s and put my shoulder to the wheel.   W. S. S.

RC (Adams Papers); written on a small sheet of paper from which a part was torn off neatly; addressed, running onto the lost end of the sheet: "Mrs. Ada[ms] G— [S?]." Originally filed and filmed at [*ca. 15 Dec.*] (Adams Papers Microfilms, Reel No. 366).

[1] The date is based on William Stephens Smith's surprise return from the Continent on "Monday Eve," in AA2 to JQA, 5 Dec., above.

[2] Two are known to the editors: 13 Aug., and 18 Sept., both above.

[3] The Lethe; see AA to William Stephens Smith, 18 Sept., above.

Lucy Cranch to Abigail Adams

My Dear Aunt   Braintree Dec. 8. 1785

I last week recieved your invaluable favour of August 27. by Mr. Storer. I wish it was in my power to return you any thing that would be any way equivelent to it, if there are any of your Letters Madam, (which I am very sure there is not) that will bear to be ranked with Whiped Sulububs Flumery &c. in what rank must *mine* be placed. Far very far below them. Believe me Madam your Letter to me was a dish of very solid food dressed in a manner the most elegant that was possible. And it must be high cultivation added to a naturally rich soil to produce fruites rich as your Letters are.

I felt flattered by your encomiums upon Richardsons works as it is what I have often thought. He was always a favourite author of mine. I think I never read any Romances, that taken alltogether were equal to his. Too many of them, if they do not directly lead to Vice, tend to eneveate the mind and robs it of the strenght which is nessesary to make it stem with resolution the torrent of folly, which too often prevails.

Yes my Dear Aunt I think it reasonable to suppose that those who shall make the highest attainments in virtue while here, and who most improve the talents alloted them by the supreme Being, will have the most elevated seats in the blissful mansions above, and even there shall we not be making constant progression toward greater perfection, and though always rising we shall yet be at an infinite distance from the infinitely perfect God.

Our dear good Aunt Tufts is now no more. She has bid an eternal adieu to this vale of tears, and has gone to take her seat with the blessed. The universal benovelence of her heart and her undesembled piety had long fited her for their company. As her Life had ever been that of virtue, and as far as in her power of ussfulness, she was able to look forward to another state with satisfaction. She bore her sickness with the resagnation of a Christion yet longing to be released from that frail tenement which had always been a sourse of pain to her. The Doctor feels his misfortune as a man and bears it as a Christion. I have not seen Mr. Storer yet, his friends in Boston cannot spare him long enough to come as far as Braintree.

My sister is now at Haverhill and has been there for two months past. She will write. Cousin JQA is there following his studies with the utmost ardour. Cousin Charles is very well, and very good. Tommy improves fast in body and mind. They all feel like Brothers to me. Charles Billy and his Chambermate L. White will keep Thanksgiving with us next week.[1]

I often my dear Aunt indulge myself in thinking of your speedy return: the idea gives me pleasure. I fear I must satisfy myself with that at present. I often think of the many happy hours we shall pass when you shall once more be fixed down in your peaceful habitation, on your native land, when Aunt Adams shall again spend the long winter evening with us and entertain her Neices with the relation of her adventures. How many pleasing anecdotes will she have to make the time pass cheererly away: how pleasing is this (at present) vissionary scene. Many years I hope will not pass before it is realised.

I think I ought to ask pardon for encroaching so long upon your time by my scribling. I will not increase my fault by making apoligies but will hasten to conclude with assureing you my ever dear Aunt of the resspectful gratitude and affection of your Niece.   L Cranch

RC (Adams Papers); endorsed by AA2: "Miss Lucy Cranch Dec 8 1785."

[1] In 1785, Massachusetts observed Thanksgiving Day on 15 December, but according to JQA's Diary, Leonard White spent the day with his family in Haverhill (JQA, *Diary*, 1:371).

Mary Smith Cranch to Abigail Adams

My dear Sister   Braintree December 10th 1785

Mr. Storer is arriv'd and I have got my Letter[1] and am very sorry to hear you have been so sick. If I had receiv'd this Letter before those by Callahan[2] I should have been very uneasey till I could have heard again. I Will hope you are by this time perfectly recover'd.

You will see by mine of November 29th that our thoughts in September and October were imploy'd about the same melancholy subjects. I felt for you as I read your account of Mr. ⟨*Erving*⟩ Erwin mistaking Colln. Smith for another of the same name.[3] I pity'd you both. We have been trying to learn what is become of this unhappy connection but we have not been able to learn any thing certain. When we can, you shall be inform'd what it is. It is said he has fled upon being suspected of making or being concern'd with those who did make counterfit money. I dread to hear least he should be brought to publick disgrace.[4]

Your Neighbours are well and desire to be kindly remember'd. I do not believe you feel more affection for them than they do for you if I may Judge from their expressions. Mrs. Field says she would give all the money in London if she had it, only to see you. It is a strong way of expressing herself, but I do not doubt her sincerity. Mr. Thaxter came here last friday from Haverhill and is gone to keep Thanksgiving with his Freinds. Next thursday is the day your son Charles and mine and his chum[5] are to keep it with us. Mr. Thaxter says that all our Freinds are well at Haverhill, but he poor man goes home with a melancholy Heart. His Friend and companion Doctor Levitt Brother to Mrs. Rice drown'd himself in the mill Pond at Hingham about ten days past. He has been wild and delirious for some time. It is a dreadful shock to the Family. Mr. Thaxter is greatly affected. By what I hear there was a connection forming between his sister Betsy and this Gentleman.[6] What misarable creatures are we when depriv'd of our Reason.

I am greatly surprisd at hearing that no more Letters have past the vast ocean as you term it from a certain gentleman.[7] I knew he did not write for the first four months. He took care to tell of that himself sufficiently for every body to know it. But since that I thought he had written by every ship and that largly. He wanted to get all her correspondents to give him their Letters that he might have the pleasure of inclosing them in his. I heard him say that he always put the last Letter aboard intimating that he writ to the last minnet, and I did not know but he did. I knew he did not write above three of [*or*] four times at home.[8] We could not help knowing it when he does, he makes such a bustle about it always. But as he has stay'd the greatest part of his time in Boston, I thought he was writing there. I am not very apt to be deceiv'd by him you know, but I certainly have been in this instance. The Doctor wished to keep the matters he had to transact a secret till they were finish'd[9] but he could not do it. The matter has been delayed as I expected it would be. Mr. Storer is come and "the cat has jump'd out of the Bag," the Docr. says, but tis known yet to but few. I beleive he thinks I know nothing of it. At least that

I did not till Mr. Storer came I am told. He says he is going immediately to London and shall settle every misunderstanding. He says also there has been foul play some where. Will he be a welcome visiter? I cannot concieve he can be in earnest when he talks of coming. What can he propose by it? Will my dear Niece again subject herself to those "suspicions doubts and fears"[10] which have so long robb'd her of her peace of mind. Indeed my sister I have been long convinc'd that whoever should be connected with him would have them to incounter through Life. True Love my dear sister always seeks the Happiness of its object and nothing can be a greater proof of its absence than a disposition to give pain.

A Satirical Lady of our acquaintance told me that when Lyde came in the Gentleman was in company where she was and was very uneasey that the Letters did not come ashoar so soon as he wish'd them too. He was in a perfect [Tear?][11] about it. Some gentlemen present told him That as The Captain could not get any other Freight he was detaining them till he could find out what he ought to charge for them. "He was sure his Letters were not upon Business. He imported nothing but Love and that ought not to be detaind for a price." She now knows there purport and if it would not be to cruil she should ask him If the *goods* came to his mind or whither his Bills came Back protested. I think I need not tell you who this is like.[12]

News News my sister. Cousin Betsy Kent is to be married this night and to go home tomorrow morning. I most sincerly wish her happy. She is very deserving of it.

The Germantown Family will write for themselves and tell you how they do.[13] Mr. Wibird is well, uncle Quincy also. They are to dine with us on the thanksgiving day. But my pen. o! my pen I will not write another page till I can get a better. I have not time to copy what I write. I trust no Eyes but yours behold them and should wish you would only read such parts of my Letter to cousin as will please her. I trust every thing however to your prudence.

My Love to Mr. Adams and my Neice tell her, that her cousin say she shall not want any intelligence they can give her for the future. They suppos'd it had been done by an abler hand.[14] Adieu.

RC (Adams Papers).

[1] AA to Mary Cranch, 11 Sept., above.

[2] AA to Mary Cranch, 30 Sept., and 1 Oct., both above.

[3] See AA to Mary Cranch, 11 Sept. and note 6, above.

[4] In her letter to AA of 22 March 1786 (Adams Papers), Mary Cranch wrote that their brother "was not found guilty upon trial, of forging those notes he pass'd. He took them in the State they Were found upon him, of another man."

[5] By "his chum," Mary Cranch apparently

meant CA's college friend and roommate Samuel Walker (Mary Cranch to AA, 23 Dec., below). Leonard White, William Cranch's "chum" (see JQA to William Cranch, 6 Nov., above), spent Thanksgiving with his family in Haverhill (JQA, *Diary*, 1:371).

⁶ Martin Leavitt of Hingham, Harvard 1773 (one year ahead of John Thaxter), drowned himself on 27 November. His sister was Meriel Leavitt, who married Martin Leavitt's classmate, Col. Nathan Rice, in 1781. John Thaxter's older sister Elizabeth Thaxter never married. *History of the Town of*

Hingham, 2:433; 3:129, 232–233.

⁷ Royall Tyler.

⁸ That is, while at the Cranch's house in Braintree, where he was boarding.

⁹ See AA to Cotton Tufts, 18 Aug., and notes 12 and 13, above; and Tufts to AA, 5 Jan., and 13 April 1786 (both Adams Papers).

¹⁰ The reference is to AA to Mary Cranch, 15 Aug., above.

¹¹ Written over an illegible word.

¹² The editors cannot identify this person.

¹³ See Mary Palmer to AA, 11 Dec., below.

¹⁴ Presumably Royall Tyler.

Thomas Jefferson to Abigail Adams

Dear Madam   Paris Dec. 11. 1785

Expecting Baron Polnitz to call every moment, I have only time to acknolege the receipt of your favor of Nov. 24. and to answer you on the subject of the bill for 319 livres drawn by Mr. Adams in favor of Mr. Bonfeild. I had never heard of it before, and Mr. Barclay calling on me this morning I asked of him if he knew any thing of it. He says that such a bill was presented to him, and he desired them not to send it back but to let it lie till he could write to Mr. Adams. He wrote. Not having Mr. Adams's answer in his pocket he can only say that from that he was discouraged from paying it by Mr. Adams's expressing a doubt whether he had not desired me to pay it. The bill therefore went back without my having ever heard a tittle of it. I told Mr. Barclay I would write immediately to Mr. Bonfeild to send it to me on an assurance that I would pay it on sight. But he desired I would not; that he would immediately see to the paiment of it, and that it would be a convenience to him to be permitted to do it, as he had a balance of Mr. Adams's in his hands. I could have urged the same reason, but he had the regular authority.¹ Between us therefore you may count on the settlement of this matter, and always on me for that of any other with which you will please to entrust me, and which may give me an opportunity of proving to you the sincere esteem with which I have the honor to be Dear Madam your most obedient humble servt.   Th: Jefferson

RC (Adams Papers); endorsed: "Mr Jefferson decem 11. 1786."

¹ Presumably as Congress' commissioner of accounts in Europe; Barclay was also America's consul general in France.

Mary Palmer to Abigail Adams

Germantown Decr. 11th. 1785

This is the fourth attempt my Dear Madam that I have made to reply to your unmerited favour of the 30th. of April last,[1] long since reciev'd, but ill health and dejection of Spirit have hinder'd me from writing, for what cou'd I write that cou'd give you half the entertainment, that excellent Letter gave us? Nothing certainly; I will not therefore attempt it. Your recollection of the Scenes of our Youth does me honour as it then gave me pleasure. We are apt perhaps to look back on those Scenes which Youth and Novelty made pleasing, as if there was nothing left equally agreable. Yet I believe there are pleasures fitted for every state of life if we had but the patience to seek for them and the humility to enjoy them; that we are not what we were, gives us unnecessary pain and aggravates our real distresses to a monstrous bulk. Perhaps this has been too much the case with your poor friend, but to be essteem'd by Mrs. Adams will lighten the burden and give me better Spirits.

Your descriptions of the Churches of France and their admirable Architecture, Statues, Paintings, Lights &c, are beyond my simple imagination grand;[2] I could wish to see them and to hear the heavenly harmony with which on certain Occasions they are fill'd. The Masses and other Ceremonials of the Romish religion must tend to solemnize the heart, while they are new, but when used to them who so indifferent As the votarys of that Church; if we may believe what History tells us, that there are more unbelievers in the dominions of those who profess that religion than in all the other Christian Countrys. Yet I dare say there are many good pious People among them, who will do honour to the Christian religion by their practise. Thank God the *religious* Inquisition is not establish'd in France, tho' the *political* one is, what a tyranny! Your Account of the unhappy Lady who suffer'd by it affected us much, poor lady! Did you ever hear any more of her?[3] Those dreadful engines the Letters de Cachet, make me tremble at the Idea of Arbitrary Power. It is for the honour of the present Monarch that he has mitigated their rigour, their absolute disuse might be still more for his honour; how glorious is it for a King to trust solely to the Affection of his people for the Safety of his person and Authority? But I suppose the Change must be by degrees, for a people born to Slavery and crouching under their burdens, if set too soon at liberty wou'd run into absurd licenciousness and really

need those fetters to restrain them from Anarchy. Perhaps by education of the Youth and by gently relaxing the reins of Government,
they may in time be as free as the rights of human Nature require
and if America can Set the example of freedom to all Mankind and
will do it by ceasing from enslaving the Africans, She will have a
glorious boast. The whole world may then thank and applaud the
virtuous people, who young as they are, cou'd thus give freedom to
the Bondslaves of every Nation. At the beginning of the Contest with
Great Britain such were, or seem'd to be the wish of us all. At this
time the fashion seems to be, each one to oppress his Neighbour, the
People Suffer, and the Lawyers thrive by fomenting divisions. Compassion and forbearance are out of taste. Yet in the year 74 and 5 we
had no need of law, and every body paid their debts as soon as they
cou'd, and seem'd more honest than they are now.

Our taxes come very heavy upon us, Our Money is very Scarce and
every one is pressing, so that with reputed freedom we are really
Slaves to each other. But I correct myself, I ought by no means to
write politicks to a lady so greatly my superiour.

Your Discription of Notre Dame, made me wish to see it, but for
all the curiosities of the Old countries, I wou'd not Suffer the fatigue
of crossing the Sea, not even to see the King of France in the
Ceremonials of giving thanks for the Birth of Prince Charles-Louis.[4]

My health and spirits wou'd not allow me to take that pleasure in
those grand parades,[5] that I shou'd if well and easy, for I am far from
pretending to despise those scenes of pageantry. You Say well my dear
Madam that "Majesty derives a Grace from State." It must be so for
what insignificant individuals wou'd most Monarchs be in the eyes
of the Multitude if they were not thus royally attended.

It is time for me to come pretty soon to a conclusion as the letters
must go I suppose tomorrow. Mr. Storer favor'd us with a visit
yesterday, he bro't his sister[6] with him, they dined with us. Mr.
Thaxter and Cousn. Lucy came in another Chaise but were engaged
to dine at their Uncle Quincys so we saw but little of Mr. Thaxter,
this was his second vis[it] to us since he return'd from Europe. He
seems entirely engaged at Haverhill, perhaps some fair Nymph has
him fast in her chains. He was told so and did not deny it. He
appear'd just as easy and agreable as he used to be and far enough
from finical.

Mr. Storer I say nothing of, as you are fully acquainted with his
amiable character. His Sister is a fine young lady, very tall and
extremely industrious at her needle—too much so I shou'd think for

her health, as she abridges herself of exercise and sleep to accomplish what she supposes to be her duty. Mr. Storer spoke highly of Miss Adams. My or rather Our Opinion of her left us no room to doubt of his praises being her due.

Master Adams I have not seen since he first went to France and I dare say shou'd not know him again, but by all accounts he bids fair to make a shining figure in the World.

Master Charles has often favour'd us with his visits in company with his Cousin Billy, in the vacations, and seems quite delighted with fishing, tho' I think both of them are liable to bad luck. They came one Morning and were to catch fish enough for our Dinner and enough to carry home besides for Supper. The wind and tide were both unfavourable, so we tho't fit to get something else⟨ *for dinner*⟩, and sent for them at half past one. They had caught nothing fit to [eat and?] had excellent Appetites for our homespun Dinn[er.]

[Master?] Tommy I have not seen for a long time, [. . . .] he is very promising, and exceedingly playful [. . . .].[7]

Our Own particular family is much as it was.

Becky Leppington has been with us near 5 Months as [. . .]ly visitor and has been of Signal Service to us, for soon After she came our Tommy Field was as it was then tho't Mortally wounded with a Scythe. The Doctor was bro't to him in less than an hour after the Accident but gave us little hopes of his life. Miss Becky constantly attended him and dress'd his Wounds for many weeks. He was unable to do any labour for 10 Weeks, but as he had no fever and was careful in his Diet he is happily recover'd, and gone to a ship Carpenters trade. He had been gone about 6 Weeks.

I am glad that John[8] makes so good a Servant, he was always faithful while with us, I hope his health may be re-establish'd. I am really oblig'd to conclude abruptly as my paper is out. My love to Miss Adams, when I can I will write to her. Every one here esteems & loves all your family. I am Madam, your obliged   Polly Palmer

RC (Adams Papers); addressed: "To Mrs. Abigail Adams—Grosvenor Square London"; endorsed by AA2: "Miss Polly Palmer Dec 11th. 1785." Some damage to the text where the seal was torn away.

[1] Not found.

[2] This may refer to a description by AA of Notre Dame, as it appeared on the occasion of the Te Deum of 1 April, celebrated in thanks for the birth, on 27 March, of Louis Charles, second son of Louis XVI and Marie Antoinette. The Adamses and Thomas Jefferson attended this service on the invitation of Mme. Lafayette. See JQA, *Diary*, 1:240–244; Jefferson, *Papers*, 8:68; and AA2, *Jour. and Corr.*, 1:65–68. AA's surviving remarks on French churches are generally brief, and not very favorable (see, for example, AA to John Shaw, 18 Jan., above).

³ This unfortunate woman, and this incident, have not been identified.

⁴ That is, Louis Charles; see note 2.

⁵ This may be a reference to the grand pre-Lenten parade from Paris to Longchamp in which the Adamses took part on 25 March; see AA to Elizabeth Cranch, 8 May, above.

⁶ Presumably Charles Storer's sister Mary (see Storer to AA, 21 Dec., note 1; and Storer to AA2, 29 Dec., note 6, both below).

⁷ Probably two or three words are lost after "long time," and "playful."

⁸ John Brisler.

John Adams to Royall Tyler

Sir   Grosvenor Square Decr. 12. 1785

I have received, your instructive and entertaining Letter of the 15. of October, and although a Change of Circumstances has rendered it improper for me, to say any Thing in answer to the first part of it, I am not the less obliged to you, for the rest.

The Pamphlets you inclosed are great Curiosities, and merit the Consideration of the Publick in Europe as well as in America. The Coin, I have presented, together with an Extract of your Letter, to the Society of Antiquaries. It has occasioned a Sensation among the learned, and all heads are employed to discover whether the Figures are Phœnician, Carthaginian or what.¹ If they are found to be ancient, they will bring into fresh Reputation, the Accounts of Diodorus Siculus and Plato, of an Atlantic Island,² and will confirm the Suspicions of many curious Persons, that the Mariners Compas, was not an Invention of the fourteenth Century, but borrowed from the Arabs in the twelfth, and that the Arabs had it from the Pheenicians. I wish We could have had more of the 300 Coins here; but I make no doubt that the Society of Arts and Sciences at Boston, will publish in their Transactions, a particular Account of the whole.³ The Antiquaries complain of the Injury done to the Coin by rubbing off the rust, which they wish to have entire, as they are able by its thickness and Colour, Sometimes to compute the Age of it. Every Particular, which you can communicate to me, relative to this Discovery, will be gratefully acknowledged, and will redound to your Reputation. It is of Importance to Mankind to ascertain the Fact, whether Arts, Sciences and Civilization have existed among ancient Nations, inhabiting Countries, where few Traces of them remain: because the Progress of the same moral and political Causes, which have desolated Tire [*Tyre*] and Sidon, Sodom and Gomorrah, may again restore Europe to a forest, the residence of Savages. And indeed if Luxury and Vice should increase for a Century to come, as they have for two Centuries past, there is nothing incredible in the supposition, that Europe might become again in time, a howling Wilderness. America I hope however will contribute to stay the Torrent both at home and abroad. When Nations are corrupted to a certain Point, Arts and Civility decline and Barbarity succeeds.

The Abby De Mablys Letters, and the Answer to Gibbons,[4] I will endeavour to send you with this. I am very happy to learn that my Sons Behaviour has been pleasing to his Countrymen, and I hope that in time he will be a valuable Man. &c.

P.S. my Bookseller informs me, that the Answer to Gibbons is out of Print. He will look out and procure me one if it is to be had.

LbC (Adams Papers).

[1] JA gave the coin to "Mr. [Edward?] Bridgen," with a note and an extract from Tyler's letter, for presentation to London's Society of Antiquaries; the extract is a nearly verbatim transcription of the fourteenth paragraph of Tyler to JA, 15 Oct., above (see note 9 there).

Bridgen presented the coin with the extract to the Society of Antiquaries on 8 December. On 15 Dec., a Dr. Combe told the Society that the inscription on the coin did not resemble Punic (Carthaginian) writing, as some Americans had supposed, but was closer to Arabic or Turkish writing. As for the inscrip-tion on Dighton (Taunton) Rock, however, a Dr. Morton assured the Society that it did indeed appear to resemble Phoenician or Carthaginian writing (*Minutes of the Society of Antiquaries of London*, 8 and 15 Dec. 1785, 21:39, 41–43).

[2] See Plato, *Timaeus*, and *Critias*; Diodorus Siculus 2.55–60.

[3] No account of the coins found at Mystic has been found in the *Memoirs of the American Academy of Arts and Sciences*.

[4] See Royall Tyler to JA, 15 Oct., and note 10, above.

Mary Smith Cranch to Abigail Adams

My dear sister   Braintree December 18th 1785

I did not design to write another line till I could get my pen mendid but not a creature can I get to do it, and I am so affraid that Captain Lyde will sail without my Pacquit that I dare not venture to wait till the children come from college tomorrow. I hope to see the dear Boys, and if the ship should not go so soon as I expect I will write again. I shall certainly write by the way of New York this winter.

Your Mother Hall din'd with me this day. I sent the chaise for her and Suky[1] to make it seem as much like coming to Daughter Adams's as I could. She desirs me to give her best Love to all of you and tell you that she thanks you for the coat but that, there is nothing in this world that she wishes for so much as to see you. She is very well and really looks charmingly. Mr. A is more attentive to her than I ever expected to see him to any woman in the world. He came and drank Tea with us and waited upon her home. She complains that she cannot get her son to write to his Brother. I wonder if Mr. Cranch does not seem quite as much like a Brother to your Friend. I had the Honour to present him with the Commission Mr. Cranch has procur'd for him—but if I should tell you he receiv'd it *very graciously* I fear you would not believe me.[2] People have different ways you know of expressing their approbation. Your Brother has a sincerity about him that I love notwithstanding he has not sacrificed much to the Graces. Suky sends her Duty to uncle and aunt and Love to cousin. They were all much gratified by your and cousins presents. Mr. Cranch had spoken for some Nuts to be brought from Bridgwater for you before you mention'd that they would be acceptable to you, but I fear they will not come soon enough for this vessel. We shall send some chocalate by Lyde, which we beg your acceptance off. I wish I could send you any thing that would bear any proportion to your present to me and our children. If there is any thing that I can send that you cannot get in Europe pray let me know it. Mrs. Quincy says she has written to cousin[3] to procure her a Black Padua Silk. The moment she knows she has done it she will pay the money to your order.

Winslow Warren surpriz'd His Friends last week by his unexpected return from Lisbon. We do not know the occation of his return. It will be a very great dissapointment to poor Charles if he should live to arrive there.[4] Did you ever find or recieve the Letters you thought you had lost of Mrs. Warrens to Mr. Adams and her son, those she deliver'd to you when you went away.[5] I have a great curiosity to know there fate. The General and Lady take it in dudgion that neither you nor Mr. Adams have written by the late vessels. "I hear he has written to Mr. Hancock." Mrs. Warren says she has written tuw very long Letters and cannot find that you have mention'd receiving them in any bodys Letters.[6] We are very jealous of any preference any where else.

You kindly desire me to tell you if I want any thing.[7] It is not for me to create wants. My task is to think what I can do without. I find the gratification of one only makes way for another. For instance your kindness has furnish'd me with a beautiful Petticoat. "Tis a Beauty mama, but you have not a thin Silk nor an apron that will do to wear With it." "I know it my dear and I know also that your Papas income will but just pay your Brothers quarter Bills and provide plain food and Raiment for us, and I will wear my old cloath's forever rather than run in debt for fine ones."[8] And so my dear sister if you will be so good as to procure me Lutstring enough for a gown suitable for my station and age and muzlain for an apron, and send me the price, it shall be placed to your account, which I shall settle as you desir'd with the Doctor. It grieves me to think of charging any thing for my Nephews Board[9] and we never shall do so if Mr. Cranch should be able to get into a little better business. As to any labour that we or the children perform for them pray my sister accept it as a small acknowledgment of the many obligations we are under to you.

I shall leave the colour of the silk to your fancy only let it be modest and not very dark.

I design'd this for a cover to my other Letters but I never know when to writ the last word. Adieu

RC (Adams Papers).

[1] Susanna Adams, daughter of Peter Boylston Adams.

[2] The editors do not know of any letters exchanged between JA and Peter Boylston Adams between 1776 and 1803. On Richard Cranch's securing a justice of the peace commission for P. B. Adams, see Cranch to JA, 19 Nov., and note 4, above.

[3] No letter written by Ann Marsh Quincy to either AA2 or AA has been found.

[4] Charles Warren did not reach Lisbon, but died near Cadiz, Spain, on 30 Nov., after Winslow had left Lisbon for Boston (Emily Warren Roebling, *Richard Warren of the Mayflower and Some of His Descendants*, Boston, 1901, p. 28).

[5] See AA to Mary Cranch, 6 July 1784, under "July 7th," above.

[6] On 14 April, JA wrote John Hancock a brief letter to introduce young Le Ray de Chaumont; on 2 Sept. he wrote Hancock a somewhat longer letter, carried to America by Charles Storer, in which he discussed Massachusetts' prospects in the whale fishery (both LbCs, Adams Papers).

JA had written to James Warren on 26 April,

to Mercy Warren on 6 May, and to both James and Mercy on 12 December. James Warren had written to JA on 28 Jan., 4 Sept., and 6 Oct.; while Mercy had written on 27 April, and (n.d.) Sept. Except for the letter to James Warren of 12 Dec. (MB), all of these letters are printed in *Warren-Adams Letters*, 2:248–269 passim. AA had written to Mercy Warren on 10 May, above; while Mercy Warren had written to AA on 30 April, above, and 18 Sept. (Adams Papers).

[7] AA to Mary Cranch, 1 Oct., above.

[8] The editors have added the quotation marks around the second sentence. Mary Cranch's conversation was probably with her daughter Lucy, who had lived most of the time in recent months in Braintree, while Betsy was in Boston and then Haverhill visiting friends and relatives and studying music.

[9] That is, for boarding JQA, CA, and TBA when they were in Braintree on visits from Haverhill or from college. Mary Cranch was also washing and mending clothes for CA while he was at college (Mary Cranch to AA, 29 Nov., above).

Abigail Adams to Thomas Jefferson

Grosvenor Square

Dear Sir   Decemr. 20th. 1785

Your favours by Colln. Smith and by the Baron Polintz[1] came safe to hand. As you have justly estimated the Worth and merit of the former, you will easily suppose we were very glad to see him, and equally so to wellcome Colln. Humphryes upon English Ground. I hope his reception here will be as agreeable to him as he expected. He will inform you I dare say that he has seen both the Lions, and His Majesty.[2]

You will find by the publick Papers what favourites we are at Court. The Prince of Wales supping with us, Mr. Adams holding frequent conferences with His Majesty, and yesterday going to Windsor for the same purpose.[3] It is said by some that these are Ministerial manvoeures to keep up the stocks. A Paragraph of this kind has certainly been attended with that effect. Others say it is to feel out the minds of the People with respect to a Treaty with America, of which if I dared to give my opinion; I should say that some simptoms have lately appeard tending to that point. But this is said in confidence Sir, as I must not betray secrets.

The affair of Capt. Stanhope has been officially taken up and his Conduct much disapproved of by the Lords of the Admirality, as Congress are informed by an official reply to them. Mr. A has also received an answer to his Demand of the Citizens of the United States sent to the East Indies, "that orders were immediately issued for their discharge." It is not probable that any thing very material will take place till the meeting of Parliament.[4]

The Pacquet arrived last week from New York, in which came Passenger Monsieur Houdon. He returns to Paris the latter End of this week. There were no official Dispatches, and only a private Letter or two to the second of November. But as Mr. A writes you I will leave Politicks with which I really have no business, and talk of that which more properly belongs to me.

The Commission you honourd me with will be compleated to send by the return of Colln. Humphryes. I received my Plateau safe about ten days since. It is a very Good one and I am much obliged by your kind attention to it. The Deities however showed that they were subject to Humane frailty and got a few Limbs dislocated in their Tour.[5]

If Mr. Barclay will be so good as to settle with Mr. Bonfeild, Mr. Adams will be obliged to him. Coll. Smith delivered me the Louis's you sent by him, and when Colln. Humphryes returns I will forward you the account of my stewardship.

Compliments to Mr. Short. We are sorry to hear of his indisposition. I once found Great benefit in the Dissorder which he complains of by taking an oz. of Castile soap and a pint of Bristol Beer, dividing it into three portions; and takeing it three Mornings, fasting.[6]

I wish you could make it convenient to let Miss Jefferson come and pass a few Months with us here.[7] I do not yet dispair of seeing you in England and in that Case you will certainly bring her with you.

I am Sir your most obedient servt. A Adams

RC in AA2's hand (DLC:Jefferson Papers); addressed: "His Excellency Thomas Jefferson Esqr. Minister Plenipotentiary from the United States of America to the Court of France Paris." Dft (Adams Papers). Major variations between the recipient's copy and the draft are noted below.

[1] William Stephens Smith brought Jefferson's letter of 20 Nov.; Baron Pöllnitz brought that of 11 Dec. (both above).

[2] Col. David Humphreys and William Stephens Smith arrived at Grosvenor Square from Paris on the evening of 5 Dec. (AA2 to JQA, 5 Dec., above). After "English Ground," in the draft, AA wrote and then struck out: "and to assure him as descendents from a people once celebrated for Hospitality we possesst a sufficient Share of it to rejoice at the sight of our Friends." And in the draft AA began a new paragraph at "I hope . . ." rather than at "You will find . . ." JA presented Col. Humphreys at Court on 14 Dec. (AA2, *Jour. and Corr.*, 1:83).

[3] In a letter of 23 Dec., to Rufus King (NHi:King Papers), JA makes clear AA's irony. The reports published in the *London Chronicle* of 6–8 Dec. were false; neither the Prince of Wales' "supping" with the Adamses on 6 Dec. nor JA's visit to George III at Windsor on 19 Dec. actually occurred.

[4] The first two sentences of this paragraph explicitly summarize the first paragraph of a letter by JA to John Jay, 9 Dec. (PCC, No. 84, VI, f. 13–16, printed in *Dipl. Corr., 1783–1789*, 2:543–544), in which JA reports on his 8 Dec. meeting with Lord Carmarthen. In that meeting, Carmarthen informed JA of the Admiralty's decision to reprimand Capt. Stanhope for his behavior in Boston in August, and to order the release of American seamen

seized by the British in the East Indies; both actions were in response to formal protests and supporting materials that JA had presented to Carmarthen. The last sentence refers to the lack of any progress in the larger disputes between the two nations—Britain's retention of forts on the American shores of the Great Lakes; America's resistance to paying debts owed to British merchants; and America's desire for a commercial treaty—to which JA made brief reference in the second and third paragraphs of his letter to Jay. See also Carmarthen to JA, 9 Dec.; and JA to John Jay, 12 Dec. (PCC, No. 84, VI, f. 27 and 17–18; printed in *Dipl. Corr., 1783–1789*, 2:545, 544–545). For the importance which Jefferson attached to AA's brief summaries of diplomatic news in London, see Jefferson to AA, 27 Dec., and note 1, below.

[5] The commission that AA intended to send with Col. Humphreys was probably the set of shirts that Jefferson had requested AA to have made for him (Jefferson to AA, 11 Oct., above). The "Deities" were the four ceramic figurines that AA requested Jefferson to buy for her (AA to Jefferson, 12 Aug., Jefferson to AA, 25 Sept., both above).

[6] William Short was "indisposed with the jaundice" (Jefferson to Francis Eppes, 11 Dec., Jefferson, *Papers*, 9:91–92).

[7] At this point in her draft, AA canceled the sentence: "If you will trust her in my care I should be happy in having her with us."

Charles Storer to Abigail Adams

Dear Madam Boston. 21st. December. 1785

I am persuaded you will be pleased with this letter, if you were not ever before with one from me, because in the first place, it will inform you of my safe arrival among my friends, and at the same time may give you some information respecting yours. I write you therefore with pleasure on my part. Our arrival here be assured was attended with much satisfaction on all sides. I need not paint to you a Parent's tears on such an occasion. Suffice it to say he pressed us to his heart. Nor were a Sister's or Brother's feelings unmoved on the occasion. In a mutual embrace we joined in one thanksgiving.[1] Since my return my time has not been mispent. From our nearest Connections we first received the flattering welcome, and since from very many others. You will readily suppose this was not unpleasing, as beleive me it was not. How shall I write you of every particular one of our friends? 'Twould be a little history. Yet I know, (for I have felt the same curiosity more than once myself,) you wish some account. But I must adopt the expression my friends have hitherto made use of to me and say "your friends are all well," or else, as I do to those who want me to tell them off ahand, at once, every thing I have heard, or seen since I left home, say ask me what questions you please and I will answer them if I can. But I must not omit telling you of one person whom I have not yet heard or seen, yet to whom I am indebted for kindness since my return, and as it comes to me thro' you, 'tis highly proper you should be made acquainted with it. I mean your Sister, *Mrs. Shaw*. She has been kind eno: to give me an invitation, from Haverhill, to make her a visit, assuring me that, having been so long one of your family, she cannot look upon me with indifference. This is a friend unexpected, and as I am indebted to you therefor I have to thank you accordingly. Betsey Cranch is and has been with her at Haverhill sometime and what is quite new to me is learning to play on the Harpsichord. They say she makes great proficiency, as Mrs. Shaw mentions that John and Thomas do also in their studies. John attends so closely he has not yet found time to write me since my arrival, tho' I wrote him from N York soon after I landed.[2] Both Mr. and Mrs. Cranch I have seen once and again: they made many enquiries about you and the family; as did Dr: Tufts. Billy Cranch and your Son Charles I have not yet seen. From Braintree I went to Germantown. The family there are distressed. *Mr. P[almer]* thinks he may be obliged even in his old age to retire to the settlements on the Ohio. He thinks he may set up the Salt works in that Country to much advantage. *Mr. Perkins* writes him encouragingly on this head. Mrs. Quincy and Nancy live quite retired at the Farms, having let their farm to their [. . .] Overseer. Mr. and Mrs. Allen remain the same they were whe[n . . .] America. Dr. and Mrs. Welsh made many enquiries about you. They have a house full of Children, who are like young Giants. I see no change either in Aunt, Uncle, or Cousins Isaac and Willm: Smith. Cousin Betsey is grown, as are all the younger of the folks in town. Many are grown quite out of my knowledge. The younger part of our family is grown also very much. As to the appearance of the town, I find it changed for the better. I mean the houses; which have been repaired and painted. But trade is extremely dull and folks are complaining. There is not therefore by any means that extravagance and dissipation I expected to find, and which there was about a twelvemonth after the peace.

But my paper bids me say no more than desire you to write me as often as you can, and *confidentially* when you can, as I love to know what's doing, and to assure you that I am with much esteem, Yrs. &c. &c.   C. S.

RC (Adams Papers); addressed: "Mrs. A. Adams. Grosvenor-Square London"; endorsed by AA2: "Charles Storer December 21st 1785." Some damage to the text where the seal was torn away.

[1] Storer evidently returned to Boston with his sister Elizabeth Atkinson. His sister Mary and brother George lived in Boston's North End with their father Ebenezer Storer and his second wife, Hannah Quincy Lincoln Storer, and their young children (*Sibley's Harvard Graduates*, 12:208–214).

[2] Not found.

Mary Smith Cranch to Abigail Adams

My Dear Sister   Braintree December 23d. 1785

I wonder whether Mr. Shaw ever wrote you an account of the good woman who was so much offendid that you were not treated with more civillity when you went to see the King and Queen. "Why I hear they did not so much as ask them to set down, but keept them standing four hours without offering them any thing to eat or drink. I thought such great Folks knew what good manners was, better than to treat such good People as Mr. and Mrs. Adams in such a manner." "I think sir you married a Daughter of Mr. Smith too?" "Yes madem." "And dont you think you was dreadful lucky? I have heard She was a fine woman." This conversation was in Mr. Tafts Parish.[1] The good Lady felt a respeect for you for having cloathed her Parson. The worthy man inquires very affectionatly after you whenever he sees any of us.

I have just reciev'd a Letter from Betsy. She Says Her uncle Shaws Family were all well, your Sons in particular. Cousin Charles and his chum[2] came the day before Thanksgiving and stay'd till the monday after. It would have gratified you to have Seen how charmingly they injoy'd themselves feasting away upon Plumb Pudding and Pyes. I furnish'd our sons with Plumb-cake and cheese enough to last them till their winter vacancy begins.

Decr. 25th

Tis a high day with you in England this day. Poor Braintree cannot get a Parson to officiate at the Church. You must send me word how and where you spent the Day? I last night reciev'd a Letter from Sister Shaw.[3] She says She has been unwell, but is better, excepting her Eyes. She has an inflamation in one of them which is very trouble-some. Your sons were well. She tells me she has been making Mr. and Mrs. Allen a visit, and that she never saw more happiness discover'd in any Persons Countinance than in hers, and she mani-fested a great degree of *Contentment*. Her House and every thing about it had an air of neatness and eleganc which was very pleasing. I have not a doubt but he will learn to esteem as he ought a Person who sincerly Loves him and studies to make him happy. If her mind is not so improv'd as he could wish, She has those Quallifications without which, if she had all the Learning that ever a woman pos-sessed, she could not make a good wife for him. She is not too old for improvment. I should think it would be a pretty amusement for him in a winter evening to imploy himself in teaching her the differ-ent meaning that is affix'd to certain words. That *exceed*, does not mean *succeed*, nor *Rebillious*, *Billious*, nor *distinguish extinguish* notwithstanding the sound is some what alike. These are things easily taught and tho they are little matters, they will mortify a man of sensibility. We ought ever to distinguish between Faults and misfortunes. It has been hers not to have had in earley life any care taken to give her a tast for any kind of Learning, but She may make as good a wife, tho not so entertaining a Companion for a man of Letters, as if she had.

Betsy is invited to stay a week or two with them and will before she returns. "Of all things in the World she says she loves to stay with *young* married People. They do look so happy."[4] It makes her quite in Love with the State. She desires I would not send for her till march. I know not how to spare her so long. The change of air Seems to have mended her Health much, but we lead a solitary kind of a Life, but not a dissagreable one. I only wish for my dear Sisters Family.

I have repeatedly told you that I know but little of the affairs or Business of ——.[5] Ever since you went away he has carefully secreted every thing he could from this Family. I sometimes hear of them abroad. The sleigh is I am told put into elegant repair and that he is going to carry Doctor Moyes five hundred mile in it as soon as the roads will admit of it. The Doctor boarded at Mrs. P[almer] at Boston where he also did all the Fall. He has been a constant attendend and assistant to Doctor through a course of Lectures upon natural Philosophy which he has deliver'd in Publick. By his manoeuvres since he reciev'd his Letters by Lyde I have thought he was going to change his Lodgings in B— and yesterday I heard that he designs too. He has not told us so yet, but I have no doubt he designs it. It is true either he or his man V-s-y[6] ought to have a Boy to take care of his stock which he keeps in their Barn. Three Horses a yoke of oxen and a Cow, will require a Boy or a man to look after them well. He has therefore provided a Boy, who he keeps at Mrs. V-s-y for the purpose. He has also placed a Negro woman there, and is to go himself soon. All this I hear from our Neighbours, who you know are intimate there. Every body wonders for his dismission is yet unknown here, exceept in one or two Familys, and *We* say nothing. You will wonder how he came by so much Stock. He took some of them for debts, where he could not get any thing else. The Horses are poor things all, but his old one, and the oxen are old. If he must keep them till spring, it would have been almost as well to have left them where they were. Not one of the Horses will do to go in a carriage with his, that which tore his sleigh last winter was never return'd, Major Miller told me, till about six weeks ago. All this may be right but it has an odd appearance. The Philedelphia chaise has made its appearence Since Lydes arrival, but all possible care has been taken that it should not come up our yard, I know not why. What a pity it is that it cannot be made to become invisible at pleasure. His dismission does not seem to trouble him much. I never saw him gayer in my Life. I write this in confidence that you will not let any mortal see it but your self, and if you should ever find it necessary to mention haveing reciev'd such intiligence, let it not be known to come from me. I thought you would be glad to know some little matter about him expecially as he is so soon to visit you, but tis a wonder if the dread of sea sickness which he so often deprecates and the horrible Idea of the Algerines catching him does not make him pospone his voyage for a few years. Pray my sister do not wound my dear Neice with a word of this. She may depend upon his being treated with all imaginable delicacy by all of us.

I have taken a Black cloth wastcoat of Mr. Adams and made cousin

Charles one. I thought I had better do it than by a new. I have taken the cinnamin for your childrens use, the other Spice we have put into cannesters, which will I hope secure them from harm. Mr. Adams Gown cousin Charles Says he must have next winter. The wine you left in the Seller cousin John says he shall make very free with when he goes into college as it will soon spoil.——If there is any thing you would wish to have done with or about your things you must let me know it. I sometimes fear I shall not do right.

Do you not take Some of the magazines. I wish when you have done with them you would send them here to amuse us in a lonely hour. We will take care of them for you against you return.——We have given Cap. Lyde a dozen of chocalate and mark'd it JA. The Nuts my dear sister we have not been able to get.[7] I hope we shall meet with some before Callahan sails, which will be soon. I shall write by him. I suppose Sister will write you particularly about your Sons and cousin John writes largly himself, I dare say. Pray my sister write often and largly. I am Sure I have not been deficient. Remember me tenderly to Mr. Adams and my Niece, tell her I have written so much to you that I cannot find any thing to say to her but that the more I reflect upon her conduct the more I am charm'd with her prudenc and discretion, and that I wish not my own Daughters more happiness than I do her.

Adieu my dear sister and believe my yours affectionatly

M Cranch

No copying for me. I hate it. I had rather write another and yet I sometimes wish to know what I have written.

RC (Adams Papers).

[1] The editors have supplied quotation marks before "I think," and after "Mr. Smith too?" and "fine woman." Rev. Moses Taft was the minister of Braintree's third church, in the South Precinct, now Randolph (see Elizabeth Shaw to AA2, 19 Nov., and note 9, above).

[2] Samuel Walker.

[3] Not found.

[4] Closing quotation mark supplied from Elizabeth Cranch to Mary Cranch, 20 Dec. (privately owned).

[5] Royall Tyler.

[6] Some member of the numerous Veasey family of Braintree.

[7] Perhaps the hickory nuts that AA requested in her letter of 5 Oct. to Cotton Tufts, above.

Thomas Jefferson to Abigail Adams

Dear Madam   Paris Dec. 27. 1785

I am this day honoured with your favor of the 20th. and an opportunity offering to acknolege it immediately, I do not fail to embrace it. I thank you for the intelligence it contains. You refered me to Mr. Adams for news; but he gives me none;[1] so that I hope you will be so good as to keep that office in your own hands. I get little from any other quarter since the derangement of the French packets.

I condole with you sincerely on the dismemberment of the gods and goddesses, and take some blame to myself for not having detained them for Colo. Smith who would have carried them safely. Can I be instrumental in repairing the loss? I will promise not to trust to a workman another time.

Mr. Short is on the recovery. I will take care to communicate to him your prescription, as soon as he returns from St. Germain's. All your friends here are well. The Abbés always desire me to remind you of them.—What shall I do for news to tell you?—I scratch my head in vain.—Oh! true.—The new opera of Penelope by Marmontel and Piccini succeeds. Mademoiselle Renaud, of 16. years of age sings, as no body ever sung before. She is far beyond Madme. Mara in her own line of difficult execution. Her sister of 12 years of age will sing as well as she does. Having now emptied my budget I have the honour of presenting my respects to Miss Adams and of assuring you of the sincere esteem with which I have the honour to be Dear Madam your most obedient & most humble servt.   Th: Jefferson

RC (Adams Papers); endorsed: "Mr Jefferson Decbr 27. 1788." The editors know of no reason for AA's endorsement error.

[1] JA had been faithfully writing to Jefferson since May, and his letters slightly outnumbered Jefferson's replies. But in his two most recent letters to Jefferson (13 and 20 Dec., Jefferson, *Papers*, 9:97–98, 116–117), JA had said nothing about his recent visits to Court, his consultations with the British ministry, the latest developments in the Stanhope affair, or the arrival of the New York packet (without dispatches), all subjects touched on by AA in her letter to Jefferson of 20 Dec., above, immediately before she said, "as Mr. A[dams] writes you I will leave Politicks with which I really have no business."

John Quincy Adams to Abigail Adams

Dear Madam   Haverhill December 28th. 1785

It is mortifying to me, to be again obliged to offer an excuse, for not having written more frequently to you, and to my father however conscious I may be, of its having been out of my Power, yet the Idea, of your suspecting me of neglecting you, worries me very much. But it has been and still is absolutely necessary for me, to apply myself with unremitting attention to my studies. About ten hours every day, are devoted to them: you will easily suppose from this, that I do not go much into Company. Many of the families in Town, have been very polite, and have given me repeated Invitations to see them often: But excepting Mr. White's, where I often pass two or three hours in the Evening, I have scarce been any where. Indeed I do not go out quite as much as I could wish too, but that would prevent me from writing at all.

The dissolution, of a certain Connection,[1] which you have been kind enough to hint in your Letters to me, and which I have also collected from other Quarters, has afforded me, as well as almost all our Friends, real consolation. My anxiety was not small before I left you, but it was greatly augmented after my return home. In Obedience to your Injunctions, I will give you with the utmost sincerity and impartiality, an account of what I have heard since my arrival concerning the Gentleman. I have no personal pique against him. I saw but little of him while I was in Braintree or in Boston, but he behaved to me in the most friendly manner; and as a transient acquaintance, I should have considered him, as a very agreeable Person. But many things I heard of him, from respectable authorities, and all agreeing perfectly, excited in my mind such fears, as I never wish to feel again, for any person, much less dear to me, than a Sister. And I cannot express how much I was relieved, when the news came, so unexpectedly, of her having so happily freed herself from an Inclination, which I considered as very dangerous. When my father's Letter came, (you know the one I mean)[2] he not only shew it about, but in some places triumphed, at his succeeding with so many of her relations and friends against him: he rather prided than otherwise, in writing so seldom as he did. He kept many of the Letters to her friends, which were inclosed to him, several months, and when he was ask'd the Reason why? he begg'd to be excused from giving any Reasons.[3] Since the last Letters,[4] he has said that it was wholly owing to *foul Play*, that every one of her friends here, had agreed to write against him; she had been thus deceived, but that he intends in a short Time to sail for Europe, and has no doubt, but that he shall bring all to rights again. For these nine months, he has spent three quarters of his Time at Boston, and from the 1st: of October to the middle of November, was not at Braintree at all.—Some of these facts are undoubtedly true: for the rest I trust to the Veracity of persons, whose honour I have not the least Reason to doubt. He Complains that all her friends are combined in a league against him. But should it be enquired, how it happened, they are so universally averse to his being connected with her, and rejoyced at her late determination, I know not what answer he would give.

I have received several Letters from you.[5] One, as late as October 5th: which came in Callahan. Accept my warmest, and sincerest thanks, my dear Mamma, for those kind attentions. It shall be the study of my Life, to follow the Instructions and the Example of my Parents, and the nearer I come to them, the greater share of happiness I shall enjoy. Three or four months more; and then I shall have time enough, to write often;[6] but never sufficient to express my love and gratitude to them.

As to Politics, this is not the place to know any thing of them; and of the public affairs even of this State, I know not so much as I did, when I was in Europe; and I should not regret it, if it did not deprive me of the Pleasure of communicating them to you. The Merchants groan sadly of the decay of trade, and failure after failure seems to justify their Complaints. Within these last Three weeks however, I hear it whispered about that *Times* are growing better, and I hope their misfortunes will in the End, prove of great Service to themselves, and to the Public.—But I can tell you a piece of private News, which will not I hope, be too sudden, and unexpected to you. On Sunday the 11th: Instant Mr. Allen, and Miss Kent, were married at Boston, and on Monday they arrived at Bradford, at the seat of Empire. She is in high Spirits, and Mr. T[haxter] says, as much pleased as a child can be with a rattle: though by the bye, he is verging towards the same State himself; and is now got so far, that he has done boasting the superlative happiness of a single Life, and begins to hint, that it is not fit for man to be alone. He has made choice of a most amiable young Lady,[7] whose least praise is, to be the prettiest girl in Haverhill.

I am as contented with my Situation, as I can be, when absent from three of the dearest Persons on Earth. If the place of Parents possibly could be supplied to me, it would be, here. And my Cousin Eliza, who has been in town ever since I came, is a Sister to me: she does not live here, but at Mr. White's, whose family have been as kind, and attentive, to me, as they always have been to my brothers: I pass many very agreeable hours, at that house. Miss Hazen, is still a boarder in this family. She has many amiable Qualities, but you have no reason to fear that she will ever prove an Omphale to your Hercules.[8]

The Winter Vacation at College, begins this day week.[9] Charles will probably spend the greater part of it here; I heard from him a few days since, when he was at Braintree to keep Thanksgiving.[10] Tommy desires I would send his Duty. He would write, but does not know what to say. Mr. and Mrs. Shaw desire to be affectionately remembered; Aunt, has had an inflammation in her Eyes, which prevents her from writing. Mr. Thaxter is so entirely absorb'd with the present, that he almost forgets the absent, and I have no great Expectations that he will write again to you before the Spring. He desires however to be remember'd.

It is now quarter of an hour after mid-night, which, as well as my Paper, bids me to subscribe myself, your dutiful and affectionate Son.

J. Q. Adams

RC (Adams Papers); endorsed: "J Q Adams Decem 28 1785."

[1] Between AA2 and Royall Tyler.
[2] The reference is probably to JA to Royall Tyler, 3 April 1784, above, the only extant letter from JA to Tyler before that of 12 Dec., above.
[3] See Mary Cranch to AA, 8 Nov., above.
[4] AA2 to Royall Tyler, [*ca. 11 Aug.*], AA to Mary Cranch, 15 Aug., AA to Cotton Tufts, 18 Aug., and see AA to Mary Cranch, 1 October. All appear above.
[5] Since JQA's last letter to AA, of 6 Oct., he had probably received AA's letters of 11 and 23 Aug., and 6 and 12 Sept., in addition to her letter of 5 Oct., which he mentions. All these letters appear above.

[6] That is, after securing admission to Harvard College; see JQA to AA2, 1 Oct., above.
[7] Elizabeth Duncan.
[8] AA, thinking of Nancy Hazen and JQA, referred to the same lovers in Greek mythology in her letter to Elizabeth Shaw of 11 Jan., above.
[9] That is, on 4 Jan. 1786; the vacation lasted five weeks (JQA, *Diary*, 1:382).
[10] CA arrived in Haverhill with William Cranch on 17 January; they left Haverhill for Braintree on 26 January (same, 1:389, 394). CA's letter to JQA from Braintree of ca. 15 Dec. has not been found.

Richard Cranch to John Adams

Dear Bror.   Boston Decr. 29th. 1785

When the Senate was last sitting I desired the Honble. Mr. Goodhue≠ of Salem, to answer your Request to me about the Cod-Fishery, and give you a Statement of it—and I learn by Capt. Geo: Williams that a Letter he deliver'd me a few Days ago (which I herewith send you)[1] contains his Observations on that Subject. The Hon: Peleg Coffin Esqr. of Nantucket, the Senator for that County, also promised me to give you a particular account of the present State of the Whale-Fishery, which I suppose you will receive from him.[2] I have been trying to get an account of the Distilleries Sugar-baking Business within this State, and hope e'er long to send you an Estimate of them. There is at present a new Valuation in hand; and, as "Truth is not to be spoken at all times," I find some Difficulty arising from that Quarter. I have sent you the Continuation of the Newspapers, and some Letters inclosed.[3] The Letter to Mr. Elworthy I wish might be carefully deliver'd as soon as possible.

Your Hond. Mother, and your Brother and Family are well. I had the Pleasure of sending your Brother a Commission for the Peace, about a fortnight ago.[4] He knew nothing of it untill it was deliver'd to him. Your Sons at Haverhill were well a few Days since, and behave so as to give you Pleasure, and do honour to their Parents and Instructors. Your dear Charles and his Chum (Mr. Walker from Bradford) kept Thanksgiving with us the Week before last, and staid untill Monday following. I keep a constant Look-out on them, and have Cousn. Charles and Billy to see me almost every Week at my Lodgings in Boston. I cannot hear that they have ever departed from the Line of Conduct that we should wish them to follow. I hope Mrs. Cranch and I have a good Share in their Confidence and Friendship; and we shall endeavour to cultivate it more and more, as, without that, Advice looses a great part of its Effect. Mrs. Cranch will write to her Sister more particularly by this Conveyance (Capt. Lyde).[5] I thank her for her most valuable Letters to our Family, they do Honour to her Sex and to Human Nature. Please to give my most affectionate Regards to her and to my amiable Niece, and believe me to be, with the highest Esteem and most cordial Friendship, your obliged Brother

Richard Cranch

P.S. I have desir'd Capt. Lyde to take a Dozn. Pound of Chocolate among his Ship-Stores. If he can be permitted to present it to Sister Adams, I beg the favour of her to accept it. The maker says it is good.

I wish to hear from you what is like to be done (if any thing) in the way of Commerce &c. Your Letters will always be esteemed by me as invaluable.

≠Mr. Goodhue is a Merchant largely concerned in the West India Trade. He was educated at the University of Cambridge, and is an active Member of the Senate. He was the Father of our Navigation-Act, and wishes to be more acquainted with you. I wish you would write to him. He was graduated in the Year 1766.[6]

RC (Adams Papers).

[1] Benjamin Goodhue to JA, 20 Dec. (Adams Papers).

[2] No letter from Peleg Coffin to JA has been found.

[3] These letters have not been identified.

[4] See Richard Cranch to JA, 19 Nov., and note 4, above.

[5] Mary Cranch had last written on 23 Dec., above; she would next write on 10 Jan.

1786 (Adams Papers), probably still in time for Capt. Lyde, who was delayed in sailing.

[6] This paragraph was written perpendicularly on the last page, and keyed to its proper location by the symbol. By "the University of Cambridge" Cranch means Harvard College (*Sibley's Harvard Graduates*, 16:359–367). JA wrote to Benjamin Goodhue on 10 March 1786 (NNS).

William Stephens Smith to Abigail Adams

Thursday Decr. 29th. 1785

An anxiety to preserve a consistancy of Character in the opinion of Mrs. Adams (in whose favourable sentiments I feel myself more and more interested) induces me to say, that I have some reason to believe, that the late Connection,[1] which appeared an insurmountable Obstacle to the accomplishment of the Wish nearest my heart—exists no longer. And from the opinion I have of the Lady, I am persuaded, that nothing dishonourable on her part could have occasioned it.

Strongly impressed with sentiments which induce a sacred attention to the Laws of hospitality, and a lively sense of Moral Obligation, I cannot postpone informing her, that her Amiable Daughter, is the only Lady of my acquaintance, either in Europe or America, that I would connect myself with for Life. With a Mind deeply impressed with her Virtues, apparently established by the principles of her education, Mrs. Adams will not be surprised at my anxiety to gain her confidence, and to lay a proper foundation for a future Connection, which must insure me all the happiness I can wish, provided it should meet with her wishes, and the approbation of her friends.

I have no inclination, My dearest Madam, to be precipitate on this Subject, but I should feel Guilty, whenever I entered your Doors, If I did not give you the earliest information of my wishes and intention. It now rests with you Madam, and her honoured Father to Object in the early stages of it, if at all, and be assured, your decission will greatly influence my Conduct. You once charged me with precipitancy, but believe me Madam, I did not merit it, as I can fully convince you, should you think proper to Converse on the Subject.

This Communication, (perhaps,) you may think, ought to be made to Mr. Adams, but I feel more easy in the communication with you. And as I do not Know that he is acquainted with my sentiments respecting the Lady, (as well as you are Madam), it would render a long and formal Letter necessary, while perhaps this mode may answer every end, as I suppose you will be in a great measure governed by his sentiments on the Subject, it is probable, you will submit this to his perusal.

I feel myself under every disadvantage. I am almost a stranger—and it might appear strange were I to say nothing of myself, but strange as it may appear, delicacy checks my pen. I can only say, my family are neither Obscure, nor unknown, and in whatever relates to them, or myself I submit freely to your investigation and you may take what time you please to satisfy yourself on the Subject. However, *I* shall neither appear the Child of fortune nor the offspring of Illustrious Ancestors, but such as I am, I seek *your* friendship, and aspire to your Daughters Love.

What has been my Conduct, and what the Lines which have marked my Character, since I entered into Life, will be better explained to you and perhaps more to your satisfaction, by the papers which accompany this,[2] than if I were to become my own Panegyrist. After the perusal of these papers, I wish it to be recollected, that altho' "it is better to marry a Gentleman alway's involved in business, than one who has no Profession at all," that I have some claim to indulgence on that point; having sacrificed that important Period of my Life in my Country's Service, which others have (perhaps more wisely) spent in their private concerns and arrangements. If Mrs. Adams knew the situation of my family before the war, she would be satisfied, that a fixed profession, was not at that time considered absolutely necessary for my support, or to enable me to move in that Circle which my Education, Conduct and Connections have hitherto entitled me to.——The Papers will convince you, that I may without presumption boast of the honourable Profession of Arms, which I have followed with success and have received my Country's acknowledgement with such assurances as the Nature of our Goverments will admit of, of Mention thro' Life.

Seperate from this, I feel myself competent to an honourable Profession, suited to the peaceful walk of Life, which with my very small fortune and moderate Abilities, will enable me to live in content and retirement, whenever I chuse to make the experiment with a *friend*, detached from the follies and vices of society.

It now rests with you Madam and Mr. Adams to determine whether I shall confine myself to the duties of my station, or whether I may be permitted to cultivate the further friendship of your family.

I am, Madam, in relation to you and Yours all that honour and inclination can make,   W. S. Smith[3]

RC (Adams Papers); docketed in JA's late hand: "Smith 1785."

[1] Between AA2 and Royall Tyler.
[2] The papers have not been found.
[3] No reply to this letter by either AA or JA has been found.

Charles Storer to Abigail Adams 2d

Boston, December 29th, 1785

I join fully with you, Amelia, that whatever is, is right. Yet I cannot but regret that the winds hurried me so soon from England. But weigh the matter, says prudence. The office was important, the task arduous, and very much expected from it.[1] Had I failed, what an everlasting blot. This is a thought, Amelia, that would have staggered me in my wish to go; nor would self-examination have aided me in the least. As it is, then, I may truly say it is right; for now, to use a common expression, I save my credit and bacon too; and have only to acknowledge myself obliged by your interest in my behalf, and your good opinion. I have written your papa about Lambe, who from all accounts is an unworthy character. I wish he may not do more hurt than good.

Believe me, Amelia, I think myself indebted to you, for your attention and remembrance of me, and return you many thanks, for your letter of the 15th October, via New-York,[2] which is just come to hand.

Surely Monsieur le Baron would regret your absence, and so I suppose would all the foreigners of the diplomatic circle, who dined with your papa, on the day of Feasts;[3] for I believe, in France, Madame la femme du ministre presides at the table. England, you know, was never remarked for politeness. But you do not say where you dined; whether in the house-keeper's room, or in your own chamber. I have heard, however, that you spent the day with Mrs. Hay, to whom I beg my compliments, as we go along. That you miss me, Amelia, I can well suppose, particularly as Colonel Smith was not returned. But how you can think this a mortifying circumstance, I am at a loss to find out. Did I not use to execute your commissions, and especially when you were with me, with much pleasure? You saw the West Indian[4] performed; a good piece 'tis called. I wish I had been with you. I hope you had not Gretna-Green[5] again for the Farce. And you saw their majesties, and the two eldest princesses. Were you near enough to be recollected by them? Apropos, methinks I see you making your reverence to them. The fashionable courtesy, you know, is very low, and slow. Have you learnt to make it gracefully? I ask because I want you to teach it here, when you return; they make such little bobs and dodges as would make you laugh most heartily. Miss Grant, sister to Betsey G., who was here some years ago, is here from England. I introduced my Maria[6] to her; of course there were

510

courtesies on both sides. Miss G. prepared her feet; Maria made a little bob; Miss G. began to sink; Maria bobbed again; Miss G. continued to sink; Maria made another bob; Miss G. was stationary; Maria bobbed again; so in the same proportion in rising again; making in the whole, about six bobs or dodges. Paint it now to yourself, Amelia, and add thereto how prettily the dodger must feel. I have been ever since trying to bend her limbs, and are [*am?*] soon going to put her into shapes, according to the frame you gave me: so I hope we shall ere long be in due form and order. * * * * * * * * * * * Why do you neglect your old friends, Amelia? Mrs. Russell, whom I love, and you too, I believe, says you promised to remember her, and to write; but that she has not received one line from you since you left this country; nor can she learn that you have once mentioned her to any one: she is a worthy woman; don't forget her—nor especially

Eugenio

MS not found. Printed from AA2, *Jour. and Corr.*, 2:40–43.

[1] Storer evidently refers to the diplomatic mission to Algiers. AA2 was confident that JA would have asked Storer to join Capt. John Lamb on this mission if Storer had stayed in England only one more week (AA2 to JQA, 18 Oct., above).

[2] Not found; it presumably contained AA2's news about the mission to Algiers.

[3] Probably 30 Sept., when JA entertained the diplomatic corps of London at his home in Grosvenor Square. Because women traditionally were excluded from such events, AA and AA2 went to the home of their good friend Mrs. Rogers for the evening (AA2 to JQA, 24 Sept.; AA to Mary Cranch, 1 Oct., both above). "Monsieur le Baron" who re-gretted AA2's absence was probably Baron de Lynden, the Dutch minister to Great Britain. Another guest who missed the Adams women, however, was the British foreign minister, the Marquis of Carmarthen (AA2 to JQA, 24 Sept., above).

[4] See AA2 to JQA, 18 Oct., note 8, above.

[5] The play *Gretna Green* by Charles Stuart was first performed in 1783. Notices appeared in London newspapers announcing many performances of the farce during the summer of 1785. Gretna Green, a village in southern Scotland, was widely known as a convenient location for quick and clandestine marriages that could not be performed in England.

[6] Probably Storer's sister Mary.

Appendix

Appendix

LIST OF OMITTED DOCUMENTS, 1761–1785

The following list includes 132 documents that have been omitted from Volumes 1 through 6 of *Adams Family Correspondence*. In the future each two-volume set will contain such a list. The general selection policy for the series set forth in volume 1:xli–xliii and in the Introduction, Part 5, above, has determined the contents. Each entry consists of the date, correspondents, form in which the letter exists (RC, LbC, Dft, Tr, FC), location, and publication, if known. All copies that exist in some form in the Adams Papers are noted. The list also includes those letters that have come to the editors' attention after the publication of the volume in which they would have appeared. These are marked with an asterisk.

1761

May 25	Abigail Smith (AA) to Hannah Storer (later Hannah Storer Green), RC (MHi:S. A. Green Papers); PRINTED: Samuel Abbott Green, *An Account of Percival and Ellen Green and of Some of Their Descendants*, Groton, Mass., 1876, p. 54–55.
June 17	Isaac Smith Sr. to Abigail Smith, RC (MHi:S. A. Green Papers).
Oct. 5	Abigail Smith to Hannah Quincy Lincoln, PRINTED: AA, *Letters*, ed. CFA, 1840, p. 3–6.

1762

Feb. 7	Abigail Smith to Isaac Smith Jr., RC (MHi:Smith-Carter Papers).
May 31*	John Adams to Mary Smith Cranch, RC (WyU).

1763

Nov. 23	Hannah Storer Green (Caliope) to Abigail Smith (Diana), RC (Adams Papers).

1764

April 22 Abigail Smith (Diana) to Hannah Storer Green (Caliope), Dft (Adams Papers).

[post Oct. 10?] John Adams to Abigail Smith, RC (Adams Papers, filmed under [Sept.–Oct.], Microfilms, Reel No. 343).

[ante Oct. 25] John Adams to Abigail Smith, RC (Adams Papers).

1766

June 29* Abigail Adams to Mary Smith Cranch, RC (Colonial Dames of America, Abigail Adams Smith House, New York).

1767

May [18] John Adams to Abigail Adams, RC (MBU).

1771

[Nov. 18] Abigail Adams to Mary Smith Cranch, RC (NAlI).

1772

n.d. [1772–1782] Mercy Otis Warren to Abigail Adams, RC (Adams Papers, Microfilms, Reel No. 601).

1773

Jan. 16 Abigail Adams to Samuel Tufts, RC (MdBJ); Tr (Adams Papers, filmed at 10 Oct. 1840, Charles Folsum to CFA, Microfilms, Reel No. 515).

Aug. 19 Elizabeth Smith (later Elizabeth Smith Shaw), to Abigail Adams, RC (Adams Papers).

Aug. 30 Mercy Otis Warren to Abigail Adams, RC (Adams Papers).

1774

Oct. 5 Hannah Storer Green to Abigail Adams, RC (MHi:S. A. Green Papers); PRINTED: Samuel Abbott Green, *An Account of Percival and Ellen Green and of Some of Their Descendants*, Groton, Mass., 1876, p. 57–58.

1775

Jan. 16	John Quincy Adams to Hannah Thaxter, Tr (Braintree Historical Society, Braintree, Mass.).
June 5	Mercy Otis Warren to Abigail Adams, RC (Adams Papers).
July 17	Mercy Otis Warren to Abigail Adams, RC (Adams Papers).
July 31	Mercy Otis Warren to Abigail Adams, RC (Adams Papers).
Sept. 11	Mercy Otis Warren to Abigail Adams, RC (Adams Papers).
Sept. 28	Abigail Adams to Mercy Otis Warren, RC (MHi:Warren-Adams Coll.).
Oct. 2	Mercy Otis Warren to Abigail Adams, RC (Adams Papers).
Oct. 6	Eunice Paine to Abigail Adams, RC (Adams Papers).
[Oct. 6]	Mercy Otis Warren to Abigail Adams, RC (Adams Papers, filmed under [Sept. 1775], Microfilms, Reel No. 345).
Oct. 24	Mercy Otis Warren to Abigail Adams, RC (Adams Papers, filmed under 25 Oct. 1776, Microfilms, Reel No. 346).
Oct. 25	Mercy Otis Warren to Abigail Adams, RC (Adams Papers).
Nov. 3	Mercy Otis Warren to Abigail Adams, RC (Adams Papers).
[post Nov. 5]	Mercy Otis Warren to Abigail Adams, RC (Adams Papers, filmed under [Nov. 1775], Microfilms, Reel No. 345).
n.d. [1775–1779]	Mercy Otis Warren to Abigail Adams, RC (Adams Papers, Microfilms, Reel No. 601).

1776

Jan. 8	Mercy Otis Warren to Abigail Adams, RC (Adams Papers).
[June]	Mercy Otis Warren to Abigail Adams, RC (Adams Papers, filmed under n.d. [ante 1782?], Microfilms, Reel No. 601.
[1776?]	Mercy Otis Warren to Abigail Adams, RC (Adams Papers).

1778

March 7	John Thaxter to Abigail Adams, RC (Adams Papers).
March 13	John Thaxter to Abigail Adams, RC (Adams Papers).
[March 21?]	James Lovell to Abigail Adams, RC (Adams Papers), probably a postscript to James Lovell to Abigail Adams, 21 March 1777 [i.e. 1778] (vol. 2:403–404); PRINTED: Smith, ed., *Letters of Delegates*, 9:322–323.
March 21	John Thaxter to Abigail Adams, incomplete Dft (MHi:John Thaxter Papers).
[April 16]*	James Lovell to Abigail Adams, incomplete(?) RC (Adams Papers, filmed under [1777–1781], Microfilms, Reel No. 347); PRINTED: Smith, ed., *Letters of Delegates*, 9:422–423.
April 24	John Thaxter to Abigail Adams, RC (Adams Papers).
April 30	John Thaxter to Abigail Adams, RC (Adams Papers).
June 3	John Thaxter to Abigail Adams, RC (Adams Papers).
June 13	John Thaxter to Abigail Adams, RC (Adams Papers).
July 21	John Thaxter to Abigail Adams, RC (Adams Papers).
July 28	John Adams to Abigail Adams, LbC (Adams Papers).
July 29	John Thaxter to Abigail Adams, RC (Adams Papers).
Aug. 5	John Thaxter to Abigail Adams, RC (Adams Papers).
Aug. 17	John Thaxter to Abigail Adams, RC (Adams Papers).
Aug. 21	John Thaxter to Abigail Adams, RC (Adams Papers).
Dec. 30	Isaac Smith Sr. to Abigail Adams, RC (Adams Papers).
Dec. 31	Abigail Adams to Cotton Tufts, Dft (Adams Papers).

1779

Feb. 23	Mercy Otis Warren to Abigail Adams, RC (Adams Papers).
March 7	Abigail Adams 2d to Elizabeth Cranch, RC (MHi:Cranch Papers).
[March]	Abigail Adams 2d to Elizabeth Cranch, RC (MHi:Cranch Papers).
April 6	Abigail Adams 2d to Elizabeth Cranch, RC (MHi:Cranch Papers).
[April–July]	Mercy Otis Warren to Abigail Adams 2d, Tr (MHi:Mercy Warren Letterbook).
May 8	Mercy Otis Warren to Abigail Adams, RC (Adams Papers).

June 15   James Lovell to Abigail Adams, RC (Adams Papers);
               PRINTED: Smith, ed., *Letters of Delegates*, 13:68–69.
[July]   Abigail Adams 2d to Elizabeth Cranch, RC
               (MHi:Cranch Papers).
[Oct.]   Abigail Adams 2d to Elizabeth Cranch; RC
               (MHi:Cranch Papers).
Nov. 24   Elbridge Gerry to Abigail Adams, Dft written on 3d
               and 4th pages of John Adams to Gerry, 8 Nov., RC
               offered for sale and PRINTED: *The Collector*, Sept.
               1909, p. 10; see also Smith, ed., *Letters of Delegates*,
               14:225.
Dec. 22   James Lovell to Abigail Adams, RC (Adams Papers);
               PRINTED: Smith, ed., *Letters of Delegates*, 14:297.
Dec. 23   James Lovell to Abigail Adams, RC (Adams Papers);
               PRINTED: Smith, ed., *Letters of Delegates*, 14:300.

1780

Jan. 21   James Lovell to Abigail Adams, RC (Adams Papers);
               PRINTED: Smith, ed., *Letters of Delegates*, 14:357–358.
Feb. 4   William Vernon Sr. to Abigail Adams, RC (Adams
               Papers).
[post Feb. 26] Abigail Adams to James Lovell, Dft (Adams Papers,
               filmed under [Feb.–March 1780], Microfilms, Reel
               No. 351).
March 18   John Adams to Abigail Adams, RC (Adams Papers).
May 2   James Lovell to Abigail Adams, RC (Adams Papers);
               PRINTED: Smith, ed., *Letters of Delegates*, 15:72–73.
[post May 4]   James Lovell to Abigail Adams, RC (Adams Papers,
               filmed under [ante 11 June 1780], Microfilms, Reel
               No. 352).
May 8   Mercy Otis Warren to Abigail Adams, RC (Adams
               Papers).
May 16   Hannah Thaxter to Abigail Adams, RC (Adams Pa-
               pers).
May 30   James Lovell to Abigail Adams, RC (Adams Papers);
               PRINTED: Smith, ed., *Letters of Delegates*, 15:216–217.
July 21   James Lovell to Abigail Adams, RC (Adams Papers);
               PRINTED: Smith, ed., *Letters of Delegates*, 15:483.
Aug. 17*   Abigail Adams to Richard Cranch(?), RC (Private
               owner, Boston, 1976).
Aug. 27   John Thaxter to Abigail Adams, RC (Adams Papers).

Aug. 29	James Lovell to Abigail Adams, RC (Adams Papers).
Nov. 30	James Lovell to Abigail Adams, RC (Adams Papers); PRINTED: Smith, ed., *Letters of Delegates*, 16:404.
Dec. 25	Abigail Adams to James Lovell, Dft (Adams Papers, filmed under 25 Dec. [1781], Microfilms, Reel No. 355).

1781

Jan. 10	John Thaxter to Abigail Adams, RC (Adams Papers).
Jan. 30	James Lovell to Abigail Adams, RC (Adams Papers); PRINTED: Smith, ed., *Letters of Delegates*, 16:647–648.
Feb. 19	James Lovell to Abigail Adams, RC (Adams Papers); PRINTED: Smith, ed., *Letters of Delegates*, 16:719–720.
April 1	John Quincy Adams to William Cranch, RC (MHi:Cranch Family Papers).
May 10	Richard Cranch to Abigail Adams, RC, fragment, written on verso of list enclosed in Abigail Adams to John Adams, 25 May (Adams Papers, see vol. 4:131).
July 27	Elizabeth and Samuel Adams to Abigail Adams, RC (Adams Papers).
[Aug. 21]	Abigail Adams to James Lovell, Dft (Adams Papers, filmed under [post 16 Aug.], Microfilms, Reel No. 355).
Sept. 10	James Lovell to Abigail Adams, RC (Adams Papers); PRINTED: Smith, ed., *Letters of Delegates*, 18:30–31.

1782

May 17	Abigail Adams 2d to John Thaxter, RC (Private owner, Boston, 1957).
May 31	James Lovell to Abigail Adams, RC (Adams Papers).
Oct. 2	Chevalier de Ronnay to Abigail Adams, RC (Adams Papers).
Nov. 8	Ingraham & Bromfield to Abigail Adams, RC (Adams Papers).
[1782?]	Abigail Adams 2d to Elizabeth Cranch, RC (MHi:C. P. Cranch Papers).
[1782?]	Abigail Adams 2d to Elizabeth Cranch, RC (MHi:C. P. Cranch Papers).

1783

Jan.	Abigail Adams 2d to Elizabeth Cranch, RC (MHi:C. P. Cranch Papers).
Jan.	Abigail Adams 2d to Elizabeth Cranch, RC (MHi:C. P. Cranch Papers).
Feb. 18	John Adams to Abigail Adams, RC (Adams Papers).
Feb. 18	John Adams to Abigail Adams, RC (Adams Papers).
Feb.	Abigail Adams 2d to Elizabeth Cranch, RC (MHi:C. P. Cranch Papers).
Sept. 10	John Adams to Abigail Adams, RC (Adams Papers).
Sept. 30	Alice DeLancey Izard to Abigail Adams, RC (DSI:Hull Coll.).
[Sept.]	Mercy Otis Warren to Abigail Adams, RC (Adams Papers).
Dec. 26	John Thaxter to Abigail Adams, RC (Adams Papers).
[Dec.]	Abigail Adams 2d to Elizabeth Cranch, RC (MHi:C. P. Cranch Papers).

1784

Jan. 3	Abigail Adams 2d to John Thaxter, RC (Private owner, Boston, 1957).
March 12	Hannah S. Green to Abigail Adams, RC (Adams Papers).
May 7	Elbridge Gerry to Abigail Adams, RC (Adams Papers).
July 3	Cotton Tufts to Abigail Adams, RC (Adams Papers).
July 25	Abigail Adams to Mary Smith Cranch, RC (MWA: Abigail Adams Correspondence).
Aug. 2	Benjamin Vaughan to Abigail Adams, Abigail Adams 2d, and John Quincy Adams, RC (Adams Papers).
Aug. 7	John Cranch to Abigail Adams, RC (Adams Papers).
Aug. 14	Anna Quincy to Abigail Adams, RC (Adams Papers).
Sept. 25	Anna Quincy to Abigail Adams, RC (Adams Papers).
Nov. 1	Katherine Farnham Hay to Abigail Adams, RC (Adams Papers).
Nov. 6	Elizabeth Cranch to Abigail Adams, RC (Adams Papers).
Nov. 18	Katherine Farnham Hay to Abigail Adams, RC (Adams Papers).

[1784?]   Anne Willing Bingham to Abigail Adams and Abigail Adams 2d, RC (DSI:Hull Coll.).

1785

Jan. 11   Mary Fitch to Abigail Adams, RC (Adams Papers).

Jan. 13   Katherine Farnham Hay to Abigail Adams, RC (Adams Papers).

March 14   The Marquis de Lafayette to Abigail Adams and Abigail Adams 2d, RC (DSI:Hull Coll.).

March 26   Katherine Farnham Hay to Abigail Adams, RC (Adams Papers).

April 22   Eunice Paine to Abigail Adams, RC (Adams Papers).

May 6   Katherine Farnham Hay to Abigail Adams, RC (Adams Papers).

May 10   The Marquis de Lafayette to [John and Abigail Adams(?)], RC (DSI:Hull Coll.).

May 12   Katherine Farnham Hay to Abigail Adams, RC (Adams Papers).

June 22   James Jarvis to Abigail Adams, RC (Adams Papers).

Aug. 17   Charles Adams' admittance to Harvard College, printed form (Adams Papers).

Aug. 19   John and Lucy Ludwell Paradise to John and Abigail Adams, RC (MQA).

Sept. 18   Mercy Otis Warren to Abigail Adams, RC (Adams Papers).

Sept. 23   Elizabeth Palmer to Abigail Adams, RC (Adams Papers).

Sept. 24   John and Katherine Farnham Hay to John and Abigail Adams, RC (Adams Papers).

Dec. 17   Anna Quincy to Abigail Adams, RC (Adams Papers).

[1785?]   Elizabeth Smith Shaw to Abigail Adams, Dft?, fragment (DLC:Shaw Family Papers).

[1785–1788]   Charles Adams to Elizabeth Cranch; Dft?, fragment (MHi:Jacob Norton Papers).

Chronology

Chronology

THE ADAMS FAMILY, 1782–1785

1782

Oct. 8: After lengthy negotiations, JA signs the first Treaty of Amity and Commerce between the Netherlands and the United States, at The Hague.

Oct. 17: JA leaves The Hague for Amsterdam and then Paris, where he arrives on 26 October.

Oct. 30–Nov. 30: JA participates in negotiating and, with his fellow commissioners, signs at Paris, on 30 Nov., the Preliminary Treaty of Peace between the United States and Great Britain.

Oct. 30: JQA leaves St. Petersburg for The Hague by way of the northern route, through Finland and across the Åland Islands to Sweden.

Nov. 8: JA tells AA to put CA and TBA in a school and come to Europe with AA2 if she can get assurances that Congress will keep him in Europe another year.

Nov. 22: JQA arrives in Stockholm.

Dec.: JA writes to Congress, asking to resign his position. He informs AA of his decision, telling her to stay in America. Royall Tyler is a serious suitor of AA2; AA informs JA.

Dec. 31: JQA leaves Stockholm to travel across Sweden to Göteborg.

1783

Jan.: AA2 visits the family of James and Mercy Otis Warren at Milton, and later in the month, the family of Samuel Allyne Otis in Boston.

Jan. 25: JQA arrives at Göteborg.

Feb. 11: JQA leaves Göteborg for Copenhagen, where he arrives on the 15th.

Feb. 23: The Shelburne ministry falls in Great Britain; shortly to be replaced by the Fox-North ministry.

March 5: JQA leaves Copenhagen for Hamburg, where he arrives on the 10th.

April: AA sends CA and TBA to live in Haverhill with their aunt, Elizabeth Smith Shaw, where they prepare for college with their uncle, Rev. John Shaw. CA remains in Haverhill until he enters Harvard in 1785. TBA lives there until he matriculates in 1786.

April 5: JQA leaves Hamburg and travels through Bremen to Holland.

April 21: JQA arrives at The Hague, where he continues his study of Latin and Greek with C. W. F. Dumas until JA's arrival in July.

April 27: JA, Benjamin Franklin, and John Jay begin conferring with David Hartley on the definitive treaty with Great Britain.

May: AA buys land in Braintree for JA from the heirs of Micajah Adams.

June: CA ill with measles. AA and AA2 go to Haverhill to visit, and to bring CA home to Braintree to recover. He returns to Haverhill in August.

July 17: AA and AA2 attend Harvard commencement.

July 19: JA leaves Paris for The Hague, where he arrives on 22 July and is reunited with JQA after two years' separation. They travel to Amsterdam on 26 July, returning to The Hague on 30 July. JQA begins serving as his father's secretary and continues in this role until his departure for America in May 1785.

July–Aug.: John Thaxter and Charles Storer travel to London. Thaxter returns to Paris on 25 Aug., but Storer remains in England, and then moves to northeastern France.

Aug. 6: JA and JQA leave The Hague for Paris, arriving on 9 August.

Sept. 3: JA, Benjamin Franklin, and John Jay sign the Definitive Treaty of Peace with Great Britain in Paris. On 7 Sept. they learn that Congress has resolved to appoint them to a joint commission to negotiate a commercial treaty with Great Britain. JA immediately asks AA, with AA2, to join him in Europe.

Sept. 14: John Thaxter, JA's private secretary since Nov. 1779, leaves Paris for America. Carrying the definitive treaty to Congress, he sails from France on 26 September. Landing at New York, he reaches Philadelphia with the treaty on 22 Nov., and Braintree on 14 December.

Sept. 17: Death of AA's father, Rev. William Smith of Weymouth, Mass.

Sept. 22: JA and JQA move to Thomas Barclay's house in Auteuil, near Paris, where JA recovers from a serious illness; they remain there until 20 October. This is the house that the Adamses will occupy in Aug. 1784.

Oct. 20: JA and JQA travel to England, where they visit London, Oxford and Bath, remaining until 2 January.

Oct.–Nov.: AA visits Haverhill to nurse TBA, who suffers from "a severe fit of the Rheumatism"; she returns on 10 November.

Dec.: AA buys land in Braintree for JA from William Adams. AA meets Francis Dana in Boston upon his arrival from St. Petersburg, over four years after his departure from Boston for Europe with JA.

Dec. 19: William Pitt the younger forms his ministry in Great Britain.

Dec.–Jan.: AA2 visits relatives and friends in Boston for over a month.

1784

Jan. 2: JA and JQA leave England and travel across the North Sea to the Netherlands, where JA seeks and secures a second Dutch loan to save America's credit. JA and JQA remain at The Hague, with brief visits to Amsterdam bankers for JA, and JQA's long trip to London, until July-August.

March: AA2 visits the Warrens in Milton.

April: AA delays arranging her departure for Europe, hoping to hear again from JA, and from Elbridge Gerry, who keeps her informed about Congress' decisions concerning America's diplomatic missions.

April–June: CA and TBA visit AA and AA2 in Braintree, before the latter depart for England.

May 7: John Jay elected secretary for foreign affairs by Congress. Thomas Jefferson elected by Congress to join JA and Benjamin Franklin to negotiate treaties of amity and commerce with over twenty European and African powers.

May 14: JQA leaves The Hague for England, reaching London on 18 May. There his purpose of meeting AA and AA2 is frustrated by their decision to delay leaving Boston. He stays in London until about 26 June and makes several visits to Parliament and to the Court of Chancery.

June 1: John Jay sails from England for America.

June 18: Thomas Jefferson arrives in Boston, too late to arrange a passage on the ship taking AA to England. He sails on 5 July, reaching England on 26 July, and Paris on 6 August.

June 20: AA and AA2 sail from Boston for England on the *Active*, landing at Deal, England on 20 July. They proceed to London, arriving on 21 July, and remain until 8 August.

July 26: JA, upon hearing from AA, and learning that Jefferson has been named a commissioner and is headed for Paris, decides to join Jefferson and Franklin there. He still plans, however, to have AA and AA2 come to The Hague first, and sends JQA to London. JQA arrives on 30 July and joins AA and AA2 after a separation of nearly five years.

Aug.: JA, having heard that Jefferson has already arrived in France, changes his plan and on 7 Aug. arrives unexpectedly in London, where he is reunited with AA after nearly five years apart. The Adamses travel from London to Paris, arriving on 13 Aug.; on the 17th they move to Auteuil, where they live until May 1785. JA, with his colleagues Franklin and Jefferson, immediately begins corresponding with several European powers to arrange commercial treaties with America.

Dec. 21: John Jay accepts Congress' appointment as secretary for foreign affairs; he is the first secretary to be in sympathy with JA's views on foreign policy.

1785

Feb. 24: Congress names JA to be the first U.S. minister to Great Britain.

March 10: Congress names Thomas Jefferson U.S. minister to France, in place of the retiring Benjamin Franklin.

May 12: JQA leaves Paris for America to attend Harvard College. On 21 May he sails from Lorient on the *Courier de l'Amérique*.

May 20: JA, AA, and AA2 leave Auteuil for England, arriving in London on 26 May. They reside in London until 1788.

June 1: JA has his first audience with King George III; he is presented to Queen Charlotte at Court on 9 June.

June 23: AA and AA2 are presented to King George and Queen Charlotte at a Court Day at St. James's Palace.

July 2: JA, AA, and AA2 move into the first American legation in London, a rented house on Grosvenor Square.

July 12: Benjamin Franklin leaves Passy, where he had lived for over eight years, to return to America. He sails from England on 28 July.

July 17: JQA arrives in New York City, where he stays with Richard

Henry Lee, president of Congress, and visits extensively with congressmen and with leaders of New York society.

mid-July: CA is admitted to Harvard College; he begins his studies in mid-August.

Aug. 4:   Col. William Stephens Smith, the secretary of the American legation in London, asks JA for leave to attend Frederick the Great's review of the Prussian army at Potsdam. He departs for Prussia on 9 Aug., and extends his stay in Europe into December, visiting Vienna and Paris.

Aug. 5:   JA signs the first Treaty of Amity and Commerce between Prussia and the United States. (Franklin and Jefferson sign in France in July; the Prussian envoy Baron von Thulemeyer signs at The Hague in September.)

Aug. 13:   JQA leaves New York for Boston, taking the overland route through central Connecticut and Massachusetts.

mid-Aug.:   AA2 breaks off her engagement with Royall Tyler; AA writes to Mary Cranch to explain this decision.

Aug. 25:   JQA arrives in Boston, after an absence of nearly six years. He visits Cambridge on 26 Aug., where he is reunited with his brother, CA, and his cousin, William Cranch, both students at Harvard. On 27 Aug. he visits his Adams and Cranch relatives in Braintree.

Aug. 31:   Harvard's President Joseph Willard advises JQA to seek further preparation to enter the college as a "junior sophister" in the spring.

Sept. 7:   JQA, with his aunt, Mary Cranch, visits Haverhill for a week to arrange for his intensive study of Latin and Greek under the guidance of his uncle, Rev. John Shaw. There he is reunited with his brother TBA. On their return from Haverhill, JQA and Mary Cranch visit his aunt Catharine Salmon Smith.

Sept. 19:   Charles Storer sails for America.

Sept. 30:   After further visits to Boston and Braintree, JQA returns to Haverhill.

Oct.:   JQA pays a short visit to the Daltons in Newbury with his cousin, Elizabeth Cranch, who lives with the John Whites of Haverhill for the entire fall. On 25 Oct., CA and William and Lucy Cranch arrive for a one-week visit.

Dec. 5:   William Stephens Smith returns to London with Col. David Humphreys.

Index

NOTE ON THE INDEX

The principles on which *The Adams Papers* indexes are compiled have been stated in a "Note on the Index" in each published unit. This Index conforms in almost all respects to that for volumes 1–4 of the *Adams Family Correspondence*. Like its counterparts, the Index is designed in some measure to supplement the annotation.

The editors have tried, not always successfully, to furnish correct spellings of proper names, to fill out names of persons mentioned incompletely or allusively in the text, to supply minimal identifying data for persons who cannot be fully named, and to distinguish by date or place of residence persons with identical names. Markedly variant spellings appearing in the MSS have been cross-referred to their most nearly standard forms, and the variant forms parenthetically recorded thereunder. In a change from previous Adams Papers indexes, the names of married women appear in the appropriate alphabetical sequence, rather than following their husbands' names. *See*-references under maiden names are used for members of the Adams and collateral families and for women who were single when mentioned in the text and were married subsequently but before January 1786.

In this Index the arrangement of items within the subentries is in the order of their first appearance, with the following exceptions:

1. under place names of particular importance in these volumes (e.g. Paris, London) there are appended separate gatherings of "Buildings, landmarks, streets, &c." in which the items are arranged alphabetically

2. all letters printed in these volumes are listed as the final element in the entries of the persons concerned, the letters divided into those written and those received, and subdivided alphabetically by correspondent and chronologically by year.

The Chronology, "The Adams Family, 1782–1785" (immediately preceding), has not been included in the Index.

The Index was compiled in the Adams Papers editorial office.

Index

AA. *See* ADAMS, ABIGAIL SMITH (1744–1818, Mrs. John Adams)

AA2. *See* ADAMS, ABIGAIL, 2D (1765–1813)

Abdee, Phoebe (Pheby, Pheebe, Mrs. William): moves into AA's house, 5:xvi, 303; offered freedom in Rev. Smith's will, 5:247–48, 249; marriage of, 5:303; provisions and duties for, 5:345–46; 6:20; bothered by neighbors, 5:420; cares well for AA's house, 5:420, 462, 476; 6:2, 87; Tufts bothered by "Spirit of the African" in, 6:87; sells produce, 6:234, 239; Tufts pays, 6:258; Tufts receives payment from, 6:259; AA offers to help support, 6:359; mentioned, 6:44, 45, 425, 459

Abdee, William, 5:303, 345, 462; 6:20, 44, 45, 87, 234, 239

Abélard, Pierre, 5:172, 173

Abingdon, Earl of. *See* Bertie, Willoughby

Abington, Frances (actress), 6:434, 436, 478, 482

Abington, Mass., 6:85, 232

Åbo, Finland, 5:79

Acrobats (in London), 6:331–32

Active (French frigate), 5:131

Active (merchant ship): AA and AA2 sail to England on, 5:xxix, 330, 350, 386, 387; location, 5:358, 374, 383, 390, 393, 396, 398; sickening cargo on, 5:359, 394; nearly run into at sea, 5:395, 396

Adam brothers (English builders), 5:386

ADAMS, ABIGAIL, 2D (1765–1813, daughter of AA and JA, later Mrs. William Stephens Smith, designated as AA2 in *The Adams Papers*)

BOOKS AND READING

studies and translates French, 5:xxxiv, 411, 428, 444; 6:24, 25, 47, 128; comments on MacKenzie's *Julia de Roubigné*, 5:32; quotes unidentified literary passage, 5:81; asks for JA's recommendations, 5:156; quotes Pope's "Ode on St. Cecilia's Day," 5:225, 226–27; Bell's *Poets of Great Britain*, 6:xv, 205; considers studying French in a convent, 6:48, 59; recounts an opera, 6:124–26; quotes *Hamlet*, 6:213, 221–22; JA buys Shakespeare for, 6:222

CHARACTER, APPEARANCE, HABITS, DOMESTIC LIFE

correspondence with Storer, 5:x; AA considers cooler than herself, 5:xxiv, 7, 56; reserved, 5:xxv, 75, 123; lack of French limits social circle, 5:xxxiii; 6:246; acts as JA's secretary, 5:xxxix; 6:180, 181, 303–304, 311, 407, 471; courted by W. S. Smith, 5:xl; 6:280, 483, 508–509; praised, 5:xl, 441, 445–46; 6:465, 469–70, 491; correspondence with Elizabeth Cranch, 5:xli, xlv–xlvi, 64, 69–70, 224–25, 226, 407, 414, 415, 429, 464, 466; 6:xvi, 90, 92, 336; correspondence with JQA, 5:xlv, xlviii, 39; 6:xv–xvi; correspondence with Thaxter, 5:xlv, 7, 27, 86, 138; as correspondent, 5:xlv–xlix; 6:18, 181, 198, 281; called Abby by CFA, 5:liii, liv; CFA alters image of courtship by W. S. Smith, 5:lvi; feels neglected, 5:2; probably not AA's "Fair American," 5:27; wants letters kept confidential or burned, 5:33, 50, 70; 6:181; remarks on Elizabeth Cranch's romantic interests, 5:50–52, 70, 225; deprived of a heart "in the days of my youth," 5:52; describes a proper journal, 5:53; characterized, 5:63, 64; friendship with Elizabeth Cranch, 5:63, 73–74; lonely and unhappy over JA's and JQA's long absence, 5:63, 64, 138–39; friendships, 5:64, 70, 374, 410, 429, 432, 434, 439, 444; 6:25, 371, 511; called a "portrait of her father," 5:67; wants Mary Cranch to be discreet, 5:72–73; Thaxter compliments, 5:77; self-appraisal, 5:80, 81–82, 207–208, 430–31; 6:183, 480; AA cuts short visit to Warrens, 5:95; offers to help aunt with domestic work, 5:106, 107; relationship with cousin William Smith, 5:119, 149, 150, 194–95; wants lutestring cloth, 5:152–53, 154, 409; desire to see Europe, 5:156; discouraged with correspondence, 5:196, 197; comments on social events and acquaintances, 5:208, 366, 395,

533

Index

ADAMS, ABIGAIL, 2D (*continued*)
6:382, 385, 467, 469; concerned about JQA's
watch, 6:387; JQA asks to be relieved of promise to write daily, 6:398–99, 405; JQA calls
letter "a most noble feast," 6:448; teases JQA
about Swedish women, 6:469

RELATIONSHIP WITH PARENTS

JA wants company of, in Europe, 5:xxvi–
xxvii, 89, 169, 202, 218, 223, 236, 238, 241, 255,
264, 265, 315; close attachment to AA,
5:xxxviii, xlv; anxious about JA's health, 5:xxxix,
294; 6:309; correspondence with JA, 5:xli, xlv,
190, 319; offers to care for JA, 5:16, 17, 47; JA
counsels, 5:29; melancholy on anniversary of
JA's departure, 5:31–32; called JA's "Image
[and] Superscription," 5:37; comments on
parents' sacrifice, 5:54–55; comments on AA's
sadness, 5:63, 297; JA thinks would dislike
Europe, 5:120, 123; JA's regard for, 5:122; receives present from JA, 5:122; family uncertain
over JA's plans for them, 5:138; feels mortified
at improper request to JA, 5:155, 156–57; con-
gratulates JA on peace, 5:156; JA says everyone
gives "a very flattering Character of," 5:161;
JA calls "princess at Pens Hill," 5:178; urges
AA to attend Harvard commencement, 5:212;
JA advises to learn Amer. history, 5:224; JA
praises exceptional "understanding and
consideration," 5:224; JA finds letters "very
agreable," 5:232; and AA's decision to go to
Europe, 5:291, 296–97; JA advises on opportunities to enjoy travel, 5:401; joyful reunion
with JA, 5:419. *See also* AA2–Courtship by
Royall Tyler

RESIDENCES

Grosvenor Square, London, 5:xxxviii;
6:204–205, 212–14; Auteuil, 5:430, 433–35, 439–
40; 6:x, 6–7; garden at Auteuil, 5:431, 433–34;
6:124; moves from Bath Hotel to Grosvenor
Square, 6:204–205

SOCIAL LIFE AND RECREATION

comments on Mme. Helvétius, 5:xviii–xix,
xxxiii, 431–32; meets Mme. Lafayette, 5:xxxiii;
6:22; attends London theater, 5:xxxvii; 6:183,
185, 326, 378, 434, 478, 510; presentation to
George III and Queen Charlotte, 5:xxxvii;
6:188–90, 195–96, 202, 324, 460–61, 462; represents AA at gatherings, 5:6, 404; 6:75; plays
whist, 5:26; visits in Germantown, 5:49–51; visits in Milton, 5:50, 52, 63–64, 225–26, 227, 308;
visits in Boston, 5:73, 74, 80–82; attends Old
South Meeting, 5:80; spends winter in Boston, 5:93, 119, 151, 276, 279, 290, 294; describes
Longchamp, 5:130; attends 4th of July celebra-

tion and Harvard commencement, 5:194, 195,
200–201, 205, 206; visits in Hingham, 5:196;
invited to visit Daltons, 5:201, 211; 6:403, 405;
holds small party in Braintree, 5:208; visits
London sights, 5:376; 6:218; dines out in London, 5:410, 412, 464, 466; 6:208, 209, 211, 300–
302, 395, 469; receives visitors in London,
5:411; 6:208, 380, 387; dines out in France,
5:419, 453; 6:81, 120; attends theater in Paris,
5:428–29, 430, 444, 451; 6:46, 47; attends opera
in Paris, 5:434; 6:124; sees Dauphin, 5:454;
sees Amer. women in Paris, 5:465; speaks with
Princess Augusta, 6:190; rides in carriage,
6:207; walks, 6:207; breakfasts out in London,
6:209; visits in London, 6:209, 261, 299, 385,
470; visits in Hempstead, 6:220; attends large
dinners at London home, 6:304–305, 479, 480,
482; would like to accept all invitations, 6:306;
attends coronation anniversary, 6:380; visits in
Clapham, 6:381; does not attend JA's dinner
for foreign ministers, 6:382, 385; declines
going to London assembly, 6:479–80; drinks
lemonade, 6:482

TRAVELS

sea voyage to Europe, 5:xxi, xxix, 350, 362,
466, 467; arrival in England and London,
5:xxxi, 368–69, 397; in Haverhill, 5:4, 182, 187,
194; decision to go to Europe, 5:298, 300, 311,
317, 325, 330; "sea Life . . . exceeds my expectations, in the disagreeable," 5:389, 390; 6:308;
brings air plant on sea voyage, 5:410; expects
to go to The Hague and then Paris, 5:412;
journey to Paris via Chantilly, 5:419; 6:28

WRITINGS

importance of letters as family chronicle,
5:xxxviii, xlvii–xlviii; 6:xvi; first publication of
letters, 5:li–lviii; probably destroyed by fire,
5:lvii–lviii; in *Adams Family Correspondence*,
5:lx; her "production" (journal?), 5:49, 51; use
of journal, 5:419; 6:85, 299, 302, 310; deliberate
removal of text from letter of, 6:474

MENTIONED

5:1, 10, 79, 115, 132, 134, 135, 137, 172, 190,
191, 231, 251, 272, 338, 349, 355, 394, 453, 462,
469, 471, 472, 477, 484; 6:3, 30, 44, 73, 81, 96,
112, 171–72, 239, 240, 294, 316, 334, 335, 339,
355, 447, 458, 464, 502, 507

LETTERS

Letters: To AA (in 1784), 5:296; to JA (in
1783), 5:155; to JQA (in 1783), 5:157; (in 1785),
6:204, 299, 378, 432, 467, 478; to Elizabeth
Cranch (in 1782), 5:2, 31, 49, 51; (in 1783),
5:63, 69, 72, 80, 194, 200, 207, 224; (in 1784),

535

ADAMS, JOHN (*continued*)
JQA mathematics, 6:47; gives books to William Cranch, 6:97–98; buys Shakespeare for AA2, 6:222; buys medical instrument for Amer. doctor, 6:286; library of, in Braintree, 6:291; commends Justinian's *Institutes* to JQA, 6:356; commends Theophilus' *Commentary* to JQA, 6:356; presented with treatise on education, 6:362; visits Royal Society, 6:384, 389; pamphlets sent to, 6:428, 492; receives and presents old coin to Society of Antiquaries, 6:430, 432, 492, 493; library in Holland and England, 6:444, 445

CHARACTER, APPEARANCE, HABITS, DOMESTIC LIFE

relationship with Charles Storer, 5:ix, 20, 30, 146; Copley's portrait of, 5:xvi–xvii, 341, 342, 373, 374, reproduced 375, 385, 403–404, 407–408; 6:216; thinks return home best for family, 5:xxiii, 15, 47, 203; plan to live with family at The Hague, 5:xxxi–xxxii, 224, 335, 399–400, 416; reunites with AA and AA2 in London, 5:xxxii, 419; 6:18; rejects moving to Vermont, 5:16, 125; AA criticizes miniature of, 5:23; Vinkeles' engravings of, 5:24; self-evaluation as virtuous man opposed by corrupt factions, 5:31, 89, 104, 126–27, 351; handwriting described, 5:76, reproduced 109, 160, 334; called "a civil Cincinnatus," 5:91; enumerates family cares, 5:124; uses Boylston seal, 5:144, 333; wants family in Europe, 5:202, 218; content to farm, be a selectman and "get a little health and teach my Boys to be Lawyers," 5:203; desire to return to private life, 5:222; "naturally inclined to be fat," 5:223; recommends brother-in-law to Dutch merchants, 5:228; laments father-in-law's death, 5:264, 265; relationship with mother, 5:301; 6:20, 95, 100, 278; values brother-in-law's opinion, 5:315; gathers possessions to be ready to return to America, 5:338; "my Life has been a Series of dissappointments, chequered with . . . a Ray of good Luck," 5:341; early romantic interest of, 5:388; has JQA buy coach for family trip to Paris, 5:416, 441; 6:42; fond of tea, 5:435; Mather Brown's portraits of, 6:xiii, xiv, 216, 222; determines to keep family together, 6:23; typical day in Auteuil, 6:24, 25, 46–47; furniture at The Hague brought to London, 6:42, 45, 194, 195, 197; tears apart Epiphany pie, 6:51–52; hospitable to relatives in Europe, 6:82, 85; green velvet cap called a "Cap of Wisdom," 6:174; and wine shipment, 6:180, 181, 264, 266; arranges for milk and cream delivery in London, 6:204; hires and dismisses a drunken coachman, 6:206; attends church,

6:283, 286; JQA's resemblance to, 6:288; sister-in-law characterizes, 6:348; referred to as "Doctor Adams" in Massachusetts, 6:52; amused by guest, 6:379; keeps food gifts confidential, 6:383; and dispute over care of house at The Hague, 6:390; Mars appropriate for table of, 6:390–91; anecdote about giving fine dinners, 6:434

CHILDREN

says Europe would "Ruin my Children forever," 5:xii, 110; correspondence with, 5:xli; prefers Amer. education for, 5:60, 102, 120, 202, 222, 232; 6:294, 327; legacy to, will be America's freedom and opportunity, 5:75; plan to put CA in school and bring AA2 and TBA to Europe, 5:89; "Boys! Work you Rogues and be free. You will never have so hard Work to do as Papa has had," 5:169; old clothes worn by sons, 6:87, 164–65, 477, 501–502; does "not know how to do, without one of my sons at least with me," 6:327

Relationship with AA2: conflict over Tyler's courtship of, 5:xxiv–xxv, xxxviii–xxxix, 59, 75–76, 88, 199, 221, 256, 301, 315, 316–17, 400, 424, 425; 6:285–86, 504; praises AA2's reserve and prudence, 5:xxv, 75, 123, 224; is touched by AA2's offer to care for him in Europe, 5:47, 120, 123; JA's ideas of a suitable partner for, 5:83, 110, 124; 6:20–21; "My dear Daughters happiness employs my Thoughts night and Day," 5:110; sends AA2 a present, 5:122, 123; gives advice to AA2 on a woman's role, 5:123, 224; "Get you an honest Man for a Husband, and keep him honest. No matter whether he is rich," 5:169; would rather pay court to AA2 than all other princesses, 5:178; advises AA2 to study Amer. history, 5:224; appreciates AA2's letters, 5:232; "I should scarcely in any Case have opposed the Final Judgment of my Daughter" [in marrying], 5:317; urges AA2 to keep journal, 5:400; reunion with AA2 in London, 5:419; characterizes AA2 as both droll and modest, 6:xiii, 216; enlists AA2 as secretary, 6:180, 181, 407, 471; gives AA2 Bell's *Poets of Great Britain*, 6:205; and courtship by W. S. Smith, 6:508–509

Relationship with JQA: concerned for JQA's safety on journey from Russia, 5:xv, xxiv, 90, 97, 110, 124; correspondence with, 5:xviii, xxii, xxix, xli, xlii, xliv–xlv, 140, 159; encourages JQA to hear speakers in Parliament, 5:xviii, 333, 334, 338, 341, 342, 350; enjoys JQA's company, 5:xxvi, 169, 197, 198, 218, 231, 233, 301–302; advises: "a young Gentleman of 17, must not talk of low Spirits for Small disappointments . . . He will meet with many," 5:xlv, 341;

Index

ADAMS, JOHN QUINCY (*continued*)
over accomplishments, 6:402; finds Americans as proud of family as Europeans, 6:410; thinks English mealtimes ridiculous, 6:444

RELATIONSHIP WITH AA2

reunites with AA2 in London, 5:xvii–xviii, xxxii, 411–12; develops correspondence with AA2, 5:xxii, xli, xlv, xlvii–xlix, 39, 294; 6:xv–xvi; agrees to write daily to AA2, 5:xlvii; 6:155; suspends writing to AA2 until admitted to college, 5:xlvii–xlviii; 6:398–99, 405; AA2 feels "as if we were growing into Life strangers to each other," 5:156; AA2: "you have become so great a traveller that much is expected from you," 5:157; criticized by AA2 for not writing, 5:196–97; 6:467; owns portrait of AA2, 6:xiii; takes pleasure in the company "of a Sister who fulfills my most sanguine expectations," 6:32; deeply moved by receiving AA2's letters, 6:150, 318; AA2's emotions on JQA's departure, 6:181–82; AA2 wants JQA's portrait and lock of hair, 6:216, 310; agrees to exchange opinions of characters with AA2, 6:244; AA2 advises, 6:307; thanks AA2 for caution and correction, 6:319; AA2 teases, 6:384–85, 469; disappointed at receiving no letters from AA2, 6:403–404; dissatisfaction with own letters to AA2, 6:443; interprets for AA2 in Paris, 6:481; approves AA2's dismissal of Tyler, 6:504

RELATIONSHIP WITH AA

reunites with AA in London, 5:xvii–xviii, xxix, xxxii, 382, 399, 408, 409; AA sends political information to, 5:xxxvi; 6:195–96, 261, 295–96, 360–61, 406; unsatisfying early correspondence with AA, 5:xlii–xliv; reassures AA of affection for, 5:xliii, 38, 39, 220–21; corrects AA's Yankee speech, 5:liii, 446, 451; AA complains at not hearing from, 5:7, 143–44, 182, 190, 213, 231, 273; AA expects great things for, 5:26–27; intends to write to AA from Holland, 5:87; writes observations on Russia at AA's request, 5:242–44, 283; AA expresses concern for JQA's moral condition, 5:273–74, 284; AA calls "Johnny," 5:277; urged by AA to have pride in own country and its leaders, 5:284; sad when AA's arrival in London is delayed, 5:335, 373; acts as AA's secretary and translator, 5:399, 446, 451, 452, 463, 472, 477, 482; 6:21, 51, 132–33, 481, 526; AA sees JQA's "Strong resemblance of his Pappa. He is the same good humour Lad he formerly was," 5:414; AA comments on, 6:30, 138, 314–15, 330; AA is happy to be with, 6:32; AA writes by fireside of, 6:51; AA calls JQA "the young Hercules," 6:56; neglects writing to AA, 6:243, 408, 502; AA

advises to prepare to serve country, 6:345; AA concerned about health of, 6:357; AA sends clothes to, 6:361; receives letters from AA, 6:403

RELATIONSHIP WITH JA

sends Copley portrait of JA to U.S., 5:xvii; correspondence with JA described, 5:xviii, xxii, xxix, xli; JA calls "greatest Traveller of his Age," 5:xviii, 399; becomes JA's closest companion, 5:xxvi; return to Holland relieves JA, 5:xxvi, 90, 97, 110, 140; writes to JA at Congress and in Europe, 5:xli, xlii, xliv–xlv; executes seal commemorating negotiations at Ghent at JA's request, 5:48; instructed by JA on residence and studies, 5:130; agrees to write JA by every post, 5:150; JA asks for account of travel expenses, 5:159–60; JA urges improvement in letterwriting, 5:160, 161, 353; JA urges to keep a journal, 5:160, 400, 401; JA urges regular distribution of time, prudence, frugality, 5:160–61; JA: "well pleased with what I hear of you," 5:161; JA longs to see, 5:169, 202; JA plans tour of England with, 5:177; tells JA he hears nothing of peace negotiations, 5:184; JA calls "a Man in Understanding as well as Stature," 5:218; as JA's secretary, 5:221; JA says people "should take him to be my younger brother, if they did not know him to be my son," 5:223; JA enjoys company of, 5:231, 233, 241, 301; JA is pleased with studies of, 5:301–302; JA sends to London to meet AA and AA2, 5:327, 328, 399; sends JA list of new congressmen, 5:330, 334; sends JA's books to Holland, 5:332, 338, 341, 343, 350–51; JA advises JQA on behavior in London, 5:333–34, 341; judges oratory of speakers in Parliament at JA's request, 5:334, 340, 341, 342, 343–44, 347–48, 350; JA wants JQA in Holland, 5:338, 341, 343, 351; JA suggests learning Dutch together, 5:341, 342; returns to JA at The Hague, 5:343, 347, 438; JA thinks JQA has greater opportunities than he had, 5:401; awaits JA's orders for bringing AA and AA2 from London, 5:414; sends JA political news from N.Y., 6:243, 248–50; hopes JA approves horse purchase, 6:253; JA says: "you must prepare yourself to get your Bread," 6:356; JA pleased with Americans' good opinion of, 6:493

RESIDENCES

house at Auteuil, 5:430; 6:x, 6; with R. H. Lee in N.Y., 6:226, 227, 248; at birthplace in Braintree, 6:291; at Shaw house in Haverhill, 6:375; boards at Cranches in Braintree, 6:495

SOCIAL LIFE

attends fair at The Hague, 5:155; sees Benjamin West's paintings, 5:415; attends theater

ADAMS, JOHN QUINCY (*continued*)
and opera in Paris, 5:430, 434, 444; 6:46, 47, 52–53; dines in London, 5:466; visits in France, 6:75; dines out in France, 6:81, 108; visits Pope's Grotto, 6:218; visits in N.Y., 6:225–26, 242, 245–46, 251, 366; dines out in N.Y., 6:226–28, 243–45, 247, 252; dines out in Boston, 6:274, 317, 321, 322, 372; visits in Boston, 6:290, 317, 321–22, 336, 371, 373; visits in Cambridge, 6:290; goes to Concert Hall in Boston, 6:322; dines out in Milton, 6:323; visits in Braintree, 6:323, 354, 370, 374; visits in Haverhill, 6:350, 351, 400, 401, 403, 450, 476; attends bachelor's wedding dinner in Haverhill, 6:351; plays cards, 6:371, 372, 403; visits Dalton's in Newbury, 6:456; visits Gov. Pownall at Richmond Hill, 6:473; hospitable social life in Haverhill, 6:503–504

TRAVELS
to Europe with JA and John Thaxter (1779–1780), 5:x, xi; returns to Holland from Russia (1782–1783), 5:xv, xxi, xxiv, 40, 46, 72, 78, 114, 124, 214–17; returns to Paris from Holland (1783), 5:xxvi, 218; in England (1783), 5:xxviii, 255, 256, 264, 266, 322–24; 6:389; in London (1784), 5:xxix, 327, 328, 348, 373; returns to Holland (1784), 5:xxix, 130, 302, 316; from London to Paris (1784), 5:xxxii, 382, 399, 408, 409, 419; returns to America (1785), 5:xxxvi; 6:120, 134, 148; at Stockholm, 5:74, 76; 6:xvi; describes journey through Sweden, 5:86–87; arrives in Copenhagen, 5:97; through Denmark to Germany, 5:104; at Hamburg, 5:124; visits Chantilly, 6:26–28; from Auteuil to Lorient, 6:143–46, 198; sea voyage to N.Y., 6:148–49, 152, 155–61, 248; arrives in N.Y., 6:161, 224–25, 234, 257; stay in N.Y., 6:225–30, 242–53, 381; from N.Y. to Boston, 6:229, 231, 232, 234, 235, 237, 250, 252, 253–55, 256, 287–91; arrives in Boston, 6:268, 274, 289; reaches Braintree, 6:290; in Boston, 6:317, 318, 352, 370; in Cambridge, 6:318, 323; in Braintree, 6:323, 353, 369–70, 373; trip to Haverhill, 6:323, 325, 336, 338; journey through Spain (1779–1780), 6:333; in Lincoln, 6:352; from Boston to Haverhill, 6:375–76; in Newbury, 6:403

WRITINGS
Published: Writings of John Quincy Adams (1913–1917), 5:li–lii; first publication of family letters, 5:li–lviii; family and non-family letters distinguished, 5:lix; letters in *Adams Family Correspondence*, 5:lx
Unpublished: essay on Russia (1781–1783?), 5:242–44; translations of classics and transcriptions of poems, 5:305–306; diary,

5:401, 469; 6:85, 462; correspondence with Lafayette family, 6:ix–x; correspondence with Storer, 6:22

MENTIONED
5:140, 166, 205, 228, 277, 300, 337, 387, 417, 460, 461, 463, 465, 469, 472, 477, 484; 6:xiii, 3, 12, 44, 108, 112, 364, 424, 458

LETTERS
Letters: To AA2 (in 1785), 6:144, 148, 155, 225, 242, 251, 287, 317, 350, 369, 398, 442; to AA (in 1783), 5:214, 220, 235, 242; (in 1785), 6:224, 408, 503; to JA (in 1783), 5:86, 97, 104, 130, 150, 155, 159, 164, 168, 184; (in 1784), 5:327, 329, 332, 335, 339, 343, 347, 412, 418; (in 1785), 6:152, 248; to Elizabeth Cranch (in 1784), 5:322; to Mary Cranch (in 1784), 6:26; (in 1785), 6:420; to William Cranch (in 1784), 6:32; (in 1785), 6:448, 449
Letters: From AA2 (in 1783), 5:157; (in 1785), 6:204, 299, 378, 432, 467, 478; from AA (in 1782), 5:37; (in 1783), 5:272, 282; (in 1784), 5:309, 325; (in 1785), 6:194, 260, 295, 360, 406; from JA (in 1783), 5:97, 140, 159, 160, 162, 166, 173, 197; (in 1784), 5:333, 338, 341, 342, 350, 353, 416; (in 1785), 6:198, 327, 355; from John Thaxter (in 1783), 5:165
Letters to, from, omitted: to William Cranch listed, 6:520; to Hannah Thaxter listed, 6:516; from Benjamin Vaughan listed, 6:521

Adams, Rev. Joseph (1689–1783, uncle of JA, of Newington, N.H.), 5:187, 188, 240
Adams, Dr. Joseph, 5:383
Adams, Louisa Catherine (1775–1852, Mrs. John Quincy, designated as LCA in *The Adams Papers*), 5:69
Adams, Love Lawrence (Mrs. Joseph), 5:360, 369, 383, 394
Adams, Mary (1769–1830, JA's niece), 5:470, 471
Adams, Micajah (1742–1769, JA's cousin), 5:154
Adams, Peter Boylston (1738–1823, JA's brother): is well, 5:10, 187, 188, 420, 423; 6:13, 162, 232; buys woodlot, 5:276; advises AA to buy woodlot, 5:285, 291; takes care of mother, 6:95, 100; inheritance from father, 6:100; JQA visits, 6:291, 323; does not correspond with JA, 6:394, 495; named justice of the peace, 6:394, 458, 459, 507; comments on, 6:493–94; mentioned, 5:468, 469, 470; 6:111
Adams, Ruth Ruggles (Mrs. William), 5:276, 278, 285

The *Adams Family Correspondence* was composed by Technologies 'N Typography of Merrimac, Massachusetts, using Xerox's Ventura Professional Publisher. The text is set in eleven on twelve and one half point, using the Linotype-Hell Postscript revival of *Fairfield Medium*, a design by Rudolph Ruzicka that includes swash characters especially designed for *The Adams Papers*. The printing and binding are by Edwards Brothers of Ann Arbor, Michigan. The paper, made by the Mohawk Paper Company, is a grade named *Superfine*. The books were originally designed by P. J. Conkwright and Burton L. Stratton.